Many Mahābhāratas

SUNY series in Hindu Studies

Wendy Doniger, editor

Many Mahābhāratas

Edited by

NELL SHAPIRO HAWLEY *and*
SOHINI SARAH PILLAI

SUNY
PRESS

Cover image: *Draupadi* by Balaji Srinivasan. © Balaji Srinivasan. Used with permission.

Published by State University of New York Press, Albany

Printed in the United States of America

For information, contact State University of New York Press, Albany, NY
www.sunypress.edu

Library of Congress Cataloging-in-Publication Data

Names: Hawley, Nell Shapiro, 1988– editor. | Pillai, Sohini, 1990– editor.
Title: Many Mahābhāratas / [edited by] Nell Shapiro Hawley, Sohini Pillai.
Description: Albany : State University of New York Press, [2021] | Series: SUNY series in Hindu studies | Includes bibliographical references and index.
Identifiers: LCCN 2020029018 | ISBN 9781438482415 (hardcover : alk. paper) | ISBN 9781438482408 (pbk. : alk. paper) | ISBN 9781438482422 (ebook)
Subjects: LCSH: Mahābhārata—Criticism, interpretation, etc. | Mahābhārata—Influence.
Classification: LCC BL1138.26 .M36 2021 | DDC 294.5/923—dc23
LC record available at https://lccn.loc.gov/2020029018

10 9 8 7 6 5 4 3 2 1

We dedicate this volume to the memory of our beloved mentor,
Anne Elizabeth Monius

Contents

List of Illustrations xi

Acknowledgments xiii

Note on Transliteration xvii

Foreword xix
Paula Richman

1 An Introduction to the Literature of the Mahābhārata 1
Nell Shapiro Hawley and Sohini Sarah Pillai

Part I
The Manyness of the Sanskrit *Mahābhārata*

2 *Ā Garbhāt*: Murderous Rage and Collective Punishment as Thematic Elements in Vyāsa's *Mahābhārata* 37
Robert Goldman

3 The Invention of Irāvān 53
David Gitomer

4 Bodies That Don't Matter: Gender, Body, and Discourse in the Narrative of Sulabhā 69
Sally J. Sutherland Goldman

Part II
Sanskrit Mahābhāratas in Poetry and Performance

5 The Remembered Self: Arjuna as Bṛhannalā in the *Pañcarātra* 91
Nell Shapiro Hawley

6 The Lord of Glory and the Lord of Men: Power and Partiality in Māgha's *Śiśupālavadha* 117
Lawrence McCrea

7 What Are the Goals of Life? The *Vidūṣaka*'s Interpretation of the *Puruṣārthas* in Kulaśekhara's *Subhadrādhanañjaya* 135
Sudha Gopalakrishnan

8 How Do We Remember Śakuntalā? The Mahābhārata and Kālidāsa's Drama on the Contemporary Indian Stage 151
Amanda Culp

Part III
Regional and Vernacular Mahābhāratas from Premodern South Asia

9 An Old Dharma in a New Age: Duryodhana and the Reframing of Epic Ethics in Ranna's *Sāhasabhīmavijaya* 171
Timothy Lorndale

10 Three Poets, Two Languages, One Translation: The Evolution of the Telugu *Mahābhāratamu* 191
Harshita Mruthinti Kamath

11 The Fate of Kīcaka in Two Jain Apabhramsha Mahābhāratas 213
Eva De Clercq and Simon Winant

12 The Power-Politics of Desire and Revenge: A Classical Hindi *Kīcakavadha* Performance at the Tomar Court of Gwalior 237
Heidi Pauwels

13 Blessed Beginnings: Invoking Viṣṇu, Kṛṣṇa, and Rāma in Two Regional Mahābhāratas 257
Sohini Sarah Pillai

Part IV
Mahābhāratas of Modern South Asia

14 How to Be Political without Being Polemical: The Debate between Bankimchandra Chattopadhyay and Rabindranath Tagore over the *Kṛṣṇacaritra* 279
Ahona Panda

15 The Epic and the Novel: Buddhadev Bose's Modern Reading of the *Mahābhārata* 305
Sudipta Kaviraj

16 Draupadī, Yājñasenī, Pāñcālī, Kṛṣṇā: Representations of an Epic Heroine in Three Novels 325
Pamela Lothspeich

17 From Excluded to Exceptional: Caste in Contemporary Mahābhāratas 343
Sucheta Kanjilal

18 A Long Time Ago in a Galaxy Far, Far Away: The Mahābhārata as Dystopian Future 361
Philip Lutgendorf

Bibliography 385

List of Contributors 411

Index 415

Illustrations

Figure 18.1	The cover of *The Kaurava Empire, Vol. 1: Abhimanyu and the Conquest of the Chakravyuha*, 2014.	370
Figure 18.2	Aśvatthāman's listener refuses to condone his crime.	373
Figure 18.3	"Hāstinapura" as capital of an intergalactic empire.	376
Figure 18.4	Droṇa is seized by a monstrous reptile.	378
Figure 18.5	Kṛṣṇa visits the Kaurava court in an effort to avert war.	379
Figure 18.6	Droṇa gives Arjuna the *brahmāstra*.	380
Figure 18.7	Poster for *Ra One*, 2011.	383

Acknowledgments

Like many of the Mahābhāratas contained within it, our account of the Mahābhārata tradition represents the work of many hands and the interweaving of many minds. This book is a result of the enthusiasm we encountered when we began to organize a "Many Mahābhāratas" symposium as part of the Annual Conference on South Asia in Madison, Wisconsin, in October 2017. The very first person to offer her unconditional support for this project was our beloved mentor, Anne Elizabeth Monius. Anne played an integral role in *Many Mahābhāratas*' journey from idea to symposium to book. As the respondent for all fourteen of the presentations at the Madison symposium, she offered insightful comments and questions that framed the book as a whole and helped develop many of the individual chapters within it. Her careful editorial eye helped us to refine the argument and broaden the scope of our book proposal and, months later, our introductory chapter. Anne unexpectedly passed away on August 3, 2019; she was only 54 years old. We dedicate this volume to her memory.

Wendy Doniger's excitement about the project really helped it materialize. As the editor of the series in which this book is published, Wendy has offered her characteristically clear-eyed leadership from the start. Her comments on our introductory chapter emboldened us to say more. To John Stratton Hawley—known to one of us as "Jack" and to the other as "Dad"—we are more grateful than we can say. Jack introduced the two of us back when each of us, individually, was quietly wondering whether she could ever bring a "many Mahābhāratas" project to fruition. He knew before we did that we could do it together. After that, he championed the project—and us—every step of the way. His editorial contributions to the introductory chapter were a special boon.

We would like to thank a remarkable group of scholars whose work on South Asia's many Mahābhāratas has contributed to this volume in truly meaningful ways. Aparna Dharwadker, Frederick Smith, and Bruce Sullivan shared magnificent presentations at the "Many Mahābhāratas" symposium—their ideas have stayed with us. The beautifully framed research questions of Arti Dhand, Chinmay Sharma, Hamsa Stainton, and Sarah Pierce Taylor helped carry the book forward through the proposal process. We are immensely excited for them to share many more Mahābhāratas with all of us.

We eagerly extend our thanks to the generous individuals who answered our questions, told us where to find things, advised us on various aspects of the manuscript, and showed their enthusiasm in so many other ways: Purushottam Agrawal, Hannah Archambault, Mrunalini Chunduri, Morgan Curtis, Christopher Diamond, Jon Keune, Priya Kothari, Archana Kumar, Raj Kumar, Kannan M., Prakash V., Bhola Varma, and Promodini Varma. Girija Jhunjhunwala and Sahadi Sharma (of Campfire Graphic Novels) and Gaurav Verma (of Red Chillies Entertainment) kindly helped us secure permission to reprint the images in Chapter 18, Philip Lutgendorf's "The Mahābhārata as Dystopian Future." Balaji Srinivasan generously allowed us to feature his painting *Draupadi* on the cover; we are grateful to Sudha Gopalakrishnan and R. Sivapriya at Sahapedia.org for connecting us with him. The Lakshmi Mittal and Family South Asia Institute at Harvard University provided valuable support in the final stages of publication. Many thanks to James Peltz and Jenn Bennett-Genthner at SUNY Press, and to Heather Grennan Gary, for supporting this book in the most tangible way of all.

We would not have been able to bring this book into being without the backing of an extremely understanding and benevolent group of advisors, teachers, and mentors: Allison Busch (who passed away in October 2019, and whom we miss dearly), Whitney Cox, Munis Faruqui, Robert Goldman, Lawrence McCrea, Vasudha Paramasivan, Parimal Patil, and Gary Tubb. They motivated us to explore the wide world of the Mahābhārata in the first place and believed that doing this project would only enhance our progress in our respective PhD programs.

Three final words of thanks. The first goes to Pamela Lothspeich, whose encouragement to transform our symposium into a collection of essays inspired us to begin down this road. The book owes so much to Pam's guidance in those first few months. Her confidence in the lasting value of the project (and in us as its orchestrators) made all the difference.

The second goes to Paula Richman, whose visionary scholarship on the Rāmāyaṇa narrative tradition has permanently shaped the field and to whose *Many Rāmāyaṇas: The Diversity of a Narrative Tradition in South Asia* (1991) this volume obviously pays tribute. We say in the introduction that the book is, in its own way, a retelling of the Mahābhārata. But we profoundly wish it to recall *Many Rāmāyaṇas* as well. There could be no better inspiration.

Finally we wish to thank our parents, Honorine Ward Pillai and Shiv Pillai, and Laura Shapiro and Jack Hawley. The joke is not lost on us: The two of us have devoted our emergent scholarly careers to a story about a world-historically unhappy family—all while coming from immensely happy families ourselves. But perhaps that is precisely the point. Through their unfailing support and boundless love, our parents have given us the strength and the courage to jump into this dark and challenging world and, we hope, make something good out of it.

Note on Transliteration

Throughout this volume, we use an italicized "*Mahābhārata*" to refer to the Sanskrit epic specifically. When referring to works outside of the Sanskrit *Mahābhārata* that take up its name, structure, narrative(s), and characters, we use an unitalicized "Mahābhārata." We also use an unitalicized "Mahābhārata" to refer to the concept of the tradition as a whole.

This book examines Mahābhāratas in a number of different South Asian languages. To make things easier for our readers, the names of characters are represented according to how their names appear in the Sanskrit *Mahābhārata* and transliterated according to the International Alphabet of Sanskrit Transliteration (IAST). For example, the name of the shared wife of the Pāṇḍavas appears as "Draupadī," not "Draupadi" (as it would be written without diacritics) or "Tiraupati" (as it would be written according to standard Tamil transliteration practices). Other characters (including characters who are clearly based on characters from the Sanskrit epic, but do not actually share their names) are represented in our essays according to how their names appear in the primary sources, with appropriate transliteration.

The names of compositions and premodern authors have been transliterated according to the standard practices for their language of origin (for example: Villiputtūr's Tamil *Pāratam*). In the case of the names of languages, modern South Asian authors, and contemporary South Asian communities, diacritics have been omitted (Kannada, Rabindranath Tagore, Nishada, etc.). We do not use italics for the Sanskrit words "dharma" or "karma" as they have become common in many European languages.

Foreword

Paula Richman

Why would a scholar of the Rāmāyaṇa tradition agree to write a foreword for a volume about diverse tellings of the Mahābhārata tradition, a work that she labeled "the other epic" decades ago when she studied it in a graduate seminar?[1] After all, as many have pointed out, in Sanskrit literary culture, the two texts do not even fall into the same category: Vālmīki's *Rāmāyaṇa* is celebrated as the first Sanskrit *kāvya* (ornate work of narrative poetry), while the Sanskrit *Mahābhārata* is often viewed as *itihāsa* (history). Moreover, the two texts differ in other ways as well. David Shulman sees the *Rāmāyaṇa* as characterized by the "poetics of perfection" but the *Mahābhārata* as informed by the "poetics of dilemma."[2] Sheldon Pollock contrasts how each text describes its particular brand of conflict, arguing that Rāma's enemy, Rāvaṇa, is "othered," but that the Kaurava and Pāṇḍava antagonists are "brothered" since they share familial bonds.[3]

Yet rather than perceiving the two as irreconcilable, let us consider that encountering the Mahābhārata and Rāmāyaṇa narrative traditions in

1. When J. A. B. van Buitenen taught it, he was translating the *Mahābhārata*'s first five books.

2. David Shulman, "Towards a Historical Poetics of the Sanskrit Epics," in *The Wisdom of Poets: Studies in Tamil, Telugu, and Sanskrit* (Delhi: Oxford University Press, 1991), 24.

3. Sheldon Pollock, "Rāmāyaṇa and Political Imagination in India," *The Journal of Asian Studies* 52, no. 2 (1993): 283. Perhaps "cousined" is more apt.

tandem yields two different—but complementary—kinds of insights about the "big questions" of existence. Moreover, as Gary Tubb reminds us, both texts are *ākhyāna* (story literature), which "edifies gently, after the fashion of a helpful friend, by presenting interesting examples of what fruit befell the actions of others in the past."[4] While the *Rāmāyaṇa* serves as a narrative of ideals, the *Mahābhārata* presents a more realistic reflection of how elites wield power and resort to violence. Today, when political leaders in many countries propagate untruths, scapegoat minorities, and engage in corruption of unprecedented magnitude, edification from narratives that have stood the test of time should be welcomed. They provide "examples of what fruit befell the actions of others in the past," but because they continue to be retold and reinterpreted, they also allow us to ask new questions.

Before moving to some of the riches of the volume you are reading, permit me to comment on a little-known retelling of a Mahābhārata episode that serves as an example of how a new telling can prompt reflection on a timely issue—in this case, how society perceives transgender individuals. Muthal Naidoo, a South African of Indian descent, wrote *Flight from the Mahabharath* in the early 1990s. The play represents an effort to dramatize the dangers that ensue when an entrenched class divides other humans into essentialized groups in order to rob them of agency.[5] Naidoo's play, which rests on the premise that specific genres allow characters more or less freedom to act, presents differences in gender, caste, and sexuality through the lens of a nearly all-female cast filled with characters from the Mahābhārata narrative. Using a play within her play, Naidoo imaginatively recasts an Indian narrative to critique the ideologies of apartheid while remaining beyond the radar screen of government censors. I chose this play to illustrate how a fresh interpretation can open up a narrative. It is not new to condemn the Sanskrit *Mahābhārata* for limiting women to the roles of wives and mothers, but Naidoo's play innovates by making such

4. Gary A. Tubb, "*Śāntarasa* in the *Mahābhārata*," in *Essays on the Mahābhārata*, ed. Arvind Sharma (Leiden: E. J. Brill, 1991), 172.

5. Muthal Naidoo, *W[orks] I[n] P[rogress] Theatre Plays* (South Africa: MN Publications, 2008), 298–338. For a close analysis of the play's clever interpretation of the Mahābhārata narrative in the South African cultural and political context, see Paula Richman, "Silence in Muthal Naidoo's 'Flight from the Mahabharath': Disrupting the Power of Categories in a South African play," *Tarikh: A Journal of History* (2011): 40–48.

criticism the starting point of her story, thereby broadening the scope and depth of the Mahābhārata tradition.

Naidoo's play opens as Draupadī leads a group of women out of the "Epic."[6] No longer do they intend to remain in a narrative that has locked them into gender roles that impel them to bear and raise sons but deprive them of the ability to prevent their boys from dying in wars provoked by their fathers. Fleeing the Epic, they enter the genre of drama. Upon arrival, they quickly change from saris to less constrictive garb and celebrate their ability as women to take control over their own lives. Yet challenges to their self-contained new world soon emerge. Two men dressed as women appear and ask to join this new created place: Bṛhannaḍā (Arjuna in makeup, jewelry, and a dancer's clothing, with a grammatically female name) and Śikhaṇḍin (Princess Ambā, reborn male in order to slay Bhīṣma). The two insist that the Epic has victimized not only Draupadī and her women companions but them as well. They demonstrate that they have rejected masculinity by pointing out that they have vowed henceforth never to shed blood. After arguing about whether to admit the two to the world that the women have worked so hard to create, the women finally decide to let the two join them.

Immediately another dilemma arises. Since epic plots rest on conflict that leads to war, how can the cast of the drama reject Epic patriarchy, which glorifies violence? Subhadrā asks whether removing violence will drain an epic of its excitement. Bṛhannaḍā responds by offering to teach the women martial arts so as to free them from depending on men for protection. Agreeing to learn self-defense, the women adopt the proposal of Rādhā (Karṇa's foster mother) to rid their drama of heroes and villains, to avoid complicity in the glorification of bloodshed. The drama's director, Draupadī, now announces that they can free themselves from Epic constraints by retelling their stories such that they align with the new identities they have embraced. Draupadī plans to alter her story so that her sole husband is Arjuna, airbrushing away her other four—but Śikhaṇḍin quickly jumps in and changes Draupadī's *svayaṃvara* (bride-groom choice ceremony) into a dance competition to showcase Bṛhannaḍā's skills. Draupadī now realizes that the women's stories are interdependent; changing one means changing others. Indeed, Bṛhannaḍā eagerly rejects his (or her) Epic roles as Arjuna the warrior and Arjuna the husband, but Bṛhannaḍā's plan means that

6. Throughout the play, "epic" is capitalized to show its dominance and power.

Draupadī cannot enact her own. Since Bṛhannaḍā left the Epic in order to escape both warfare and wife, he (or she) threatens to withdraw from the drama. Immediately, Draupadī withdraws, too.

The play continues without them. What's more, the Mahābhārata's male roles are now played by women in disguise. During the scene in the assembly hall, the actress playing Duryodhana pulls off Draupadī's sari—but Draupadī, having left the scene, is now played by Śikhaṇḍin. Although many tellings of this episode show Kṛṣṇa saving Draupadī from humiliation by lengthening her sari indefinitely, no divine intervention occurs here. Instead, Duryodhana strips off her sari and attempts to shame her by placing her on his lap. When Śikhaṇḍin's wig falls off, Duryodhana discovers that "she" is a man, and flees in homophobic terror. By the next scene, Bṛhannaḍā has rejoined the drama and narrates Arjuna's story: male gender constructs, Bṛhannaḍā says, were forced on Arjuna since boyhood; he escaped gender entrapment only when he took on the guise of Bṛhannaḍā, in effect "coming out of the closet." This admission incites a debate with Śikhaṇḍin about the best way to win respect for same-sex love. Śikhaṇḍin argues that if all the cast members recount their stories, they will form a community where they all accept one another. Disagreeing, Bṛhannaḍā proposes to make Vyāsa's authority serve their cause. Since the author created characters that depart from heterosexuality, people will realize that "Vyāsa invented transsexuality" and accept it.[7] When Draupadī overhears the debate, she realizes that the two are lovers, and returns to the Epic. After more challenges to the drama,[8] Draupadī, returns from the Epic and admits she had been duped by patriarchal notions of romance to believe that she should marry only a successful warrior. Her experiences in the drama, she says, enabled her to see through such constructs. The cast welcomes her back and the play ends with singing and dancing to music of the rainbow nation, South Africa.[9]

The twists and turns of Mahābhārata and Rāmāyaṇa traditions multiply as one moves past the prodigious Sanskrit telling to encompass each story's

---

7. Naidoo explained to me that their difference in viewpoint safeguards the play from tokenizing a single character to represent all non-heterosexual voices (interview 2007).

8. These incidents include the scapegoating of Hiḍīmbā as a witch, during a drought.

9. It is conventional in some popular genres of South Indian musical dramas to end a play with the whole cast returning to the stage to sing one of the songs from it together.

many tellings in different genres, regional languages, and performance traditions—including works such as Muthal Naidoo's play, which was written in English from South Africa. Over time, rigid boundaries between and within narrative traditions become more permeable. That accounts for the Sanskrit *Mahābhārata*'s brief account of how Bhīma searches for a *saugandhika* flower to give Draupadī and, along the way, encounters his half-brother, Hanumān—Rāma's devotee and a major figure in the *Rāmāyaṇa* in his own right (3.3.146–50).[10] Kōṭṭayam Tampurān (ca. 1675–1725) transforms this short incident into the night-long *Kalyāṇasaugandhikam* ("The Flower of Good Fortune"), a beloved work from the *Kathakaḷi* dance-drama repertoire in southeast coastal India.[11] Both the textual account and the dance-drama center on this encounter between Bhīma and Hanumān, each a hero in a separate text but through whose interaction boundaries between narrative traditions appear more elastic. Another example is a Tamil epistolary story published in 1948 by Kumudini, the *nom de plume* of Ranganayaki Thatham (1905–1986).[12] Adopting the voice of a *rākṣasī* (demoness), a grandmother proposes that her granddaughter Hiḍīmbā (a *rākṣasī* from the *Mahābhārata*) would make a good bride for the grandson of Rāvaṇa's brother, Kumbhakarṇa (a *rākṣasa* or "demon" from the *Rāmāyaṇa*). The story's humor derives from the fantastical notion of a marital alliance between non-human characters from two different texts. In this way, hard and fast distinctions between these two narrative traditions begin to lose their bite.

---

10. All references to the Sanskrit *Mahābhārata* in this foreword are to the critical edition: *The Mahābhārata for the First Time Critically Edited*, ed. V. S. Sukthankar et al. 19 vols. (Poona: Bhandarkar Oriental Research Institute, 1933–66).

11. V. R. Prabodhachandran Nayar, M. P. Sankaran Namboodiri, and Phillip B. Zarrilli have translated this performance text, which appears in Phillip B. Zarrilli, *Kathakali Dance-Drama: Where Gods and Demons Come to Play* (London and New York: Routledge 2000), 103–17. There is also a popular Sanskrit play by the same name by Nīlakaṇṭha that is a part of the *Kūṭiyāṭṭam* performance tradition repertoire. See Nīlakaṇṭha, *Bhīma in Search of Celestial Flower: Nīlakaṇṭhakavi Kalyāṇasaugandhikavyāyoga*, trans. K. G. Paulose (Delhi: Bharatiya Book Corporation, 2000).

12. "Kumudini" [Raṅkanāyaki Tātam], *Cillaṟaic Caṅkatikaḷ Limiṭeṭ* (Tricchi: Natesan Books Ltd., 1948), 84–86. For a close analysis of this work, see Paula Richman, "Why Did Bhima Wed Hidimbaa? A Comparative Perspective on Marriage to the Other," in *Reflections and Variations on The Mahabharata*, ed. T. R. S. Sharma (Delhi: Sahitya Akademi, 2009), 190–93.

Readers, I heartily commend *Many Mahābhāratas* to you for its range of essays by authors trained in diverse academic disciplines, including literature (literary theory, poetics, Sanskrit aesthetics), theater and performance studies, gender studies, politics, and history. When we compare it to a volume of similar scope from 1991, *Essays on the Mahābhārata* (edited by Arvind Sharma), we see striking shifts in the field.[13] *Many Mahābhāratas* marks a moment in South Asian studies when a new generation of scholars has emerged—a number of them at early stages of their careers, which bodes well for future research on the Mahābhārata tradition. In addition, the volume's purview not only includes new essays on the Sanskrit *Mahābhārata* but moves beyond it to analyze the richness of Mahābhārata-inspired Sanskrit dramas, among them some rich examples of classical *kāvya*. Essays on regional and vernacular Mahābhāratas demonstrate the breadth of retellings that emerged between the ninth century and the eighteenth. The volume's prioritizing of less accessible Mahābhāratas provides a service to those exploring texts about which little has been written in English. The section on modern Mahābhāratas provides a selective yet wide-ranging orientation to materials such as graphic novels, nineteenth-century debates about Indian history, nationalism, and modernism, as well as postcolonial representations of Draupadī and Ekalavya. This volume demonstrates not only the ongoing energy and creativity of the Mahābhārata tradition but also the energy and creativity of those who study it. I invite you to enjoy the feast of Mahābhāratas that follows.

13. Sharma's volume contains twenty-three essays, more than half of which focus on the Sanskrit *Mahābhārata*. See Arvind Sharma, ed. *Essays on the Mahābhārata* (Leiden: E. J. Brill, 1991).

Chapter One

An Introduction to the Literature of the Mahābhārata

Nell Shapiro Hawley and Sohini Sarah Pillai

Those who hear *Mahābhārata* in many languages,
in many styles,
from many tellers,
always wanting these stories,
all the rewards of many offerings will forever
be theirs.

—Nannaya, *Mahābhāratamu*

Always Wanting These Stories

As soon as you begin to ask questions about what the Mahābhārata is, does, and says, you find yourself staring at some of the most daunting and irresistible challenges in the study of South Asian literature and religion. The earliest and largest Mahābhārata, a Sanskrit epic[1] poem of some 100,000

1. Finding the right genre description for the Sanskrit *Mahābhārata* has been as tricky for readers in the modern West as it was for those in early South Asia. As Alf Hiltebeitel points out, the *Mahābhārata* refers to itself using several different

verses[2] that was composed and compiled early in the Common Era, narrates the events of a catastrophic fratricidal war and, along with it, nearly everything else in Hindu mythology, philosophy, and story literature. Since a certain darkness haunts the events of the Sanskrit *Mahābhārata*'s core narrative—the protagonists' family splinters; the characters hurl accusations of moral failing at one another in infinite regress; the main figures die vividly and poignantly; everything is subject to deconstruction, dilemma, and decay—it is sometimes, in India, considered inauspicious to read the entire text or to keep it inside one's house.[3] Yet even its own sinister power

---

genre designations: *itihāsa* (history), *ākhyāna* (narrative), *purāṇa* (an extended myth narrative), *kathā* (story), *carita* (biography), *śāstra* (treatise), *saṃhitā* (collection), *upākhyāna* (tale), Upaniṣad, and Veda. See "Not without Subtales: Telling Laws and Truths in the Sanskrit Epics," in *Argument and Design: The Unity of the Mahābhārata,* eds. Vishwa Adluri and Joydeep Bagchee (Boston: Brill, 2016), 20. We find "epic" to be a useful descriptor because it signals that we are talking about a very long verse narrative. Some scholars have embraced the "epic" genre designation for the *Mahābhārata*. For example, Shubha Pathak convincingly argues that we can group together "the *Iliad* and the *Rāmāyaṇa* as affirmative epics that depict the ready realization of *kléos* [heroic glory] and *dharma*, respectively, and the *Odyssey* and the *Mahābhārata* as interrogative epics that portray the difficulties in achieving these religious ideals," in *Divine Yet Human Epics: Reflections of Poetic Rulers from Ancient Greece and India*, Hellenic Studies Series 62 (Washington, DC: Center for Hellenic Studies, Harvard University, 2014), 174. But we also realize that "epic" means different things for different thinkers, and one can easily contest its applicability to the Sanskrit *Mahābhārata*. Sheldon Pollock discusses several important ways in which the *Mahābhārata* diverges from major Western notions of epic literature in *The Language of the Gods in the World of Men: Sanskrit, Culture, and Power in Premodern India* (Berkeley: University of California Press, 2006), 554–55. For more on the relationship between epic poetry and political ideology in the West, see David Quint, *Epic and Empire: Politics and Generic Form from Virgil to Milton* (Princeton, NJ: Princeton University Press, 1993).

2. This figure is the Sanskrit *Mahābhārata*'s own estimate. The Bhandarkar Oriental Research Institute puts the verse count of its critical edition at around 75,000. See *The Mahābhārata for the First Time Critically Edited*, ed. V. S. Sukthankar et al. 19 vols. (Poona: Bhandarkar Oriental Research Institute, 1933–66). The fourteenth-century commentary of Vidyāsāgara, known as the *Jayakaumudī*, arrives at a total verse count of 102,555. See Dinesh Chandra Bhattacharya, "Vidyāsāgara's Commentary on the Mahābhārata," *Annals of the Bhandarkar Oriental Research Institute* 25, no. 1/3 (1944): 102.

3. Translating the *Mahābhārata* has also been considered a cursed enterprise. The eleventh-century Telugu poet Nannaya is said to have passed away after translating

cannot contain it. Triumphalist readings of the *Mahābhārata* have made it India's "national epic."[4] The *Bhagavadgītā* ("The Song of the Blessed Lord"), a series of chapters in the Sanskrit epic's sixth book, now constitutes a sacrosanct strand of many Hindu worldviews.[5] But the clearest indicator of the epic's allure is the fact that for the last two thousand years, the most common response to the *Mahābhārata* has been to recreate it. From medieval Telugu poetry to transnational Twitter, Mahābhāratas flood the languages, localities, and literary genres of South Asia and beyond. How is it that a story so disquieting has also proven so attractive?[6]

Each of the eighteen chapters in this book presents its own answer to that question.[7] Here is ours. The Mahābhārata story inherently invites more Mahābhāratas. Because of the relentless complexity of its worldview and the ensuing magnitude of its scope, the Mahābhārata persists in leaving

---

only the first two and a half books of the Sanskrit poem. More recently, in 1978, J. A. B. van Buitenen died after completing less than one third of his English translation of the *Mahābhārata*. See Velcheru Narayana Rao, "Multiple Literary Cultures in Telugu: Court, Temple, and Public," in *Text and Tradition in South India* (Ranikhet: Permanent Black, 2016), 86 n18; and Wendy Doniger, "How to Escape the Curse: The *Mahabharata* translated by John Smith," *London Review of Books* 31, no. 19 (2009): 18.

4. See Pamela Lothspeich, *Epic Nation: Reimagining the Mahabharata in the Age of Empire* (Delhi: Oxford University Press, 2009).

5. On the diversity and popularity of the Bhagavadgītā tradition, see Richard H. Davis, *The Bhagavad Gita: A Biography* (Princeton, NJ: Princeton University Press, 2015); and Winand M. Callewaert and Shilanand Hemraj, *Bhagavadgītānuvāda: A Study in Transcultural Translation* (Ranchi: Satya Bharati Publications, 1983).

6. One possible answer is that violent and fantastical narratives often prove popular. In this respect, we cannot help but notice the striking resemblance the Sanskrit *Mahābhārata* bears to the hit television series *Game of Thrones* (2011–19), an adaption of George R. R. Martin's series of fantasy novels *A Song of Ice and Fire*. Both the *Mahābhārata* and *Game of Thrones* feature endless numbers of characters, major family drama, royal succession disputes, queens who literally emerge from fire, and gruesome depictions of violence including but not limited to rape, beheading, maiming, and cannibalism. And both have inspired voluminous second-order literature, including commentarial and theoretical works, produced by professionals as well as amateurs.

7. In the Mahābhārata tradition, the number eighteen itself holds a certain weight: the battle of Kurukṣetra lasts eighteen days; the *Bhagavadgītā* has eighteen chapters; and the critical edition and vulgate recension of the Sanskrit *Mahābhārata* each consist of eighteen *parvans*, or books.

its interpreters more to tease out, more to experience, more to complicate or to resolve.[8] After all, as belief has it, there is something dangerous about a complete Mahābhārata. And so there are many of them; one is never enough. There are Mahābhāratas in Apabhramsha, Arabic, Assamese, Bengali, Gujarati, Hindi, Kannada, Konkani, Malayalam, Marathi, Nepali, Oriya, Persian, Prakrit, Punjabi, Sanskrit, Sindhi, Tamil, Telugu, Urdu, and countless other South Asian languages. They testify to the fact that when it comes to this story, there will always be more to say. And there will always be more ways to say it. The many Mahābhāratas that emerge from the Indian subcontinent include poems, plays, sculptures, paintings, novels, folk tales, short stories, comic books, essays, television shows, and films.

This desire for more—"always wanting these stories," in the words of passage from Nannaya's eleventh-century Telugu *Mahābhāratamu* quoted above[9]—is baked into the Sanskrit *Mahābhārata*'s own creation myth. There Gaṇeśa, the elephant-headed deity and the text's divine scribe, demands that the sage Vyāsa, the text's mythical author (and the grandfather of the story's main figures), dictate the *Mahābhārata* to him without interruption so that Gaṇeśa will not have to stop writing, even for a moment. Gaṇeśa, "always wanting these stories," becomes not only the *Mahābhārata*'s original hungry audience but also its original reteller, its transmitter from one medium to another. Already the myth links the desire for more of the *Mahābhārata* with the act of retelling it. And Gaṇeśa never finds satisfaction. Vyāsa makes a counteroffer (in the world of this *Mahābhārata*, everything is up for negotiation) and demands that Gaṇeśa comprehend each passage before writing it down. When Gaṇeśa seems to be getting ahead of the dictation, Vyāsa interrupts the flow of the narration with an especially complicated

8. As others have pointed out, the fact that the Mahābhārata evokes unending layers of dilemma, crisis, and struggle has contributed to the narrative's perpetual and universal relevance. If the Sanskrit *Mahābhārata* was, as David Gitomer argues, "the repository of crisis in classical India," then the work's robust survival in South Asia resulted (as both Gitomer and Sheldon Pollock suggest) from the perpetual relevance of its "war fought at home [in which] both sides must lose." See "King Duryodhana: The *Mahābhārata* Discourse of Sinning and Virtue in Epic and Drama," *Journal of the American Oriental Society* 112 (1992): 222; and Pollock, *Language of the Gods*, 225.

9. This is Velcheru Narayana Rao and David Shulman's translation in *Classical Telugu Poetry: An Anthology* (Berkeley: University of California Press, 2002), 59.

passage.[10] This call for perpetual interpretation—that Gaṇeśa make meaning out of each verse—would seem to be disruptive enough. But there is also the literary strategy of rupture per se—what Emily Hudson calls a "gap of meaning" in the narrative, a moment in the Mahābhārata story when a palpable "presence of absence" disorients the listener from her emotional and intellectual expectations.[11] The two outermost frame stories of the Sanskrit epic employ this idea of rupture in a more literal way.[12] In both frames, the narration of the *Mahābhārata* takes place during the pauses in an ongoing ritual: the *Mahābhārata* interrupts the ritual, and the ritual interrupts the *Mahābhārata*. All of these meta-narratives teach us that an essential part of reading (or hearing) the Mahābhārata is never getting quite enough of it, at least not as soon as one wants it—the story remains interrupted, incomplete, and maybe a little incomprehensible. That the epic claims to include "whatever exists"[13] and at the same time runs on the fuel of unfinished, unstable, unsatisfied things—stories, rituals, lineages, truths, audiences—is one of the tantalizing incongruities that propels the *Mahābhārata* forward into endless tellings.

What's more, the chapters in this book demonstrate that any Mahābhārata represents many Mahābhāratas. We have retellings inside retellings: four chapters explore Mahābhāratas that reconstruct the events of the *Virāṭaparvan*

---

10. Paul B. Courtright, *Gaṇeśa: Lord of Obstacles, Lord of Beginnings* (Oxford: Oxford University Press, 1985), 151–53. Courtright notes that this creation myth most likely postdates (by many centuries) the compilation of the Sanskrit *Mahābhārata.*

11. Emily T. Hudson, *Disorienting Dharma: Ethics and the Aesthetic of Suffering in the Mahābhārata* (New York: Oxford University Press, 2012), 22–23, 100–04.

12. On the frame stories of the Sanskrit *Mahābhārata*, see C. Z. Minkowski, "Janamejaya's *Sattra* and Ritual Structure," *Journal of the American Oriental Society* 109, no. 3 (1989): 401–20; and James W. Earl, *Beginning the Mahābhārata: A Reader's Guide to the Frame Stories* (Woodland Hills, CA: South Asian Studies Association, 2011).

13. *dharme cārthe ca kāme ca mokṣe ca bharatarṣabha |*
yad ihāsti tad anyatra yan nehāsti na tat kvacit || *MBh* 1.56.33, 18.5.38 ||

"When it comes to dharma, *artha* (wealth or power), *kāma* (desire), and *mokṣa* (liberation from the cycle of rebirth), what is here is elsewhere—but what is not here is not anywhere else." All references to the Sanskrit *Mahābhārata* (*MBh*) in this chapter are to the critical edition. Unless noted otherwise, all translations of the Sanskrit *Mahābhārata* and other primary texts cited in this chapter are our own.

("The Book of Virāṭa's Court"), a book of the Sanskrit *Mahābhārata* that self-consciously mirrors the epic as a whole. Other authors find it impossible to stop at one Mahābhārata, even though they know that the volume addresses over a dozen more. The process of organizing this book has taught us that when it comes to understanding the Mahābhārata, comparison—which drives every chapter in one way or another—becomes a particularly fruitful tool for interpretation. Clearly a comparative approach complements the multivocality that many Mahābhāratas embody.[14] Mahābhāratas often unfold through multiple narrative voices that diverge from and question one another. This intrinsic multivocality allows Mahābhāratas to mirror, on a formal level, the various conflicts that they depict. Even Mahābhāratas that present the narrative in an ethically and aesthetically straightforward manner, as some of the works in this volume do, are in some sense responding to this multivocal, "interrogative" mode of storytelling.[15]

---

14. The multivocality of the Mahābhārata tradition is beautifully illustrated in Balaji Srinivasan's painting *Draupadi* (2015), which is featured on the cover of this volume. *Draupadi* is painted in the style of the *Citrakathī* picture storytelling tradition that was once practiced in Maharashtra, Karnataka, and Andhra Pradesh. Srinivasan's painting displays five different forms of the Mahābhārata heroine Draupadī. The first two forms of Draupadī would be familiar to a pan-South Asian audience. First she appears as the fire-born princess of Pañcāla during her *svayaṃvara* (bridegroom-choice ceremony). Then, in what the artist has called "the oath," Draupadī appears as the queen of Indraprastha—surrounded by yards of miraculously replenished clothing, hair flowing freely—vowing not to rebind her hair until she can comb into it the blood of Duḥśāsana (and/or, in certain tellings, Duryodhana). This second Draupadī would be recognized particularly in South India, where the oath has long been a feature of Draupadī's storyline. See Alf Hiltebeitel, "Draupadī's Hair," in *Essays by Alf Hiltebeitel*, vol. 2, *When the Goddess was a Woman: Mahābhārata Ethnographies*, eds. Vishwa Adluri and Joydeep Bagchee (Leiden: Brill, 2011), 3–7. The other three forms in the painting are inspired by unique representations of Draupadī from the *Terukkūttu* performances of the Draupadī goddess cult in Tamil Nadu. At the center of the painting, Srinivasan presents Draupadī as a *kuṛavañci* (fortune teller) preparing to tell the Kaurava women their fortunes. (Sahadeva is disguised as a baby on her hip.) Then we see Draupadī as the fearsome goddess Kālī, who sucks blood from the battleground of Kurukṣetra at night. On the far right, we arrive at Draupadī Amman̲, a beautiful local deity with a parrot on her hand who is worshiped in northern Tamil Nadu. See Alf Hiltebeitel, *The Cult of Draupadī*, vol. 1, *Mythologies: From Gingee to Kurukṣetra* (Chicago: University of Chicago Press, 1988), 303, 291, and 263.

15. "Interrogative" is Shubha Pathak's term. See *Divine Yet Human Epics,* 174.

There are no categorical boundaries that the Mahābhārata does not overstep. The chapters in this book show that the Mahābhārata has been both elite and popular, Hindu and non-Hindu, classical and vernacular, orthodox and heterodox, constructive and destructive, textual and performative, fragmented and whole, normative and subversive, and affirmative and surprising. For some of the interpretive communities featured in this book, the Mahābhārata defines these categories. For others, the Mahābhārata dismantles these terms of analysis entirely. To anyone who insists that the Mahābhārata is one thing or another, we present the astounding magnitude and heterogeneity of this literary cosmos. If there is "a" Mahābhārata, it is transhistorical, translinguistic, transmedial; it is a Mahābhārata that insists on engendering more Mahābhāratas.

The Story

We first conceived of this book as one answer (among many, of course) to the enduring questions of just what the Mahābhārata is, does, and says. There will be many answers to this mega-question, and many of them will presume many Mahābhāratas. Even the title, "Mahābhārata," suggesting a unified body of text, hides a plural behind its ever-so-gossamer veil. "Mahābhārata," after all, means "the Great Bhāratas." Still one might ask: Is there not a single core story of these great Bhāratas? Let's begin by expounding the story most people assume.[16]

The nuclear tale of most well-known Mahābhāratas goes something like this. After the death of Pāṇḍu, the former ruler of the Bhārata empire, a fierce rivalry is born between two sets of royal cousins, all in the Kuru family: the five Pāṇḍavas (Yudhiṣṭhira, Bhīma, Arjuna, Nakula, and Sahadeva) and the one hundred Kauravas, who are led by the formidable Duryodhana and the obsequious Duḥśāsana.[17] While "Pāṇḍava" literally means "son of Pāṇḍu," the five princes are actually the offspring of Pāṇḍu's

16. For detailed summaries of the story of the Sanskrit *Mahābhārata*, we recommend: *The Mahābhārata: An Abridged Translation*, trans. John D. Smith (London: Penguin Books, 2009), xv–xviii; and Hudson, *Disorienting Dharma*, 10–20.

17. For a hilarious song that lists the names of all one hundred Kauravas, see SnG Comedy, "SnG: The Kaurava Song," YouTube video, 2:52, June 24, 2014, https://www.youtube.com/watch?v=t1whAeFHW_s.

two wives, Kuntī and Mādrī, as impregnated by five Vedic deities. (Pāṇḍu himself is unable to father children—the result of a curse.)[18] The Kauravas are the sons of King Dhṛtarāṣṭra, Pāṇḍu's blind elder brother, and his wife, Gāndhārī.[19]

After the Pāṇḍavas survive a fiery assassination attempt in a lac palace and jointly marry an equally fiery princess named Draupadī,[20] Dhṛtarāṣṭra divides the kingdom among his sons and nephews. The Pāṇḍavas build a magnificent city called Indraprastha, where Yudhiṣṭhira, the son of the god Dharma (Righteousness), asserts his universal kingship through an elaborate consecration ritual. The prosperous rule of the Pāṇḍavas comes tumbling down, however, when Yudhiṣṭhira gambles and loses to the Kauravas. In a game of dice played against Duryodhana and Duryodhana's maternal uncle Śakuni, Yudhiṣṭhira forfeits his wealth, his brothers, himself, and Draupadī. In most Mahābhāratas, Draupadī emotionally anchors the dicing scene. Some have argued that she is really the center of the story, its linchpin. Let's be agnostic about that as a general statement, but because this aspect of the overall story sits at the core of several Mahābhāratas discussed in this book, we must pause to review it in some detail.

Duryodhana and Duḥśāsana force Draupadī to appear before the kings, elders, and family members who have gathered in the assembly hall to observe the dicing. There, the most prominent Kaurava warriors attack Draupadī verbally and harm her physically; Duḥśāsana drags her by the hair,

---

18. In most Mahābhāratas, Nakula and Sahadeva are the twin sons of the Aśvins (the twin Vedic deities of medicine) and Mādrī. In the *Pāṇḍavlīlā* performance tradition in Uttarakhand, however, Nakula is regarded as the biological son of Pāṇḍu and Mādrī. Similarly, in Sabalsingh Cauhān's Hindi *Mahābhārat*, Sahadeva is the actual son of Pāṇḍu and Mādrī. See William S. Sax, *Dancing the Self: Personhood and Performance in the Pāṇḍav Līlā of Garhwal* (New York: Oxford University Press, 2002), 63; and Sabalsingh Cauhān, *Sabalsingh Cauhān-Viracit Mahābhārat* (Lucknow: Tej Kumar Book Depot, 2015), 23.

19. While the term "Kaurava" means "descendent of Kuru" and can therefore technically refer to the Pāṇḍavas, who also belong to the Kuru clan, the name "Kaurava" usually refers to the one hundred sons of Dhṛtarāṣṭra.

20. As Jonathan Geen has shown, Mahābhāratas from the Digambara Jain religious tradition "insist that Draupadī married Arjuna alone, and that the rumour of her marriage to five men must be considered absurd, scandalous, and unequivocally false." See "The Marriage of Draupadī in the Hindu and Jaina Mahābhārata," (PhD diss., McMaster University, 2001), 173.

and Duryodhana shows her his thigh (a sexual advance). Draupadī protests not only the insults that the Kaurava warriors hurl at her, but also everyone else's failure to intervene.[21] The most iconic part of the story unfolds when Duḥśāsana attempts to remove the garment that Draupadī is wearing. He tries to strip it away, but another one always appears in its place. Over and over he tries, but a new garment appears every time. Many Mahābhāratas attribute this wonder to the intervention of Kṛṣṇa (an incarnation of the Hindu deity Viṣṇu, who is also the Pāṇḍavas' maternal cousin and closest advisor); the critical edition of the Sanskrit *Mahābhārata* does not. In any case, after this ordeal, Dhṛtarāṣṭra restores to the Pāṇḍavas all that was lost. But this reinstatement of an earlier balance is short-lived. Yudhiṣṭhira loses in a second game of dice. According to the terms of *this* game, the five brothers and Draupadī are forced to live in exile in the forest for twelve years followed by another year of living incognito, which they elect to do at the court of King Virāṭa.

After several failed peace negotiations, the Pāṇḍavas and the Kauravas prepare for war. But before the battle commences, Arjuna, the most skilled warrior in the Pāṇḍava army, holds back. In response, his charioteer Kṛṣṇa tells him a great deal about philosophy and social theory and persuades him to fight. This is the famous *Bhagavadgītā*. In the course of a brutal eighteen-day war, which takes place at Kurukṣetra (literally "the field of the Kurus"), Bhīma, the strongest of the Pāṇḍava brothers, kills all one hundred Kauravas. Under the guidance of Kṛṣṇa, the Pāṇḍavas and their allies also defeat the four generals of the Kaurava army: Bhīṣma (the patriarch of the Kuru clan), Droṇa (the Pāṇḍavas and the Kauravas' teacher), Karṇa (Duryodhana's closest friend, who, unbeknownst to the Pāṇḍavas, is the eldest son of their mother, Kuntī), and Śalya (the Pāṇḍavas' maternal uncle through their other mother, Mādrī).

By the end of this apocalyptic war, nearly all of its participants—including Bhīma's son, Ghaṭotkaca, and Arjuna's sons, Irāvān and Abhimanyu—are dead. Yet the carnage does not stop. In the night, Droṇa's son Aśvatthāman sneaks into the Pāṇḍava camp and slaughters the remaining survivors, including Draupadī's brothers Dhṛṣṭadyumna and Śikhaṇḍin and all of her five sons, each one begotten with one of the Pāṇḍavas. In

21. "The old, eternal dharma of the Kurus has been destroyed," she says in *MBh* 2.62.9.

order to wipe out the lineage completely, Aśvatthāman releases a celestial weapon into the womb of Abhimanyu's pregnant widow, Uttarā. Kṛṣṇa later intervenes in this disaster. He revives Uttarā's stillborn son and the Pāṇḍavas' heir, Parikṣit.

Several Mahābhāratas—from Kumāravyāsa's fifteenth-century Kannada poem *Karṇāṭabhāratakathāmañjarī* ("The Essence of the Bhārata Story in Kannada") to the 2013 animated Bollywood film *Mahābhārat*—end with the conclusion of the battle at Kurukṣetra. The Sanskrit *Mahābhārata* and many other tellings, however, explore the aftermath of this bloody war. After the Kuru women mourn the dead, Kṛṣṇa brings Yudhiṣṭhira to the dying Bhīṣma, who gives Yudhiṣṭhira an extensive lecture on kingship, dharma, and *mokṣa* (freedom from the cycle of rebirth). After Yudhiṣṭhira's brothers, together with Draupadī and Kṛṣṇa, exhort him to reassert his political power, Yudhiṣṭhira performs a horse sacrifice to atone for his wrongdoing in battle and establish rulership once again.

Many years later, Dhṛtarāṣṭra, Gāndhārī, and Kuntī retire to a hermitage in the forest, where they eventually die in a fire. All the members of Kṛṣṇa's clan, the Vṛṣṇis, murder one another in a drunken brawl; Kṛṣṇa himself is accidentally killed by a hunter. The Pāṇḍavas and Draupadī embark on a final journey during which all but Yudhiṣṭhira perish. Yudhiṣṭhira reaches heaven, where he finds Duryodhana—the most meager of happy endings. But when he learns that the other Pāṇḍavas and Draupadī are suffering in hell, he insists on joining his loved ones there. It is then revealed that hell is an illusion, and Yudhiṣṭhira is reunited with his family in heaven.[22] Thus a sense of ambiguity reigns over the story to the end: What is real, and what is not?

The Mahābhārata Genre

Does a composition need to tell this story in order to be considered a Mahābhārata, and does it need to tell *only* this story? Consider, for example, the Jain narratives that integrate the story of the Pāṇḍavas into their

22. On the endings of the Sanskrit epic and other Sanskrit Mahābhārata tellings, see Naama Shalom, *Re-ending the Mahābhārata: The Rejection of Dharma in the Sanskrit Epic* (Albany: State University of New York Press, 2017).

more sweeping accounts of the lives of Kṛṣṇa and his cousin, Neminātha, the twenty-second *tīrthaṅkara* (Jain teacher). In the earliest of these texts, Jinasena Punnāṭa's Sanskrit *Harivaṃśapurāṇa* ("The Legend of Hari's Lineage," ca. 783), after the Kauravas are defeated (but not killed) by the Pāṇḍavas in the great war, the hundred brothers renounce their earthly possessions and become ascetics.[23] Two remarkably similar poems, Bhīm Kavi's Hindi *Ḍaṅgvaikathā* ("The Story of Ḍaṅgvai," ca. 1493) and Carigoṇḍa Dharmanna's Telugu *Citrabhāratamu* ("The Peculiar Bhārata," ca. 1500), depict the Pāṇḍavas and the Kauravas joining forces to wage battle with Kṛṣṇa in order to save the life of a local king.[24] The Sanskrit drama *Pañcarātra* ("The Five Nights," ca. 200–800) is still more radical in its departure from the central story line. There the feuding cousins avoid the war at Kurukṣetra entirely. Still other works ignore all but one or two characters—Karṇa, for example, or Aśvatthāman, Kuntī, or Ghaṭotkaca—and others engage shorter, more self-contained installments from the Mahābhārata narrative corpus, such as the stories of Śakuntalā, Sāvitrī, or Nala and Damayantī.[25]

23. Eva De Clercq, "The Jaina *Harivaṃśa* and *Mahābhārata* Tradition: A Preliminary Survey," in *Parallels and Comparisons in the Sanskrit Epics and Purāṇas*, ed. P. Koskikallio (Zagreb: Croatian Academy of Sciences and Arts, 2008), 404.

24. See Francesca Orsini, "Texts and Tellings: *Kathas* in the Fifteenth and Sixteenth Centuries," in *Tellings and Texts: Music, Literature and Performance in North India*, eds. Francesca Orsini and Katherine Butler Schofield (Cambridge, UK: Open Book Publishers, 2015), 337–46; and E. Vasumati, *Telugu Literature in the Qutub Shahi Period* (Hyderabad: Abul Kalam Azad Oriental Research Institute, n.d., ca. 1960), 19–53. We find similar stories in Haḷēmakki Rāma's seventeenth-century *Yakṣagāna* play *Gaya Carite*, the Tamil ballad poems *Pañcapāṇṭavar Vaṉavācam* and *Kurukṣēttira Mālai*, and the 1963 Telugu film *Śrīkṛṣṇārjuna Yuddhamu*. See K. Shivarama Karantha, *Yakṣagāna* (Delhi: Abhinav Publications, 1997), 245–46; and M. Arunachalam, *Ballad Poetry* (Thanjavur: Saraswati Mahal Library, 1976), 108.

25. For some examples of this, see Ahona Panda, "What Karna and Kunti Talked about the Night before the Battle of Kurukshetra," *Scroll.in*, November 8, 2015, https://scroll.in/article/767802; Amruta Patil, *Sauptik: Blood and Flowers* (Noida: HarperCollins Publishers India, 2016); Romila Thapar, *Śakuntalā: Texts, Readings, Histories* (London: Anthem Press, 1999); Amanda Louise Culp, "Searching for Shakuntala: Sanskrit Drama and Theatrical Modernity in Europe and India, 1789–Present," (PhD diss., Columbia University, 2018); and Aurobindo, *Savitri: A Legend and a Symbol* (Twin Lakes, WI: Lotus Press, 1995).

Are these compositions, so many of which refrain from calling themselves anything resembling "Mahābhārata," in fact Mahābhāratas?

Sometimes being a Mahābhārata means that a work shares certain motifs (characters, structures, relationships, themes) with the story we have outlined here—a story with which all of the audiences we consider in this book would have been (or are) intimately familiar. Perhaps we can be content with the idea that sometimes being a Mahābhārata means being a work that relates to the central "core" story, or to other Mahābhāratas that embody it. But there are many different ways in which this can be done. To follow in A. K. Ramanujan's deeply imprinted footsteps, we might delineate these relationships as responsive, reflexive, or self-reflexive;[26] or again, following Ramanujan, we might call them iconic, indexical, or symbolic.[27] In the end, we would propose, the novels, plays, poems, essays, chronicles, and short stories studied in this book become most meaningful when we leave aside these formal constraints and experience them first and foremost *as Mahābhāratas*, that is, when we embed them in the ever-growing ecosystem of Mahābhārata-related works. The important thing isn't whether a composition "is" a Mahābhārata or calls itself one, but whether the value of interpreting that work increases as a result of putting it into conversation with other Mahābhāratas. We would argue that it almost always does, and often with a sense of discovery that feels like crystallization.

We are not the first to propose that this is so. This is precisely the move that the Sanskrit literary theorist Ānandavardhana (ca. 850 CE) made in relation to the *Harivaṃśa*—"Hari's Lineage," a 16,000-verse Sanskrit account of the lives of Kṛṣṇa and his descendants, along with related cosmological myths. Ānandavardhana described the interpretive advantage of reading in close relation to the Sanskrit *Mahābhārata* by taking the *Harivaṃśa*'s own claim that it continues the epic and going a step further.[28] "It is true," he writes, that

26. A. K. Ramanujan, "Where Mirrors are Windows: Toward an Anthology of Reflections," *History of Religions* 28, no. 3 (1989): 189.

27. A. K. Ramanujan, "Three Hundred *Rāmāyaṇas*: Five Examples and Three Thoughts on Translation," in *Many Rāmāyaṇas: The Diversity of a Narrative Tradition in South Asia*, ed. Paula Richman (Berkeley: University of California Press, 1991), 44–45.

28. The *Harivaṃśa* (probably composed over the early centuries CE) takes on the same two outermost frame stories of the Sanskrit *Mahābhārata*. Like the *Mahābhārata*, the *Harivaṃśa* falls into a number of genre categories. Explorations

> the principal role of serenity in the *Mahābhārata* and the importance of *mokṣa* over all human aims are not displayed in the *Mahābhārata*'s initial listing of its subject matter, at least not in so many words. But they are displayed through suggestion . . . And this very meaning that was beautiful and hidden is made perfectly clear (when it was not before) by the creator of the poem, Vyāsa, when he himself creates a resolution at the end of the *Mahābhārata* by offering us the *Harivaṃśa*.[29]

For Ānandavardhana, the *Harivaṃśa* brings out the *Mahābhārata*'s subtextual Kṛṣṇa-centricity, which allows the audience to appreciate the most "beautiful and hidden" meanings of the epic: its ethos of serenity[30] and its lessons about release from the cycle of existence.[31] It is not the individ-

---

of its participation in the major contenders—*mahākāvya*, *purāṇa*, and *khila* (an appendix)—along with critical essays on its poetic style, structural features, narrative contents, and history can be found in Daniel H. H. Ingalls, "The *Harivaṃśa* as a *Mahākāvya*," in *Mélanges d'Indianisme à la mémoire de Louis Renou* (Paris: Éditions de Boccard, 1968), 381–94; and André Couture, *Kṛṣṇa in the Harivaṃśa*, 2 vols. (Delhi: D.K. Printworld, 2015–17). For a recent translation, see *Krishna's Lineage: The Harivamsha of Vyāsa's Mahābhārata*, trans. Simon Brodbeck (New York: Oxford University Press, 2019).

29. *satyaṃ śāntasyaiva rasasyāṅgitvaṃ mahābhārate mokṣasya ca sarvapuruṣārthebhyaḥ prādhānyam ity etan na svaśabdābhidheyatvenānukramaṇyāṃ darśitaṃ, darśitaṃ tu vyaṇgyatvena . . . ayaṃ ca nigūḍharamaṇīyo 'rtho mahābhāratāvasāne harivaṃśavarṇanena samāptiṃ vidadhatā tenaiva kavivedhasā kṛṣṇadvaipāyanena samyak sphuṭīkṛtaḥ* | *Dhvanyāloka*, 276 (*vṛtti* on 4.5). All references to the *Dhvanyāloka* in this chapter are to Ānandavardhana, *The Dhvanyāloka of Ānandavardhana*, ed. K. Krishnamoorthy (Dharwad: Karnatak University, 1974).

30. A working translation of *śānta-rasa* in this context. See Gary A. Tubb, "*Śāntarasa* in the *Mahābhārata*," in *Essays on the Mahābhārata*, ed. Arvind Sharma (Leiden: E. J. Brill, 1991), 171–203. Lawrence McCrea writes that *śānta-rasa* "has as its emotional basis the cessation of all desires" and, later on, clarifies that indifference is still an emotional response. See *The Teleology of Poetics in Medieval Kashmir* (Cambridge, MA: Harvard University Press, 2008), 132 and 243. For more on the paradox of feeling non-feeling, see Edwin Gerow, "Abhinavagupta's Aesthetics as a Speculative Paradigm," *Journal of the American Oriental Society* 114, no. 2 (1994): 186–208.

31. See *Dhvanyāloka*, 272–82 (*vṛtti* on 4.5). For a full translation of this section, see Ānandavardhana, *The Dhvanyāloka of Ānandavardhana with the Locana of Abhinavagupta*, trans. Daniel H. H. Ingalls, Jeffrey Moussaieff Masson, and M. V.

ual works but the conversation between them that speaks to this deeper understanding. Over a millennium later, Wendy Doniger used the concept of conversation to describe the value of reading intertextually. Whether it involves "conscious quotation" or a more unconscious kind of representation, she writes, the idea of intertextuality enables us to "eavesdrop on the conversations between storytellers centuries and continents apart."[32]

How we listen to this conversation matters, too. Ramanujan speaks of genre as a special way of listening, one that requires hearing "radially" so as to take in other works even when listening to one in particular. Here is how he describes classical Tamil poems:

> Every poem resonates with the absent presence of others that sound with it, like the unstruck strings of a sitar. So we respond to a system of presences and absences; our reading then is not linear but what has been called "radial." Every poem is part of a large self-reflexive paradigm; it relates to all others in absentia, gathers ironies, allusions; one text becomes the context of others. Each is precisely foregrounded against a background of all the others.[33]

In the spirit of Ramanujan's model, above, we propose to read the Mahābhārata tradition as if it constituted a genre of its own. (Ramanujan himself said something similar of the Rāmāyaṇa tradition: it is "not merely a set of individual texts, but a genre with a variety of instances."[34]) Mahābhāratas shape "a system of presences and absences" based on recurring characters, relationships, stories, themes, and aesthetics; when we experience a Mahābhārata, we respond—whether we are aware of it or not—to the presence, absence, inversion, subversion, or reformation of these shared features that frame our expectations. Engaging with the

---

Patwardhan (Cambridge, MA: Harvard University Press, 1990), 690–96.

32. Wendy Doniger, *The Woman Who Pretended to Be Who She Was: Myths of Self-Imitation* (New York: Oxford University Press, 2005), 7.

33. Ramanujan, "Where Mirrors are Windows," 197. On the term "radial," Ramanujan cites Jerome J. McGann, "Theory of Texts," *London Review of Books* 10, no. 4 (1988): 21.

34. Ramanujan, "Three Hundred *Rāmāyaṇas*," 45.

Mahābhārata as a genre would prompt us to listen for such resonances across languages, regions, religions, cultures, and all kinds of historical contexts. The broader goal of *Many Mahābhāratas*, then, is to facilitate this kind of listening. By representing the Mahābhārata as a transmedial, transhistorical, translinguistic, and transdisciplinary mode of expression in South Asia, this book will, we hope, enable the reader to listen closely to a given interpretation of the Mahābhārata while hearing a polyphony of absent tellings in the background.

A Contextual Introduction to the Essays

The sections of this volume reflect a roughly chronological progression of Mahābhārata representations that appear across a range of South Asian literary, religious, historical, social, and political contexts. Of course, we cannot include reflections on *every* Mahābhārata; such a book would end up being longer than the Sanskrit *Mahābhārata* itself. In order to keep the length of the book in check—and to escape the long-standing curse that is said to befall those who take on the epic as a whole—we explore but a tiny fraction of extant Mahābhāratas. For one thing, we restrict the scope of our primary sources to Mahābhāratas of South Asian origin. Also, we tend to prioritize less "accessible" Mahābhāratas—works that a reader might seek help understanding or appreciating if she happened to come across them on her own, or simply to hear of their existence. For this reason, the volume contains a significant number of essays on premodern Mahābhāratas in less commonly known languages—Apabhramsha, Old Kannada, Sanskrit, and so on—many of them as yet untranslated into English. Within those bounds, we have endeavored to make our collection of sources representative of different languages, historical periods, media, and genres. We have also been eager to exhibit a range of disciplinary and interdisciplinary approaches to the material—reflective, we believe, of the Mahābhārata's remarkable reach across the field of South Asian studies.

Part I: The Manyness of the Sanskrit *Mahābhārata*

Taken together, the chapters in the first part of the volume argue that themes of multiplicity and retelling emerge from, and indeed define, the Sanskrit *Mahābhārata* itself. It is important to point out that while we speak of "the" Sanskrit epic *Mahābhārata*—something that we say not only for convenience but also to honor the aesthetic cohesion of the Sanskrit *Mahābhārata* corpus—there are, in fact, many Sanskrit *Mahābhāratas*. First we have the epic's northern and southern recensions, which themselves represent multi-branch manuscript traditions rather than single texts.[35] Then we find that the text we nowadays call the "vulgate" *Mahābhārata*, produced by the seventeenth-century scholar Nīlakaṇṭha, is not just that, but also an exhaustive commentary that he composed to accompany it.[36] Nīlakaṇṭha's was not the earliest commentary on the epic, but it is the only complete commentary to which we have access. Then comes the twentieth-century critical edition of the epic, constructed at the Bhandarkar Oriental Research Institute under the direction of V. S. Sukthankar.[37] And there are many more "thens" we could add to the list. The Sanskrit *Mahābhārata* thus presents us with multiples beyond measure. The hundreds of written and oral accounts of the Sanskrit epic demonstrate that it "flickers back and forth between Sanskrit manuscripts and village storytellers, each adding new gemstones to the old mosaic, constantly reinterpreting it," Doniger writes.[38] In the volume's third chapter, David Gitomer leads us through a spectacular exam-

---

35. See Thennilapuram P. Mahadevan, "On the Southern Recension of the *Mahābhārata*, Brahman Migrations, and the Brāhmī Paleography," *Electronic Journal of Vedic Studies* 15, no. 2 (2008): 43–147; and Wendy J. Phillips-Rodriguez, "Unrooted Trees: A Way around the Dilemma of Recension," in *Papers of the 13th World Sanskrit Conference,* vol. 2, *Battle, Bards and Brāhmins*, ed. John Brockington (Delhi: Motilal Banarsidass, 2012), 217–29.

36. See Christopher Minkowski, "What Makes a Work 'Traditional'? On the Success of Nīlakaṇṭha's *Mahābhārata* Commentary" in *Boundaries, Dynamics, and Construction of Traditions*, ed. Federico Squarcini (Florence: Firenze University Press, 2005), 225–44; and C. Minkowski, "Nīlakaṇṭha's Mahābhārata," *Seminar* 608 (2010): 32–38.

37. For some different perspectives on the critical edition of the epic, see M. A. Mehendale, "The Critical Edition of the Mahābhārata: Its Constitution, Achievements, and Limitations," in *Texts and Variations of the Mahābhārata: Contextual, Regional, and Performative Traditions,* ed. Kalyan Kumar Chakravarty (Delhi: National Mission for Manuscripts, 2009), 3–23; Simon Brodbeck, "Analytic and Synthetic Approaches in Light of the Critical Edition of the *Mahābhārata* and *Harivaṃśa*," *Journal of Vaishnava Studies* 19, no. 2 (2011): 223–50; and Vishwa Adluri and Joydeep Bagchee, *Philology and Criticism: A Guide to Mahābhārata Textual Criticism* (New York: Anthem Press, 2018).

38. Wendy Doniger, *The Hindus: An Alternative History* (New York: Viking Penguin, 2009), 263–64.

ple of how one such "gemstone"—the story of Irāvān, Arjuna's half-serpent son—both reflects the stories connected with a better-known figure in the epic, Bhīma's half-*rākṣasa* or "demon" son, Ghaṭotkaca, and also develops the narrative structure of the epic's sixth book, the *Bhīṣmaparvan* ("The Book of Bhīṣma").

Whether mammoth or miniature, the many versions of the Sanskrit *Mahābhārata* reflect a profound awareness of one another. "Anyone who added anything to the *Mahabharata* was well aware of the whole textual tradition behind it," Doniger explains, "and fitted his or her own insight, or story, or long philosophical disquisition, thoughtfully into the ongoing conversation."[39] Sheldon Pollock highlights the epic's remarkable uniformity throughout the first millennium when he observes that "the unmistakable impression given by hundreds of medieval manuscripts copied time and again for centuries on end is that the *Mahābhārata*, just like Sanskrit itself, existed in a quasi-universal trans-regional space and spoke across this space in an entirely homogenous voice."[40] In this sense, one might speak of the Sanskrit *Mahābhārata* as embodying a single authorial voice, as Sally J. Sutherland Goldman does in the fourth chapter, when she draws upon multiple sources of the Sanskrit epic—the critical edition, the vulgate, Nīlakaṇṭha's commentary, and two English translations—to analyze the relationship between gender and character narration in "Vyāsa's" *Mahābhārata*.

Yet we must always keep the manyness in view, as Robert Goldman does in the book's second chapter. Taking seriously Ramanujan's assertion that narrative reflexivity forms the aesthetic architecture of the epic,[41] he explores a mode of repetition in the Sanskrit *Mahābhārata* that has so far escaped the commentator's eye. Goldman analyzes two of the most prominent motifs in the epic's narrative framework—revenge and attempted genocide—and shows how they are replicated through the Sanskrit epic. Later in the book we will see that many Mahābhāratas beyond the Sanskrit orbit confront these centrally positioned themes, evoking a world helplessly caught up in the momentum of its own self-destruction.[42] Some try to rescue that world from its downward spiral—a seemingly monumental task.

39. Doniger, 264.

40. Pollock, *Language of the Gods*, 229.

41. A. K. Ramanujan, "Repetition in the *Mahābhārata*," in *Essays on the Mahābhārata*, ed. Arvind Sharma (Leiden: E. J. Brill, 1991), 421–26.

42. We thank Robert Goldman for the language and the idea in the second part of this sentence.

Part II: Sanskrit Mahābhāratas in Poetry and Performance

The chapters that form the second part of this volume expand our definition of "Sanskrit Mahābhārata" far beyond the early epic poem. This is a necessary task, for the characters and stories of the Mahābhārata virtually saturate the fabric of Sanskrit literature. Some of the best-known works of classical Sanskrit *kāvya*, comprising the arena of poetry and drama, focus their attention on some of the relatively self-contained stories that emerge from the Mahābhārata corpus. Kālidāsa's drama *Abhijñānaśākuntala* ("The Recognition of Śakuntalā," ca. 400 CE) is one particularly famous example, but three celebrated *mahākāvya*s (ornate, multi-chapter poems that follow narrative arcs) do the same. We have Bhāravi's *Kirātārjunīya* ("Arjuna and the Hunter," sixth century), Māgha's *Śiśupālavadha* ("The Slaying of Śiśupāla," seventh century), and Śrīharṣa's *Naiṣadhīyacarita* ("The Adventures of the Naiṣadha King," twelfth century).[43] Meanwhile, many Mahābhāratas were voiced in Sanskrit literary genres with which readers are ordinarily less familiar: epitomes, bitextual poems (many of which narrate the Mahābhārata and the Rāmāyaṇa simultaneously), and mixed prose-poems (*campū*s).[44]

43. See Bhāravi, *Arjuna and the Hunter*, ed. and trans. Indira Viswanathan Peterson, Murty Classical Library of India (Cambridge, MA: Harvard University Press, 2016); Indira Viswanathan Peterson, *Design and Rhetoric in a Sanskrit Court Epic: The Kirātārjunīya of Bhāravi* (Albany: State University of New York Press, 2003); Māgha, *The Killing of Shishupala*, ed. and trans. Paul Dundas, Murty Classical Library of India (Cambridge, MA: Harvard University Press, 2016); and Deven Patel, *Text to Tradition: The Naiṣadhīyacarita and Literary Community in South Asia* (New York: Columbia University Press, 2014).

44. A few examples in roughly chronological order: Vāsudeva's *Nalodaya* and *Yudhiṣṭhiravijaya* and Dhanañjaya's *Dvisandhānakāvya* (ninth century); Trivikrama Bhaṭṭa Bāṇa's *Nalacampū*, Nīlakaṇṭha's *Kalyāṇasaugandhika*, and Rājaśekhara's *Bālabhārata* (tenth century); Kṣemendra's *Bhāratamañjarī* and Anantabhaṭṭa's *Bhāratacampū* (eleventh century); Kavirāja's *Rāghavapāṇḍavīya*, Śrutakīrti Traividya's *Rāghavapāṇḍavīya*, and Hemacandra's *Saptasandhānakāvya* (twelfth century); Rāmacandra's *Nalavilāsa* and *Yādavābhyudaya*, Amaracandrasūri's *Bālabhārata*, and Agastya Paṇḍita's *Bālabhārata* (thirteenth century); Viśvanātha's *Saugandhikāharaṇa* (fourteenth century); and Melputtūr Nārāyaṇa Bhaṭṭa's *Bhārataprabandha* (seventeenth century). For more on these works, see Yigal Bronner, *Extreme Poetry: The South Asian Movement of Simultaneous Narration* (New York: Columbia University Press, 2010), 91–152; and Shalom, *Re-ending the Mahābhārata*, 70–80.

Other compositions take on the Mahābhārata's central narrative and engage with its themes of dilemma and decay. In one influential study, Yigal Bronner shows how Nītivarman's *Kīcakavadha* ("The Slaying of Kīcaka," ca. 600) transposes the epic's evocation of fragmented identities into the "disguised language" of *śleṣa* (simultaneous narration) in poetry.[45] The same fragmentation casts its shadow across Bhaṭṭa Nārāyaṇa's *Veṇīsaṃhāra* ("The Binding of the Braid," ca. 700), a play that depicts events from the epic in alternating perspectives. One act unfolds from the perspective of the Kauravas, the next from that of the Pāṇḍavas, back and forth. David Gitomer has argued that this play really consists of two plays: one in which the Pāṇḍavas are victorious heroes, and one in which the Kauravas are tragic heroes. This is *śleṣa* again, but in a markedly different way. The fact that the *Veṇīsaṃhāra* presents not a single dramatic path but something more like a dramatic discourse, or conversation between plots, allows the drama to import (in Gitomer's words) "at least something of that epic's eschatology which, on its more original socio-political level, is [an eschatology] of disintegration and human failure."[46] Meanwhile, Lawrence McCrea has shown that a similar ethos governs the twelfth-century Kashmiri poet Kalhaṇa's *Rājataraṅgiṇī* ("The River of Kings"). While Kalhaṇa does not use the figures and stories of the Sanskrit *Mahābhārata* in the *Rājataraṅgiṇī* directly, he consciously applies the *Mahābhārata*'s illustrations of immorality and decline to the kings whose reigns he describes.[47]

These studies bring us to the threshold of the fifth chapter in our volume. There, Nell Shapiro Hawley directs our attention to one of the six anonymous Mahābhārata plays that were recovered in Kerala in 1910 and initially attributed to Bhāsa (ca. 200), the *Pañcarātra*.[48] These Bhāsa

45. Bronner, *Extreme Poetry*, 58–81.

46. David L. Gitomer, "The 'Veṇīsaṃhāra' of Bhaṭṭa Nārāyaṇa: The Great Epic as Drama," (PhD diss., Columbia University, 1988), 495.

47. Lawrence McCrea, "*Śāntarasa* in the *Rājataraṅgiṇī*: History, Epic, and Moral Decay," *Indian Economic and Social History Review* 50 (2013): 179–99.

48. On the date and authorship of these six Mahābhārata-inspired dramas, see Heidrun Brückner, "Manuscripts and Performance Traditions of the so-called Trivandrum Plays ascribed to Bhāsa—A Report on Work in Progress," *Bulletin d'études indiennes* 17–18 (1999–2000): 501–50; and Herman Tieken, "The So-Called Trivandrum Plays Attributed to Bhāsa," *Wiener Zeitschrift für die Kunde Südasiens und Archiv für Indische Philosophie* 37 (1993): 5–44. A counterpoint

dramas, like others we have described, demonstrate a strong commitment to representing both the ethos of disintegration and the aesthetics of mirroring and repetition that characterize the Sanskrit epic itself. Of the six plays, five give life to the Kaurava experience of the events surrounding the war at Kurukṣetra. The *Karṇabhāra* ("Karṇa's Burden") dramatizes the story in which Karṇa severs from his body his inborn armor and earrings and gives them to Indra (the king of the gods and Arjuna's father), who disguises himself as a *brāhmaṇa* (Brahmin) begging for alms.[49] In the *Dūtavākya* ("The Messenger's Words"), Duryodhana and Kṛṣṇa rehearse the events that have led their respective sides of the family to the brink of war. Kṛṣṇa ultimately reveals his cosmic powers to Duryodhana, but the revelation only leads them closer to war. The second messenger play in the corpus, the *Dūtaghaṭotkaca* ("Ghaṭotkaca the Messenger"), brings Ghaṭotkaca to the Kaurava camp near the end of the war. In the *Dūtaghaṭotkaca*, the anger of the *Dūtavākya* morphs into a series of laments over the war's many deaths. Ghaṭotkaca then takes center stage in the *Madhyamavyāyoga* ("The Middle Brother"), the only one of the dramas to follow only the Pāṇḍavas. It is set during the Pāṇḍavas' period of exile and sets in motion a recognition drama between Ghaṭotkaca and Bhīma.[50] Bhīma (or at least the idea of him, since he does not stand among the play's *dramatis personae*) reappears in the *Ūrubhaṅga* ("The Breaking of the Thighs"), which takes the theme of brokenness as its starting point and its endpoint. The first half of the drama unfolds through the eyes of three soldiers who witness Bhīma breaking Duryodhana's thighs (and, figuratively, breaking dharma). The second half features a series of emotional separations between Duryo-

---

to the positions of Brückner and Tieken, if one that predates their research, can be found in V. S. Sukthankar, "Studies in Bhāsa" in *V. S. Sukthankar Memorial Edition*, vol. 2, *Analecta*, ed. P. K. Gode (Bombay: Karnatak Publishing House, 1945), 82–184.

49. See *Karṇabhāra: The Trial of Karṇa,* trans. Barbara Stoler Miller in *Essays on the Mahābhārata*, ed. Arvind Sharma (Leiden: E. J. Brill, 1991), 57–67.

50. See Sally J. Sutherland Goldman, "The Monstrous Feminine: Rākṣasīs and Other Others—The Archaic Mother of Bhāsa's *Madhyamavyāyoga*," in *On Meaning and Mantras: Essays in Honor of Frits Staal*, eds. George Thompson and Richard K. Payne (Moraga, CA: Institute of Buddhist Studies and BDK America, Inc., 2016), 247–74.

dhana and his loved ones: he separates from his teacher, from his parents, from his child, and from his drive to win the war.[51]

And that brings us to the longest of the six, the *Pañcarātra*. In a manner that befits its greater length, it reconstructs the events of the *Virāṭaparvan*, which in turn, as we pointed out earlier, encapsulate the narrative arc of the Mahābhārata as a whole. The plot of the *Pañcarātra*, in accordance with the story of the *Virāṭaparvan*, is fueled by disguises, costumes, and performances. As Hawley shows, the *Pañcarātra* lends a profound interiority to a famously doubled persona that emerges in the *Virāṭaparvan*—Arjuna, whom we meet in disguise as the dance teacher Bṛhannalā. The *Pañcarātra* takes the *Virāṭaparvan*'s expression of disguise as a performance—something that Arjuna, as Bṛhannalā, directs toward an audience—and turns it into a portrayal of disguise as an experience, something that Arjuna feels to be transforming his very self.

Next comes another famously multifaceted Mahābhārata figure, Kṛṣṇa, and an entirely different Sanskrit literary genre. This time it is the *mahākāvya*, and Lawrence McCrea introduces us to the masterful ways in which the seventh-century poet Māgha orchestrates a relationship between Kṛṣṇa and the eldest Pāṇḍava brother, Yudhiṣṭhira, within that genre. McCrea shows that the emotional intensity of the interactions between Kṛṣṇa and Yudhiṣṭhira in the *Śiśupālavadha* contributes to Māgha's aestheticized vision of rulership while adding further complications to the ever-paradoxical figure of Kṛṣṇa, the poem's hero.

In the following chapter Sudha Gopalakrishnan presents a detailed snapshot of Mahābhārata literature as it is brought to life in the *Kūṭiyāṭṭam* theater tradition of Kerala. Gopalakrishnan's discussion of the *Kūṭiyāṭṭam* performance of Kulaśekhara's medieval Sanskrit drama *Subhadrādhanañjaya* ("Subhadrā and Arjuna") illuminates one of the play's most distinctive figures: the *vidūṣaka*, the hero-king's comic sidekick. In the *Kūṭiyāṭṭam* performance of *Subhadrādhanañjaya* he is a ravenous Malayalam-speaking

51. See *Ūrubhaṅga: The Breaking of the Thighs*, trans. Edwin Gerow in *Essays on the Mahābhārata*, ed. Arvind Sharma (Leiden: E. J. Brill, 1991), 68–83; Edwin Gerow, "Bhāsa's Ūrubhaṅga and Indian Poetics," *Journal of the American Oriental Society* 105, no. 3 (1985): 405–12; Gitomer, "King Duryodhana," 222–32; and Bruce M. Sullivan, "Dying on Stage in the *Nāṭyaśāstra* and *Kūṭiyāṭṭam*: Perspectives from the Sanskrit Theatre Tradition," *Asian Theatre Journal* 24, no. 2 (2007): 422–39.

brāhmaṇa who executes much of the play's humor and who, by way of that humor, vocalizes much of its social criticism. Gopalakrishnan demonstrates that through the figure of the *vidūṣaka*, the *Kūṭiyāṭṭam* portrayal of *Subhadrādhanañjaya* subverts the Sanskrit *Mahābhārata*'s vision of the aims of human life. Here we have, then, not an accentuation of an earlier pattern, as in the prior two chapters, but an open reversal—testimony, nonetheless, to the tensile strength of the world the epic spawns.

Finally, Amanda Culp showcases the staying power of Mahābhārata literature in Sanskrit by analyzing three contemporary productions of Kālidāsa's *Abhijñānaśākuntala*. Culp explores how these productions of *Abhijñānaśākuntala* navigate the tension between Kālidāsa's demure heroine and her far more disruptive (and, to many, far more satisfying) *Mahābhārata* counterpart. Culp makes the point that these contemporary productions looked to the Sanskrit epic's portrayal of the Śakuntalā figure as a feminist corrective to Kālidāsa's vision of his heroine. Again we see the lasting importance of the epic's way of framing the world—a capaciousness even Kālidāsa failed to attain.

Part III: Regional and Vernacular Mahābhāratas from Premodern South Asia

The third part of this book is dedicated to premodern Mahābhāratas that were composed in languages other than Sanskrit. Between 800 and 1800 CE, nearly every South Asian literary culture orchestrated at least one retelling of the Mahābhārata. The earliest (albeit incomplete) extant regional Mahābhārata was Peruntēvaṉār's ninth-century Tamil *Pārataveṇpā* ("The Bhārata in Veṇpā Meter").[52] As Pollock points out in his study of the vernacularization of premodern India, the first work of literature (*ādikāvya*) in each of a number of regional South Asian languages—for instance, Pampa's tenth-century Kannada *Vikramārjunavijaya* ("The Victory of Heroic Arjuna"), Nannaya's portion of the Telugu *Mahābhāratamu*, and Sāraḷādāsa's fifteenth-century Oriya *Mahābhārata*—was a retelling of the

52. See Kambalur Venkatesa Acharya, *Mahabharata and Variations: Perundevanar and Pampa; A Comparative Study* (Kurnool: Vyasaraja Publications, 1981), 57–181; and Kamil Zvelebil, *Companion Studies to the History of Tamil Literature* (Leiden: E. J. Brill, 1992), 66–69.

epic.[53] One of the earliest literary texts composed in Marathi was Jñāndev's thirteenth-century *Jñāneśvarī*, an elaborate nine-thousand-verse devotional meditation on the *Bhagavadgītā*.[54]

Often a single premodern literary culture would produce many different Mahābhāratas.[55] After parts of the Mahābhārata were incorporated into the Persian *Ādāb al-Mulūk* ("The Etiquettes of Kings") in the eleventh century,[56] scholars in the court of the Mughal emperor Akbar (r. 1556–1605) continued to tell the Mahābhārata in Persian, most notably in the *Razmnāmah* ("The Book of War," ca. 1582).[57] Beyond the Indian subcontinent, the Mahābhārata inspired many poems in Old Javanese, including Kaṇwa's *Arjunawiwāha* ("The Marriage of Arjuna") and Panuluh's *Ghaṭotkacāśraya* ("Ghaṭotkaca

53. Pollock, *Language of the Gods*, 396. It is also worth noting that the author of the sixteenth-century Malayalam *Bhāratam*, Tuñcattŭ Ĕḻuttacchan, is often called the "father of Malayalam." See Rich Freeman, "The Literature of Hinduism in Malayalam," in *The Blackwell Companion to Hinduism,* ed. Gavin Flood (Oxford: Blackwell Publishing Ltd. 2003), 173.

54. See Davis, *The Bhagavad Gita*, 65–71; and Christian Lee Novetzke, *The Quotidian Revolution: Vernacularization, Religion, and the Premodern Public Sphere in India* (Columbia University Press, 2016), 213–84.

55. For example, see M. S. H. Thompson, "The Mahābhārata in Tamil," *Journal of the Royal Asiatic Society of Great Britain and Ireland* 92, no. 3/4 (1960): 115–23; M. R. Joshi, "*Mahābhārata* and Marathi Vernacular Writers," in *Mahābhārata: The End of an Era (Yugānta)*, ed. Ajay Mitra Shastri (Shimla: India Institute of Advanced Study, 2004), 367–80; Shrinivas Ritti, "*Mahābhārata* in Early Kannada Literature," in *Mahābhārata: The End of an Era (Yugānta)*, ed. Ajay Mitra Shastri (Shimla: India Institute of Advanced Study, 2004), 353–66; Bharati Shelat, "*Mahābhārata* and its Study in Gujarati," in *Mahābhārata: The End of an Era (Yugānta)*, ed. Ajay Mitra Shastri (Shimla: India Institute of Advanced Study, 2004), 381–99; and P. P. Raveendran "Fiction and Reception: Reconstructions of the *Mahabharata* in Malayalam," in *Reflections and Variations on The Mahabharata*, ed. T. R. S. Sharma (Delhi: Sahitya Akademi, 2009), 287–300.

56. Finbarr Barry Flood notes that in this text, "Alexander the Great keeps company with both the great warriors of the *Mahābhārata* and *Shāhnāma* (the Persian national epic), in a transcultural congeries of heroic personalities and deeds." See *Objects of Translation: Material Culture and Medieval "Hindu-Muslim" Encounter* (Princeton, NJ: Princeton University Press, 2009), 251.

57. See Audrey Truschke, *Culture of Encounters: Sanskrit at the Mughal Court* (New York: Columbia University Press, 2016), 181–249.

to the Rescue") in the eleventh century.[58] Certain Mahābhārata episodes, such as the story of Nala and Damayantī, were particularly popular among regional poets.[59] The Sanskrit *Jaiminibhārata* ("The Bhārata of Jaimini," ca. 1100), which reimagines the events of Yudhiṣṭhira's horse sacrifice in the Sanskrit *Mahābhārata*, was repeatedly invoked throughout South Asia in Assamese, Bengali, Gujarati, Kannada, Malayalam, Marathi, Nepali, Oriya, Persian, Tamil, and Telugu.[60]

Some premodern regional Mahābhārata retellings have inspired living performance traditions in South Asia.[61] For example, the *Terukkūttu* ("street theater") plays and the *Piracaṅkam Pāratam* ("discourse on the Bhārata") recitations of the Draupadī goddess cult in Tamil Nadu draw heavily from Villiputtūr's fifteenth-century Tamil *Pāratam*.[62] In present-day Chhattisgarh, Sabalsingh Cauhān's seventeenth-century Hindi *Mahābhārat* can be heard in the *Paṇḍvānī* ballad performances of the Gond community and in the chants of the Rāmnāmī religious sect.[63]

We realize that it is impossible to present investigations of a truly representative selection of premodern non-Sanskrit Mahābhāratas in terms of language, region, or period. Therefore, in this part of the volume, we chose to strike a balance between essays on Mahābhāratas in more com-

58. For translations of these poems, see Mpu Kaṇwa, *Arjunawiwāha: The marriage of Arjuna of Mpu Kaṇwa*, trans. Stuart Robson (Leiden: Koninklijk Instituut, 2008); and Mpu Panuluh, *The Kakawin Ghaṭotkacāśraya by Mpu Panuluh*, trans. Stuart Robson (Tokyo: Tokyo University of Foreign Studies, 2016).

59. See Susan Wadley, ed. *Damayanti and Nala: The Many Lives of a Story* (Delhi: Chronicle, 2011).

60. W. L. Smith, "The Jaiminibhārata and its Eastern Vernacular Versions," *Studia Orientalia* 85 (1999): 389–406; and Petteri Koskikallio and Christophe Vielle, "Epic and Puranic Texts Attributed to Jaimini," *Indologica Taurinensia* 27 (2001): 71.

61. For a detailed list of Mahābhārata performance traditions, see M. L. Varadpande, *Mahabharata in Performance* (Delhi: Clarion Books, 1990), 129–33.

62. Hiltebeitel, *Draupadī* 1, 137–38; and Richard Armando Frasca, *The Theatre of the Mahābhārata: Terukkūttu Performances in South India* (Honolulu: University of Hawaii Press, 1990), 54–55.

63. Niranjan Mahawar, *Folk Theatre Pandwani* (Delhi: Abhinav Publications, 2013), 32; and Ramdas Lamb, *Rapt in the Name: The Ramnamis, Ramnam, and Untouchable Religion in Central India* (Albany: State University of New York Press, 2002), 118–19.

monly studied languages (Hindi, Tamil) and religious textual traditions (Hindu) and scholarship that brings to light works from major literary (Apabhramsha, Kannada, Telugu) and religious (Jain) cultures that have tended to stand closer to the margins of South Asian studies.

Timothy Lorndale's essay investigates one of the oldest regional Mahābhārata poems: Ranna's Kannada *Sāhasabhīmavijaya* ("The Victory of Bold Bhīma," ca. 1000).[64] Lorndale contends that while this text has generally been understood as a panegyric to Ranna's royal patron, Satyāśraya Cāḷukya, likening him to Bhīma, the *Sāhasabhīmavijaya* in fact retells the Mahābhārata from the perspective of Duryodhana, the epic's supposed antihero. Through a close reading of Duryodhana's extended critique of the Pāṇḍavas in the poem's third canto, Lorndale shows that in the *Sāhasabhīmavijaya*, Duryodhana's revisionist interpretation of the Mahābhārata opposes the normative "pro-Pāṇḍava" account of the epic story by identifying and pronouncing Duryodhana's moral code as the proper conduct for *kṣatriya*s (warriors).

The *Mahābhāratamu*—the Telugu translation of the Sanskrit *Mahābhārata* that was begun by Nannaya in the eleventh century, continued by Tikkana around the thirteenth century, and completed by Ĕṟṟāpragaḍa roughly another century later—is the subject of the chapter by Harshita Mruthinti Kamath. Kamath traces the evolution of the dynamic relationship between Telugu and Sanskrit soundscapes, prosody, characterization, and style in the *Mahābhāratamu*. Through a careful examination of different sections of the text by each of its three composers, Kamath reveals the immense complexities of the process of vernacularization in the *Mahābhāratamu*.

The following chapter, by Eva De Clercq and Simon Winant, presents us with a comparison of two Jain Apabhramsha Mahābhāratas: Svayambhūdeva's *Riṭṭhaṇemicariu* ("The Biography of Neminātha," ca. 850–950) and Raïdhū's *Harivaṃsapurāṇa* (ca. 1400). While these works were composed several centuries apart, there is evidence that both the *Riṭṭhaṇemicariu* and the *Harivaṃsapurāṇa* were read in fifteenth-century Jain literary circles in Gwalior (in present-day Madhya Pradesh). By comparing each of these Apabhramsha poems' depictions of Kīcaka—Virāṭa's brother-in-law, who attempts to rape Draupadī during the Pāṇḍavas' thirteenth year of

64. For an in-depth study of this text, see Timothy Lorndale, "Epic Translation: Ranna's *Sāhasabhīmavijaya* and the Mahābhārata's Afterlife in Medieval Karṇāṭa," (PhD diss., University of Pennsylvania, forthcoming).

exile—De Clercq and Winant highlight the remarkable diversity of the Jain Mahābhārata tradition.

Heidi Pauwels complicates our study of Mahābhāratas in fifteenth-century Gwalior by bringing into focus the oldest extant Hindi retelling of the epic, Viṣṇudās' *Pāṇḍavcarit* ("The Story of the Pāṇḍavas," 1435). As De Clercq and Winant do in the previous chapter, Pauwels focuses on the portrayal of Kīcaka and his gruesome murder at the hands of Bhīma. Drawing on methods from micro-history and performance studies, Pauwels' examination of the *Pāṇḍavcarit* interrogates the relationship between emotion and literary performance at the historical moment in which the vernacular emerged as a mode of literary expression at the Tomar court in Gwalior.

In the final chapter in this section, Sohini Sarah Pillai compares Villiputtūr's Tamil *Pāratam* and Sabalsingh Cauhān's Hindi *Mahābhārat*. Although these texts were composed in two different regional languages that are distinct in terms of their linguistic, geographic, and literary trajectories, these Mahābhāratas share a striking feature: both poems describe themselves as the *carita* or "deeds" of the Hindu deity Kṛṣṇa. Pillai argues that one of the most effective methods that both Villi and Cauhān use to recast the Mahābhārata as the deeds of Kṛṣṇa is the insertion of elaborate invocations to various forms of the god in the beginnings of different sections of their respective compositions.[65]

Part IV: Mahābhāratas of Modern South Asia

The final section of *Many Mahābhāratas* examines the spectacularly variegated ways in which the Mahābhārata and the idea of the Mahābhārata have inspired South Asian literary, religious, artistic, and political thought from the late nineteenth century until the twenty-first. In the late colonial period, as Pamela Lothspeich has observed, the Mahābhārata narrative "conveniently captured the essence of the struggle between Indian nationalists and the colonial regime."[66] In this vein, several acclaimed works in regional languages from the early twentieth century use the Mahābhārata to allegorize the oppression of India by the British Raj. The following quickly come to

65. Recall that Ānandavardhana anticipated this turn of events with his embrace of the *Harivaṃśa*.

66. Lothspeich, *Epic Nation*, 213.

mind: K. P. Khadilkar's Marathi play *Kīcak Vadh* ("The Slaying of Kīcaka," 1907),[67] Maithilisharan Gupt's Hindi poem *Jayadrath Vadh* ("The Slaying of Jayadratha," 1910),[68] and C. Subramania Bharati's Tamil poem *Pāñcāli Capatam* ("Draupadī's Vow," 1912, 1924).[69]

Since India's independence in 1947, literally hundreds of Mahābhāratas have been produced in a myriad of languages and literary genres.[70] Prominent plays based on the epic include Dharamvir Bharati's Hindi *Andhā Yug* ("Age of Darkness," 1954),[71] Girish Karnad's Kannada *Yayāti* (1961),[72] Jean-Claude Carrière's French *Le Mahabharata* (1985),[73] and Peter Brook and Marie-Hélène Estienne's English *Battlefield* (2015). Shivaji Sawant's Marathi *Mṛtyuṃjaya* ("Conqueror of Death," 1967),[74] Sunil Gangopadhyay's Bengali *Arjun* (1971),[75] S. L. Bhyrappa's Kannada *Parva* (1979),[76] M. T.

---

67. For a translation, see K. P. Khadilkar, *Globalization, Nationalism and the Text of 'Kichaka-Vadha': The First English Translation of the Marathi Anticolonial Classic, with a Historical Analysis of Theatre in British India,* trans. and ed. Rakesh H. Solomon (London: Anthem Press, 2014).

68. See Lothspeich, *Epic Nation*, 106–37.

69. For a translation, see C. Subramania Bharati, *Panchali's Pledge*, trans. Usha Rajagopalan (Gurgaon: Hachette India, 2012).

70. For extensive studies of post-independence Mahābhāratas, see Aparna Bhargava Dharwadker, *Theatres of Independence: Drama, Theory, and Urban Performance in India since 1947* (Iowa City: University of Iowa Press, 2005), 165–217, 418–19; Sucheta Kanjilal, "Modern Mythologies: The Epic Imagination in Contemporary Indian Literature," (PhD diss., University of South Florida, 2017); and Chinmay Sharma, "Many Mahabharatas: Linking Mythic Re-Tellings in Contemporary India," (PhD diss., University of London: SOAS, 2017).

71. For a translation, see Dharamvir Bharathi, *Andha Yug*, trans. Alok Bhalla (Delhi: Oxford University Press, 2010).

72. For Karnad's own English translation, see Girish Karnad, *Yayati* (Delhi: Oxford University Press, 2008).

73. For Peter Brook's well-known English translation, see Jean-Claude Carrière, *The Mahabharata: A Play Based on the Indian Classic Epic*, trans. Peter Brook (London: Methuen, 1987).

74. For a translation, see Shivaji Sawant, *Mrityunjaya: The Death Conqueror*, trans. P. Lal and Nandini Nopany (Calcutta: Writer's Workshop, 1989).

75. For a translation, see Sunil Gangopadhyay, *Arjun*, trans. Chitrita Banerji-Abdullah (New York: Viking Penguin, 1987).

76. For a translation, see S. L. Bhyrappa, *Parva: A Tale of War, Peace, Love, Death, God, and Man,* trans. K. Raghavendra Rao (Delhi: Sahitya Akademi, 1994).

Vasudevan Nair's Malayalam *Raṇṭāmūḻam* ("Second Turn," 1984),[77] and Shashi Tharoor's *The Great Indian Novel* (1989), written in English, represent but a handful of the best-selling novels inspired by the Mahābhārata. Roshani Chokshi's "Pandava Novels" cast the Mahābhārata's characters in a fantasy series for young adult readers. (If you've ever wondered where the Pāṇḍava *sisters* are, they appear in *Aru Shah and the Tree of Wishes* (2020), the third novel in the collection.)[78] An impressive number of Mahābhārata titles were published between 1970 and 1989 in the beloved *Amar Chitra Katha* ("Immortal Picture Stories") comic book series, with the originating language always being English.[79] But that was hardly the end. In the past decade, for example, we have witnessed the emergence of several English Mahābhārata graphic novels, including Amruta Patil's *Adi Parva: Churning of the Ocean* (2012) and *Sauptik: Blood and Flowers* (2016) and Krishna Udayasankar's trilogy, *The Aryavarta Chronicles* (2012–14). We also have *Vyasa: The Beginning* (2017), written and illustrated by Sibaji Bandyopadhay and Sankha Banerjee.

The poetry of so many premodern Mahābhāratas finds a contemporary counterpart in Arun Kolatkar's *Sarpa Satra* (2004), which reimagines one of the Sanskrit *Mahābhārata*'s frame stories—the snake sacrifice (*sarpa-sattra*) orchestrated by Janamejaya, Arjuna's great-grandson. Here are a few irreverent lines (spoken by the snake woman Jaratkāru) on the subject of Vyāsa: "I mean 24000 verses, Lord have mercy! / what it badly needs / is a good editor . . . But what did you expect of / an old man / who saw it as no part of his business / to interfere, let alone try / and stop / the madness of his grandchildren."[80] The incisive, expressive narration of Kolatkar's poem is answered by Karthika Naïr's *Until the Lions: Echoes from the Mahabharata* (2015), a stunning collection of poems that brings voice to the epic's quieter

77. For a translation, see M. T. Vasudevan Nair, *Bhima: Lone Warrior,* trans. Gita Krishnankutty (Delhi: Harper Perennial, 2013).

78. Roshani Chokshi, *Aru Shah and the End of Time* (New York: Disney Hyperion, 2018); *Aru Shah and the Song of Death* (New York: Disney Hyperion, 2019); *Aru Shah and the Tree of Wishes* (New York: Disney Hyperion, 2020); and *Aru Shah and the City of Gold* (New York: Disney Hyperion, forthcoming 2021).

79. Frances W. Pritchett, "The World of *Amar Chitra Katha,*" in *Media and the Transformation of Religion in South Asia*, eds. Lawrence A. Babb and Susan S. Wadley (Philadelphia: University of Pennsylvania Press, 1995), 85–89.

80. Arun Kolatkar, *Arun Kolatkar: Collected Poems in English*, ed. Arvind Krishna Mehrotra (Tarset: Bloodaxe, 2010), 192.

figures: Ulūpī (Arjuna's serpentine lover, mother of Irāvān), Duḥśalā (the lone Kaurava sister), and Satyavatī (whose poetic narration serves as the work's frame story), for example, not to mention the epic's foot soldiers and dogs.[81] Through Akram Khan's dance company, *Until the Lions* finds expression in modern dance, too—a new phase of the Mahābhārata's long life on stage.[82]

Perhaps the most famous modern Mahābhārata is the immensely popular Hindi *Mahābhārat* serial, which was broadcast on India's national television network, Doordarshan, from 1988 to 1990.[83] But again, it hardly exhausts the field. In the past fifteen years there have been many other Hindi Mahābhārata TV shows, including *Draupadī* (2001–02), *Kahānī Hamāre Mahābhārat Kī* ("Our Story of the Mahābhārata," 2008), *Mahābhārat* (2013–14), *Dharmakṣetra* ("Field of Dharma," 2014–15), *Sūryaputra Karṇ* ("Son of the Sun, Karṇa," 2015–16), and *Karṇ Saṅginī* ("Karṇa's Wife," 2018–19).[84] The epic has also enjoyed an active life on the big screen ever since the first Indian feature film, *Rājā Hariścandra* ("King Hariścandra," 1913), which retells a story found in various Sanskrit texts including the *Mahābhārata*.[85] Along with several well-known "mythological" films[86] such as *Māyābazār* ("Marketplace of Illusions," 1957) in Tamil and

81. Karthika Naïr, *Until the Lions: Echoes from the Mahābhārata* (Delhi: HarperCollins India, 2015).

82. *Until the Lions*, directed and choreographed by Akram Khan, first performed at Roundhouse, London, January 12, 2016.

83. See Ananda Mitra, *Television and Popular Culture in India: A Study of the Mahabharat* (Delhi: Sage, 1993); and Purnima Mankekar, *Screening Culture, Viewing Politics: An Ethnography of Television, Womanhood, and Nation in Postcolonial India* (Durham: Duke University Press, 1999), 224–56.

84. It should be noted that *Kahānī Hamāre Mahābhārat Kī* was a flop that was canceled after only four months. See Reed Ethan Burnam, "Not Simply for Entertainment: The Failure of *Kahani Hamare Mahabharat Ki* and its Place in a New Generation of Televised Indian Mythology," (master's thesis, University of Texas at Austin, 2010). Most of the Hindi Mahābhārata television shows mentioned here, however, enjoyed lengthy runs on major Hindi television networks.

85. Rachel Dwyer, *Filming the Gods: Religion and Indian Cinema* (New York: Routledge, 2006), 22. For the story of Hariścandra in the Sanskrit epic, see *MBh* 2.11.

86. On the "mythological" genre, see Dwyer, *Filming the Gods*, 12–62. Prem Chowdhry notes that in the years between 1916 and 1944, there were eleven Indian mythological films made on Draupadī alone. See *Colonial India and the Making of Empire Cinema: Image, Ideology and Identity* (Manchester: Manchester University Press, 2000), 143.

Telugu, *Karṇaṉ* ("Karṇa," 1964) in Tamil, and, most recently, *Kurukṣētra* (2019) in Kannada, a number of Mahābhārata movies have been set in contemporary India. These productions include *Paḍuvāraḷḷi Pāṇḍavaru* ("The Pāṇḍavas of the Village of Paḍuvāra," 1978) in Kannada, *Taḷapati* ("Commander," 1991) in Tamil, and *Kalyug* ("Age of Discord," 1980) and *Rājnīti* ("Politics," 2010) in Hindi.[87]

Finally, the internet has hosted a variety of innovative Mahābhāratas. The venue is fitting: Doniger compares the Sanskrit *Mahābhārata* to "an ancient Wikipedia."[88] From July 2009 to October 2014, the journalist Chindu Sreedharan retold the epic on Twitter using 2682 tweets, each no longer than 140 characters.[89] B. Jeyamohan, a Tamil author, has posted a chapter of his massive Mahābhārata novel, *Veṇmuracu* ("White Drum") to his website every day since January 1, 2014.[90] In September 2016, a short film called *Mama's Boys* was released on YouTube. The sixteen-minute movie tells the story of a sexually assertive, modern woman (Draupadī) navigating her role as the shared wife of an alcoholic gambler (Yudhiṣṭhira), a dim-witted bodybuilder (Bhīma), a whining man-child (Arjuna), and twin gay fashion designers (Nakula and Sahadeva). Not surprisingly, perhaps, it was only a few days after its release that *Mama's Boys* was removed from YouTube. There had been complaints from a right-wing political organization called the Hindu Sena.[91] Indeed, we often think of the Rāmāyaṇa as the primary literary touchpoint for conservative Hindu political movements' attempts to cast a certain type of Hinduism as the sole and rightful seat of political

87. On *Kalyug* and the 1980 Hindi remake of *Paḍuvāraḷḷi Pāṇḍavaru, Ham Pāñc* ("We Five"), see Philip Lutgendorf, "Bending the *Bhārata*: Two Uncommon Cinematic Adaptations," in *Popular Indian Cinema and Literature: Recasting the Tradition*, ed. Heidi Pauwels (London: Routledge, 2008), 19–41.

88. Doniger, *The Hindus,* 264.

89. These tweets are now available as: Chindu Sreedharan, *Epic Retold. #Mahabharata #TwitterFiction #Bhima #140Characters* (Noida: HarperCollins Publishers India, 2014).

90. Jeyamohan estimates that *Veṇmuracu* will be over 30,000 pages long when it is complete. See Jeyamohan, "Viyācaṉiṉ pātaṅkaḷil," January 1, 2014, https://www.jeyamohan.in/43681#.XDNAuKeB1N0.

91. Geeta Pandey, "Mama's Boys: An Irreverent Take on India's Mahabharat," *BBC*, September 14, 2016, https://www.bbc.com/news/world-asia-india-37340277.

and cultural power in India.[92] Who is thereby excluded? Islamic, lower-caste, or otherwise non-Brahmanical Hindu cultures, representing just the sort of range that earlier Mahābhāratas have often happily included.

Hence it is not surprising that several local religious traditions in contemporary South Asia challenge hegemonic Brahmanical readings of the Mahābhārata. Alf Hiltebeitel has documented how Draupadī is worshiped in Tamil Nadu as a powerful virgin goddess who is guarded by a Muslim devotee named Muttāl Rāvuttaṉ.[93] Certain indigenous communities in Chhattisgarh and Orissa regard Bhīma as a rain god and a creator deity.[94] Ehud Halperin has shown how Haḍimbā, a local goddess in Himachal Pradesh, is frequently identified with Hiḍimbā, the demoness wife of Bhīma.[95] And William Sax has revealed that there are temples in the Garhwal region of Uttarakhand dedicated to two of the Mahābhārata's supposed villains: Karṇa and Duryodhana.[96]

The chapters in this section explore recent models of a two-thousand-year-old phenomenon. When many individuals and communities in South Asia ask what it means to be political, to be literary, to be religious, to be social, to be gendered, or to be artistic *today* (whether "today" is in 2021 or 1886), they turn, more often than not, to the Mahābhārata. It provides a handsome and expansive vocabulary for constructing the answers they seek. Each of the chapters in Part IV of the book illustrates an instance in

92. On this topic, see Linda Hess, "Marshaling Sacred Texts: Ram's Name and Story in Late Twentieth-Century Indian Politics," Academia, June 2020, https://www.academia.edu/43473803/Marshaling_Sacred_Texts_Rams_Name_and_Story_in_Late_Twentieth_Century_Indian_Politics, previously published as "Marshalling Sacred Texts: Ram's Name and Story in Late Twentieth-Century Indian Politics," *Journal of Vaishnava Studies* 2, no. 4 (1994): 175–206.

93. Hiltebeitel, *Draupadī* 1, 101–27.

94. Mahendra Kumar Mishra, "A Hero of Mahābhārata in Folklore of Central India," in *Mahābhārata in the Tribal and Folk Traditions of India,* ed. K. S. Singh (Shimla: Indian Institute of Advanced Study, 1993), 162; and N. K. Das, "Adivasi Theatre Pandavani and Persona of Bhima in Folklore of Chhattisgarh-Gondwana Region," *Irish Journal of Anthropology* 18, no. 2 (2015.): 80.

95. Ehud Halperin, *The Many Faces of a Himalayan Goddess: Haḍimbā, Her Devotees, and Religion in Rapid Change* (New York: Oxford University Press, 2019).

96. Sax, *Dancing the Self,* 157–200.

which the Mahābhārata is deployed as an expression of modernity—and each is different from the others.

Ahona Panda analyzes two very different accounts of the Sanskrit *Mahābhārata*—and particularly Kṛṣṇa's role in it—that were articulated by two seminal Bengali litterateurs and political thinkers, Bankimchandra Chattopadhyay (Chatterjee) and Rabindranath Tagore. In 1886, when Bankim was actively engaged in fostering the cause of Hindu nationalism, he wrote the *Kṛṣṇacaritra* ("The Nature of Kṛṣṇa"), which presents Kṛṣṇa as a historical figure and the embodiment of the perfect king and householder. In her essay Panda provides a close reading of Tagore's harsh 1896 review of the *Kṛṣṇacaritra* and asserts that, in contradistinction to Bankim, Tagore believes that the *Mahābhārata* is politically relevant not because it is "historical" but because of its value as literature, the best of which, in Tagore's view, explores the concept of flawed heroism.

In the next chapter Sudipta Kaviraj turns to a more contemporary Bengali literary engagement with the Sanskrit *Mahābhārata*: Buddhadev Bose's prose study of the epic, *Mahābhārater Kathā* ("About the *Mahābhārata*," 1974). Using Mikhail Bakhtin's essay "Epic and Novel" (1941) as a point of entrance, Kaviraj shows that Bose detects certain aspects in the *Mahābhārata*—such as its distorted aesthetic vision and its presentation of Yudhiṣṭhira as a fallible human being—that suit the sensibility of a modern reader. Ultimately, Kaviraj argues that Bose's aesthetically bold reading of the epic articulates a modern *bildungsroman* (that is, a coming-of-age story) through the figure of Yudhiṣṭhira.

Pamela Lothspeich traces postcolonial literary representations of Draupadī in three novels by women authors: Jyotirmayi Devi's Bengali *Epar Gaṅgā, Opar Gaṅgā* ("This Bank of the Ganges, That Bank of the Ganges," 1968), Pratibha Ray's Oriya *Yājñasenī* (1984), and Chitra Banerjee Divakaruni's English *The Palace of Illusions* (2008). Indebted to and invigorated by theoretical work on global feminisms, Lothspeich's chapter demonstrates how, in the last fifty years, Draupadī has become a multivalent figure in modern Indian literature.

In the penultimate chapter Sucheta Kanjilal draws our focus to modern representations of marginalized lower-caste and tribal characters from the Mahābhārata tradition, focusing especially on Ekalavya. The Sanskrit *Mahābhārata* presents Ekalavya as an archer so skilled that Droṇa, the Pāṇḍavas' teacher, feels compelled to force him to cut off his own thumb so that Arjuna can retain his position as the world's greatest bowman. Kanjilal considers two Bengali short stories by Mahasweta Devi (1926–2016) and the English play *Bedtime Story* by Kiran Nagarkar (b. 1942) as she investigates what happens to Ekalavya and other more muted Mahābhārata figures in modern times. She demonstrates just how complicated it is to represent social marginalities in contemporary India within the narrative context of the Mahābhārata. Kanjilal also reveals that these retellings by Devi and Nagarkar, who themselves come from upper-caste backgrounds, at times reflect the very oppressive structures that they work to overturn.

In the book's final chapter, Philip Lutgendorf examines a trilogy of graphic novels titled *The Kaurava Empire* (2014–15) that are illustrated by the Delhi-based artist Sachin Nagar, written in English by the British author Jason Quinn, and published by Kalyani Navyug Media for an Indian audience. Lutgendorf shows how the *Kaurava Empire* trilogy adapts the international visual code of the science-fiction graphic novel in order to texturize the Mahābhārata's tale of fratricidal conflict. He finds that the trilogy draws upon another trilogy—the original *Star Wars* movie trilogy—so as to create a Mahābhārata that will be simultaneously archaic and dystopian.[97] In doing so, Lutgendorf brings the Mahābhārata squarely into the intimately well-known world of many readers of this book—or rather, suggests how it has been there all along.

A Story's Cycle of Rebirth

If, as Ramanujan writes of the Sanskrit *Mahābhārata*, "one thing is certain . . . total destruction,"[98] then it is just as certain that retelling the Mahābhārata—continuing the story, leaving it unfinished—is a way of counteracting that destructive bent. When we recycle the Mahābhārata—whether we do so artistically, as many of the works we study in this book do, or scholastically, as the book itself does—we insist that the whole story has not yet been told. In this way our various retellings allow us to do our part in forestalling the Mahābhārata's famous curse. Each return to the story responds to the Mahābhārata's ethos of disintegration and decay

97. For another study of the relationship between *Star Wars* and the Mahābhārata, see Steven J. Rosen, *The Jedi in the Lotus: Star Wars and the Hindu Tradition* (Huntingdon, UK: Arktos Media Ltd., 2010), 67–88.

98. Ramanujan, "Repetition in the *Mahābhārata*," 436.

with the equally powerful force of creativity. So long as we continue to make something new of the Mahābhārata, we stay safe. When we keep the Mahābhārata alive, the Mahābhārata keeps *us* alive. This is part of the epic's mysterious power.

It is tempting to think, indeed, that the kaleidoscopic Mahābhārata tradition occupies its own kind of cycle of rebirth. Each telling gives the Mahābhārata a new body, a new life. Desire—"always wanting these stories"—keeps the cycle in motion. This is what we call *saṃsāra*. When it comes to the lives of humans and other creatures, various South Asian religious traditions speak of *saṃsāra* as something to be escaped or transcended. But when it comes to stories—and particularly when it comes to the Mahābhārata—we seem to find an altogether different paradigm. The Mahābhārata's cycle of narrative rebirth is not one from which any of us seem to want to be free. Frightening it may be, and complex and bewildering as well. But is it a *saṃsāra* from which we hope to be released? What the Mahābhārata tells is by and large gruesome and deeply difficult. And yet in order to find in this story something more, something different, we must enter its stream—we know it is our own—and not let go. And so, like all accounts of the Mahābhārata, ours is by necessity an unfinished one. We must keep our Gaṇeśas wanting more.

Ramanujan once said that no person belonging to South Asia ever reads the Mahābhārata—or the Rāmāyaṇa, in another version of the story—for the first time. Let us propose a codicil. No one ever reads the Mahābhārata for the last time.

PART I

The Manyness of the Sanskrit *Mahābhārata*

Chapter Two

Ā Garbhāt

Murderous Rage and Collective Punishment as Thematic Elements in Vyāsa's *Mahābhārata*

Robert Goldman

The old order changeth, yielding place to new,
And God fulfils himself in many ways,
Lest one good custom should corrupt the world.

—Tennyson, *Idylls of the King*

Great, popular, and enduring works of literature must, one imagines, achieve their popularity and longevity in substantial part by responding to the aspirations and anxieties of the cultures that give rise to them and sustain them. Many of these works, from many cultures and many eras, are centrally concerned with violence—organized, massive violence. In short, war. This mass, largely tribal, violence, which our species appears to have inherited from our primate forbears, has been frequently textualized: it has been both recorded as history and aestheticized as literature, although the boundary between the two is often tenuous. In these forms, it appeals to our desire for violence and the gains we may obtain from it; it also appeals to our apprehension and fear of what it may cause us to lose.

In the West, the literary and performative traditions of representing real and fictive violence extend from the Bible, the Homeric epics, Herodotus' *Histories*, and Thucydides' *History of the Peloponnesian War* through the early medieval *Chanson de Roland* and into the modern era's *The Red Badge of Courage* (1895), *All Quiet on the Western Front* (1929), *Star Wars* (1977), and *Saving Private Ryan* (1998). In India, it begins in the Vedas—recall the divine, mythological narration of the never-ending *devāsura-yuddha* (the war between gods and anti-gods) and the *daśarājakīya* (the battle of the ten kings)—and extends through the Rajput epics,[1] emerging in modern Hindi films such as *LOC Kargil* (2003) and *Wagah* (2016). But in the Indian literary-historical tradition, the *śiromaṇis* (the "crest jewels") of the textualization of armed conflict come in the form of the great Sanskrit epic poems: the *Rāmāyaṇa* and the *Mahābhārata*. As Upinder Singh points out in her recent study of the idea and practice of violence in early premodern India, these two works stand among the principal sources for our understanding of how violence was conceptualized and represented as a critical element in the construction of Indian kingship.[2] In parallel to her work on violence in the epics, in this chapter I will investigate a very specific and characteristic kind of violence that is endemic (but not restricted) to the *Mahābhārata* and speculate on what this particular representation of violence might tell us about the ethos of the composers and audiences of the great saga that describes the ancient civil war of the Kuru-Pañcālas.

The *Mahābhārata*, by which I mean the monumental Sanskrit epic attributed to Vyāsa, has long been an object of ambivalence in its diverse receptive communities. On the one hand, it is revered as India's national epic and as a repository of the nation's normative constructions of social, political, and religious codes. Its large cast of characters provides striking exemplars of positive and negative ethical behavior, and the work has stimulated profound contemplation on what it means to act in accordance with dharma in a contingent and complex world. The *Mahābhārata* also provides

---

1. On the epic poems of the Rajput community in South Asia, see John D. Smith, *The Epic of Pābūjī: A Study, Transcription, and Translation* (Cambridge: Cambridge University Press, 1991); and Cynthia Talbot, *The Last Hindu Emperor: Prithviraj Chauhan and the Indian Past, 1200–2000* (Cambridge: Cambridge University Press, 2016), 107–45.

2. Upinder Singh, *Political Violence in Ancient India* (Cambridge, MA: Harvard University Press, 2017), 57–94.

the narrative context for the *Bhagavadgītā*, which is perhaps the single most universally recognized and cherished work in the vast Hindu canon. Because of the poem's extraordinary pervasion along every geographical, social, and generic axis, it becomes difficult to refute A. K. Ramanujan's famous observation that "No Hindu ever reads the *Mahābhārata* for the first time."[3] In fact, we could extend the aphorism to all Indian communities, Hindu or otherwise. Indeed, the popularity of the epic tale and its characters has only increased in recent years as a result of its television serializations.

There is, however, another side to the *Mahābhārata's* receptive history, and it is not a comfortable one. For all the reverence that the *Mahābhārata* and Kṛṣṇa, its divine *sūtradhāra* or "stage manager," receive, there are communities in which the poem is kept at arm's length.[4] For some it is an "outside" book, copies of which should not be kept inside one's home. This practice exists, no doubt, because in India's cultural imaginary, the work's central narrative, the history of a bitter and sanguinary civil war, is a disturbing example of *bheda*, "divisiveness," that tears apart a great royal dynasty and ends a heroic age. The *Mahābhārata*'s theme of internecine conflict and violence is deeply unsettling to a culture that considers itself grounded in tolerance and that strongly valorizes *ahiṃsā* (non-violence), social integration, *ānṛśaṃsya* (non-cruelty), and, above all, the harmonies of caste, class, and family. Indeed, some families believe that to keep a manuscript or printed text of the poem in the house is to invite the kind of internal feuding and fraternal violence that destroyed the great Bhārata lineage into one's own domestic realm.[5] In some communities, this anxiety is even directed toward the figure of Kṛṣṇa himself. Friends who grew up in South India have told me that their families never give the name or an epithet of Kṛṣṇa to a son for fear that he might somehow cause the death

3. A. K. Ramanujan, "Repetition in the *Mahābhārata*," in *Essays on the Mahābhārata*, ed. Arvind Sharma (Leiden: E. J. Brill, 1991), 419.

4. On Kṛṣṇa's role as the "ringmaster" of the *Mahābhārata*, see Alf Hiltebeitel, "Krishna in the *Mahabharata:* The Death of Karna," in *Krishna: A Sourcebook*, ed. Edwin F. Bryant (New York: Oxford University Press, 2007), 23.

5. A number of years ago after a lecture I had given on this issue at the Asiatic Society of Bombay, the discussant, Professor Sardesai, then president of the Society, remarked that he now understood why the meetings of the Society's board were so contentious since its library contained many manuscripts of the Bhārata. His jocular remarks were quoted the next morning in the City pages of *The Times of India*.

of an uncle, just as the *Mahābhārata*'s Kṛṣṇa does. (In the critical edition of the *Mahābhārata*, Kṛṣṇa narrates an abbreviated version of this story.[6])

But there is more at work here than the dread of *bheda* and internecine violence. From beginning to end, and from its outermost framing and the setting of its narration to its core narrative, the *Mahābhārata* is a profoundly dark and violent work, the chronicle of a shattered world. As Sheldon Pollock notes, "The *Mahābhārata* ends in anomie, ascetic suicide, and apocalypse."[7] The ninth-century Kashmiri *alaṅkaraśāstrin* (theorist of literature) Ānandavardhana, who was the first to read the epic as a consistent work of literature that embodies an overarching emotional-aesthetic tenor, makes note of the epic's *virasāvasāna*—the "miserable ending" of its protagonists—which "inspires only despondency in our hearts."[8] What is undeniably the darkest recurrent theme in this grim history emerges from its author's (or authors') evident preoccupation with tales of slaughter, vengeance, collective punishment, and, as we would say today, genocide and ethnic cleansing. By the term "collective punishment," I refer to practices such as those to which the Nazis resorted, where, in retaliation for the killing of a single person, the population of an entire village or an entire ethnic or religious community might be attacked. This has happened throughout history; another example is the 1984 anti-Sikh pogrom in Delhi that followed the assassination of Prime Minister Indira Gandhi. Throughout the vast and complex narrative of the *Mahābhārata*, we find repeated examples of the extermination or attempted extermination of entire ethnic groups, classes of society, and even non-human species.

Wherever we look in the poem, there is no escaping this theme. The central event of the epic is, no doubt, the exterminatory Bhārata War.

6. *Mahābhārata* (henceforth *MBh*) 2.13.30–34. All references to the *Mahābhārata* are to the critical edition: *The Mahābhārata for the First Time Critically Edited*, ed. V. S. Sukthankar et al. 19 vols. (Poona: Bhandarkar Oriental Research Institute, 1933–66).

7. Sheldon I. Pollock, "Introduction" in *The Rāmāyaṇa of Vālmīki: An Epic of Ancient India*, vol. 2, *Ayodhyākāṇḍa*, trans. Sheldon I. Pollock (Princeton: Princeton University Press, 1986), 71.

8. *vṛṣṇipāṇḍavavirasāvasānavaimanasyadāyinīṃ samāptim* | Ānandavardhana, *Dhvanyāloka*, *vṛtti* on 4.5. See Ānandavardhana, *Dhvanyāloka of Shri Anandavardhanacharya with the Lochan Commentary by Shri Abhinava Gupta*, 2 vols. (Delhi and Varanasi: Motilal Banarsidass, 1973).

This event does not represent a normal military-political war of conquest, nor is it a routine conflict between contending factions over land, wealth, and women—the proverbial *zamīn, zāli, zenāna*—although it is also that. This cataclysmic struggle is an epoch-ending, mass-extinction event. For, of the many elite heroes who take part in the barely three-week clash of royal cousins, only ten are said to have survived the war. Before the epic ends, most of these survivors are slain or simply die. The casualties, which the poem itself calculates, are truly staggering. Including the (generally overlooked) rank-and-file soldiery of the war's eighteen legendarily vast armies, Yudhiṣṭhira reckons the combined losses of both sides come to 1,660,020,000 dead and 24,165 missing—perhaps more individuals than populated the earth at the time the epic was composed.[9]

Whether it was known to the combatants or not, the slaughter at Kurukṣetra was never exclusively about who would rule the Kuru kingdom. As the mythical and theological framing of the *Mahābhārata* makes clear, the political and military conflict between the sons of Pāṇḍu and those of Dhṛtarāṣṭra is merely the occasion for a cosmic event that Lord Nārāyaṇa (Viṣṇu) orchestrates in the guise of Kṛṣṇa, the warrior-sage. The real purpose of the war is the massive extermination of the kings of the *dvāpara-yuga* (the third of four ages in the cosmic cycle of time), whose excesses and depredations have become too great for the Earth goddess herself to bear.[10] The purpose of Viṣṇu's incarnation (as Kṛṣṇa), along with those of the gods who father the Pāṇḍava brothers, is to carry out but one battle in real, historical time; this battle is set amid the never-ending struggle for dominance between (those superhuman half-brothers) the *devas* and the *asuras*, to which the Vedas first attest. As Indra (the king of the gods and Arjuna's father) makes clear, the purpose of the incarnation of Kṛṣṇa and his subordinate divinities is not only *jaya* (victory) but a literal cleansing of the earth (*bhuvaḥ śodhanāya*)[11]—an extermination of the warrior class not

9. *daśāyutānām ayutaṃ sahasrāṇi ca viṃśatiḥ* |
koṭyaḥ ṣaṣṭiś ca ṣaṭ caiva ye'smin rājamṛdhe hatāḥ ||
alakṣyāṇāṃ tu vīrāṇāṃ sahasrāṇi ca caturdaśa |
daśa cānyāni rājendra śataṃ ṣaṣṭiś ca pañca ca || *MBh* 11.26.9–10 ||

Compare this extraordinary number with the seventy million military and civilian casualties said to have been caused during World War II.

10. *MBh* 1.58.25–51.

11. *MBh* 1.58.51.

only down to the last man, but, as it is often described, *ā garbhāt*: "down to the very embryos in the womb."[12]

Students in my class on the Indian epics often ask why Kṛṣṇa does not intervene to prevent such horrific slaughter. In fact, a former Indian ambassador to the United States once told me that his colleagues see Kṛṣṇa as the prototypical diplomat, and an exemplary one, because of the negotiations that he undertakes between rival clans in the *Mahābhārata*. But given the work's framing narrative, asking why Kṛṣṇa fails to prevent the violent events that unfold is like asking why the fox did not prevent the carnage in the henhouse. Kṛṣṇa makes perfectly clear his purpose as an *avatāra* (incarnation) and his *rôle* in the Great War in the epic's most widely read and deeply revered section, the *Bhagavadgītā*. There he famously explains that the specific reason that he takes on various incarnations (i.e., as the different *avatāra*s of Viṣṇu) over the long course of the *yuga*s (cosmic eras) specifically to annihilate evildoers (*vināśāya ca duṣkṛtām*).[13] More to the point, he states that he is the world-destroying power of time itself who has come to carry out that mission. Arjuna, who is about to fight in the war, is, in Kṛṣṇa's analysis, merely an instrumental cause (*nimitta-mātram*) of the slaughter of the *kṣatriyas*, since they all have already been destroyed by Kṛṣṇa himself.[14] Indeed, the whole Bhārata War is but a *nimitta*, "a mere instrument," through which the Lord (Kṛṣṇa) accomplishes his grim but nonetheless divine purpose.

The author or authors of the *Mahābhārata* were deeply entwined in this theme. The *Mahābhārata* tells of the crisis of the *dvāpara-yuga*'s *ancien régime* in such a way as to keep it ever-fresh in the minds of the work's audiences. In the next section of the essay, I will examine the architecture of the poem from this perspective in an attempt to clarify the nature and extent of the work's repeated examples of and emphasis on massive violence. Then, in the concluding section, I will offer a few words on why I think the *Mahābhārata* persistently focuses on murder, retaliation, and genocide.

When considering themes of murderous rage and collective punishment, the specific context in which the *Mahābhārata* describes itself being

---

12. *MBh* 1.169.18.

13. *Bhagavadgītā* (henceforth *BhG*) 4.8. All references to the *Bhagavadgītā* are from *The Bhagavad-Gita with Eleven Commentaries*, ed. Pandit Gajanana Shastri Sadhale, 3 vols. (Bombay: Gujarati Printing Press, 1935).

14. *BhG* 11.32–34.

narrated proves just as significant as the poem's mythological-theological framing. The version of the epic tale that has come down to us as the *Mahābhārata* is the one that is said to have been recited by the bard Ugraśravas to a group of sages who had gathered to attend a sacrifice in the Naimiṣa Forest.[15] The bard tells them that earlier he had been at yet another sacrifice, one that had been performed on behalf of Janamejaya, a monarch in the lineage of the last great Kaurava dynast, the Dharmarāja (king of dharma) Yudhiṣṭhira. During the intervals in the performance of Janamejaya's ritual, the *brāhmaṇa* Vaiśaṃpāyana, a disciple of the great seer Vyāsa himself, had entertained and edified the gathering with various tales of glory relating to the king's ancestors—in other words, with his *guru*'s great composition, the *Mahābhārata*.[16] Two details in Ugraśravas' account of Janamejaya's sacrifice and Ugraśravas' subsequent journey to the Naimiṣa Forest are noteworthy here. First, Ugraśravas refers to the sacrifice as a *sarpasattra*, a snake sacrifice, although he does not pause to explain exactly what such a ritual might entail. Then he remarks that on his way to the Naimiṣa Forest, after leaving the *sarpasattra*, he visited many pilgrimage spots and shrines. Of these shrines, he singles out only one by name: the *tīrtha*, or holy pilgrimage spot, called Samantapañcaka, which, he notes, was the very battleground of the Bhārata war.[17]

As Ugraśravas explains, the critical point about Janamejaya's sacrifice is that its entire purpose is genocidal. Janamejaya undertakes the sacrifice in order to exterminate an entire race of beings: the great *nāga*s, or serpent lords, along with their terrestrial cousins, ordinary snakes. In this aspect, Janamejaya's sacrifice becomes the prototype for many of the tales of near-total genocide that follow it. Janamejaya's sanguinary ritual along with its causes and consequences are described at great length in seventeen chapters of the epic's first book, the *Ādiparvan* ("The Book of Beginnings").[18] In subsequent tales, one individual's offense is avenged with a killing, which, in turn, provokes a genocidal rampage against the class, race, or species of the killer. The genocide is never total, as it is ultimately stopped by an authoritative person, normally a *brāhmaṇa*, after a slaughter of massive

15. *MBh* 1.1.1–7.

16. *MBh* 1.1.8–19.

17. *MBh* 1.1.11.

18. *MBh* 1.36–53.

proportions.[19] In this case, the precipitating cause is the death of the Kaurava dynast Parikṣit, Janamejaya's father, when the *nāga* lord Takṣaka bites him. Janamejaya's response is the snake sacrifice, which he designs to exterminate all the serpents of the world. Before the sacrifice accomplishes this mission, however, the Bhārgava *brāhmaṇa* sage Āstīka puts a stop to the slaughter. The detailed account of Janamejaya's *sarpasattra* is framed in multiform[20]: Ugraśravas foreshadows the story of the *sarpasattra* with another tale of near-annihilation of serpents; Ruru vows a genocidal vendetta against snakes after his beloved dies by snake bite. He is only dissuaded, like Janamejaya, by a *brāhmaṇa* sage.[21] These accounts establish a motif, or tale-type, that will be followed many times throughout the poem.

The sages also inquire about the holy site of Samantapañcaka. Ugraśravas reports that although the great slaughter of the Bhārata war took place there at the *sandhyā*, the "twilight" between the *dvāpara-* and *kali-yuga*s, it was not the only noteworthy extermination that occurred at that spot, nor was it the original reason for site's sanctity. For, he informs the sages, it was there that—an entire *yuga* before the Bhārata war, during the "twilight" between the *tretā-* and *dvāpara-yuga*s—the fearsome Bhārgava *brāhmaṇa* warrior Rāma Jāmadagnya repeatedly exterminated all the *kṣatriya* kings of the earth. This narrative conforms to the motif that I describe above. The sons of a king kill Rāma's father; Rāma retaliates first by slaughtering that king's entire lineage and then, his genocidal rage still unappeased, by wiping out the entire *kṣatriya* class twenty-one times—including the children and, finally, even the newborns as they emerge from their mothers' wombs.[22] Rāma fills five lakes with the *kṣatriyas*' blood, which he uses to make sanguinary offerings to his ancestors until he is finally stopped by a delegation of his

19. *sahasrāṇi bahūny asmin prayutāny arbudāni ca* |
na śakyaṃ parisaṃkhyātuṃ bahutvād vedavittama || *MBh* 1.52.2 ||

In the case of the snake sacrifice, the victims are said to be beyond count but number at least in the tens of millions.

20. Wendy Doniger O'Flaherty, "Horses and Snakes in the Ādi Parvan of the *Mahābhārata*," in *Aspects of Essays in Honor of Edward Cameron Dimock, Jr*, eds. Margaret Case and N. Gerald Barrier (Delhi: American Institute of Indian Studies and Manohar, 1986), 24–25.

21. *MBh* 1.8–12.

22. *MBh* 12.49.54–55.

ancestors, headed by (once again) a sage, Ṛcīka. It is these bloody libations that, we learn, have lent Samantapañcaka its aura of sanctity.[23] The legend of Bhārgava Rāma, which Ugraśravas recounts only briefly at this point in the epic, represents a transparent effort to link the two grand massacres of the ruling class to a particular place (Samantapañcaka). Soon, however, Rāma's slaughter of the warrior class emerges as a kind of leitmotif throughout the poem. The tale is narrated at length at several points in the work,[24] and various characters make allusions to it throughout.

Later in the first book we find yet another nexus of ethnic cleansing. The sage Parāśara, upon learning that his father, the sage Śaktin, had been killed by a *rākṣasa* (demon), decides to carry the idea of collective punishment to its ultimate limit and destroy the entire world.[25] His grandfather, the great seer Vasiṣṭha, dissuades him from his apocalyptic plan by recounting yet another tale of genocide in which an earlier project of world-ending vengeance was aborted. This time it is the *kṣatriya*s of the Haiheya lineage who, angered that the Bhārgava *brāhmaṇa*s have hidden their wealth from them, launch a great massacre and slaughter the Bhṛgus *ā garbhāt*, down to the embryos in the womb—a point that the narrative stresses throughout. As the Bhārgava widows flee, one of them, in an effort to save her unborn child, somehow transfers her embryo from her womb to her thigh. When the pursuing *kṣatriya*s catch up with her, the infant, Aurva, literally a "son of the thigh," bursts forth, blinding them with his blazing radiance. They sue for mercy, and the child at first relents—but then, like Parāśara, he vows to destroy the entire world. Just as he begins to carry out his dreadful holocaust, his ancestors, as in the tale of Rāma Jāmadagnya, appear to him and compel him to desist. He then casts the fire of his vengeful rage into the sea, where it remains in the form of the horse-headed submarine fire.[26]

Although dissuaded from his plan to destroy the entire world, Parāśara is by no means free from his exterminatory fury. He now reverts to the

---

23. *MBh* 1.2.2–8.

24. As at *MBh* 3.116–117 and 12.49.27–60. See also Robert P. Goldman, *Gods, Priests, and Warriors: The Bhṛgus of the Mahābhārata* (New York: Columbia University Press, 1977).

25. *MBh* 1.169.9.

26. *MBh* 1.169–171.

standard model, as it were: he initiates a *sarvarākṣasasattra* sacrifice, one that is analogous to Janamejaya's *sarpasattra*, in order to destroy the entire race of *rākṣasas*. But once again, sages—including Pulastya, a son of Brahmā and an ancestor of the *rākṣasas*, who is distraught at the extermination of his progeny (*prajoccheda*)—arrive and persuade Parāśara to relent and to cast his blazing anger into the wilderness.[27]

The poem's first book concludes with yet another account of a mass extermination of creatures (*bhūtānāṃ kadanaṃ mahat)*, in the form of the burning of the Khāṇḍava Forest, during the course of which Arjuna and Kṛṣṇa burn to death (or slaughter with their arrows) virtually every living creature of the virgin woodlands in a vast holocaust to sate Agni, the god of fire.[28]

The narrative pauses once more in the third book, the *Āraṇyakaparvan* ("The Book of the Forest"), to recount Rāma Jāmadagnya's serial exterminations of the *kṣatriyas* and his gory oblations with their blood[29] before proceeding with its central narrative, the carnage on the killing field of Kurukṣetra-Samantapañcaka, which unfolds in the four battle books of the epic (books six through nine).[30] But although this battle represents the culmination of the epic's recurrent framing narratives of genocidal violence, it is hardly the last. It is important to note that even the massive slaughter on the killing field of Kurukṣetra does not complete the war's toll. The epic provides a series of grim codas.

On the side of the war's victors, only the five Pāṇḍava brothers, their five sons with Draupadī, and Kṛṣṇa, along with a few allies, survive the battle. Of the vanquished, aside from the mortally wounded Duryodhana, there are but three survivors: the Kaurava elder Kṛpa, the warrior Kṛtavarman, and Aśvatthāman. Aśvatthāman, like Rāma Jāmadagnya, nurses a bitter rage at the deceitful killing of his father and forms a plot to avenge it.[31] With his two companions, he steals into the camp of the sleeping victors with the intent of exterminating the entire Pāṇdava lineage. The three effect a

27. *MBh* 1.172.

28. *MBh* 1.214–219.

29. *MBh* 3.116–117.

30. *MBh* 6–9.

31. On a depiction of Aśvatthāman's revenge in a modern graphic novel, see the chapter by Philip Lutgendorf in this volume.

grand slaughter of the sleeping warriors, including the five surviving sons of the Pāṇḍavas. But, like the earlier attempts at the extermination of a race, species or lineage, this one, too, proves incomplete as the Pāṇḍava brothers themselves are absent from the camp during the attack.[32] The conspirators, however, virtually assure the end of the Pāṇḍava lineage. Just as in the story of Aurva and the slaughter of the Bhārgavas, hope comes in the form of an embryo. Uttarā, the widow of Arjuna's son Abhimanyu, who was killed earlier during the main battle, is pregnant. But yet again, Aśvatthāman acts on his burning desire to exterminate the entire Pāṇḍava clan. He unleashes the fearsome *brahmāstra* (a celestial projectile weapon) directly at the embryo in her womb, killing it. The child is stillborn; but Kṛṣṇa magically restores him to life as prince Parikṣit.[33] It is Parikṣit whose eventual death by snakebite will, in the *Mahābhārata*'s endless round of violence, impel his son Janamejaya to undertake the genocidal snake sacrifice with which the poem begins, bringing the cycle to a close. Of course, all of this fits in with the tradition's placement of the Bhārata War at the transition between the chivalric era of the *dvāpara-yuga* and the impending degeneracy and chaos of the *kali-yuga*. In this way its history becomes imbricated in the epic-purāṇic tradition's larger cosmological frame of cyclical time and, especially, of decline and destruction.

But even these ghastly events do not exhaust the poet's (or poets') fascination with genocidal violence. After the holocaust of Kurukṣetra and Aśvatthāman's attempt to complete the extirpation of the Kaurava lineage, aside from the Pāṇḍavas themselves, the only *kṣatriya* survivors of the civil war are their distant cousins, Kṛṣṇa and his kinsmen, the Yādavas, who have returned to their western coastal stronghold of Dvārakā. As a group, they alone have managed to escape the internecine slaughter of the Kurus, but not for long. Inevitably, their own internecine rampage of self-destruction

32. *MBh* 10.1–9.

33. *MBh* 14.68. At this point it becomes apparent that the epic authors have a particular fascination with the theme of the killing of embryos and newborns, which violates both the *dharmaśāstraic* prohibition of abortion and revulsion for an abortionist. For example, in *Manusmṛti* 4.208, 5.90, 8.317, etc. See *Manusmṛti with the Commentary Manvarthamuktāvalī of Kullūka*, ed. N. R. A. Kaavyatirtha (Bombay: Nirnaya Sagara Press, 1946). It may be that this theme—the slaughter of the innocents—with its shock value is intended to graphically signify the importance attached to the idea of total extermination of the target class, race or species.

takes place a scant thirty-six years after the Great War. Provocatively, this, the epic's final genocidal episode, also begins with an embryo—or, rather, with an imaginary embryo—that is transmuted by Brahmanical rage into a monstrous weapon of mass destruction that brings about the near-extermination of the last surviving Somavaṃśa clans and draws the epic tale to a close.[34]

When a group of *brāhmaṇa* sages visit Dvārakā, the young men of the town, apparently as a prank to mock their supposed supernormal knowledge, dress Kṛṣṇa's son Sāmba as a pregnant woman and ask the visitors to predict what "she" will give birth to, presumably referring to the false embryo's gender. But in keeping with ancient India's well-known trope of the omniscience and irascibility of ascetics, the sages easily see through the foolish deception and, in a rage, they proclaim that Sāmba will, indeed, give birth, not to a child, but to a fearsome iron club that will annihilate all the Yadu warriors, sparing only Kṛṣṇa and Balarāma. Following the clan's mutual slaughter, the sea will rise and inundate the city as the two divine brothers abandon their earthly forms and return to their heavenly abodes.[35]

The very next day Sāmba gives birth to a dreadful iron club. In a futile effort to save his people from the inevitable consequences of a *brāhmaṇa*'s curse, the Yādava king Ugrasena has the weapon ground into a powder and cast into the sea. But, the particles, like seeds, grow into a field of metallic marsh grass. Later, during a drunken feast at the beach, the Yādava warriors begin to taunt one another for their unchivalrous conduct during the great war. They all seize bunches of the grass, which turn into fearsome war clubs. An extremely violent, internecine brawl ensues, with fathers killing sons and sons killing fathers. Kṛṣṇa himself becomes enraged at the slaughter of his own sons and personally exterminates most of his surviving kinsmen.[36] When it is over, Kṛtavarman, Kṛṣṇa's sons, and virtually all of the Vṛṣṇi warriors have been slaughtered. The sea begins to rise, ultimately inundating Dvārakā. Kṛṣṇa and Balarāma abandon their earthly forms, inaugurating the disastrous Kali Age.[37]

---

34. For the genealogies and relationship of the Yadus to the Kurus lineage, see *MBh* 1.79.5–7. See also Simon Brodbeck, "Solar and Lunar Lines in the *Mahābhārata*," *Religions of South Asia* 5, no. 1–2 (2012): 127–52.

35. *MBh* 16.1.2–10.

36. *MBh* 16. 16–46.

37. *MBh* 16.5.11–25.

Ultimately, Arjuna, alerted by dire portents, will arrive and lead the doomed city's women, children, and elderly on a sad journey back to Hāstinapura.[38] It is the news of the extermination of the Vṛṣṇis and the passing of Kṛṣṇa from the earthly realm that finally convinces the Pāṇḍavas that their world is in ruins and their age has ended. Yudhiṣṭhira then sets his mind on their ritual *mahāprasthāna*, their departure from the world, amidst the very "anomie, ascetic suicide, and apocalypse" of which Pollock writes.[39]

This terrifying, culminating episode in many ways appears to draw in and encapsulate several of the grim threads of the *Mahābharata* episodes sketched out above—and even the entire epic itself. With its grotesque, transgressive, and antic performance of the false embryo which becomes the means of a universal slaughter and its theme of the final inundation of Dvārakā, this last internecine brawl both mirrors and anticipates, in miniature, the cosmic destruction of the world (*pralaya*). For, in many *śruti* and *smṛti* texts ("revealed" and "remembered" texts, respectively), each cycle of creation arises from the undifferentiated cosmic waters and returns to it at the end of its time.

The significance of the extreme violence of the *Mahābhārata* has long been a matter of scholarly debate and has given rise to widely divergent opinions. Several of the violent episodes that I have discussed here—and indeed the central battle of Kurukṣetra—are depicted literally or figuratively as sacrifices. In this way, they mirror the early Vedic *karmakāṇḍa* ("section on rituals") view that sacrifice is critical to the maintenance of the world order. In this view, dharma and many of the rituals that sustain it require the immolation of victims. When the eighth-century Hindu philosopher Śaṅkarācārya uses the analogy of sacrifice to justify the violence of the Bhārata war, his analysis reflects this Vedic understanding of violence as sacrifice.[40] This idea has also been discussed at length in modern scholarship.[41]

38. *MBh* 16.8.33–74.

39. *MBh* 17.1.2.

40. Śaṅkarācārya on *BhG* 2.10. See *Bhagavad-Gita Eleven Commentaries*, 75.

41. For example, see Alf Hiltebeitel, *The Ritual of Battle: Krishna in the Mahābhārata* (Albany: State University of New York Press, 1976); and Danielle Feller Jatavallabhula, "Raṇayajña: The Mahābhārata War as a Sacrifice" in *Violence Denied: Violence, Non-Violence, and the Rationalization of Violence in South Asian Cultural History*, eds. Jan E. M. Houben and Karel R. Van Kooij (Leiden: Brill, 1999).

More recently, the theme of mass violence in the *Mahābhārata* became the subject of a critical disagreement between two of the epic's influential modern interpreters, themselves important political actors. Lokamanya B. G. Tilak famously understood the violence of the poem, and specifically Kṛṣṇa's exhortation in the *Gītā* to abandon faintheartedness and passivity in the interest of acting violently against one's enemies, as a call to his contemporaries to take militant action against India's colonial rulers.[42] Mahatma Gandhi, on the other hand, saw the *Mahābhārata* as a warning against violence. Not only does the *Mahābhārata* display the sorrow and misery of the war's victors but it also, Gandhi reasoned, intends to present an allegorical reading of humanity's inner conflict between its beneficent and malefic drives.[43] We might trace Gandhi's interpretation to Śaṅkara's commentary on the *Chāndogya Upaniṣad*, in which he argues that the *deva*s represent the refined organs of sense that are illuminated by the teachings of the *śāstra*s (scriptures), while their rivals, the *asura*s, are, in reality, the natural, unrefined human senses that are constituted of darkness. Through this allegorical interpretation, Śaṅkara represents the perpetual conflict between the *deva*s and the *asura*s—of which, after all, the *Mahābhārata* war is but one battle—as the endless struggle between the positive and negative elements of our nature, which constantly strive to overcome one another.[44] This position finds a measure of support from the contemporary scholar Vishwa Adluri, who reads the epic as a guide toward the attenuation of violence.[45]

Still, we ought to ask: How does a work that is grounded in and pervaded by a form of cosmic and totalizing violence truly work toward its attenuation in the emotional life of its audience? What, in other words,

42. On Tilak and the *Gītā*, see Richard H. Davis, *The Bhagavad Gita: A Biography* (Princeton, NJ: Princeton University Press, 2015), 130–34.

43. On Gandhi and the *Gītā*, see Davis, 136–43.

44. *devāsurā devāś cāsurāś ca | dīvyater dyotanārthasya śāstrodbhāsitā indriyavṛttayaḥ | asurās tadviparītāḥ sveṣv evāsuṣu viṣvagviśayāsu prāṇanakriyāsu ramaṇāt svābhāvikyastamaātmikā indriyavṛttaya eva. . . . yatra yasmin nimitta itaretaraviṣayāpahāralakṣaṇe saṃyetire saṃpūrvasya yatateḥ saṃgrāmārthatvam iti saṃgrāmaṃ kṛtavanta ity arthaḥ |* Śaṅkarācārya on *Chāndogya Upaniṣad* 1.2.1. See Śaṅkarācārya, *The Upanishadbhashya*, ed. Hari Raghunath Bhagavat, 2 vols. (Poona: Ashtekar & Co., 1927–28).

45. Vishwa Adluri, "Literary Violence & Literal Salvation: Śaunaka Interprets the *Mahābhārata*," *EXEMPLAR: The Journal of South Asian Studies* 1, no. 2 (2012): 47.

can we make in real, human terms of the *Mahābhārata's* pervasive concern with and representation of extreme mass violence? What does it mean when authors and audiences fantasize about and/or engage, directly or vicariously, in acts of ethnic cleansing or genocide? There are probably few, if any, major works of world literature that even remotely approach the level of the *Mahābhārata's* obsession with this theme. But unfortunately, world history—especially in modernity—stands as a rich source of all-too-real examples of it. If we look at the cases of Turkey (the Armenian genocide), Nazi Germany (the Holocaust), Myanmar (the ethnic cleansing of the Rohingya), Rwanda (the Hutu-Tutsi massacres), the Balkans (expulsion and killings of Bosnian Muslims), and the genocide of the Native Americans,[46] it is clear that, as authorities on political psychology have observed, movements to define specific groups, classes, ethnicities, or religions as other than or at odds with a settled majority generally arise "at times of stress from factors like war, major political changes, or economic collapse."[47] The sense of apocalypse that certain groups take on when they believe that their sense of self and security has been undermined by other communities—a feature of stressed and anxious populations such as those that we see in contemporary Europe, Asia and, now, the United States, with its resurgence of nativism, anti-immigration movements, and white supremacy—may well have been at the root of the pessimism, anxiety, and sense of the end of a familiar world order that so deeply characterizes the *Mahābhārata*.

It is illuminating to compare the ethos of the literal "end of days" scenario of the poem—of the sense of *yugānta*, as the familiar world slips into the feared chaos, whether of the Kali Age or of "American carnage"—with that of the *Mahābhārata's* twin epic, the *Rāmāyaṇa*. The two works have much in common structurally and thematically. But where the former ends with the wretched survivors, victorious though they may be, trekking grimly into the mountains as their world, impelled by all-powerful Time, grinds inexorably on into a degenerate future, the latter ends on a note of great cultural optimism. For there, in the Tretā age, when Rāma recovered his rightful throne, it was as if the downward spiral of cosmic time was reversed

46. See, for example, Benjamin Madley, *An American Genocide: The United States and the California Indian Catastrophe, 1846–1873* (New Haven: Yale University Press, 2016).

47. Amanda Taub, "Myanmar Follows Global Pattern in How Ethnic Cleansing Begins," *New York Times*. September 19, 2017. A4.

and the world was returned once again to its pristine state of perfection, just as in the golden age (*kṛtayuge yathā*).[48]

It remains, of course, an ongoing matter of debate as to when exactly the *Mahābhārata* as we know it was composed and over how long a period. But it seems likely that the archetypal form of the text was basically settled between the last century BCE and the first two centuries CE. This was a period of increasing foreign contact; exogenous groups such as the Greeks, Kuṣāṇas, and Śakas increasingly immigrated into the Indian subcontinent, where they both confronted and co-opted late- and post-Vedic civilization. During the same period, the burgeoning *śramaṇa* monastic communities of the Buddhists and the Jains posed a continuing challenge to the *vaidika* (Vedic) social order such as it was. This was the so-called "age of invasions," and of the social and political disruptions and dislocations that the subcontinent's "second urbanization" would likely have produced. All of this social and cultural instability, I believe, might well have provoked the kinds of cultural anxiety we have seen over the course of history that has not infrequently generated genocidal ideation, fantasies, and, far too often, action. The *Mahābhārata*, with its constantly repeated tales of mass exterminations and accounts of the slaughter of one's perceived enemies and "others" *ā garbhāt*, "down to the embryos in the womb," presents an unsettling scenario that has been all too familiar throughout humanity's shared history. Perhaps the poem itself—imbibed, recited, and performed publicly—stimulated, through a vicarious and mixed sense of horror and gratification, a kind of catharsis on the part of its audiences. For, at least as far as history has been able to uncover, we have no record of such massive killings in Indian antiquity other than, perhaps, Emperor Aśoka's famous third-century BCE account of the many hundreds of thousands who perished in the course of his conquest of Kalinga.[49] But sadly, as we learn from our own history and our daily media, we know that these things are no mere fantasies.

48. *Rāmāyaṇa* 1.1.73. See Vālmīki, *The Vālmīki Rāmāyaṇa: Critically Edited for the First Time*, eds. G. H. Bhatt and U. P. Shah, et al. 7 vols. (Baroda: Oriental Institute, 1960–75).

49. Romila Thapar, *Early India: From the Origins to AD 1300* (Berkeley: University of California Press, 2002), 180–81.

Chapter Three

The Invention of Irāvān[1]

David Gitomer

Introduction

Many Mahābhāratas evokes *Many Rāmāyaṇas* and *Questioning Rāmāyaṇas*, two volumes (both of them edited by Paula Richman) that explore the diversity of the other major South Asian epic tradition, the Rāmāyaṇa.[2] Yet there is at least one sense in which the notion of "many Mahābhāratas" is more plural and expansive than that of "many Rāmāyaṇas," and it emerges even when we focus on the Sanskrit epic alone. If we consider the critical edition—with its apparatus and various supplements—to be a kind of library of Sanskrit Mahābhāratas, then this library, because of its significant variations in regional recensions and interwoven popular narratives, appears to represent an even more lavish narrative diversity than what one finds

1. Many thanks to Nell Shapiro Hawley and Sohini Sarah Pillai for their support of this project. I am also grateful to the Kannada scholar Timothy Lorndale for generously answering my research questions about the tenth-century *Vikramārjunavijaya* of Pampa.

2. See Paula Richman, ed. *Many Rāmāyaṇas: The Diversity of a Narrative Tradition in South Asia* (Berkeley: University of California Press, 1991); and Paula Richman, ed. *Questioning Rāmāyaṇas: A South Asian Tradition* (Berkeley: University of California Press, 2000).

within the corpus of Vālmīki's *Rāmāyaṇa*. Most striking are the *Mahābhārata*'s authors[3] who produce new narrative channels out of tributary streams that are otherwise mere trickles. In other words, they introduce stories that strongly resonate with epic themes, even if these stories are not consistently stitched into the primary narrative. This essay concerns one such channel: the story of Irāvān, Arjuna's mysterious half-*nāga* (snake) son, to whom a chapter of the *Bhīṣmaparvan* ("The Book of Bhīṣma," the sixth book of the Sanskrit *Mahābhārata*) is dedicated.[4]

Irāvān resembles the figure of Aravāṉ, who appears not only in the premodern Tamil Mahābhāratas of Peruntēvaṉār and Villiputtūr but also in

3. Whether we see it through careful reading or through computational linguistics, it is clear that the epic on the whole represents many styles and interests in composition. One could argue that the epic does not have a single "unity," but a variety of "unities." I hold no orthodoxy about the "stages" or time frames of the epic's composition, but I observe signs of both disjunction (what Oliver Hellwig calls "change points") in the introduction of different material and also a creative sensitivity to context. See "Stratifying the Mahābhārata: The Textual Position of the Bhagavadgītā," *Indo-Iranian Journal* 60, no. 2 (2017): 132–69. It is important to point out that the notion that some materials are "spurious" or "interpolated" often reflects biased ideologies or preconceptions about the origin and growth of the text. My argument is about literary structure and meaning, what was once called "the higher criticism." Yet my way of thinking about the epic's composition is not resolutely ahistorical; it may ultimately affect how we understand processes of composition and intertextuality in premodern South Asia.

4. Unless otherwise stated, cited passages are from the *Mahābhārata* (*MBh*) as constituted in the critical edition: *The Mahābhārata for the First Time Critically Edited*, ed. V. S. Sukthankar et al. 19 vols. (Poona: Bhandarkar Oriental Research Institute, 1933–66). But owing to the perspective described in the first paragraph and the previous note, I also make use of passages appearing in the vulgate edition with the *Bhāvadīpa* commentary of Nīlakaṇṭha and the southern recension (Kumbakonam edition). See *Śrī Mahābhāratam with the Bhāratabhāvadīpa Commentary of Nīlakaṇṭha*, ed. Ramchandrashastri Kinjawadekar, 6 vols. (Poona: Chitrashala Press, 1929–36); and *Sriman Mahābhāratam: A New Edition Mainly Based on the South Indian Texts*, eds. T. R. Krishnacharya and T. R. Vyasacharya, 7 vols. (Kumbakonam: Madhva Vilas Book Depot, 1906–10). Many thanks to Dominik Wujastyk for his assistance in stimulating the completion of the Romanized IAST version of the southern recension as part of the SARIT project. See SARIT, "Mahabharata: Machine Readable Transcription in IAST Encoding," *Archive*, 2016, https://archive.org/details/Mahabharata-MachineReadableTranscriptionInIastEncoding; and SARIT, "Śrīman Mahābhāratam," *Indology*, 2014, http://sarit.indology.info/exist/rest/db/apps/sarit-pm/sarit-data/mahabharata-devanagari.xml

the Kūttāṇṭavar (Aravāṉ) and Draupadī cults of present-day Tamil Nadu.[5] David Shulman and Alf Hiltebeitel have studied the relationship between the Sanskrit *Mahābhārata*'s Irāvān and Aravāṉ of the Tamil texts and rituals; this chapter expands on these studies by analyzing the resonance of the Irāvān story within the Sanskrit *Mahābhārata* itself.[6] The fact that this story ushers in a series of narratives about *rākṣasa* battles (I soon discuss the term *rākṣasa*)—all of which are linked, in one way or another, to Bhīma's half-*rākṣasa* son Ghaṭotkaca—presents us with the opportunity first to consider the relationship between Irāvān and these *rākṣasa* stories, particularly the story of Ghaṭotkaca, and then to come to a better understanding of the affection that the Pāṇḍava fathers Arjuna and Bhīma express toward their quarter-human sons.

The Texture of Battle Narration in the *Bhīṣmaparvan*

The *Bhīṣmaparvan* begins with Janamejaya (the Pāṇḍavas' descendent) asking the sage Vaiśaṃpāyana (one of the epic's frame narrators), "How did those heroes fight?"[7] Inside Janamejaya's frame story, the Kaurava king Dhṛtarāṣṭra asks the same question of his own storyteller, Sañjaya. Yet the interrogative word *katham*—"How?"—also expresses astonishment, and so this question represents not only a request for narration ("In what manner did the war unfold?") but also reflects a moral question: How can it be

5. In several Tamil Mahābhārata traditions, Aravāṉ is the son of Arjuna who willingly offers himself to the Pāṇḍavas for a human sacrifice to the goddess Kālī before the battle at Kurukṣetra. In certain tellings of this story, Aravāṉ is married to Mohinī (Kṛṣṇa in female form) before he is sacrificed. Because of his marriage to Mohinī, Aravāṉ has become an important figure for the transgender community in Tamil Nadu. See David Shulman, "The Serpent and the Sacrifice: An Anthill Myth from Tiruvārūr," *History of Religions* 18, no. 2 (1978): 107–37; Alf Hiltebeitel, *The Cult of Draupadī*, vol. 1, *Mythologies: From Gingee to Kurukṣetra* (Chicago: University of Chicago Press, 1988); Alf Hiltebeitel, *The Cult of Draupadī*, vol. 2, *On Hindu Ritual and the Goddess* (Chicago: University of Chicago Press, 1991); and Alf Hiltebeitel, "Dying Before the *Mahābhārata* War: Martial and Transsexual Body-building for Aravāṉ," *The Journal of Asian Studies* 54, no. 2 (1995): 447–73.

6. Shulman, "Serpent and Sacrifice," 131–33; Hiltebeitel, *Draupadī* 1, 317–32; *Draupadī* 2, 283–319; and Hiltebeitel, "Dying before the War," 447–73. Both Shulman and Hiltebeitel seem careful not to imply the priority of the Sanskrit epic.

7. *kathaṃ yuyudhire vīrāḥ* || *MBh* 6.1.1||

that events are turning out this way? How is that with all our might, we Kauravas are losing? What moral and divine vectors bear on the outcome of the war? This doubly resonant *katham* constitutes a recurring device that provides both the practical armature of storytelling and the moral armature of the meaning of violent action. The latter plays a special role in the *Bhīṣmaparvan* specifically: it invokes the ideal of devotional yogic detachment that Kṛṣṇa discusses in the *Bhagavadgītā* (a series of chapters early in the *Bhīṣmaparvan*), which makes for the most grandiose reflection on ethical meaning in the war books (books six through nine of the Sanskrit epic), and perhaps in the epic as a whole.[8]

The initial verses of the *Bhīṣmaparvan* model the battle rhetoric for the entire narration of the war. The armies of the world amass under ominous portents: blood and flesh rain down on them. They are flushed with the excitement of battle, jangling their armor and blowing their conches; they are like two oceans roiling against each other at the hour of apocalypse. In fact, Sañjaya's narration of the battles models an entire battle aesthetic. The battlefield—resplendent with toppled banners, carpeted with lopped-off limbs that gleam with ornaments and weapons—captures the beauty of a garden blossoming with spring flowers. Bhīma—lacerated with arrows, blood flowing from his wounds—is as beautiful as a flowering *kiṃśuka* tree. Repeated frequently, these images contribute to the highly formulaic language for which the battle books have become famous.[9]

Initially, there are no significant deaths during the *Bhīṣmaparvan*. This absence is important to note because the death of a major figure—a character to whom audiences have become attached—typically occasions

8. In particular the assertion of an earlier, martially-oriented oral epic against the devotional, philosophical, and hieratic concerns of the *Bhagavadgītā* have been endlessly and contentiously theorized. See the arguments in Vishwa Adluri and Joydeep Bagchee, *The Nay Science: A History of German Indology* (New York: Oxford University Press, 2014), 156–313.

9. See Georg von Simson, "Text Layers in the *Mahābhārata*: Some Observations in Connection with *Mahābhārata* VII.131," in *The Mahābhārata Revisited*, ed. R. N. Dandekar (Delhi: Sahitya Akademi, 1990), 38; *The Mahābhārata: An Abridged Translation,* trans. John D. Smith (London: Penguin Books, 2009), liv–lx; John Brockington, *Epic Threads: John Brockington on the Sanskrit Epics,* eds. Greg Bailey and Mary Brockington (Delhi: Oxford University Press, 2000),115–16, 341; and *Mahabharata, Book Seven: Drona,* vol. 1, trans. Vaughn Pilikian, Clay Sanskrit Library (New York: New York University Press, JJC Foundation, 2006), 19–22.

a lament, which constitutes an indispensably engaging element of the epic battle genre. (Consider, for example, the heart-rending laments for Arjuna's [other] son Abhimanyu and Bhīma's son Ghaṭotkaca, which hold such emotional weight later in the epic.) In the *Bhīṣmaparvan*, at least at first, the named warriors who die are obscure and their deaths perfunctory. The dramatic death of Irāvān in the eighty-sixth chapter marks a major shift.

The Birth of Irāvān

In general, our capacity to be moved by the battle narration depends on a pre-existing connection to the warriors whose conflicts the battle books depict. For this reason, the story of Irāvān reflects not only a virtuoso epic composition but also an ingenious narrative illusion: it presents itself as a sequel of an earlier story, but it is not. Our narrator introduces Irāvān (who initially appears attacking a part of the Kaurava army) as "Arjuna's virile heir, Irāvān by name, son of the *nāga* king's daughter and the intelligent Pārtha [Arjuna]."[10] This introduction prompts the audience to recall the story of Arjuna meeting Ulūpī in the *Ādiparvan* ("The Book of Beginnings," the first book of the Sanskrit *Mahābhārata*).[11] The context for Arjuna and Ulūpī's encounter in the *Ādiparvan* is that Arjuna has violated his marriage contract by "seeing" Draupadī with Yudhiṣṭhira and thus is required to live as an ascetic in exile for a year. Ulūpī, meanwhile, is a *nāga* princess. While Arjuna bathes in the Gaṅgā, she pulls him underwater and asserts that while dharma may require that Arjuna remain in exile for a year from Draupadī, this particular dharma has nothing to do with her. In fact, she explains, dharma demands that Arjuna satisfy her lust. So, of course, he does. At this point, the southern recension of the *Mahābhārata* says that the two have a son named Irāvān, but neither the name nor the birth of a son occurs in the *Ādiparvan* of the critical edition of the epic, nor does it appear in the vulgate.[12]

10. *MBh* 6.86.6.

11. *MBh* 1.206.

12. The southern recension of the epic inserts the birth of Irāvān by adding a verse between what are the first and second lines of 1.206.34 of the critical edition. The vulgate ends the tale of Arjuna and Ulūpī's sexual union with the *nāga* princess granting Arjuna a boon of invincibility in water (1.216.36).

In fact, Irāvān appears nowhere in the epic except for in this chapter of the *Bhīṣmaparvan*. Our "Irāvān author" elaborates on the tale of Irāvān's birth:

> Childless and wretched in mind, the miserable creature [Ulūpī] had been given in marriage by the high-souled Airāvata, her father, when her husband was killed by Suparṇa [Garuḍa]. Pārtha took her to wife, since she was consumed by passion.[13] And thus was Arjuna's own son born from another's wife. [Irāvān] grew up in the realm of the *nāgas*, secretly guarded by his mother, as he had been rejected by an evil paternal uncle who hated Arjuna.[14]

Here in the *Bhīṣmaparvan*'s account, Ulūpī—whom the narrative does not name at this point—is widowed when her husband is killed by the celestial eagle Garuḍa (who, like all birds, is known for his enmity with *nāgas*). These details do not emerge in the *Ādiparvan*'s account of Arjuna and Ulūpī's encounter.

Just as the author exploits the story of Arjuna's relationship with the *nāga* princess in the *Ādiparvan* to create Irāvān here in the *Bhīṣmaparvan*, so, too, does the author use the story of Arjuna's sojourn in Indra's heaven (which is narrated in the third book of the Sanskrit epic, the *Āraṇyakaparvan*, or "The Book of the Forest") to construct a reunion between Irāvān and Arjuna. We hear nothing of a visit from Irāvān in any recension of

13. Previous translators, against grammar and against the very point of the story, have construed Arjuna as the one consumed by passion.

14. *MBh* 6.86.7–9. *Pitṛvya* definitely means a relative on the father's side and this passage is translated both by Alex Cherniak (6.90) and K. M. Ganguli (6.91) as "his paternal uncle," but who would this be? I think it might more likely refer to a paternal uncle of his mother's. See *Mahabharata, Book Six: Bhishma,* vol. 2, trans. Alex Cherniak, Clay Sanskrit Library (New York: New York University Press, JJC Foundation, 2009); and *The Mahabharata of Krishna-Dwaipayana Translated into English Prose*, trans. K. M. Ganguli, ed. P. C. Roy, 12 vols. (Calcutta: Bharat Press, 1883–96). Nīlakaṇṭha, on the corresponding passage in the southern recension (6.90.10), plausibly glosses *pitṛvyena* as Aśvasena—not the son of Dhṛtarāṣṭra but the son of the mighty snake Takṣaka, who manages with the help of his snake mother, and then Indra, to escape Arjuna's burning of the Khāṇḍava Forest, making Arjuna furious (1.218–19).

the *Āraṇyakaparvan*; this story exists exclusively in the *Bhīṣmaparvan*.[15] Here is the *Bhīṣmaparvan*'s account of the encounter between Irāvān and Arjuna in Indra's heaven:

> Handsome in form, endowed with virility, full of good qualities, valorous in truth, Irāvān quickly went to Indra's realm, hearing that Arjuna had gone there. He approached his great-souled father, valorous in truth. His focus unwavering, he saluted him in accordance with proper behavior, his hands folded, saying: "I am Irāvān, your son. I wish you well, mighty lord!" Irāvān then communicated everything about his father's union with his mother, and Arjuna recollected it all just as it occurred. Arjuna embraced his son, quite like himself in his qualities, and became filled with gladness there in the dwelling of the king of the gods. There in the realm of the gods Arjuna became filled with love and briefed mighty-armed Irāvān about his duties: "In wartime, you must give us your assistance." "For certain!" he replied. So when it was wartime, he arrived surrounded by many horses, desirable in their colors and speed.[16]

It's a charming wisp of a story: Arjuna spends time with his father (Indra), so Irāvān wants to spend time with *his* father, Arjuna. More important, however, is the fact that this vignette puts in parallel three different father-son relationships. The most straightforward parallel sits between Indra and Arjuna, on the one hand, and Arjuna and Irāvān, on the other: two sons undertake journeys on which they encounter their fathers. But Irāvān's promise to Arjuna echoes another father-son relationship—that which exists between Bhīma and Ghaṭotkaca. A crucial detail in this respect is that soon after Ghaṭotkaca is born, Ghaṭotkaca promises Bhīma that he will come to his aid when Bhīma needs it.[17] Here, through Irāvān's parallel promise ("In

15. Nīlakaṇṭha says nothing about the tale of the visit to the Indraloka. Nor is this event described in the extensive mythologies of Irāvān/Aravāṉ reported in Hiltebeitel's two volumes on the Draupadī cult. Hiltebeitel gives only a cursory acknowledgement of the story in "Dying Before the War," 448.

16. *MBh* 6.86.10–15.

17. *MBh* 1.143.36.

wartime, you must give us your assistance"—"For certain!"), the narrative constructs Irāvān as an explicit reflection of Ghaṭotkaca. Both Irāvān and Ghaṭotkaca are born from nonhuman mothers (Ulūpī the *nāga*, in Irāvān's case, and Hiḍimbā the *rākṣasa*, in Ghaṭotkaca's); both of them promise to come to the aid of their human (or, rather, half human, half divine) fathers when necessary. We will see how the stories surrounding Irāvān and Ghaṭotkaca weave together even more tightly as the battle books continue.

The Death of Irāvān

When Duryodhana sees Irāvān wreaking havoc on the Kaurava army, he summons a *rākṣasa* named Ārśyaśṛṅgi (not to be confused with the ascetic Ṛśyaśṛṅga of the *Āraṇyakaparvan*[18]), whom the epic eventually calls Alambusa[19] and who, as Alambusa, becomes the first of two major Kaurava *rākṣasas*.[20] It seems that this story of the confrontation between Ārśyaśṛṅgi and Irāvān has been introduced in order to illustrate an exhilarating *rākṣasa* battle replete with illusions and supernatural combat feats. Until this point, everything in the *Bhīṣmaparvan*'s battles has been rather grimly human, if exaggerated (in true *Mahābhārata* style). But Irāvān, being the son of a *nāga*, can almost match this *rākṣasa* in magical violence:

18. Still, Hiltebeitel declares that this Ārśyaśṛṅgi is a descendent of the sage Ṛśyaśṛṅga in "Dying Before the War," 450.

19. In the critical edition, Alambusa is first mentioned at 6.43, where he fights Ghaṭotkaca in the first battle, and then again in a series of combats in 6.59, 6.77, and 6.78. These appearances illustrate von Simson's principle (demonstrated in his essay on *MBh* 7.131) that "one of the means to illustrate the importance of a given hero of the Mahābhārata in relation to other heroes is to make him fight several single combats, including one or more encounters with his main enemy by whom he is finally killed." See "Text Layers," 38. In the vulgate, this *rākṣasa* is always called Alambuṣa (rather than Alambusa as in the critical edition). In the critical edition, he is called only Ārśyaśṛṅgi during the fight with Irāvān; he is not identified as Alambusa. It is only in 6.96.41–6.97 (in a fight with Abhimanyu) that he is once again called Alambusa. Abhimanyu defeats but does not kill him. In the critical edition, Ghaṭotkaca kills him in the 149th chapter of the seventh book (7.174 in the vulgate).

20. *MBh* 6.86.44.

> Then Irāvān also jumped into the sky confounding the *rākṣasa* with his illusions. Irāvān—knowing all the vulnerable spots of the body, shape-shifting at will, and impossible to overpower—cut off the *rākṣasa*'s limbs with arrows. But as he was being sliced by arrows again and again, that best of *rākṣasa*s renewed himself in a youthful form. For illusion is innate in *rākṣasa*s—age and form are whatever they will. And so the *rākṣasa*'s body grew out even when sliced and sliced again. Yet Irāvān, too, boiling with rage, sliced away at the *rākṣasa* with a razor-sharp axe again and again. While that virile *rākṣasa* was being chopped down like a tree by his strong foe, he bellowed fiercely, and the sound became a tumultuous blast. Great quantities of blood poured out of the *rākṣasa*'s wound from the battle axe but, being strong, he gathered his rage and renewed his vehemence in battle. Ārśyaśṛṅgi, beholding his enemy resurgent, assumed a huge dreadful form, and rushed forward to lay hold of him at the front of the battle, while everyone looked on. When he saw this illusion that the great-souled *rākṣasa* had fashioned, Irāvān became enraged and he, too, started to conjure an illusion. Never retreating from battle, fully under the sway of his anger, relief came to him in the form of his mother's *nāga* kin. Surrounded in battle by multitudes of snakes, he assumed a vast body like that of the divine cobra Ananta with his hood spread wide, and he smothered the *rākṣasa* with snakes of every kind. But even while smothered by serpents, that bull of a *rākṣasa* figured out what to do: Taking on the form of divine vulture Garuḍa, he devoured the snakes.[21]

In the battle between Irāvān and Ārśyaśṛṅgi, each of the combatants uses illusion to transform himself into an aspect of Viṣṇu's cosmic apparatus: Irāvān, being part *nāga*, turns himself into the divine serpent Ananta, on whom Viṣṇu reclines; when Irāvān summons an onslaught of snakes, Ārśyaśṛṅgi transforms himself into Garuḍa, Viṣṇu's winged mount, a natural enemy of snakes. When Ārśyaśṛṅgi, as Garuḍa, kills all of Irāvān's snakes, we recall how, in the story of Irāvān's birth, Garuḍa slays Ulūpī's first

---

21. *MBh* 6.86.58–68.

husband. Irāvān can almost match Ārśyaśṛṅgi, but not quite: "Then, just as the snakes—his mother's kinfolk—were being devoured by the *rākṣasa*'s illusion of Garuḍa, the *rākṣasa* struck down the swooning Irāvān with his sword. Ārśyaśṛṅgi knocked Irāvān's head to the ground, his earrings and diadem glowing like moon lotuses."[22] Writing of the possible connections between the Sanskrit *Mahābhārata*'s Irāvān and the extensive mythology of Aravāṉ in Tamil myths, literature, and ritual theater, both Shulman and Hiltebeitel identify the centrality of the motif of sacrifice in the story of Irāvān's death. Hiltebeitel points out the alternate derivation of Irāvān's name from *iḍā*, the "sacrificial essence," while Shulman declares that Aravāṉ "lives today as a folk hero because he embodies the idea of self-sacrifice."[23] The motif of sacrifice is heightened in the *Mahābhārata*'s account of Irāvān's death when, crucially, Ghaṭotkaca—who himself dies fighting on behalf of the Pāṇḍavas later in the epic story—is the first to react to the death of his "brother" Irāvān. His "terrible roar" shakes the earth and paralyzes the legs of the Kaurava army: "The *rākṣasa* bellowed out his roar like a thunderstorm, brandished his blazing pike, and assumed a terrifying form. Surrounded by the foremost *rākṣasa* troops wielding all kinds of dreadful missiles, he concentrated his fury and went at [the Kaurava] forces like Yama [Death] at the end of time."[24]

Arjuna, meanwhile, discovers Irāvān's death eight chapters later. His brief but intense lament for Irāvān represents the first significant lament for a dead hero in the Kurukṣetra war.[25] But beyond the fact that eight chapters have elapsed since the death of Irāvān, there is something curious about this lament. Arjuna learns of Irāvān's death from Bhīma at the end of the previous chapter ("at last, Bhīmasena told Kṛṣṇa and Arjuna about the killing of Irāvān just as it had happened"[26]). Then only a single verse describes the part of the lament that references Irāvān specifically: "When

22. *MBh* 6.86.69–70.

23. Hiltebeitel, *Draupadī* 1, 320; and Shulman, "Serpent and Sacrifice," 132. Timothy Lorndale has informed me that Irāvān is called Iḷāvanta in the Kannada *Vikramājunavijaya*.

24. *MBh* 6.87.2–7.

25. *MBh* 6.92. This is a striking contrast to the Draupadī cult battlefield rituals, in which Arjuna witnesses Aravāṉ's sacrificial death. See Hiltebeitel, *Draupadī* 2, 237.

26. *bhīmaseno 'pi samare tāv ubhau keśavārjunau |*
āśrāvayad yathāvṛttam irāvadvadham uttamam || *MBh* 6.91.81 ||

Arjuna heard that his son Irāvān was killed, he became mightily grieved, exhaling like a hissing snake."[27] Arjuna's sigh represents a brief (perhaps playful) tribute to his half-*nāga* son, but the remainder of the lament takes a much broader focus. Arjuna bemoans the terrible destruction of the war and the greed that caused it; he damns the *kṣatriya* (warrior) life. Then he emboldens himself to fight the next battle.[28] Given that the remainder of this lament fails to reference Irāvān specifically, it may be that one or more of the epic's authors situated the two verses about Irāvān—first Bhīma's news, then Arjuna's serpentine sigh—before a pre-existing lament (about the moral failings of the war and its warriors) in order to support the insertion of the story of Irāvān's death earlier in the narrative.

As a whole, the Irāvān episode—the origin story, the promise between Irāvān and Arjuna, the combat with Ārśyaśṛṅgi, Irāvān's death, Ghaṭotkaca's dramatic reaction, and Arjuna's lament—lends both an extravagant battle narrative and a certain degree of pathos to a part of the epic that otherwise lacks these key features that make the remainder of the war story so engaging. Moreover, when it comes to the overall construction of the battle narrative, Irāvān's death activates Ghaṭotkaca's *rākṣasa* nature—a *rākṣasa* horde materializes to accompany Ghaṭotkaca when he becomes enraged at Irāvān's death—and provides a key link in the war's chain of *rākṣasa* revenge killings. The death of Irāvān causes Ghaṭotkaca to kill the Kaurava *rākṣasa*s Alambusa (whom we know as Ārśyaśṛṅgi) and Alāyudha. These slayings eventually lead to Ghaṭotkaca's own death at the hands of Karṇa: because Karṇa uses on Ghaṭotkaca the special weapon that he had been planning to unleash on Arjuna, Ghaṭotkaca's death preserves the life of Arjuna, Irāvān's father, and so the circle leads back to Irāvān.[29]

Irāvān and the *Rākṣasa*s

*Rākṣasa*s echo from every corner of Irāvān's story. Not only does Irāvān battle a *rākṣasa* to the death, but he uses *rākṣasa*-specific powers in this fight; shape-shifting and illusions, both of which Irāvān engages in combat,

27. *putraṃ tu nihataṃ śrutvā irāvantaṃ dhanaṃjayaḥ* |
duḥkhena mahatāviṣṭo niḥśvasan pannago yathā || *MBh* 6.92.1 ||

28. *MBh* 6.92.2–10.

29. *MBh* 7.155.

constitute the classic weapons of a *rākṣasa*. The narrative then deepens Irāvān's *rākṣasa* undertones by linking him to Ghaṭotkaca in a number of important ways.[30] As we have seen, Ghaṭotkaca expresses an emotional connection to Irāvān in his anger at Irāvān's death; this anger then ties Irāvān's death to Ghaṭotkaca's eventual death later in the revenge cycle. Both Irāvān and Ghaṭotkaca, two figures whose mothers live far outside the Pāṇḍavas' *kṣatriya* orbit, sacrifice their lives to fight in their Pāṇḍava fathers' war. The two figures' origin stories connect them, too: the story of Bhīma and the *rākṣasa* Hiḍimbā's marriage, from which Ghaṭotkaca emerges, clearly serves as a template for Arjuna and Ulūpī's. In this way, although Irāvān is a *nāga*, the *Mahābhārata* also formulates him as a pseudo-*rākṣasa*, or more specifically, a pseudo-Ghaṭotkaca.

*Rākṣasa*s—excremental wreckers of sacrifice, libidinous shape-shifters, and conjurers of illusions—can be characterized as the psychological and cultural opposites of *brāhmaṇa*s, who typically exhibit a great deal of concern for purity (ritual and otherwise) and maintenance of the social order.[31] As a group, *rākṣasa*s are morally ambivalent rather than evil. While there are *rākṣasa*s of varying moral complexions in both of the Sanskrit epics, *rākṣasa*s in the *Rāmāyaṇa* are the narrative's central villains—emblematic figures who live in a fantastic remote kingdom. Since the evil in the *Mahābhārata* resides among human brothers, the *rākṣasa*s play a secondary role there. Nonetheless, in all of our received texts of the *Mahābhārata*, *rākṣasa*s have become integral to the story.[32]

Tales of marauding *rākṣasa*s abound in the early books of the epic, and it is typically up to Bhīma—who embodies certain *rākṣasa*-like quali-

30. On the depiction of Ghaṭotkaca in a modern graphic novel, see Philip Lutgendorf's chapter in this volume.

31. For an examination of the pre-epic and epic typology of these figures, see Sheldon Pollock, "*Rākṣasas* and Others," *Indologica Taurinensia* 13 (1985–86): 263–81. See also Adheesh Sathaye, *Crossing the Lines of Caste: Viśvāmitra and the Construction of Brahmin Power in Hindu Mythology* (New York: Oxford University Press, 2015), 88–95.

32. This part of the essay is not intended to be a comprehensive study of *rākṣasa*s in the *Mahābhārata,* but a sketch of the extent of participation of *rākṣasa*s in the central narrative, in particular as they interact with the major characters. There are indeed many other *rākṣasa* appearances in subnarratives of the epic.

ties himself—to destroy them.[33] His first encounter with *rākṣasas* has far-reaching consequences: He comes upon the *rākṣasa* Hiḍimba, who wants to eat him, and Hiḍimba's sister, Hiḍimbā (also called Hiḍimbī), who desires him. Their union produces the unambiguously "good" Ghaṭotkaca, who is half *rākṣasa*, a quarter divine (through Bhīma's father, Vāyu, the god of the wind), and a quarter human.[34] Later, Bhīma battles *rākṣasas* when retrieving the *saugandhika* flower for Draupadī in the *Āraṇyakaparvan*.[35] At the end of the war, *rākṣasas* help Aśvatthāman's crew swarm the remaining Pāṇḍavas in the surprise murder from which the *Sauptikaparvan* ("The Book of the Night Massacre") gets its name. Then there are the individual members of the *rākṣasa* clan who remain true to type in their vicious hatred of ritual order and human community.[36] The Pāṇḍavas especially draw their ire: Bhīma kills the *rākṣasas* Baka, Hiḍimba, Kirmira, and Jaṭāsura in the early parts of the epic. There are traces of "redeemed" *rākṣasas*, such as the followers of Baka, who, on Bhīma's admonition, agree to behave.[37]

The epic presents us with one final parallel between Irāvān and Ghaṭotkaca, this time set in an entirely *rākṣasa* context. In the *Droṇaparvan* ("The Book of Droṇa," the seventh book of the Sanskrit *Mahābhārata*), Ghaṭotkaca avenges Irāvān's death by slaying Ārśyaśṛṅgi, who is, at that point, known as Alambusa.[38] Then, on the fourteenth day of battle, the fighting continues into the night—the ideal time for *rākṣasas*' cannibalistic cruelty and illusions to hold sway. (*Rākṣasas* are frequently called *niśācaras*,

33. For a detailed examination of ambiguous motifs concerning *rākṣasas* and Bhīma's distinctive intimacy with the creatures, see David L. Gitomer, "Rākṣasa Bhīma: Wolfbelly among Ogres and Brahmans in the Sanskrit *Mahābhārata* and the *Veṇīsaṃhāra*," in *Essays on the Mahābhārata*, ed. Arvind Sharma (Leiden: E. J. Brill, 1991), 296–323.

34. *MBh* 1.139–42.

35. *MBh* 3.151–2, 3.157.

36. They do present themselves as a clan. The named evil *rākṣasas* know each other, and the last appearing *rākṣasa*, Alāyudha, claims that other *rākṣasas* who appear in earlier parts of the epic, Baka, Hiḍimba, and Kirmira, are his *jñāti* and *bāndhava*, or kin-relatives (*MBh* 7.151.3, 6). Various communities or "tribes" of *rākṣasas* are named in the Sanskrit *Mahābhārata*.

37. *MBh* 1.152.1–5.

38. *MBh* 7.83–84.

"night stalkers.") In this section, another *rākṣasa*, Alāyudha, appears (with thousands of other *rākṣasas*) and offers to assist Duryodhana: he wishes to exact revenge on Bhīma, he says, since Bhīma killed the *rākṣasas* Baka, Hiḍimba, and Kirmira.[39] The confrontation between Alāyudha and Ghaṭotkaca, breathlessly narrated, ends with Ghaṭotkaca beheading Alāyudha, just as Alambusa had beheaded Ghaṭotkaca's brother Irāvān.[40]

When we pull back from the *Bhīṣmaparvan* and look at the entire epic, especially at the entire war, we see that there is a narrative stream focusing on *rākṣasas* in battle that somewhat separates *rākṣasas* from their recurring role as despoilers of Brahmanical ritual and order.[41] This stream is inaugurated with the birth of Ghaṭotkaca, who promises to return when he is needed. Unlike Ghaṭotkaca, who is deeply embedded in many areas of the epic, Irāvān has been invented in the *Bhīṣmaparvan* to echo this same relationship with Arjuna and the *nāga* princess Ulūpī. Moreover, it is only when Irāvān dies that Ghaṭotkaca's role in the war comes to the fore. The death of Irāvān catalyzes Ghaṭotkaca's *rākṣasa* rage. Through Ghaṭotkaca's drive for revenge, Irāvān's death eventually beckons a chain of *rākṣasas* who engage in spectacular combat with him (and with Ghaṭotkaca's human associates). For this reason, we can say that Irāvān's story ushers in a whole series of narratives about nonhumans in the Kurukṣetra war.

Conclusion

As Aravāṉ, Irāvān lives a much more vigorous life in the regional and popular Tamil Mahābhārata cosmos than he ever lives in the Sanskrit epic. The story of Irāvān in the Sanskrit *Mahābhārata* prompts us to reconsider the commonly-held belief that figures such as Irāvān/Aravāṉ were "minor characters in the Sanskrit epic" who then acquired bigger, more complex, and wildly altered roles in regional traditions. When we look more closely at the textual evidence of all the Sanskrit materials available to us and

39. *MBh* 7.151. Like Alambusa, Alāyudha has only brief textual antecedent. In *MBh* 7.70.46 and 7.71.27 Alāyudha is mentioned briefly when he fights with Ghaṭotkaca.

40. *MBh* 7.153.

41. It is possible that further investigations may demonstrate that there was an author or group of authors who had a special interest in writing about these other kinds of *rākṣasas*.

examine the textual dynamics internally—rather than as antecedents or variants of later, more developed traditions in Tamil—we are more likely to see both the features of a dialogic, sometimes collaborative, process of narrative development.

The textual evidence shows that the story of Irāvān is consistently found only in the eighty-sixth chapter of the *Bhīṣmaparvan*. (Some manuscript traditions scatter single verses about Irāvān, or about Arjuna and Ulūpī's initial encounter, elsewhere in the narrative.) Even Irāvān's visit to Arjuna in Indra's heaven is narrated exclusively in the *Bhīṣmaparvan*; it never appears among Arjuna's other encounters in Indra's heaven, which the *Āraṇyakaparvan* describes at length. The considerable narrative gap between Irāvān's death and Arjuna's reaction to it further indicates that the figure of Irāvān is not completely integrated into the fabric of the epic. In the other major story featuring Irāvān's mother Ulūpī—her dramatic role in the killing and revival of Arjuna in the *Āśvamedhikaparvan* ("The Book of the Horse Sacrifice," the fourteenth book of the Sanskrit epic), which we would be well within our rights to call the "main" story of Ulūpī—there is no mention of a son named Irāvān.[42] For this reason, we can speak of the "invention" of Irāvān in the *Bhīṣmaparvan*. The question is: Why?

First, we ought to consider the possibility that regional stories about Irāvān (or Aravāṉ) are a source for the Sanskrit *Mahābhārata* material rather than the other way around. We might ask: Does the Irāvān story represent a stage in the assembly of the epic when an epic author or editor might have felt prompted to acknowledge a burgeoning regional interest in Irāvān? We should be open to the possibility that other stories in the Sanskrit *Mahābhārata* may represent regional traditions during the later periods of assembly and editing.

Moreover, we can see that there are a number of compelling literary reasons for the figure of Irāvān to emerge within the *Bhīṣmaparvan* itself and then to resound, narratively speaking, in the battle beyond. Irāvān's death lends both excitement and emotional gravity to the battles of the *Bhīṣmaparvan*, which otherwise lack the drama of those in later battle books, mostly because no one of significance is killed. As we can see on a larger scale during the *rākṣasa* battles of the *Droṇaparvan* (such as those

42. *MBh* 14.78–82. It is worth noting, however, that Babhruvāhana, Arjuna's son with Princess Citrāṅgadā of Maṇipūra, does play an important role in this episode.

between Ghaṭotkaca, Alambusa, and Alāyudha), conflicts that involve *rākṣasas* impart striking and unpredictable color and variety to the texture of the storytelling.

The most poignant deaths in the war are those of Bhīma's and Arjuna's younger sons—sons who are not born of Draupadī. The deaths of Irāvān and Ghaṭotkaca precede and follow (respectively) the death of Abhimanyu, Arjuna's son with Subhadrā (Kṛṣṇa's sister).[43] All three of them—Ghaṭotkaca, Irāvān, and Abhimanyu—are far more individualized, developed figures than the Pāṇḍavas' other sons. Irāvān is the first son of Arjuna to die and to receive a lament; he actually seems to be the first patrilineal Pāṇḍava child to die. By contrast, the five sons of Draupadī (often termed a collective, the Draupadeyas) play no major role in the epic and receive no laments or expressions of affection from their fathers. While each of the five is the son of a different Pāṇḍava, and while they are occasionally named individually, during the most horrific massacre of the war—the night raid of the *Sauptikaparvan*—they are named as a group and slaughtered as a group.[44] Why would the epic's authors create two highly individual, nonhuman sons for Bhīma and Arjuna and then tell the stories of these sons, Ghaṭotkaca and Irāvān, right up to their deaths? Do Irāvān and Ghaṭotkaca give the *Mahābhārata* a way of appropriating the monstrous, the alien? There is, it seems, a deep empathy on the part of the epic authors for these half-monstrous, half-human sons who die for the clans of their human fathers.

43. *MBh* 7.49.

44. *MBh* 10.8–9.

Chapter Four

Bodies That Don't Matter

Gender, Body, and Discourse in the Narrative of Sulabhā

SALLY J. SUTHERLAND GOLDMAN

In the *Śāntiparvan* ("The Book of Peace") of Vyāsa's *Mahābhārata*, Bhīṣma narrates to Yudhiṣṭhira a fascinating and challenging discourse between Sulabhā, a female ascetic, and King Janaka, ruler of Videha.[1] The episode, with its proto-*sāṃkhya*[2] underpinnings, focuses on Sulabhā's challenge to King Janaka's claim that he can simultaneously be both a liberated man (*mukta*) and a householder (*gṛhastha*). The narrative has been studied by a number of scholars,[3] but only James Fitzgerald, in his 2002 article entitled

---

1. The episode occurs at *MBh* 12.308. All references to the *Mahābhārata* (*MBh*) are to the critical edition unless specified otherwise: *The Mahābhārata for the First Time Critically Edited*, ed. V. S. Sukthankar et al. 19 vols. (Poona: Bhandarkar Oriental Research Institute, 1933–66).

2. *Sāṃkhya* refers to an early, dualist philosophical worldview that separates all of existence into a passive, unchanging pure awareness or consciousness (*puruṣa*) and an active, manifest material existence (*prakṛti*).

3. See, for example, V. M. Bedekar, "Studies in Sāṃkhyā: The Teachings of Pañcaśikha in the Mahābhārata," *Annals of the Bhandarkar Oriental Research Institute* 38, no 3/4 (1957): 233–44; Nicolas Sutton, "An Exposition of Early Sāṁkhya, A Rejection of the *Bhagavad-Gītā* and a Critique of the Role of Women in Hindu Society: The *Sulabhā-Janaka-Saṁvāda*," *Annals of the Bhandarkar Oriental Research Institute* 80

"Nun Befuddles King," provides a detailed analysis of the text, context, and philosophical implications.[4] This he does admirably, while still admitting that much more could and should be done.

Hinted at but not developed within Fitzgerald's discussion is one of the more fascinating aspects of this story: its construction of gender and the body, which serves to structure the narrative and enhance the passage's philosophical arguments.[5] As Ruth Vanita has noted in her insightful reading of this episode, gender forms a critical dynamic of the story.[6] Yet Vanita's discussion does not address how the language and structure of the narrative construct, deconstruct, and reconstruct the very notions of gender and body that permeate the episode.

The relationship between gender and body has become a focal point of feminist theory,[7] and as the story of Sulabhā unfolds, it becomes clear that the theoretical debates that form the underpinnings of this dynamic are hard to ignore. Western masculinist tradition, however, has long posited a singular, static body,[8] while many South Asian religious and philosophical constructs—also masculinist—posit the possibility, and in fact the likelihood, of multiple different corporal identities over multiple births. Given these diverse, culturally normative base assumptions, incorporation of Western theoretical frames must be made judiciously and cautiously.

(1999): 53–65; Ruth Vanita, "The Self Is Not Gendered: Sulabha's Debate with King Janaka," *NWESA Journal* 15, no. 2 (2003): 76–93; Arti Dhand, "Paradigms of the Good in the *Mahābhārata*: Śuka and Sulabhā in Quagmires of Ethics," in *Gender and Narrative in the Mahābhārata*, eds. Simon Brodbeck and Brian Black (London: Routledge, 2007), 258–78; and Brian Black, "Dialogue and Difference: Encountering the Other in Indian Religious and Philosophical Sources," in *Dialogue in Early South Asian Religions: Hindu, Buddhist, and Jain Traditions*, eds. Brian Black and Laurie Patton (New York: Routledge, 2015), 243–57.

4. James Fitzgerald, "Nun Befuddles King, Shows *Karmayoga* Does Not Work: Sulabhā's Refutation of King Janaka at *MBh* 12.308," *Journal of Indian Philosophy* 30, no. 6 (2002): 641–77.

5. Fitzgerald, 643.

6. Vanita, "The Self Is Not Gendered," 76–93. But see, also, Sutton, "An Exposition of Early Sāṁkhya," 61–64; Dhand, "Paradigms of the Good," 263–65; and Black, "Dialogue and Difference," 249–50, 254–55.

7. Margrit Shildrick and Janet Price, "Openings on the Body," in *Feminist Theory and the Body*, eds. Janet Price and Margrit Shildrick (New York: Routledge, 1999), 1–14.

8. Shildrick and Price, 2–3; and Judith Butler, *Bodies that Matter: On the Discursive Limits of "Sex"* (New York: Routledge, 1993), 2.

Additionally, the passage's underlying philosophy, while it appears to have *sāṃkhya* leanings, is rather murky. Janaka twice names his teacher as Pañcaśikha, whom the later tradition identifies as a foundational teacher of *sāṃkhya*.[9] Fitzgerald understands Sulabhā's own philosophy to align with *sāṃkhya*, or rather argues that it "says nothing that is inconsistent with *sāṃkhya* teaching."[10] Fitzgerald has also convincingly argued that in light of the new ideologies of the *Bhagavadgītā* and the role of *karmayoga* (the performance of one's duties without attachment) in it, the suitability of the second *āśrama* (stage of life), *gārhasthya* (the state of being a householder), as a state from which or during which *mokṣa* (liberation) might be obtained and retained emerges as a cultural concern, and that it is with this possibility that the narrative is concerned.[11]

The narrative opens with a focused, if brief, description of King Janaka. He is described as learned and is said to be advanced in his study of the Vedas, of the science of *mokṣa*, and of kingship. Moreover, he has controlled his senses. From the outset, however, the passage is ambiguous. For the king is also called *dharmadhvaja*, "he whose banner is dharma." Although somewhat rare, the compound elsewhere is used euphemistically to refer to "a hypocrite *or* imposter."[12] We also learn that other wise men are jealous of him.[13]

---

9. *MBh* 12.208.24, 79.

10. Fitzgerald, "Nun Befuddles King," 644–46, esp. 646. On the gendering of *sāṃkhya* see Kanchana Natarajan, "Gendering of Early Indian Philosophy," *Economic and Political Weekly* 36, no. 17 (2001): 1398–1401.

11. Fitzgerald, "Nun Befuddles King," 641–42.

12. The compound *dharmadhvaja* is found sporadically in Sanskrit literature, not uncommonly as the name of a king (for example, in Somadeva's eleventh-century *Kathāsaritsāgara*, 12.18.3ab). See Somadeva, *Kathāsaritsāgara,* ed. Jagadishalala Shastri (Delhi: Motilal Banarsidass, 2008; first published 1889, Nirnaya Sagara Press (Bombay), eds. Pandit Durgaprasad and Kashinath Pandurang Parab). It occurs elsewhere in the *MBh* (7.166.19) and in the *Rāmāyaṇa* (4.17.18). All references to Vālmīki's *Rāmāyaṇa* (*VR)* are from the critical edition: Vālmīki, *The Vālmīki Rāmāyaṇa*: *Critically Edited for the First Time*, eds. G. H. Bhatt and U. P. Shah et al. 7 vols. (Baroda: Oriental Institute, 1960–75). Also, see Vālmīki, *The Rāmāyaṇa of Vālmīki: An Epic of Ancient India*, vol. 4, *Kiṣkindhākāṇḍa*, ed. and trans. Rosalind Lefeber (Princeton, NJ: Princeton University Press, 1994), note to 4.17.18; and Pandurang V. Kane, *History of Dharmaśāstra,* vol. 5, pt. 2 (Poona: Bhandarkar Oriental Research Institute, 1962), 1368 n2237.

13. *MBh* 12.308.4–6.

Of Sulabhā we are told nothing of a physical nature. At the opening of the story, she is described only as "one who engages in the practice (*dharma*) of *yoga*"[14] and as a *bhikṣuṇī*,[15] a female mendicant, who wanders the earth alone.[16] Her actions tell us more: she is not gullible and possesses keen insight. For, upon hearing of Janaka's claims, she calls them into question and decides to discover for herself whether Janaka truly is *mukta* (liberated) even while remaining engaged in the kingly duties that constitute his responsibilities as a householder.[17]

From these few opening verses, we can see that the author or composer of the passage has skillfully constructed the passage in anticipation of the remaining narrative. Janaka's description is ambiguous and allows space for suspicions over his claims to fester. On the other hand, Sulabhā's character is confusing. The Sanskrit literary tradition normally defines a woman by her sexuality, and the author plays on this assumption with his choice of names: Sulabhā, which means "easily obtained." As Fitzgerald notes, the sexual overtones of the name cannot be ignored.[18] The absence of any standard identifiers—place, social status, family, physical attributes, or even a proper name—so crucial to the definition of a "good" woman disrupts the audience's expectations. Similarly disruptive is the presence of the modifiers *bhikṣuṇī* and *ekā* (solitary). Such descriptors typically belong to a traditional masculine construct; however, the fact that Sanskrit genders such words to agree with the referent undermines this inherent bias. Yet it is Sulabhā alone who possesses the insight and knowledge to confront the king; the others who might, that is, the wise men, are merely jealous. Additionally, these opening verses use gender to challenge our understanding of *āśrama-dharma*, the system of four life-stages. For it is the king who is a *gṛhastha* (householder) and, despite his claims of being simultaneously *mukta*, he is still active in the material world, while it is Sulabhā who is the *vanavāsinī* (forest dweller). Such inversions haunt much of the narrative.

14. See *MBh* 12.306.83 and 15.33.29 where the term *yogadharma* is used similarly.

15. The term *bhikṣuṇī* is rare. It is listed only twenty times in *The Digital Corpus of Sanskrit*, which gives four citations for it in the *MBh*. It occurs three times in this story and once at 1.73.11. See Oliver Hellwig, *The Digital Corpus of Sanskrit*, 2010–12, http://kjc-sv013.kjc.uni-heidelberg.de/dcs/

16. *MBh* 12.308.7.

17. *MBh* 12.308.9.

18. Fitzgerald, "Nun Befuddles King," 668.

In order to test whether or not King Janaka is truly *mukta*, Sulabhā transforms herself into a beautiful young woman through her yogic power (*yogataḥ*). Of particular import here is the vocabulary that the author employs to describe her transformation: "Then having abandoned her previous form (*pūrvarūpaṃ*) through *yoga*, she took on an excellent form, a faultless body (*anavadyāṅgī rūpam anyad anuttamam*)."[19] Here the term *rūpa* appears twice: as *pūrva-rūpa*, or "previous form," and as *rūpa*: "form," "shape," "body," or "lovely body."[20] The choice of the term *rūpa* to refer to both her prior, unmarked body and to her new, "beautiful body" plays on the word's multiple semantic realms.[21]

Through her yogic powers, Sulabhā arrives instantly at Janaka's court. Under the pretext of begging for alms, she gains an audience with the king.[22] Immediately upon seeing her lovely, youthful form (*vapus*),[23] the king, filled with amazement, asks the culturally requisite, gendered questions: "Who is she? Whose is she? Where does she come from?"[24]

---

19. *MBh* 12.308.10. On similar transformations, see Frederick M. Smith, *The Self-Possessed, Deity and Spirit Possession in South Asian Literature and Civilization* (New York: Columbia University Press, 2006), 256.

20. Fitzgerald translates this as "body." See "Nun Befuddles King," 655. K. M. Ganguli, however, renders "form . . . features." See *The Mahabharata of Krishna-Dwaipayana Translated into English Prose*, trans. K. M. Ganguli, ed. P. C. Roy, 12 vols. (Calcutta: Bharat Press, 1883–96), 10:468; and *A Prose English Translation of The Mahabharata: Translated Literally from the Original Sanskrit Text,* trans. M. N. Dutt, 2 vols. (Calcutta: Oriental Publishing Co., 1962; first published 1903, H. C. Dass, Elysium Press (Calcutta)), 2:500. Note that Ganguli translated the entire *Mahābhārata* into English, which was subsequently published by Roy, who took credit for the translation. This translation was then edited by Dutt, who made minor changes in the translation, and published it under his name.

21. Compare other pre-*sāṃkhya* passages such as *MBh* 12.298.12–13 and 20, where *rūpa* is understood as the object of sight and as one of the *bhautika*s (gross elements).

22. *MBh* 12.308.12.

23. *MBh* 12.308.13ab. Used here and at *MBh* 12.308.54. Fitzgerald translates "beauty" in "Nun Befuddles King," 655, 658. Ganguli translates "delicate form" at 12.308.13 and "shapely form" at 12.308.54. *Mahabharata Krishna-Dwaipayana,* 10:469, 472; and *Prose English Mahabharata,* 2:500, 502.

24. *keyaṃ kasya kuto veti. . . .* The centrality of such phrases to a normative cultural identity is evidenced by their use some five times in the passage. See *MBh* 12.308.13, 20, 96, 124, 127.

Once she has assumed a gender normative body, that is, a sexualized one, Sulabhā is provided numerous standard descriptors of a young woman. She has a faultless body; the form that she has assumed is unsurpassed (*anuttamam*); she has lovely eyebrows (*subhrūḥ*) and lotus-like eyes (*kamalekṣaṇā*). Yet despite these sexualized markers, she remains a *bhikṣuṇī*, traditionally an asexual figure. Sulabhā's transformation can, in part, be understood as a mechanism to further undermine Janaka's claim of being *mukta* and to heighten the irony of the passage. The inescapable implication is that if she had not transformed herself, Janaka would not have granted her an audience. The passage also makes clear that Janaka is incapable of comprehending a reality beyond the normative gendered binary. A true *mukta* would have transcended consciousness of both physical form and gender. The fact that he has not is further reinforced by the king's own words in his questions to Sulabhā, words that indicate he can recognize her only in a normative sexualized context.[25]

Sulabhā, having first confronted Janaka with her doubts, literally enters into the being or body of the king. The vocabulary used for this entry as well as for the mechanics of that entry presents a challenge, for the original intent of the author is unknown. But a careful examination of internal and external contexts can help shed light on the author's understanding. After Sulabhā first accepts the king's hospitality, we are told that "She who knew *yoga* entered [his] *sattva* with her *sattva*, your majesty."[26]

The term *sattva*, here intentionally left untranslated, is, like so many other Sanskrit words, polysemic. In his commentary to this passage, Nīlakaṇṭha understands the term to be a synonym for *buddhi*, or "intellect," glossing: "she entered the *sattva*, that is to say, the *buddhi* of Janaka by means of her own *sattva*, that is to say, her *buddhi*."[27]

---

25. The discourse eerily anticipates many of Butler's ideas of the materiality of the body and the performativity of gender. See *Bodies that Matter*, 1–16.

26. *sattvaṃ sattvena yogajñā praviveśa mahīpate* || *MBh* 12.308.16cd ||

The phrase "your majesty (*mahīpate*)" harks back to the outer frame, where Bhīṣma is addressing Yudhiṣṭhira. Fitzgerald renders *sattva* as "being" and provides an informative note on the term in "Nun Befuddles King," 656 and 673, note to *MBh* 12.308.104.

27. *janakasya sattvaṃ buddhiṃ sattvena svayā buddhyā praviveśa* | Nīlakaṇṭha on 12.320.16 (*MBh* 12.308.16). All quotations from Nīlakaṇṭha's commentary are

The verb *praviveśa*, "she entered," too, carries a nuanced message to its audience, especially when "entry" is a type of possession. As Frederick Smith notes, the *Mahābhārata* generally employs the verb *pra√viś* when there is an "external" possession—that is, the possession of an individual by an external agent—accompanied by an element of surprise.[28] This is certainly true of Sulabhā's possession of Janaka.

The mechanism of this possession is then described: "Having united (*saṃyojya*) the beams (*raśmi*) of [his] two eyes with the rays of [her own] two eyes, she bound him—who was about to challenge her—with her *yoga*-bonds."[29] The following verse, which describes Janaka's defensive strategy, parallels the previous one, yet employs different vocabulary: "King Janaka, that best of kings, smirking and keeping separate her *bhāva*, in turn took hold (*pratijagrāha*) of her *bhāva* with his *bhāva*."[30] Nīlakaṇṭha understands the vocabulary shift as significant. Prior to tackling the specific terminology, he clarifies the process with some rather extended comments:

> The *buddhi-sattva*, an elemental substance, like the radiance of the sun, is subtle, and, having gone outside from the openings [of the body], the eyes etc., it makes pots, etc., visible; just like that light from a lamp that emerges through the openings in a pot. Now it is said that the eyes are a sense organ. In this instance, in one place simultaneously, the rays of two [individual] *buddhi*s like [the light of] two lamps, are mixed. It is well known in the world, that concerning this, males such as *yakṣa*s

from: *Śrī Mahābhāratam with the Bhāratabhāvadīpa Commentary of Nīlakaṇṭha*, ed. Ramchandrashastri Kinjawadekar, 6 vols. (Poona: Chitrashala Press, 1929–36). On *sattva* in this sense, see J. A. B. van Buitenen, "Studies in Sāmkhya (III)," *Journal of the American Oriental Society* 88, no. 2 (1957): 88; and Fitzgerald, "Nun Befuddles King," 673, note to *MBh* 12.308.104. Ganguli, likely influenced by Nīlakaṇṭha, translates "understanding." *Mahabharata Krishna-Dwaipayana*, 10:469; and *Prose English Mahabharata*, 2:500.

28. Smith, *The Self Possessed*, 263.

29. *netrābhyāṃ netrayor asya raśmīn saṃyojya raśmibhiḥ* |
sā sma saṃcodayiṣyantaṃ yogabandhair babandha ha || *MBh* 12.308.17 ||

30. *janako 'py utsmayan rājā bhāvam asyā viśeṣayan* |
pratijagrāha bhāvena bhāvam asyā nṛpottamaḥ || *MBh* 12.308.18 ||

> (a class of supernatural beings), and *rākṣasa*s (a class of demonic beings), having overpowered the *buddhi*s of others, which become mixed by means of their own [the *rākṣasas*' and *yakṣas*'] *buddhyastra*s (mind-weapons)—through those very bodies [i.e., the ones of others]—carry on in life. But if two *yogavīra*s (men of *yoga*) are conversant with both the discharging and retrieval of *buddhyastra*s, like the two *buddhyastra*s, two minds cannot overpower each other. Thus, this dispute occurs between the two in one body.[31]

Focusing on the phrase *bhāvam asyā viśeṣayan*, "keeping separate her *bhāva*," Nīlakaṇṭha glosses *viśeṣayan*, normally "separating" or "distinguishing," as *abhibhavan*, "overpowering," and explains *bhāvam asyāḥ* as "her, that is, Sulabhā's, *bhāvam*, that is, intention, which takes the form of 'I will make him speechless.'"[32]

Given the proto-*sāṃkhya* persuasion of this passage, both *sattva* and *bhāva*, should, it seems, be viewed at least partially in terms of how they are understood within the corpus of texts of that philosophical system. And while there is no absolute agreement on the definitions of these terms, *sattva* is, there, sometimes identified with the *buddhi*, and sometimes understood in its more common sense as the first of the three *guṇa*s (qualities) of which the *prakṛti* (material world) is made up. According to C. Sharma, *sattva* is "responsible for the manifestation of the objects in consciousness."[33] Later, in her response to Janaka, Sulabhā articulates a slightly different priority, where *buddhi* is the twelfth evolute within which *sattva* resides.[34] Fitzgerald, however, notes that the narrative is silent on the three *guṇa*s, but he

31. Nīlakaṇṭha on 12.320.17 (*MBh* 12.308.17).

32. *asyāḥ sulabhāyā bhāvam āśayam enaṃ mūkaṃ kariṣyāmīty evaṃrūpam* | Nīlakaṇṭha on 12.320.18 (*MBh* 12.308.18). Fitzgerald understands *bhāva* as "thought," while Ganguli translates, "defeating the intentions of Sulabha, seized her resolution with his own resolution," using the term *bhāva* to mean both "intention," following Nīlakaṇṭha, and "resolution." See "Nun Befuddles King," 656; *Mahabharata Krishna-Dwaipayana*, 10:469; and *Prose English Mahabharata,* 2:500.

33. Chandradhar Sharma, *A Critical Survey of Indian Philosophy* (London: Rider & Company, 1960), 154.

34. *MBh* 12.308.103–104.The term *buddhi* is used in the passage five times (12.308.30, 78, 81, 103, 187), but it is only in 12.308.103 that this sense is found.

is tempted to understand the use of the term here in this way.[35] *Sattva* is associated with luminosity, power of reflection, upward movement, and other similar positive constructions.[36] Note that the comparisons upon which Nīlakaṇṭha draws refer primarily to light, lamps, luminescence, and the like. Nīlakaṇṭha, in his gloss of *sattva* as *buddhi*, likely understands this term in its technical meaning of the psychological aspect of the *mahat*, the first evolute of the *prakṛti*.

The term *bhāva*, too, is polysemic in the *sāṃkhya* context. According to Michael Hulin, in early Sanskrit literature, *bhāva* is commonly used in the sense of *guṇa*, "quality," or the "successive stages of a cosmic process of evolution."[37] But more commonly it refers to the "psychic states" that are numbered at either eight or fifty (under four sub-divisions) and are invariably concomitant with what A. B. Keith calls the physical apparatus, until a spirit is freed from the latter.[38] In either case the *bhāvas* are clearly inferior to the *sattva*/*buddhi* and seem to represent different levels of spiritual sophistication. Again, in what must be seen as an inversion, it is the woman who is aligned with a "higher," more evolved state—a state that is associated with an absence of physical qualities—while the king still functions through *bhāvas*, in a level of consciousness that is understood as highly differentiated and aligned with physical objects (often understood to be *rūpas*).[39]

It is here, apparently within the *sattva* of Janaka's *buddhi*, that Sulabhā and King Janaka—separate but at the same time intimately conjoined—carry out their conversation, much to the king's dismay. The dialogue is constructed in two separate segments: Janaka speaks first, then Sulabhā responds. Note that the narrative reflects the physical relationship between

35. Fitzgerald, "Nun Befuddles King," 673, note to 12.308.104.

36. Sharma, *Indian Philosophy*, 154.

37. Michael Hulin, *Sāṃkhya Literature* (Wiesbaden: Otto Harrassowitz, 1978), 133.

38. A. B. Keith, *The Sāṃkhya System* (London: Oxford University Press, 1918), 93–95.

39. Simon Brodbeck notes that salvation is conceptualized in "gendered terms" and suggests the subversive nature of the Sulabhā episode. See "Husbands of Earth: *Kṣatriyas*, Females, and Female *Kṣatriyas* in the *Strīparvan* of the *Mahābhārata*," in *Papers of the 12th World Sanskrit Conference*, vol. 2, *Epic Undertakings*, eds. Robert P. Goldman and Muneo Tokunaga (Delhi: Motilal Banarsidass, 2009), 49 n55.

the two participants: the two discourses are intimately tied together and yet separate.[40]

Janaka once again seeks to objectify Sulabhā: "Where have you been wandering? Where will you go? Whose are you and whence are you?"[41] He admits that he does not have a good sense (*sadbhāva*) of her learning, age, or birth.[42] Once more, the author aligns Janaka with the term *bhāva*. Janaka proclaims, then, that he is liberated and condescends to instruct Sulabhā. Janaka explains, somewhat eclectically and with a fair degree of inconsistency, the philosophy that he claims to have acquired from his teacher Pañcaśikha.[43]

Janaka then turns to the issue of Sulabhā's occupation of his body. This he sees in purely sexualized terms. He has doubts that appear to parallel hers: How is it possible that a young, delicate, and beautiful woman could also be an ascetic?[44] Yet his doubts are subtly different. Janaka is bound in the world of the *gṛhastha*—an existence delimited by bodily concerns—and his mind is tied to the physical world. He chastises Sulabhā as he would a promiscuous woman. Here too, the specific language of the passage is informative. First, the king accuses Sulabhā of assaulting his body.[45] The phrase employed to describe the assault—"because of this, my corporal entity (*parigraha*) is abused [or attacked] (*asmad dharṣito matparigrahaḥ*)"—is ambiguous, since both words, *dharṣita* and *parigraha*, are, again, polysemic.[46] Throughout the passage, the term *parigraha* is employed only by Janaka or in reference to him. In his dialogue it occurs some seven times and carries multiple semantic connotations, including "possessions."[47] Fitzgerald tries

40. This articulation of the spatial positioning between Sulabhā and Janaka can be understood as a reflection of *sāṃkhya*'s own negotiation of the relationship between *puruṣa* and *prakṛti* through the positing of *samyogābhāsa*, "the [mere] appearance of contact." See Sharma, *Indian Philosophy*, 159.

41. *bhagavatyāḥ kva caryeyaṃ kṛtā kva ca gamiṣyasi* |
kasya ca tvaṃ kuto veti papracchaināṃ mahīpatiḥ || *MBh* 12.308.20 ||

42. *MBh* 12.308.21ab.

43. *MBh* 12.308.22–53.

44. *MBh* 12.308.54.

45. *MBh* 12.308.55.

46. *asmad dharṣito matparigrahaḥ* || *MBh* 12.308.55c ||

47. *MBh* 12.308.35, 41, 42, 43, 51, 55, 57.

to encompass its polysemy, rendering "polite reception, household, retinue, and body."[48]

Nīlakaṇṭha is more restrictive in his interpretation of the passage, but clearly acknowledges a sexually aggressive component. He understands *dharṣitaḥ* to mean "overpowered by your (i.e., Sulabhā's) *rūpa* (beauty, or beautiful form)" and glosses *parigraha* as "the state of taking on a future form (*bhāvikṛtaveśatvam*) and the overpowering by another; the idea is that this is not characteristic of a liberated person."[49] Nīlakaṇṭha associates the word *parigraha* with something that is subject to future manifestations, i.e., rebirths, as well as being subject to ownership or possession by another (i.e., Sulabhā's overpowering of Janaka). He also emphasizes that the term is not consistent with liberation. This understanding of the use of the term is applicable in all of its uses in this passage, and thus ties Janaka's body to his other "possessions." That such susceptibility to both ownership and the need for ownership applies only to Janaka in the narrative both defines and limits the use of the term. Thus, Janaka's possessions and his body, as one of these possessions, are both encompassed by the term *parigraha*.

One must also consider that the term *dharṣita* is a common word in the epics for "rape," and its usage in Vyāsa's *Mahābhārata*, where it appears some forty times, supports this.[50] When both the subject and object of the verbal participle are masculine, the context invariably indicates that an assault or attack is understood to be a violent physical confrontation or battle. Yet when the subject is male and the object is female, the context clearly indicates either an explicit or implicit, unwanted penetration of a sexual nature, that is, rape.[51] Here, of course, the author of the passage,

48. On *parigraha*, see Fitzgerald "Nun Befuddles King," 671–72, note to 12.308.55.

49. *parigrahaḥ sa bhāvikṛtaveṣatvaṃ parābhibhāvaś ca, na muktalakṣaṇam iti bhāvaḥ* | Nīlakaṇṭha on *MBh* 12.320.55 (*MBh* 12.308.55).

50. See Sally J. Sutherland Goldman, "Against Their Will: Sexual Assault and the *Uttarakāṇḍa*." *Studies in History* 34, no. 2 (2019): 169; and Vālmīki, *The Rāmāyaṇa of Vālmīki: An Epic of Ancient India*, vol. 7, *Uttarakāṇḍa*. ed. and trans. Robert P. Goldman and Sally J. Sutherland Goldman (Princeton, NJ: Princeton University Press, 2017), passim.

51. The definitions used for "rape" and "sexual assault" follow Merriam-Webster [s.v.]. I take exception, however, to the use of "unlawful" in the first definition and "illegal" in the second.

once again playing on his thematic of inverted roles, has the woman as the subject, that is, the perpetrator, of the assault and the male as its victim.[52]

Fitzgerald is more cautious, noting, "With this last suggestion [i.e., that *parigraha* means body] the king is making a charge akin to what we today might call rape; but while he will later explicitly charge her with the inappropriate mingling of their bodily substances, he does not cry 'rape,' but rather accuses her of wantonness."[53] Given the cultural context—where a female victim is held equally guilty as her male assailant and understood to be the *de facto* instigator of a sexual assault—such a distinction is not terribly meaningful.

That the assault is sexual in nature is reinforced by the fact that Sulabhā physically "possesses" Janaka. This is the only occurrence in either the *Mahābhārata* or the *Rāmāyaṇa* where the term *dharṣita* is employed to mark such a role reversal. Given the ongoing theme of role reversal in this story (and despite Fitzgerald's concern that King Janaka fails to cry "rape"), it seems that the author intended the audience to associate the phrase with a non-consensual sexual encounter of a violent nature. Note, too, that sexuality is closely associated with the state of being a *gṛhastha*—as Janaka is—and stands in contrast with that of being a *mukta*. That Janaka understands this as a sexual assault is further supported by the following half-verse, where he reminds Sulabhā of the incompatibility of libidinal desire and liberation: "This triple-staff [of an ascetic] is only for one who is liberated; not for one who is attached to desire (*kāmasamāyukte*)."[54] The word *kāma* (desire) here reinforces the sexual focus of the preceding verse. The disruptive and disturbing nature of Sulabhā's action is further made clear in the following verses, where Janaka complains that she improperly flaunts the signs of an ascetic and does not defend those things for which they stand. But it is

52. That women are inherently sexualized beings and that this sexual nature poses a threat to the patriarchy are deep-seated beliefs of the traditional Brahmanical world.

53. Fitzgerald "Nun Befuddles King," 672, note to *MBh* 12.308.55.

54. *na ca kāmasamāyukte mukte 'py asti tridaṇḍakam* || *MBh* 12.308.56ab ||

The verse could also be rendered as: "This triple-staff is only for one who is liberated; not for one who is attached to desire." Fitzgerald renders: "The triple staff is not for a person who still loves, even if the love is for one who has gained Freedom." See "Nun Befuddles King," 658–59.

her violation of his body on which he is most focused: "And because of [your] connection with my *pakṣa,* hear your transgression—you who have taken recourse to my *pūrva-parigraha* through your *svabhāva*."[55] The verse's meaning is obscure, as is the intent of the terms *pakṣa*, *pūrva-parigraha*, and *svabhāva*. Nīlakaṇṭha glosses "because of connection with my *pakṣa*" (*matpakṣasaṁśrayāt*) as "because of [your] entry into my body" (*maccharīrapraveśāt*) and *parigraha* as "body" (*śarīram*). He is silent on the force of the *pūrva* in the passage. Fitzgerald translates the former as "from my side of it," and the second as "my first enclosure." K. M. Ganguli renders the first and second, respectively, "in consequence of thy contact with me" and "gross body."[56] Nīlakaṇṭha understands that Janaka is suggesting that Sulabhā has resorted to the sin of magic.[57]

The third term, *svabhāva*, "one's own *bhāva*," is similarly unclear in its meaning. Note, too, that Janaka uses the term *bhāva* to describe the instrument through which Sulabhā has entered him. This is the very term used above to describe Janaka's own mechanism of containment and isolation of her. But the narrative has made it clear that Sulabhā enters him with her *sattva*, not her *bhāva*. Nīlakaṇṭha apparently attempts to correct Janaka by glossing *bhāvena* as *cittena*, a term commonly equated to *buddhi*, especially in the closely aligned *yoga* tradition.[58]

---

55. *matpakṣasaṁśrayāc cāyaṃ śṛṇu yas te vyatikramaḥ* |
āśrayantyāḥ svabhāvena mama pūrvaparigraham || *MBh* 12.308.57 ||

56. *svabhāvena svena cittena mama parigrahaṃ śarīram āśrayantyāḥ* | Nīlakaṇṭha on 12.320.57 (*MBh* 12.308.57). He glosses *matpakṣa* as "because of (your) entry into my body (*matpakṣeti maccharīrapraveśāt*)" and understands the third and fourth quarters of the verse to mean "by [your] *svabhāva*, that is to say, by your intellect (*cittena*)—[you] taking recourse in my *parigraha*, that is to say, my body." Fitzgerald translates: "Hear now from my side of it (*matpakṣasaṃśrayāt*) what transgression you commit by resorting to my first enclosure (*pūrvaparigraham*) with your being (*svabhāvena*)." "Nun Befuddles King," 659. While Ganguli offers: "Listen now to me as to what thy transgression has been in consequence of thy contact with me (*matpakṣasaṃśrayāt*) and thy having entered into my gross body (*pūrvaparigraham*) with the help of thy understanding (*svabhāvena*)." *Mahabharata Krishna-Dwaipayana*, 10:473; and *Prose English Mahabharata*, 2:502.

57. *atas tvayi vyabhicāradoṣa iti bhāvaḥ* | Nīlakaṇṭha on 12.320.57 (*MBh* 12.308.57).

58. S. N. Dasgupta and R. R. Agarwal, *History of Indian Philosophy* (Allahabad: Kitab Mahal, 1969), 73.

Janaka does not merely use the word *bhāva*, he uses *svabhāva*—a term that is laden with cultural resonances in its sense of "inherent nature." The *Mahābhārata* uses the compound some 148 times, overwhelmingly in this sense. A woman's *svabhāva*, as the epic tradition and the *dharmaśāstras* ("treatises on dharma") make abundantly clear, is *cala* (fickle), *pauṃścalya* (whorish), and the like.[59] This resonance further reinforces the suggestion that Janaka understands Sulabhā's invasion of his body as not merely a transgression but a sexual assault of which he feels himself to be the victim.

This inappropriate sexualized invasion of his body, the king argues, gives rise to four potential transgressions, *saṃkaras* (mixings): first, *varṇa-saṃkara*, the "mixing of *varṇas*" (he is a *kṣatriya* and she is a *brāhmaṇa*);[60] second, *āśrama-saṃkara*, the "mixing of *āśramas*" (he is a householder and she is a renunciant);[61] third, a potential *gotra-saṃkara*, "the mixing of clans";[62] and fourth, *dharma-saṃkara*, the "mixing of *dharmas*," here, unlawful relations with another man's wife.[63] These potential *saṃkaras*, particularly the last, leave little doubt as to Janaka's understanding of Sulabhā's behavior. The word *saṃkara* alone suggests "commingling arising from inappropriate marriages."[64]

Janaka further disparages her apparent freedom, noting that perhaps she is independent through some self-inflicted flaw.[65] He accuses her of either being ignorant or having false knowledge, and threatens that any knowledge she might have acquired will be useless.[66] Janaka then notes

59. See, for example, verse 9.15 in *Manusmṛti with the Commentary Manvarthamuktāvalī of Kullūka*, ed. N. R. Acharya (Bombay: Nirnaya Sagara Press, 1946). See, too, *MBh* 1.211.21 and Robert P. Goldman, "Carried Away: Abduction and Marriage in Sanskrit *Itihāsa* and *Purāṇa*," *Sanskrit Studies*, vol. 4, ed. Upendra Rao (Delhi: D. K. Printworld, 2015), 153 on this verse.

60. *MBh* 12.308.59.

61. *MBh* 12.308.60.

62. *MBh* 12.308.61. Whether or not this *saṃkara* is applicable is debatable since Sulabhā's *gotra* is never mentioned.

63. *MBh* 12.308.62.

64. Sir Monier Monier-Williams, *Sanskrit English Dictionary* (Oxford: Clarendon Press, 1899), s.v., *saṃkara*.

65. *svantatrāsi svadoṣeṇeha kenacit* || *MBh* 12.308.63–64 ||

66. Fitzgerald renders *svatantrāsi* as "you are on your own, free of a husband." See "Nun Befuddles King," 659.

a third and final impediment arising from her invasion of his body—she is marked with the signs of a corrupted woman,[67] that is, a promiscuous one.[68] He remarks: "The enjoyment of a man and woman, each desiring [the other], is like nectar. But for a man who has no passion (*arakta*), there is no enjoyment; and in this circumstance, the sin is like poison."[69] Note that the verse marks the male as *arakta*, "passionless," an innocent victim, and assumes the unmarked woman is the aggressor. This attitude reinforces the cultural presuppositions that understand women to be inherently (*svabhāva*) sexually threatening and aggressive, especially when they are independent (that is, beyond the control of a man), as Sulabhā is.

Immediately thereafter, Janaka cries out: "Do not touch [me] (*mā sprākṣīḥ*)! You know what is proper. Protect your own discipline. This investigation as to whether I am liberated or not is completed. You must not keep secret from me all that has been hidden."[70] Here, Janaka's words resonate with the pleas of a rape victim. His protest "Do not touch me (*mā sprākṣīḥ*)!"[71] is reminiscent of that of Vālmīki's Vedavatī, who cries out in a similar manner as Rāvaṇa assaults her.[72] These words make it clear that Janaka does not merely understand Sulabhā to be a wanton woman, since all women are inherently understood to be so, but the perpetrator a sexual assault—an unwanted penetration of a sexual nature, a rape.

Janaka's words are ironic in that his very accusations against Sulabhā reveal his own failures. His virtual obsession with Sulabhā as a sexual object permeates his entire discourse and interaction with her—both externally and internally. Absent her transformation into a sexualized being, Janaka would have not admitted her to the court, nor offered her hospitality. He is unable to see her as anything but a sexualized object and threat. Once

67. *duṣṭāyā lakṣyate liṅgam* || *MBh* 12.308.65 ||

68. Fitzgerald understands the prior two transgressions to be stated in *MBh* 12.308.54–56. See "Nun Befuddles King," 672, note to 12.308.65.

69. *icchator hi dvayor lābhaḥ strīpuṁsor amṛtopamaḥ* |
alābhaś cāpy araktasya so 'tra doṣo viṣopamaḥ || *MBh* 12.308.69||

70. *mā sprākṣīḥ sādhu jānīṣva svaśāstram anupālaya* |
kṛteyaṃ hi vijijñāsā mukto neti tvayā mama |
etat sarvaṃ praticchannaṃ mayi nārhasi gūhitum || *MBh* 12.308.70 ||

71. *mā sprākṣīḥ* || *MBh* 12.308.70 ||

72. *mā mā evam* || *VR* 7.17.22 || Also see Sutherland Goldman, "Against Their Will," 166–67.

she has entered and possessed part of his *sattva*, he can understand that occupation only in sexualized terms, demonstrating that he is still bound to the life of a *gṛhastha* both externally and internally.

The narrative further concretizes Janaka's inability to move beyond a sexualized objectification of Sulabhā when Janaka demands that she reveal her caste, education, occupation, state of mind (*bhāva*), natural state (*prakṛti*), and purpose in coming.[73] Note, again, his use of the term *bhāva* here. These attempts simultaneously serve to force a gendered conformity on her and delegitimize her non-normative status as *bhikṣuṇī*.

As it provides a normative, if negative, construction of femaleness, Janaka's response to Sulabhā's invasion of his *parigraha*, "something that can be possessed," reveals his own shortcomings. That the space within which this is done is the male body suggests the male containment of the female. Moreover, the use of the male body as the site of sexual assault rather than the vehicle for it both reflects and reinforces a cultural normativity that marks the female as sexually uncontrolled that is, dangerous. Nevertheless, such a construction of the male body demonstrates that Janaka is confined to and limited by his gross physical body. His body is both a possession and subject to ownership; it does not function beyond his *bhāva*. These are not the signs of a liberated man (*mukta*).

It is here—a space where she is able to dominate the discourse and occupy his body—that Janaka will be able to hear Sulabhā's words. Here, too, Sulabhā, demonstrating her non-attachment to the physical world, is able to deconstruct Janaka's construction of both gender and body. It is not without irony that only here, inside of Janaka, does the author give Sulabhā voice to expound upon philosophical matters traditionally controlled by males. Simultaneously, this space is conceived as uterine as it is inhabited by another "unseen" body. Sulabhā's response, which occupies some 112 verses,[74] is substantially longer than King Janaka's verbal attack. Her refutation, which addresses linguistic, philosophical, and worldly issues, largely parallels Janaka's attack. For our purposes, Sulabhā's response is particularly notable for three reasons. One is that the first eighteen verses constitute a fairly technical lesson in rhetoric,[75] during which the text makes clear

73. *MBh* 12.308.75.

74. *MBh* 12.308.78–190.

75. *MBh* 12.308.78–95.

Sulabhā's rhetorical skill and Janaka's lack of it.[76] Thus, near the end of her refutation, Sulabhā describes Janaka as *mokṣa-vātikaḥ*: "a man who prattles on about *mokṣa* [without knowing anything about it]."[77]

The second is that Sulabhā, through her rhetorical skills, deconstructs Janaka's argument. This she carries out in part through a detailed description (a reconstruction, if you will) of what constitutes "body" and "embodiment." After articulating the thirty or thirty-one base elements of which the gross body (*śarīra*) is constituted,[78] Sulabhā provides a step-by-step analysis of how the gross, that is, physical, body is gendered, created, and born, and finally how it matures and grows old. It is through this that Sulabhā identifies two types of people: those who see only what is manifested in gross physical form (*sthūladarśī*) as the *prakṛti* and those who realize that the *prakṛti* is unmanifested (*avyakta*).[79]

Explaining to Janaka that it is through these component parts that the non-manifest *prakṛti* becomes manifest, Sulabhā reminds him that they are both merely embodied beings (*śarīriṇaḥ*).[80] Sulabhā lists eight stages of the embodied being, which begin from a union of blood and semen,[81] as well as three fetal states (the zygote [*kalala*], the fetus in the second half of the first month of pregnancy [*arbuda*], and the fetus after that [*peśī*]).[82] After nine months the *nāmarūpa*—the individual being or specific embodiment—comes about. At this stage, the gender, that is, maleness or femaleness, is assigned. It is important to note that starting with the term *nāmarūpa*, the element that embodies a being is termed *rūpa* (body, form). Immediately following birth, the body is identified as *tāmranakhāṅguli*, "hav-

76. Fitzgerald "Nun Befuddles King," 645, 651–52, n13.

77. *MBh* 12.308.175.

78. *MBh* 12.308.112. See Fitzgerald, "Nun Befuddles King," 673, note to 12.308.112. The first fourteen correspond to traditional *sāṃkhya* lists of the *tattva*s, which here are termed *kalās*, "[component] parts."

79. *MBh* 12.308.113.

80. *MBh* 12.308.115.

81. *MBh* 12.308.116.

82. Caraka, the author of the medical treatise, the *Carakasaṃhitā*, identifies the second month as "*ghana*." When shaped as a tight ball, it is male; when elliptical, female; and when a sphere, of indeterminate gender. See Frances Garrett, *Religion, Medicine and the Human Embryo in Tibet* (New York: Routledge, 2008), 20.

ing red nails and fingers." Three additional bodies—childhood (*kaumāra),* youthful (*yauvana*), and aged (*sthāvirya*)—are identified.[83] This appears to be the only place in Vyāsa's *Mahābhārata* that such a description of fetal and post-fetal development occurs.

This enumeration is, of course, in part a mechanism through which to establish the existence of a "subtle body" (*liṅga-śarīra*) distinct from the gross body (*sthūla-śarīra*). This subtle body is necessary to provide physical support for the individual self (*jīva* or *ātman*) during transitional intervals between death and rebirth. But in the context of this narrative, it is a clear demonstration of how the gross or physical body is transitory and distinct from the *sattva*/*buddhi*. What we see here, then, is a very cleverly structured narrative through which Janaka has constructed a limited understanding of "body" that takes cognizance merely of the gross physical body (*parigraha*), while Sulabhā's response deconstructs that "body" and offers a reconstruction of an entity that consists of both manifest and subtle components of the *prakṛti*. The uterine imagery of Janaka as the locus of Sulabhā's reconstruction of this complex entity completely disrupts normative notions of female corporality and maternity. That this disruption is central to the narrative is further enhanced by Sulabhā's own lack of both.

The third reason that Sulabhā's response is remarkable is that with it, the narrative ends. Once she has finished her discourse, Sulabhā informs the king that she will depart in the morning after spending the night inside him.[84] The narrator tells us that Janaka does not respond, and the story ends.[85] What appears to some as a rather abrupt conclusion is, in fact, an acknowledgment on the part of the author, and perhaps even the audience, that nothing more need be explained. Sulabhā has convincingly demonstrated that Janaka still remains bound in the physical world and cannot therefore be a liberated being.

As the narrative plays with the construction of corporality to reflect the larger philosophical concerns of the passage, so, too, does the vocabulary of corporality used throughout the narrative become meaningful. Janaka

83. *MBh* 12.308.115–22.

84. *MBh* 12.308.190.

85. *MBh* 12.308.190.

uses the terms *rūpa*[86] and *vapus*[87] either in the sense of "form," "body," or "beautiful body," as well as the problematic term *parigraha*[88] discussed above. Sulabhā, too, employs a number of semantically similar terms that potentially reflect what might encompass the word "body": *rūpa,*[89] *śarīra,*[90] *śarīrin,*[91] *ātman,*[92] (*sva*)*deha,*[93] (*para*)*parigraha.*[94] The narrator uses only the term *rūpa.*[95]

The terms *parigraha* and *deha* are used, or said to be used, only by Janaka. At one point, the term *parigraha,* in the compound *paraparigrahe,* "in the body of another," is employed in contrast with *svadehe,* "in my own body," and, though spoken by Sulabhā, these are her quotes of Janaka's words.[96] The word *śarīra* refers to "the gross (or physical) body" that is constantly in transition, that is, the body that is born, grows old, decays, and dies, while the term *śarīrin* refers to an "embodied being" or a "soul." These terms are used exclusively by Sulabhā. The use of the word *rūpa* in the passage is equally noteworthy. While Janaka employs both this term and the word *vapus* exclusively in the sense of physical beauty,[97] both the narrator and Sulabhā use it more restrictively and seemingly more in a philosophical sense as one of the five *indriyas*[98] (sense organs) and/or one of the three causes of sight.[99] In both these meanings, *rūpa* is only one mutable component of what constitutes beings, and it cannot function

86. *MBh* 12.308.10, 54.

87. *MBh* 12.308.54.

88. *MBh* 12.308.55, 57.

89. *MBh* 12.308.98, 101, 118, 119.

90. *MBh* 12.308.112, 115, 189.

91. *MBh* 12.308.115.

92. *MBh* 12.308.126.

93. *MBh* 12.308.162.

94. *MBh* 12.308.162.

95. *MBh* 12.308.10.

96. *MBh* 12.308.162.

97. *MBh* 12.308.13, 54, 73.

98. *MBh* 12.308.98.

99. *MBh* 12.308.101.

in isolation. Thus when Sulabhā describes the various "stages" of a being's physical development, she consistently employs the term *rūpa*, reminding us that its referent is both impermanent and mutable.[100] In this way, too, at the opening of the narrative, when we are told that Sulabhā exchanges a *rūpa* for her *pūrvarūpa*, the phrase anticipates that her *rūpa* is only one of multiple elements that create her "being," and that this *rūpa* is exchangeable, mutable, temporary, and does not equate to her "being" (*bhūta*).[101] Because of this, such questions as: "Who is he? Whence is he? Whence is he not? Whose is this? Whose is this not? Whence is this? Whence is this not?" are meaningless.[102] Sulabhā is uninterested in and unattached to her own gross body, let alone someone else's.[103]

What becomes apparent through such a reading of the Sulabhā episode is that the author or composer has carefully and intentionally both crafted a narrative and employed vocabulary that reflects and enhances the religio-philosophical concerns of the passage. The narrative is amusing for its choice of theme and its numerous inversions of normative roles and cultural norms. At the same time, the narrative is meaningful, as it constructs a dialogue on the nature of corporality. The narrator thus provides his audiences with a spatial demonstration of the discourse and linguistic cues and examples to help them navigate that space, simultaneously invoking, inverting, and challenging normative cultural frames of gender and body.

---

100. See, for example, *MBh* 12.308.98 (*pṛthagātmā daśātmānaḥ saṃśliṣṭā jatukāṣṭhavat*), and 12.308.125.

101. *MBh* 12.308.119–21.

102. *kaḥ kuto vā na vā kutaḥ* |
kasyedaṃ kasya vā nedaṃ kuto vedaṃ na vā kutaḥ || *MBh* 12.308.123c–124ab ||

103. *MBh* 12.308.162.

PART II

Sanskrit Mahābhāratas in Poetry and Performance

Chapter Five

The Remembered Self

Arjuna as Bṛhannalā in the *Pañcarātra*

Nell Shapiro Hawley

The many Mahābhāratas of this book form a notoriously prismatic landscape, but even against that landscape the *Pañcarātra* ("The Five Nights"), a three-act play that many attribute to the Sanskrit poet Bhāsa (ca. 200 CE),[1] stands out as extreme. Through plot and poetry, the play adds layers of complexity to the (already, and famously) fraught *Mahābhārata* story: rituals are mismanaged, battles go awry, relationships deteriorate, gambles are lost, and disguises become reality. The *Pañcarātra* adopts the Sanskrit epic's polyperspectivity—a central feature of the *Mahābhārata*'s "inter-

1. On the date and authorship of the *Pañcarātra* and its five *Mahābhārata*-inspired sister dramas (*Ūrubhaṅga*, *Karṇabhāra*, *Dūtaghaṭotkaca*, *Dūtavākya*, and *Madhyamavyāyoga*), see Heidrun Brückner, "Manuscripts and Performance Traditions of the So-Called Trivandrum Plays Ascribed to Bhāsa—A Report on Work in Progress," *Bulletin d'études indiennes* 17–18 (1999–2000): 501–50; and Herman Tieken, "The So-Called Trivandrum Plays Attributed to Bhāsa," *Wiener Zeitschrift für die Kunde Südasiens und Archiv für Indische Philosophie* 37 (1993): 5–44. A counterpoint to the positions of Brückner and Tieken, if one that predates their research, can be found in V. S. Sukthankar, "Studies in Bhāsa" in *V.S. Sukthankar Memorial Edition*, vol. 2, *Analecta*, ed. P. K. Gode (Bombay: Karnatak Publishing House, 1945), 82–184.

rogative" style, or its "poetics of dilemma"[2]—by allowing the audience to experience the fourth book of the epic, the *Virāṭaparvan* ("The Book of Virāṭa's Court"), through the eyes of multiple figures. Duryodhana, Śakuni, Bhīṣma, Yudhiṣṭhira, Arjuna, and Abhimanyu all have their stories to tell. Not only does the play reframe the narrative in this way, but it supplies it with a new and extraordinary conclusion. At the end of the *Pañcarātra* the Pāṇḍavas and the Kauravas split the kingdom and avert the very war that is the *Mahābhārata*'s defining feature. Yet even this unusual ending is faithful to the *Virāṭaparvan*'s ethos. Just as the *Virāṭaparvan* encapsulates the epic's central story in a series of inversions that allow it to layer an impression of harmony over the *Mahābhārata*'s more pressing ethical and emotional discordances, so too does the *Pañcarātra* offer its audience the illusion of a resolution, one that masks a more fragmented interior.[3] Like the story of the *Virāṭaparvan*, then, the *Pañcarātra* is fueled by the imagery of disguises, costumes, and performances from start to finish.

The figure of a character in disguise—an utterly ubiquitous, transhistorical, world-literary trope—presents an array of interpretive knots for readers and audiences to untangle. New selves blanket old ones, outer layers of selfhood contradict inner ones, fragmented selves find surface-level

---

2. David Gitomer makes a similar observation about the drama *Veṇīsaṃhāra* ("The Binding/Catastrophe of the Braid," ca. 700 CE) in "The 'Veṇīsaṃhāra' of Bhaṭṭa Nārāyaṇa: The Great Epic as Drama" (PhD diss., Columbia University, 1988), 341. On "poetics of dilemma," see David Shulman, "Toward a Historical Poetics of the Sanskrit Epics," in *The Wisdom of Poets: Studies in Tamil, Telugu, and Sanskrit* (Delhi: Oxford University Press, 2001), 24. On the *Mahābhārata* as an "interrogative" epic, see Shubha Pathak, *Divine Yet Human Epics: Reflections of Poetic Rulers from Ancient Greece and India*, Hellenic Studies Series 62 (Washington, DC: Center for Hellenic Studies, Harvard University, 2014), 174. Gregory Bailey points out that fundamental dichotomies of values and worldviews might be granted theoretical resolutions in the *Mahābhārata*, but that such resolutions are never "in consonance with what happens on the narrative level of the epic." See "Suffering in the *Mahābhārata*: Draupadī and Yudhiṣṭhira," in *Inde et Littératures: Études Réunies par Marie-Claude Porcher* (Paris: École des Hautes Études en Sciences Sociales, 1983), 126.

3. In this respect, it is worth noting one more mirror. The entire *Mahābhārata* has a false ending of its own: Yudhiṣṭhira goes to hell, only to discover that it is an illusion. On the ending of the *Mahābhārata*, see Bruce M. Sullivan, "The *Mahābhārata*: Perspectives on its Ends and Endings," *International Journal of Hindu Studies* 15, no. 1 (2011): 1–7.

expression, and so on down the hall of mirrors. In this chapter I study the *Pañcarātra*'s portrayal of a famous character in disguise, the epic hero Arjuna posing as a dance teacher named Bṛhannalā. This is a mantle that Arjuna elects to adopt while the Pāṇḍavas live in Virāṭa's court for the final year of their exile.[4] What makes the play's expression of Arjuna as Bṛhannalā so distinctive—and so relevant to a book about the relationships between Mahābhāratas—is that the *Pañcarātra*'s rendering of Arjuna-as-Bṛhannalā lends a real sense of interiority to the Sanskrit *Mahābhārata*'s depiction of the same disguised figure. While it is of course impossible to know which telling(s) of the Mahābhārata story the *Pañcarātra*'s author(s) had in mind when orchestrating the play—nor would a tracing of "influence" necessarily amount to the most valuable analysis of the work[5]—I would argue that the way in which the play untangles the knot of Arjuna-as-Bṛhannalā represents a studied reflection on the portrait of this figure that is given in the *Virāṭaparvan* of the Sanskrit *Mahābhārata* itself. It is exegesis, then, not eisegesis.

Those who know how Sanskrit names are formed already know that Bṛhannalā is a woman. The matter of Bṛhannalā's gender is quite crucial, since in the *Pañcarātra*, Arjuna expresses a sense of becoming Bṛhannalā on the inside—in his body, in his mind—in addition to pretending to be her on the outside. His limbs lose their familiar qualities, so his body changes; as he forgets his old self, his mind changes too. Even after Arjuna recovers the parts of himself that he loses over the course of being Bṛhannalā, the play continues to present Arjuna as a bifurcated character, a person split between two personae. The *Mahābhārata*'s *Virāṭaparvan*, quite by contrast, presents Bṛhannalā (or, as she is called there, Bṛhannaḍā) as an extrinsic costume that Arjuna layers over himself. This still-very-present self is Arjuna the Pāṇḍava. Bṛhannaḍā, meanwhile, is a role he consciously performs. The *Virāṭaparvan* evokes this sense of costumery and its companion, performance, by drawing the audience's attention to Arjuna's changes of jewelry, clothes, and hairstyles as he transitions between his familiar self, Arjuna,

4. On the epic's narrative rationale(s) for Arjuna's particular disguise, see Wendy Doniger, *Splitting the Difference: Gender and Myth in Ancient Greece and India* (Chicago: University of Chicago Press, 1999), 280–81.

5. On intertextuality and the idea of influence, see Wendy Doniger, *The Woman Who Pretended to Be Who She Was: Myths of Self-Imitation* (New York: Oxford University Press, 2005), 6–7.

into his pretend self, Bṛhannaḍā. These transformations unfold on the surface of Arjuna's body but remain external to it. It is all quite different in the *Pañcarātra*.

The *Pañcarātra* takes this idea of disguise as a performance—something that Arjuna directs toward others, an audience—and turns it into an expression of disguise as an experience, something that Arjuna feels unfolding within himself. The representation of "himself" becomes a particularly important point on which the *Pañcarātra* responds to the *Virāṭaparvan*. The *Virāṭaparvan* ascribes to Arjuna a selfhood that remains consistent throughout the narrative—even while performing Bṛhannaḍā—whereas the *Pañcarātra* transforms Arjuna-as-Bṛhannalā into a splintered self. David Shulman writes of Nala, another famously doubled character in the *Mahābhārata*, that "Nala's primary experience . . . is that of watching reality—his reality, inner and outer—splinter and reproduce itself . . . Nala is driven into a series of utterly alien dislocations, of disjoined *vaiṣamya* ['unevenness'] states."[6] Shulman's analysis points to the idea that doubled characters can embody certain negativities; they can reveal losses of self and fragmentations of self rather than abundances of self—or selves, as it were.[7] I believe that this is true of the *Pañcarātra*'s Arjuna.

Arjuna as Bṛhannaḍā in the *Virāṭaparvan*

To appreciate the ways in which the *Pañcarātra* counters the *Virāṭaparvan*'s vision of Arjuna in disguise, let us turn to the passages in the *Virāṭaparvan* that most vividly articulate the idea that Arjuna performs Bṛhannaḍā while retaining an intact sense of self. I want to begin with the most literal expression of this idea, the place where the narrative describes Arjuna as "self-possessed" (*ātmavān*) during his time as Bṛhannaḍā:

---

6. David Shulman, "On Being Human in the Sanskrit Epic: The Riddle of Nala," *Journal of Indian Philosophy* 22, no. 1 (1994): 14–15.

7. As David Shulman writes elsewhere, there is a gleam of "intense self-alienation" in each of the *Virāṭaparvan*'s main personalities. See *The King and the Clown in South Indian Myth and Poetry* (Princeton, NJ: Princeton University Press, 1985), 259.

So Dhanaṃjaya lived in disguise:
Self-possessed, doing sweet things with the ladies.
No one at the palace, inside or outside it,
Discovered who he really was.[8]

Although there is an obvious subtext to this *ātmavān*, which is that Arjuna (here called Dhanaṃjaya, an epithet) remains sexually unavailable—self-controlled, if you will—to Virāṭa's daughter and her friends, the rest of the verse demonstrates that Arjuna's self-possession represents more than sexual unavailability. The verse posits a self that is accessible to Arjuna alone ("no one discovered who he really was"). The sentiment lingers in the narrative. Later in the *Virāṭaparvan*, Arjuna reminds Draupadī that she "doesn't know" Bṛhannaḍā.[9] I believe there is a significance to the verse's final image, too, the one that describes the "outsiders" and "insiders" of the palace—that is, those who work around the periphery of the palace and those who live inside it—going about their business while remaining unaware of who Arjuna "really is" (*tathāgata*). This last part of the verse invites the reader (or listener, as the case may be) to picture Arjuna as if he were somewhat like the palace in which he resides. He has a kind of multi-layered dynamism that emerges out of his transformations from Arjuna to Bṛhannaḍā and back again, but there is something immovable to him—like the structural foundation of the palace itself—that withstands all of the commotion and that might well go unnoticed.

Finally, the verse describes Bṛhannaḍā not as a character or an identity but as a costume. For Arjuna, to be Bṛhannaḍā is to "live in [literally 'through'] disguise" (*sattreṇa avasat*). The text does not equate Arjuna with the disguise; rather, the disguise becomes a mode (in Sanskrit's instrumental

8. *tathā sa sattreṇa dhanaṃjayo 'vasat priyāṇi kurvan saha tābhir ātmavān* |
tathāgataṃ tatra na jajñire janā bahiścarā vāpy atha vāntarecarāḥ || *MBh* 4.10.13 ||

Note that *tābhir*, in this verse, refers to Uttarā and her ladies-in-waiting. All quotes from the Sanskrit *Mahābhārata* (*MBh*) are taken from the electronic edition of *The Mahābhārata for the First Time Critically Edited*, ed. V. S. Sukthankar et. al. 19 vols. (Poona: Bhandarkar Oriental Research Institute, 1933–66) that was prepared by Muneo Tokunaga and revised by John Smith in 1999. Unless noted otherwise, all translations of the *Mahābhārata* and the *Pañcarātra* are my own.

9. *MBh* 4.23.23.

case *sattreṇa*), a way of living that exists separately from Arjuna and that he can harness as he wants, for his own benefit, just as he does everything else—his bow, Gāṇḍīva, and his arrows and various celestial weapons. Mythologically speaking, he inherits this capability from his father, the god Indra, who frequently appears in disguise in the *Mahābhārata*.[10]

Here, in Arjuna's voice, the epic describes his transfiguration into Bṛhannaḍā as a matter of finding the right costume:

> My lord, this is my vow: I'll dress in drag
> Since my great bowstring scars are hard to disguise.
> Fastening rings bright as fire to my ears,
> And doing up my hair into a braid, king,
> I will take the name Bṛhannaḍā.[11]

In this passage, Arjuna narrates a series of changes that take place on the surface of the body. He speaks of how he'll wear ornaments—which we later discover to be bangles, an image that the *Pañcarātra* will go on to spotlight—that cover the bowstring scars on both of his forearms. (Another aspect of Arjuna's doubled identity: his ambidexterity.) He describes himself putting on dazzling earrings. (Might it be more than a coincidence that Arjuna introduces his costume in terms of doubles—the two bowstring scars, the two earrings?) And once we see him put his hair into a braid, the transformation is complete: we arrive at Bṛhannaḍā, the last word in the passage. It is important to note that while the text describes this transformation as an external one, we ought not to consider it superficial, at least not in the sense of being meaningless. Costumes, jewelry, and hair always matter. (This is especially true in the world of Sanskrit literature, where poetic figures are described in theoretical texts as *alaṅkāra*s—ornaments, decorations.) As James McHugh observes, "The way we normally use the

10. Three examples of Indra's disguises in the *Mahābhārata*: a *brāhmaṇa* in the story of the robbing of Karṇa's earrings (*MBh* 2.284–94); a *brāhmaṇa* in the story of Arjuna's encounter with Śiva as a *kirāta* (*MBh* 3.38); a hawk in the story of Śibi (*MBh* 3.131).

11. *pratijñāṃ ṣaṇḍhako 'smīti kariṣyāmi mahīpate* |
jyāghātau hi mahāntau me saṃvartuṃ nṛpa duṣkarau ||
karṇayoḥ pratimucyāhaṃ kuṇḍale jvalanopame |
veṇīkṛtaśirā rājan nāmnā caiva bṛhannaḍā || *MBh* 4.2.21–22 ||

word 'superficial' reflects our 'depth ontology,' according to which our being is inside us and opposed to our exteriors. This metaphorical way of understanding the inner self might not be the same everywhere . . . Clothes are not mere symbols but can constitute the self."[12]

Nowhere does this idea shine through more clearly than at the end of the *Virāṭaparvan*, when Arjuna—still dressed as Bṛhannaḍā, at first—must fight to protect Virāṭa's cattle from a Kaurava raid. Here we learn that even for the self-possessed Arjuna, "Arjuna" is a costume. As Arjuna prepares for battle, the narrative returns to images of ornaments and hair. And once again we see Arjuna undergo an external transformation. But here, Arjuna sheds one costume (Bṛhannaḍā's ornaments, Bṛhannaḍā's hair) and puts on another one (Arjuna's ornaments, Arjuna's hair):

> Then the hero loosened the bangles from his arms
> And fastened shining, splendid guards to his forearms—
> like kettledrums they boomed.
> He tied up his dark curls with a white cloth,
> Quickly strung Gāṇḍīva, and drew the bow.[13]

The passage reiterates the idea that Bṛhannaḍā is a costume—this time a costume that can be taken *off*, bangles loosened and braid taken out. But crucially, the passage also sets up Arjuna's customary garb (forearm guards, hairstyle, Gāṇḍīva) as a second costume. In that second costume "Arjuna" takes the place of "Bṛhannaḍā." On one level, this turn of the narrative deconstructs (with a wink, perhaps) the trope of the epic hero donning his armor: warriors don't typically have to move their bangles out of the way.[14]

---

12. James McHugh, *Sandalwood and Carrion: Smell in Indian Religion and Culture* (New York: Oxford University Press, 2012), 4. Here, McHugh draws upon the arguments of the anthropologist and scholar of material culture Daniel Miller.

13. *tato nirmucya bāhubhyāṃ valayāni sa vīryavān* |
citre dundubhisaṃnāde pratyamuñcat tale śubhe ||
kṛṣṇān bhaṅgīmataḥ keśāñ śvetenodgrathya vāsasā |
adhijyaṃ tarasā kṛtvā gāṇḍīvaṃ vyākṣipad dhanuḥ || *MBh* 4.40.23–24 ||

14. For example, Achilles arming himself for battle in *Iliad* 19.368–79. See Homer, *Iliad*, vol. 2, *Books 13–24*, trans. A. T. Murray, rev. William F. Wyatt, Loeb Classical Library 171 (Cambridge, MA: Harvard University Press, 1999), 360–61. In the *Mahābhārata*, see, for example, 5.71.35–39.

More specifically, however, it uses the figure of Bṛhannaḍā to defamiliarize the iconography of Arjuna. It does this by describing Arjuna's transformation *into Arjuna* in such a way that it closely parallels his transformation into Bṛhannaḍā, which we witnessed in the previous passage. Both of these costume-change passages begin with the image of his arms; both passages show him fastening (with the same word, *prati√muc*) two bright ornaments to his body, first earrings and now forearm guards; in both passages, he manipulates his hair. By the time we reach Gāṇḍīva, we realize that this weapon, too, is an ornament, a crucial part of Arjuna's "Arjuna" costume.[15] Arjuna's body stays the same throughout; it's only the costume that changes.

The adverb "quickly" (*tarasā*) suggests that Arjuna maintains control of these costumes—that he switches between them with ease, never getting stuck in any one of them for too long. (The *Pañcarātra*'s figuration of Arjuna-as-Bṛhannalā will hinge on distorting this feature.) We see this dexterity most plainly when Arjuna pretends not to have it. Compelled to go into battle to defend Virāṭa's cattle, Arjuna acts as if he has never worn armor before:

> The Pāṇḍava made a great game of it in front of princess Uttarā.
> (Listen, tamer of enemies: in fact he knew how to do it all!)
> He set up his armor upside-down[16] and fastened it to his body—
> All the princesses, wide-eyed, saw him there and laughed.[17]

Here the *Virāṭaparvan* frames the figures of Bṛhannaḍā and Arjuna not as costumes but as full performances. To begin with, there is an audi-

---

15. The construction of this costume begins in an earlier passage, when Uttara holds up Arjuna's hidden weapons and asks of each one "Whose is this?" See *MBh* 4.38.20–36.

16. J. A. B. van Buitenen interprets the line as Bṛhannaḍā donning the armor upside-down (*ūrdhvam*), but it could also be that Bṛhannaḍā tries on the upper part (*ūrdhvam*) of the armor and jokingly parades around in it. See *The Mahābhārata*, vol. 3, *4. The Book of Virāṭa, 5. The Book of the Effort*, trans. J. A. B. van Buitenen (Chicago: University of Chicago Press, 1978), 81.

17. *sa tatra narmasaṃyuktam akarot pāṇḍavo bahu* |
uttarāyāḥ pramukhataḥ sarvaṃ jānan ariṃdama ||
ūrdhvam utkṣipya kavacaṃ śarīre pratyamuñcata |
kumāryas tatra taṃ dṛṣṭvā prāhasan pṛthulocanāḥ || *MBh* 4.35.17–18 ||

ence: Virāṭa's daughter Uttarā and her friends, in front of whom Arjuna puts Bṛhannaḍā on display and through whose wide eyes we take in the spectacle. Then the passage sketches Arjuna playing a role, Bṛhannaḍā, for that audience: he plays at not knowing how to wear armor, when really he knows how to do everything. But "Arjuna," too, becomes a production. He fastens the armor on top of his Bṛhannaḍā costume and in doing so creates a new character, the warrior. (Again the term *prati√muc* signals the costume change.) The image of him layering the armor over the clothes that he wears as Bṛhannaḍā sets up the later point in the narrative at which Arjuna will put on his "Arjuna" costume in earnest. This moment was described in the passage that I shared earlier: "Then the hero loosened the bangles from his arms . . ."

As it happens, when the princesses laugh at Arjuna's double performance here—Arjuna pretending to be Bṛhannaḍā pretending to be a warrior—the scene prefigures one of the most memorable vignettes in the *Virāṭaparvan*. Later, during the narration of the cattle raid, the *Virāṭaparvan* describes Arjuna (still dressed as Bṛhannaḍā) running after the terrified prince Uttara, whose chariot Bṛhannaḍā is supposed to be driving. In a marvelous inversion of the *Bhagavadgītā*, here it is Arjuna who plays Kṛṣṇa, the humble charioteer who must persuade his charge to fight. (The *Virāṭaparvan* unfurls the *Bhagavadgītā* reflection at some scale. Following the chasing and urging, there is a theophany of sorts—Bṛhannaḍā reveals herself to be Arjuna the Pāṇḍava—for which Uttara, mimicking Arjuna's role in the *Gītā*, serves as the amazed and initially disbelieving witness.) As Arjuna-Bṛhannaḍā races after Uttara, admonishing him to take up arms, we see him through the eyes of the soldiers watching him: "Arjuna scampered after the running prince, expertly tossing about his long braid and his red dress. Not knowing that it was Arjuna running and tossing his braid about, some of the soldiers laughed."[18] And so, as the *Virāṭaparvan* continues, Bṛhannaḍā's audience only grows larger; her stage broadens from the inner rooms of the palace to the pastures that become her battlefield.

18. . . . *tam anvadhāvad dhāvantaṃ rājaputraṃ dhanaṃjayaḥ* |
dīrghaṃ veṇīṃ vidhunvānaḥ sādhu rakte ca vāsasī ||
vidhūya veṇīṃ dhāvantam ajānanto 'rjunaṃ tadā |
sainikāḥ prāhasan kecit . . . || *MBh* 4.36.27–28 ||
Note that some of the soldiers recognize Arjuna beneath (or above) the costume.

Amid these more subtle cues, we ought not forget that the *Virāṭaparvan* explicitly integrates the motif of performance into its representation of Bṛhannaḍā—after all, she is a dancing teacher. Here Arjuna describes Bṛhannaḍā's livelihood to his brother, Yudhiṣṭhira (the "Kaunteya" of the last line):

> Over and over, as a woman—telling little stories, you see—
> I'll delight the king, who protects the earth, and everyone
> else in the zenana, too.
> Songs and dances of all kinds, and so many musical
> instruments,
> My king, will I teach the women in Virāṭa's palace—
> While I talk at length of his people's triumphs, won by their
> own deeds.
> Listen, Kaunteya: Through illusion, I will disguise myself
> with myself.[19]

It is a vivid passage, and two of its features will prove particularly relevant to our study of the *Pañcarātra*. If we look at the phrase in the first line, "over and over, as a woman" (*strībhāvena punaḥ punaḥ*), we find the image of Arjuna behaving repeatedly and consistently as a woman does. The phrase expresses an idea that eventually appears among the founding principles of performance studies, namely, that performance involves behavior that has been rehearsed.[20] Note, however, that the *Virāṭaparvan*'s Arjuna repeatedly behaves as a woman while still being able to switch back into his "Arjuna"

---

19. *paṭhann ākhyāyikāṃ nāma strībhāvena punaḥ punaḥ* |
ramayiṣye mahīpālam anyāṃś cāntaḥpure janān ||
gītaṃ nṛttaṃ vicitraṃ ca vāditraṃ vividhaṃ tathā |
śikṣayiṣyāmy ahaṃ rājan virāṭabhavane striyaḥ ||
prajānāṃ samudācāraṃ bahu karmakṛtaṃ vadan |
chādayiṣyāmi kaunteya māyayātmānam ātmanā || *MBh* 4.2.23–25 ||

Note that in the line following this one, Arjuna compares himself to Nala. In making this comparison, Arjuna frames himself as the double of a double. Note, too, that the *ātmanā* of this last verse could be working reflexively with *māyayā* ("I disguise myself with *māyā* itself) or with Arjuna himself, if in a different way from that which I sketch in the essay ("By myself, I disguise myself with *māyā*").

20. See, for example, Richard Schechner, *Performance Studies: An Introduction* (New York: Routledge, 2002), 22.

costume at the end of it all. The *Pañcarātra*'s Arjuna, quite by contrast, will find it difficult to unlearn this behavior.

As a culmination to all this, if we look at the very end of the passage, we find a direct articulation of the idea that Bṛhannaḍā represents a full, second self with which Arjuna disguises his "Arjuna" self. Arjuna announces that "Through illusion, I will disguise myself with myself" (*chādayiṣyāmi kaunteya māyayātmānam ātmanā*). The two reflexives in a row (*ātmānam ātmanā*) cannot possibly be a coincidence. The two *ātmans* represent a doubled self, one *ātman* ("self") piled on top of another—Arjuna as Bṛhannaḍā. Through *ātmānam ātmanā*, the *Virāṭaparvan* frames Arjuna's experience in disguise not in negative terms (that is, as a self-splintering or self-fragmentation) but in positive ones. He gains an additional self during his period as Bṛhannaḍā; the second self attaches in some sense to the first. In the *Virāṭaparvan*, this is the special magic of playing pretend.

Arjuna as Bṛhannalā in the *Pañcarātra*

The *Pañcarātra* adopts these two expressions from the passage—both the concept of "over and over, as a woman" and the language of *ātman*—when it approaches the matter of Arjuna as Bṛhannalā. This, we recall, is the *Pañcarātra*'s name for her, slightly different from the *Virāṭaparvan*'s Bṛhannaḍā (although they mean the same thing: "Big-Reed," a phallic joke and thus a nod to the idea that Arjuna becomes a drag-queen-like figure, a persona that explicitly invokes layers of gender expression and performance).[21] But the distance between the two extends far beyond the matter of names. If the *Virāṭaparvan* presents a self-controlled Arjuna who wears Bṛhannaḍā as a costume and performs her at will, then the *Pañcarātra* responds to this depiction by evoking a deeper ambivalence about the stability of Arjuna's selfhood during his time in disguise. In the *Pañcarātra* Arjuna describes the experience of being doubled not as a state of convergence, which is to say, being two things at the same time, but rather as a state of divergence—being split, being neither one thing nor another. The *Pañcarātra*'s Arjuna gives full expression to the internal dimensions of this divergence. The transitions between Arjuna and Bṛhannalā unfold on the interior, both in Arjuna's body

21. See Doniger, *Splitting the Difference*, 281.

and in his mind, rather than on the exterior—that is, through costumery and ornamentation—as they do in the *Virāṭaparvan.*

We can hear these dynamics most clearly in a four-verse soliloquy that Arjuna voices when he first arrives on the *Pañcarātra*'s stage—verses 2.29–32. Other verses in the play speak to Arjuna's experience in disguise, and I will make use of some of them later in my analysis, but these four verses offer what I believe is the play's most intimate portrait of this doubled and, in this case, truly split character. The soliloquy evokes in stunning detail Arjuna's experience of being both Arjuna and Bṛhannalā at the same time. This imagining of what it actually *feels* like for a character to live as a doubled figure is unique in the play. Neither Yudhiṣṭhira nor Bhīma, the other disguised Pāṇḍava brothers who play significant roles in the drama, reflects on the feeling of living in costume.[22] Such introspection belongs only to Arjuna. His soliloquy also lends a depth to the affective expression of the Arjuna character, whose emotional landscape the *Virāṭaparvan* tends to cloud over. In the epic we know how Arjuna, as Bṛhannaḍā, makes *others* feel—delighted, amused, bewildered, brave—but the epic imparts little of how Arjuna himself feels. The *Pañcarātra*, by contrast, dives right in.

The first three verses of the soliloquy relate Arjuna's experience in disguise as a series of self-separations. In the first verse, Arjuna talks about the feeling of no longer being Arjuna. He recalls the moment in the cattle raid at which he first strings Gāṇḍīva and speaks of the difficulty of inhabiting Arjuna's body after living as Bṛhannalā for so long. He describes this experience through images of loss and contrast. Different parts of Arjuna's body disarticulate themselves from their familiar qualities; Arjuna's weapons turn against him; he forgets Arjuna and then remembers him. Then, in the following verse, Arjuna talks about not really being Bṛhannalā, either. Having "remembered himself" at the end of the first verse, Arjuna goes on to describe the experience of pretending to be Bṛhannalā—while presumably still feeling more like Arjuna on the inside. Here he captures some of the performative aspect of his disguise that we see in the *Virāṭaparvan.* The third verse envisions another self-separation, namely, the gap between

22. Perhaps because the play presents Yudhiṣṭhira as continuous with his costumed self (an idea that I discuss in the final paragraphs of this section) and presents Bhīma as essentially uncostumed. The play positions Arjuna-as-Bṛhannalā in a middle ground.

Arjuna's appearance of success in battle and his feeling that he has missed a more important target. And the fourth verse introduces a new perspective: Arjuna contrasts his experience in disguise with what he understands to be Yudhiṣṭhira's experience in disguise. Whereas Arjuna undergoes these various self-alienations, Yudhiṣṭhira—in Arjuna's imagination—embodies a continuity between his "real" self and his disguise. In this way, as if in a final twist, Arjuna evokes yet another separation, this one not a self-separation but a separation between brothers.

So, to begin with, what does it feel like for Arjuna not to be Arjuna? Arjuna recounts this experience largely but not exclusively in terms of his body, which, in his account, has separated from its conventional characteristics. His fist is neither compact nor efficient; his forearm has no skill; his stance has none of its natural grace. Here, then, is the first of our four verses (2.29):

When I pulled Gāṇḍīva's string,
there was a moment when it fought me.
My fist was not clenched enough,
not deft enough,
to spin the arrows.
Skill escaped my forearm;
balance was stolen from my stance.
Because I had become a woman,
practicing it for so long, I grew soft—
But later, I remembered myself.[23]

Notably, the verse does not describe Arjuna's body in positive terms but articulates these instances of separation in negative particles (*na*), negative prefixes (*a-*), and in other kinds of negative vocabulary (for instance, *hṛta*,

23. *gāṇḍīvena muhūrtam ātataguṇenāsīt pratispardhitam*
bāṇānāṃ parivartaneṣv aviśadā muṣṭir na me saṃhatā |
godhāsthānagatā na cāsti paṭutā sthāne hṛtaṃ sauṣṭhavaṃ
strībhāvāc chithilīkṛtaḥ paricayād ātmā tu paścāt smṛtaḥ || *PR* 2.29 ||

All quotes from the Sanskrit text of the *Pañcarātra* (*PR*) are taken from the digital edition of the *Pañcarātra*, critically edited by the Bhāsa Projekt Würzburg: *Pañcarātra*, ed. Bhāsa Projekt Würzburg, Multimediale Datenbank zum Sanskrit-Schauspiel, 2007, http://www.bhasa.indologie.uni-wuerzburg.de/rahmen.html.

"stolen"). All this illustrates Arjuna's sense of loss. In this way, the *Pañcarātra* takes a transformation that the *Virāṭaparvan* presents as eminently external—nothing changes about Arjuna except for his jewelry, clothes, and hair—and shows how it unfolds internally, in the musculature and carriage of Arjuna's physical body. The language of motion ("balance was stolen," "I grew soft") adds further dynamism to the internal metamorphosis that the verse evokes.

This verse also serves to illuminate a second kind of division, one between Arjuna and his most familiar weapons, the bow Gāṇḍīva and the arrows of his inexhaustible quiver. Not only do Arjuna's body parts lose their distinctive features, but his weapons refuse to cooperate: Gāṇḍīva's string fights against his pull; the arrows won't release. The passage inverts the epic's description of Arjuna seamlessly ("quickly," *tarasā*) stringing Gāṇḍīva and asks: "What if it weren't so easy?" Or perhaps it asks: "What if, for Arjuna, it's never quite as easy as it seems?" The image of Arjuna's weapons failing him is a striking one, especially considering how the *Mahābhārata* devotes chapter after chapter to Arjuna's acquisition and manipulation of weapons. It reminds us of a handful of stories in the Sanskrit epic where we are prompted to think twice about Arjuna's skills. For instance, there is the time when Arjuna discovers that the tribal prince Ekalavya can shoot arrows faster than he can. There's also the famous moment when he loses his nerve at the beginning of the war (this occasions the *Bhagavadgītā*); or when he shoots at opponents who are unable to fight back (Karṇa, Bhīṣma, Bhūriśravas); or even when he exhausts his inexhaustible quiver in combat with Śiva.[24] All of these stories come naturally to mind when the *Pañcarātra* presents its audience with an Arjuna who doesn't quite live up to his own mythology.

Even more powerfully, perhaps, the image of Arjuna being unable to use his body and his weapons inverts a *Virāṭaparvan* sketch to which we are far more accustomed—Arjuna, as Bṛhannaḍā, pretending not to know how to use the armor of a warrior:

> He set up his armor upside-down and fastened it to his body—
> All the princesses, wide-eyed, saw him there and laughed.[25]

---

24. On running out of arrows, see *MBh* 3.40.35–39 and *MBh* 16.8 (where Arjuna struggles in other ways, too).

25. *MBh* 4.35.18.

The *Pañcarātra* captures this image and takes the joke out of it. Instead of Arjuna pretending not to be able to use his battle apparatus while really "knowing everything," the *Pañcarātra*'s Arjuna struggles with this same task. What the *Pañcarātra*'s Arjuna knows is the state of "being a woman" (*strībhāva*), to which he has grown accustomed after long practice (*paricaya*). With Arjuna's concession that "Because I had become a woman, practicing it for so long," verse 2.29 recalls the way in which Arjuna in the *Virāṭaparvan* describes the things that he will do "over and over, as a woman" (*strībhāvena punaḥ punaḥ*). But in harnessing the *Virāṭaparvan*'s image of performance as rehearsed behavior, the *Pañcarātra* presents Arjuna's womanly body as a reality that offers more immediacy than the firmness of his fist or even Gāṇḍīva's string: "I grew soft" is the first positive statement about Arjuna's selfhood that we hear in this verse.[26] The *Pañcarātra*'s Arjuna actually becomes the thing that he is pretending to be.

We might call him one of the "actors who become the characters they impersonate" that Wendy Doniger recalls in *The Woman Who Pretended to Be Who She Was*:

> Some films depict actors who become the characters they impersonate . . . In *The Legend of Lylah Clare* (Robert Aldrich, 1968), an actress becomes possessed by the spirit of the actress whom she is portraying and repeats in her own life the fatal errors of the film character. Someone in the film comments, "Actors don't know who they are until someone writes some lines to tell them who they are," and his companion replies, "But we are all impersonating an identity." Some of us more than others, perhaps.[27]

The *Pañcarātra* anticipates such films. Instead of Arjuna being possessed of himself (*ātmavān*) during this period of living in disguise—this, we have seen, is how the *Virāṭaparvan* depicts him—the *Pañcarātra* gives us something like the actress above. Possessed by the spirit of Bṛhannalā, he becomes the actress (or dancer, if you will) whom he is portraying. After

26. The *cvi* formation *śithilīkṛta* communicates its own sense of loss: "I grew soft (when I wasn't before)."

27. Doniger, *Woman Who Pretended*, 21.

all, the transformation turns out to be as much mental as it is physical. The verse's final phrase, "But later, I remembered myself," suggests that so long as these features—the qualities of being compact, dextrous, skillful, or steady on his feet—depart from Arjuna's body, and so long as his familiar ornaments—Gāṇḍīva and the arrows—fail to attach to him as they are supposed to, then something happens in Arjuna's mind, too: he loses or forgets himself. Thus we come to feel that Arjuna's entire sense of self is wrapped up in the particular qualities of his body and the relationship with his weapons. Without those qualities and those weapons, he forgets himself. Looking back, we can see that the verse displays Arjuna's internal transition to Bṛhannalā in three stages. It begins with repeated, rehearsed behavior; it seeps into the musculature and carriage of his body; and it spills over into Gāṇḍīva and his arrows. At the end of this transition, Arjuna's self lands in the quiet corner of the mind where memories go to wait until they can be recovered. "I remembered myself," *ātmā smṛtaḥ,* he says.[28]

This conclusion ("I remembered myself") takes the *Pañcarātra*'s presentation of Arjuna in a more familiar direction. The following verse finds Arjuna no longer in the state of not being Arjuna, but rather in the state of not being Bṛhannalā. Instead, he *pretends* to be her (verse 2.30):

> Assuming this appearance among the kings of men,
> I drew the bow as if I were bashful about it.
> But the next thing we knew, there was war, in a storm of arrows—
> Quickly the dust settled and bloodied.[29]

Here we can see more immediate reflections of the Arjuna-as-Bṛhannaḍā that we know from the *Mahābhārata*. He makes use of a costume or a dress (*anena veṣeṇa*, reflecting the *Virāṭaparvan*'s *sattreṇa*); he pretends to be bashful when he isn't. Gāṇḍīva, the subject of so much distress in the first verse, becomes almost an afterthought here. This second verse grants

28. One could construe *paricayāt* with *ātmā tu paścāt smṛtaḥ*—i.e., that Arjuna remembers himself because of his previous "long practice" *as Arjuna*—but my reading takes into account the *Mahābhārata*'s "over and over again, as a woman" and also accounts for the caesura.

29. *mayā hi*
anena veṣeṇa narendramadhye lajjāyamānena dhanur vikṛṣṭam |
yātrā tu tāvac charadurdineṣu śīghraṃ nimagnaḥ kaluṣaś ca reṇuḥ || *PR* 2.30 ||

us a new perspective in another way, too. We see not only a different Arjuna but a different world ("there was war, in a storm of arrows") because Arjuna no longer looks inward, searching for a lost self, but outward, past his costume—just a costume once more—and over the bloodied landscape. Putting Bṛhannalā back on the exterior allows Arjuna, and therefore the audience, to awaken to a whole world outside.

In this way the second verse really sets up the third in the series, which takes that same outside world—the field of battle, or in this case, a pasture of battle—and suggests to the audience that Arjuna puts on a certain kind of performance there, too (2.31):

> Winning cattle,
> Winning victory for the king—
> In all this winning
> My heart doesn't feel a single thrill.
> No taking Duḥśāsana today,
> No capturing him at the battle's head.
> Still, I entered Virāṭa's city.[30]

Here Arjuna expresses an inconsistency between the victory that he wins on the outside (that is, his defense of Virāṭa's cattle) and the loss that he feels on the inside (in his heart, *manasi*), the missed opportunity to capture his enemy Duḥśāsana during the conflict. If the previous verse conveys the idea that Arjuna pretends to be Bṛhannalā while "really" having been restored to Arjuna on the inside, then this verse implies that there is a discontinuity even within Arjuna's "Arjuna" self. The external victory (*vijaya*) masks an internal numbness (*naivāsti me . . . manasi praharṣaḥ*, "my heart feels not a single thrill").

As I see it, this verse lends a certain complexity to the phrases in the *Virāṭaparvan* that position "Arjuna as warrior" as a costume that replaces "Arjuna as Bṛhannaḍā." The present verse carries forward the idea that "Arjuna as warrior"—at least a warrior who wins—represents an external layer of

30. *jitvāpi gāṃ vijayam apy upalabhya rājño*
naivāsti me jayagato manasi praharṣaḥ |
duḥśāsanaṃ samaramūrdhani sannigṛhya
baddhvā yad adya na virāṭapuraṃ praviṣṭaḥ || *PR* 2.31 ||

Arjuna's experience. But here the *Pañcarātra* does something that the *Mahābhārata* does not. It tells us what might lie beneath this layer: a warrior who lacks something, who fails to do something. In this sense the verse echoes the first we heard in the soliloquy ("When I pulled Gāṇḍīva's string, there was a moment when it fought me"), which also presents us with an Arjuna who expresses a feeling of having failed to fulfill his storied heroism.

I believe that the verse's play on the verbal root √*ji* ("to win")—which emerges twice in the first line (*jitvā*, *vijayam*) and once in the second (*jayagata*)—is intended to convey this idea, too. *Vijaya* is a common word for victory, yes, but it is also one of Arjuna's ten names.[31] When Arjuna says that he "won victory" (*vijayam upalabhya*) for the king, he also, in this subordinated sense, expresses the sentiment that he has found himself: *vijayam upalabhya*, "I found Vijaya." The verse's triple use of √*ji* draws our attention to the word *vijaya*—it might have slipped under the radar otherwise—and then, just as the *Pañcarātra* does to other aspects of Arjuna's character, fragments it. In the second line, we find that Arjuna feels no thrill that is "*jayagata*"—"in (or connected to) the victory." This is surely true, but the phrase could also mean that he finds no joy "in being [*Vi*]*jaya*," that is, in some sense, himself.

And who is this Vijaya? In the *Virāṭaparvan* of the Sanskrit *Mahābhārata*, Arjuna takes on the name Vijaya as the secret name that his brothers and wife use to address him while they live incognito in Virāṭa's court.[32] In the *Virāṭaparvan* "Vijaya" becomes the piece of the "old" Arjuna that he carries with him into Virāṭa's court. It seems to symbolize the way Arjuna holds on to his "real" self while living in disguise. Recall that in the *Virāṭaparvan* he remains *ātmavān*—self-possessed, self-controlled, self-aware. This verse in the *Pañcarātra* calls exactly that into question. Here Arjuna is no longer able to retain the old self named "Vijaya" on an interior level of experience. He may perform "Vijaya" in his defense of Virāṭa's land, but he also makes it clear,

31. These names play an important role in the *Virāṭaparvan*: before Arjuna can emerge in battle as Arjuna, he must recite to the doubtful Uttara the stories of how he earns each of his ten names. The narration of his names makes it possible for Arjuna to become "Arjuna" in public. See *MBh* 4.39.

32. *MBh* 4.5.30. In fact, all of the Pāṇḍava brothers' secret names involve √*ji*. Arjuna's, however, is the only secret name that is used both in Virāṭa's court and in the Pāṇḍavas' "real" lives.

afterward, that the thrill of the victory—the thrill of "being [*Vi*]*jaya*" (*jaya-gata*)—escapes his heart (*manasi*).

By illuminating a part of Arjuna that is somehow missing, the third verse in the series returns to the theme of the first. Both verses communicate the challenge of moving between selves: certain parts get lost or forgotten along the way. Where the first verse expresses a divergence between a past and a present self—the old Arjuna and the current Bṛhannalā—the third verse expresses a divergence between a present self and a future self. In the first *pāda* (quarter of the verse), we see the current Arjuna, who enacts a limited "Vijaya," or victory; but in the other three *pāda*s, we see the future Arjuna, an imagined Arjuna, who will fulfill the promise of that name when he captures Duḥśāsana.

The final verse in the soliloquy creates a different kind of split from the previous three. Here, instead of expressing contrasts between Arjuna's various expressions of self, the *Pañcarātra* juxtaposes the fragmentation of Arjuna's experience in disguise against what Arjuna perceives to be a remarkable sense of unity or consistency in Yudhiṣṭhira's experience of disguise. Arjuna looks at Yudhiṣṭhira and notices that his present disguise—a *brāhmaṇa*[33]—reflects an element of Yudhiṣṭhira's character that has been present since his youth. Arjuna tells us in verse 2.32:

> When he was a boy, he desired
> only the lovely *tapas* groves.[34]
> Now a lord of men, he finds solace
> in a *brāhmaṇa*'s ways.
> He let his kingdom go—
> still he grows in royal glory.
> He holds a triple staff,
> and wields no scepter.[35]

---

33. Yudhiṣṭhira does not take on the name Kaṅka in the *Pañcarātra* (as he does in the *Virāṭaparvan* and some other retellings). In the play, Yudhiṣṭhira is only ever called Bhagavān ("the blessed one"), a name that suggests he represents a more generalized *brāhmaṇa* figure.

34. The term "*tapas* groves" conveys the image of forested areas in which people engage in ascetic practice (*tapas*).

35. *sayauvanaḥ śreṣṭhatapovane rato nareśvaro brāhmaṇavṛttam āśritaḥ* |
vimuktarājyo 'py abhivardhitaḥ śriyā tridaṇḍadhārī na ca daṇḍadhārakaḥ || *PR* 2.32 ||

Shulman calls Yudhiṣṭhira the "reluctant ruler" of the *Mahābhārata,* for the epic depicts him as uneager to engage in conflict. It is not an admirable trait. Time and again he must be persuaded to rule.[36] Yudhiṣṭhira's choice of disguise in the *Virāṭaparvan* forms a part of this pattern. It reflects his disinclinations toward *kṣatriya* responsibilities (martial power, social power) and his identification, instead, with a kind of idealized renunciant *brāhmaṇa* lifestyle in which power is redirected toward the self through enacting control over one's own body and mind. The "triple staff" takes note of this shift of weight; it marks the renunciant *brāhmaṇa*—a wanderer, an ascetic—rather than the householding *brāhmaṇa,* who carries a single staff. In the *Virāṭaparvan* the façade of ascetic *brāhmaṇa*-hood falls away quickly for Yudhiṣṭhira. Rather than letting him move into this idealized role and therefore somehow enjoy his period in exile, the *Virāṭaparvan* awards Yudhiṣṭhira the disguise of being a different kind of *brāhmaṇa*: the king's dice game master. He becomes a comic figure, the king's *brāhmaṇa* sidekick—a standard figure in the literature of kingship in early South Asia.[37] Once again the *Pañcarātra* takes a second, more reflective look at the scene. Arjuna gives voice to what he sees as Yudhiṣṭhira's long-awaited ability fully to express this idealized *brāhmaṇa* side of himself. He restores Yudhiṣṭhira to his inner nobility—an expression, perhaps, of the depth of Arjuna's own feeling.

But there is a bittersweet taste to all this. Arjuna's observations deliberately contrast Yudhiṣṭhira's experience in disguise with his own. In Arjuna's eyes, Yudhiṣṭhira loses his kingdom but still manages to grow in the essence of kingship—*śrī,* the divine kind of royal glory that attends a king as if it (indeed, She) were a consort to him. In other words, Yudhiṣṭhira looks even more royal and even more glorious without a kingdom there to distract whoever might be looking at him. Arjuna, however, gains nothing; he only loses. He loses his strength, his skill, his balance, himself. Arjuna presents the icon of Yudhiṣṭhira's disguise, the renunciant's triple staff (*tridaṇḍa*), as a kind of natural outgrowth of the centerpiece of Yudhiṣṭhira's royal apparatus, the scepter (*daṇḍa*). For Yudhiṣṭhira, *daṇḍa* becomes *tridaṇḍa.* For Arjuna, by contrast, the apparatus always stands apart, whether it is the bowstring that resists his pull or the women's ornaments that slightly

36. Shulman, *King and the Clown,* 28–30.

37. On which, see Shulman, 152–54.

discomfit him: "I'm a little embarrassed for the kings to see me like this, decked out in the ornaments that Uttarā gave me so affectionately," he says to himself just before he notices Yudhiṣṭhira.[38] Likewise, in the previous verse, Arjuna says that he feels no joy (*naivāsti me . . . praharṣaḥ*), which marks a striking difference from his description of Yudhiṣṭhira. Yudhiṣṭhira is doing what he has always loved and desired (*rata*). While both Yudhiṣṭhira and Arjuna become, in some way, the people they are pretending to be, Yudhiṣṭhira's transition—as Arjuna sees it—lacks the fragmentation and self-forgetfulness of his own. What is it to be a brother but to be distant from one's brother? Here we find a mark of the complex and heightened interiority that the *Pañcarātra* discovers in Arjuna.

Arjuna as Śiva, Arjuna as *Śleṣa*

Taken together, the final three verses of the monologue demonstrate that even once Arjuna "remembers himself" at the end of the first verse, he continues to experience a series of disjunctions—between his remembered self and his disguised self Bṛhannalā (in the second verse), between an external victory and an internal lack thereof (in the third), and between himself-as-Bṛhannalā and Yudhiṣṭhira-as-a-*brāhmaṇa* (in the fourth). But if the *Pañcarātra* allows the audience to survey the full panorama of self-fragmentation that the play creates for Arjuna in disguise as Bṛhannalā, then it also grants the audience certain ways of making sense of this splintering—ways of rendering it more expected and more familiar than it seems when we compare it with the self-possession that the Sanskrit *Mahābhārata* sketches for its own Arjuna-in-disguise.

One of these methods calls upon the audience to see Arjuna-as-Bṛhannalā through the lens of the mythology and iconography of Śiva. This becomes a motif as the play continues its second act, the act in which our soliloquy appears. One might draw many parallels between Arjuna and Śiva, but the most important for our present purposes, and for the *Pañcarātra* as a whole, is that the image of being split is baked into the mythology of both Arjuna and Śiva. In both cases, the split is dramatic: one side of the character directly contradicts the other.

---

38. *uttarāprītidattālaṅkārenālaṅkṛto vrīḍita ivāsmi rājānaṃ draṣṭum* | *PR* 2.31.1

The *Pañcarātra* takes clear notice of this. It invokes two distinct correspondences between its split Arjuna and a split Śiva. The play invites the audience to compare Arjuna-as-Bṛhannalā with the image of Śiva merged with his consort, the goddess Pārvatī. We see this likeness from the perspective of Arjuna's son Abhimanyu, whom the play introduces as a central character.[39] Abhimanyu sees Arjuna for the first time in twelve years and remarks, without recognizing him, that (2.44):

> With your women's ornaments that don't quite fit,
> You're like an elephant bull, painted like an elephant cow!
> Light in clothes, hefty in muscle,
> You're resplendent! Like Śiva—dressed as Pārvatī.[40]

His remark suggests that in his disguise as a woman, Arjuna reflects Śiva Ardhanārīśvara ("the lord who is half woman"), the iconic formulation of the intermingling of Śiva and the goddess.[41]

An oft-retold story in the third book of the Sanskrit *Mahābhārata* (commonly called the *Kairātaparvan*, "The Tale of the Hunter") connects a paradoxical Arjuna to a paradoxical Śiva more explicitly. In the story, Arjuna, a virile figure in two senses—he is both a warrior and a ladies' man—lives as an ascetic in order to win the favor of the original "erotic ascetic," Śiva.[42] Their encounter results in a battle of increasingly pedestrian weapons until the two figures, both of whom now represent not only erotic ascetics but also warrior-ascetics,[43] wrestle one another. When Arjuna reveals himself to Virāṭa in the *Pañcarātra*, he identifies himself as the Arjuna of the *Kairātaparvan*, whose body was "licked by Śiva's arrows" (verse 2.65):

---

39. This feature presents a fascinating contrast with Abhimanyu's peripheral role in the *Virāṭaparvan*.

40. *ayujyamānaiḥ pramadāvibhūṣaṇaiḥ kareṇuśobhābhir ivārpito gajaḥ* |
laghuś ca veṣeṇa mahān ivaujasā vibhāty umāveṣam ivāśrito haraḥ || *PR* 2.44 ||

41. For more on this idea, see Alf Hiltebeitel, "Śiva, the Goddess, and the Disguises of the Pāṇḍavas and Draupadī," *History of Religions* 20, no. 1/2 (1980): 147–74.

42. On Śiva as the original erotic ascetic, see, of course, Wendy Doniger O'Flaherty, *Śiva: The Erotic Ascetic* (New York: Oxford University Press, 1981).

43. On the figure of the warrior ascetic, particularly in its more recent incarnations, see William R. Pinch, *Warrior Ascetics and Indian Empires* (New York: Cambridge University Press, 2006).

If I am Arjuna the Bhārata,
My body licked by Śiva's arrows,
Then isn't it just as clear
That Bhīmasena is this man here?
And this one is Yudhiṣṭhira, the king.[44]

There are countless descriptors that the *Pañcarātra* could have used to illustrate Arjuna in this pivotal moment of self-revelation. This one links our fragmented Arjuna to another splintered Arjuna, the *Kairātaparvan*'s erotic-warrior-ascetic, whose contradictory aspects fade into the background only once they meet their divine doubles in Śiva. In this phrase, the *Pañcarātra* offers the audience a way to see Arjuna's various internal conflicts as familiar, even essential, parts of his character. The mythology and iconography of Śiva, which are themselves charged with the imagery of contrast and paradox, prompt the audience to find a cosmic—and therefore familiar—resonance in Arjuna's fragmentation.

The play's second way of showing the audience how to make sense of Arjuna's splintered self is quite different. It turns away from the mythological and toward the literary. It invites the audience to see the bifurcated Arjuna as a kind of personified *śleṣa*—a pun, or, as Yigal Bronner calls it in his book on this ubiquitous feature of Sanskrit literature, an expression of "bitextuality."[45] In an incidence of *śleṣa*, a verbal expression—whether it is a word, a phrase, a verse, a passage, or a multi-chapter work—can be read in at least two ways at once such that each reading remains meaningful within the expression's broader context. Although the *Pañcarātra* does not, as far as I can tell, make use of *śleṣa* as a literary device, I believe that the play calls for us to use the concept of the *śliṣṭa* (bitextual) expression to bring a sense of coalescence to the figure of Arjuna-as-Bṛhannalā.

The play extends this invitation by taking a single image, Arjuna's bowstring scar, and using it in two successive verses, each of which tells a

44. *rudrabāṇāvalīḍhāṅgo yady ahaṃ bhārato 'rjunaḥ |*
avyaktaṃ bhīmaseno 'yam ayaṃ rājā yudhiṣṭhiraḥ || *PR* 2.65 ||

45. Bronner connects the work of *śleṣa* to the exploration of fragmented selfhood in Sanskrit literature specifically and to the expression of multivalence in classical South Asian art forms more generally. See Yigal Bronner, *Extreme Poetry: The South Asian Movement of Simultaneous Narration* (New York: Columbia University Press, 2010), 1–19, 57–90, 122–54, and 242–46.

different story about what the scar signifies, and each of which therefore gives a different account of who Arjuna-as-Bṛhannalā "really" is. Initially, Uttara points to the scar as proof that Bṛhannalā is actually Arjuna (2.63):

> Tucked inside his forearm:
> The scar struck by Gāṇḍīva's string.
> After twelve years
> It still hasn't lost its color.[46]

But Arjuna, in response to Uttara, tells a different story about that same scar. For him, the scar proves that he is Bṛhannalā, not Arjuna (2.64):

> Oh, this? My bracelets turned
> And made the scar.
> The pressure left its mark—
> Just the spot for a leather guard.[47]

Arjuna's account of the scar—that it was created by his bracelets—recalls the reasoning that the *Virāṭaparvan*'s Arjuna uses to support his choice of costume: "My lord, this is my vow: I'll dress in drag / Since my great bowstring scars are hard to disguise."[48] But it resonates with the *Virāṭaparvan*'s depiction of Arjuna in another way, too. The *Virāṭaparvan* shows Arjuna preserving a kind of core identity as he transitions into his "Bṛhannaḍā" costume and then back into his "Arjuna" costume—the self stays the same (*ātmavān*) while the costume changes. So, too, do these verses prompt the audience to see a certain consistency in the Arjuna-as-Bṛhannalā figure. The scar stays the same, but the story one tells about it can change. Together the two verses position the scar as a *śliṣṭa* image, a single shape that conjures two different target meanings.

Since the scar constitutes a significant part of Arjuna's iconography, these two verses cast Arjuna in the same mold—a figure who might look

46. *prakoṣṭhāntarasaṅgūḍhaṃ gāṇḍīvajyāhataṃ kiṇam |*
yat tad dvādaśavarṣānte naiva yāti savarṇatām || *PR* 2.63 ||

47. *etan me pārihāryāṇāṃ vyāvartanakṛtaṃ kiṇam |*
sannirodhavivarṇatvād godhāsthānam ihāgatam || *PR* 2.64 ||

48. *MBh* 4.2.21.

unchanged on the outside but about whose inner workings very different stories might be told. By now these stories are familiar to us. They are the stories that Arjuna tells when he first comes on stage and speaks of forgetting himself, remembering himself, hiding himself, enacting himself, and splitting himself from himself. Just as the dynamics of *śleṣa* unfold underneath the surface of a verbal expression, so Arjuna narrates various shifts that he feels on the inside but that other characters cannot perceive. This framing of Arjuna inverts the one found in the *Virāṭaparvan*. In the *Virāṭaparvan*, as we have seen, Arjuna remains the same on the inside but changes on the outside. In the *Pañcarātra*, Arjuna remains the same on the outside but expresses a series of dramatic changes and self-separations on the inside.

So when the *Pañcarātra*'s Arjuna picks this exact moment—the moment at which everyone on stage gathers around to look at this bivalent bowstring scar—to reveal himself as "Arjuna the Bhārata, my body licked by Śiva's arrows," the play makes a very powerful statement. It implies that if there is a "real" Arjuna in the drama, an Arjuna who would remain consistent with his self-presentation earlier in the play, then it is an Arjuna who, like his bowstring scar and like the variegated literature of the *Mahābhārata* itself, brings multivalence to life. He is his own *śleṣa* and his own Śiva. In a way, he is his own *Mahābhārata*. But it takes a side-step into drama—a move into a different refractive world—to make the point in a way you can't forget.

Chapter Six

The Lord of Glory and the Lord of Men

Power and Partiality in Māgha's *Śiśupālavadha*

Lawrence McCrea

While the Sanskrit genre of *mahākāvya* (literally "great poem," often translated as "court epic") is generally presumed to have been closely connected with the arena of royal power and self-presentation, and to have been produced and consumed mainly within royal or court settings, one of the most celebrated and canonized examples of the genre, Māgha's seventh-century *Śiśupālavadha* ("The Slaying of Śiśupāla"), appears to display a surprising level of ambivalence and even hostility toward royalty and royal power. The poem often deliberately goes out of its way to emphasize the non-royal status of its hero, Kṛṣṇa, and places him in conflict with an adversary—his cousin Śiśupāla, the king of Cedi—whose extended attack on Kṛṣṇa presents him as not merely non-royal but as regicidal (due to his killing of his uncle Kaṃsa, who had seized the throne of Mathurā from his own father Ugraśravas).[1] The poem can hardly be seen as an unqualified endorsement or ideological prop for kingship in general.

1. See Yigal Bronner and Lawrence McCrea, "To Be or Not to Be Śiśupāla: Which Version of the Key Speech in Māgha's Great Poem Did He Really Write?" *Journal of the American Oriental Society* 132, no. 3 (2012): 439.

Even given the poem's seeming ambivalence about kings and kingship, however, the poem offers us at least one clear positive model of royalty: Kṛṣṇa's cousin Yudhiṣṭhira, eldest of the five Pāṇḍava brothers who serve as the central heroes of the Sanskrit *Mahābhārata*. The plot of the poem revolves around Kṛṣṇa's extended journey to Yudhiṣṭhira's city of Indraprastha to attend his *rājasūya* sacrifice, a ritual that confirms Yudhiṣṭhira as an imperial or universal monarch (*saṃrāj*), dominant over the other kings of the earth. In Māgha's poem, as in the *Mahābhārata* episode on which it is based,[2] it is the elevation of Kṛṣṇa as the guest of honor at this sacrifice that provokes Śiśupāla to challenge the Pāṇḍavas, threatening Yudhiṣṭhira's sacrifice and provoking the military confrontation with Kṛṣṇa that culminates in Śiśupāla's own death. Hence, while Māgha has pointedly chosen a non-royal (albeit divine) figure as the hero, his plot places a contest over royal power at its center. Nevertheless, despite the seemingly central relevance of this political struggle to Māgha's poem, the actual interactions between Yudhiṣṭhira and Kṛṣṇa as depicted in the poem foreground not the political or tactical aspects of their relationship, but rather concentrate on their emotional bond.

The poem builds toward Kṛṣṇa's meeting with Yudhiṣṭhira almost from its beginning. In the second *sarga* (canto), Kṛṣṇa decides, after consultation with his advisors Balarāma and Uddhava, to attend Yudhiṣṭhira's *rājasūya* sacrifice rather than move immediately to attack Śiśupāla (as he had agreed to do at the urging of the divine messenger, Nārada, in the first *sarga*). But Kṛṣṇa's journey from his home city of Dvārakā to Yudhiṣṭhira's capital Indraprastha occupies the bulk of the poem, and the actual meeting of the two is put off until fairly late. When the two finally do meet, nothing is said about Yudhiṣṭhira's sacrifice or about the ostensible political mission of either figure. Instead, the focus is placed entirely on their personal relationship and the sheer delight of both at their reunion.

I have argued elsewhere that a basic structuring feature of Māgha's poem is his portrayal of Kṛṣṇa as a model of physical, verbal, and emotional restraint, presented as an ideal and deliberately contrasted to the uncontrolled

2. *MBh* 2.33–42. All references to the Sanskrit *Mahābhārata* are to the critical edition: *The Mahābhārata for the First Time Critically Edited*, ed. V. S. Sukthankar et al. 19 vols. (Poona: Bhandarkar Oriental Research Institute, 1933–66).

emotional excess of his antagonist, Śiśupāla.[3] I still believe that this holds true as a general characterization of Kṛṣṇa's presentation in the poem, but the depiction of Yudhiṣṭhira's attitude toward Kṛṣṇa and Kṛṣṇa's reaction upon their first meeting in the poem stands as a startling exception in its ascription of intense and uncontrolled emotion to the normally taciturn and restrained Kṛṣṇa—an exception that, as we shall see, appears to be significantly linked to Yudhiṣṭhira's status as a king.

Kṛṣṇa's Meeting with King Yudhiṣṭhira

It is only in the thirteenth *sarga*, after the long description of the journey from Dvārakā, that Kṛṣṇa and the reader at last arrive at Indraprastha, capital city of King Yudhiṣṭhira and scene of the poem's principal action. After the long digression of the "descriptive cantos,"[4] Māgha now pointedly returns our attention to the main frame of the narrative, deliberately beginning this *sarga* by taking us back to the scenario of the initial *sarga*s and telling us how Yudhiṣṭhira himself has been occupied since the events of the poem's opening. He has been waiting expectantly for Kṛṣṇa to arrive, just as the reader has:

> Not only did the son of Dharma [Yudhiṣṭhira] learn of it as soon as Kṛṣṇa had crossed the Yamunā; from the very moment [Kṛṣṇa] had left his city the king had news of Him brought to him night and day.[5]

In refocusing our attention on Kṛṣṇa's decision to attend Yudhiṣṭhira's sacrifice at the close of the second *sarga*, and Kṛṣṇa's departure from his home city

---

3. Lawrence McCrea, "The Conquest of Cool: Theology and Aesthetics in Māgha's *Śiśupālavadha*," in *Innovations and Turning Points: Toward a History of Kāvya Literature*, eds. Yigal Bronner, David Shulman, and Gary Tubb (Delhi: Oxford University Press, 2014), 130–35.

4. *ŚV* 4–12. All references to the *Śiśupālavadha* (*ŚV*) are from the following edition: Māgha, *Śiśupālavadha*, eds. Pandit Durgaprasad and Pandit Shivadatta (Bombay: Nirnaya Sagara Press, 1888).

5. *yamunām atītam atha śuśruvān amuṃ tapasas tanūja iti nādhunocyate* |
sa yadācalan nijapurād aharniśaṃ nṛpates tadādi samacāri vārtayā || *ŚV* 13.1 ||

of Dvārakā in the third *sarga*, Māgha draws the reader's attention to the main line of the plot, reminding us that Kṛṣṇa chose to attend Yudhiṣṭhira's sacrifice rather than immediately proceeding to fulfill his promise to Nārada to attack Śiśupāla. This backward glance emphasizes Yudhiṣṭhira's emotional state in relation to Kṛṣṇa, highlighting not any action on his part, but rather his all-consuming anxious waiting and hunger for news of Kṛṣṇa's approach. The focus on Yudhiṣṭhira's emotional state is intensified as the text proceeds; the specific character of his expectancy is further developed in the second verse of the *sarga*:

> As if there was no longer room for him in his vast city, due to [the great expanse of his] joy born from the arrival of the leader of the Yadus [Kṛṣṇa], the lord of the earth [Yudhiṣṭhira] suddenly came out from the city, together with his younger brothers, looking out for Him.[6]

Yudhiṣṭhira's unnamed brothers are kept very much in the background; the poet focuses resolutely on Yudhiṣṭhira himself, and specifically on his sheer delight in Kṛṣṇa's arrival (rather than any expectation of political support or counsel).

After establishing the narrative and emotional context of Yudhiṣṭhira's and Kṛṣṇa's encounter in this way, Māgha pulls back to paint the larger scene, describing in four verses the joyful and raucous union of their two armies as Kṛṣṇa's forces arrive outside the city.[7] Only then does he depict the actual moment of contact between the divine hero and his royal cousin:

> Even though the king wanted to descend from his chariot instantly at the very moment he saw Him in the distance, Kṛṣṇa Himself hurriedly got down from his own chariot first, emphasizing His own humility.[8]

The two cousins' competition as to who will show the greater deference emerges as a major theme here: Yudhiṣṭhira, a king, ostensibly of higher

6. *yadubhartur āgamanalabdhajanmanaḥ pramadād amān iva pure mahīyasi | sahasā tataḥ sa sahito 'nujanmabhir vasudhādhipo 'bhimukham asya niryayau* || *ŚV* 13.2 ||

7. *ŚV* 13.3–6.

8. *avaloka eva nṛpateḥ sma dūrato rabhasād rathād avatarītum icchataḥ | avatīrṇavān prathamam ātmanā harir vinayaṃ viśeṣayati sambhrameṇa saḥ* || *ŚV* 13.7 ||

status, seeks to humble himself before to his guest, while Kṛṣṇa, tacitly or even subconsciously recognized as divine by Yudhiṣṭhira, as he is by most other characters in the poem, seeks to preempt this honor by showing his own humility first.

This back-and-forth of mutual self-deprecation and deference between guest and host serves as another thematic and structural echo of the poem's opening, recalling the similar exchange between Kṛṣṇa and Nārada in the first *sarga*.[9] There too both guest (Nārada) and host (Kṛṣṇa) glorified each other while simultaneously abasing themselves. But despite this formal similarity, the emotional tone of the two meetings is radically different. When Nārada and Kṛṣṇa meet, the exchange is entirely verbal, and played out as a heightened form of politeness—rhetorically inflated and only semi-sincere. Here the encounter is depicted through the physical actions of the two characters, rather than through words, with a visceral intensity seemingly deliberately avoided in the earlier meeting, with its hyper-refined etiquette. Kṛṣṇa's encounter with Yudhiṣṭhira deliberately plays against this prior sense of decorum, emphasizing the attempt of each figure to discard the expectations dictated by his social status, to the point of literally getting "down in the dirt":

> That Primordial Person, even though all the worlds bowed down to Him, prostrated Himself before His father's sister's son [Yudhiṣṭhira] with His whole body, so that the cord of His long necklace became piled up on the ground in front of Him.
>
> As the dirt in front of Him was made red by the light from the jewels in His crown, but before He had actually touched the earth with His head, the king [Yudhiṣṭhira], ignoring all decorum, forcefully grasped Him in the cage of his arms.[10]

Kṛṣṇa's immediate attempt to prostrate himself before the king, vividly illustrated by the image of the necklace piling up on the ground as he lowers himself, together with Yudhiṣṭhira's desperate effort to stop him

9. On which, see McCrea, "The Conquest of Cool," 125–29.

10. *vapuṣā purāṇapuruṣaḥ puraḥ kṣitau paripuñjyamānapṛthuhārayaṣṭinā* |
bhuvanair nato 'pi vihitātmagauravaḥ praṇanāma nāma tanayaṃ pitṛṣvasuḥ ||
mukuṭāṃśurañjitaparāgam agrataḥ sa na yāvad āpa śirasā mahītalam |
kṣitipena tāvad anapekṣitakramaṃ bhujapañjareṇa rabhasād agṛhyata ||
ŚV 13.8–9 ||

before he actually touches his head to the ground, rapidly and effectively highlights both the uncharacteristic emotional intensity of Kṛṣṇa and Yudhiṣṭhira's relationship and its specifically political dimension: Kṛṣṇa immediately strives to show not merely affection but deference for his royal cousin, while Yudhiṣṭhira (often simply referred to as "the king" here and in following verses) seeks to prevent him from lowering himself in this way. And the emotional intensity of the encounter is all the more heightened and physical as the two embrace one another in the immediately succeeding verses:

> The chest of [the demon] Mura's enemy, wide as a door-panel, was too large for the smaller chest of the king. Still, stretching out his two long arms, he embraced Him all around.
>
> Surely Śrī [the Goddess of beauty], who had always made her home on His chest, now left behind the lotus growing out of His navel and climbed up to His face, afraid of being crushed by the Kuru king's pitilessly strong embrace.[11]

The physical intensity of the king's "pitiless" embrace of Kṛṣṇa elevates the emotional pitch of their bond to a nearly erotic level, as certainly seems to be deliberately suggested by the idea that Yudhiṣṭhira, through this embrace, has driven away Kṛṣṇa's consort Śrī from her customary position on Kṛṣṇa's chest and has himself taken her place there. And this is only augmented by the verses that conclude Māgha's description of this initial encounter, which again play on both the emotional and the political dimensions of Kṛṣṇa and Yudhiṣṭhira's bond:

> The king then affectionately smelled Him on the head—Him who had become a false dwarf to subdue the enemy of the gods, and who now became a dwarf [by bowing down] in humility; and

11. *na mamau kapāṭataṭavistṛtaṃ tanau muravairivakṣa urasi kṣamābhujaḥ* |
bhujayos tathāpi yugalena dīrghayor vikaṭīkṛtena parito 'bhiṣasvaje ||
gatayā nirantaranivāsam adhyuraḥ parinābhi nūnam avamucya vārijam |
kururājanirdayanipīḍanābhayān mukham adhyarohi muravidviṣaḥ śriyā ||
ŚV 13.10–11 ||

> the hair on His head was perfumed by the aroma of the divine *Pārijāta* tree He had won with His valor, as if [perfumed] by fame.
>
> Even after the son of Vasudeva had been released, the Kuru king's slender body remained as beautiful as a blooming cluster of *kadamba* flowers, as all his hairs still stood on end from the sheer delight of Kṛṣṇa's touch.[12]

The description of Yudhiṣṭhira's body hairs standing up with delight and the resultant comparison with a bristling *kadamba* flower heighten the quasi-erotic dimension of his encounter with Kṛṣṇa, as both the physical reaction and the simile are standard in (and largely confined to) descriptions of romantic encounters. But, again, the political—or, broadly, status—dimension is also highlighted in the above verse, which uses the standard affectionate gesture of smelling the head to show Kṛṣṇa's formal submission to Yudhiṣṭhira, and also to stress the authenticity of this self-humbling. In the past, Kṛṣṇa deceptively lowered himself by incarnating as a dwarf to trick the demon Bali, but here, through his bowing down, he "becomes a dwarf" out of genuine humility.

So intense mutual affection between Kṛṣṇa and Yudhiṣṭhira as well as Kṛṣṇa's deliberate humbling of himself in deference to Yudhiṣṭhira's authority are emphasized throughout this extraordinary passage. Stress is continually laid lexically on Yudhiṣṭhira's status as king, but the characterization of both Yudhiṣṭhira and Kṛṣṇa highlights their eminently personal and emotional bond. While Yudhiṣṭhira's politically elevated position is kept in view, neither political objectives nor tactics (either Kṛṣṇa's or Yudhiṣṭhira's) are addressed or even alluded to. There seems to be no calculus of advantage in play here on either side. In the end, it is attraction and the sheer joy of each in the other's presence that seems to define their relationship. This relationship is left to stand as the implied ideal model for relations between political authority and divinity within the poem.

---

12. *śirasi sma jighrati surāribandhane chalavāmanaṃ vinayavāmanaṃ tadā* |
yaśaseva vīryavijitāmaradrumaprasavena vāsitaśiroruhe nṛpaḥ ||
sukhavedanāhṛṣitaromakūpayā śithilīkṛte 'pi vasudevajanmani |
kurubhartur aṅgalatayā na tatyaje vikasatkadambanikurambacārutā ||
ŚV 13.12–13 ||

Kingship and Kingdom in the *Śiśupālavadha*

This persistent lexical focus on Yudhiṣṭhira's kingship actually represents a significant departure from what we find earlier in Māgha's poem. In the earlier *sargas* of the *Śiśupālavadha*, engagement with the theme of royalty is conspicuous by its near total absence, and the political status of Kṛṣṇa and his antagonist go largely unmentioned. Strikingly, for example, the opening *sarga* of the poem not only avoids discussion of the political status of Kṛṣṇa or his rival, it is almost wholly devoid of any terms for king (unusual for any comparably long stretch of Sanskrit poetry, but especially for a *mahākāvya*). There are only three occurrences of terms for kings in the *sarga*, and of these, two[13] are used non-anthropomorphically to refer honorifically to animals, both peripheral to the main subjects being described.[14] The single use of a term for king applied anthropomorphically occurs in the seventieth verse of the *sarga*, where Śiśupāla is punningly identified with the sun, who extends his rays (*kara*) over the mountains (*bhūbhṛt*), just as Śiśupāla extracts tribute (*kara*) from the kings (*bhūbhṛt*).[15] At no point are Śiśupāla or any of his (or Kṛṣṇa's) incarnations described in terms indicative of their royalty or social status.[16]

This silence regarding kings and kingship in the *Śiśupālavadha*'s first *sarga* may seem no more than an odd coincidence, but it forms part of a larger pattern of avoidance or suppression of royalty and related themes in the opening *sargas* of Māgha's poem. Kṛṣṇa's city of Dvārakā, the setting for the first three *sargas*, is itself presented as something of an apolitical space. The actual sovereign of Dvārakā at the time of the poem, Kṛṣṇa's

13. *ŚV* 1.7 and 1.56.

14. In *ŚV* 1.7, the golden filaments that make up Nārada's sacrifical thread are compared to "the feathers of the king of birds (Garuḍa)" (*vihaṅgarājāṅgaruhaiḥ*). In 1.56, the god Varuṇa fails to subdue Śiśupāla's prior incarnation Rāvaṇa after the "snake-king ropes" (*uragarājarajjavaḥ*) he tries to bind him with instead turn back in fear and bind Varuṇa himself.

15. *ŚV* 1.70.

16. Kṛṣṇa's prior avatar Rāma was of royal status, as were all three of Śiśupāla's incarnations discussed in the poem—Hiraṇyakaśipu (the demon ruler defeated by Narasiṃha, the half-man, half-lion *avatāra* of Viṣṇu), Rāvaṇa (the demon king of Laṅkā and Rāma's nemesis), and Śiśupāla himself. But there is no allusion to the royalty of any of these figures, and their status can only be known from external sources.

maternal grandfather, Ugrasena, is mentioned only once in the poem, during Śiśupāla's tirade against Kṛṣṇa in the fifteenth *sarga*, and even then only obliquely, as Śiśupāla refers to Kaṃsa, the usurping king of Mathurā whom Kṛṣṇa (Kaṃsa's nephew) killed, as "the son of Ugrasena."[17] Ugrasena, though at least nominally the ruling king of Kṛṣṇa's realm of Dvārakā during the time of the poem, plays no role whatsoever, and is not even vaguely alluded to anywhere else. If one did not know from the *Mahābhārata* or other sources, there would be no way to tell from Māgha's poem itself who is the sovereign in Dvārakā, or even if there is one.

The opening of the second *sarga*, in which Kṛṣṇa's older brother, Balarāma, and his uncle debate whether to immediately attack Śiśupāla or instead go to attend Yudhiṣṭhira's sacrifice, seems to deliberately highlight this political and social void. It plays on the emptiness of the Yādavas' assembly hall:

> Those three human sacrificial fires, come together for pacifying the world, shone blazing in the sacrificial enclosure that was the assembly hall.
>
> Although they were alone, with their images reflected in the jeweled pillars, they looked as if they were surrounded with people on all sides.[18]

The assembly hall where Kṛṣṇa and his advisors meet is imaginatively configured as a sacrificial space (mirroring the setting of Yudhiṣṭhira's actual sacrifice later in the poem) through the metaphorical identification of Kṛṣṇa and his two counselors as the three sacrificial fires. But this hall is an empty space, populated only by their reflections (again in contrast to Yudhiṣṭhira's assembly hall, where the entirety of the world's royalty will gather for his sacrifice).

In the ensuing debate between Kṛṣṇa's advisors, references to kings are not wholly suppressed, but they are still significantly downplayed or avoided. As a debate on the proper policy to adopt toward Kṛṣṇa's rival

17. *ŚV* 15.38.

18. *jājvalyamānā jagataḥ śāntaye samupeyuṣī*
vyadyotiṣṭa sabhāvedyām asau naraśikhitrayī ||
ratnastambheṣu saṃkrāntapratimās te cakāśire |
ekākino 'pi paritaḥ pauruṣeyavṛtā iva || *ŚV* 2.3–4 ||

Śiśupāla, the argument between Balarāma (who argues for immediate war) and Uddhava (who counsels delay) naturally enough turns on disputes over the principles of diplomatic and political strategy. Such debates (a fixture of *mahākāvyas*), drawing heavily as they do on the political and military science literature of *arthaśāstra*, normally take the form of a discussion of how kings should act to gain supremacy over their rivals. And the advice given by Kṛṣṇa's advisors is occasionally cast in the form of recommendations as to how a "king" should act to counter his rivals.[19] But far more often these maxims are cast generically as prescribing the best course of action for a "wise person," a "successful," "prideful," or "powerful person," or simply for "a person."[20] The passage as a whole, like the preceding chapter, conspicuously avoids mention or discussion of kings. Both the pronounced thematic and lexical avoidance of references to royalty and governance, and the curious circumspection regarding the governing structure of Dvārakā itself, then, would seem to reflect a general and (for a court-centered *mahākāvya*) highly atypical avoidance of kings and kingship as a thematic focus in the opening *sargas* of Māgha's poem.

All of this is in marked contrast with the *Śiśupālavadha*'s most prominent intertext (apart from the *Mahābhārata* itself): Bhāravi's sixth-century Sanskrit *mahākāvya*, the *Kirātārjunīya* ("Arjuna and the Hunter").[21] Bhāravi's poem, especially in its early *sargas*, is almost obsessed with the nature and dynamics of kingship. Its first *sarga* opens with a spy's report to Yudhiṣṭhira on the actions of his cousin and rival for the throne, Duryodhana, detailing his effective rulership and the success of his royal policy. The remainder of the first *sarga* and all of the second are devoted to an internal debate

19. See for example *ŚV* 2.28, 2.82, 2.83, 2.88.

20. For "wise person," see, for example, *ŚV* 2.48 (*manasvin*), 2.54 (*prājña*), 2.79 (*kṛtadhī*), 2.86 (*vidvān*); for "successful," 2.30 (*kṛtin*); for "prideful," 2.33, 2.61 (*mānin*); for "powerful," 2.51 (*tejasvin*), 2.76 (*svāmin*), 2.89 (*prabhu*), 2.90 (*vibhu*). For simply "person," see 2.42, 2.50 (*nara*), and 2.44, 2.47 (*puṃs*). Other non-royal terms used are "great souled" (*mahātman*– 2.31), "steadfast person" (*dhīra*– 2.77), and "fierce person" (*tīkṣṇa*– 2.78). In many other verses the advice is phrased impersonally so as to avoid using any term for the agent of the prescribed policy—see, e.g., *ŚV* 2.34, 2.35, 2.37, 2.52, 2.63, 2.85, and 2.93.

21. On Māgha's close and contestatory relationship with Bhāravi, see Hermann Jacobi, "On Bhāravi and Māgha," *Wiener Zeitschrift für die Kunde des Morgenlandes* 3 (1889): 121–45.

among the Pāṇḍavas over how Yudhiṣṭhira should respond to Duryodhana's prosperity. Yudhiṣṭhira's wife, Draupadī, and his brother Bhīmasena advocate for an immediate attack on Duryodhana (despite the family's vow to remain in the forest for twelve years); Yudhiṣṭhira counsels patience and preparation instead. The nature, obligations, and prerogatives of royalty are explicitly thematized everywhere throughout this debate. In contrast to their near total absence in the opening *sarga* of the *Śiśupālavadha*, words for "kings" and "kingship" occur thirty-one times in the first *sarga* of the *Kirātārjunīya* (even though it runs to only forty-five verses, whereas the *Śiśupālavadha* has seventy-five).

Later in Bhāravi's poem, this near obsessive focus on kingship is increasingly muted and largely dropped as the narrative focus shifts from the deposed king Yudhiṣṭhira to his younger brother Arjuna, who proceeds into the wilderness to perform austerities. By the time of his climactic battle with the god Śiva in the concluding *sarga*s of the poem, Arjuna's social identity has largely been stripped away; he is often referred to simply as "the ascetic" (*muni*).[22] One might almost see the two poems as pursuing precisely and deliberately opposite trajectories. Bhāravi follows Arjuna as he journeys away from his royal brother (and the kingdom-centered debate that surrounds him) into the wilderness, where his social identity and, in his final encounter with the god Śiva, all his weapons are stripped away. Māgha, on the other hand, charts the progress of his hero from the curiously depoliticized space of Dvārakā to the kingdom of Yudhiṣṭhira to the assembly of the world's kings at the sacrifice—the arena for his final confrontation with the aggressively royalist Śiśupāla.

It seems likely that Māgha's choice to foreground Kṛṣṇa's relationship with Yudhiṣṭhira, and to keep Arjuna almost entirely in the background, marks a deliberate contrast with Bhāravi's poem, decentering and eclipsing not only Bhāravi's chosen deity, but his central hero as well. If so, Māgha's choice of the Śiśupāla episode of the *Mahābhārata* as his source is particularly apt, as it is one of the few major narrative moments of the poem that focuses closely on Yudhiṣṭhira's interactions with and responses to Kṛṣṇa, to the relative exclusion of Arjuna. But it is also, not coincidentally, a particularly

22. See *Kirātārjunīya* 17.19, 33, 49, 54. I am following: Bhāravi, *Kirātārjunīya*, eds. Pandit Durgaprasad and Kashinath Pandurang Parab (Bombay: Nirnaya Sagara Press, 1895).

apt selection for exploring the theme of royal power, and Kṛṣṇa's somewhat oblique relation to it. The royal consecration and the events surrounding it represent the high point of Yudhiṣṭhira's political ascension: He has only recently gained possession of his own kingdom (split off from the larger realm of Hāstinapura, still ruled by his uncle Dhṛtarāṣṭra, to forestall an intrafamilial conflict over the inheritance of the kingdom). He will shortly lose this kingdom in a dice-match with his cousin, Duryodhana, and enter a lengthy period of forest exile. When he ultimately does regain his kingdom, and Dhṛtarāṣṭra's, after the intrafamilial war that forms the centerpiece of the *Mahābhārata*, his predominant post-war mood, like that of the epic as a whole, is one of resignation and despair. It is this pre-war episode of the *rājasūya* sacrifice that stands as the single great moment of royalist triumph for Yudhiṣṭhira and his brothers. And Kṛṣṇa plays a pivotal role not only in the sacrifice itself but during the events that lead up to it. Apart from his selection as the guest of honor at the sacrifice, it is specifically Kṛṣṇa to whom Yudhiṣṭhira turns for advice in his doubts about whether to perform the *rājasūya* at all, and how to go about it. It is Kṛṣṇa who raises the problem of the rival effort of Jarāsandha, the king of Magadha, to attain the role of universal monarch, and it is Kṛṣṇa who convinces Yudhiṣṭhira that Jarāsandha must be destroyed before the sacrifice can begin.[23]

But this makes Māgha's evident suppression of royalty and related themes in the opening of his poem all the more striking. The *Mahābhārata* passage on which it is based is saturated with considerations of the imperatives of royal sovereignty and the rivalries with other kings that must be addressed for Yudhiṣṭhira's sacrifice to succeed. We see Kṛṣṇa himself counseling Yudhiṣṭhira to perform the *rājasūya* sacrifice to confirm his royal supremacy, advising him on the steps he must take against his rival claimant to world sovereignty, Jarāsandha, and even offering a brief history and enumeration of the 101 royal dynasties of the Dvāpara age.[24] All this is firmly off the table in Māgha's poem. Instead, we are told only that Kṛṣṇa has been invited to Yudhiṣṭhira's sacrifice—nothing about the nature or

23. See *MBh* 2.12–14.

24. *MBh* 2.13–15. The death of Jarāsandha at the hands of Bhīma is alluded to once in the *Śiśupālavadha* (2.60), but Kṛṣṇa's role in orchestrating his death and the ostensible reason for it—Jarāsandha's own attempt to perform the *rājasūya* and the threat it poses to Yudhiṣṭhira's rival sacrifice—are neither mentioned nor alluded to.

circumstances of the sacrifice, and certainly nothing to suggest that Kṛṣṇa played any role in arranging it.[25] In Māgha's depiction of Kṛṣṇa's entry into the royal assembly, the arena of the world conqueror's sacrifice, the focus remains resolutely on the present and the personal.

Sharing a Single Throne

After describing Kṛṣṇa's meeting with Yudhiṣṭhira and his entry into Indraprastha, and a brief physical description of the Pāṇḍavas' wondrous assembly hall, the thirteenth *sarga* concludes with Yudhiṣṭhira and Kṛṣṇa's entry into the hall, where the two finally sit down together in conversation. This closing section builds on and reinforces the themes developed in earlier portions of the *sarga*. The social and emotional bond between the two is forcefully and directly represented by their sitting together on Yudhiṣṭhira's throne:

> Then those two, the king and Acyuta [Kṛṣṇa], sat on that great glorious throne, taking on the beauty, never seen before, of the sun and the full moon simultaneously shining their light on the peak of the Rising Mountain.[26]

The motif of two male kin or allies sitting on a single throne is not new—it occurs, for example, in the *Mahābhārata* itself, when Arjuna visits his father Indra in heaven[27]—and recurs in later *kāvya* compositions as well: Whitney Cox, in particular, has studied the use of this motif in the work of the eleventh-century court poet Bilhaṇa in his *Vikramāṅkadevacarita*

---

25. *MBh* 2.1.

26. *udayādrimūrdhni yugapac cakāsator dinanāthapūrṇaśaśinor asambhavām* |
rucim āsane ruciradhāmni bibhratāv alaghuny atha nyaṣadatāṃ nṛpācyutau ||
ŚV 13.64 ||

The "Rising Mountain" (*udayādri*) is a mythical mountain in the east behind which both the sun and the moon are thought to rise. Normally both would not be visible there at the same time, and hence the beauty of this union has never before been seen.

27. *MBh* 3.44.22–27.

("The Deeds of the Lord Vikramāṅka").[28] Cox argues that Bilhaṇa uses the articulation of intense male-male friendship between royal allies as a way of suppressing or displacing the more calculating logic of *arthaśāstra*-based political strategy. A similar dynamic seems evident here, as Māgha's depiction of Yudhiṣṭhira and Kṛṣṇa's union again emphasizes the personal and emotional aspect of their relationship, to the complete exclusion of any consideration of political advantage either may hope to gain from it. Still, while the intimacy of the two first seen in the opening verses of the *sarga* is reinforced, this close personal relation is again given a tacit political dimension by the public setting, and by the labeling of Yudhiṣṭhira as king (*nṛpa*)—in addition, of course, to the obvious political symbolism of the throne itself.

The following three verses emphasize the joy of the people at Kṛṣṇa's arrival and the public celebrations thereof. After that, his direct interaction with the crowd is presented in a single verse:

> Hari [Kṛṣṇa] knew the names of everybody, down to the smallest child; and He asked after news of their kinfolk. Good people who are not proud, even if they attain great glory, never forget anything.[29]

There is no further detail given regarding this exchange—we are not told to whom he speaks, or what news he receives—but brief as it is, this emphasis on his personal attention and concern for the people of Indraprastha stands in stark contrast to his far more distant and idealized relations with the abstract and unindividualized populace of Dvārakā in the third *sarga*.[30] He knows their names and engages with them as individuals, and again, as in his meeting with Yudhiṣṭhira himself, his humility is highlighted. The verse

---

28. Whitney Cox, "Sharing a Single Seat: The Poetics and Politics of Male Intimacy in the *Vikramāṅkakāvya*," *Journal of Indian Philosophy* 38, no. 5 (2010): 488–94.

29. *harir ākumāram akhilābhidhānavit svajanasya vārtam ayam anvayuṅkta ca* | *mahatīm api śriyam avāpya vismayaḥ sujano na vismarati jātu kiṃcana* || *ŚV* 13.68 ||

30. The third *sarga* describes Kṛṣṇa's departure from Dvārakā, but apart from a few verses describing the city women's attraction to Kṛṣṇa (3.13–15) and a handful describing the general crowding as his army departs (3.27–31), there is nothing to suggest any verbal or social interaction between Kṛṣṇa and the completely generalized populace.

depicts his nearness to the people, while his procession through Dvārakā emphasized his distance from them.

The thirteenth *sarga* concludes by returning specifically to the relationship between king Yudhiṣṭhira and his divine cousin. Once again the emotional intensity of their relationship is emphasized:

> The lord of Śrī and that lord of men both savored the nectar of speech with one another, in which they found the arising of *rasa* hard to obtain in this world, and, through its continuing intensification, renewing itself with every word.[31]

This culminating moment of conversational union is explicitly presented as a source of "*rasa*"—the "emotional flavor" or mood that has already by Māgha's time become a pivotal term in literary and aesthetic theory. Thus, in an explicitly meta-literary flourish, Māgha likens the two characters' shared emotional experience of their own conversation to the experience of readers of the poem itself. Thus the *sarga* concludes with a moment of full harmony—almost a merging—between Yudhiṣṭhira, the king, and Kṛṣṇa, the divine (but decidedly not royal) hero of the poem.

While this at last brings a figure of royal standing into the center of the poem, and thereby touches on the divine central hero's relation with political power, this encounter is conspicuous for the extent to which questions of political objectives and strategies are suppressed. This is again a contrast to the earlier portions of the poem, as the debate between Kṛṣṇa's counselors Uddhava and Balarāma, while downplaying themes of royalty per se, turned largely on questions of strategic calculation: What will be the most effective way to confront Śiśupāla? In the conclusion of that debate, Kṛṣṇa's advisor Uddhava offers a strategic rationale for avoiding direct confrontation with Śiśupāla and proceeding instead to attend Yudhiṣṭhira's sacrifice:

> The dissension produced by [Śiśupāla], though slight, will inflame those already angry with you, as the wind does to kindling after it's set on fire.

31. *martyalokaduravāpam avāptarasodayaṃ nūtanatvam atiriktatayānupadaṃ dadhat* | *śrīpatiḥ patir asāv avaneś ca parasparaṃ saṃkathāmṛtam anekam asisvadatām ubhau* || *ŚV* 13.69 ||

> His allies, and your enemies—both sorts of kings will join him if you engage with him [now]; only those in neither group will come to you.[32]

A direct attack on Śiśupāla should be avoided, as it will draw both his own allies and Kṛṣṇa's enemies to his side. On the other hand, proceeding to Yudhiṣṭhira's sacrifice—where all potential allies and rivals will be in attendance—allows an opportunity to turn others to their side:

> The enemy's associates can be alienated from him by double agents, who know his faults without revealing their own, when they make his [secret] orders known.
>
> The hordes of kings that have come to Yudhiṣṭhira's city will be made to have a purpose united [with yours] by your agents.[33]

Uddhava's rationale for proceeding to Yudhiṣṭhira's sacrifice, rather than directly attacking Śiśupāla, is thus entirely tactical. He sees it as politically and diplomatically advantageous, charting a course that will draw them more allies in preparation for their eventual military confrontation. But, very much in line with the dynamic that Cox sees at play in Bilhaṇa's *Vikramāṅkadevacarita*, the actual arrival of Kṛṣṇa in Yudhiṣṭhira's city totally displaces this *arthaśāstra*-like calculus of political advantage in favor of an idealized presentation of the disinterested personal affection between the two. It is this "poetics of male intimacy," rather than the tactical logic of Uddhava's and Balarāma's earlier debate, that predominantly characterizes Kṛṣṇa's relation with worldly political authority in Māgha's poem. In a characteristic turn, Śiśupāla will later, in his tirade against Kṛṣṇa and the Pāṇḍavas' decision to offer him the chief honors at the sacrifice, single out precisely this affective foundation of their relationship as a basis for criticism; the only possible explanation for

32. *upajāpaḥ kṛtas tena tān ākopavatas tvayi |*
āśu dīpayitālpo 'pi sāgnīn edhān ivānilaḥ || *ŚV* 2.99 ||
tasya mitrāṇy amitrās te ye ca ye cobhaye nṛpāḥ |
abhiyuktaṃ tvayainaṃ te gantāras tvām ataḥ pare || *ŚV* 2.101 ||

33. *ajñātadoṣair doṣajñair uddūṣyobhayavetanaiḥ |*
bhedyāḥ śatror abhivyaktaśāsanaiḥ sāmavāyikāḥ ||
upeyivāṃsi kartāraḥ purīm ājātaśatravīm |
rājanyakāny upāyajñair ekārthāni carais tava || *ŚV* 2.113–14 ||

Yudhiṣṭhira's selection of the obviously inferior Kṛṣṇa over the many great kings attending the sacrifice is an overwhelming personal favoritism that distorts his understanding of true worth:

> Since you honor here the conqueror of Mura, whom good people do not honor, I think this is great affection showing itself. Indeed, people always imagine that their friends are people of merit![34]

But, as always, Śiśupāla's sarcastic critique, while in a sense cogent and even perceptive, is seen to be fundamentally misguided. The deep and intense emotional fellowship between Kṛṣṇa and Yudhiṣṭhira that underwrites his selection does indeed displace the ordinary political and social logic that would reflexively elevate kings over commoners. Yet this displacement is precisely held up as a counter-ideal to the royalism represented most vocally in the poem by Śiśupāla himself. It is precisely his valuation of his personal bond with Kṛṣṇa over any ordinary political calculus that seems to mark Yudhiṣṭhira as worthy of the divine favor he enjoys and the worldly sovereignty he aspires to.

Conclusion

Engagement with the theme of royalty and its relation to the divine emerges as a principal focus in the thirteenth *sarga* of the *Śiśupālavadha* and lays the groundwork for the court setting that will dominate the later part of the poem—the setting for Yudhiṣṭhira's sacrifice, and the climactic confrontation with Śiśupāla that follows from it. In placing its iconic, mythic, and heretofore deliberately depoliticized hero in a more recognizably royal and courtly setting, it sets out, for the first time in the poem, to define Kṛṣṇa's relationship to the political and royal world order, through his relationship with the aspiring world-sovereign Yudhiṣṭhira. It presents us with a vision of a harmonious and almost blissful union of the royal and the divine, spontaneous and wholly lacking in the calculus of worldly advantage, and thereby grounds the relationship between worldly and divine power in affect, rather than in calculations of advantage.

34. *yad apūpujas tvam iha pārtha murajitam apūjitaṃ satām* |
prema vilasati mahad tad aho dayitaṃ janaḥ khalu guṇīti manyate || *ŚV* 15.14 ||

Chapter Seven

What Are the Goals of Life?

The *Vidūṣaka*'s Interpretation of the *Puruṣārthas* in Kulaśekhara's *Subhadrādhanañjaya*

Sudha Gopalakrishnan

The oil lamp is lit, with two wicks facing the stage and one directed toward the audience. The stage is set. There is much anticipation as the sound of the *miḻāvŭ* drum reverberates, and then he appears, holding a banana leaf folded in the shape of a bowl, begging for alms. He is hungry, dejected, and pathetic-looking, as he has not managed to eat even a morsel of food for the last few days. He rubs his belly and wanders around the stage, begging imaginary donors.

This is how Kauṇḍinya the *vidūṣaka* (jester) is introduced, for the first time, on the fourth day of the *Kūṭiyāṭṭam* performance of the Sanskrit drama *Subhadrādhanañjaya* ("Subhadrā and Arjuna").[1] For the following five days he will single-handedly occupy the stage with his verbal narration of the

1. See Kulaśekhara, *The Subhadrādhananjaya of Kulasekhara Varma with the Commentary of Sivarāma*, ed. T. Ganapati Sastri (Trivandrum: Travancore Government Press, 1912).

Puruṣārtha Kūttu ("The Theater of the *Puruṣārthas*").[2] The hero's elaborate performance finds a parody in the ludicrous actions of the *vidūṣaka*, who appears on the stage as a friend and advisor to the king in matters of love and sport, indulging in jokes and sometimes mildly ridiculing the king. His incongruous appearance, comic demeanor, and, above all, his freedom to use the Malayalam language set him apart from other characters in the play. During the five-day performance of *Puruṣārtha Kūttu*, the *vidūṣaka* turns upside-down the norms of the everyday world and builds alternative domains of experience, with the power of his words disrupting the concept of the *puruṣārtha*s (goals of life)—*dharma* (righteous duty), *artha* (material wealth, political power), *kāma* (desire) and *mokṣa* (liberation from worldly existence)—as they are described in early prescriptive texts. This chapter examines the *vidūṣaka*'s *Puruṣārtha Kūttu* within *Subhadrādhanañjaya*, a play composed and choreographed by Kulaśekhara (a medieval king[3] in southwest India, today the state of Kerala) that continues to be performed in the *Kūṭiyāṭṭam* Sanskrit drama performance tradition in Kerala.[4]

Singling out an episode from the Mahābhārata tradition, Kulaśekhara's play describes the courtship and marriage of Subhadrā (Kṛṣṇa's sister)

2. For a transcription of an oral performance of the *Puruṣārtha Kūttu*, see V. R. Krishnachandran, *Puruṣārtthakkūttu* (Trichur: Kerala Sahitya Akademi, 1978). All references to this performance in this chapter are to Krishnachandran's text. For ease of reading, this essay refers to this type of performance as *Puruṣārtha Kūttu* throughout.

3. *Subhadrādhanañjaya* has been dated as early as the ninth century. N. P. Unni and Bruce Sullivan date it to the twelfth century. See the introduction to Kulaśekhara, *The Wedding of Arjuna and Subhadrā: The Kūṭiyāṭṭam Drama Subhadrā-Dhanañjaya: Text with Vicāratilaka Commentary, Introduction, English Translation, and Notes*, trans. N. P. Unni and Bruce M. Sullivan (Delhi: Nag, 2001).

4. On the *Kūṭiyāṭṭam* performance tradition, see Diane Daugherty, "Subhadra Redux: Reinstating Female Kutiyattam," in *Between Fame and Shame: Performing Women—Women Performers in India,* ed. Heidrun Brukner, Hanne M. de Bruin, and Heike Moser (Wiesbaden: Otto Harrassowitz, 2011), 153–67; Sudha Gopalakrishnan, *Kutiyattam: The Heritage Theatre of India* (Delhi: Niyogi Books, 2011); and Bruce M. Sullivan, "Kerala's Mahābhārata on Stage: Texts and Performative Practices in Kūṭiyāṭṭam Drama," *Journal of Hindu Studies* 3, no. 1 (2010): 124–42). See, also, Heike Oberlin and David Shulman, eds. *Two Masterpieces of Kūṭiyāṭṭam: Mantrāṅkam and Aṅgulīyāṅkam* (Delhi: Oxford University Press, 2019), in which *Kūṭiyāṭṭam* actor-performers and scholars analyze the art form in depth.

and Arjuna.[5] At the beginning of the play, Arjuna reaches the land of Prabhāsatīrtha after a year-long pilgrimage; accompanying him is his friend Kauṇḍinya, the *vidūṣaka*, who is a *brāhmaṇa*. Already in love with Subhadrā although he not yet seen her, Arjuna becomes enchanted with a woman whom he rescues from a demon. Of course, he does not know that this woman is Subhadrā herself. Subhadrā's experience mirrors Arjuna's: she falls in love with her rescuer, but she, too, already loves someone whom she has never met—Arjuna. A series of complications follow. Disguised as a hermit, Arjuna gains entry into Subhadrā's chambers. Plagued by guilt at her love for "two" men at the same time, Subhadrā tries to commit suicide. Upon learning that Subhadrā and the woman he rescued are the same person, Arjuna appears on the scene and clears the confusion. The couple marries—with Kṛṣṇa's blessing and with Indra (the king of the gods and Arjuna's father) as witness—and returns to Indraprastha. Kuntī and Draupadī accept Subhadrā, but, at Duryodhana's bidding, the demon Alambuṣa kidnaps her. This time, however, the goddess Kātyāyanī rescues her. Arjuna and Subhadrā live a happy life and are blessed with a son, Abhimanyu.

Subhdrādhanañjaya forms a significant part of the *Kūṭiyāṭṭam* repertoire for several reasons. Apart from being one of the earliest plays that is still performed on the *Kūṭiyāṭṭam* stage, *Subhdrādhanañjaya*—along with Kulaśekhara's other Mahābhārata drama, *Tapatīsaṃvaraṇa* ("Tapatī and Saṃvaraṇa")[6]—is credited with launching a series of innovative theater practices that developed into what is now known as *Kūṭiyāṭṭam*. There is also a commentarial text by Kulaśekhara, called the *Vyaṅgyavyākhyā* ("Commentary on Suggested Meanings"), in which the author details his concept of *dhvani* ("suggestion" or "implicature," a Sanskrit literary theoretical term[7])

5. A version of this story appears in *Mahābhārata* 1.217–20. All references to the Sanskrit *Mahābhārata* in this chapter are to the southern recension (Kumbakonam edition): *Sriman Mahābhāratam: A New Edition Mainly Based on the South Indian Texts,* eds. T. R. Krishnacharya and T. R. Vyasacharya, 7 vols. (Kumbakonam: Madhva Vilas Book Depot, 1906–10).

6. In the first book of the Sanskrit epic, we learn the story of Tapatī and Saṃvaraṇa, the parents of Kuru, the founder of the Kuru clan and the ancestor of the Pāṇḍavas and the Kauravas (*Mahābhārata* 1.171–73).

7. On the concept of *dhvani* and its vibrant life in Sanskrit poetics, see Lawrence J. McCrea, *The Teleology of Poetics in Medieval Kashmir* (Cambridge, MA: Harvard University Press, 2009).

and explains the subtleties of acting by discussing literal and deeper layers of meaning. The *Vyaṅgyavyākhyā* underscores the complexity of *abhinaya* (acting) and anticipates several *āṭṭaprakārams* (performance manuals) that survive in *Kūṭiyāṭṭam.*

Second, *Subhdrādhanañjaya* and *Tapatīsaṃvaraṇa* introduced into *Kūṭiyāṭṭam* (perhaps for the first time) the *vidūṣaka* as a character of crucial importance. This character developed into one as important as the hero. The figure of the *vidūṣaka* even spurred an independent (yet allied) performance genre called *Prabandha Kūttu* ("the narration of *prabandhas*"), otherwise known as *Cākyār Kūttu*, in which the *vidūṣaka* is the sole protagonist-actor.[8] While the language and theatrical grammar of the codified art of *Kūṭiyāṭṭam* may be less accessible to those without prior or informed knowledge, the speech and actions of the *vidūṣaka* are directed toward more popular tastes. Though his own lines in the text of the play are in Prakrit (whereas the hero speaks in Sanskrit), on stage the *vidūṣaka* may speak in Malayalam, which he uses to interpret the hero's verses for the audience. Early on, the convention that the *vidūṣaka* would serve as a commentator on the action of the play meant that the *vidūṣaka* could address the audience directly; sometimes this meant that he could reference audience members personally and sometimes it even meant that he could ridicule them.

When the *vidūṣaka* speaks in Malayalam, he adopts the dialect and mannerisms of the high-caste Nampūtiri *brāhmaṇa* community; these behaviors both localize him and identify him with the *brāhmaṇa* figure whom he represents in the play. We might therefore see the role of the *vidūṣaka* as a sort of social and aesthetic inversion that was deliberately integrated into the "high" art of *Kūṭiyāṭṭam.* The *vidūṣaka* caricatures social norms, using humor to levy social criticism. Though the *vidūṣaka* employs a highly metaphoric language of intratextual reference within the play, his dramatic liberties are so great that in the early days, he could even criticize the local king during a performance. This freedom on the stage was accepted, tolerated, and even appreciated by the dominant classes as a hegemonic sanction. The comic protagonist's venting of repressed emotions allowed the community at large to let out steam; at the same time,

8. On *Cākyār Kūttu* and the Mahābhārata, see Naama Shalom, *Re-ending the Mahābhārata: The Rejection of Dharma in the Sanskrit Epic* (Albany: State University of New York Press, 2017), 154.

it allowed the upper classes to reassert their power through an attitude of humane tolerance.

The *vidūṣaka* appears in many classical Sanskrit plays as a stock character; he has prototypes and counterparts in many folk, popular, and ritualistic performances in India. His primary function is to evoke laughter by being both a wit and also the target of jokes. As a professional court jester, he is represented in Sanskrit dramas as the hero's friend (*vayasya*), a minister of games (*narmasaciva*), and a great *brāhmaṇa* (*mahābrāhmaṇa*). Most classical plays emphasize the *vidūṣaka*'s silliness or idiocy: they augment his gluttony, nonsensical behavior, unruly mannerisms, and lewd remarks (usually directed toward the maids). The figure deftly combines the seemingly disparate traits of wit and stupidity.

The *Puruṣārtha*s in *Kūṭiyāṭṭam*: A Counterpoint Narration of the Goals of Life

The *vidūṣaka*'s performative commentary on the *puruṣārtha*s within *Subhadrādhanañjaya* counters the concept of the "goals of life" that is enshrined in parts of the Sanskrit *Mahābhārata*, the *dharmaśāstra*s (treatises on dharma), and political texts such as Kauṭilya's *Arthaśāstra* ("Treatise on Political Power"). Of course, these works themselves present nuanced, multilayered, and often contradictory visions of the terms *dharma*, *artha*, *kāma*, and *mokṣa*; the *vidūṣaka*'s *Puruṣārtha Kūttu*, however, responds to the most straightforwardly orthodox of those visions.

Early in the *Puruṣārtha Kūttu* section of *Subhadrādhanañjaya*, the *vidūṣaka* explains why he must reformulate the *puruṣārtha*s. The starting point is that the play's *vidūṣaka*, Kauṇḍinya, represents the *brāhmaṇa* community in the village of Anadhītimaṅgalam. (Anadhīti literally means "un-studying," a reference to what happens—or, rather, doesn't happen—there.) Over the years, he explains, the village and his community have become so debased, quarrelsome, illiterate, and anarchical that they do not even perform the ordained "six actions" of Brahmanical Hinduism (the *ṣaṭkarma*s—performing sacrifices, giving instructions on how to conduct them, learning, teaching, giving donations, and accepting aid) and have no interest in pursuing the *puruṣārtha*s anymore. During this time of total moral collapse, the *vidūṣaka* says, there is no other way forward but to substitute the *puruṣārtha*s with another set of goals—goals that the villagers can actually attain.

He enumerates the four "alternative" *puruṣārtha*s:

For a *brāhmaṇa*, *dharma* is eating food,
and he accumulates *artha* by serving a king.
A *veśya* (courtesan) helps him fulfill *kāma*,
while deceit and treachery lead him to *mokṣa*.[9]

With this verse, the *vidūṣaka* presents an interpretation of the *puruṣārtha*s within "a" Mahābhārata that subverts the *puruṣārtha*s as they are presented in major parts of "the" *Mahābhārata*, the Sanskrit epic. For example, in the *Śāntiparvan* ("The Book of Peace"), Bhīṣma presents what is essentially a guidebook to moral leadership for the ruler of a kingdom.[10] Accordingly, the *Śāntiparvan* is replete with advice on *rāja-dharma* (kingly duties), *āpad-dharma* (how to act in times of catastrophe), *mokṣa-dharma* (the path to liberation), and *dāna-dharma* (the rules of gift-giving). It appears that Bhīṣma's advice in the *Śāntiparvan* voices a marked inclination toward a Brahmanical order, which the *vidūṣaka* then undermines in his reworking of the *puruṣārtha*s.

Each of the five days of the *Puruṣārtha Kūttu* is devoted to one of several themes that govern the *vidūṣaka*'s unconventional expression of the *puruṣārtha*s: *vivādam* (dispute), *vinodam-vañcanam* (entertainment and deceit), *aśanam* (eating) and *rājaseva* (service under a king). The *vidūṣaka* enacts these themes by telling one story after another in quick succession and voicing imagined dialogues between people. The performance employs a conversational and argumentative mode—the actor always presents his narration as though there were two people enagaged in a dialogue. This device of an "imagined interlocutor"—a performative take on articulations of the *pūrvapakṣa* (the "prior," or opposing, point of view) that constitute a standard rhetorical strategy in classical Indian philosophical discourse—affords him the opportunity to express contrasting viewpoints, enact heated discussions, mock the vices or foolishness of his imagined interlocutor, and,

9. *āmantraṇaṃ brāḥmaṇānāṃ hi dharmaḥ*
sevā rājñām arthamūlaṃ narāṇām |
veśyāstriṣu prāptir evātra kāmo
bhūyas tāsāṃ vañcanaṃ mokṣahetuḥ || *Puruṣārtthakkūttu*, 112.

10. On one of the stories Bhīṣma uses to impart wisdom in the *Śāntiparvan*, see the chapter by Sally Sutherland Goldman.

finally, validate his own point, which inevitably and deliberately represents a subversive interpretation of a particular incident or story. He offers commentaries, indulges in apparently nonsensical speech, elaborates on stories of deceit, lust, and transgression, and parodies and ridicules the extravagances and pompousness of people from all sections of society.

Donald Davis Jr. writes that the *vidūṣaka*'s role in *Kūṭiyāṭṭam* exploits "the gap between the normative ideal of the *puruṣārtha*s and the reality of what people pursue."[11] Yet there is another way of seeing this. It could be that the *vidūṣaka*'s vision of the *puruṣārtha*s sketches not a polarity but a *reciprocity* between idealized, righteous principles and the impulses that govern our daily lives. Rather than being straightforwardly instructional, the *vidūṣaka*'s portrayal of the *puruṣārtha*s reconciles the realistic and the aspirational. The loquacity of its language, the animation of ideas, and the potency of meanings that it generates have the power to reach beyond constricting definitions; it is from this perspective that this wondrous five-day performance makes the most sense. Like that of Falstaff, the comic character found in several plays by Shakespeare (and who rejects "grinning honour" in *Henry IV, Part 1*), the *vidūṣaka*'s double role of being both a wit and a target creates a mood of mirth, which makes the entire performance a joyous activity.[12] In this way, although *Puruṣārtha Kūttu* represents a digression from the main drama, it suffuses the entire play with the spirit of its stories of greed, lust, deceit, gluttony, and servility.

The narration contains many illustrative sub-stories. Some of these stories elaborate on the oddities of different gods and goddesses, who hardly seem divine; rather, the *vidūṣaka* describes them behaving as ordinary (human) members of his community do. Other figures appear in *Puruṣārtha Kūttu*: foolish, arrogant *brāhmaṇa*s; scheming *veśya*s; and members of temple-serving communities such as the Poduvāls, the Mārārs, the Vāriers, and the Nambīśans. A member of the community of Cākyār actors—bearing his heavy knapsack full of costumes and other useless things, always eager to stage a performance—is not spared. Through highlighting specific social contexts and customary occupations, the *vidūṣaka*'s long narrative—full of

11. Donald Richard Davis, Jr., "Satire as Apology: The *Puruṣārtthakkūttŭ* of Kerala," in *Irreverent History: Essays for M. G. S. Narayanan*, eds. Kesavan Veluthat and Donald Richard Davis, Jr. (Delhi: Primus Books, 2014), 9.

12. William Shakespeare, *Henry IV, Part 1*, ed. Adam Frost (Mineola: Dover Publications, 1997), Act V, Scene 3.

satire and mockery—underscores the importance of the role of the comic protagonist as an institutionalized commentator and critic of society. The pleasure of knowing the inquisitorial role of the *vidūṣaka* and the flair of his narration in the familiar setting of the *Kūttu* stage have for centuries, made him a favorite with audiences of all kinds. That the *vidūṣaka* communicates with those audiences in the local language of Malayalam makes his engagement with his listeners even more profound. Through the *vidūṣaka*'s excursus, the art of storytelling in Malayalam dovetails with the "high" Sanskrit theater of *Kūṭiyāṭṭam*—an ingenious method of reaching people of all tastes among the audience. (Just the same, we ought to remember that only a limited audience—mainly people from the higher castes of Kerala—has historically been able to access *Kūṭiyāṭṭam* in the first place.)

Day One: Preparations

In the light of the core principles of *Kūṭiyāṭṭam* aesthetics, the *vidūṣaka* in *Subhadrādhanañjaya* represents the prototypical comic character. From the first act (where the *vidūṣaka* makes his entry, introducing the context and setting of the play) to several stages of the plot, including the confusion between the "real" identities of the heroine and the hero—Subhadrā and Arjuna—and the subsequent blossoming of love between them, the *vidūṣaka* maintains an active presence throughout. Apart from his presence as a character in the play—the friend of Arjuna—his duty as an actor (*naṭa-dharma*) is to demonstrate the interpretive potential of the play's multilayered meanings. He transforms the hero's Sanskrit verses into Malayalam, offering comments on the hero's words and actions, and acts as a foil to the romantic extravagances of the hero—for example, by reciting parodic verses (*pratiśloka*) about Cakki, the maid, when the hero describes the heroine in fervent terms.

On the first day, Kauṇḍinya appears weary, hungry, and begging for food. After performing the preliminary rituals for a performance, entering into his role (a dramatic convention[13]), and reciting a verse about fate,

13. *Vidūṣakastobham*, the stock characteristics of a *vidūṣaka* in *Kūṭiyaṭṭam*, consist of actions such as chewing betel leaves, cleaning his sacred thread, untangling the tuft of his hair (also conventional for a *brāhmaṇa*), and fanning himself with his vest cloth.

Kauṇḍinya describes his past life—his comfortable position at the court of the Pāṇḍavas—and how he reached this state of impoverishment. This backstory allows him to recapitulate the story of the play so far: Arjuna's arrival at Prabhāsatīrtha, Arjuna falling in love with Subhadrā, and the situation in which Arjuna must disguise himself as a wandering mendicant in order to gain access to Subhadrā. Over the course of attending to Arjuna, Kauṇḍinya has become impoverished. In fact, he has come to a state of such utter destitution that he has now to beg for alms.

Much like the storytelling in the Sanskrit *Mahābhārata*, the stories in the *vidūṣaka*'s performance do not follow a linear progression but, rather, digress from the main narrative and mesh with other stories. Often we find one narrative stemming from another and assuming multiple layers, sometimes branching out further or closing unexpectedly, but ultimately coming back to the main branch and taking the reader back to the original narrative. The stories are not merely told, but illustrated, demonstrated, and developed, spiced up with sparkling dialogue within each story and episode, all in meticulous detail and with great humor.

Day Two: *Vivādam*—Dispute and Settlement

The second day of the *Puruṣārtha Kūttu* presents a series of disputes and their subsequent reconciliations. It begins with the *vidūṣaka* paying tribute to the quarrel between Gaṅgā and Pārvatī over Śiva.[14] Here the *vidūṣaka* describes the rivalry between the goddess Pārvatī and the river Gaṅgā over the love of Śiva, their shared husband, which develops into a vicious competition and war of words between the two women. The *vidūṣaka's* extended oral illustration of the dispute provides immense entertainment to the audience because it depicts this celestial argument as an everyday quarrel among people in a love triangle. Gaṅgā, the perpetual "other woman," keeps pestering Śiva to caress and make love to her; the suspicious Pārvatī, ever vigilant of potential threats to her marital bliss, tries to thwart any such dalliance at all costs. Śiva plots to keep Pārvatī out of the way for some time in order to make love to Gaṅgā: he beckons *apsaras*es (celestial women) from heaven to take Pārvatī for a bath in the divine Mānasa lake. (*Apsaras*es are particularly

14. This is an independent verse used by the actors in *Kūṭiyāṭṭam* performances and is not found in the text of the *Subhadrādhanañjaya*.

fond of water.) When the *apsaras*es arrive at Śiva's door, the dim-witted gatekeeper, Bhṛṅgīraṭi, has immense difficulty pronouncing their names, and this slip-up delays their entry. Though Pārvatī is keen to go with them for a bath by the lake, she is extremely suspicious about her husband, so she instructs her sons, Subrahmaṇya and Gaṇapati, and daughter, Kālī, to accompany their father during her absence. (Keep in mind that the *vidūṣaka* enacts this entire story himself; he portrays every character.)

Gaṇapati takes his mission seriously because he is tempted with a large portion of sweetmeats as compensation; though Śiva tries to outdo the promised gift, Gaṇapati refuses to budge. An irritated Śiva pushes his son and he falls down the hill, grievously injuring himself. Nārada, the well-known sage and mischief-maker, reports the incident to Pārvatī. Pārvatī comes rushing back, only to get a glimpse of Śiva's active flirtation with Gaṅgā. This enrages her to no end. She squabbles with Gaṅgā, who claims Śiva for herself with equal relentlessness. In a fit of scorn and outrage, Pārvatī mocks Gaṅgā for her watery state and her lack of knowledge of the pleasures of love. At last Pārvatī gives up, realizing that love and truth do not always align.

Then Kauṇḍinya narrates a more local altercation: the story of the dispute (*vivādam*) between Mēkkāntala and Kīḷkkāntala, the heads of two families. (A comic Mahābhārata in miniature?) The patriarchs argue, for example, about who should walk in front of whom. Kauṇḍinya serves as a mediator, in which capacity he recalls the story of a Vedic teacher and his student, both of whom are attracted to a local courtesan, Iṭṭuṇṇūli. Kauṇḍinya narrates their failed attempts to seduce her. Iṭṭuṇṇūli's grandmother, a celebrated courtesan (she supposedly wrecked the lives of men from sixty-four different villages), is ashamed that her granddaughter does not possess the same skills in seducing men and extracting money from them. Rising to the challenge, Iṭṭuṇṇūli beckons the Vedic teacher and two of his disciples to her house around the same time. Through various comic twists and turns they come face-to-face with one another, which prompts them to squabble and eventually leads to blows.

Kauṇḍinya's disputes now include those between Pārvatī and Gaṅgā, Śiva and Gaṇapati, Mēkkāntala and Kīḷkkāntala, the Vedic teacher and his student (or students), and Iṭṭuṇṇūli and her grandmother. What is the nature of the debates here? Why do they occur at all? I would argue that the *vidūṣaka* presents these disputes as evidence of the steady disintegration of a society where everyone automatically situates themselves in polemical relationships with others. Life, after all, is a web of interrelationships: each individual is an entity in oneself, but individuals are also constantly defined by one another. Kauṇḍinya narrates the comic side of this mutual inter-definition. Even after much counsel and persuasion, the dispute between Mēkkāntala and Kīḷkkāntala does not come to a settlement: the two patriarchs simultaneously retract their arguments and each one decides to walk behind the other, which once again causes a dispute over protocol.

They agree to end the fight only if their mediator, Kauṇḍinya, composes and recites a verse to their satisfaction. Here the *vidūṣaka* enjoys a lengthy digression on the art and science of how to write good poetry.[15] It is not until he recites a paronomastic (*śleṣa*) verse that praises their favorite gods (Śiva and Viṣṇu) simultaneously that they agree to walk together, assured of their own distinctive positions in society and the world. Their acceptance of the mediating agency and mutual agreement to walk side by side symbolically reaffirms reconciliation for the society at large. Rather than serving as a simplistic satire, this seemingly comical narration articulates a complex transactional process.

Day Three: *Vinodam* and *Vañcanam*—Amusement and Deceit

By the third day of the *vidūṣaka*'s monologue, it is possible for the audience to gain better access into this world of stories that pour out one after (and inside) another. The stories narrated in the *vinodam* (entertainment, enjoyment) and *vañcanam* (deceit) segments, while seemingly farcical and couched in a language of unrestrained humor, elucidate societal absurdities, critique established institutions, and reveal interpretive, visionary insights into complex situations. The questions being probed are fundamental: What is the purpose of life? What is reality, and how do we perceive it?

In order to restore the moral dignity of Anadhītimaṅgalam, Kauṇḍinya argues, the villagers need to take collective action. All worldly actions

15. David Shulman sees the discussion on the making of poetry as metapoetic text, and a parodic description of "what it means to be a poet and what a poet's tasks might be and how language operates and how language relates to the world." (Personal communication.)

must lead toward *mokṣa*, the supreme goal of the *puruṣārtha*s—the other three *puruṣārtha*s are pathways to it. Since these *puruṣārtha*s are not easily achievable, however, one may substitute a lighter package of aspirations. This argument leads Kauṇḍinya to elaborate on the principles of *vinodam* and *vañcanam*, both of which may be achieved in the realm of worldly desires, the first through enjoying the company of a *veśya* and the second through cheating her of her wealth.

Marriage, Kauṇḍinya says, sustains one's lineage, without which life cannot be deemed complete. Yet one need not fulfill all of life's sensual pleasures with one's wife alone, and this is where the *veśya* steps in. Many compositions in early Malayalam literature discuss *veśya*s, and here, the *vidūṣaka*'s *Puruṣārtha Kūttu* elaborates on what makes a *veśya* inappropriate for a man to pursue. A man should not go after a woman who is only after money, he says, nor should he pursue one who is lonely and unsupported in life, one who lacks a house of her own, who is easily accessible to all kinds of people, who is deeply attached to another person, who has an unattractive body, who gets pregnant often, or who is a great deal older or younger. Kauṇḍinya illustrates these arguments with stories about what would happen if a man were to find himself partnered with any of these inappropriate *veśya*s.

The *vidūṣaka* also lends an account of the ideal courtesan, as an example of which he describes a celebrated *veśya* in the area, Uṇṇimañjarī. In order to fulfill the *puruṣārtha* of *vinodam*, men in the village of Anadhītimaṅgalam from all castes and communities make a beeline for the house of Uṇṇimañjarī. (Who better to lead them there than Iṭyāsu, the ardent Vedic student from the previous day's performance?) This procession presents an occasion for the *vidūṣaka* to describe these individuals in relation to the quirks of their castes and occupations: the gluttonous Vedic teacher who lumbers toward the house with his protruding belly preceding him; the temple priests whose dishonesty drives even the god out of the shrine; the community leaders, revenue collectors who pocket a large chunk of the collection; a Cākyār actor laden with a huge knapsack of old and worthless costumes. Finally comes the *viḍḍhi*, the village buffoon, accompanied by the *naṅṅyār*, the *Kūṭiyāṭṭam* actress. Since her presence does not suit the occasion, she is sent back home, and the rest of the men enjoy the night in the delightful company of Uṇṇimañjarī—well, all except the *viḍḍhi*, who has no idea what is happening. He is so tired that he sleeps through the night and when he wakes up, everyone else has left. Seeing him weeping and desolate, Uṇṇimañjarī takes pity on him and introduces the pleasures of *vinodam* to him as well. Before he leaves the house, however, he manages to deceive and swindle (*vañcanam*) the woman by stealing her precious golden *aḍappan*: a small vessel that stores lime paste, which she uses along with betel leaves, pieces of areca nut, and other fragrant substances. He gobbles up the contents and leaves the scene, but when this deception is noticed by the others in the community, he is rewarded (not chastised) because of his success in achieving another *puruṣārtha*, "deception."

Day Four: *Aśanam*—Feasting

The next day's performance of *aśanam* (eating) is a favorite with audiences and actors alike. We might also view it as a compendium on the culinary arts of the medieval Nampūtiri community. The narration opens with the worship of Gaṇapati, the elephant-headed god, who is a true food enthusiast. Kauṇḍinya recounts the famous story of Gaṇapati's breakfast, in which the conceited King Vaiśravaṇa invites Śiva and all of his family and friends, including his ever-hungry son, Gaṇapati, to a hearty meal at his house. The circumstances leading up to the event—Śiva's words of caution about Gaṇapati's appetite, Vaiśravaṇa's overconfident disregard of the warning, the elaborate preparations for the gargantuan feast, and Gaṇapati's arrival for breakfast—are performed in detail with great verve and humor. These qualities continue to ripen as Kauṇḍinya narrates how Gaṇapati devours not only the food but also the foodstalls and vessels in his host's house.

Nuanced, experiential, and evocative, the narration of *aśanam*—food and eating—demands that the actor employ immense skill, craft, and knowledge to communicate the aesthetics of food. Deploying this knowledge, the *vidūṣaka* says that the very word *aśanam*, in this context, refers to the three types of food to be devoured in a grand feast: food that fills up a person as far as the neck, food that fills a person up to the nose, and food that fills a person to the head. A well prepared meal, he says, is like a beautiful woman: just as it is difficult to keep away from a lovely woman, it is difficult to abstain from good food. Kauṇḍinya describes different kinds of hosts (various combinations of cordial and hostile) and elaborates on the best times to eat.

The best occasion for a feast, he says, is the grand celebration on the anniversary of the death of the head of a family. On such an occasion, all the people of the Anadhītimaṅgalam village set out for the house where the feast is being held. There is great excitement in the air. Once the group reaches the venue, they are a bit dismayed at the large crowds, but are reassured when they tour the storehouse and granary inside the house, where ample food is being prepared. (In case it bears remembering: the *vidūṣaka* enacts this entire tableau himself.) Many verses are devoted to describing each element of the feast: large mounds of rice, huge piles of vegetables, enormous pots of oil, heaps of fruits, towers of coconuts, and massive cooking vessels. With the depiction of each item in graphic, elaborate terms, the crowd's craving for food increases. There are charged accounts of how the food is served. When the distribution of the food starts from the first row, the anticipation grows, and the *vidūṣaka*, picturing himself in the story, almost swoons in excitement by the time the food reaches him. He honors the dishes one by one. He speaks directly to the bitter gourd:

> Spattered with green along the fields, as an embellishment to the hedge,
> Wafting and billowing in the breeze, like blessed favors from nature,
> Capable of crushing the arrogance of nectar—please come to my hands now,
> The young babies of bitter gourd clusters, germinating from the vines![16]

He pays homage to a mixed vegetable curry called *olan*:

> Pumpkin, along with cucumber and eggplant
> Combined well with fresh string beans,
> If lovely blue-eyed women would cook them for me,
> *Olan, olan* is enough—why go for a hundred other foods?[17]

He worships *pāyasam*, Kerala's much beloved dessert:

---

16. *pāṭattinkarĕ nīḷĕ nīlaniramāy, veliykkŏrāghoṣamāy*
āṭittūṇṇiyalaññulaññu sukṛtaṃ kaikkŏṇṭu vāḻuṃ vidhau |
pārāte varikĕnṭĕ kayyil adhunā pīyūṣaḍambhattĕyuṃ
bhediccanpŏṭu kaippavaḷḷi tarasā pĕttuḷḷa paitaññaḷe || *Puruṣārtthakkūttu*, 220.

17. *mattañña nallŏriḷavan bṛhatīsametaṃ*
puttan maṇippayarum aññatinotu certtŭ |
ālolanīlamiḻimār atu vĕccu tannāl
ololan ŏnnu mati ĕntinu nūrukūṭṭaṃ || *Puruṣārtthakkūttu*, 222.

When the superb sugar mingles exquisitely
With the purest milk, *pāyasam* is born.
When immortal nectar wanted a contest,
Pāyasam was judged superior, and nectar fled to the heavens
 in shame![18]

When the grand feast concludes, our gluttonous *brāhmaṇa* is so pleased that he blesses (or, rather, curses) the eldest member of the family to "conduct another such event in the house exactly twelve months from now!"

Day Five: *Rājaseva*—Serving a King

Rājaseva—to serve as a companion to a king—is the *vidūṣaka*'s fourth and final *puruṣārtha*, and perhaps the most difficult one. Once again Kauṇḍinya represents the public cause of salvaging the lost moral authority of his village, this time by finding favor with royalty. The *vidūṣaka* uses his signature humor to illustrate the challenge of forging a connection with the king: he likens it to the licking the sharp side of a sword from one end to the other, embracing an irate lion, and kissing the mouth of a poisonous serpent. Of course, the *vidūṣaka* finds ample time to mock the different kinds of kings and their manners. Kauṇḍinya knows not to approach a king who has fallen on hard times, nor one who has miserly habits, but ironically (and, presumably, intentionally), Kauṇḍinya's *rājaseva* brings him little satisfaction. At the end of the five-day *Puruṣārtha Kūttu*, Kauṇḍinya decides to serve Yudhiṣṭhira—a king who famously falls on hard times—though he later shifts his allegiance to Arjuna. But Arjuna falls on hard times of his own, and so, too, does Kauṇḍinya: when Arjuna chooses to disguise himself as a mendicant, Kauṇḍinya becomes ravenous and has to beg for alms to satisfy his hunger. This account brings us full circle: the *Puruṣārtha Kūttu* ends and the *Kūṭiyāṭṭam* performance returns to the main story of *Subhadrādhanañjaya*. Arjuna comes on stage the very next day, and the action continues.

---

18. *nalppārnna mādhuriyĕḻunnŏru pañcasāra-*
ppālppāyasaṃ paṭayilūkkŏṭaṭutta neraṃ |
nilppān prayāsam itinoṭĕtiriṭṭitĕnnor-
ttippāru viṭṭamṛtu pukkitu nākalokaṃ || *Puruṣārtthakkūttu*, 231.

Chapter Eight

How Do We Remember Śakuntalā?

The Mahābhārata and Kālidāsa's Drama on the Contemporary Indian Stage

Amanda Culp

From a contemporary perspective, the storyline of Kālidāsa's celebrated Sanskrit drama, the *Abhijñānaśākuntala* ("The Recognition of Śakuntalā," henceforth *Śākuntala*), is not always easy to palate as a romance. The plot begins when an innocent girl is seduced by a king who subsequently abandons her to return to his kingdom. When she discovers she is pregnant and appeals to him to accept her and her child in front of his court, he rejects her (the result of a curse) and sends her away. Her companions, who have accompanied her on her journey, refuse to take her back, insisting instead that she fulfills her marital responsibilities to her husband, regardless of his rejection of her. Years later, after she has given birth to and has begun to raise their son, the king returns (the curse has been broken) and begs her forgiveness; the family is reunited, and Śakuntalā's abandonment and humiliation are wiped away—a happy ending. Dramaturgically, the play is driven by the goal of romantic resolution, predicated on the moral exoneration of the king, Duṣyanta, for both his deeds within the play and of those enacted by his epic counterpart.[1] Modeled on the Śakuntalā narrative from the Sanskrit *Mahābhārata* (attributed to Vyāsa, a mythical sage and one of the characters in the epic itself), Kālidāsa's play makes a number of significant adjustments to the story's plot order to redeem the character of Duṣyanta—an ancestor of the epic's protagonists—and produce an acceptable, unflawed, felicitous *dénouement*.[2] In Vyāsa's iteration of the story, for example, there is no curse that causes the king to forget his romance with Śakuntalā, and no ring to help him remember—he simply chooses to reject her, knowing that no one could (or would dare to) contradict his account of events. By inserting the sage Durvāsas into the play to produce said curse and its antidote, the signet ring, Kālidāsa gives depth and color to an otherwise cruel character. Act Six of *Śākuntala* exists almost exclusively to expound on Duṣyanta's regret at losing his wife, building an audience's sympathy for him so that by the time the lovers are reunited in Act Seven, they—and Śakuntalā—are prepared to forgive his betrayal and accept his apology.

Of all the changes that Kālidāsa makes to Vyāsa's telling of the story, however, it is his characterization of the story's eponymous heroine that has given contemporary theater artists the most pause. Unlike her epic counterpart who, in Romila Thapar's words, is "a forthright, free, assertive, high spirited young woman who demands that her conditions, as stipulated at her marriage, be fulfilled,"[3] the Śakuntalā of Kālidāsa's drama is a provincial girl whose inexperience defines her early interactions with the king. She demands no conditions, negotiates no terms, and seems to accept unquestioningly the fate that the drama allots her. She does have one assertive moment that cannot be overlooked: after being definitively rejected by Duṣyanta in Act Five, Śakuntalā upbraids the king's behavior as *anārya* (dishonorable). Given the social, historical, and literary contexts of the play, Kālidāsa's audience would have considered such an insult monumental. Mere moments before she disparages him, Śakuntalā respectfully addresses the king as *āryaputra*, a common term of endearment between a

1. In the Sanskrit *Mahābhārata*, the king's name is Duḥṣanta (not Duṣyanta, as Kālidāsa calls him). For simplicity I will be referring to both as Duṣyanta.

2. This episode is found in the first book of the Sanskrit epic (1.62–69). See *The Mahābhārata for the First Time Critically Edited,* ed. V. S. Sukthankar et al. 19 vols. (Poona: Bhandarkar Oriental Research Institute, 1933–66).

3. Romila Thapar, *Śakuntalā: Texts, Readings, Histories* (London: Anthem Press, 1999), 38.

wife and her husband, as well as an honorific epithet that conveys civility, respectability, and nobility. To call a man *āryaputra,* literally "son of a noble person (*ārya*)," is to pay him and his family a great honor. Then to call Duṣyanta *anārya* to his face, before his court, as he sits on the throne of Hāstinapura (the seat of the Kurus' empire in the Sanskrit *Mahābhārata*), is not only an insult to his character but also to his very legitimacy. It would have carried extraordinary dramatic weight.

Still, when contextualizing the play for twentieth- and twenty-first century audiences, this one moment of strength feels increasingly insufficient to convey a sense of agency for Śakuntalā; her willing reconciliation with the king at the play's end feels far from happy when considered from a feminist perspective. The issue of squaring early modern portrayals of women with contemporary gender politics is not an uncommon one for those who work in theater to encounter when they adapt classical works for performance in contemporary contexts. With regard to the Greek tragedies, feminist critic Sue-Ellen Case notoriously suggests that feminist artists and scholars may ultimately want to excise the plays from the broader performance canon on account of their patriarchal prejudices, which Case finds irreconcilable with contemporary feminist values.[4] Yet I have found that many artists have been drawn to such texts precisely because of these tensions in transposition: these artists stage classical works in order to call attention to the very issues of representation they present.

Within the canon of Sanskrit drama, there is a long tradition of not only retelling but also revising the epics.[5] In addition to *Śākuntala,* which reflects Kālidāsa's significant revisions to a story from the Sanskrit *Mahābhārata* (as described above), Bhavabhūti's *Uttararāmacarita* ("Rāma's Last Act," ca. 700 CE, which reimagines the Rāmāyaṇa) and the *Ūrubhaṅga* ("The Shattered Thighs," ca. 200–800 CE, attributed to Bhāsa, which interprets a story from the Mahābhārata) serve as two of the more vigorous examples of this practice. The productions that I address in this essay represent the modern manifestation of this tradition. They perpetuate a centuries-old practice of reinventing familiar narratives onstage through the medium of

4. Sue-Ellen Case, "Classic Drag: The Greek Creation of Female Parts," *Theatre Journal* 37, no. 3 (1985).

5. For example, see the chapters in this volume by Nell Shapiro Hawley and Sudha Gopalakrishnan.

performance, and they offer an array of possible resolutions, including the provocative lack thereof, to Śakuntalā and Duṣyanta's complicated courtship. Ensemble 86's 1987 production of *Śākuntala*, directed by Prasanna, draws the play into the twentieth century in performance style while preserving the source text. Rita Ganguly's 1995 production, by contrast, embraces the classical performance idiom and radically alters the source text. And Kirtana Kumar's 2006 *Shakuntala Remembered* abandons Kālidāsa altogether, critiquing the alterations that the illustrious *kavi* ("poet," Kālidāsa) made to the myth by returning to the epic source material for inspiration.

Despite differences in the aesthetics used by the productions that I discuss here, all three productions make a similar tactical shift in the play's narrative to establish Śakuntalā as its protagonist in place of Duṣyanta. It is important to remember that although the common English shorthand for the play's title is "Shakuntala," an abbreviation that suggests that the play is about her, the full Sanskrit title is *Abhijñānaśākuntala*, "The Recognition of Śakuntalā," the agent of which is the play's protagonist, the king.[6] So when the king is exonerated in Act Seven and reunited with his family, it *is* a happy ending according to Kālidāsa's narrative: Duṣyanta's romantic exploits have reached a felicitous resolution, and Śakuntalā is the means by which that resolution is attained. For contemporary artists and audiences, however, this ending has become a source of anxiety. We are less willing to accept the curse as justification for Duṣyanta's actions, and we are less content to let Śakuntalā be an accessory to his story. In response to this discomfort, the following productions of the play have embraced its abbreviated title as a mandate to make Śakuntalā the heroine of her own story. Renouncing the perennial happy endings of Sanskrit theater, these artists have opted instead to permit the leading lady the tragedy of her circumstances by placing the structural focus of the play not on the couple's reconciliation, but on Śakuntalā's abandonment.[7]

6. Even if one translates the title as "Śakuntalā and the Ring of Recognition (*abhijñāna*)," as some do, the ring remains the king's, as does the recognition that it prompts.

7. Tragedy, as a genre, is unknown in premodern Indian dramaturgy. All plays from this period, be they romances, comedies, or political intrigues, end felicitously, meaning they end in a union of some kind, the hero's objectives having been successfully attained. As Edwin Gerow elaborates, "The tragic view [. . .] presumes a notion of the individual whose existence and moral status are separable from,

The Three Śakuntalās of Ensemble 86

In the summer of 1987, a group of recent graduates from the National School of Drama (NSD) in New Delhi conceived of a production of *Śākuntala* that would adapt Kālidāsa's narrative in order to reframe the play from a feminist perspective. Calling themselves Ensemble 86, after the year in which they had graduated, the actors recruited celebrated director Prasanna, who had been their teacher at NSD, to join them on this endeavor. Working with a Hindi translation of the play, Ensemble 86 and Prasanna's point of entry to the text was simple: to track Śakuntalā's evolution as a character from the naïve forest dweller of Act One to the abandoned, but resilient, single mother of Act Seven.[8] They did not read the play as a love story; the love story was simply the catalyst for Śakuntalā's journey. A fundamental challenge they faced in dramatizing this interpretation, however, was the dearth of text afforded to their lead. As written, Kālidāsa's play features remarkably little of its heroine's voice. Unlike the epic, in which Śakuntalā owns her narrative—she speaks on her own behalf in marital negotiations with the king, as well as in her defense upon their reunion—Kālidāsa's iteration of the character is often spoken for. Her friends Priyaṃvadā and Anasūyā intervene on her behalf in Act One, Kaṇva's disciples do almost all the speaking for her in Act Five (until she has no choice but to address the king herself), and in their long-awaited seventh-act reunion, Śakuntalā speaks a grand total of thirteen lines. By contrast, the king speaks fifty-nine.

With limited textual options to emphasize Śakuntalā's character development, Prasanna and company faced a choice: they could add new language to their production, lending their heroine the voice that she lacks in the original; or they could leave the text as-is, critiquing her silence by

---

and possible irreconcilable with, the community in which he finds himself [. . .] In this sense, tragedy seems antithetical to the basic Indian notion that the ultimate good of an individual is integrally bound to the good of all. In drama this means that any separation of the protagonist is a temporary and resolvable condition." See "Dramatic Theory and Kālidāsa's Plays," in *Theater of Memory: The Plays of Kālidāsa*, ed. Barbara Stoler Miller (New York: Columbia University Press, 1984), 48.

8. I spoke to Prasanna about the production in February 2016. When I asked him if he viewed the project as explicitly feminist or explicitly political, he answered, "If you think of women's issues as political, then yes, my 'Shakuntala' would be political." Prasanna in conversation with the author at Shravajivi Ashrama, February 19, 2016.

calling attention to it. They chose the latter. They marked the character's development over the course of the play through shifts in casting, employing three separate actresses to portray Śakuntalā in succession. The first played Śakuntalā in Acts One and Three—a naïve *āśrama* girl who falls in love with Duṣyanta and marries him in secret. As most critics remarked, this Śakuntalā is the one that tracks with the romantic ideal of the character. The second Śakuntalā, who takes the stage in Acts Four and Five, progresses from an abandoned but hopeful young bride preparing to leave home to a fiery heroine who steps out on her own, finally finds her voice, and chooses exile over enduring "slavery in [her] husband's house."[9] And finally, the third actress portrayed the Śakuntalā of Act Seven—a single mother raising her son in isolation. By articulating the character's development visually—through these shifts in the performer—Ensemble 86 protests Śakuntalā's relative absence from Kālidāsa's text, projecting the character's fragmentation across multiple embodiments.

In the director's own words, the production was a critique of genre that was designed to illuminate the differences between Sanskrit drama and the permutations of Western realism which were, and for the most part remain, far more popular with his Delhi audience.[10] "It is possible," Prasanna remarked to critic Reeta Sondhi, "to convey the growth of a character through one actress only if the text is as dramatically complete and as character oriented as in western drama." He went on to cite Henrick Ibsen's Nora from *A Doll House* as a prime example of such character orientation, as well as Mallikā from Mohan Rakesh's 1958 Hindi play *Āṣāḍh Kā Ek Din* ("One Day in Autumn"), suggesting that Indian dramaturgy was also capable of producing such characters, but only in its contemporary output.[11] Structurally, Sanskrit drama is neither plot- nor character-driven, but is designed toward the successful evocation of *rasa*, sentiment, in the audience. In this quote, however, Prasanna makes clear that he is not interested in directing *Śākuntala* in a historicist mode that is intended to replicate

9. Kālidāsa, *Abhijñānaśākuntala,* eds. Narayana Balakrishna Godabole and Kasinatha Panduranga Paraba (Bombay: Nirnaya Sagara Press, 1883), 76. All references to the play in this essay are to this edition.

10. In the late 1980s, when this production took place, the National School of Drama in Delhi did not yet have a classical Indian component to their curriculum.

11. Reeta Sondhi, "Demystifying Shakuntalam," *The Economic Times*, July 5, 1987 (accessed at the Natarang Pratishthan).

some kind of original stage practice. Instead, his production queries how to apply theatrical training in psychological realism—and character-based critique—to a character that far predates such practices. Do the specifics of the Sanskrit dramatic canon, in other words, forestall the possibility of a feminist interpretation of an underdeveloped female character?

For their audience even to consider seeing Śakuntalā in this way, Ensemble 86 needed to subvert the genre, and so the production began by disrupting any expectation the audience may have had that it would adhere to classical aesthetics or dramaturgy. As described by Sunit Tandon, the performance commences with the entrance of

> a bare-chested actor in traditional dance costume [who] salutes the audience and the stage elaborately, Kuchipudi [*Kūcipūḍi*] style, in the best traditional manner, accompanied by a percussion ensemble. When he finally addresses the audience, it is in the accepted idiom of the *sutradhar* [usually featured only in the *prastāvanā*, or prologue, the *sūtradhāra* is a director-character in classical Sanskrit drama who introduces the evening's play to the audience]. But this elaborate opening is only a sly dig at the traditionalists for it is torn apart when the young lady who is supposed to assist the *sutradhar* enters, dressed in a skirt and a bright red shirt."[12]

This plainly-clothed *naṭī* (the actress and director's assistant, another standard figure in Sanskrit drama) then goes on—in the only piece of text added to the script—to inform the *sūtradhāra* that the costume trunk has been left behind at the play's previous venue, and so the company will have to go ahead and perform in the clothes and with the props that they have on their persons.

These costume choices immediately established Kālidāsa's characters as contemporaries with their twentieth-century audience. Instead of keeping these characters at arm's length—in other words, by enshrining them in an antiquated idiom—Prasanna attempted to move them closer

12. Sunit Tandon, "A Directors' Play," *The Sunday Observer*, August 30, 1987 (accessed at the Natarang Pratishthan). *Kūcipūḍi* is a classical dance form from South India.

to the audience, overcoming the play's antiquity in a bid for emotional recognition. The company's selection of contemporary dress also worked against the classical production aesthetic typically associated with the play. As Mandakranta Bose remarks, costumes were an essential design element used by producers to attempt to replicate the play's original stage practice. Describing a production of the play from 1958 in which she played the role of Anasūyā, Bose notes that the costume designs were "derived from available illustrations of what [were] purported to be typical ancient Indian dress."[13] The traditional dress approach to the play was, in fact, so expected at the time of Ensemble 86's production that Romesh Chander's review in the *Times of India* noted that this was the "first time that anyone had attempted a Sanskrit classic in jeans and shawls."[14]

To depict Śakuntalā in contemporary dress also therefore worked against the character's iconographic limitations, depicting her for the first time not as a rarefied figure of mythology, but as a peer to members of the audience. There is something particularly democratic about these costumes. What could be a more empowering feminist statement than to allow a contemporary audience of women to see themselves in this figure from the epic canon and quite literally to put her in their shoes? To drive home this point, the production kept Duṣyanta bound to the classical idiom. His were the only costumes that were not "left behind" (or, perhaps more poignantly, the male actor's street clothes simply conformed to the revivalist aesthetic—the approximation of ancient Indian dress that Bose describes—that was traditionally afforded the play in performance). His mannerisms and performance style further reflected the aesthetic of his wardrobe. Had another character been sartorially isolated in this way, the choice would simply have preserved the audience's historical distance from the play throughout the performance, providing a counterpoint to their emotional identification with Śakuntalā. The choice of Duṣyanta as this anchor genders that distance. Having shifted the narrative focus to its modern heroines, the production's depiction of their interactions with a classical Duṣyanta acts as a constant reminder of the enduring associations,

13. Mandakranta Bose, "Staging *Abhijñānaśākuntalam*," in *Revisiting Abhijñāna-śākuntalam: Love, Lineage and Language in Kālidāsa's Nāṭaka*, eds. Saswati Sengupta and Deepika Tandon (Delhi: Orient Blackswan Private Limited, 2011), 46.

14. Romesh Chander, "Vivid New Shades to Shakuntala," *The Times of India*. September 2, 1987 (accessed at the Sangeet Natak Akademi).

biases, and cultural predilections that have, for centuries, cast Śakuntalā as instrumental to his story rather than as agent of her own. This Duṣyanta embodies the persistence of such stereotypes, traditions, and taboos, and his interactions with each Śakuntalā simultaneously display how antiquated such perspectives have become and also how persistent they remain.

All of this work—the subversion of the classical dramatic idiom, the contemporary dress, the multiple heroines—crescendos in Act Seven when Śakuntalā reunites with Duṣyanta. The closest that Kālidāsa comes to expressing Śakuntalā's misgivings in not only forgiving Duṣyanta, but returning to him, is in her refusal to reclaim the ring. "I do not trust that," she replies when Duṣyanta goes to place it on her finger once more. "Please, my husband, you wear it."[15] The moment is interrupted, however, by the arrival of the sage Mārīca and his wife, Aditi, who soon allay Śakuntalā's reservations with their account of the curse. In the only other substantial change to the source text, Prasanna's production eliminates this interruption, and the play's dramatic action stalls on Śakuntalā's refusal to take back the ring. Though she does not reject Duṣyanta outright, the moment indicates that all is not so easily forgotten or forgiven. "Prasanna does not quite wrap up the denouement," Sondhi observes in her review, "though [Vibha Chhiber's performance] suggests [Śakuntalā's] rejection of [Duṣyanta] in the frigidity of her final glance."[16] The final choice of the play is Śakuntalā's and, after so much interpolation, Prasanna and Ensemble 86 refuse to supply the audience with her decision. Instead, they present a question: Does Śakuntalā take Duṣyanta back? And perhaps more important: Why do we assume that she should?

Śakuntalā Alone—Rita Ganguly's *Tridhara*

When National School of Drama professor Rita Ganguly directed *Śākuntala* in 1995, she conceived of an even more aggressive rejection of Kālidāsa's happy resolution than that which the Ensemble 86 production offered, but subsumed her commentary on the play in a production that was aesthetically classical. A renowned dancer, singer, and overall proponent of India's

15. Kālidāsa, *Abhijñānaśākuntala*, 117. Full Text (from the *chāyā*): *nāsmai viśvasimi | āryaputra evaitad dhārayatu |*

16. Sondhi, "Demystifying Shakuntalam."

classical arts, Ganguly was instrumental in implementing a Sanskrit theater track at the NSD, and her *Śākuntala* was part of the inaugural season of that curricular shift. One of three Sanskrit plays performed by the school's second-year students under the umbrella title *Tridhara*, Ganguly's *Śākuntala* was staged in a temporary theater that had been constructed to adhere as closely as possible to the description of the *vikṛṣṭamadhyama* (medium/rectangular) theater hall that is articulated in the *Nāṭyaśāstra* (the earliest known Sanskrit treatise on drama).[17] The play was also performed entirely in Sanskrit (although not in the original text's mix of Sanskrit and Prakrit).[18] With no supertitles to translate the play's dialogue into a more familiar or contemporary language, this production relied on the physical and gestural performances of the actors to convey narrative and emotional states, as well on the audience's presumed familiarity with *Śākuntala's* basic plot structure. Ganguly's interpretation of the play, however, departs from Kālidāsa's text from the very first moment after the preliminary rituals beginning the performance are completed.[19] In lieu of the *prastāvanā* (a prologue that is traditional to this genre of drama) and in advance of the king's entrance (which commences the action of the play itself), Ganguly's production begins with a scene that features Śakuntalā and her two friends at play in the forest. The lights come up on a hand-held rectangular curtain, which conceals three sets of legs behind it.[20] A single hand appears on the upper rim of the curtain, then another, before the curtain finally lowers to reveal Śakuntalā's face staring at the audience—a deer not in headlights but in

17. The other two plays were Mahendravarman's one-act farce *Mattavilāsaprahasana* and Viśākhadatta's political drama *Mudrārākṣasa*.

18. To call this canon of plays "Sanskrit" dramas is, in fact, a misnomer, as the plays often feature multiple languages in addition to Sanskrit. In *Śākuntala*, for example, Duṣyanta speaks in Sanskrit, as do Kaṇva and his disciples, while Śakuntalā speaks Shauraseni. The languages Maharashtri, Magadhi, and Ardhamagadhi are also featured in the play.

19. My descriptions of the production are based on video recordings of performance held by the National School of Drama Audio-Visual Archives

20. The curtain is similar to that which is used in *Kathakaḷi* (an Indian classical dance-drama form native to the South Indian state of Kerala) and *Kūṭiyāṭṭam* (a theatrical form that utilizes Sanskrit dramatic texts, also native to Kerala) when a new character is revealed in a scene. On *Kūṭiyāṭṭam*, see the chapter by Sudha Gopalakrishnan in this volume.

spotlights. She performs a short *abhinaya*, a form of gestural acting that conveys a sentiment or idea through the coordinated movement of the hands, eyes, and face as well as of the strategic positioning of the body's limbs. The whole scene is extratextual, in fact. Once she has finished her *abhinaya*, Śakuntalā is joined by the other two women, Priyaṃvadā and Anasūyā, who abandon the curtain to perform a "ball dance" together with their friend in the style of *Bharatanāṭyam* (a classical dance form originating in South India).[21] The king enters about fifteen minutes into this scene, interrupting a game in which Śakuntalā is blindfolded while her friends hide from her. When she inadvertently collides with the king, he grabs her wrist, prompting her to remove her blindfold. The two hold one another's gazes for a prolonged moment before Śakuntalā pulls free and runs offstage. The king then spots a deer and pursues it off stage. He returns with his chariot, effectively returning the audience to Kālidāsa's text.

From the start, Ganguly, like Prasanna, framed her production around Śakuntalā and not the king. I use the word "frame" intentionally here, since Ganguly literally framed Śakuntalā throughout the play, forming a white picture frame with cloth that was brought onstage to highlight key moments in her narrative: the mirroring of Śakuntalā and the deer in the aforementioned prologue; when the king first interrupts the women in the forest; lovesick Śakuntalā at the start of Act Three; as she is being cursed by Durvāsas in Act Four; the moment she realizes the ring is gone in Act Five; and throughout the reunion scene with Duṣyanta in Act Seven. The moments that Ganguly chose to highlight are significant in the way that they shaped the arc of the play to highlight the tragedy of Śakuntalā rather than the romantic exploits of Duṣyanta. They provided a supertext to her emotional life in the same way that Prasanna's triple casting did, imposing a more complex arc on the character than the one that exists in Kālidāsa's play.

These moments are, for the most part, applied to the play's text. They comment on Kālidāsa's story but do not markedly change it until the fifth

21. In this dance, the performers use the kind of gestural acting described above (*abhinaya)* to give the impression of having a small ball. Throughout the dance they "throw," "bounce," and "catch," the ball, passing it amongst themselves. The exercise is a perfect way to demonstrate the coordination of hands, eyes, face, etc., as through this enactment, the audience comes to believe there to be a physical ball onstage.

act, when Śakuntalā is rejected by the king. Here Ganguly abruptly cuts the scene short: Duṣyanta laughs at Śakuntalā's inability to produce the proof she claims to have, Kaṇva's disciples abandon her, and she is left alone onstage, in all of her wedding finery, behind the frame. She takes off her veil, her wedding clothes, and her wedding jewelry to reveal her *āśrama* clothing concealed underneath. She performs this removal slowly, heartbreakingly; she takes her time before collapsing to the ground. There is no celestial miracle here, and the earth does not swallow her, but instead another woman comes to her aid, picks her up, and invites Śakuntalā to seek refuge with her: a salvation in the kindness of strangers, in communities of women. The scene then shifts to Śakuntalā with her infant child cradled in her arms—no fisherman, no painting, no redemption for Duṣyanta.

The final act of Ganguly's production is the most poignantly different, as Duṣyanta re-appears without any of the emotional development that Kālidāsa attributes to him in Act Six, which has been cut from Ganguly's production. The scene parallels the first, only here, in the final act, Śakuntalā is blindfolded by her son when she runs into Duṣyanta in the forest. He is apologetic, but the sentiment does not seem genuine. She is indifferent, and her decision unambiguous: when Duṣyanta asks her to come with him, she flatly refuses, though she still allows him to take their son. Her final line, to Bharata and not to Duṣyanta, is "My son, in this world everyone is on their own, and I will remain alone. You go." (The line, spoken in Sanskrit, was added to Kālidāsa's text.)[22] Bharata follows Duṣyanta offstage, and Śakuntalā remains by herself, framed, performing the same *abhinaya* that she did at the very top of the show. No longer the deer in spotlights, she is world-wearied but not broken, sadder and wiser, standing on her own two feet. She has walked out of Kālidāsa's narrative and into a completely new context.

Igniting Cultural Memory in Kirtana Kumar's *Shakuntala Remembered*

For Kirtana Kumar, actor, director, and artistic director of Little Jasmine Theatre Project in Bangalore, the only way to stage *Śākuntala* for the

22. *Putra, jagati sarve 'py ekākinaḥ, ahaṃ tv ekākinī sthāsyāmi. Anugaccha.* (Recording viewed at the National School of Drama.)

twenty-first century was to abandon Kālidāsa (almost) altogether and to return to the play's epic roots. Commissioned to produce the play as part of an international collaboration with Trestle Theatre Company of the UK, Kumar found herself searching for a way to approach what felt like a static, unapproachable text. "I love Kalidasa's language," Kumar admitted in hindsight, "but the device he uses—the ring and curse—didn't interest me at all."[23] Kālidāsa's interpretation of the story felt in some ways too familiar to her, and in other ways completely unknown—a story that everyone remembers but that no one truly understands. In her research, Kumar discovered Śakuntalā in the Sanskrit *Bhāgavatapurāṇa*, a compilation of myths and legends pertaining to the Hindu god Kṛṣṇa that scholars date to between the ninth and thirteenth centuries.[24] Going back to the play's mythological roots—in both the *Mahābhārata* and the *Bhāgavatapurāṇa*—reignited the character for Kumar by revealing a bold, assertive alternative to the familiar image of the heroine that Kālidāsa imagined. "Ninety percent of India knows Shakuntala through Kalidasa," she remarked in an interview. "For them Shakuntala means Kalidasa's Shakuntala. She, and her story, have permeated the national consciousness, through calendar art and Raja Ravi Varma, and she's always the Sita-like passive ideal."[25] Reading a contrasting portrayal of Śakuntalā in the *Bhāgavatapurāṇa* prompted Kumar to wonder where the monolithic associations of the character originate, and how revisiting variant readings might provoke an audience to interrogate the cultural means by which divergent narratives are so efficiently obscured. Beginning with the story's recapitulation in the *Bhāgavatapurāṇa* and ultimately returning to the Sanskrit *Mahābhārata* as Śakuntalā's point of origin, Kumar unpacked

23. Venetia Ansell, "Interview with Kirtana Kumar," *Sanskrit Literature Blog*, May 21, 2008. https://venetiaansell.wordpress.com/2008/05/21/interview-with-kirtana-kumar/

24. See Edwin F. Bryant, "Introduction," in *Krishna: The Beautiful Legend of God: Śrīmad Bhāgavata Pūrāṇa, Book X*, trans. Edwin F. Bryant (London: Penguin Books, 2003), xvi. The story of Śakuntalā is found in the ninth book of the *Bhāgavatapūrāṇa* (9.9). See *Bhāgavata Purāṇa of Kṛṣṇa Dvaipayana Vyāsa*, ed. J. L. Shastri (Delhi: Motilal Banarsidass, 1983).

25. Ansell, "Interview with Kirtana Kumar." Raja Ravi Varma, whom Kumar mentions here, was a renowned painter in the second half of the nineteenth century and is remembered for utilizing European techniques to depict Indian subjects. Among other mythological themes and characters, Śakuntalā was a particular favorite of his.

the layered history of this character, unseating Kālidāsa's interpretation of the story as the sole authoritative one.

Suddenly the play's popularity became a boon for engaging what Marvin Carlson would call the "binocular vision" of Kumar's audience: their "familiarity with the previous treatment of the same material and their ability to draw comparisons between that and the new, rival treatment."[26] This dual vision is key to any critical artistic adaptations designed to comment on and/or significantly alter an original text. As David Gitomer reminds us, "although *we* in the twenty-first century may not be thinking of [the] older harsher stor[y] when we read or watch [*Śākuntala*], the audiences of the author's day surely were,"[27] and that therefore in order to fully appreciate the layers the text intended, we need to imagine the ancient myth always superimposed on the drama. To do so, however, is to invite the memory of the heartless Duṣyanta from the Sanskrit *Mahābhārata* (where he is called Duḥṣanta) to compete for our attention with the softer Duṣyanta of the play. "Why," Gitomer asks, "did Kālidāsa select [a story] that he knew would remind his audiences of cruelty in love? [. . .] Because he wanted the cruel, problematic nature of love to remain present in the imagination of his audiences; they should remain present in our imaginations as well."[28] Though perhaps less focused on the cruelty of love in the story than on the cruelty to women, Kumar is also interested in having her audience grapple with competing iterations of the story that are difficult to reconcile. The irony, and innovation, of Kumar's production rests in the inversion of source and adaptation. If Kālidāsa relied on his audience's familiarity with the epic to appreciate his interventions with the story, Kumar relies on her audience's familiarity with Kālidāsa to be shocked by her return to the source.

For Prasanna and Ganguly, the source of comparison was the play itself. Each director pits his and her theatrical interpretation of Kālidāsa's play against other, more "traditional" productions. The *Mahābhārata* may have been invoked indirectly by each production's insistence on a more

26. Marvin Carlson, *The Haunted Stage: The Theatre as Memory Machine* (Ann Arbor: University of Michigan Press, 2003), 27.

27. David L. Gitomer, "Can Men Change? Kālidāsa's Seducer King in the Thicket of Sanskrit Poetics," in *Revisiting Abhijñānaśākuntalam: Love, Lineage and Language in Kālidāsa's Nāṭaka*, eds. Saswati Sengupta and Deepika Tandon (Delhi: Orient Blackswan Private Limited, 2011), 174.

28. Gitomer, 174.

outspoken heroine, but audiences needn't have registered those subtleties in order to be able to discern the ways in which the production deviated from previous dramatic interpretations. Kumar, on the other hand, makes the citation explicit in the form as well as in the content of the narrative. Performed in English, the structure of *Shakuntala Remembered* is far more epic than dramatic. The play is built around three performers who step in and out of a number of different parts, a style of performance more akin to oral narration than character-based acting. As the roles were assigned for production, Kumar herself played both Śakuntalā and the *sūtradhāra* (the director), whose role is drastically expanded from Kālidāsa's play. Present throughout the duration of the action, including at the play's end, Kumar's *sūtradhāra* situates the story in a broader mythological framework that incorporates some the *Mahābhārata* back into the action. As our narrator, this *sūtradhāra* takes her place as the intermediary, providing commentary on the play. She is not impartial, either—her position as a woman on the outside of the story allows her to see it more clearly than Śakuntalā does, and she has opinions about it. By playing both roles, however, Kumar subsumes both women, both perspectives. In her first scene, the *sūtradhāra* claims her place in the story by recounting her relationship with the *Mahābhārata*'s Vyāsa: "My father's *guru* was the great Vyāsa," she tells the audience. "In one story, he tells us about Duṣyanta, the warrior king, and the forest dweller, Śakuntalā. Do you know why? You don't? Then listen to the story unfold. For when humanity sleeps and will not awake, will not remember, then will Kali play mischief with the world."[29] The scene differs vastly from Kālidāsa's prologue, yet still fulfills its primary dramaturgical function: she gives us key information about the play and introduces a central theme. She turns that theme directly around onto the audience, however, by informing them that the memory in question in this production is not Duṣyanta's but their own.

The basic narrative of the play is also structured on that of the epic. Though there are vignettes that Kumar steals from the play—notably Duṣyanta's verses as he watches Śakuntalā being attacked by a bee—she does not keep any of Kālidāsa's structural changes: no ring, no Durvāsas, no curse, no painting. The king simply departs, and twelve years pass before Śakuntalā finally confronts him at Hāstinapura. This scene serves as the heart of Kumar's production. Rejected by the king, Śakuntalā spends the night on

29. Kirtana Kumar, *Shakuntala Remembered* (unpublished manuscript, PDF file).

the streets of the city. She dreams of what she *should* have said to the king but did not; it's the argument she wishes she had made. In the dream, she resolves to return to the palace and make herself heard. The next morning, she returns with her son; Duṣyanta rejects her yet again, pushing her and the child to the floor. She does not give in, however, but rises to makes her case, building her righteous indignation syllable by syllable through the use of *koṉṉakkōl*, a system of vocal percussion used in south Indian music. Her non-verbal anger reaches a crescendo and erupts out of her, expanding the one word Kālidāsa has given her—*anārya*—into a fierce monologue: "Ignoble man, you do remember: I know that you remember everything and yet here you are, like a cornered rat. You liar!"[30] she decries. In performance, this verbal confrontation escalates into a physical altercation, choreographed in the vocabulary of *Kaḷarippayattu*, a martial art form native to Kerala. As they battle, Śakuntalā continues her indictment:

> Listen to me, O Liar-King, and I will help you remember. I am your lawful wedded wife and it is despicable that you should so humiliate me in the presence of your court [. . .] Drunk with power I might have known that you were steeped in treachery. You can tell yourself "I am safe, no one knows, I will not be found out." Look around you! Look around you! But they *all* know.[31]

She precedes to list her witnesses: the *deva*s (the gods), the *bhūta*s (the creatures), the sun, the moon, and Agni (Fire), heaven and earth and Yama (Death) and Dharma—they all know.

In this climactic scene, Kumar's production becomes more than a critique of Kālidāsa's play and its depiction of Śakuntalā. Here, *Shakuntala Remembered* evolves into a broader conversation about cultural memory and its counterpoint, cultural amnesia. What are the repercussions of not remembering? Who is hurt when those who do remember don't speak up, and those who know don't hold them accountable? For Kumar this shift had a topical reference point: the 2006 Mumbai train bombings had taken place just days before Kumar had begun work on the project, which gave her a hook into the material. "I love cyclical structure—this is set in the

30. Kumar, *Shakuntala Remembered.*

31. Kumar, *Shakuntala Remembered.*

Kaliyuga [the age of dissonance]—and of course in Indian thought everything is a cycle just as with these terrible things which keep happening," Kumar explained. "I'm interested in the manner in which we forget."[32] The stakes of forgetting are scaled, of course, but are ultimately the product of a similar, and dangerous, cultural trajectory. Forgetting the epic heroine behind Kālidāsa's Śakuntalā speaks to a persistent cultural amnesia that obscures divergent or alternative narratives and subsequently renders those narratives too weak to stand, or to be stood up for. Kumar's Śakuntalā, in retaliation, does not let Duṣyanta or the audience forget. She calls the audience as a witness, while citing others—natural forces and social structures—who are always witnesses, a move that suggests that cultural memory is a communal action: individuals can't forget if the social order keeps truths alive. "The manner in which we forget," to borrow Kumar's phrase, is entrenched in systems of power. Duṣyanta gets away with rejecting Śakuntalā only if everyone who knows the truth turns a blind eye, if their reticence intimidates her into silence. In a provocation that feels, unfortunately, timelier than ever, Kumar seems to ask if Kālidāsa's ring would still be necessary if we all were better at helping, and sometimes even compelling, one another to remember.

Conclusion

As much as these productions of *Śākuntala* differ from one another, all of them betray a desire among contemporary theater artists to place Śakuntalā at the center of her drama: a *Śakuntalā-nāṭaka*, if you will, in place of the *Abhijñānaśākuntala*. The artistic choices made in service of these ends necessarily rupture the dramatic structure within which Kālidāsa wrote his famous play, permitting for tragedy in a tradition in which tragedy is not traditionally recognized. In doing so (whether explicitly, as Kumar does, or more subtly, as Ensemble 86 and Rita Ganguly do), each of these productions calls the Śakuntalā of the Sanskrit *Mahābhārata* to stand alongside Kālidāsa's heroine—to lend her some of her assertiveness, yes, but also to illuminate the many interpretations of the character that exist simultaneously. Just as there are many Mahābhāratas, so are there many Śakuntalās. The memory of one is enriched by remembering them all.

32. Ansell, "Interview with Kirtana Kumar."

PART III

Regional and Vernacular Mahābhāratas from Premodern South Asia

Chapter Nine

An Old Dharma in a New Age

Duryodhana and the Reframing of Epic Ethics in Ranna's *Sāhasabhīmavijaya*

Timothy Lorndale

This essay examines Ranna's *Sāhasabhīmavijaya*[1] ("The Victory of Bold Bhīma"; *SBhV*), or *Gadāyuddha* ("The Battle of Clubs"), an early retelling of the Mahābhārata in Old Kannada. It was composed at the Western Cāḷukya court, most likely during the reign of Satyāśraya (ca. 997–1008 CE).[2] In its preface, the poet Ranna describes his patron, Satyāśraya, as the

1. This chapter draws on arguments made in my forthcoming PhD dissertation, "Epic Translation: Ranna's *Sāhasabhīmavijaya* and the Mahābhārata's Afterlife in Medieval Karṇāṭa." All translations are my own, unless otherwise noted. Quotations from the *Sāhasabhīmavijaya* are from: Ranna, *Sāhasabhīmavijaya*, eds. B. S. Sannayya and Ramegauda (Mysore: University of Mysore Prasaranga, 1985).

2. The Western Cāḷukyas, also known as the Kalyāṇi Cāḷukyas, rose to prominence following the fall of the Rāṣṭrakūṭas (ca. 973 CE). The dynasty ruled over large parts of South India and the Deccan Plateau between the tenth and twelfth centuries of the Common Era. For more on the Western Cāḷukyas, see B. R. Gopal, *The Chalukyas of Kalyana and the Kalachuris* (Dharwad: Karnatak University Prasaranga, 1981). For the clearest discussion on the *SBhV*'s dating, see N. S. Tharanatha, "Ranna: Itivṛtta, Paraśurāmacarita, Cakreśvaracarita," in *Kannaḍa Sāhitya Caritrĕ: Mūrunĕya*

hero of the story and identifies him with Bhīma.[3] He then declares that this work will tell the story of Bhīma's defeat of Duryodhana in the Battle of Clubs, which secures the Pāṇḍavas' victory in the Mahābhārata war. The text, however, rapidly veers away from a narrative that is centered on Bhīma (and therefore Satyāśraya). Instead, the *SBhV* retells the Mahābhārata through the alternate perspective of Duryodhana, the traditional antihero of the epic.[4] He is the epic's primary narrator, *focalizor*, and interpreter. As readers, we receive a Mahābhārata narrative that is filtered through his interpretive lens, values, and character biases.[5]

I focus on Duryodhana's first extended monologue, which he addresses to Sañjaya (Dhṛtarāṣṭra's charioteer, who narrates the entire battle at Kurukṣetra to the blind king).[6] Over the course of this speech, Duryodhana outlines his particular take on *kṣatriya* dharma (the warrior's code of conduct), which serves as the interpretive lens for the *SBhV*'s presentation of the Mahābhārata as a whole. By defining his guiding moral code and

---

Saṃpuṭa, eds. H. M. Nayak and T. V. Venkatachala Sastry (Mysore: Institute of Kannada Studies, University of Mysore, 1976), 575–83.

3. As Heidi Pauwels notes in her chapter in this volume, the fifteenth-century poet Viṣṇudās also compares his patron to Bhīma in the Hindi *Pāṇḍavcarit.*

4. Duryodhana has long been a person of interest in the Mahābhārata tradition. The *SBhV* is part of a larger network of narratives that seek to explore his characterization and point of view. For a discussion of Duryodhana's role in Sanskrit works such as Bhāsa's *Ūrubhaṅga* and Bhaṭṭa Nārāyaṇa's *Veṇīsaṃhāra,* see David Gitomer, "King Duryodhana: The Mahābhārata Discourse on Sinning and Virtue in Epic and Drama," *Journal of the American Oriental Society* 112, no. 2 (1992): 222–32. For a discussion of Duryodhana in the Garhwali *Pāṇḍavlīlā* performance tradition, see William S. Sax, "Worshiping Epic Villains: A Kaurava Cult in the Central Himalayas," in *Epic Traditions in the Contemporary World: Poetics of Community*, eds. Margaret Beissinger, Jane Tylus, and Susanne Wofford (Berkeley: University of California Press, 1999), 169–86.

5. The concept of focalization was originally theorized by Gerard Genette, and then further refined by Mieke Bal, who defines it as "the relationship between the vision, the agent that sees, and that which is seen." Bal's notion, therefore, provides a useful model to consider the relationship between the narrative and the perspective through which it is narrated. See *Narratology: Introduction to the Theory of Narrative*, trans. Christine von Boheemen (Toronto: University of Toronto Press, 1985), 104–5.

6. *SBhV* 3.23–44.

character in opposition to that of his cousins, Duryodhana contributes to the dismantling and undermining of pro-Pāṇḍava interpretations of the epic. He retells familiar stories, but his perspective often differs from—even challenges—how the events found in other versions of the epic are perceived. Through his retelling, Duryodhana presents an altogether new take on the Mahābhārata conflict: the Pāṇḍavas have forsaken dharma and must be stopped.

In what follows, I analyze the *SBhV*'s intervention into the Mahābhārata discourse on dharma by examining three passages that demonstrate how Duryodhana re-narrates well known stories from the Mahābhārata in order to argue that the Pāṇḍavas consistently fail to abide by *kṣatriya* dharma. The first narrative that Duryodhana retells centers on Droṇa's murder at the hands of Yudhiṣṭhira and Arjuna. The second juxtaposes Bhīma's heroic failures and so-called triumphs. Duryodhana's third narrative, a retelling of the famous wrestling match between Śiva and Arjuna, characterizes Arjuna as an unlawfully ruthless competitor. In order to highlight the *SBhV*'s interventions into the epic narrative, I offer a close and comparative reading of the *SBhV* alongside two earlier tellings of the Mahābhārata: the Sanskrit *Mahābhārata* attributed to Vyāsa (*MBh*) and Pampa's Old Kannada *Vikramārjunavijaya* ("The Victory of Heroic Arjuna," *VAV*), also known as the *Pampabhārata*.[7]

Dharmic Tension in the Mahābhārata

The nature and limits of *kṣatriya* dharma have been challenged and redefined throughout the Mahābhārata tradition. The Sanskrit *MBh* narrative presents

7. Quotations from the Sanskrit *Mahābhārata* are from: *The Mahābhārata for the First Time Critically Edited*, ed. V. S. Sukthankar et al. 19 vols. (Poona: Bhandarkar Oriental Research Institute, 1933–66). Quotations from the *Vikramārjunavijaya* are from: Pampa, *Vikramārjunavijaya*, ed. Bellave Venkatanarayanappa (Mysore: University of Mysore Prasaranga, 2013; first published 1931, Kannada Sahitya Parishattu (Bangalore)). The *VAV* of Pampa (ca. 942 CE) is the first of the Old Kannada Mahābhāratas. For more on the *SBhV*'s relationship with this work, see T. N. Srikanthayya, "Gadāyuddhavū Svīkaraṇavicāravū," in *Ranna Kavi Praśasti* (Bangalore: Kannada Sahitya Parisat, 1978), 73–97; and B. S. Sannayya and Ramegauḍa, *Prastāvanĕ* (introduction) to the *Sāhasabhīmavijaya* (Mysore: University of Mysore Prasaranga, 1985), xxviii–xxxiv.

a growing tension between an older and a newer notion of dharma. The former emphasizes a model of behavior according to *varṇāśrama* dharma (a set of duties and laws that are specific to one's caste and stage of life), while the latter, which some Indologists see as a Brahmanical response to the Buddhist emperor Aśoka (268–232 BCE), emphasizes the practice of *yoga*, cultivation of *gnosis* (*jñāna*), non-violence (*ahiṃsā*), theistic devotion (*bhakti*), and non-attachment toward one's duty. As Adam Bowles, James L. Fitzgerald, and Alf Hiltebeitel argue, the character of Kṛṣṇa plays a significant role in this shift.[8] His actions and advice throughout the epic are particularly instrumental in indoctrinating the surviving *kṣatriya*s into the new dharma.[9] At key moments in the *MBh*, Kṛṣṇa downplays the duties of an individual and, instead, emphasizes the collective need to uphold the "greater good." But this new *kṣatriya* dharma is certainly met with resistance within the epic. As David Gitomer argues, this same dharmic tension can be seen in the contentious relationship between Duryodhana (the old *kṣatriya*) and Kṛṣṇa (the *avatāra* or "incarnation" of Viṣṇu), wherein the former is the paradigmatic exemplar of old *kṣatriya* dharma and the latter is the representative of the new. The Pāṇḍavas will ultimately triumph over Duryodhana, in spite of his devotion to correct conduct, because of their association with Kṛṣṇa.[10]

Unlike the *MBh*, the *SBhV* frames dharma exclusively in the realm of the mundane and human. Duryodhana does not engage with Kṛṣṇa's new

8. James Fitzgerald, "Introduction" in *The Mahābhārata*, vol. 7, *11. The Book of the Women, 12. The Book of Peace, Part One* (Chicago: University of Chicago Press, 2004), 100–42; James Fitzgerald, "Making Yudhiṣṭhira King: The Dialectics and the Politics of Violence in the *Mahābhārata*," *Rocznik Orientalisticzny/Polskie Towarzystwo Orientalistyczne* 54, no. 1 (2001), 71–72; Adam Bowles, *Dharma, Disorder, and the Political in Ancient India: The Āpaddharmaparvan of the Mahābhārata* (Leiden: Brill, 2007), 133–54; Paul Hacker, "Dharma in Hinduism," trans. Donald Davis Jr., *Journal of Indian Philosophy* 34, no. 4 (2006): 479–96; Alf Hiltebeitel, *Dharma: Its Early History in Law, Religion, and Narrative* (Oxford: Oxford University Press, 2011), 35–50; and Patrick Olivelle, "The Semantic History of Dharma: The Middle and Late Vedic Periods," *Journal of Indian Philosophy* 32, no. 5–6 (2004): 505–6.

9. Fitzgerald, "Introduction," 128–29, 140–41; Bowles, *Dharma, Disorder and the Political*, 133–54; and Hiltebeitel, *Dharma*, 553–62.

10. Gitomer, "King Duryodhana," 229.

dharma. His only concern is the Pāṇḍavas. For that matter, Duryodhana does not criticize Kṛṣṇa until the very end. Yet unlike Duryodhana in the Sanskrit *MBh*, the Kaurava king in the *SBhV* is anything but blind to Kṛṣṇa's divinity.[11] For example, he says:

> They call him one of the *trimūrti*,[12] the destroyer of *asura*s (demons), and a *guru* for the world.
> So why is he driving a chariot for someone else? Why is he Arjuna's servant?
> And why is he such a big wimp?
> How is it appropriate for Kṛṣṇa to be called "*Ādideva*—Primordial God"?
> Surely, words like *driver*, *servant*, or *coward* are far more fitting![13]

Humor aside, Duryodhana, in this stanza, draws a striking contrast between Viṣṇu, God with a capital "G," and Kṛṣṇa, his earthly *avatāra*. Though he is mindful of Kṛṣṇa's divinity, Duryodhana clearly does not see him as a threat to dharma, since dharma is a matter for humans alone. From his point of view, *kṣatriya*s should speak the truth, practice good conduct on the battlefield, never retreat, and die in battle. As will be seen in the three passages that highlight Duryodhana's dharmic reinterpretation, the Pāṇḍavas stand in opposition to the acts and duties required of the *kṣatriya varṇa* (class).

---

11. See Gitomer, 224, 229–232; and Robert P. Goldman, "Gods in Hiding: The Virāṭa Parvan and the Divinity of the Indian Epic Hero," in *Modern Evaluation of the Mahābhārata (Professor R. K. Sharma Felicitation Volume),* ed. Satya Pal Narang (Delhi: Nag Publishers, 1995), 81–82.

12. This is a reference to the trinity of Hindu deities composed of Brahmā, Viṣṇu, and Śiva.

13. *puruṣar mūvarŏḷ ŏrban ĕṃbar asurapradhvaṃsiy ĕṃbar jagad-*
guruv ĕṃbar pĕṟarg' ekĕ teran ĕsapaṃ dharmānujaṅg' ekĕ kiṃ-
karan ādaṃ karaveḻiy ādan adaṟiṃ sūtaṃ bhaṭaṃ peḻim ĕṃ-
bara māt' ŏppugum ādidevan ĕnisal kṛṣṇaṅg' ad' ĕnt' ŏppuguṃ || *SBhV* 3.43 ||

Who Killed Droṇa?[14]

At the beginning of the *SBhV*'s second *canto*, Duryodhana and Sañjaya are on Kurukṣetra, surrounded by dead friends, allies, and relatives. Sañjaya tries to reason with Duryodhana that the war is futile, arguing that he should give up, and describes some of the Pāṇḍavas' heroic feats to illustrate his point. Duryodhana attempts to refute Sañjaya's argument. The first story he recounts to Sañjaya is about the murder of Droṇa, the archery teacher of the Kauravas and the Pāṇḍavas. It spans a total of five stanzas. The first four stanzas[15] concern Yudhiṣṭhira's actions in orchestrating Droṇa's death, and the final verse[16] accuses Arjuna of being involved in this brutal murder. Duryodhana's account of Droṇa's death, which focuses especially on the Pāṇḍavas' deceit, makes no attempt to alleviate the ethical tensions of the plot. In fact, it rejects many of the standard events found in works like the *MBh* and *VAV*.

The murder of Droṇa, head of the Kaurava forces, is one of the most controversial events in the Sanskrit *MBh*. While Droṇa is decimating the Pāṇḍava army, Kṛṣṇa concocts a plan and pitches it to Arjuna in order to trick Droṇa into leaving the battle. He suggests starting a rumor that Droṇa's son, Aśvatthāman, has died. Unlike Arjuna, Bhīma and Yudhiṣṭhira agree to help Kṛṣṇa. Bhīma then slays an elephant by the name of Aśvatthāman and spreads the word to Droṇa that "Aśvatthāman" has been killed. Yet his words do not cause Droṇa to withdraw from battle. After Droṇa unleashes the *brahmāstra* weapon on the Pāñcālas, the Pāṇḍavas' allies, a host of sages appear and make him leave the war. They tell him that releasing a divine weapon in battle is against the rules of combat.[17] He then goes to Yudhiṣṭhira, the truthful son of Dharma, to get the real answer about his son's condition. Yudhiṣṭhira mumbles that "he was slain . . . the elephant."[18] After hearing about his "son's" death, Droṇa becomes listless. Facing an

---

14. For other tellings of Droṇa's death, see *MBh* 7.155–65 and *VAV* 12.25V–30V. V stands for *vacana* (prose).

15. *SBhV* 3.23–26.

16. *SBhV* 3.31.

17. *MBh* 7.164.87–92.

18. *tam atathyabhaye magno jaye sakto yudhiṣṭhiraḥ* |
avyaktam abravīd rājan hataḥ kuñjara ity uta || *MBh* 7.164.106 ||
Yudhiṣṭhira, overwhelmed from fear of lying to Droṇa, but intent upon winning, mumbled: "my lord, he was slain . . . the elephant."

attack, however, he fights a little longer, before dropping his weapons and undertaking a self-willed death, or *prāya*. Finally, while Droṇa sits in meditation, Dhṛṣṭadyumna (the son of the Pāñcāla king Drupada) beheads him.

The *VAV*'s telling of the story generally follows that of the Sanskrit *MBh*. Yet Pampa's text alters the narrative slightly, so that Yudhiṣṭhira does not have to lie. Upon hearing the news of his son's death, Droṇa's character undergoes a profound change. He immediately abandons not only his bow, but also his heroic masculine identity.[19] His character also experiences an aesthetic change. His innate heroic *rasa* is described as broken, and a new sorrowful *rasa* is born in its place.[20] He then goes to Yudhiṣṭhira and inquires about what happened to his son. But unlike in the *MBh*, Yudhiṣṭhira, in the *VAV*, speaks truthfully and tells him about the elephant. Even knowing that his son is alive, Droṇa resolves to give up his life because he already abandoned his weapons and he cannot go back on his word.[21] After this exchange, the narrative ends much as it does in the Sanskrit *MBh*.

In the *SBhV*, the story of Droṇa's downfall starts with Yudhiṣṭhira's deceit, not Kṛṣṇa's plot (as it does in the Sanskrit *MBh* and Pampa's *VAV*). Duryodhana expands upon the lie that defeated Droṇa and he outlines the story as follows:

> People say:
> "His vow to the truth is firm;"
> "He is devoted to *dharma*"; and
> "That Yudhiṣṭhira, Dharma's son, is oh, so compassionate;"

---

19. *ŏgĕda sutaśokadind' āvagĕyant' ŏḷag' uriyĕ bhoṅkan' ĕrdĕ tĕṟĕyal hā magane ĕnd' aśrujalārdragaṇḍan ā gaṇḍin' ŏḍanĕ bisuṭaṃ billaṃ* || *VAV* 12.28 ||

> As sadness for his son sprung up,
> His mind burned, rapidly, like a potter's kiln,
> And his heart burst.
> Saying, "Oh, my son!"
> Droṇa, eyes wet with tears,
> Threw down his bow, along with his virility.

The term *gaṇḍu* (*gaṇḍina,* gen.) denotes not only strength and bravery, but also masculinity.

20. *VAV* 12.28V.

21. *VAV* 12.29.

> But these *clichés* are now false!
> He lied and at that moment killed Droṇa,
> Our archery master, *guru*, and a *brāhmaṇa*.
> It is said that "lying is the greatest offense,"
> So is Yudhiṣṭhira then not a sinner?[22]

In order to lay stress upon the import of Yudhiṣṭhira's lie to the ensuing narrative, Duryodhana begins by detailing his reputation through a series of epithets. Truthful, dharmic, and compassionate, Yudhiṣṭhira's former image is now nothing but a façade (*pusi*).

After examining Yudhiṣṭhira's public persona, Duryodhana describes the devastating results of his lie. He positions two very important phrases together: *todaḷ nuḍidu* and *kond' āgaḷ*. The former means: [Yudhiṣṭhira] told (*nuḍidu*) a lie (*todaḷ*); the latter: and at that moment killed him (Droṇa). Through the ordering of these phrases, Duryodhana creates a causal relationship between these two acts: Yudhiṣṭhira tells a lie and, as a result, Droṇa is killed. Duryodhana also notes that killing Droṇa is not the same as killing another *kṣatriya*. Droṇa is the *guru*, or teacher, of the Pāṇḍavas; he is also a *brāhmaṇa*. Therefore, Yudhiṣṭhira is liable for three crimes. Not only did he lie—the lesser offense—but he slayed his own *guru* and killed a *brāhmaṇa*.[23]

After outlining Yudhiṣṭhira's transgressions, Duryodhana turns to the exact details of the lie that killed Droṇa.

> Is it right for him to say, "Aśvatthāman has been slain"?
> Will he say, ". . . the big elephant,"
> At the time when Droṇa is going to Yama's city,
> Just for the sake of pleasing people?
> There is no knowing Dharma's son.[24]

---

22. *sthirasatyavratiy ĕndu dharmaruciy ĕnd' ā dharmaputran dayā-*
paran ĕnd' ĕllara peḻda mātu pusiy āyt' ī kārmukācāryanaṃ
guruvaṃ brāhmaṇanaṃ tŏdaḷnuḍidu kŏnd' āgaḷ mṛṣāpātakaṃ
param ĕṃb' ī nuḍiyiṃ pṛthāpriyasutan pāpakkĕ pakk' āgane || *SBhV* 3.23 ||

23. This stanza overstates the severity of Yudhiṣṭhira's falsehood, referring to it as the worst crime, while, in reality, the crime of killing a *brāhmaṇa* is far graver.

24. *tanagĕ hato śvatthāmo*
yĕnal akkumĕ yamapurakkĕ guru pop' ĕḍĕyŏḷ

In this stanza, Duryodhana focuses on Yudhiṣṭhira's lie about the dead elephant. The narrative details concerning what and when Yudhiṣṭhira tells Droṇa about his "dead son" differ from those that appear in the Sanskrit *MBh* and Pampa's *VAV*. In the *SBhV*, Yudhiṣṭhira neither mumbles (as he does in the Sanskrit *MBh*) nor tells the truth (as he does in the *VAV*). According to Duryodhana, Yudhiṣṭhira lies outright: he never even breathes the word *kuñjara* (elephant) to Droṇa. After quoting Yudhiṣṭhira (*hato 'śvatthāmo*), who, curiously, speaks in ungrammatical Sanskrit, not Kannada, Duryodhana queries: when and for what purpose will Yudhiṣṭhira admit that only an elephant has died? Speaking in a hypothetical future tense (signified by *ĕṅgumĕ*), he speculates that Yudhiṣṭhira will dare to finish that sentence only once Droṇa has safely reached the realm of Yama (that is, death), because the eldest Pāṇḍava is concerned only with his precious reputation as a truth teller. In the final line of the above verse, Duryodhana tells Sañjaya that Yudhiṣṭhira is truly an enigma. He is the son of the god Dharma, but lies to his *guru*'s face in order to trick him into leaving the war—a decidedly non-dharmic act.

Duryodhana then debates with Sañjaya about the possible reasons that Droṇa chooses to give up his life. He says:

> His weapons tossed aside,
> Droṇa went to the netherworld in order to confront Dharma:
> "Look! Even Yudhiṣṭhira,
> The so-called '*son of Dharma,*' is a liar!"
> Or, do you, actually, think Droṇa went there to find his son?[25]

Here, Duryodhana imagines two reasons behind Droṇa's choice to die. One option is that he dies in order to tell Dharma, Yudhiṣṭhira's divine father, that his son lied. The other is that he went to the afterlife in order to find his own son. It might seem like an obvious choice that Droṇa, as a father who is devastated by the death of his son, would choose death in order to

---

ghanakuñjaran ĕnd' ĕṅgumĕ
janarañjanĕg' ar̲iyal ādudill' ar̲amaganaṃ || *SBhV* 3.24 ||

25. *ī dŏrĕy ar̲amaganuṃ mṛṣa-*
vādaṃ noḍ' ĕndu dharmanaṃ mūdalisal
podan putranan ar̲asal
podanĕ yamapurakĕ muktabāṇaṃ droṇaṃ || *SBhV* 3.25 ||

reunite with Aśvatthāman. Duryodhana's language and tone, however, present an altogether different opinion. As he sees it, Droṇa dies not as a grieving father, but as a warrior intent upon upholding a correct dharma. Duryodhana expresses the first option, that is, that Droṇa chooses to die because he wants to confront the god Dharma, as a statement of fact: "he went to confront Dharma (*dharmanaṃ mūḍalisal podan*)." The second option, on the other hand, comes across as if it were an afterthought. Here, Duryodhana speaks with hesitation, as is indicated by the interrogative particle, "*ĕ*," which is affixed onto the verb (*podanĕ*). By adding this particle, Duryodhana questions the assumption that Droṇa threw down his weapons and gave up his life because of Aśvatthāman's death. Instead, he privileges the alternate narrative—a narrative that does not feature Aśvatthāman at all. It is a story about dharma and the choice of Dharma's son, Yudhiṣṭhira, to discard it.

The next stanza concludes Duryodhana's interpretation of Yudhiṣṭhira's role in the death of Droṇa. Thus far, he has argued that Yudhiṣṭhira is nothing but a liar who falsified Aśvatthāman's death in order to deprive his former teacher of his will to fight. Now, Duryodhana looks beyond Yudhiṣṭhira's bad conduct and considers his inappropriate epithet, "the son of Dharma."

> That wicked man, who caused Droṇa to be killed,
> Is none other than Dharma's son.
> But it is like how calling Tuesday "auspicious day" and Saturday "great day"
> Causes the names of the inauspicious days of the week to be forgotten.[26]

In the two earlier stanzas, Duryodhana refers to Yudhiṣṭhira as *aṟamagan* (an Old Kannada equivalent of *dharmaputra*, "the son of Dharma").[27] In

26. *kaḷaśajanan intu kŏlisida*
khaḷanĕ gaḍaṃ dharmanandanaṃ krūradinaṅ-
gaḷa pĕsaraṃ maṟĕyisi maṅ
gaḷavāraṃ vaḍḍavāram ĕṃbantĕ valaṃ || *SBhV* 3.26 ||

Here I follow D. L. Narasimhacar's decision to emend *kaḍḍavāra* (*kaṣṭavāra*) to the variant reading *vaḍḍavāra* (*vṛddhavāra*). *Vaḍḍavāra* is another name used for Saturday (*śanivāra*) in South Indian epigraphy, and it bolsters Duryodhana's argument about using overly auspicious names for inauspicious things. See "Gadāyuddhada Ŏndu Padyada Arthavicāra," in *Pīṭhakĕgaḷu, Lekhanagaḷu*, ed. D. L. Narasimhacar (Mysore: D. V. K. Murthy Prakashan, 2015), 929–33.

27. *SBhV* 3.24–25.

this stanza, Duryodhana notes that bearing a title like the "son of Dharma" masks Yudhiṣṭhira's true nature. Despite Yudhiṣṭhira's ambiguous character, Duryodhana spells out one thing clearly: Yudhiṣṭhira may not have delivered the final blow to Droṇa, but he caused it. Duryodhana's employment of the causative participle *kŏlisida* (to cause someone to be killed) in the first line of this stanza makes the point straightforwardly. In these concluding thoughts, Duryodhana reaffirms his belief about Yudhiṣṭhira's central role in Droṇa's death: to him, the name *Dharmanandana* (son of Dharma) does not suit a man who betrays his *guru*.

Over the past few stanzas, one of the key details of this narrative has remained unstated: who actually murdered Droṇa? In the stanza below, Duryodhana adds another plot twist to his revisionist telling of Droṇa's death. He declares that Arjuna slew his former teacher.

> Arjuna, Indra's son, killed Droṇa,
> His *guru* and a *brāhmaṇa*.
> A man who was weaponless and
> Consumed by fire—the separation from his son.
> But was it just the crime of murdering his teacher
> That caused Arjuna's reputation to be destroyed?[28]

Arjuna's part in Droṇa's death represents a truly new take on this famous episode. In both the *MBh* and *VAV*, it is Dhṛṣṭadyumna, Drupada's son, who beheads Droṇa while he is sitting in meditation, not Arjuna. I disagree with the noted Kannada philologist T. N. Srikanthayya when he argues that Duryodhana merely superimposes Dhṛṣṭadyumna's actions upon Arjuna.[29] On the contrary, Duryodhana does not simply substitute Arjuna for Dhṛṣṭadyumna, since Duryodhana still holds Drupada's son responsible in some capacity. In the *SBhV*'s fourth *canto*, when Duryodhana sees Droṇa's corpse, he describes Arjuna as his teacher's killer and Dhṛṣṭadyumna as the

28. *guruvaṃ dvijanmanaṃ suta-*
virahāgnigrastanaṃ nirāyudhanaṃ saṃ-
harisida śakrasutaṅg' ā
guruvadhamĕ yaśovadhakkĕ kāraṇam alte || *SBhV* 3.31 ||

29. Ranna, *Gadāyuddhasaṅgraha*, ed. T. N. Srikanthayya (Bangalore: Vasantha Prakashana, 2015), 95.

one who desecrated his body after death.[30] Furthermore, this account of events appears to be unique to Duryodhana because no other character in the *SBhV* knows it. The question remains: why make Arjuna Droṇa's killer?

I argue that Duryodhana's reinterpretation of this part of the episode ultimately keeps Droṇa's death "in the family." In Duryodhana's understanding, there are no interventions made by anyone other than the Pāṇḍavas. Those brothers alone are accountable for their actions. This alteration underscores Duryodhana's larger argument that the Pāṇḍavas are willing to transgress any and all notions of *kṣatriya* dharma. In his extended description of Droṇa's state at the time of his death, Duryodhana demonstrates how far Arjuna is willing to go in order to defeat the Kauravas. Duryodhana attributes four transgressions to him.[31] In the above stanza, four adjectives qualify Droṇa: *guru* (teacher), *dvija* (*brāhmaṇa*), *nirāyudha* (weaponless), and *sutavirahāgnigrastana* (consumed by fire that is separation from his son). Duryodhana uses each of these adjectives to describe Arjuna's three other breaches of *kṣatriya* dharma. By killing Droṇa, Arjuna is, by default, guilty of murdering a *brāhmaṇa* (*brahmahatyā*), attacking a man who is weaponless, and killing a man who appears to be afflicted or pained by something (*ārtaṃ*).[32] To these accusations Duryodhana adds another: *guruvadha* (slaying one's teacher). And yet, in Duryodhana's account, the

30. *adaṭina pārthan ĕccu kŏlĕ jātabalaṃ drupadātmajātan o-*
vadĕ puḍiyŏḷ pŏraḷci talĕyaṃ tĕgĕvalli pinākav' ĕttavo-
dudŏ śarav' ĕttavodudŏ lalāṭadin iṅgaḷagaṇṇad' ĕttavo-
dudŏ gurusūnu tānum aṇam amman' alaṃpum ad' ĕttavodudo || *SBhV* 4.51 ||
When mighty Arjuna shot and killed [Droṇa], and strong Dhṛṣṭadyumna,
Cruelly, caused him to roll on the ground and cut off his head,
Where did your bow, *Pināka,* go? Where were your arrows?
Where was the fiery eye on your forehead? Aśvatthāman, where did your love for your father go?

31. Subraya Bhaṭ's analysis of this stanza differs from my own. He contends that Arjuna is guilty of only three offenses (slaying one's guru, a *brāhmaṇa*, and a weaponless person). See *Gadāyuddhadarpaṇa* (Kasaragodu: Subraya Bhaṭ, 1975), 100.

32. "He must never slay . . . a sleeping man, a man without his armor, a naked man, a man without his weapons, a non-fighting spectator, a man engaging with someone else, a man with damaged weapons, a man in distress, a badly wounded man, a frightened man, or a man who has turned tail—recalling the Law followed by good people." *Manusmṛti* vv.7.91–93. See *Manu's Code of Law: A Critical Edition and Translation of the Mānava-Dharmaśāstra*, ed. and trans. Patrick Olivelle (New York: Oxford University Press, 2005), 159.

severity of these violations does not seem to stop Arjuna from finishing the job that Yudhiṣṭhira started.

The death of Droṇa is the first of several episodes that Duryodhana employs to describe how the Pāṇḍavas infringe upon dharma. His narration highlights Yudhiṣṭhira and Arjuna's willingness to transgress any and all rules of proper conduct in order to win the war. In this manner, Duryodhana is able to weave a new interpretation of this episode that holds the Pāṇḍavas solely accountable for their own actions. There is no "greater good" that divine agents (such as Kṛṣṇa or even the Pāṇḍavas, with their divine fathers) must uphold through nefarious means. Rather, Duryodhana builds a narrative in which the Pāṇḍavas have completely abandoned dharma.

Bhīma's Heroic "Triumphs"

Without stopping for a breath after detailing Yudhiṣṭhira's role in Droṇa's death, Duryodhana continues down the Pāṇḍava line and reflects on the second eldest Pāṇḍava, Bhīma. When he takes Bhīma's *kṣatriya* conduct into consideration, Duryodhana juxtaposes Bhīma's multiple heroic failures with his one so-called victory: the massacre of Duryodhana's younger brothers. The Kaurava king calls attention to Bhīma's inconsistency as a *kṣatriya* and the monstrous tactics that Bhīma employs to compensate for it. He says:

> Bhīma did not become a hero
> When my brother Duḥśāsana pulled Draupadī's hair there in the court;
> Nor when Supratīka, Bhagadatta's elephant, pressed down upon him until his rib broke;
> And certainly not when Karṇa choked him out with just his bow, not wanting to kill him;
> So did Bhīma then become a hero just by murdering Kaurava children!?[33]

In this stanza, Duryodhana characterizes Bhīma's conduct by recalling four vignettes: Draupadī's assault in the Kaurava court; Bhīma's battle with

33. *vanitĕya keśamaṃ sabhĕyoḷ ĕnn' anujaṃ tĕgĕvalli gaṇḍan ā-*
ganĕ bhagadattan' ānĕ bariyĕlvuḍivannĕgam ŏttĕ gaṇḍan ā-
ganĕ kŏlal ŏllad' aṅgapati billŏḷĕ kŏṇḍĕḻĕvalli gaṇḍan ā-
ganĕ kurubālasaṃharaṇamātradĕ māruti gaṇḍan ādane || *SBhV* 3.27 ||

Bhagadatta's elephant, Supratīka; his duel with Karṇa; and the slaughter of Duryodhana's younger brothers. In each of these illustrations, Duryodhana recalls a moment in which Bhīma fails to uphold his duty as a *kṣatriya*. The first three lines are nearly identical in terms of their construction: each contains a dependent and independent clause. The former tells the actual episode and the latter houses a "refrain" found at the end of each line: "he certainly did not become a hero (*gaṇḍan āganĕ*)." This independent clause contains the finite verb, suffixed with an emphatic particle (*ĕ*), for each story: *āgan* (3rd p. sing. neg. *āgu*-to become). In the fourth line, however, this pattern is broken and the tone changes. Duryodhana switches from negative to affirmative and his choice of particle goes from emphatic to interrogative.

The first story, Draupadī's molestation at the hands of Duḥśāsana during the dice match, is arguably the incident that incites the whole war.[34] During the ill-fated dice match against the Kauravas, Yudhiṣṭhira foolishly gambles away his kingdom, his brothers, and eventually his wife. At the command of Duryodhana, Duḥśāsana drags a menstruating Draupadī by the hair in front of the entire court. A debate then ensues about the legality of Yudhiṣṭhira's wager, and Bhīma vows to avenge his wife. Draupadī's molestation is a scene that haunts the *SBhV*, lurking in the narrative's background. But this stanza is, in fact, the first time that Duryodhana directly reflects upon the episode. His version of events stands in stark contrast to the two earlier renditions by Bhīma[35] and Sañjaya,[36] both of which focus on Yudhiṣṭhira's perceived indifference to the ordeal and the reactions of anger and shame of all who witnessed it, Kaurava and Pāṇḍava alike. When Duryodhana tells the story, he lacks interest in the violent, sexually aggressive nature of Duḥśāsana's act. He neither censures his brother's actions nor praises them. For Duryodhana, only Bhīma's inaction is really worthy of note. Though earlier tellings of this episode in the *SBhV* highlight Bhīma's outrage, the present stanza calls into question whether or not Bhīma actually did anything to protest his wife's assault. In this respect, Duryodhana's eyewitness account flies in the face of the earlier versions of the story. As

34. For other tellings of Draupadī's assault, see *MBh* 2.60–61 and *VAV* 7.1–15.

35. *SBhV* 1.59.

36. *SBhV* 3.22.

Duryodhana tells it, Bhīma is guilty of idly standing by during the attack. Furthermore, Duryodhana makes no acknowledgment of Bhīma's famous vows to avenge Draupadī. Just a few lines later, he elaborates further on the event: it is not only Bhīma, but the whole Pāṇḍava brood who failed to do anything at that occasion. He says, "While my younger brother Duḥśāsana beat Pāñcāla's daughter, Draupadī, the beloved of those five men, there in the court, before their eyes, those 'valorous' men stared in awe."[37] For Duryodhana, Bhīma and the Pāṇḍavas are silent observers who failed to act according to dharma and protect their queen when she needed it most.

In the second line, Duryodhana turns to Bhīma's wartime record, recalling his fight with Supratīka, the war elephant of Bhagadatta, the king of Prāgjyotiṣa.[38] Duryodhana now offers a counter-narrative to Sañjaya's earlier praise of Bhīma's prowess on the battlefield and especially his history of fighting war elephants. In describing Bhīma's battle with Supratīka, Duryodhana amplifies how Bhīma falls victim to the elephant's great strength and size, noting that the animal pushes down (*ŏttĕ*) hard upon Bhīma's ribs (*bariyĕlvu*) until they break (*uḍivannĕgam*). Interestingly, this detail occurs in neither the *MBh* nor the *VAV*. Perhaps, by drawing attention to the elephant's physical power over Bhīma, Duryodhana's statement suggests a narrative detail that is common to other tellings: in other accounts, Bhīma is unable to defeat Supratīka or Bhagadatta; his younger brother, Arjuna, has to save him. With each example, Duryodhana methodically picks apart Bhīma's façade as a mighty warrior.

In the stanza's next line, Duryodhana mentions another fight in which Bhīma fails to prove himself.[39] Shortly after his battle with Supratīka, Bhīma squares off against Karṇa in a duel.[40] In both the *MBh* and the *VAV*, Karṇa defeats Bhīma in battle, but Karṇa also remembers the vow he made to Kuntī not to slay his brothers (other than Arjuna) and refuses to kill Bhīma. In

37. *sabhĕyŏḷ tammaya pakkad' ĕnn' anujan ā pāñcāliyaṃ pañcava-llabhĕyaṃ modĕyum alli miḷmiḷanĕ noḍuttirda ballāḷgaḷ* || *SBhV* 3.36 ab ||

38. For other tellings of the fight with Supratīka, see *MBh* 7.25–28 and *VAV* 11.68V–75.

39. *SBhV* 3.27.

40. For other tellings of Bhīma's duel with Karṇa, see *MBh* 7.106–114 and *VAV* 11.142V–144.

the *SBhV*, however, Karṇa makes a slightly different decision. According to Duryodhana, Karṇa defeats Bhīma and has the opportunity to kill him, but ultimately decides that he does not want to do so (*kŏllal ŏlladĕ*). He simply chokes Bhīma with his bow. It is noteworthy that Duryodhana completely elides Karṇa's vow to Kuntī. Rather than imagining Karṇa begrudgingly upholding an old promise, Duryodhana depicts Karṇa humiliating Bhīma by sparing him. Karṇa deprives the Pāṇḍava of a death in battle, the highest achievement for any *kṣatriya*.[41]

Reaching the final line of the quatrain, Duryodhana still doubts Bhīma's status as a formidable hero (*gaṇḍan*), adopting an incredulous tone. Of all of Bhīma's supposed heroisms, Duryodhana gives the most adharmic one: he killed all of the Kaurava children! "Can Bhīma be considered a hero (*gaṇḍan ādan-e*) for this?" Duryodhana asks. Over the course of the war, Bhīma kills all of Duryodhana's younger brothers. At this point in the narrative, Duryodhana is the very last of the Kauravas still standing. Careful in his choice of words, he refers to his brothers as *bāla*, or children. In the same way that Duryodhana accused Yudhiṣṭhira and Arjuna of *brahmahatyā*, Duryodhana, here, accuses Bhīma not only of killing his brothers, but also of doing so when they were but children. He ultimately argues that Bhīma is so incapable as a *kṣatriya* male that he has to stoop to infanticide to gain any repute.

Wrestling Gone Wrong: A New Winner in the *Kirātārjunīya*

The next event that Duryodhana narrates, and the final episode that I will examine, takes place long before the war. This stanza concerns one of Arjuna's exploits during the Pāṇḍavas' exile.[42] It addresses Arjuna's wrestling match with the deity Śiva, who disguises himself as a mountain man, or

41. The honor that attends death in battle is constantly alluded to in the *MBh*, *VAV*, and *SBhV*. One also finds references to its importance in *dharmaśāstras*, such as the *Manusmṛti*: "When kings fight each other in battles with all their strength, seeking to kill each other and refusing to turn back, they go to heaven" (v.7.89). See *Manu's Code of Law,* 159.

42. *SBhV* 3.39.

kirāta.[43] Before turning to Duryodhana's unique take on this narrative, I want briefly to contextualize this famous story within the larger epic tradition. As the story goes in the Sanskrit *MBh*, Arjuna's brothers send him on a mission to acquire divine weapons that the Pāṇḍavas can use to reassert their claim to the kingdom. Arjuna goes to Mount Indrakīla, where he meets Indra in the guise of an ascetic. After testing Arjuna, Indra offers him a boon and the Pāṇḍava requests divine weapons. Indra tells him that he will receive them after his encounter with Śiva. Arjuna then performs *tapas* (acts of asceticism, penance) on the mountain. While there, he gets into an argument with a local hunter, the *kirāta* (who is actually Śiva in disguise). Both hunting the same boar, they disagree on who shot it first. A wrestling match ensues and Arjuna is defeated.[44] In a moment of realization, Arjuna sees Śiva for who he really is and honors him.[45] Praising Arjuna's heroism, Śiva then awards him the *pāśupata* weapon.[46] In Pampa's *VAV*, the fight unravels in a slightly different manner. Arjuna actually wins the wrestling match by throwing Śiva onto the ground and stepping on his neck.[47] It is only after Arjuna has physically bested him that Śiva reveals his third eye and his divine form.[48] This vision, in turn, inspires Arjuna to surrender himself to God. The deity then awards Arjuna the *pāśupata* weapon[49] and Śiva's wife Pārvatī gives him the *añjarika* weapon.[50] Both of these tellings highlight Arjuna's prowess as a warrior who is both capable of fighting honorably and humbling himself before God.[51]

---

43. For Arjuna's wrestling match with Śiva, see *MBh* 3.40–41; and *VAV* 8.16V–8.27.

44. *MBh* 3.40.50–51.

45. *MBh* 3.40.55–60.

46. *MBh* 3.41.13–16.

47. *VAV* 8.22–22V.

48. *VAV* 8.23–24.

49. *VAV* 8.25V–26.

50. *VAV* 8.26V.

51. Bhāravi's Sanskrit *mahākāvya*, the *Kirātārjunīya* ("Arjuna and the Hunter," ca. sixth century), also tells the story of Arjuna's wrestling match with Śiva. At the fight's climax, in the eighteenth *sarga* (canto) of Bhāravi's work, Śiva rewards Arjuna's martial prowess with a vision of his divine form. Arjuna proceeds to bow before his opponent and then sings a series of *stotra*s (hymns) in his honor. After Arjuna begs for Śiva forgiveness, the god instructs him in the ways of the *pāśupata* weapon.

In the *SBhV*, Duryodhana's version of the wrestling match paints an altogether different picture of Arjuna. Duryodhana deploys this episode in order to foreground Arjuna's brutish behavior. He recalls:

> At first, when Arjuna continuously propitiated him,
> Śiva would not give it.
> But afterward, when Arjuna trod on his throat,
> Śiva, who was in a difficult position,
> Gave the *pāśupata* weapon to him,
> As if conceding victory.[52]

As we can see, Duryodhana's narrative is barebones: Arjuna performs *tapas* in honor of Śiva, but unsuccessfully; as a result, Śiva refuses to grant him divine weapons. Arjuna then responds violently and receives the weapons as a sign of Śiva's surrender. Skipping from *tapas* to Arjuna's victory over Śiva cuts out quite a few plot points. Duryodhana jumps over large parts of the narrative, like Arjuna's initial disagreement with the *kirāta* and the subsequent wrestling match. The fact that Duryodhana does not actually make reference to Śiva's guise as a *kirāta* is perhaps the most jarring divergence. According to the Kaurava king, Arjuna does not fight another hunter (who then happens to be Śiva). Rather, he knowingly fights Śiva and forces him to submit in order to earn the divine weapons.

These are not the only emendations in Duryodhana's story. Surrender to God is a key aspect of the other *kirāta* narratives. In the MBh, Śiva, upon defeating Arjuna, rewards him with a vision of his true form. Falling before the god, Arjuna propitiates him and is given the *pāśupata* weapon for his unflinching heroism.[53] As previously noted, in the *VAV*, Arjuna becomes acutely aware that the *kirāta* is Śiva at the very moment he steps on Śiva's neck. He first surrenders, bowing and saluting Śiva with reverence.

---

52. *biḍad' ārādhisĕ munnamĕ*
kuḍal āṟadĕ baḻikĕ gaṇṭalaṃ mĕṭṭidŏḍ'
iṭṭ' ĕḍĕyŏḷ kŏṭṭaṃ gĕllaṃ-
guḍuvantĕ naraṅgĕ pāśupatamaṃ rudraṃ || *SBhV* 3.39 ||

53. For further discussion of this episode in both the *MBh* and Bhāravi's *Kirātārjunīya*, see Indira Viswanathan Peterson, *Design and Rhetoric in a Sanskrit Court Epic: The Kirātārjunīya of Bhāravi* (Albany: State University of New York Press, 2003), 167–78.

He then asks him what he can do to make up for his transgression. As a result, Śiva rewards him for both his heroism in hand-to-hand combat (*parākrama*) and his restraint (*vinaya*) afterwards. In Duryodhana's account of the event in the *SBhV*, Arjuna experiences neither a moment of revelation nor subsequent remorse. Instead, it is Śiva who surrenders to Arjuna, giving up the *pāśupata* weapon. In telling the story this way, Duryodhana inverts the traditional themes of surrender and devotion; the inversion amplifies Arjuna's ruthlessness. Situated near the end of his discussion of *kṣatriya* dharma, Duryodhana, in this stanza, argues that Arjuna will stop at nothing to win, even when he fights against God.

Conclusion: A Different Dharma

As his speech goes on, Duryodhana starts to draw conclusions about the Pāṇḍavas that drastically affect his behavior in the *SBhV*'s remaining narrative. If the Pāṇḍavas continually fight without any sense of honor and refuse to act in ways that accord to their *kṣatriya* status, the question begs to be asked: what are they?

To sum up, I argue that Duryodhana in his first major speech of the *SBhV* presents a radical reinterpretation of the Mahābhārata. Duryodhana's retelling of key episodes from the epic draws out the Pāṇḍava's repeated transgression of dharma, tracing their lapsed conduct from the dice match up through the war. The Kaurava king interprets their actions through the lens of *kṣatriya* dharma, and as a result, comes to see them as warriors without a moral code to guide them. This interpretation of the Pāṇḍavas' actions sets up the narrative's major conflict and presents Duryodhana's solution: the Pāṇḍavas, who eschew dharmic norms, must be defeated. Duryodhana, the last Kaurava on the battlefield, will continue to fight them in order to uphold dharma. He calls on us readers to reassess the deteriorating *kṣatriya* ethics of his enemies:

Heroism
Lied and killed Droṇa,
Who had already laid down his bow;
Might
Angrily took aim and shot Bhīṣma,
Who had fallen upon a bed of arrows;

Valor
　　Shot and decapitated Karṇa,
　　Without considering that he had no chariot, bowstring or weapons;
Those are the qualities the Pāṇḍavas certainly are capable of displaying.
But am I, despite my own wealth of violence?[54]

54. *guruvaṃ projjhitacāpanaṃ pusidu kŏnd' ā bīramaṃ bhīṣmaraṃ śaraśayyāgataraṃ kaṟuttu guṟiyĕcc' ā pŏccaṟaṃ karṇanaṃ virathajyāyudhan ĕnnad' ĕccu talĕgŏṇḍ' ā śauryamaṃ pāṇḍuputrarĕ ballar mĕṟĕyalkĕ sāhasadhanaṃ duryodhanaṃ ballane* || *SBhV* 3.33 ||

Chapter Ten

Three Poets, Two Languages, One Translation

The Evolution of the Telugu *Mahābhāratamu*[1]

Harshita Mruthinti Kamath

The history of Telugu literature begins with the Mahābhārata. Composed by three poets later known as the *kavitrayamu* (Trinity of Poets)—Nannaya, Tikkana, and Ĕṛṛāpragaḍa—over the course of four centuries in the early second millennium, the Telugu *Mahābhāratamu* marks the entry of Telugu language into the literary sphere. Even prior to its completion by these three poets, the *Mahābhāratamu* immediately usurped its Sanskrit counterpart to occupy center stage in the Telugu literary imagination. As it was composed by the *kavitrayamu,* the *Mahābhāratamu* represents a breadth of possibility for the Mahābhārata: it reflects explicitly on the Sanskrit epic and, at the same time, lays the foundation for a distinctly Telugu mode of literary expression. My study of the *Mahābhāratamu* shows

1. Thanks to Karri Ramachandra Reddy for reading the Telugu *Mahābhāratamu* with me in the summer of 2017. Thanks also to Velcheru Narayana Rao, Nell Shapiro Hawley, Sohini Sarah Pillai, Anne Monius, and the attendees of the "Many Mahābhāratas" Symposium at the Annual Conference on South Asia in October 2017 for their feedback on this chapter.

that the evolution of the Mahābhārata epic from Sanskrit to the vernacular was far from straightforward; rather, the *Mahābhāratamu* embodies a dynamic relationship between Sanskrit and Telugu soundscapes, prosody, characterization, and style.

This chapter explores the contours of vernacularization in the Telugu *Mahābhāratamu* by reading closely from sections of the text that each of its three authors composed. At the beginning of the essay, I show how the first verse in Nannaya's *Mahābhāratamu* makes use of Sanskrit—not Telugu—poetics when it introduces the Mahābhārata into Telugu literature. Nannaya also inaugurates unique metrical and poetic conventions in his *Mahābhāratamu* that are adopted by Telugu poets centuries after his composition. I then argue that Tikkana, the second of the three poets, articulates a distinctively Telugu mode for the Mahābhārata by fundamentally altering the poetic soundscape of the text, reshaping the expressivity of its central characters, and lending performative elements that are exclusive to the Telugu vernacular. Finally, I demonstrate that Ĕṟṟāpragaḍa (more commonly known as Ĕṟṟana), the third poet, reasserts the value of the Sanskrit *Mahābhārata* and its moral paradigms into the expanding world of Telugu literature.

Before turning to Telugu *Mahābhāratamu* in detail, it is important to identify the distinctions and similarities across Telugu and Sanskrit literary realms. Telugu arises from a class of Dravidian languages in South India and dates to the first millenium CE in inscriptional sources.[2] Sanskrit, by contrast, belongs to the Indo-European family of languages and is the oldest literary language in South Asia. Sanskrit has long been considered the most powerful language of the South Asian arena, extending across vast domains of poetic and discursive literature. The very name of Sanskrit seeks to convey its intellectual prowess: *saṃskṛta* means "perfectly executed" and the language is often called *devavāṇī,* or the language of the gods. The distinction of Sanskrit and the vernacular must be situated against the backdrop of Sheldon Pollock's influential study of the Sanskrit cosmopolis and the cosmopolitan vernacular.[3] Pollock argues that the second millennium gave rise to a host of written, literary vernacular languages—including Telugu, Kannada, and Marathi—that grew to replace

2. Velcheru Narayana Rao and David Shulman, *Classical Telugu Poetry: An Anthology* (Berkeley: University of California Press, 2002), 2. See also Sheldon Pollock, *The Language of the Gods in the World of Men: Sanskrit, Culture and Power in Premodern India* (Berkeley: University of California Press, 2006), 289.

3. Pollock, 381.

Sanskrit in regional courtly settings and yet were modeled on the norms of Sanskrit poetry.[4] This period of the second millennium is what Pollock characterizes as the "cosmopolitan vernacular," which represents an era in which poetry (*kāvya*) and kingship (*rājya*) combined within the context of the court. Power, for Pollock, is expressed both through Sanskrit courtly literatures and also through later "classical" vernacular poetry that mirrors Sanskrit literary aesthetics.[5]

Telugu literature reflects this shifting of power from Sanskrit *kāvya* to the cosmopolitan vernacular, particularly through the genres of *mārga* and *deśī.* As Velcheru Narayana Rao writes: "To have any status as a literary language, [Telugu] needed the support of Sanskrit. If Sanskrit is the *mārga,* the 'path,' Telugu could only hope to be *deśī,* 'local' or 'regional,' if it did its job right."[6] The analogy, however, is not simply that Telugu is to Sanskrit as *deśī* is to *mārga.* Telugu court poetry, including the *kavitrayamu*'s Telugu *Mahābhāratamu,* fits within the broader genre of *mārga*, which is a term that can broadly refer to classical Telugu poetry. By contrast, poetic works composed in couplets (*dvipada*), such as the writings of thirteenth-century Śaiva poet Pālkuriki Somanātha, are designated as *deśī.*[7]

Mārga poetry, beginning with Nannaya's Telugu *Mahābhāratamu,* reflects the shift from Sanskrit *kāvya* to the cosmopolitan vernacular. In many *mārga* Telugu texts, spanning from Telugu *Mahābhāratamu* to the sixteenth-century *mahāprabandha*s of the Vijayanagara period, it is difficult to determine where a Sanskrit word ends and a Telugu one begins. As Narayana Rao and David Shulman observe, "Telugu must have swallowed Sanskrit whole, as it were, even before Nannaya. . . . [Every] Sanskrit word is potentially a Telugu word as well, and literary texts in Telugu may be lexically Sanskrit or Sanskritized to an enormous degree, perhaps sixty percent or more."[8] Many Telugu words are formed by taking a Sanskrit word

4. Pollock, 283–329.

5. Pollock, 6.

6. Velcheru Narayana Rao, "Coconut and Honey: Sanskrit and Telugu in Medieval Andhra," in *Text and Tradition in South India* (Ranikhet: Permanent Black, 2016), 158.

7. Narayana Rao, 157–59. Pingala Lakshmikantham characterizes *mārga* as "classical" and *deśī* as "vernacular." See *Āndhra Sāhitya Caritra* (Hyderabad: Andhra Pradesh Sahitya Academy, 1974), 33.

8. Narayana Rao and Shulman, *Classical Telugu Poetry*, 3.

and then adding a Telugu case-ending, such as *-ḍu, -mu, -vu,* or *-lu*. But the relationship between Sanskrit and Telugu is an uneasy one. According to one legend, when the fourteenth-century poet Śrīnāthuḍu showed his Telugu translation of Śrīharṣa's Sanskrit *Naiṣadhīyacarita* (which itself is a Mahābhārata retelling), to a group of Sanskrit *paṇḍitas* (learned people), they exclaimed: "Take your Telugu case-endings—*ḍu*, *mu*, *vu*, and *lu*—and give our Sanskrit text back to us."[9]

Despite such views, and despite the ostensible overlap between Telugu and Sanskrit, it would be a mistake to characterize Telugu as derivative of or secondary to Sanskrit. In fact, it is only when Telugu breaks away from Sanskrit's poetic constraints that we find an entirely unique vernacular soundscape, one that belies the simplicity of a straightforward trajectory from the Sanskrit cosmopolis to the cosmopolitan vernacular. This "breakthrough into full performance," to borrow the language of Dell Hymes, presents an alternative configuration not only of poetry but also the power of language.[10] In order fully to examine power and its relationship to the vernacular, we must look beyond the sphere of Sanskrit poetry and kingship and direct our attention to more minute expressions of power—what Michel Foucault terms the "polymorphous techniques of power."[11] Power does not simply flow from Sanskrit to the vernacular; rather, it manifests through the textures of the vernacular, which is to say that the recited word, the mimetic gesture, or even the silent caesura in a verse can express power in a Telugu medium. In what follows, I foreground the oral-performative dimensions of Telugu *Mahābhāratamu* in order to trace the emergence of the vernacular and its relationship with Sanskrit.

Telugu *Mahābhāratamu*

The Sanskrit *Mahābhārata* is considered a dangerous narrative in the Telugu literary imagination. In fact, as Narayana Rao notes, "the text was

9. Narayana Rao and Shulman, 27.

10. Dell Hymes, *Breakthrough into Performance* (Rimini: Guaraldi, 2015), 31.

11. Michel Foucault, *The History of Sexuality*, vol. 1, *An Introduction,* trans. Robert Hurley (New York: Vintage Books, 1990), 11.

felt to generate a disturbing power (*ōjas*) that needed to be brought under control through appropriate rituals of pacification."[12] Telugu people long believed that the Sanskrit epic should not be read inside the home nor be read from beginning to end; the reader who breaks this convention risks death. This lingering feeling of superstition extends across India; as Shulman observes, the Mahābhārata "is not recited (or even stored) inside a house, lest it consume the building and its inhabitants; one reads it outside, on the porch—and even then not from beginning to end, since that progression, too, is felt to be potentially disastrous."[13]

Nannaya, a *brāhmaṇa* writing in the eleventh-century Cāḷukya court of King Rājarājanarendra, is said to have died midway through his composition because he flouted this taboo and sought to translate the text from beginning to end.[14] Nannaya completed a Telugu retelling of only the first two and a half books of the Sanskrit *Mahābhārata,* leaving the latter half of the *Āraṇyaparvamu* ("The Book of the Forest," his translation of the Sanskrit epic's third book, the *Āraṇyakaparvan*) unfinished. Later, in the mid-thirteenth century, Tikkana avoided completing the *Āraṇyaparvamu* and instead began his composition with the *Virāṭaparvamu* ("The Book of Virāṭa's Court," equivalent to the fourth book of the Sanskrit epic, the *Virāṭaparvan*). Tikkana composed a staggering fifteen books of the *Mahābhāratamu,* but—fearful, perhaps, of meeting the same fate as his predecessor—he left that small section of the *Āraṇyaparvamu* untouched. Ĕṛṛana finally completed the epic in the fourteenth century when he composed the latter section of the *Āraṇyaparvamu* that Nannaya had left unfinished.[15] Together, the *kavitrayamu* composed all eighteen books of the Sanskrit *Mahābhārata* in Telugu, surpassing the small subsection of the Sanskrit epic that is reflected in Pampa's tenth-century Kannada

12. Velcheru Narayana Rao, "Multiple Literary Cultures in Telugu: Court, Temple, and Public," in *Text and Tradition in South India* (Ranikhet: Permanent Black, 2016), 43.

13. David Shulman, "Toward a Historical Poetics of the Sanskrit Epics," in *The Wisdom of Poets: Studies in Tamil, Telugu, and Sanskrit* (Delhi: Oxford University Press, 2001), 29.

14. Narayana Rao, "Multiple Literary Cultures," 86 n18.

15. Narayana Rao and Shulman, *Classical Telugu Poetry*, 8–23. See also Narayana Rao, "Multiple Literary Cultures," 86 n18.

Vikramārjunavijaya, which is often considered to be a precursor to Nannaya's composition.[16]

Unlike many of the Mahābhāratas discussed in this volume, the *Mahābhāratamu* largely represents an effort—three efforts, rather—to transform the Sanskrit *Mahābhārata* verse-by-verse and event-by-event into a poetic narrative that a Telugu-speaking audience would relish. Because each of the three poets insists, in his own way, on preserving the poetic and narrative details of the Sanskrit epic in his Telugu (or, as the case may be, Telugu-*cum*-Sanskrit) portrayal, each of the poet's compositions embodies something remarkably close to what we would commonly call a "translation" today. All three poets are closely aligned with the model of *iconic translation* laid out by A. K. Ramanujan in his discussion of the Rāmāyaṇa, with Tikkana's retelling moving between an *iconic* and *indexical* translation.[17] And yet, the application of the term "translation" to the *Mahābhāratamu* is problematic; as Narayana Rao and Shulman observe:

> The vehemence and wildness of the Sanskrit *Mahābhārata* are softened and partly tamed, even as the inner world of the characters become more familiar. In this sense . . . the existence of the Sanskrit prototype becomes a relatively abstract presence that hardly impinges upon the dynamic world of the Telugu text. Only the modern misapplication of the notion of "translation" to Telugu literary creation could see Nannaya—and a host of other Telugu poets—as primarily "translators."[18]

The Sanskrit *Mahābhārata,* like the Sanskrit *Rāmāyaṇa,* should not be considered the urtext for vernacular retellings.[19] For the Telugu reader,

16. R. V. S. Sundaram, in discussion with author, October 18, 2017. For a discussion of Pampa, see Pollock, *Language of the Gods*, 356–63. See also the chapter by Timothy Lorndale in this volume.

17. A. K. Ramanujan, "Three Hundred *Rāmāyaṇas*: Five Examples and Three Thoughts on Translation," in *Many Rāmāyaṇas: The Diversity of a Narrative Tradition in South Asia* (Berkeley: University of California Press, 1991), 44–45.

18. Narayana Rao and Shulman, *Classical Telugu Poetry,* 11.

19. Paula Richman makes this claim in "Introduction: The Diversity of the *Rāmāyaṇa* Tradition," in *Many Rāmāyaṇas: The Diversity of a Narrative Tradition in South Asia,* ed. Paula Richman (Berkeley: University of California Press, 1991), 5.

the *kavitrayamu*'s text is not a translation of the Sanskrit epic; rather, the Telugu *Mahābhāratamu* is *the* Mahābhārata.

Nannaya: Early Experimentations in Telugu

As the first poet and supposedly the first grammarian of Telugu literature, Nannaya is accorded a particular prominence in the Telugu literary imagination.[20] I will not belabor the uniqueness of Nannaya's contributions as *ādi-kavi* (the first poet) of Telugu literature, which Narayana Rao, Shulman, and Pollock have all documented in detail.[21] For the purposes of this discussion, however, I will point out that Nannaya established a new literary style: writing an epic narrative in *campū,* a Sanskrit-based genre that consists of metrical stanzas interspersed with prose.[22] The *campū* style is dizzying in its metrical and syntactical variety, particularly in the range of meters used. *Campū* serves as a bridge across Sanskrit and Telugu literary realms and it became the norm of Telugu literature for seven hundred years after Nannaya's Telugu *Mahābhāratamu.*

Although most scholars consider Nannaya to be Telugu literature's foundational poet, it is telling that Nannaya composes the very first verse of the Telugu *Mahābhāratamu* entirely in Sanskrit—and in the meter *śārdūlavikrīḍita* ("tiger's play"), an extremely popular meter in classical Sanskrit poetry that is also found in Telugu prosody.[23] In this verse, the poet,

20. Nannaya is the attributed author of the first Telugu grammar, written in Sanskrit, the *Āndhraśabdacintāmaṇi*. The dating of this text, however, is speculative and likely from the seventeenth century. See Narayana Rao and Shulman, *Classical Telugu Poetry* 55–56; and Pollock, *Language of the Gods*, 364 n73 and 398. For a recent translation, see *Āndhraśabdacintāmaṇi*: *A Grammar of Telugu Language in Sanskrit,* trans. Deven M. Patel and R. V. S. Sundaram (Mysore: Central Institute of Indian Languages, 2016).

21. See Narayana Rao and Shulman, *Classical Telugu Poetry*; Pollock, *Language of the Gods*; and Narayana Rao, "Multiple Literary Cultures."

22. As Pollock notes, Nannaya's text "was composed according to the formal requirements of Sanskrit literature and in a new cosmopolitan idiom that would remain the dominant literary register in Telugu for the next seven hundred years." *Language of the Gods*, 381. See also Narayana Rao, "Coconut and Honey," 157.

23. For a discussion of Telugu prosody, see Malliyarecana, *Kavijanāśrayamu* (Hyderabad: Telangana Sahityaparishodana Kendram, 2016). This text is written

Nannaya, addresses his patron, King Rājarājanarendra, while simultaneously praising the three gods Viṣṇu, Brahmā, and Śiva:

śrīvāṇīgirijā'ścirāya dadhato| vakṣomukhāṅgeṣu ye
lokānāṃ sthiti'māvahantyavihatāṃ| strīpuṃsayogodbhavām
tevedatrayamūrtaya'stripuruṣā| 'ssampūjitā vassurai-
rbhūyāsuḥ puruṣottamāmbhujabhava|śrīkandharā'śśreyase

Lakṣmī, Sarasvatī, and Pārvatī have resided on
Viṣṇu's chest, Brahmā's mouth, and Śiva's body
since the beginning of time.
In this world created by the union of women and men,
Viṣṇu, Brahmā, and Śiva,
who take the form of the three Vedas,
are worshipped by the gods.
May they exist for your welfare.[24]

The Sanskrit of the poem is straightforward in its recitation and composition: the poem's metrical pattern is exactly what one would expect from a *śārdūla* verse in Sanskrit. According to the norms of Sanskrit prosody, the caesura—the break within a metrical foot, or *pāda*—of a *śārdūla* verse should occur after the twelfth of the *pāda*'s nineteen syllables.[25] (In my notation, the caesura, also known as the *yati,* is marked in the verse by a vertical line in each of the four metrical feet.) In Nannaya's verse, above, the caesura falls neatly at the end of a word (as caesuras in Sanskrit poetry generally should), which allows the reciter of this *śārdūla* verse to pause naturally in the middle of each rhythmic unit. In Nannaya's careful arrangement, the verse strictly follows the conventions of Sanskrit metrics. As a Sanskrit verse embedded in a classical Telugu text, Nannaya's *śārdūla* literally bridges the Sanskrit and Telugu literary domains through his Sanskritized soundscape.

by a Jain author and is very likely from the tenth century, thus predating Nannaya. *Kavijanāśrayamu* 2.117 discusses the *śārdūla* meter. See the forthcoming translation of this text by R. V. S. Sundaram and Harshita Mruthinti Kamath.

24. Nannaya, *TM* 1.1.1. All references from the Telugu *Mahābhāratamu* (*TM*) in this essay are from: *Āndhramahābhāratamu*, ed. G. V. Subrahmanyam, 15 vols. (Tirupati: Tirumala Tirupati Devasathanams, 2014).

25. Martha Ann Selby, *Grow Long, Blessed Night: Love Poems from Classical India* (New York: Oxford University Press, 2000), 77.

In its firm adherence to the norms of Sanskrit prosody, this verse—the very first poem of what is considered to be the first classical Telugu text—is *not* emblematic of the oral soundscape of much of classical Telugu literature, including Nannaya's retelling of the Mahābhārata. In a classical Telugu text, almost every single poem is written in a different meter: sometimes they are Sanskrit meters, like *śārdūla*; sometimes they are vernacular meters that can be found across Telugu or Kannada texts, such as *kanda* or *sīsa*. This variety in meter provides a sharp contrast to Sanskrit poetic works, one of which can be written entirely in a single meter. Even when a Telugu poem is written in a Sanskrit meter, the poet often explicitly flouts Sanskrit metrical conventions, such as the coincidence of a caesura with a break between words and a metrical foot with a semantic unit. Words spill beyond the line breaks and caesuras of Telugu poems, which results in a complex enjambment of meaning and sound. This convention "made it possible for Telugu poets to borrow a four-line Sanskrit meter, such as *śārdūla* or *mattebha,* and play with it in a variety of intricate syntactic twists not allowable in Sanskrit."[26] In addition, a Telugu poem must be read out loud, and when this event occurs, the poem can be read according to syntax (*artham prakāram*) or to meter (*candas prakāram*), which means that the reciter must already be initiated into the complexities of Telugu prosody.[27]

Despite adhering to Sanskrit metrical conventions in his very first verse, Nannaya quickly departs from such strictures early in his text. In a section known as the *avatārika,* or colophon of the text, Nannaya describes the context in which his patron, King Rājarājanarendra, asks him to compose the Mahābhārata in Telugu. The king says to the poet:

jananuta kṛṣṇadvaipā | yanamunivṛṣabhābhihita mahābhārataba-
ddhanirūpitārtham'erpaḍan | 'dĕnuguna raciyimpum'adhikadhīyuktimĕyin

Nannaya,
with your great intellect,
compose in Telugu
the intent of the Mahābhārata
spoken by Vyāsa, the best of sages.[28]

26. Narayana Rao, "Multiple Literary Cultures," 41.

27. Narayana Rao and Shulman, *Classical Telugu Poetry*, 10.

28. Nannaya, *TM* 1.1.16.

The verse is written in *kanda,* a *jāti* meter unique to Telugu and Kannada literary traditions.[29] The *yati* (also known as *vaḍi* in Telugu) does not indicate the end of the word; for example, *kṛṣṇadvaipāyana* (another name for Vyāsa) is split across the *yati* in the first line. And, as in many other Telugu verses, there is complex enjambment across the lines; the compound *mahābhāratabaddhanirūpitārthamu* (simply translated here as "the intent of the Mahābhārata") extends across the first and second lines of the verse.

In addition to experimenting with metrical conventions, Nannaya also inaugurates a new style of contextualizing the speaker and the patron of the text, a practice that is adapted by later Telugu poets.[30] The context of the relationship of power seems clear in this early *avatārika* verse: the king requests, the poet agrees, and the text is commissioned. We must remember, however, that Rājarājanarendra was not a powerful ruler of a large empire. Instead, he was a small regional king of the Veṅgi, or eastern, Cāḷukya courts in present-day Rajamahendravaramu, Andhra Pradesh. It is likely that the king would have been entirely forgotten had it not been for Nannaya's colophon, which includes several praise poems in dedication of Rājarājanarendra.[31] If we consider Nannaya's dedication to be not only a literary text but a historical archive, it seems that the poet is the patron of the king, rather than the other way around.

Based on this cursory survey of these early verses of the Telugu *Mahābhāratamu,* it seems evident that Nannaya's experiments with prosody and poetic conventions set the stage for his successor Tikkana, who adapts these standards but recreates them into a highly idiomatic Telugu mode. In Tikkana's hands (or, perhaps more aptly, from Tikkana's tongue), the Mahābhārata evolves into a uniquely dramatic Telugu text.

Tikkana: Dramatic Flair in Virāṭa's Court

By listening to a Telugu poem, we find a distinctly vernacular soundscape that unfolds through the manipulation and even violation of the rules of Sanskrit prosody. This distinct vernacular soundscape is most resonant in the

29. See *Kavijanāśrayamu* 3.3–6 for a discussion of *kanda* meter.

30. Narayana Rao, "Multiple Literary Cultures," 36.

31. Narayana Rao, 37–38.

compositions of Tikkana, the second of the *Mahābhāratamu* poets.[32] Tikkana stands apart from his contemporaries in that he employs dramatic literary style, which modern literary critics refer to as *naṭakīyata* or *nāṭakamu*.[33] By "dramatic," I mean that Tikkana's verses are dialogical and oftentimes abrupt; they blend lengthy Sanskrit compounds with short Telugu words. Tikkana often employs indexicals—such as "now" (*ippuḍu*) or "here" (*ikkaḍa*)—to create a conversational style in his verses, one that demands an oral mode of recitation.[34] The poet himself emphasizes the orality of his work: in the colophon that begins the *Virāṭaparvamu,* Tikkana describes his Mahābhārata as *bhāratāmṛtamu karṇapuṭambulan 'āragroli* or "nectar that is drunk by the ears."[35] While Tikkana's dramatic style certainly affects the soundscape of the Telugu verse, it also has a distinctly performative dimension, which I will highlight in my discussion of Draupadī's dialogue in Virāṭa's court.

One of the most compelling sections of Tikkana's text is his rendering of the slaying of Kīcaka in the *Virāṭaparvamu*.[36] In the *Virāṭaparvamu*, the five Pāṇḍavas and Draupadī are living in hiding in the court of King Virāṭa. Each of the six main characters takes on a menial role in the king's court, one that provides a foil to his or her role in "real" life. Draupadī assumes the role of a hairdresser to the queen. While serving the queen, Draupadī is spotted by Kīcaka, the queen's younger brother, who immediately becomes infatuated with her. Kīcaka begs Draupadī to become his lover, but she refuses. Ultimately, Draupadī solicits Bhīma and together, they devise a secret plan to draw out Kīcaka in the middle of the night and kill him. In the final, climactic scene, Kīcaka gullibly comes to meet Draupadī for a late-night tryst, only to find Bhīma hiding in her place. After an intense wrestling match in total darkness, Bhīma kills Kīcaka, "forcing his head, arms, and feet, into his torso and pounding it in a dense, neat lump."[37]

---

32. In the words of Narayana Rao and Shulman, Tikkana "stands alone in the whole history of Telugu literature, a figure of remarkable individual creativity." *Classical Telugu Poetry*, 82. For a discussion of the orality of Tikkana's composition, see pages 17–18.

33. Lakshmikantham, *Āndhra Sāhitya Caritra,* 54.

34. Velcheru Narayana Rao, in discussion with author, October 25, 2017.

35. Tikkana, *TM* 4.1.30.

36. On other depictions of this episode in regional Mahābhāratas, see the chapters by Eva De Clercq and Simon Winant, and Heidi Pauwels in this volume.

37. Tikkana, *TM* 4. 2.353.

Tikkana's version of the slaying of Kīcaka is dramatically compelling and reshapes the emotive force of the Sanskrit narrative by positioning an oral-performative dimension at the forefront of the composition. Tikkana certainly stays close to the Sanskrit epic in terms of both plot and imagery. For example, the "dense, neat lump" mirrors the Sanskrit *Mahābhārata*'s description of the same event.[38] And yet, despite being an ostensibly iconic retelling, Tikkana's rendering reads like the transcript of a spoken dialogue, which further enhances both Draupadī's anger and Kīcaka's passion. Tikkana's verses are rarely narrative (*ākhyānamu*) or descriptive (*varṇanamu*) renditions of events; rather they are dramatic verses that are positioned from the perspective of a character who speaks the verses as dialogues to those around her.[39] A popular verse in the *Virāṭaparvamu* illustrates this aspect of Tikkana's uniquely dramatic style. The verse is set in Draupadī's voice during one of her initial attempts to stave off Kīcaka's lustful advances:

*d**urv**ārodyama-bāhu-vikrama-rasā|stoka-pratāpa-sphura*
*d-g**arv**āndha-prativīra-nirmathana-vi|dyā-pāragul mat-patul*
*g**īrv**āṇākṛtul'evur'ipḍu ninu dor|līlan vĕsaṅ giṭṭi gan-*
*dh**arv**ul mānamu prānamun konuṭa ta|thyamb'ĕmmĕyiṅ kīcakā*

My husbands—
invincible in their strength,
shining with great splendor,
skilled in destroying their enemies blinded by pride—
are *gandharva*s with the bodies of gods.
All five of them will easily destroy you
and your pride.
Depend on that, Kīcaka.[40]

38. *Mahābhārata* 4.22.80–85. For this episode, I am following the vulgate edition of the Sanskrit epic: *Mahabharata, Book Four: Virata,* trans. Kathleen Garbutt, Clay Sanskrit Library (New York: New York University Press, JJC Foundation, 2006), 127.

39. See Lakshmikantham, *Āndhra Sāhitya Caritra*, 54–55 for a discussion of narrative, dramatic, and descriptive styles.

40. Tikkana, *TM* 4.2.55. For another translation of the verse, see Narayana Rao and Shulman, *Classical Telugu Poetry*, 15 and 85. The verse also parallels the Sanskrit *Mahābhārata* (4.14.45–50) in some ways. See *Virata*, 113.

The first two lines of the poem are populated by a lengthy Sanskrit compound extolling the heroic qualities of the five Pāṇḍavas. The density of the compound—*durvārodyama-bāhu-vikrama-rasāstoka-pratāpa-sphurad-garvāndha-prativīra-nirmathana-vidyā-pāragul*—physically expands the breadth of the Pāṇḍavas' heroism. The second half of the verse, by contrast, is infused with short snappy units: it combines Sanskrit loan words and Telugu case endings in order to express the urgency of Draupadī's spoken appeal. The pause for Telugu words like *evuru, ipḍu,* and *ninu* in the third line adds to the conversational tone in this verse. Draupadī's words are playful in their belittling of Kīcaka, but remain fierce in asserting her intention. She brings the verse to a dramatic conclusion with a straightforward command to her aggressor: *Tathyamb'ĕmmĕyiṅ kīcakā*—"Depend on that, Kīcaka."

The meter of this verse, like that of Nannaya's first poem, is *śārdūla-vikrīḍita.* But unlike Nannaya's eminently Sanskrit *śārdūla* verse, Tikkana's takes a marked turn toward the vernacular. First, Tikkana's verse includes the characteristic Telugu feature of *prāsa,* which is the repetition of the same syllable in the second position of each line. (I mark these repetitions in bold above.) Second, the complex enjambment that is inimical to Telugu prosody readily appears in the first and third lines of Tikkana's verse, in which the words *sphurad* and *gandharvul* spill across the line break. Although the first two lines consist primarily of a long Sanskrit compound, Tikkana breaches the conventions of Sanskrit metrics when he splits the word *sphurad* between the first and second line. It is as if Tikkana's Sanskrit speaks Telugu.

So, too, does Tikkana's placement of the caesura signal a distinctly Telugu poetics. The caesura of this poem, which is marked here by a vertical line, also violates Sanskrit metrical norms. Instead of occurring at a word break (as it would in a more Sanskrit-attuned *śārdūla* verse), the caesura falls in the middle of a word in all four lines of the verse. This positioning for the caesura is actually the norm in Telugu literature: in Telugu prosody, there is no rule that the caesura must land at a break between words, a point that is also evident in Nannaya's *kanda* verse cited earlier.[41] The resulting enjambment is ubiquitous in Telugu poetry; in fact, a poet whose words divide along the lines of a metrical foot or a caesura is said to lack mastery in composing a Telugu verse, a point that directly violates the standards of Sanskrit poetics.

41. The syllable at the caesura should be "friendly" with the first syllable of each *pāda,* which is known as *yati maitri.*

Tikkana's dramatic flair is not simply encompassed by a conversational, dialogical tone, but also includes literal references to performance and acting. Take the following verses in which Draupadī denounces Yudhiṣṭhira after he publicly castigates her in the court of Virāṭa. She says:

nādu vallabhuṇḍu naṭuḍ'inta nikkambu pĕddavāri aṭla pinnavāru
gāna'batula vidhamakākaye śailūṣin' gānanangarādu kankabhaṭṭa

aṭlaguṭañ'jesi nāku nāṭyambunu paricitamba matpati śailūṣuṇḍa kāḍu kitavuṇḍunuṅ kāvuna jūdari yāliki garuvacandamb'ĕkkaḍidi anucun'ac-coṭu vāsi tana cittambuna[42]

"Yudhiṣṭhira,
it's true that my husband is an actor.
Youngsters naturally follow
the footsteps of their elders.
So I too am a performer,
just like my husbands.

Sure, I know all about acting.
But my husband's not only a performer.
He's a gambler too.
Can the wife of a gambler
keep her pride?"
saying this, she fled.

Notably, there is a similar conversation in the Sanskrit *Mahābhārata*'s *Virāṭaparvan*, in which Yudhiṣṭhira disparagingly refers to Draupadī as an actress who is unaware of the appropriate time to speak: *akālajñāsi sairandhri, śailūṣīva virodisi.*[43] In the Sanskrit text, Draupadī responds rather briefly to Yudhiṣṭhira when he critiques her in Virāṭa's court; she says: "I believe that I am a virtuous wife to compassionate husbands, but the eldest of them is

42. Tikkana, *TM* 4.2.152–53. *TM* 4.2.152 is composed in *teṭagīti*, a Telugu meter that often immediately follows a *sīsa* verse. *TM* 4.2.153 is composed as a *vacanam*, or prose. For another translation of the verse, see Narayana Rao and Shulman, *Classical Telugu Poetry*, 91.

43. *Mahābhārata* 4.16.40–45. See *Virata*, 127.

addicted to dice and so they are humbled by one and all."[44] Following this single line, Draupadī runs to the chambers of Queen Sudeṣṇā.

Tikkana's Telugu rendering contrasts with the Sanskrit epic's by giving far more scope to the development of Draupadī's anger and amplifying her bitter reprisal of Yudhiṣṭhira. Draupadī chastises her (unnamed) husband for his acting skills, referring to him pejoratively as *naṭuḍu* (actor) and *śailūṣunḍu* (performer), while also boldly referring to herself as a *śailūṣin* (performer) who is knowledgeable of *nāṭyambunu* (acting). Through these references to acting and drama, Draupadī alludes to the costumes that she and her husbands don during their year in Virāṭa's court. The dramatic flourish of Tikkana's verbal craft is evident in these direct allusions to *nāṭya* (drama or performance). Coupled with these overt allusions to acting is the heightened emotional state of the dialogue, which convey Draupadī's anger at her husband's lack of appeal on her behalf.

A. K. Ramanujan famously quips, "In India and in Southeast Asia, no one ever reads the *Rāmāyaṇa* or the *Mahābhārata* for the first time."[45] In the case of Telugu South India, this adage applies to the *Mahābhāratamu* rather than to its Sanskrit predecessor. In fact, whereas the Sanskrit *Mahābhārata* is still considered to be a dangerous text in the Telugu imagination, the Telugu *Mahābhāratamu* still holds enormous popular appeal: its verses appear in Telugu films and are memorized by scholars and schoolchildren across South India today. For example, the 1963 Telugu film *Nartanaśāla* ("Dance Pavilion"), which features extremely popular actor N. T. Rama Rao as Arjuna and actress Savitri as Draupadī, focuses entirely on *Virāṭaparvamu.* Draupadī dramatically sings the aforementioned *śārdūla* verse in a final attempt to stave off Kīcaka before his physical assault on her.[46] The selection of this verse is not happenstance; rather, Tikkana's dramatic flair and aesthetic intensity is evident in the crafting of his verses through this section of *Virāṭaparvamu,* arguably making them not only apt for Telugu

44. *Mahābhārata* 4.16.45. See *Virata,* 127.

45. Ramanujan, "Three Hundred *Rāmāyaṇas,*" 46.

46. Shalimar Telugu & Hindi Movies, "Narthanasala Telugu Full Length Movie," YouTube Video, 2:14:42, December 10, 2013, https://www.youtube.com/watch?v=c68L_IONQvU. The scene is found at time stamp 1:36:03. The verse appears out of order from Tikkana's text, in which it is mentioned during Draupadī's initial encounter with Kīcaka. In the film, the verse appears in a later scene in which Draupadī is sent back to Kīcaka's quarters by Sudeṣṇā.

poetry but also translatable to the Telugu silver screen. The soundscape of Tikkana's poetry, which the poet forges at the juncture of Sanskrit poetics and Telugu idiom, domesticates the Sanskrit *Mahābhārata,* making it accessible to a broader Telugu audience and readership. One could even suggest that Tikkana, perhaps even more than Nannaya, is responsible for popularizing the Mahābhārata into a vernacular Telugu mode. Once the Sanskrit *Mahābhārata* is ushered into the Telugu vernacular by the oral-performative elements of Tikkana's dramatic literary style, the Sanskrit version of the epic becomes superfluous.

Ĕṛṛana: An Iconic Return to the Sanskrit *Mahābhārata*

Something curious happens in the context of Ĕṛṛana's Telugu *Mahābhāratamu* that does not fit neatly within the literary evolution from Sanskrit to Telugu. We recall that Ĕṛṛana was a fourteenth-century poet who completed the *Mahābhāratamu* by composing the latter section of the *Āraṇyaparvamu* that Nannaya left unfinished. Rather than develop the oral-performative qualities of Tikkana's *Mahābhāratamu* that set the work in a distinctively Telugu poetic sphere, Ĕṛṛana sets his composition within the framework of Nannaya's *Mahābhāratamu.* He does so not only through his particular literary choices (which we will soon examine) but also in two formal gestures: In the early colophons of his work, Ĕṛṛana signs Nannaya's name instead of his own; he also extends the dedication to Rājarājanarendra, Nannaya's patron.[47] Ĕṛṛana, perhaps even more than Nannaya, relies on Sanskrit poetics and conventions: his portion of the Telugu *Mahābhāratamu* models the Sanskrit *Mahābhārata* in its tone, structure, and characterization of the narrative's major figures.

The Sanskrit-centrism of Ĕṛṛana's translational style—especially as a counterpoint to Tikkana's renegade interpretation of the Sanskrit epic within a Telugu idiom—appears most clearly in Ĕṛṛana's translation of the dialogue between Draupadī and Satyabhāmā, Kṛṣṇa's wife. In Ĕṛṛana's *Āraṇyaparvamu,* Satyabhāmā has a private conversation with Draupadī about her ability to manage all five of her husbands. Satyabhāmā naively asks Draupadī to reveal the secrets of her success; she asks whether some

47. Narayana Rao and Shulman, *Classical Telugu Poetry,* 106. Ĕṛṛana is also credited with composing a Telugu *Harivaṃśamu* and a *purāṇa,* the *Nṛsiṃhapurāṇamu,* although his completion of the *Mahābhāratamu* and subsequent inclusion into the *kavitrayamu* is certainly what has given him lasting fame.

special drug or spell has given Draupadī power over her husbands. In a series of rapid-fire questions, Satyabhāmā asks:

vratamu pĕmpo
mantrauṣadha vaibhavambo
sarasa naipathyakarma kauśalamo
catura vibhramollāsa rekhayo
vĕladi nīviśeṣa saubhāgya hetuvu
sepuma nāku

Is this the effect of a vow?
Or the power of some mantra or drug?
Is this the way you dress up?
Or is it the beauty of your graceful charms?
Woman, tell me the reason behind
your uniquely fortunate position.[48]

Appalled at Satyabhāmā's direct line of questioning, Draupadī responds by asking if it is proper for her to speak like an evil-minded woman, a *duṣṭavanitā*. Draupadī characterizes herself as the ideal *pativratā,* a Sanskrit term that refers to a virtuous married woman. Draupadī then launches into a laundry list of the various acts she does to gain her husbands' favor as a *pativratā*. According to Draupadī's remarkable self-assessment, she eats only after her husbands eat, she never tarries too long in front of her house, she never laughs too long, she always follows the orders of her mother-in-law, and she successfully manages all the expenses of the household, including feeding 8,000 *brāhmaṇa*s and 10,000 ascetics every day.[49] Clearly embarrassed by this response, Satyabhāmā recants her direct line of questioning, saying that she was only joking. Draupadī responds by directing Satyabhāmā always to serve Kṛṣṇa, honor his relations, and associate only with women from good families.[50] Satisfied, Satyabhāmā pays her respects to Draupadī and departs from the forest with Kṛṣṇa.

The Telugu version of the Satyabhāmā-Draupadī dialogue appears to be virtually identical to its Sanskrit counterpart in tone and structure;

48. Ĕṟṟana, *TM* 3.5.291.

49. Ĕṟṟana, *TM* 3.5.299–309.

50. Ĕṟṟana, *TM* 3.5.313–21.

in his rendering of the text, Ěṛṛana employs many of the same images and directives that appear in the Sanskrit epic.[51] For example, when Satyabhāmā approaches Draupadī in the Sanskrit text, she asks almost exactly the same questions as those found in Ěṛṛana's aforementioned Telugu verse:

> Was it a religious vow, austerities, ablutions, *mantras*, or magical herbs, the power of secret spells, or the power of roots, or repetition of sacred words, or offerings of drugs? Tell me, lady of Pāñcāla, the lucky secret that brings you [matrimonial] good fortune.[52]

As another example, the Sanskrit epic states that women who use deceitful means of controlling their husbands are like snakes in the house.[53] Similarly, in the Telugu text, Draupadī says that a husband will view a woman who uses the efforts of mantra, tantra, or various medicines as "friendship with a snake."[54] Ěṛṛana's version of this dialogue is paradigmatic of Ramanujan's notion of an "iconic translation" in which "Text 1 and Text 2 have a geometrical resemblance to each other as one triangle to another."[55] What does it mean for Ěṛṛana's rendering of the Telugu epic to replicate its Sanskrit counterpart, especially considering the revolutionary work of Ěṛṛana's predecessor, Tikkana? While Tikkana is credited for ushering the Mahābhārata into the realm of the Telugu vernacular, Ěṛṛana relies heavily on the Sanskrit text as the iconic

51. See Sally J. Sutherland Goldman, "Sītā and Draupadī: Aggressive Behavior and Female Role-Models in the Sanskrit Epics," *Journal of the American Oriental Society* 109, no. 1 (1989): 67–68; Laurie L. Patton, "*Samvada* as a Literary and Philosophical Genre: An Overlooked Resource for Public Debate and Conflict Resolution?" *Evam* 3 (2004): 182–84; and Laurie L. Patton, "How Do You Conduct Yourself? Gender and the Construction of a Dialogical Self in the *Mahābhārata*," in *Gender and Narrative in the Mahābhārata,* eds. Simon Brodbeck and Brian Blackburn (London: Routledge, 2007), 97–109.

52. *Mahābhārata* 3.222.4–7. Translated by Sutherland Goldman in "Sītā and Draupadī," 67–68. Note that Sutherland Goldman is translating the critical edition of the Sanskrit epic.

53. *Mahābhārata* 3.222.11. Cited in Patton, "How Do You Conduct Yourself?" 102. Patton is following the critical edition of the epic.

54. Ěṛṛana, *TM* 3.5.296.

55. Ramanujan, "Three Hundred *Rāmāyaṇas,*" 44.

model for composing each and every verse of this particular section. Ĕṟṟana, at least within the context of the Satyabhāmā-Draupadī dialogue, manages to re-posit the Sanskrit *Mahābhārata* as the urtext from which he operates.[56]

Ĕṟṟana's rendering departs from the Telugu idiomatic imagination not only on the level of poetic resonance but also on the level of character development. Let me turn briefly to the character Satyabhāmā, who begs Draupadī for any drugs, potions, or spells that will charm her husband, Kṛṣṇa. Ĕṟṟana's translation replicates in full force the *pativratā* ideology that this particular dialogue in the Sanskrit *Mahābhārata* espouses: Draupadī schools Satyabhāmā in every detail of proper wifely behavior. Yet if we look beyond the *Mahābhāratamu* to later Telugu literary productions, this model of the good wife unravels. For example, in the sixteenth-century poem *Pārijātāpaharaṇamu* ("Theft of a Tree"), the Vijayanagara court poet Nandi Timmana does not mention the term *pativratā* when describing the methods that Satyabhāmā uses to trick Kṛṣṇa into stealing the *pārijāta* (wish-giving tree) from Indra's garden. Like Tikkana, Timmana takes great creative liberties in re-composing a Sanskrit narrative—this one from the *Harivaṃśa*—into a vernacular Telugu text, particularly when it comes to the characterization of Satyabhāmā.[57] In the *Pārijātāpaharaṇamu*, Timmana separates Satyabhāmā from the discourse of the *pativratā* that surrounds her in both the Sanskrit *Mahābhārata* and the Sanskrit *Harivaṃśa*.[58] By eliding talk of the *pativratā*, Timmana symbolically removes Satyabhāmā from her life in Sanskrit literature and recreates her in the Telugu vernacular. Moreover, it is Timmana's vernacularized Satyabhāmā, not Ĕṟṟana's chastened *pativratā*, who becomes a major figure in the Telugu literary world in the centuries that follow.

56. See Sutherland Goldman, "Sītā and Draupadī," 67–68; Patton, "*Samvada*," 182–84; and Patton, "How Do You Conduct Yourself?" 97–109.

57. For a full discussion of Timmana's text, see Harshita Mruthinti Kamath and Velcheru Narayana Rao, "Introduction," in Nandi Timmana, *Theft of a Tree,* trans. Harshita Mruthinti Kamath and Velcheru Narayana Rao, Murty Classical Library of India (Cambridge, MA: Harvard University Press, forthcoming).

58. The *pārijāta* narrative is briefly mentioned in the critical edition of the *Harivaṃśa* (2.92.63–70). For a discussion of the *pārijāta* episode in the critical edition and appendices of the *Harivaṃśa*, see Christopher Austin, "The Fructification of the Tale of a Tree: The *Pārijātaharaṇa* in the *Harivaṃśa* and Its Appendices," *Journal of the American Oriental Society* 33, no. 2 (2013): 249–68.

Ĕṛṛana's *Āraṇyaparvamu* presents us with a rupture to the teleological progression of the vernacular millennium when it reasserts the literary importance of the Sanskrit *Mahābhārata* over the Telugu idiom. By examining Tikkana and Nannaya alongside Ĕṛṛana, it becomes clear that vernacularization does not unfold in a straight line from Sanskrit epic to Telugu text; rather it is an uneven, oftentimes meandering, process that eventually produces uniquely vernacular formulations of poetics and prosody. The poet Ĕṛṛana and, on a larger scale, the Telugu *Mahābhāratamu*'s elastic relationship with the Sanskrit *Mahābhārata,* provide us with a fruitful starting point for thinking through the complexities of the literary-cultural transformations of the vernacular world in premodern South India.[59]

Conclusion

Vernacularization is not simply about the development of Telugu as a language but the emergence of Telugu as a form of discourse, one that has the power to shape how its speakers hear and envision the world around them. According to linguist J. L. Austin, speech has a performative power: it not only describes but also creates the very thing that it names.[60] Drawing on Austin as well as philosopher Jacques Derrida,[61] Judith Butler goes on to argue that the performative utterance is never circumscribed merely to the moment in which it is spoken; rather, she suggests, speech is an iterative and performative act that "exceeds itself in past and future directions."[62]

59. Pollock, *Language of the Gods*, 380.

60. In *How to Do Things with Words* (Oxford: Oxford University Press, 1975; first published 1962, Harvard University Press [Cambridge, MA]), J. L. Austin makes an important linguistic distinction between a constative statement and a performative utterance. Austin suggests that a constative statement describes the state of affairs and can be verifiable as either true or false (2–3). Rather than simply describing a state of affairs, Austin states that speech has the power to act through the performative utterance (6–7).

61. Jacques Derrida, "Signature Event Context," in *Margins of Philosophy*, trans. Alan Bass (Chicago: University of Chicago Press, 1982), 307–30.

62. Judith Butler, *Excitable Speech: A Politics of the Performative* (New York: Routledge, 1997), 3.

Like the performative utterance, the emergence of the Telugu vernacular represents an iterative process, one that spans a thousand years. Each iteration of Telugu in the *Mahābhāratamu*—whether it is captured in the uniquely Telugu poetic conventions of Nannaya's *kanda* verse, Tikkana's departure from the Sanskrit *Mahābhārata* in his representation of Draupadī, or Ĕṛṛana's replication of Sanskrit typologies of the *pativratā*—creates a new possibility for the vernacular that exceeds the boundaries of Sanskrit. Therefore, it is important not to view the *Mahābhāratamu* as a simple translation of the Sanskrit epic. As Narayana Rao and Shulman observe:

> A good "translation" . . . creates a new original. This is not a matter of adapting, imitating, or following. The new original preexists in the "old" original, before the translation, but it needs the translator to reveal it . . . This also explains why "translation," understood in this manner, can be the beginning of an entirely new literary culture.[63]

By thinking through the micro-textures of the language of the *Mahābhāratamu* and considering the specific poetic choices of its three authors as they move between Sanskrit and Telugu literary spheres, we can both see and hear the development of the Telugu vernacular in an entirely new literary frame. And yet it is Tikkana, over and above his counterparts, who uniquely illuminates Telugu in its vernacular form.

In this vein, I will conclude with an orally circulated poem, or *cāṭu,* that describes the tangibility of Telugu, a language that can be approached by all the senses. The *cāṭu*, titled *The Definition of Poetry* by translators Narayana Rao and Shulman, is attributed to the Vijayanagara court poet Allasāni Pĕddana:

> Is poetry a surface sheen,
> the green delusion of unfolded buds? . . .
> If you sink your teeth into it, it should be succulent
> as the full lips of a ripe woman from another world,
> sitting on your knees. It should ring

63. Narayana Rao and Shulman, *Classical Telugu Poetry*, 23.

as when godly Sound strokes her fingernails
the strings of her *vīṇā*, with its golden bulbs resting
on her proud, white, pointed breasts,
so that the *rāga*-notes resound.
That is the pure Telugu mode.[64]

It is Tikkana's Telugu *Mahābhāratamu*, with its multiplex soundscape and its vision of the Mahābhārata as both a reflection of the Sanskrit literary world and the projection of a Telugu vernacular one, that inaugurates what we can now call a "pure Telugu mode."

64. Velcheru Narayana Rao and David Shulman, *A Poem at the Right Moment: Remembered Verses from Premodern South India* (Berkeley: University of California Press, 1998), 34–35.

Chapter Eleven

The Fate of Kīcaka in Two Jain Apabhramsha Mahābhāratas

Eva De Clercq and Simon Winant

As a minority religion for most of its existence, Jainism, when confronted with the rising popularity of the Sanskrit epics and the Hindu *purāṇas* and their heroes (especially Rāma and Kṛṣṇa), sought active engagement with these narratives. The result is a voluminous corpus of texts telling the stories of these heroes from a distinct Jain viewpoint.[1] As a collection of complete Mahābhārata tellings that do not focus on a specific episode or character, the Jain Mahābhārata tradition is exceptional in both number and scope. Premodern Jain authors composed their works in different styles and languages, from the transregional literary languages of Sanskrit, Prakrit, and Apabhramsha to regional languages such as Kannada and Hindi. Jain

1. Not all tellings of the epics composed by Jain authors are from a Jain viewpoint. Notable exceptions are Amaracandrasūri's thirteenth-century *Bālabhārata* in Sanskrit, and Pampa's *Vikramārjunavijaya* (ca. 941) and Ranna's *Sāhasabhīmavijaya* (ca. 993) in Kannada. See Jonathan Geen, "The Marriage of Draupadī in the Hindu and Jaina Mahābhārata," (PhD diss., McMaster University, 2001), 85–97; and B. N. Sumitra Bai and Robert Z. Zydenbos, "The Jaina *Mahābhārata*," in *Essays on the Mahābhārata*, ed. Arvind Sharma (Leiden: E. J. Brill, 1991), 264–65.

Mahābhāratas also vary in content. Here, we explore this diversity as it is exemplified in two Apabhramsha accounts of the character Kīcaka.[2]

The first Kīcaka narrative that we discuss appears in the *Harivaṃsapurāṇa* ("The *Purāṇa* on the Dynasty of Hari"), an Apabhramsha work that includes a Jain Mahābhārata that was composed by the lay religious teacher Raïdhū in fifteenth-century Gwalior. Over the course of this discussion, we relate Raïdhū's account in the *Harivaṃsapurāṇa* to three intertexts in three different languages: Jinasena Punnāṭa's eighth-century Sanskrit *Harivaṃśapurāṇa*, which includes a Jain Mahābhārata; the *Nāyādhammakahāo* ("Stories of Knowledge and Righteousness"), an earlier text that is written in Ardhamagadhi Prakrit and that constitutes part of the Jain scriptural canon; and Viṣṇudās' Hindi *Pāṇḍavcarit* ("The Life of the Pāṇḍavas"), a Hindu Mahābhārata that, like Raïdhū's *Harivaṃsapurāṇa*, was composed in fifteenth-century Gwalior. The second Kīcaka narrative that we analyze is the one in Svayambhūdeva's Apabhramsha *Riṭṭhaṇemicariu* ("The Life of Ariṣṭanemi"), a Jain Mahābhārata from the ninth or tenth century that also circulated in fifteenth-century Gwalior.

Early and Medieval Jain Mahābhāratas: An Overview

The Jain Mahābhāratas are part of a corpus of texts that is commonly called the Jain Universal History; in reality, it consists of the biographies (*carita*s) of the sixty-three *mahāpuruṣa*s or *śalākāpuruṣa*s, "great men" who are each responsible for some heroic feat. This illustrious group of heroes consists of the twenty-four *tīrthaṅkara*s ("fordmakers" or Jain prophets), twelve *cakravartin*s (universal emperors) and nine triads of figures, each triad consisting of a *baladeva*, a *vāsudeva* (the *baladeva*'s half-brother), and a *prativāsudeva* (their archenemy). In testimony to their (partial) purpose as a counter-tradition, these texts are also called *purāṇa*s. As such, the Jain

2. The selection of this episode was largely inspired by a collaborative project with Heidi Pauwels on emotion and memory construction in Gwalior under the Tomar dynasty, examining the evocative Kīcaka episode in the various Mahābhāratas composed there as reflecting Rajput martial valor. The present chapter will not go into the other Jain Mahābhāratas circulating in this environment that were examined for the project, such as the one by Yaśaḥkīrti.

Mahābhārata tradition is linked—initially as a secondary story—to the biographies of the twenty-second *tīrthaṅkara* Neminātha and his cousin Kṛṣṇa, the ninth *vāsudeva*. In Jain Mahābhārata narratives, the feud between the Pāṇḍavas and Kauravas is integrated into the main conflict of Nemi (that is, Neminātha) and Kṛṣṇa with Jarāsandha, the ninth *prativāsudeva*. (In the second book of the Sanskrit *Mahābhārata*, Kṛṣṇa, Bhīma, and Arjuna work together to bring down this same Jarāsandha, a Māgadha king, in the interest of consolidating political power behind Yudhiṣṭhira.)

Jain Mahābhārata tellings are found in works bearing titles such as the *Harivaṃśapurāṇa*[3] or the *Nemināthacarita* ("The Life of Neminātha") in addition to the *Pāṇḍavacarita* ("The Lives of the Pāṇḍavas") or *Pāṇḍavapurāṇa* ("The *Purāṇa* on the Pāṇḍavas"). Yet regardless of the titles used to describe them, nearly all of these compositions integrate narrative material from four sources: (1) the biography of Neminātha, (2) the biography of Kṛṣṇa, (3) a version of the *Bṛhatkathā* ("The Great Story"), a famous story collection about the adventures of the emperor of the *vidyādharas* (a class of supernatural beings), which, in this context, is narrated as the wanderings of Kṛṣṇa's father Vasudeva, and (4) the biography of the Pāṇḍavas. A distinctive feature of the Jain *purāṇas* is that they may exhibit instances of "moral cleansing," whereby morally ambiguous episodes from their more orthodox counterparts are transformed so that they conform with stricter Jain codes of ethics.[4]

Certain aspects of the Mahābhārata are also present in the oldest layer of Jain literature, the canonical texts (*āgamas*), the extant versions of which are tentatively dated to the fifth century or earlier. These *āgamas* are recognized only by the Śvetāmbara branch of Jainism. The Digambara branch believes that the original *āgamas* are now lost. We find stories of

3. The title *Harivaṃśapurāṇa* for these Jain works is a clear reference to the better-known non-Jain composition of the same name dealing with the life of the non-Jain Kṛṣṇa. This non-Jain *Harivaṃśa* describes itself as a *khila* (supplement) to the Sanskrit *Mahābhārata*.

4. For more on Jain *purāṇas*, see John E. Cort, "An Overview of the Jaina Purāṇas," in *Purāṇa Perennis: Reciprocity and Transformation in Hindu and Jaina Texts*, ed. Wendy Doniger (Albany: State University of New York Press, 1993), 185–206; and Padmanabh S. Jaini, "A Purāṇic Counter Tradition," in *Purāṇa Perennis: Reciprocity and Transformation in Hindu and Jaina Texts*, ed. Wendy Doniger (Albany: State University of New York Press, 1993), 207–49.

the previous lives of Draupadī and the Pāṇḍavas in the *Nāyādhammakahāo* and the *Maraṇasamāhi*, two texts in the *āgama* corpus.[5]

Leaving aside these stray canonical references, the first complete Jain rendering of the lives of the Pāṇḍavas appears over the course of seven chapters of the seminal *Harivaṃśapurāṇa* (783 CE), a Sanskrit narrative that its Digambara author, Jinasena Punnāṭa, composed in Saurāṣṭra (present-day Gujarat).[6] Jinasena Punnāṭa was the first poet to integrate the four distinct sources noted above into one narrative. His *Harivaṃśapurāṇa* develops the stories of Kṛṣṇa and Neminātha with special interest and at great length. By contrast, the author devotes around only 500 of 10,000 verses to the Pāṇḍavas.

In addition to compositions such as Jinasena Punnāṭa's that focus on Kṛṣṇa, Neminātha, and the Pāṇḍavas, Jain Mahābhāratas were also composed as part of the *mahāpurāṇas*: *purāṇas* narrating the lives of all sixty-three *mahāpuruṣas*. The oldest extant *mahāpurāṇa* is the *Triṣaṣṭilakṣaṇamahāpurāṇasaṃgraha* ("The Compendium of the *Mahāpurāṇa* Describing the Sixty-Three"), which consists of two parts: the *Ādipurāṇa* ("The *Purāṇa* of Ādinātha"), which was composed by one of the greatest Digambara authors, Jinasena (not to be confused with Jinasena Punnāṭa), in the second half of the ninth century in present-day Malkheda (in Karnataka); and its supplement, the *Uttarapurāṇa* ("The *Purāṇa* of the Subsequent [Great Men]"), which was composed by Jinasena's pupil, Guṇabhadra. While dealing with the biographies of Neminātha, Kṛṣṇa, and the Jain *Bṛhatkathā* in the seventieth to seventy-second chapters, Guṇabhadra also gives an account of the *Pāṇḍavacarita*, albeit a short one. (It consists of fewer than a hundred verses.) Another *mahāpurāṇa*, the *Caüpaṇṇamahāpurisacariya* ("The Lives of the Fifty-Four Great Men") was composed in 867 CE in literary Maharashtri Prakrit by a Śvetāmbara mendicant from Gujarat who was known as Śīlāṅka (or Śīlācārya).[7] Śīlāṅka reduced the Pāṇḍava story even further by narrating it in about thirty-five lines; like his predecessors, Śīlāṅka devotes

5. See Geen, "The Marriage of Draupadī," 35–36.

6. *JPH* 45–47, 54, and 63–65. All references to Jinasena Punnāṭa's *Harivaṃśapurāṇa* (*JPH*) are from: Jinasena Punnāṭa, *Harivaṃśapurāṇa*. ed. and trans. P. Jain (Delhi: Bharatiya Jnanpith, 1978).

7. The nine *prativāsudevas* are not considered *mahāpuruṣas* by Śīlāṅka, hence the number fifty-four instead of sixty-three.

most of his attention to the stories of Kṛṣṇa and Neminātha. Far more significant as a Śvetāmbara *mahāpurāṇa* is the renowned *Triṣaṣṭiśalākāpuruṣacaritra* ("The Lives of the Sixty-Three Illustrious Men"), a Sanskrit narrative that was composed by Hemacandra (1160–1172) at the request of King Kumārapāla in Gujarat. Here, too, the story of the Pāṇḍavas is rather limited: Hemacandra narrates it in about 240 verses.

The first composition after Jinasena Punnāṭa's *Harivaṃśapurāṇa* that specifically relates the narratives of Kṛṣṇa, Neminātha, the Pāṇḍavas, and Vasudeva in a Jain *Bṛhatkathā* is Svayambhūdeva's *Riṭṭhaṇemicariu* ("The Life of Ariṣṭanemi"), which was composed in Apabhramsha, a late Middle Indic literary language. This work, which Svayambhūdeva composed between the ninth and tenth centuries in a Kannada-speaking area in South India, is also called the *Harivaṃsapurāṇa* and the *Bhārahapurāṇa* ("The *Purāṇa* on the Bhārata") in its colophons. As far as main titles go, the latter designation seems more appropriate than either the *Riṭṭhaṇemicariu* or the *Harivaṃsapurāṇa*, since the majority of the work's 112 chapters narrate the story of the Pāṇḍavas, in particular the battle of Kurukṣetra. Unlike the earlier compositions that we discussed, which grant narrative priority to the lives of Neminātha and Kṛṣṇa, the *Riṭṭhaṇemicariu* moves away from these figures. Given this refocusing of attention, the *Riṭṭhaṇemicariu* may be considered the first proper Jain Mahābhārata.

From the thirteenth century onward, a number of Jain authors followed in Svayambhūdeva's footsteps by composing a corpus of texts, mostly in Sanskrit, called *Pāṇḍavapurāṇa*s or *Pāṇḍavacarita*s. Although these texts contain the narratives of Kṛṣṇa and Neminātha, their main focus, like that of the *Riṭṭhaṇemicariu*, remains the story of the Pāṇḍavas. The first of these works is a *Pāṇḍavacarita* in eighteen[8] chapters which was composed in 1214 by the Śvetāmbara mendicant Maladhāri Devaprabhasūri. In 1552, the Digambara poet Śubhacandra produced a very popular *Pāṇḍavapurāṇa*[9] and

8. Note that the critical and vulgate editions of the Sanskrit *Mahābhārata* contain eighteen books.

9. Śubhacandra's *Pāṇḍavapurāṇa* was infamously plagiarized by Śrībhūṣaṇa. See Padmanabh S. Jaini, "Bhaṭṭāraka Śrībhūṣaṇa's *Pāṇḍavapurāṇa*: A Case of Jaina Sectarian Plagiarism," in *Middle Indo-Aryan and Jaina Studies: Proceedings of the VIIth World Sanskrit Conference*, eds. J. Bronkhorst and C. Caillat (Leiden: E. J. Brill, 1991), 59–68.

in 1598, the mendicant Vādicandra wrote another Digambara *Pāṇḍavapurāṇa* of eighteen chapters in southern Gujarat.[10]

Jain manuscript catalogs list compositions called the *Harivaṃśapurāṇa*, the *Neminātbacarita*, the *Pāṇḍavapurāṇa*, and so on, in great numbers in vernacular languages as well. Very few of these works have been edited, let alone studied critically. One example of a particularly significant poem is Bulākīdās' Hindi *Pāṇḍavapurāṇa* (1697) of which Kasturcand Kaslival notes that over fifty manuscripts exist in libraries in Rajasthan alone.[11]

Two Jain Mahābhāratas in Apabhramsha

The two texts that this chapter discusses, Svayambhūdeva's *Riṭṭhaṇemicariu* and Raïdhū's fifteenth-century *Harivaṃsapurāṇa,* are composed in Apabhramsha, originally an ecumenical language that, over time, became associated with Jainism in particular.[12] Both compositions are *sandhibandhas* ("bound in *sandhis*"), a form that was favored specifically by Digambara authors and in which chapters (*sandhis*) are roughly divided into between fifteen and twenty sections (*kaḍavakas*), each of which consists of eight or more rhyming couplets (*yamakas*) and each of which is concluded by a longer verse (*ghattā*). Although today we consider Apabhramsha a classical literary language—its grammar is fixed and its lexicon is nearly identical to that of classical Prakrit (Maharashtri)—the *kaḍavaka* structure of the *sandhibandha* is found in an almost identical form in later Old Hindi literature, which demonstrates the proximity of Apabhramsha, as a literary idiom, to newer vernaculars. The preferred themes of *sandhibandhas* are the lives of the *mahāpuruṣas* and of various spiritual, royal, or merchant heroes who appear elsewhere in Jain narrative literature.

10. For a more exhaustive overview of Jain Mahābhāratas, see Eva De Clercq, "The Jaina *Harivaṃśa* and *Mahābhārata* Tradition-A Preliminary Survey," in *Parallels and Comparisons in the Sanskrit Epics and Purāṇas*, ed. P. Koskikallio (Zagreb: Croatian Academy of Sciences and Arts, 2008), 399–421.

11. Kasturcand Kaslival, *Kavivar Bulākhīcand Bulākīdās aur Hemrāj (Śrī Mahāvīr Granth Akādamī 6)* (Jaipur: Sri Mahavir Granth Akadami, 1983), 116.

12. For an introduction to Apabhramsha literature, see Eva De Clercq, *The Apabhramsa of Svayambhudeva's Paumacariu*, Pandit Nathuram Premi Research Series, vol. 17 (Mumbai: Hindi Granth Karyalay, 2009), 5–32.

Even though Svayambhūdeva predates Raïdhū by several centuries, we have clear evidence that the Mahābhāratas of both these poets were read in fifteenth-century Jain literary circles in Gwalior (in present-day Madhya Pradesh) because the *Riṭṭhaṇemicariu*, which was apparently left unfinished by Svayambhūdeva, was completed by one of Raïdhū's preceptors, Yaśaḥkīrti. Despite the fact that both texts were composed in the same language and circulated in the same community, these retellings differ in many ways. In particular, the approaches to the fate of Kīcaka in these two Jain Mahābhāratas could not be more distinct from one another.

Introducing Kīcaka

The character of Kīcaka appears in the Sanskrit *Mahābhārata*'s *Virāṭaparvan* ("The Book of Virāṭa's Court"), which describes the Pāṇḍavas' and Draupadī's thirteenth year in exile. Donning various disguises, the Pāṇḍavas live in the service of the Matsya king, Virāṭa. Their stay is trouble-free until the general Kīcaka, brother-in-law to Virāṭa, becomes obsessed with Draupadī, who is disguised as a maidservant (*sairaṃdhrī*, which Draupadī also takes as a name during this period), and attempts to rape her. Frustrated with the unresponsiveness of Virāṭa and Yudhiṣṭhira after the attack, Draupadī approaches Bhīma in the interest of exacting revenge on Kīcaka. She invites Kīcaka for an evening rendezvous at a secluded location, where Bhīma awaits and kills him in a most gruesome fashion, reducing him to a lump of flesh. Following Kīcaka's death, his clansmen want to burn Draupadī on his funeral pyre, but Bhīma intervenes again and kills them.

Later authors and poets have recast this episode in various molds to satisfy particular cultural needs and sensibilities.[13] During the British Raj, many writers adapted the Kīcaka episode in the context of the struggle for Indian independence. The famous Hindi author Maithilisharan Gupt composed a poem titled "Sairandhrī" (1927) that highlights the social struggles of Indian women at the time.[14] Similarly, K. P. Khadilkar wrote the anti-imperialist Marathi play *Kīcak Vadh* (1907), an extensive allegory

13. On premodern regional renderings of this episode, see the chapters by Harshita Mruthinti Kamath and Heidi Pauwels in this volume.

14. See Pamela Lothspeich, *Epic Nation: Reimagining the Mahabharata in the Age of Empire* (Delhi: Oxford University Press, 2009), 185–86.

on British colonial rule in India, in which Kīcaka represents Lord Curzon, Viceroy of India, and Draupadī represents Mother India.[15] Just as modern Indian writers used the Kīcaka episode as an allegory for unjust British rule or as a means to address contemporary issues of Indian womanhood, premodern Jain authors retold the story of Kīcaka in various ways.

Raïdhū's *Harivaṃsapurāṇa*

The first text that we will investigate is the *Harivaṃsapurāṇa* of Raïdhū, of which there is one (attested) manuscript that is kept at the Jain Siddhant Bhawan in Arrah in Bihar.[16] Undoubtedly the most renowned author of the Gwalior Digambara community in the fifteenth century, Raïdhū was a *paṇḍita*, a lay religious teacher, who worked in the service of several monastic heads (*bhaṭṭāraka*) in Gwalior. Raïdhū composed over thirty works, mostly in Apabhramsha, for various patrons from the affluent Digambara merchant community. In addition to composing literature, he is also famed for masterminding the large-scale carvings of *jina* or "peaceful conqueror" images in the walls of Gwalior Fort during this period.[17] His *Harivaṃsapurāṇa*, which, in the colophons of the first two chapters, is called the *Riṭṭhanemicariu* (the same title as Svayambhūdeva's work) consists of fourteen

15. K. P. Khadilkar, *Globalization, Nationalism and the Text of 'Kichaka-Vadha': The First English Translation of the Marathi Anticolonial Classic, with a Historical Analysis of Theatre in British India,* trans. and ed. Rakesh H. Solomon (London: Anthem Press, 2014).

16. Rajaram Jain, *Raïdhū Sāhitya kā Alocanātmak-pariśīlan* (Vaisali: Prakrit, Jainsastra aur Ahimsas-samsthan, 1974), 180. The manuscript is dated 1987 Vikram Saṃvat (1930 CE; Vikram Saṃvat is a traditional South Asian calendar system which has a zero point of approximately 57 BCE). Digital copies of the Jain Siddhanta Bhawan manuscripts are available online at "Book Manuscripts," *International Digambar Jain Organization*, http://idjo.org/site/Books_Manuscript.aspx. The *Harivaṃsapurāṇa* of Raïdhū is listed under Jha 83. All references to Raïdhū's *Harivaṃsapurāṇa* (*RH*) in this essay are from this manuscript.

17. For an overview of Raïdhū's works, see Jain, *Raïdhū Sāhitya*; and Phyllis Granoff, "Mountains of Eternity: Raidhū and the Colossal Jinas of Gwalior," *Rivista di Studi Sudasiatici* 1 (2006): 31–50.

chapters and 302 sections. The work itself is undated, but the *praśasti* (the eulogizing sections at the beginning and the end of a composition in which kings and patrons are described at length) of another of Raïdhū's texts, the *Sukosalacariu*, composed in 1439 CE, mentions that Raïdhū had already written a biography of Nemi. Hence the *Harivaṃsapurāṇa* must have been composed prior to 1439 and possibly around the same time as Viṣṇudās' Hindi *Pāṇḍavcarit* (1435), which Heidi Pauwels analyzes in the next chapter of this volume. From the *praśasti* of the *Harivaṃsapurāṇa* itself, we learn that Raïdhū wrote the work for Loṇa Sāhu, a member of the mercantile Agravāla caste[18] whose family hailed from Jhuṇujhuṇupura, north of Delhi (*joiṇipura*).[19] We learn that the patronage was arranged by a novice monk named Khelhā, but the passage makes no specific reference to the text's place of composition or to any rulers.

The account of Kīcaka's death is found in the ninth chapter, in *kaḍavakas* fifteen through eighteen, and extends over approximately fifty couplets. In a typically Jain fashion, Raïdhū transforms the Sanskrit epic's depiction of the lecherous Kīcaka being gruesomely killed by a vengeful Bhīma into one of Kīcaka becoming a Jain monk after realizing that his lust for Draupadī emerges from their karmic connections in previous existences.

The fifteenth *kaḍavaka* introduces Kīcaka as the eldest of the hundred sons of King Cūlika and the brother-in-law of King Virāṭa. One day, in passing, he beholds Draupadī and falls madly in love with her as a result of the power of his karma (*kammaha vaseṇa*).[20] He proclaims: "Your beauty agitates my heart. If you wish it so, I will make you chief queen."[21] Yet Draupadī rebukes him, lecturing him on the sinfulness of lusting after another man's wife.[22]

Until the point at which Bhīma attacks Kīcaka (which, in this text, takes place at a secret location outside the city), Raïdhū's account more or less follows the one found in the Sanskrit *Mahābhārata*, albeit in a very abridged

18. *RH* 1.4.8, 14.24.1.

19. *RH* 1.4.3.

20. *RH* 9.15.3. The meaning of this phrase becomes clear later in the story.

21. *taü rūvi majhu saṃkhuhiu cittu | vaṃchahi karemi jeṭṭhaü kalattu* || *RH* 9.15.4 ||

22. *RH* 9.15.4–7.

fashion.[23] But now the story takes a very different turn. Bhīma violently beats and kicks Kīcaka until he lies unconscious on the ground. Assuming that he killed him, Bhīma then leaves. When Kīcaka comes to, he feels deeply ashamed, goes to the forest, and takes initiation from the sage Ratavardhana in order to become a Jain monk.[24] When Kīcaka's brothers seek revenge, Bhīma kills them.[25] Raïdhū then refocuses the narrative on Kīcaka, describing him in terms that are typical for an ideal sage: "His mind averse to the sensory objects, the sage Kīcaka shone with his steadfast body and mind, standing in meditation, his mind absorbed, unwavering like the mountain of the gods."[26] It is more or less a standard in classical Jain narratives that the protagonist renounces the world after a life filled with adventures, sometimes (though not always) after meeting a Jain monk. To a Jain audience, therefore, the transformation of Kīcaka would not come as a big surprise.

That night, a *yakṣa* (a superhuman being common in South Asian folklore), intent on testing Kīcaka's commitment, assumes the form of Draupadī and tries to seduce him.[27] Kīcaka does not even glance at her; instead, he attains omniscience.[28] The *yakṣa* asks Kīcaka the reason behind his infatuation with Draupadī.[29] In response, Kīcaka narrates the story of his and Draupadī's connection in previous births. Once, Kīcaka was born

---

23. Unless noted otherwise, all references to the Sanskrit *Mahābhārata* (*MBh*) in this essay are to the critical edition: *The Mahābhārata for the First Time Critically Edited,* ed. V. S. Sukthankar et al. 19 vols. (Poona: Bhandarkar Oriental Research Institute, 1933–66). The parallel passage in the *Mahābhārata* up to this point extends over nine chapters of the *Virāṭaparvan* (*MBh* 4.13–21.50). Raïdhū does not mention any involvement of Queen Sudeṣṇā, Kīcaka's sister, described at length in the *Mahābhārata* (4.13–15), nor does Raïdhū's Kīcaka at any point physically harm Draupadī, as he does in the Sanskrit epic (4.15). The lengthy complaints of Draupadī during her nightly visit to Bhīma (*MBh* 4.16–20) are reduced to the three verses (*RH* 9.15.12–14) and equally include the threat of suicide.

24. *RH* 9.16.9–11.

25. *RH* 9.16.12–13.

26. *kiccaü muṇi visayavirattaü ji thirasarīramaṇi bhāvaïṃ* |
ṭhiu jhāṇeṃ eyaggamaṇu acalu amaragiri ṇāvaïṃ || *RH* 9.16.14 ||

27. *RH* 9.17.1–6.

28. *RH* 9.17.7–8.

29. *RH* 9.17.9.

as Sukumāra, the son of a woman named Sukumārā. After poisoning a sage, Sukumārā was reborn in hell, as was Sukumāra, because his mother never taught him the Jain teachings.[30] The two souls remained connected for many existences, sometimes as animals, sometimes as mother and child, sometimes as lovers.[31] After somehow breaking this cycle, Sukumāra eventually was born as Madhu, who was to become an ascetic, erasing his bad karma by giving alms to a sage. After Madhu died, he was reborn in heaven and then reborn as Kīcaka.[32] The woman suffered greatly in all of her existences, and eventually became a nun who took on a *nidāna* (sinful resolution), and was reborn in heaven, and then again as Draupadī.[33] Kīcaka's explanation of his multi-lifetime connection to Draupadī satisfies the *yakṣa*, who then accepts the Jain faith.[34] Eventually Kīcaka attains final emancipation.[35]

This interesting twist is again a common device in Jain narrative literature, which seeks to educate the audience on the workings of karma. Reminiscent of the *yakṣa* who famously tests Yudhiṣṭhira during the Pāṇḍavas' forest exile in the Sanskrit epic,[36] this *yakṣa* tests Kīcaka's resolve, thereby setting up an opportunity for the new monk to explain his behavior. The account of his and Draupadī's connection through previous existences offers nuance to Kīcaka's character. The Jain audience now comes to understand Kīcaka not as a shameless villain (as he appears in the *Mahābhārata*) but as a man overcome by an irrational, blinding passion for Draupadī resulting from the accumulation of karma in previous existences.

This is by no means an innovation on Raïdhū's part. Raïdhū was inspired by a very similar account of the Kīcaka episode in Jinasena Punnāṭa's *Harivaṃśapurāṇa*.[37] Yet one notable difference between the accounts of Jinasena Punnāṭa and Raïdhū is that in Jinasena Puṇṇāṭa's narrative, Bhīma, while beating Kīcaka, is overcome with compassion and releases him:

---

30. *RH* 9.17.10–18.2.

31. *RH* 9.18.3–5.

32. *RH* 9.18.6.

33. *RH* 9.18.7–9.

34. *RH* 9.18.10.

35. *RH* 9.18.11.

36. *MBh* 3.297–98.

37. *JPH* 46.23–62.

> After he had fully satisfied [Kīcaka's] desire for another man's
> wife, noble-minded [Bhīma]
> took pity and let him go, saying: "Go away, you wretch!"[38]

Although Raïdhū's account of the Kīcaka story otherwise follows Jinasena Punnāṭa's, it is striking that the two authors' visions of Bhīma diverge so dramatically. It could be argued that Raïdhū's choice to represent Bhīma as a fierce warrior through and through—rather than as a combatant whose compassion eventually gets the better of him, as Jinasena Punnāṭa portrays him—may demonstrate a consistence with Raïdhū's literary and political context, namely, the Tomar court of fifteenth-century Gwalior. As Pauwels shows elsewhere in this volume, the Tomar court held martial values in high esteem, and these values permeate Viṣṇudās' Hindi *Pāṇḍavcarit*. Like Viṣṇudās, Raïdhū may been inspired by a desire to accommodate these ideals of behavior, such as protecting the honor of a female relative, in his portrait of Bhīma.

Although Raïdhū also draws the story of Draupadī's previous lives from Jinasena Punnāṭa's *Harivaṃśapurāṇa*, this narrative has a longer history in Jain literature. A variant of the story is found in a number of Śvetāmbara texts, including the Prakrit *Nāyādhammakahāo*, the sixth book of the Śvetāmbara canon, in order to explain why Draupadī is married to five husbands.[39] The *Nāyādhammakahāo* story begins with Draupadī's former birth as Nāgaśrī, a *brāhmaṇa* woman who unintentionally prepares a poisonous curry. The Jain monk Dharmaruci eats all of the curry in order to save innocent animals from consuming it and subsequently dies. When Nāgaśrī dies, she suffers many rebirths in hell and as a lower being, until she is reborn as Sukumārikā, a frustrated woman who becomes a nun after two unsuccessful marriages. One day, Sukumārikā sees a courtesan flirting with five men. The envious Sukumārikā then takes on a *nidāna* to attract the attention of men in her next life. After a birth in heaven, she is born

38. *JPH* 46.36.

39. The problematics of Draupadī's marriage to five men in Jain Mahābhāratas are discussed extensively in the works of Jonathan Geen. See "The Marriage of Draupadī"; "The Evolution of Draupadī's Marriage in the Jaina Tradition," *Asiatische Studien-Etudes Asiatiques* 59, no. 2 (2005): 443–97; and "Jaina Origins for the Mahābhārata Story of Draupadī's Past Life," *Asiatische Studien-Etudes Asiatiques* 60, no. 3 (2006): 575–606.

as Draupadī and ends up marrying the five Pāṇḍavas. This early Śvetāmbara account seeks to explain Draupadī's polyandrous marriage.[40]

These previous birth stories in the *Nāyādhammakahāo* and the ones described above from Raïdhū's and Jinasena Punnāṭa's tellings are considerably different: the first deals with Draupadī's past lives, the second with Kīcaka's. Because the *Nāyādhammakahāo* story is concerned only with explaining Draupadī's polyandry, it does not include any reference to Kīcaka or his previous births. Nevertheless, these different accounts do agree that Draupadī was a woman called Sukumārikā or Sukumārā who became a nun and was reborn as Draupadī as the result of a *nidāna*.[41] The fact that these two Digambara authors take up a story found in the Śvetāmbara canonical story of Draupadī's past lives and adapt it in order to explain Kīcaka's infatuation with Draupadī seems to suggest that the origins of the Jain story of Draupadī's previous births, or at least the story of Sukumārikā's *nidāna*, predates the hardening of the Śvetāmbara-Digambara divide in the first centuries of the Common Era.

In many ways, the Kīcaka story in Raïdhū's *Harivaṃsapurāṇa* could not be more different from the one that appears in Viṣṇudās' *Pāṇḍavcarit*, even though both works appear to have been composed around the same time in Gwalior. Viṣṇudās largely follows the narrative of the Sanskrit *Mahābhārata*, with Bhīma mercilessly reducing Kīcaka to a lump of flesh,[42] whereas Raïdhū's Kīcaka survives and becomes a Jain monk. Nevertheless, there are several striking coincidences between them. For example, as Pauwels notes in her chapter, unlike in the Sanskrit *Mahābhārata,* in both of these poems, Bhīma disguises himself as a woman before meeting Kīcaka.[43]As we discussed earlier, another similarity is that both authors narrate Bhīma following through on his promise to kill Kīcaka (a portrayal that may seem standard to many Mahābhārata readers, but that contrasts with Jinasena Punnaṭa's Bhīma, who ultimately releases Kīcaka). Both authors refer to the Pāṇḍavas' host as Vairāṭa (Apabhramsha: Vairāḍa), rather than Virāṭa (as the character is known in many other Mahābhāratas).

---

40. See Geen, "The Marriage of Draupadī," 109–12.

41. In Digambara versions, Draupadī is married to Arjuna alone. See Geen, 173.

42. *PC* 4.3. All references to the *Pāṇḍavcarit* (*PC*) in this essay are to: Viṣṇudās, *Mahākavi Viṣṇudās Kṛt Mahābhārat (Pāṇḍav-carit),* ed. Harihar Nivas Dvivedi (Gwalior: Vidya Mandir Prakasan, 1973).

43. *RH* 9.16.3–4, *PC* 4.3.118–21.

What's more, both Raïdhū and Viṣṇudās give Arjuna's alter ego a name other than Bṛhannaḍā (or Bṛhannalā), which is what appears in the Sanskrit *Mahābhārata* and elsewhere.[44] Raïdhū names this character Vihaṃṭali; Viṣṇudās calls her Bihaṃdari.[45] Neither of these two names are straightforward phonological derivatives from the Sanskrit Bṛhannaḍā, but they are cognate with one another. The similarity between the names suggests that Viṣṇudās possibly knew Raïdhū's *Harivaṃsapurāṇa* and adapted the name from it. (If Viṣṇudās' work was composed earlier than Raïdhū's, then the reverse could be true.) Another possibility is that both authors were inspired by another local version of the narrative, perhaps in performance, that made use of the name Vihaṃtali (or Bihaṃdari).[46]

Svayambhūdeva's *Riṭṭhaṇemicariu*

The *Riṭṭhaṇemicariu* (Sanskrit: *Ariṣṭanemicarita*) is Svayambhūdeva's most voluminous work, consisting of 1937 *kaḍavaka*s and 112 *sandhi*s that extend across four books: (1) *Yādavakāṇḍa* ("The Book of the Yādavas"), (2) *Kurukāṇḍa* ("The Book of the Kurus"), (3) *Yuddhakāṇḍa* ("The Book of War") and (4) *Uttarakāṇḍa* ("The Book of the Epilogue"). By using the term *kāṇḍa* for the division of his work, Svayambhūdeva continues the practice of his first *magnum opus*, the *Paümacariu* ("The Life of Padma"), an Apabhramsha Rāmāyaṇa retelling. (The Sanskrit *Rāmāyaṇa* is also divided into *kāṇḍas*.) Of the 112 *sandhi*s in the *Riṭṭhaṇemicariu*, only the first ninety-nine were composed by Svayambhūdeva himself. From the colophons of the extant manuscripts, we learn that *sandhi*s 100–104 were added by his son Tribhuvana. The final eight chapters were composed in fifteenth-century Gwalior by the *bhaṭṭāraka*-poet Yaśaḥkīrti. Yaśaḥkīrti figures prominently among the *bhaṭṭāraka*s who mediated with patrons for Raïdhū's endeavors. Unlike later poets such as Raïdhū, who embed their

44. *MBh* 4.2.22. On Bṛhannaḍā in the Sanskrit epic as well as in the Sanskrit drama *Pañcarātra*, see Nell Shapiro Hawley's chapter in this volume.

45. *PC* 4.3.19.

46. Ronald Stuart McGregor argues for a possible influence of Jain Apabhramsha Mahābhāratas in Viṣṇudās' truncated version of the Bhagavadgītā in the *Pāṇḍavcarit.* See *Hindi Literature from Its Beginnings to the Nineteenth Century* (Wiesbaden: Otto Harrassowitz, 1984), 37.

sandhibandhas in lengthy *praśastis* with valuable sociocultural references, we have little direct evidence of Svayambhūdeva's historical context. The colophons mention a certain Dhavalaïya as his patron but lack any further information. A commentarial remark on another work may suggest that Svayambhūdeva adhered to the Yāpanīya sect, a now-extinct branch of Jainism.[47] Svayambhūdeva's works, however, circulated heavily among Digambaras.

Svayambhūdeva is the first Jain author of a Harivaṃśa or Mahābhārata to use a frame story to criticize more authoritative versions of the narrative. (This rhetorical strategy is inspired by one that frequently appears in Jain Rāmāyaṇas and of which Svayambhūdeva makes use in his own Rāmāyaṇa, the *Paümacariu.*) The frame story begins in the same way that Jain Mahābhāratas (and Rāmāyaṇas) typically do: Śreṇika, the king of Rājagṛha, attends the holy assembly of Mahāvīra, the last *tīrthaṅkara*, who lived in the sixth century BCE. Earlier Jain texts dealing with the Mahābhārata depict Śreṇika asking to hear the story of the Hari dynasty, the Kuru dynasty, and so on; in this text, by contrast, Śreṇika motivates his request with a *kaḍavaka* of critical statements and almost disdainful questions about the major events of the story he is about to hear:

> Today doubt permeates my mind. Everyone hears things that are wrong:
> [They say] Nārāyaṇa (Kṛṣṇa) served Nara (Arjuna): he steered his chariot and kept his horses in check.[48]
> Dhṛtarāṣṭra and Pāṇḍu were fathered by a bachelor. Kuntī is said to have had five husbands.[49]
> When [they say that] the five Pāṇḍavas [were the husbands] of Draupadī, should we say it is true or false?
> Bad behavior is a source of joy for people; they do not think of how it destroys one's reputation.

47. The reference is said to occur in a gloss on Puṣpadanta's *Mahāpurāṇa*. See Nathuram Premi, *Jain Sāhitya aur Itihās* (Bombay: Hindi Granth Ratnakar, 1942), 374.

48. Svayambhū here rejects the idea that, Kṛṣṇa, a god, would act as the charioteer of Arjuna.

49. Vyāsa, an unmarried sage, is the biological father of Dhṛtarāṣṭra and Pāṇḍu (*MBh* 1.100), and Kuntī is the wife of Pāṇḍu but has children with four Vedic deities and thus has five "husbands."

If Bhīṣma had the ability to die at his own wish, then why did he die at all?[50]
If Droṇa were invincible with his arrow and bow, then how come he perished in battle?[51]
If Karṇa was born from her ear, then how come Kuntī did not die giving birth?[52]
Can a man be born from pitcher? Did the Kauravas' teacher Droṇa arise from a pitcher?[53]
Even if relatives are angry, surely they do not drink[54] each other's blood![55]

In these lines, Śreṇika rejects a series of narrative events that occur in the Sanskrit *Mahābhārata*.[56] The author's aim is to discredit the entire

50. Bhīṣma receives a boon allowing him to pick the time of his own death (*MBh* 1.94).

51. This is a reference to Droṇa possessing many divine, invincible weapons (*MBh* 1.121).

52. While this is not found in the Sanskrit epic, multiple regional Mahābhāratas, including Peruntēvaṉār's ninth-century Tamil *Pāratavenpā*, Kabi Sañjay's fifteenth-century Bengali *Mahābhārata*, Cĕṟuśśeri's fifteenth-century Malayalam *Bhāratagātha*, and Sabalsingh Cauhān's seventeenth-/eighteenth-century Hindi *Mahābhārat* describe Karṇa being born from Kuntī's ear. See Kambalur Venkatesa Acharya, *Mahabharata and Variations: Perundevanar and Pampa; A Comparative Study* (Kurnool: Vyasaraja Publications, 1981), 113; Pradip Bhattacharya, "Variations on Vyasa: The First Bengali Mahabharatas," *Boloji*, April 29, 2011, https://www.boloji.com/articles/10910/variations-on-vyasa; A. Harindranath and A. Purushothaman, "*Mahābhārata* Variations in Malayalam," *Mahabharata Resources*, May 22, 2005, http://mahabharata-resources.org/variations/mvm_v2.pdf; Sabalsingh Cauhān, *Sabalsingh Cauhān-Viracit Mahābhārat* (Lucknow: Tej Kumar Book Depot, 2015), 17; and Devdutt Pattanaik, *Jaya: An Illustrated Retelling of the Mahabharata* (Delhi: Penguin Books, 2010), 69. Note that *karṇa* also means "ear" in Sanskrit.

53. When the sage Bharadvāja spills some semen in a pitcher (*droṇa*), his son (Droṇa) is born from it (*MBh* 1.121).

54. This refers to Bhīma drinking the blood of his cousin, Duḥśāsana (*MBh* 8.61).

55. *SR* 1.3. For Svayambhūdeva's *Riṭṭhaṇemicariu* (*SR*), we have consulted: Svayambhūdeva, *Riṭṭhaṇemicariu—Yādavakāṇḍa*, ed. and trans. D. K. Jain (Delhi: Bharatiya Jnanpith, 1985); and Svayambhūdeva, *Riṭṭhaṇemicariya*, ed. R. S. Tomar, 5 vols. (Ahmedabad: Prakrit Text Society, 1993–2000).

56. The one exception is the story of Karṇa being born from Kuntī's ear. See note 52 above.

Mahābhārata by illuminating the narrative's internal inconsistencies. If Bhīṣma and Droṇa were basically immortal, how come they died? If Kṛṣṇa is a god, then how come he acts as Arjuna's servant? They further reject episodes that go against common South Asian mores in later ages, such as Vyāsa's levirate and Draupadī's polyandry, or that defy common sense (How could the hero of a narrative drink a relative's blood?). This practice of criticizing the authoritative *Mahābhārata* is adopted by subsequent authors of Jain Mahābhāratas, such as the sixteenth-century poets Śubhacandra and Vādicandra. They seem to occur only in works where the Mahābhārata narrative is dominant over the other subjects (the biographies of Kṛṣṇa and Neminātha and the *Bṛhatkathā*).[57] By putting forth such criticisms (which, again, can also be found in Jain Rāmāyaṇa tellings) into the mouth of Śreṇika as part of the narrative frame, the Jain authors create a Jain *purāṇic* setting that parallels that of the Hindu *purāṇas*; in this shared setting, a character asks an authoritative figure to clarify certain things in a question-and-answer session.

In the *Riṭṭhaṇemicariu*, the events of the Sanskrit epic's *Virāṭaparvan* are narrated in condensed form over the course of twenty sections in chapter twenty-eight. Despite the critique of the *Mahābhārata* in the *Riṭṭhaṇemicariu*'s frame story, the *Virāṭaparvan* narrative within the *Riṭṭhaṇemicariu* follows that of the Sanskrit epic (and not that of Jinasena Punnāṭa's *Harivaṃśapurāṇa*). Characteristic of Svayambhūdeva's work is its evocative poetic style: Svayambhūdeva uses classical literary embellishments to the degree that its author has the tendency to abridge narrative content in order to allow more space for expansive descriptions in which similes and metaphors enhance the poetic experience of the text. At the outset of the episode, Svayambhūdeva echoes much of the imagery and narrative framework of the Sanskrit *Virāṭaparvan*: for instance, the action begins with the Pāṇḍavas discussing which disguises they should don and transitions when Nakula hides their weapons in a *śamī* tree near the edge of the city.[58] Yudhiṣṭhira and Bhīma take on the names Kaṅka and Ballava, just as they do in the *Mahābhārata*. Later on, most of the details of the interactions between Draupadī and Kīcaka remain consistent between the

57. For a comparison and further discussion on these rejections, see Eva De Clercq and Tine Vekemans, "Rejecting and Appropriating Epic Lore," in *Jaina Narratives*, ed. Peter Flügel (London: Routledge, forthcoming).

58. *SR* 28.1–4.

Riṭṭhaṇemicariu and the Sanskrit *Virāṭaparvan*; in both accounts, Draupadī and Bhīma plot for Bhīma to kill Kīcaka by surprise in Virāṭa's dance hall.

Donning their disguises, the group introduce themselves to the gatekeeper and are invited to enter and stay there. Then Kīcaka is introduced:

> [The Pāṇḍavas] spent eleven months there, all performing the duties they were familiar with.
> The twelfth month arrived like Death's bludgeon that fell on Kīcaka.
> His body burning, he caught the fever of love. [Kāma's][59] flower arrow tortured and pierced him.
> Draupadī's wide eyes speared him, igniting his lust.
> Her exquisite breasts gave him joy. The fire of Kāma, the bodiless one, scorched his body.
> Prince [Kīcaka] waned, his face completely white, like a forest elephant separated from his mate.
> Wherever the woman went, he would drop hundreds of compliments.[60]

The very first mention of Kīcaka encapsulates Kīcaka's fate: in the second line, the poet compares the arrival of the twelfth month of the Pāṇḍavas' stay to Death's bludgeon falling on Kīcaka. With this simile (and a few other similar devices described below), the poet prepares the audience for the climactic battle between Bhīma and Kīcaka further in this chapter.

Unable to bear Kīcaka's advances, Draupadī rejects him and threatens that her five *gandharva* (semi-divine attendants of the god Indra) husbands will kill him.[61] Boasting about his powers, Kīcaka utters contempt for her husbands, subjects himself to Draupadī, and offers her half the kingdom.[62] Again rejected by her, Kīcaka now turns to his sister (here named Kaïkaï)[63]

59. Kāma is the god of love.

60. *SR* 28.6.1–7.

61. *SR* 28.6.8–9.

62. *SR* 28.7.1–4.

63. Kaïkaï is the Apabhramsha form of Kaikeyī. In the vulgate recension of the Sanskrit *Mahābhārata*, Sudeṣṇā is referred to as Kaikeyī twice (4.9.6–7 and 4.15.1). See *Mahabharata, Book Four: Virata,* trans. Kathleen Garbutt, Clay Sanskrit Library (New York: New York University Press, JJC Foundation, 2006).

and asks her to intervene by ordering Draupadī to bring some unguent to his quarters. When Draupadī does so, Kīcaka grabs her by the hand. She manages to escape and runs to Virāṭa and Yudhiṣṭhira.[64] As the men in the royal assembly look on, Kīcaka grabs Draupadī by the hair and kicks her with his feet.[65] Bhīma wants to intervene, but is held back by Yudhiṣṭhira.[66] Draupadī despondently cries for her *gandharva* husbands.[67] When night falls, she visits Bhīma and bemoans the state of servitude to which the Pāṇḍavas have been reduced and threatens to kill herself.[68] Bhīma's reply betrays the poet's Jain inclinations:

> Why do you cry, my dear? Wipe your eyes, vessels of past suffering and pain!
> Did you not observe the law of *saṃsāra*? To what extent do we get happiness? To what extent pain?
> The tree of our past actions bears both types of fruit, Draupadī. Was Sītā's suffering any less, when Rāvaṇa abducted her?[69]

In the Sanskrit *Mahābhārata*, after Draupadī's drawn-out complaint, a dejected Bhīma first voices his own frustrations and then attempts to comfort and encourage her to persevere just a little while longer by reminding her of famous women who endured suffering while following their husbands.[70] In the *Riṭṭhaṇemicariu*, Svayambhūdeva transforms Bhīma's words into concepts more consistent with Jain ideology: all beings caught in *saṃsāra* (the eternal cycle of birth, death, and rebirth) are subject to the laws of karma; suffering is the result of one's own past actions. Svayambhūdeva's reference to Sītā reflects Bhīma's words from the Sanskrit *Mahābhārata*, which reveals the poet's familiarity with the text.[71]

---

64. *SR* 28.7.5–9.

65. *SR* 28.8.1–2.

66. *SR* 28.8.3–6.

67. *SR* 28.8.7–9.2.

68. *SR* 28.9.3–11.4.

69. *SR* 28.11.7–9. Sītā is Rāma's wife and Rāvaṇa is the demon king who abducts her in the Rāmāyaṇa tradition.

70. *MBh* 4.20.

71. *MBh* 4.20.9–10.

Bhīma then promises Draupadī that he will kill Kīcaka, despite Yudhiṣṭhira's order to desist.[72] Draupadī goes back to her quarters, and dawn breaks. Analogous to the simile of Death's bludgeon falling on Kīcaka, the closing verse of the *kaḍavaka* below hints at Kīcaka's impending doom: "Because [Kīcaka] yesterday pulled Draupadī's hair, the sun came up, as if to discover: 'Is he dead yet?' "[73] Anthropomorphized as a spectator, the sun takes on imagined behavior that suggests the audience's anticipation of Kīcaka's death.

Draupadī approaches Kīcaka, who addresses her once more. This time, instead of rejecting him, Draupadī invites him to come to the dance hall at night, where they will make love.[74] Thereafter Draupadī reports back to Bhīma, who prepares for the fight, while Kīcaka prepares for a rendezvous.[75] Bhīma enters the dance hall, later followed by Kīcaka:

> The place where Bhīma had entered—where a lion set himself up to attack a deer—there his enemy, the paramour, came in, acting as if it were his own home.
>
> He was not aware that it was a chessboard of death that had been set up.[76]

Bhīma grabs Kīcaka by the hair. Kīcaka, thinking he is being attacked by one of Draupadī's *gandharva* husbands, manages to escape his grip and tells his adversary that fighting him is useless, since he is destined to die at the hand of Bhīma.[77] This motif of Kīcaka being predestined to die at Bhīma's hand, apparently an innovation of Svayambhūdeva, on the one hand rationalizes the outrageousness of Kīcaka's behavior toward Draupadī. Kīcaka probably thinks he is immortal, having assumed that Bhīma and his brothers have perished during their banishment in the forest. On the other

72. *SR* 28.12.

73. Svayambhūdeva's focus here on Kīcaka pulling Draupadī's hair highlights the parallel of this episode with the one in the Sanskrit epic where Duḥśāsana drags Draupadī into the assembly by pulling her hair (*MBh* 2.60.25).

74. *SR* 28.13.1–14.2.

75. *SR* 28.14.3–5.

76. *SR* 28.14.6–7. There are very similar images in the parallel passage in the Sanskrit epic (*MBh* 4.21.38).

77. *SR* 28.14.8–15.4.

hand, this is a popular narrative device that enhances the dramatic effect. Kīcaka's confrontation with his destiny is completely unexpected.

Bhīma reveals his true identity as well as that of his brothers and Draupadī,[78] and a fierce fight erupts between the two.[79] Bhīma takes a severe hit in the chest:

> As he observed [Kīcaka], the general of unequalled power,
> Bhīma's lotus face withered.
> [He reflected:] "Will I lose my reputation in battle? Will the drums of infamy resound in the world?
> Will people speak of disgrace?" Somehow, he collected himself,
> And he exerted his strength with both his arms and struck [Kīcaka] in the chest with a blow of his fists.
> The impact sent him to the city of Yama, the god of death. That Kīcaka was reduced to the shape of a tortoise.[80]

Bhīma then brings Kīcaka's corpse outside, and Draupadī announces that her *gandharva* husbands killed him.[81] When they hear of this, Kīcaka's 105 brothers, without permission from Virāṭa, decide to burn Draupadī along with the body of Kīcaka.[82] Draupadī calls for her *gandharva* husbands, and Bhīma comes to her rescue. He uproots a tree and chases away the brothers. In an interesting deviation from the Sanskrit *Mahābhārata*[83] and many other Jain Mahābhāratas, Bhīma does not appear to kill Kīcaka's brothers.[84] Afraid of future *gandharva* attacks, Virāṭa asks Kaïkaï to send her servant girl away. After Draupadī returns from a visit with Vihaṃdala (Bṛhannaḍā), the queen asks her to leave. Threatening the destruction of the city, Draupadī begs her to be allowed to stay for thirteen more days.[85]

78. *SR* 28.15.5–9.

79. *SR* 28.16.1–8.

80. *SR* 28.17.1–5.

81. *SR* 28.17.6–8.

82. *SR* 28.18.

83. *MBh* 4.22.

84. *SR* 28.19.

85. *SR* 28.20. Note the resemblance between the names Vihaṃdala in the *SR*, Vihaṃtali in the *RH*, and Bihaṃdari in the *PC*.

Svayambhūdeva breaks with the tradition of earlier Jain Mahābhāratas: not only is he the first Jain author to present this episode in a violent way, but he is also the first to lay the focus on the Pāṇḍavas and the battle of Kurukṣetra, instead of Kṛṣṇa or Neminātha, in a work titled the *Nemināthacarita* or the *Harivaṃśapurāṇa*. Given the status of Jinasena Punnāṭa's *Harivaṃśapurāṇa* as a work of great authority among Digambaras, it is difficult to conceive that the poet was unaware of this specifically Jain version. It is more likely that he made a deliberate choice to distance himself from these earlier versions and to compose a work closer to the Sanskrit *Mahābhārata*. If we assume that Svayambhūdeva's audience, more precisely his patron Dhavalaïya, like the poet himself, were Jain laypeople, then this audience may have preferred a detailed account of hand-to-hand combat over the more moralistic Mahābhārata of Svayambhūdeva's predecessor, Jinasena Punnāṭa. This preference is also reflected in his treatment of the Kīcaka episode, where the poet deliberately builds up the anticipation to the fight, culminating in Kīcaka's death. Except in his words of comfort to Draupadī on the nature of *saṃsāra*, Svayambhūdeva's Bhīma is just as violent as the Bhīma of the *Mahābhārata*: as the above passage suggests, Bhīma is uniquely concerned with losing his reputation as a warrior if he were to lose the fight with Kīcaka. Svayambhūdeva even extends the violence of the episode, describing how a fierce Draupadī threatens to have Virāṭa's city destroyed if she were forced to leave, a motif that is absent in the *Mahābhārata*.

The choice of Apabhramsha—a medium that is, on the one hand, a classical language of literature, and on the other, already close to regional languages and literatures in many ways and possibly informed by popular performances—similarly reflects Svayambhūdeva's choice to situate the *Riṭṭhaṇemicariu* adjacent to the Sanskrit epic. Apabhramsha allows Svayambhūdeva to echo the classical literary qualities of the *Mahābhārata* and, at the same time, reach a lay audience that would have resisted the overt moralizing of earlier Jain Mahābhāratas and that may have preferred the more violent telling of the *Mahābhārata* with which they may have been familiar. Authors of subsequent *Pāṇḍavapurāṇa*s and *Pāṇḍavacarita*s, such as Śubhacandra and Devaprabhasūri, followed in Svayambhūdeva's footsteps by presenting Kīcaka's fate in a similar way.

Nevertheless, other Jain Apabhramsha authors such as Raïdhū revert to Jinasena Punnāṭa's "moral cleansing" of the violent episode, transforming

Kīcaka into an exemplar whose fate is explained karmically. The choice for either variant cannot be explained along sectarian or monastic lines. In practice, even when Jain Mahābhāratas circulated in the same limited environments (such as fifteenth-century Gwalior), they exhibited a narrative variety that illustrates the extraordinary diversity, complexity, and flexibility of the Mahābhārata tradition as a whole.

Chapter Twelve

The Power-Politics of Desire and Revenge

A Classical Hindi *Kīcakavadha* Performance at the Tomar Court of Gwalior[1]

Heidi Pauwels

Why was the Mahābhārata retold in the vernacular? This chapter presents a reconsideration of the case of the first complete extant classical Hindi Mahābhārata retelling, usually called the *Pāṇḍavcarit* ("The Story of the Pāṇḍavas"), which was composed by Viṣṇudās in 1435 CE in Gwalior in present-day Madhya Pradesh.[2] Little is known about Viṣṇudās,[3] but his epic

1. This research has been made possible thanks to a visiting professorship at the University of Ghent in Belgium, with a Royalty Research Foundation Grant of the University of Washington in Seattle.

2. This is the name under which the work has been edited on the basis of two manuscripts. See Harihar Nivas Dvivedi's introduction in Viṣṇudās, *Mahākavi Viṣṇudās Kṛt Mahābhārat (Pāṇḍav-carit),* ed. Harihar Nivas Dvivedi (Gwalior: Vidya Mandir Prakasan, 1973), 26–29. All references to the *Pāṇḍavcarit* (*PC*) in this essay are to this edition.

3. On the basis of his reference to a Sundarnāth as Viṣṇudās' *guru* in his Rāmāyaṇa, Ronald Stuart McGregor asserts that Viṣṇudās was a Nāth Yogī in "An Early Hindi (Brajbhāṣā) Version of the Rāma Story," in *Devotion Divine: Bhakti Traditions from the Regions of India,* eds. Diana Eck and Françoise Mallison (Groningen: Egbert

recreations in classical Hindi (he also composed a Rāmāyaṇa in 1442) are sometimes characterized as assertions of Hindu identity during a period that followed an interlude of Sultanate-installed overlordship.[4] In this essay, I question this assumption via a two-pronged approach: first, inspired by micro-history, I situate the *Pāṇḍavcarit* against the background of the specific historical circumstances at the time of its composition at the Tomar court in Gwalior,[5] and second, inspired by performance studies, I analyze the emotional appeal of this Mahābhārata recreation, asking what work it does as a public performance. I focus on one episode, a tale of desire and revenge, the *Kīcakavadha* ("The Slaying of Kīcaka,") from the *Virāṭaparva* ("The Book of Virāṭa's Court"), in which King Virāṭa's brother-in-law, Kīcaka, is gruesomely murdered by Bhīma after accosting Draupadī.

I first highlight how the vernacular epic presents itself within a Sanskrit tradition and analyze the emotional regimes that are mobilized in its preamble. Next I ask what ends may have been served by this poem given the historical context of its creation, and how the performance of the work indexes and alters social paradigms during that particular time. Zooming in on the emotional development in Viṣṇudās' long rendering of the *Kīcakavadha* episode, with its twin themes of desire and violent revenge, I investigate how it can be construed as a critique of existing power relations. By searching for theatrical traditions that may have inspired this epic, I then

---

Forsten, 1991), 182. The evidence for this, however, is weak, as pointed out by Imre Bangha in "Early Hindi Epic Poetry in Gwalior: Beginnings and continuities in the Rāmāyan of Vishnudas," in *After Timur Left: Culture and Circulation in Fifteenth-Century North India*, eds. Francesca Orsini and Samira Sheikh (Delhi: Oxford University Press, 2014), 370 n13.

4. Thus Dvivedi reads his sources anachronistically from a communalist perspective, a stance that has sometimes been uncritically adopted by other scholars.

5. Besides the multiple path-breaking works of Dvivedi and the aforementioned essays, see also the following essays by Ronald Stuart McGregor: "Vishnudas and his *Rāmāyan-kātha,*" in *Studies in Early Modern Indo-Aryan Languages, Literature and Culture*, eds. Alan Entwistle and Carol Salomon with Heidi Pauwels and Michael C. Shapiro (Delhi: Manohar, 1999); "A Narrative Poet's View of his Material: Viṣṇudās's Introduction to his Brajbhāṣā *Pāṇḍav-carit* (AD 1435)" in *The Banyan Tree: Essays on Early Literature in New Indo-Aryan Languages*, ed. Mariola Offredi (Delhi: Manohar, 2000); and "The Progress of Hindi, Part 1: The Development of a Transregional Idiom," in *Literary Cultures in History: Reconstructions from South Asia*, ed. Sheldon Pollock (Berkeley: University of California Press, 2003).

draw comparisons between the *Pāṇḍavcarit* and the contemporaneous (and similarly named) folk genre of *Paṇḍvānī*. In the conclusion, I discuss the implications of this case study for vernacular epics more broadly.

A *Kauravādi-Vadha*: Foregrounding the Martial Mood

The fifteenth-century classical Hindi *Pāṇḍavcarit* places itself in the lineage of the Sanskrit *Mahābhārata*. In his preface, Viṣṇudās pays obeisance to the legendary sage Vyāsa, stating that his own work is based on having "heard" the "old version."[6]

> Then I bow my head for that Vyāsa, [thanks to] whom the faults
> of human weakness do not show.
> I have brought to the year of 1435 CE (1492 VS)[7] the old story
> of the Pāṇḍavas, as I have heard it.[8]

By claiming the sage as his inspiration, Viṣṇudās cements the relationship between his retelling and the Sanskrit *Mahābhārata*. At the same time, he explains that he updated his rendering of the epic to be relevant to the time of its production. The use of the word "heard" indicates the author was not working from a written copy of the Sanskrit text, but rather from an oral tradition. It is possible that he refers to a recitation of the *Mahābhārata*, but more likely to a performance, as I will discuss below.[9]

The prestige of the Sanskrit model is further acknowledged through the inclusion of a lengthy Sanskrit preamble, which ends with a line that sets

6. While it is not impossible that the term *purānā* refers to the genre of the *purāṇa* literature, I decided to translate it here literally, as the most neutral option.

7. The Vikram Saṃvat (VS) calendar system, which was used extensively in premodern North India, has a zero point of approximately 57 BCE.

8. *puni tihi vyāsa navani kiya sīsā tā nara rogu kalaṅku na dīsā*
caudaha sai ru bānavai ānā paṇḍucaritu meṃ sunyo purānā || *PC* 1.1.34 ||

9. One possibility is that he heard a contemporaneous Jain retelling of the epic. The Apabhramsha authors Yaśaḥkīrti and Raïdhū were active in Gwalior around this time and composed on the topic just shortly after Viṣṇudās, perhaps influenced by the same sources. I have been engaged in collaborative research with Eva De Clercq on the topic.

the tone for the work as a whole: "Listen now to the supremely delightful story of the slaughter of the Kauravas and their allies on the occasion of the story of the Mahābhārata."[10] Importantly, the work here is designated a *kauravādi-vadha*: "slaughter of the Kauravas, et cetera." This strongly suggests a martial focus for this particular epic retelling as a whole.

The predominance of the martial mood is also strong in the classical Hindi preamble to the work that immediately follows the Sanskrit one. Viṣṇudās begins, of course, by paying obeisance to the elephant-headed remover of obstacles, Gaṇeśa, who is described as carrying a stainless axe.[11] Next he praises Viṣṇu: first as Narasiṃha, the half-man, half-lion slayer of the demon Hiraṇyakaśipu,[12] and then as Kṛṣṇa, the charioteer on the battlefield.[13] While the poet goes on to inform us that his telling of the Bhārata has been accomplished only through Kṛṣṇa's grace,[14] he does not evoke the romantic cowherd form of Kṛṣṇa, but rather his persona as an advisor in times of war.

Even the traditional praise to Sarasvatī, the goddess of learning, takes on a martial tone, as her warrior-goddess aspects are stressed in the couplet (*dohā*) that precedes the longer eulogy: "Worship the Remover of Obstacles, and then again bow your head to Śāradā (Sarasvatī), Protectress of the Gods [against] the hordes of demons, by whose grace this story is completed."[15] The eulogy itself is remarkably martial for this Brahmanical (*sāttvika*) goddess:

> Who carries on her chest the world with all nine divisions, on which powerful demons were slaughtered.[16]

10. *paramaramyā śrīmadbhāratakathāprasaṅge kauravādivadhakathā śrinvitām* (sic) || *PC* Sanskrit Preamble || In contrast to the highly accomplished Sanskrit of the preceding verses, the Sanskrit of this verse is deficient, but it occurs in both recensions of the text as extent. It is possible that this line might be a scribal error or a later interpolation.

11. *pharasā niramala sauhe pānī* || *PC* 1.1.2 ||

12. *PC* 1.1.5.

13. *rana mahaṃ jantā* || *PC* 1.1.9 ||

14. *bhārathu bhākhoṃ tohi pasāī* || *PC* 1.1.10 ||

15. *bhakti vināyaka kī karau puni sārada sira nāī*
sura racchaka asvara nikara jinha taiṃ kathā sirāī || *PC* 1.1, *dohā* 1 ||

16. *jihi ura dharai pahumi navakhaṇḍa aganita asura badhe balabaṃḍa* || *PC* 1.1.18 ||

Who manifested herself as Sītā and defeated Rāvaṇa . . .[17]
Creator of the eighty-four [Rajput][18] families, in your primordial
form you are the primordial maiden.[19]

Viṣṇudās unmistakably succeeds in setting the martial mood for his Mahābhārata right from the start.

The Martial Context: Claiming a *Kṣatriya* Status for the Tomars

The martial character of the work befits the occasion of its composition, which occurred in the month of Kārtik, at the beginning of the campaigning season after the monsoon rains stop and the roads are traversable again. This occasion is typically marked by ritual displays of military pomp. The auspicious moment of composition given within the text (not the colophon) of the *Pāṇḍavcarit* clues us in to its performance context. It is specified to be the *ekādaśī* (eleventh lunar day) of the dark half of Kārtik,[20] which is known as *Ramā-ekādaśī*; the event is celebrated by telling the story of King Mucukunda's daughter and her husband, Śobhan.[21] The theme of the story is how to make one's kingdom permanent, a concern preoccupying the still-new Tomar dynasty in Gwalior, which, at the time of the *Pāṇḍavcarit*'s composition, had succeeded in holding on to power for around four decades.

The poet describes the circumstances of how he was commissioned to compose a Mahābhārata, in the same breath asserting the Tomars' descent from the Pāṇḍavas:

The Tomars in Pāṇḍu's lineage are brave and strong, their king
Dūṅgar Singh is a grand hero.
Their fort, Gopācala, is a thorn in their enemies' eye.

17. *siyā rūpa rāvana saṃghāryau* || *PC* 1.1.19 || Sītā is the wife of Rāma and Rāvaṇa is the demon king who abducts her in the Rāmāyaṇa tradition.

18. The term Rajput refers to a martial social class/caste/community in South Asia.

19. *caurāsī kula sirajana hārī ādi rūpa tū ādi kuvārī* || *PC* 1.1.20 ||

20. *PC* 1.1.35.

21. The story of *Ramā-ekādaśī* is told in the Sanskrit *Padmapurāṇa* (6.60). See *Padmapurāṇa*, eds. J. L. Shastri, G. P. Bhatt, and N. A. Deshpande (Delhi: Motilal Banarasidass, 1951), 2534–38.

> A Muscular Bhīma, not afraid of anyone! Brandishing his sword,
> he inspires fear.[22]

This seems to be the first time that a Pāṇḍava genealogy is suggested for the Tomars. What better way to claim *kṣatriya* status for the newly established dynasty than by performing a Mahābhārata at the very beginning of the campaigning season?[23] Moreover, Viṣṇudās goes on to compare his patron, Dūṅgar Singh (r. ca. 1429–59),[24] with the fierce epic hero Bhīma.[25] Here the bard comes up with a situational construction of his patron: he invites his audience to read his selective Mahābhārata retelling allegorically and, in that allegory, to find local Gwalior martial ambitions that are centered around the figure of the king. The passage unmistakably points to an intent to legitimize and reconstruct existing power relations via the ritual performance of this Mahābhārata.

The reference to Gwalior (Gopācala) being a thorn in the enemies' eye may well have reminded its local audience of their recent confrontations

---

22. *paṇḍuvaṃsa tauvara dhuradhīrū ḍauṃgara singhu rāu bara bīrū*
gaṛha gopācala bairini sālū haya gaya nara pati ṭoḍara mālū
bhujabala bhīu na saṃkai kāsū asivara āni dikhāvai trāsū || *PC* 1.1.36–37 ||

23. Perhaps it is not coincidental either that the name of the fort becomes the more militaristic Gopācaladurgā (as opposed to the earlier Gopagiri or Gopācala) for the first time in one of Dūṅgar Singh's inscriptions (dated 1453 or 1510 VS). See Michael D. Willis, *Inscriptions of Gopakṣetra: Materials for the History of Central India* (London: British Museum Press, 1996), 32.

24. Dvivedi gives this range of dates as established on the basis of analysis of dated manuscripts and inscriptions in manuscripts mentioning him as ruler. Harihar Nivas Dvivedi, ed. *Gvāliar ke Tomār*, vol. 2 (Gwalior: Vidya Mandir Prakasan, 1976), 77–78. The 1429 (1486 VS) date of Yaśaḥkīrti's writing the *Bhaviṣyadattacaritra* is confirmed in the catalogue of manuscripts preserved in Naya Mandir, Dharmpura, Delhi. See Kundanlal Jain, *Dillī-Jina-grantha-ratnāvalī: Dig. Jaina Sarasvatī Bhaṇḍāra, Nayā Mandira, Dharmapurā, Dehalī ke Saṃskṛta, Prākṛta, evaṃ Apabhraṃśa kī hastalikhita pāṇḍulipiyoṃ kī sūcī* (Delhi: Bharatiya Jnanpith Prakasan, 1981), 1.4 no 20 and the colophon quoted on 2.6. Dvivedi extrapolates from other sources that his rule would have started in 1425, but that seems highly speculative. See *Gvāliar ke Tomār*, 75.

25. As Timothy Lorndale notes in his chapter in this volume, Ranna does something very similar in his Kannada *Sāhasabhīmavijaya*.

with the Delhi Sultan as well as with neighboring Malwa in 1424.[26] Some have read this as a resurgence of Hinduism against Muslim onslaught, but such a view considerably reduces the complexities of the political situation; enmity and alliances were expedient and not necessarily drawn along religious lines. Rather, as the Sultanate had weakened, Gwalior could afford to neglect to pay its tribute to Delhi; from 1426 through 1432, the Delhi Sultan had to campaign annually to receive his dues. Gwalior represented just one stop among many; neighboring principalities, including ones that were occupied by Muslim rulers, similarly revolted when they saw their chance.[27] Significantly, the Tomar Mahābhārata was first performed at the beginning of the campaigning season in 1435, shortly after the murder of the Delhi Sultan, Mubārak Shāh, and the death of Hoshang Shāh of Malwa—in other words, a period of instability in the region. Taking advantage of this political climate, Dūṅgar Singh tried to occupy the nearby stronghold of Bhander but he was rebuffed and had to sue for peace.

As described by contemporaneous Persian chronicler Muḥammad Bihāmad Khānī in the fourteenth chapter of the *Tārīḳh-i Muḥammadī*,[28] the affluent Seths of Gwalior had to pay considerable amounts to bail out their ruler. Gwalior was a flourishing center of commerce with a very active Jain trading community,[29] which, during Dūṅgar Singh's reign, conspicu-

26. C. E. Luard and Dwarka Nath, *Gwalior State Gazetteer*, 3 vols. (Calcutta: Superintendent Government Printing, 1908), 232. See, also, Heidi Pauwels, "The Tomars' New Emotional Regime: Martial Hindu Identity?" *South Asian History and Culture* 11, no. 1 (2020): 32–33.

27. See, for instance, the descriptions of these campaigns of the Sayyid sultans as well as those of the Lodis in Mohammad Habib and Khaliq Ahmad Nizami, eds. *Comprehensive History of India,* vol. 5, *The Delhi Sultanate* (Delhi: People's Publishing House, 1970), 637–40, 645–48, 650, 654, 684.

28. Muḥammad Bihāmad Khānī, *Tarikh-i-Muhammadi by Muhammad Bihamad Khani,* trans. Muhammad Zaki (Aligarh: Aligarh Muslim University, 1972), 79–80. This is related in a communalist vein by Dvivedi in *Gvāliar ke Tomār,* 81. See also McGregor, "Narrative Poet's View," 340.

29. See for instance the description of the city by the Apabhramsha poet Raïdhū, as translated in Eva De Clercq, "Apabhramsha as a Literary Medium in Fifteenth-Century North India," in *After Timur Left: Culture and Circulation in Fifteenth-Century North India,* eds. Francesca Orsini and Samira Sheikh (Delhi: Oxford University Press, 2014), 343–44. Raïdhū also reports on a conversation where the

ously displayed its wealth by sponsoring the huge Jain images of "peaceful conquerors" or *jinas* that still line the access road to the fort.[30] One can imagine that the rich merchants were not too keen on their ruler's adventurous campaigns. Dūṅgar Singh, however, did not give up. A few years later, in 1438, he felt emboldened enough to attack the stronghold Narwar that belonged to Malwa, again to no avail. In short, rather than project this Mahābhārata against a clash of religious identities, the "thorn in the eye" fits a pattern of neighborly aggression and revolt to feudal overlordship interspersed with tactical submission to the central power of the time.

Similarly, Khaḍagrāy's mid-seventeeth century classical Hindi chronicle *Gopācalākhyāna* ("The Tale of Gwalior") depicts the Tomars' takeover of Gwalior not as a victory over Muslim rulers but, rather, as an advance that was supported by an insecure, newly appointed Sultan in order to dislodge the local stakeholders.[31] Rather than enact a grand moral victory for dharma, the Tomars overcame their desperate position via a clever but morally dubious stratagem that involved mass murder of the hereditary Sayyid occupants of the fort and their families.[32] It was a breach of trust and hospitality. In that respect, the episode in which Bhīma kills his host's brother-in-law, Kīcaka, thus breaking the rules of hospitality, takes on a special resonance.

What preoccupied the Tomar court when the classical Hindi Mahābhārata was commissioned in 1435 was not dharmic warfare against Muslims, but, rather, how to prevail when outperformed by the enemy's superior military strength. The poet, Viṣṇudās, describes his commission as follows:

---

king casts himself as a generous sponsor, like the Gujarati Vīsaladeva and Sultan Firoz Shāh. See De Clercq, 357–58, 362. The positive evaluation of the Delhi Sultan also belies a simplistic Hindu-Muslim antagonism with the Tomars, as anachronistically read by Dvivedi.

30. See the inscriptions from Dūṅgar Singh's rule on or near Jain images, two of which are dated 1450 (1497 VS), another two dated 1510 VS, and one perhaps dated 1505 VS in Willis, *Inscriptions of Gopakṣetra,* 40–43. On the Jain images themselves, see Phyllis Granoff, "Mountains of Eternity: Raidhū and the Colossal Jinas of Gwalior," *Rivista di Studi Sudasiatici* 1 (2006): 31–50. Granoff also speculates about their significance within a Hindu-Muslim antagonistic context.

31. Khaḍagrāy, *Gopācal Ākhyān*, ed. Harihar Nivas Dvivedi (Gwalior: Jivaji Visvavidyalay, 1980), 89–92.

32. See Pauwels, "Tomars' New Emotional Regime," 30–31.

Dūṅgar the king commissioned this poet (by the ritual gift of *tambul*), asking:

> Tell with verve, O poet, the true gist of the Kauravas' and Pāṇḍavas' [conflict].
> [If] there were five Pāṇḍavas and one hundred Kauravas, how come Duryodhana was destroyed?[33]

In the *Pāṇḍavcarit*'s account of its own commission, then, we see that the king looks to the Mahābhārata narrative for advice on how to overcome an enemy whose forces outnumber his own. The poet does not cast the king as the Dharmarāja (king of dharma) Yudhiṣṭhira, as he might have done if he were setting out to claim moral victory for his king. Instead, he casts him as the formidable Bhīma.[34] This is not just a rhetorical device in the introduction; rather, he consistently foregrounds Bhīma's exploits throughout the work.[35] It seems that Bhīma's violent approach is central to the way in which he answers the king's quandary. As we shall see, the poet's retelling

33. *PC* 1.1.38–39.

34. Yudhiṣṭhira figures prominently in Viṣṇudās' later work, the *Svargārohaṇ*, which is a retelling of the final book of the *Mahābhārata*. (Not to be confused with the *Pāṇḍavcarit*, this is a separate work, with its own preface.) In this text, due to the nature of the topic of the looming *kali-yuga* (age of discord), indeed dharma takes on a more important role. The *Svargārohaṇ* is included as an appendix to Dvivedi's edition of the *PC*.

35. The lengthy *Ādiparva* ("The Book of Beginnings") revolves around attacks on the strongman Bhīma and his remarkable survival skills, starting when he was a baby and targeted by Gāndhārī in her jealousy of Kuntī's children (*PC* 1.2.51–60). It dwells on his slow-witted desire to play with his Kaurava cousins who know how to manipulate him to their advantage, culminating in his duel with Duryodhana (1.3). It foregrounds his role in the escape from the burning lac house (1.34–44) and tells at length the Hiḍimbā episode (1.4.45–62). In the *Sabhāparva* ("The Book of the Assembly Hall"), Bhīma's role in killing Jarāsandha is foregrounded (2.1). In the *Vanaparva* ("The Book of the Forest"), Bhīma's adventures while fetching a lotus for Draupadī, including the meeting with Hanumān and his massacre of the magical beings, the *yakṣa*s and *kiṃnara*s, are told extensively (3.3), and he plays a major role in saving the Kauravas from *gandharva*s (celestial musicians) (3.5). The *Virāṭaparva* is one of the longest books, and again foregrounds Bhīma's exploits—his fight with two wrestlers (4.2) and with an elephant (4.3)—before the *Kīcakavadha* described further below.

reveals that Bhīma's rashness causes terrible upheaval. I will suggest that there is something else going on in this text beyond the programmatic Rajputization that one might initially be led to emphasize.

Questioning Masculine Prowess in the *Kīcakavadha*

While Bhīma is at the center of several episodes throughout the *Pāṇḍavcarit*, I will focus here on the expansive retelling of Bhīma's slaughter of Kīcaka, the brother-in-law of Virāṭa, who is the Pāṇḍavas' host during their year of living undercover at the end of their exile. The *Virāṭaparva* of Viṣṇudās' retelling devotes nearly two chapters to this episode of desire and revenge, where Bhīma stealthily murders Kīcaka in retaliation for his sexual assault of Draupadī.[36] When compared to the Sanskrit epic's account of the episode, as well as those of other vernacular retellings (such as in Tikkana's portion of the Telugu *Mahābhāratamu*),[37] Viṣṇudās' version of the episode stands out for the prevalence of comedy (*hāsya rasa*). There are several indications that the transmitted text was the transcript of a performance that included slapstick comedy, which is exploited here to maximum effect. For example, when Kīcaka visits his sister, Queen Sudeṣṇā, Draupadī's mistress, and sees Draupadī for the first time, he is completely floored:

> He sat down, speaking of other things, but his eye dwelled over and over on the woman's body.
> When she (Sudeṣṇā) saw how helpless her brother was, she fanned him to relieve his heat.
> Longing for the beautiful lady (Draupadī) to glance at him, his body was already struck oblivious,

36. Out of five chapters (thirty-seven pages in Dvivedi's edition), the episode takes up nearly two whole chapters (*PC* 4.3.20–135–4.4.54) totaling thirteen pages (pages 119–32).

37. Harshita Mruthinti Kamath describes Tikkana's rendering on this episode in her chapter in this volume. See also the translation of this episode in Velcheru Narayana Rao and David Shulman, *Classical Telugu Poetry: An Anthology* (Berkeley: University of California Press, 2002), 83–101.

> Unable to utter a word to the queen, he was sweating profusely,
> His lips dry, his eyes rolling, his mouth wilted like a lotus,
> Moaning "Alas, alas." The Matsya queen forbade her clever maid.
> She grabbed his ponytail, warned him to control his body,
> As she understood his feelings, that he had fallen for the maid![38]

From a performance standpoint, it is important to note that this sequence of events is described with reference to the actors' expressions (*abhinaya*), such as Kīcaka's rolling eyes. We also see the queen pull her brother's hair—an action that ridicules Kīcaka's hypermasculinity and is sure to have elicited amused responses from the audience.

Sudeṣṇā then teaches Kīcaka a lesson, introducing a didactic element to the performance. Her advice turns the audience's laughter into a learning experience by citing a wide range of mythological antecedents about how blind lust can cause even those who have the most physical and political power to lose it:

> Brother, let me teach you a lesson. You are a fool taking out your anger on me.
> Your eyes have become blinded with desire! How could I express sins in words?
> Like you, so many have ruined their house, so many kings I've heard were destroyed,
> When they fell in love with the wives of others. Stones knocked their feet out from under them.
> Like you, Rāvaṇa made his choice, and for Sītā's sake, Rāma routed him.
> For the sake of Tārā, Vālin was destroyed by the exiled Sugrīva, [after the episode of] the king of the demons (Dundubhi).[39]
> Śumbha and Niśumbha were defeated by a woman.[40] Indra, on account of the sage, lost his body

38. *PC* 4.3.23–26.

39. A reference to the story of Vālin and Sugrīva in the Rāmāyaṇa tradition. Dundubhi is Rāvaṇa's brother-in-law.

40. A reference to the story of Śumbha and Niśumbha as told in the Sanskrit *Devīmāhātmya*.

When he enjoyed the wife (Ahalyā) of the *guru* (the sage Gautama);[41] And the Moon on account of [excessive love for] Rohiṇī became diseased.[42]
Viśvāmitra's austerities were spoiled when he kept company with the likes of a divine *apsaras*.[43]
Exposing the body of his wife, [Nala] became a cripple [at the court of] Rituparṇa.[44]
He who willingly abducts another's wife knows the path that lies before him."[45]
Thus she spoke, trying to make King Kīcaka understand.[46]

This type of instruction through negative examples is characteristic of advice literature of the period and is evident in the roughly contemporaneous Sanskrit *Puruṣaparīkṣā* by Vidyāpati of Tirhut (ca. 1410–1420). Sudeṣṇā evokes briefly what in Vidyāpati's text are called "counterexample stories" (*pratyudāharaṇa-kathā*) about how not to get ensnared with women.[47] The *Pāṇḍavcarit* narrative goes on to illustrate that council as well-intended as Sudeṣṇā's did not always fall on fertile ground: Kīcaka scoffs and goes on to accost Draupadī anyway.

All of this edutainment may have been intended to instruct not only the characters within the story, but also their audience in Gwalior in 1435, in particular the king himself. The idea that a king's lust can have disastrous effects on his kingdom was also a prominent theme in contem-

41. A reference to the Ahalyā story from the Rāmāyaṇa tradition.

42. A reference to the myth of the Moon's excessive love for the star, Rohiṇī.

43. In the Mahābhārata tradition, the sage Viśvāmitra's penance is broken by the *apsaras* (celestial woman) Menakā and famously results in the birth of Śakuntalā. On Śakuntalā, see the chapter by Amanda Culp in this volume.

44. A reference to the story of Nala and Damayantī in the Mahābhārata tradition.

45. Literally: "walks his own, knowing himself." Thanks to Professor Raj Kumar of Banaras Hindu University for suggesting this translation.

46. *PC* 4.3.41–46.

47. Interestingly, rather than blaming the women, as Vidyāpati does, the queen here foregrounds the folly of the men. See Pankaj Kumar Jha, "Beyond the Local and the Universal: Exclusionary Strategies of Expansive Literary Cultures in Fifteenth Century Mithila," *The Indian Economic and Social History Review* 51, no. 1 (2014): 16–19. Christopher Diamond addressed this in an paper presented at the European Conference on South Asian Studies in Paris in 2018.

poraneous Sanskrit works produced at the Tomar court, such as the play *Rambhāmañjarī* and the poem *Hammīramahākāvya*, both composed by the Jain author Nayacandra Surī perhaps a few years earlier.[48] The general intent of the *Hammīramahākāvya* has sometimes been interpreted through the lens of Hindu-Muslim conflict. The text, however, situates itself within a complex historical setting of multi-ethnic confrontations and shifting alliances, reflecting a strong concern with social mobility, perhaps an early form of Rajputization, not unlike the *Pāṇḍavcarit*.[49] At the same time, certain episodes seem to critique Rajput codes of compulsion toward aggression at any cost. The warnings against a king's lustful and impulsive behavior in the *Hammīramahākāvya* are strikingly similar to the interaction between Kīcaka and Sudeṣṇā in the *Pāṇḍavcarit*. While the reference may be to incidents in the Gwalior harem that we cannot reconstruct in its 1435 context, one could also read this as veiled criticism against the rash new campaign that Dūṅgar Singh had planned to encroach on Malwa territory. In that case, the humor in the episode may be construed as a subtle counter-current to broader preoccupations with emerging Rajput codes.

The story continues to make fun of hypermasculine aggression. When approached by Kīcaka, Draupadī pretends to be flattered, but warns him that it is for his own good to stay away from her, as her five superhuman (*gandharva*) husbands are sure to take bloody revenge. Her advice, too, falls on deaf ears: Kīcaka just laughs, boasting about his virility. Since everyone in the audience knows Kīcaka's fate, it is clear that the poet intended Kīcaka's hyperbolic boasting to have a comic effect:

> Hearing this much Kīcaka burned with anger: "What *gandharva* would you choose over me?
> First let them get wind of it, O woman! I will disarm them, kill them, and destroy them.
> Even if all the demons, gods, *yakṣa*s, and *gandharva*s would join forces, I'd vanquish them all!

48. Sander Hens, "Beyond Power and Praise: Nayacandra Sūri's Tragic-historical Epic Hammīra-mahākāvya as a Subversive Response to Hero Glorification in Early Tomar Gwalior," *South Asian History and Culture* 11, no. 1 (2020): 48.

49. Michael Bednar, "Mongol, Muslim, Rajput: Mahimāsāhi in Persian Texts and the Sanskrit *Hammīra-Mahākāvya*," *Journal of the Economic and Social History of the Orient* 60, no. 5 (2017): 585–613.

Are you not ashamed to show such fear for me, pretty lady?
I have conquered the forces of all four countries, have punished the kings of Malwa!
All kings that have clashed with me, I have crushed their arrogance on the battlefield.
Now just look: I will kill any *gandharva* that would come," he said, laughing loudly.[50]

For the contemporaneous audience, Kīcaka's claim that he has punished the kings of Malwa (*mālaeṃ naresā*) would have brought to mind the Tomars' confrontations with Malwa that had occurred only a few years earlier. A subtle message to the poem's patron may therefore be buried in this mirth. Is Dūṅgar Singh being discouraged from overestimating his military might, even as he and his court are chuckling about Kīcaka's hubris inviting his own fall?

The implication that the king's own hubris is the object of the passage's humor becomes evident when not only the villain, Kīcaka, is cast in a comic light, but also Bhīma, to whom the Tomar king had been likened at the outset of the text. When Draupadī complains to her husbands one by one about the outrage that she has to endure, they are reluctant to defend her: they express that they are afraid to upset the power balance at their host's court and hesitate to expose themselves before their year in exile is over. By contrast, Bhīma, to whom she appeals last, swings into action right away in an overly zealous way that is played for comic effect:

"Do not despair in your heart, woman, right now I will prevail and destroy Kīcaka.
Every breath I take fills me with anger. Even today I will send him on his way to the city of Death!
I will arrange for his end, or else renounce Kuntī as mother!
He's a frog seated on the head of a snake, a jackal enraged with a lion;
When the donkey is rutting, the elephant pushes it away. He's a dog playing with the muskrat!
When he grabbed your arm, O queen, he invited his own death upon him!"
Bhīma was shivering, his lips quivering, his eyes seemed to fill up red with vermilion (*sindūr*).

50. *PC* 4.3.57–61.

He sat in the assembly, but when he got the chance, Bhīma, greatly upset, set off to kill him (Kīcaka).
"I will not flee anywhere. I will kill Kīcaka, or else my name is not Bhīmasena!"[51]

This fragment provides not only the direct speech but also hints of inexplicit stage directions: the expressions (*abhinaya*) for the actor in Bhīma's role. The detail includes the comic description of the eyes of the virile hero as filling "up red with vermilion (*sindūr*)." The powder of *sindūr* is associated with women's marital status, so this image is very aptly used here to demonstrate that Draupadī's honor is at stake. At the same time, the hero's hypermasculinity is being feminized, which lends the description a comic tone. Bhīma does not totally escape the fate of his co-husbands, all of whom the *Pāṇḍavcarit* portray as overly cautious cowards. The poem's reference to *sindūr* implies that Bhīma, too, undergoes a process of emasculation.

This transformation becomes even more apparent in the actual killing of Kīcaka, which involves Bhīma posing as Draupadī:

The son of the wind could not suppress his anger, like *ghee* thrown on fire.
At the end of the day, when it became dark, Bhīma prepared by attiring himself.
He put on a dress and tied on a bustier. He looked in the mirror to make a *tilak*;
Coloring his hair-parting, he completed his transformation into a pretty woman.
He put on his jewel-studded earrings, made his eyes luscious with kohl.
He wore a garland, adorned his arms with bracelets,
He put anklets on his feet that would softly tinkle.
And swaying like an elephant in rut, he set off, casting amorous glances from his eyes;
Thus, Bhīma went and sat down in the arena, and there arrived Kīcaka, the wrestler.[52]

51. *PC* 4.3.109–14.

52. *PC* 4.3.118–21.

The angry Bhīma, then, prepares for his revenge not by donning a warrior's attire but instead by elaborately disguising himself as a woman. Notably, as Eva De Clercq and Simon Winant point out in the previous chapter of this volume, Bhīma also dresses up as a woman in this episode in another fifteenth-century Gwalior Mahābhārata: Raïdhū's Apabhramsha *Harivaṃsapurāṇa*. Even though the gruesome murder of the offender and proper extraction of revenge follows this scene and the rest of the story regales the audience with Bhīma's prowess, the martial mood is subverted by the humor of the situation since Bhīma is dressed like a woman. The deflation of the male bravado of both Kīcaka and Bhīma through humor seems intentional. I would argue that it is meant to serve as a warning at the beginning of the campaigning season.

The Performative Tradition of *Paṇḍvānī*

The presence of these performative elements in the text suggests that this old vernacular retelling may very well be located within a local performance tradition. Mahābhārata theatrical traditions remain largely understudied; for North India, we have only William Sax's work on the Garhwali *Pāṇḍavlīlā*.[53] Parallel with what we see in our text, Sax analyzes *Pāṇḍavlīlā* as an assertion of Rajput identity linked with claims of descent from the Pāṇḍavas.[54] Less has been written on the related genre *Paṇḍvānī*, a storytelling genre by a lead performer to musical accompaniment, which is popular in the broader areas of Madhya Pradesh and Uttar Pradesh even today.[55]

One could make the case that *Pāṇḍavcarit* is related to *Paṇḍvānī*. Since *Paṇḍvānī*'s origins are in present-day Chhattisgarh, in central India,

53. William S. Sax, *Dancing the Self: Personhood and Performance in the Pāṇḍav Līlā of Garhwal* (New York: Oxford University Press, 2002).

54. William S. Sax, "Worshiping Epic Villains: A Kaurava Cult in the Central Himalayas," in *Epic Traditions in the Contemporary World: The Poetics of Community*, eds. Margaret Beissinger, Jane Tylus, and Susanne Wofford (Berkeley: University of California Press, 1999), 172–73.

55. I am grateful to Professor Archana Kumar (Banaras Hindu University) for directing my attention to this genre during one of our reading sessions at Ghent University, Belgium, in 2016 and for providing me with a recording of a *Paṇḍvānī* performance of *Kīcakavadha* by Ritu Verma.

and are associated with Gond tribes, *Paṇḍvānī* may seem at first to be irrelevant to Viṣṇudās' Gwalior text. There are, however, some fascinating intersections. First, as in Viṣṇudās' poem, Bhīma plays an important role in *Paṇḍvānī,* partly due to its association with local tribes who claim to be the descendants of Bhīma and a tribal woman.[56] The *Pāṇḍavcarit* and the *Paṇḍvānī* performance tradition are connected in another way: through Sabalsingh Cauhān's *Mahābhārat,* a narrative poem that was composed in the late seventeenth and early eighteenth centuries and that forms part of the *Paṇḍvānī* repertoire (in its recitation style, called Vedmatī).[57] Both texts are composed in the same metrical structure, mostly in *caupāī*s (quatrains), punctuated with *dohā*s (couplets).[58] According to Harihar Nivas Dvivedi, a 1738 manuscript from Datiya combines parts of Viṣṇudās' text with that of Cauhān's to render a complete eighteen-book Mahābhārata.[59] The *Pāṇḍavcarit*'s strong links with this tribal performative tradition also translate to the level of storytelling. Just as she does in Viṣṇudās' retelling, in *Paṇḍvānī*, Draupadī seeks help from each of her husbands in turn before Bhīma finally agrees to avenge her honor.[60] Here, too, as in the *Pāṇḍavcarit* and Raïdhū's *Harivaṃsapurāṇa*, Bhīma dresses up as a woman.[61] These narrative similarities are striking because neither one is found in the Sanskrit

56. Niranjan Mahawar, *Folk Theatre Pandwani* (Delhi: Abhinav Publications, 2013). It is also worth mentioning that in this style of folk theatre the lead singer holds a stringed instrument called *tuṃvara* (*tambura*) and uses this mostly as a prop for the narration. The similarity of the instrument's name to that of Gwalior's dynasty, Tomar, is suggestive.

57. Soumya Mohan Ghosh and Rajni Singh, "Demythologizing Draupadī: A Comparative Study of Saoli Mitra's *Nāthavatī anāthavat* ("Five Lords, Yet None a Protector") and Teejan Bai's *Draupadī cīrharaṇ*," *Archiv Orientalni* 82, no. 3 (2014): 513–14, n15. On Cauhān's poem, see the chapter by Sohini Sarah Pillai in this volume.

58. In one manuscript of *Pāṇḍavcarit* in Dvivedi's collection that preserves a more archaic spelling, the older metrical form of *pālhurī*s are found rather than *dohā*s.

59. See page 26 of Dvivedi's introduction to his edition of the *PC.*

60. *CM* 4.17–19. For Cauhān's *Mahābhārat* (*CM*), I am following: *Sabalsingh Cauhān-Viracit Mahābhārat* (Lucknow: Tej Kumar Book Depot, 2015). The same is true for the performance of Ritu Verma referenced above.

61. This is elaborated in the performance of Ritu Verma, though it is less stressed in the text of Cauhān. See *CM* 4.20.

Mahābhārata.[62] Nor, for that matter, does either feature appear in Tikkana's section of the Telugu *Mahābhāratamu.*[63]

The similarities between the "first" Hindi Mahābhārata and the contemporary performances of *Paṇḍvānī* are highly suggestive of some form of symbiosis. It seems likely that this performance-oriented classical text was part of or influenced by a forerunner of the contemporary theatrical tradition of *Paṇḍvānī.* Given the latter's tribal correlations, the connection invites us to ask new questions about the Gwalior Tomar dynasty. Did the Tomars have a tribal past, or did they displace or incorporate tribal groups? Perhaps we can see the *Pāṇḍavcarit* as a case of appropriation of tribal technologies for "dynastic" legitimation, not unlike what the kings in Puri did with the worship of the originally tribal deity Jagannātha[64] or the Kacchvāhā Rajputs from Amer (later Jaipur) did with the worship of the Mīṇā tribal deity Jaṃvā Mātājī.[65] The discovery of close links between the *Pāṇḍavcarit* and the tribal performance tradition of *Paṇḍvānī* may point to the co-opting of local tribal groups for the Tomar community-building process. To appreciate the intervention of this vernacular Mahābhārata fully,

---

62. 4.13–23 in *The Mahābhārata for the First Time Critically Edited,* ed. V. S. Sukthankar et al. 19 vols. (Poona: Bhandarkar Oriental Research Institute, 1933–66).

63. M. V. Subramanian notes that a humorous impersonation of Bhīma as a woman is found in Villiputtūr's fifteenth-century Tamil *Pāratam* and Tuñcattū Ĕḻuttacchan's sixteenth-century Malayalam *Bhāratam.* See *The Mahabharata Story: Vyasa & Variations* (Madras: Higginbothams (Private) Ltd., 1967), 151. Similar scenes have also been reported for the South Indian performance tradition of *Yakṣagāna,* including in a play called *Kīcaka Vadhe,* as reported for a performance in South Kanara in 1970. See Martha Bush Ashton and Bruce Christie, *Yakṣagāna: A Dance Drama of India (*Delhi: Abhinav Publications, 1977), 43. Based on the forty-fourth verse of his Sanskrit *Kīcakavadha* (ca. 600), Nītivarman seems to also be aware of this impersonation, but he does not seem to exploit its humorous potential. See Nītivarman, *The Kīcakavadha of Nītivarman with the Commentary of Janārdanasena,* ed. S. K. De (Dacca: Dacca University, 1929).

64. Herman Kulke, "*Jagannath* as the state deity under the Gajapatis of Orissa," in *The Cult of Jagannath and the Regional Tradition of Orissa,* eds. A. Eschmann, H. Kulke, and G. C. Tripathi (Delhi: Manohar, 1986), 199–208.

65. Monika Horstmann, *Der Zusammenhalt der Welt: Religiöse Herrschaftslegitimation und Religionspolitik Mahārājā Savāī Jaisinghs (1700–1743)* (Wiesbaden: Otto Harrassowitz, 2009), 4.

we can appreciate its double move: beyond invoking the sophistication of the cosmopolitan Sanskrit tradition (in the preamble), there is also an appeal to the hyper-local tribal (in the chosen genre).

Conclusion

Situating Viṣṇudās' *Pāṇḍavcarit* within its micro-historical milieu in Gwalior has shown that it represents a claim for *kṣatriya* status on the part of the (relatively) newly established Tomar dynasty, rather than a call for a Hindu revivalist anti-Muslim campaign. Its preoccupations are not with the defense of dharma, but rather with overcoming a numerically stronger enemy. The emotional regime that the poem as a whole activates is overwhelmingly martial: it focuses on the hero Bhīma, whom it likens at the outset to the king Dūṅgar Singh. This fits the ritual context of the poem as the Tomar military is embarking on the campaigning season in 1435, taking advantage of the political instability occasioned by the murder of the last sultan and the death of the neighboring Malwa ruler.

Yet that is not the whole story. The analysis of the work as a performance has uncovered a counter-current that subtly critiques the patron's programmatic intent. Picking up on clues in the *Kīcakavadha* episode and reading it in tandem with other literary production at the court, we find that the poet pokes fun at the masculine prowess not only of Bhīma's enemies but also of Bhīma himself. By extension, he critiques—under the cover of slapstick—the rash Dūṅgar Singh for undertaking military adventures in Malwa once again. The poet seems to be hinting that the Tomar ruler's ambitions were greater than what his military could, and his financiers would, support at the time. Through deft use of humor and slapstick, this criticism could be voiced, even if history shows it fell on deaf ears. Finally, the discovery of similarities with the contemporary theatrical tradition of *Paṇḍvānī* associated with tribal communities raises the possibility that the very genre of the text may have been important. It raises a new question: was this Mahābhārata involved an attempt to co-opt local tribal groups in the interest of strengthening the Tomar hegemony? This case study of the first extant complete classical Hindi Mahābhārata suggests two fruitful methodological interventions for approaching other vernacular Mahābhāratas: (1) carefully studying their micro-historical contexts and (2) taking an analytical approach to text as performance. This will draw attention not only to such texts' relationships with the cosmopolitan Sanskrit universe they index, but also to local concerns, such as, in this case, attempts to mobilize the energy of regional communities for the king's martial expeditions, and resistance to such military adventurism by local stakeholders.

Chapter Thirteen

Blessed Beginnings

Invoking Viṣṇu, Kṛṣṇa, and Rāma in Two Regional Mahābhāratas[1]

Sohini Sarah Pillai

Despite his pivotal role as the advisor of the Pāṇḍavas and the bestower of the *Bhagavadgītā*, the divine diplomat, Kṛṣṇa, is not the protagonist of the Sanskrit *Mahābhārata*. Unlike Vālmīki's Sanskrit *Rāmāyaṇa*, which narrates the adventures of the warrior-prince Rāma, or the *Harivaṃśa*, the *Viṣṇu-purāṇa*, or the *Bhāgavatapurāṇa* (three Sanskrit texts that describe Kṛṣṇa's birth, adolescence, and adulthood in great detail), the critical edition of the Sanskrit *Mahābhārata* does not revolve around a major incarnation of the Hindu deity Viṣṇu.[2]

---

1. I am very grateful to Anne E. Monius and John Stratton Hawley for carefully reading this chapter and offering many valuable suggestions. I plan to build on the arguments presented in this essay in my doctoral dissertation: "Region and Religion in Retellings of the Mahābhārata," (PhD diss., University of California, Berkeley, forthcoming).

2. Some scholars have questioned Rāma's status as an incarnation of Viṣṇu in Vālmīki's text. For one example, see Luis González-Reimann, "The Divinity of Rāma in the *Rāmāyaṇa* of Vālmīki," *Journal of Indian Philosophy* 34, no. 3 (2006): 203–20.

Yet while the Sanskrit *Mahābhārata* does not center on Viṣṇu, the same is not true for at least two premodern regional retellings of the epic. In the author's own introduction (*taṟciṟappuppāyiram*) to his fifteenth-century Tamil *Pāratam*, Villiputtūr states that he is retelling the Mahābhārata out of his desire for "the deeds of the eternal Mādhava (Kṛṣṇa)."[3] Similarly, in the opening prologue of his seventeenth-century *Mahābhārat*, Sabalsingh Cauhān proclaims: "I cannot comprehend any of the mysteries of the deeds of Hari (Kṛṣṇa), [but] I will summarize some of them in Bhasha (Old Hindi)[4] and sing."[5]

Villiputtūr and Sabalsingh Cauhān composed their Mahābhāratas more than two hundred years apart in distinctly different languages at opposite ends of the Indian subcontinent. That both poets describe their retellings as the *carita* or "deeds" of Kṛṣṇa is thus striking.[6] How does one transform an epic about a cataclysmic internecine war into the story of Kṛṣṇa's deeds?

In this essay, I demonstrate that one of the most effective methods that both Villi and Cauhān use to reframe the Mahābhārata as the deeds of Kṛṣṇa is the insertion of elaborate invocations to different forms of Viṣṇu at

3. *maṉṉum mātavaṉ caritamum* || *VP taṟciṟappuppāyiram* 8 ||

For Villi's *Pāratam* (*VP*), I am following: Villiputtūr, *Villiputtūrār Iyaṟṟiya Makāpāratam*, ed. V. M. Gopalakrishnamachariyar, 7 vols. (Madras: 1963–68). All translations in this chapter are my own.

4. The North Indian vernacular language used by Sabalsingh Cauhān is sometimes referred to as "Old Hindi," "Early Hindi," or "Classical Hindi" and many scholars also use dialect designations like "Avadhi" and "Brajbhasha" to qualify texts in this language. I choose to use the term "Bhasha" (*bhāṣā*, literally: "language"), which is the name used by a number of poets (including Cauhān, Tulsīdās, and Viṣṇudās) in their own compositions.

5. *haricaritra kou bheda na pāvahiṃ kai bhāṣā saṅkṣepa kachu gāvahiṃ* || *CM* 1.2 ||

For Cauhān's *Mahābhārat* (*CM*), I am following: Sabalsingh Cauhān, *Sabalsingh Cauhān-Viracit Mahābhārat* (Lucknow: Tej Kumar Book Depot, 2015). References are to the book (*parv*) and page number of the Tej Kumar edition.

6. I should point out that the names of Kṛṣṇa that Villi and Cauhān use in the opening prologues of their poems (Mādhava and Hari) are also associated with Viṣṇu. See Steven P. Hopkins, *An Ornament for Jewels: Poems for the Lord of Gods by Vedāntadeśika* (New York: Oxford University Press, 2007), 163; and John Stratton Hawley, *The Memory of Love: Sūrdās Sings to Krishna* (New York: Oxford University Press, 2009), 9.

the beginnings of different sections of their texts. By carefully examining the invocations, I reveal how the opening verses in praise of a "layered" Kṛṣṇa in the Tamil *Pāratam* and Rāma in the Bhasha *Mahābhārat* distinctly align these Mahābhāratas with local devotional traditions. I conclude this chapter by briefly discussing the prologues of some other regional Mahābhāratas in order to demonstrate how the poems of Villi and Cauhān are participating in larger patterns of retelling this epic in premodern South Asia.

Layering Kṛṣṇa in Villi's *Pāratam*

Kṛṣṇa first appears in the critical edition of the Sanskrit *Mahābhārata* as a spectator at the contest for Draupadī's hand in marriage.[7] In the Tamil *Pāratam*, however, Villiputtūr chooses to introduce Kṛṣṇa 320 verses before the bride-choice episode with a salutation (*vaṇakkam*) that opens the second chapter of his *Ātiparuvam* ("The Book of Beginnings"):

> In utter darkness, becoming a respected woman,
> transforming her own form into that of a mother,
> overflowing with love, coming and picking him up,
> embracing him, her heart rejoicing,
> and caressing him with affection,
> the demoness with great breasts of milk melted.
> The red lotus feet of Gopāla,
> whose dark body is among
> the young ones who sucked life from her,
> never leave my mind.[8]

7. *MBh* 1.178.8–10. All references to the Sanskrit *Mahābhārata* (*MBh*) are to the critical edition: *The Mahābhārata for the First Time Critically Edited*, ed. V. S. Sukthankar et al. 19 vols. (Poona: Bhandarkar Oriental Research Institute, 1933–66).

8. *ariya kaṅkuliṉ aṉṉai taṉ vaṭivu koṇṭu alakai ākiya naṅkai*
parivu poṅka vantu eṭuttu aṇaittu uvantu uḷam parintu uṭaṉ pārāṭṭa
urukum mā mulai pāluṭaṉ avaḷ uyir uṇṭu aḻum muruku ār mey
kariya kōvalaṉ ceyya tāḷ malarkaḷ eṉ karuttai viṭṭu akalāvē || *VP* 1.2.1 ||

Notably, the Kṛṣṇa being introduced here is not the enigmatic advisor to the Pāṇḍavas, but the charming "cow protector," Gopāla, who is raised in the forests of Vṛndāvana. This invocation tells the story of Pūtanā, the child-slaughtering demoness who tries to kill Kṛṣṇa by nursing him from her poisoned breast. While some incidents from Kṛṣṇa's childhood in Vṛndāvana (including the Pūtanā episode) are briefly alluded to in the critical edition of the *Mahābhārata*,[9] the earliest detailed accounts of Kṛṣṇa's adolescence are found in the *Harivaṃśa* and the *Viṣṇupurāṇa*, which are both roughly dated to the first four centuries of the common era.

Tales of Kṛṣṇa's youth are also found throughout the Tamil *Nālāyirativiyappirapantam* ("The Four Thousand Divine Works"), the collected poems of the twelve Vaiṣṇavas (Viṣṇu devotees) known as the Āḻvārs who likely lived in the eighth and ninth centuries. By the twelfth century, the *Nālāyirativiyappirapantam* was revered as the "Tamil Veda" by the Śrīvaiṣṇava community in South India. Friedhelm Hardy argues that, unlike the Sanskrit *Bhagavadgītā*, which espouses philosophical or "intellectual" *bhakti* (devotion), the Āḻvārs' poetry is filled with "emotional" *bhakti* focused on a personal relationship between the divine and the devotee.[10]

Several of the Āḻvārs use the idiom of the relationship between a mother and a child to express their love for Viṣṇu in an intimate and familiar way.[11] This mode of *bhakti* would eventually be termed the emotion of parental love (*vātsalya-bhāva*) by sixteenth-century Vaiṣṇava theologians in North India. Periyāḻvār, the first poet that readers encounter in the *Nālāyirativiyappirapantam*, frequently adopts the persona of Kṛṣṇa's foster mother, Yaśodā.[12] In one particularly lovely set of ten verses in Periyāḻvār's *Tirumoḻi* ("Divine Speech"), Yaśodā is overcome with the

9. *MBh* 2.38.4, 5.128.45.

10. Friedhelm Hardy, *Viraha-Bhakti: The Early History of Kṛṣṇa Devotion in South India* (Delhi: Oxford University Press, 1983), 36–38.

11. See Vasudha Narayanan, *The Way and the Goal: Expressions of Devotion in the Early Śrī Vaiṣṇava Tradition* (Washington, DC: Institute for Vaishnava Studies, 1987), 31–33.

12. It is worth noting that Villi may have been named after Śrīvilliputtūr, the town Śrīvaiṣṇavas revere as the hometown of Periyāḻvār and the only female Āḻvār poet, Āṇṭāḷ.

urge to nurse Kṛṣṇa, and each verse ends with her begging the baby to eat.[13]

Villi, who is remembered today as Villiputtūrāḻvār or "Villiputtūr the Āḻvār," is clearly playing with the emotion of parental love in his invocation on Pūtanā. Although she has been sent to murder Kṛṣṇa by his wicked uncle, Kaṃsa, Pūtanā is completely enchanted by the irresistible infant, and the immensely affectionate physical reaction she has to Kṛṣṇa mirrors that of Yaśodā in Periyāḻvār's *Tirumoḻi*. In both the *Tirumoḻi* and the *Pāratam*, the love that Villi's Pūtanā and Periyāḻvār's Yaśodā have for the adorable Kṛṣṇa causes their breasts to overflow with milk. Pūtanā thus almost seems to be a Kṛṣṇa devotee herself in Villi's invocation.

This salutation about Kṛṣṇa's encounter with Pūtanā commences the *Campavaccarukkam* or "Origins Chapter." Starting the chapter that describes the births of major characters, such as the Pāṇḍavas and the Kauravas, with an episode from Kṛṣṇa's own infancy is no accident. With this introductory invocation, Villi reminds his South Indian audience of the lovable Kṛṣṇa of Vṛndāvana who exists outside of the Sanskrit epic and who pervades the *Nālāyirativiyappirapantam* and other South Indian Vaiṣṇava *bhakti* compositions, such as the *Bhāgavatapurāṇa* (ca. tenth century) and the works of the Śrīvaiṣṇava poet-philosopher Vedāntadeśika (traditional dates: 1268–1369).[14] Thirty-seven of the fifty chapters of the *Pāratam* begin with a salutation or a benediction (*vāḻttu*). While some of these verses are solely in praise of the adult Kṛṣṇa of the Mahābhārata,[15] others exclusively retell episodes featuring the child Kṛṣṇa, including his splitting of two trees with

---

13. Periyāḻvār, *Tirumoḻi* 2.2.1–10. All references to compositions in the *Nālāyirativiyappirapantam* are to the following edition: *Nālāyirativviyappirapantam*, ed. P. P. Annangarachariyar (Kanchi: V. N. Tevanatan, 1971). For a translation of these verses, see Lynn Ate, *Yaśodā's Songs to Her Playful Son, Kṛṣṇa: Periyāḻvār's 9th Century Tamil Tirumoḻi* (Woodland Hills, CA: South Asian Studies Association, 2011), 101–103.

14. Like the *Pāratam,* the *Bhāgavatapurāṇa* and the compositions of Vedāntadeśika are clearly in conversation with and responding to the *Nālāyirativiyappirapantam.* See Hardy, *Viraha-Bhakti*, 488; and Hopkins, *Ornament for Jewels*, 119–26.

15. For example: *VP* 2.1.1, 5.5.1, 6.2.1, 7.4.1.

a mortar,[16] his antics with the local *gopī*s (herdswomen),[17] and his victory over Kaṃsa.[18] By beginning different chapters with these invocations, Villi ensures that his readers do not forget the early deeds of Kṛṣṇa.

As Steven Hopkins points out, in the *Nālāyirativiyappirapantam* and the later compositions of the Śrīvaiṣṇava *ācārya*s (teachers), "Krishna comes, as it were, layered with other forms (*avatāras* or 'incarnations') of Vishnu."[19] A close examination of all thirty-seven invocations of the *Pāratam* reveals that this is also true for Kṛṣṇa in Villi's text. Many of Villi's salutations and benedictions are addressed not to Kṛṣṇa, but to Māl, the distinctly Tamil form of Viṣṇu who is also known as Māyaṉ, Māyavaṉ, and Māyōṉ.[20] For example, right before his rendering of the Bhagavadgītā, Villi presents his audience with the following invocation:

> Our King is
> the flood of joy, the overflowing, rare wisdom,
> the first god among the three, the foremost among those three,[21]
> everyone, each and every person,
> the deity before whom many many enemies bow,
> Māl with enduring, lovely eyes.[22]

By inserting this verse in praise of the thoroughly Tamil deity, Māl, right before his version of what is easily the most famous episode involving Kṛṣṇa in the Sanskrit *Mahābhārata*, Villi firmly places the Kṛṣṇa of the *Pāratam* in a markedly South Indian religious landscape.

---

16. *VP* 6.7.1.

17. *VP* 5.2.1.

18. *VP* 8.1.1.

19. Hopkins, *Ornament for Jewels*, 115.

20. For example: *VP* 1.3.1, 3.8.1.

21. This is a reference to the trinity of Hindu deities comprised of Brahmā, Viṣṇu, and Śiva.

22. *mēvu aru ñāṉam āṉantam veḷḷam āy vitittōṉ āti*
mūvarum āki anta mūvarkkuḷ mutalvaṉ āki
yāvarum yāvum āki iṟaiñcuvār iṟaiñca pal pal
tēvarum āki niṉṟa cemkaṇ māl eṅkaḷ kōvē || *VP* 6.1.1 ||

Villi also often describes Kṛṣṇa alongside other forms of Viṣṇu in the same invocation.[23] Take the salutation of the fourth chapter of the *Vīṭṭumaparuvam* ("The Book of Bhīṣma"):

> The feet ended the curse placed on the searching Ahalyā.
> The extensive feet measured all of the expansive worlds.
> The lovely feet kicked and killed the broken cart and danced on top of the snake.
> The feet ruled me.[24]

Like the very first invocation in the *Pāratam* about Pūtanā, the final two lines of this salutation praise the child Kṛṣṇa of Vṛndāvana with references to his defeat of the cart-demon, Śakaṭa, and his dance on the head of the poisonous serpent, Kāliya. With the opening lines of this invocation, however, Villi is also layering Kṛṣṇa with Rāma, the prince of Ayodhyā whose touch releases the beautiful woman Ahalyā from a terrible curse, and Vāmana, Viṣṇu's dwarf incarnation who spans the earth, heavens, and netherworld in just three steps. This invocation also strongly resembles the beginning of a verse from the *Tiruppāvai* ("The Divine Vow") of the Āḻvār poetess, Āṇṭāḷ, in which the dwarf who covers the worlds is layered with the prince who attacks Laṅkā (the kingdom of the demon king Rāvaṇa) and the cowherd who slays Śakaṭa:

> You measured these worlds that time. Hail your feet.
> You went there to the South and destroyed Laṅkā.
> Hail your courage.
> You kicked and murdered Śakaṭa. Hail your fame.[25]

---

23. For example: *VP* 5.1.1, 5.7.1, 8.2.1, 9.1.

24. *tēṭiya akalikai cāpam tīrtta tāḷ*
nīṭiya ulaku elām aḷantu nīṇṭa tāḷ
oṭiya cakaṭu iṟa utaittu pāmpiṉ mēl
āṭiyum civanta tāḷ eṉṉai āṇṭa tāḷ || *VP* 6.4.1 ||

25. *aṉṟu i ulakam aḷantāy aṭi pōṟṟi*
ceṉṟu aṅku teṉ ilaṅkai ceṟṟāy tiṟal pōṟṟi
poṉṟa cakaṭam utaittāy pukaḻ pōṟṟi || Āṇṭāḷ, *Tiruppāvai* 24 ||

Along with following the Āḻvārs' practice of layering Kṛṣṇa with different forms of Viṣṇu, Villi also uses the invocations in his text to pay homage to the Āḻvārs themselves. The benediction of the final chapter of the *Vīṭṭumaparuvam* praises the sacred name, Nārāyaṇa (Viṣṇu).[26] While Villi begins this invocation with the story of how the uttering of this name brings Narasiṃha (the half-man/half-lion *avatāra* of Viṣṇu) to the aide of his devotee, Prahlāda, he ends the benediction with a tribute to Tirumaṅkaiyāḻvār, whose first ten verses of his massive work, the *Periyatirumoḻi* ("The Grand Divine Speech"), are dedicated to the power of Nārāyaṇa's name.[27] Similarly, in the salutation in the last chapter of his *Turōṇaparuvam* ("The Book of Droṇa"), Villi praises Nammāḻvār, the paradigmatic devotee of the Śrīvaiṣṇava tradition.[28]

These invocations that extol Tirumaṅkaiyāḻvār and Nammāḻvār commence the chapters of the *Pāratam* in which Bhīṣma and Droṇa are defeated by the Pāṇḍavas and their allies. In Villi's poem (as in the Sanskrit *Mahābhārata*),[29] Kṛṣṇa orchestrates the deaths of both these powerful generals.[30] By beginning these chapters that showcase Kṛṣṇa's involvement in the battle at Kurukṣetra with invocations to two of the Āḻvārs, Villi once again positions his version of Kṛṣṇa in a distinctly Tamil-speaking, Śrīvaiṣṇava devotional world.

Villi also strategically places invocations at the beginning of chapters in which Kṛṣṇa is absent from the narrative. Both Villi and Sabalsingh Cauhān insert several scenes highlighting Kṛṣṇa's divinity into their retellings that are not found in the critical edition of the Sanskrit *Mahābhārata*. For example, in the *Pāratam*, Yudhiṣṭhira does not lose the second dice game with the Kauravas (as he does in the Sanskrit epic)[31] because he prays to Kṛṣṇa before the match.[32] In the Bhasha *Mahābhārat*, it is not Bhīma[33] but

26. *VP* 6.10.1.

27. Tirumaṅkaiyāḻvār, *Periyatirumoḻi* 1.1.1–10. On these ten verses, see Archana Venkatesan, "Speared through the Heart: The Sound of God in the Worlds of Tirumaṅkai," *Journal of Hindu Studies* 10, no. 3 (2017): 275–300.

28. *VP* 7.5.1.

29. *MBh* 6.103, 7.164.

30. *VP* 6.10.9–10, 7.5.19–20.

31. *MBh* 2.67.

32. *VP* 2.2.280.

33. *MBh* 1.136.

Kṛṣṇa who rescues the Pāṇḍavas during the fire in the lac palace.[34] There are some episodes in the Mahābhāratas of Villi and Cauhān, however, such as those in which Bhīma murders the demons, Hiḍimba and Bakāsura, in which Kṛṣṇa does not make an appearance. Yet by starting his chapter on the deaths of Hiḍimba and Bakāsura with an invocation, Villi provides his audience with an example of Viṣṇu's legendary compassion for his devotees. In this benediction, Villi recounts a story that is alluded to several times in the *Nālāyirativiyappirapantam*, in which Viṣṇu grants salvation to the elephant Gajendra after he is almost killed by a crocodile.[35]

> Let us worship the feet of
> the lotus of the cold season, the one who fills up heaven,
> the lord of beautiful Śrī,[36] the lord of the gods,
> the lord of the Vedas, the lord of living beings,
> the lord of vows, the lord of scholars,
> the primordial lord who came before the king of elephants
> who in the mouth of the crocodile, his strength growing weak,
> meditated and in front of everyone called out
> "Primordial Cause!"[37]

By inserting intricate invocations throughout the different sections of their Mahābhāratas, both Villi and Cauhān guarantee that their audiences are constantly thinking of Viṣṇu. In the Tamil *Pāratam*, the Viṣṇu on display in Villi's salutations and benedictions is a Kṛṣṇa layered with several other

34. *CM* 1.39. Kṛṣṇa's rescue of the Pāṇḍavas in this episode is also alluded to in the *Bhāgavatapurāṇa* (1.8.24) and in at least two Bhasha compositions by the sixteenth-century Kṛṣṇa devotee, Sūrdās. See *Bhāgavata Purāṇa: Selected Readings*, trans. Ravi M. Gupta and Kenneth R. Valpey (New York: Columbia University Press, 2017), 53–55; and Sūrdās, *Sur's Ocean: Poems from the Early Tradition,* trans. John Stratton Hawley, ed. Kenneth E. Bryant, Murty Classical Library of India (Cambridge, MA: Harvard University Press, 2015), 652–55.

35. There are fifty-three references to the story of Gajendra in the *Nālāyira-tiviyappirapantam*. See Narayanan, *Way and the Goal*, 163.

36. Śrī (Lakṣmī) is Viṣṇu's consort.

37. *cītam nāḷ malar kōyil mēvu cem tiruviṉ nāyakaṉ tēva nāyakaṉ*
vētam nāyakaṉ pūtam nāyakaṉ viratam nāyakaṉ viputa nāyakaṉ
pōtaka atipaṉ mutalai vāyiṭai poṟai taḷarntu muṉ potuvilē niṉaintu
āṭi mūlamē eṉṉa muṉ varum āti nāyakaṉ aṭi vaṇaṅkuvām || *VP* 1.4.1 ||

forms of Viṣṇu who would be immensely familiar to members of the Śrīvaiṣṇava religious community in fifteenth-century South India. In the Bhasha *Mahābhārat*, however, the main form of Viṣṇu that Cauhān praises in his invocations is not Kṛṣṇa, but Rāma.

Remembering Rāma in Cauhān's *Mahābhārat*

Eleven out of the eighteen books of Sabalsingh Cauhān's *Mahābhārat* begin with prologues, all of which include invocation (*maṅgalācaraṇ*) verses. At first glance, the prologue of the second book, the *Sabhāparv* ("The Book of the Assembly Hall"), seems to have little to do with Kṛṣṇa since he is just one of five divine figures being invoked in the opening couplets.

> Meditating on Vyāsa, the feet of Gaṇapati (Gaṇeśa),
> Girijā (Pārvatī), Hara (Śiva), and Bhagavān (Kṛṣṇa),[38]
> Sabalsingh Cauhān tells the *Sabhāparv* in Bhasha.
> In Vikram Saṃvat[39] 1727 (1670 CE), in the auspicious month of Caitra, the ninth day,
> Thursday, in the light half of the lunar month,
> this story was illuminated.[40]

This prologue to the *Sabhāparv* and the prologues to seven other books in Cauhān's text have caught the interest of Hindi scholars because they all contain dates ranging between 1661 and 1724 CE.[41] Five of these dated prologues also praise Aurangzeb (Awrangzīb), the sixth ruler of the

38. Ramlagan Pandey states that Bhagavān modifies Hara. See Sabalsingh Cauhān, *Sabalsingh Cauhān Kṛt Mahābhārat*, ed. Ramlagan Pandey (Varanasi: Shri Thakur Prasad Pustak Bhandar, 2014), 160. I think it is more likely that Bhagavān refers to Kṛṣṇa given the way this title has been used in seminal Vaiṣṇava texts such as the *Bhagavadgītā* and the *Bhāgavatapurāṇa*.

39. The Vikram Saṃvat calendar system, which was used extensively in premodern North India, has a zero point of approximately 57 BCE.

40. *sumiri vyāsa gaṇapati caraṇa girijā hara bhagavāna*
sabhāparva bhāṣā bhanata sabalasiṃha cauhāna
satrah sau sattāisai saṃvata śubha madhu māsa
navamī aru guru pakṣa sita bhai yaha kathā prakāsa || *CM* 2.1 ||

41. *CM* 2.1, 6.1, 7.1, 8.1, 9.1, 16.1, 17.1, 18.1.

Mughal Empire.[42] Given that seven out of the eight dates in the prologues are within the dates accepted as Aurangzeb's reign (1658–1707 CE), many prominent Hindi literary historians assert that the prologues document the exact composition dates for these eight books.[43]

A closer look at the date in the *Sabhāparv* prologue, however, reveals that it is not simply a random composition date, but a paramount festival for devotees of Rāma in North India. The ninth day of the month of Caitra in the Hindu lunar calendar, known as Rāmnavamī, is celebrated throughout North India as Rāma's birthday. This date also aligns Cauhān's Bhasha *Mahābhārat* with Tulsīdās' Bhasha *Rāmcaritmānas* ("The Lake of the Deeds of Rāma"), the *bhakti* Rāmāyaṇa retelling that has been labeled the "Bible of North India."[44] In the opening prologue to his poem, Tulsīdās states:

> With respect, I bow my head to Lord Śiva and begin to sing
> of Rāma's pure attributes.
> In Vikram Saṃvat 1631 (1574 CE), I begin this story, placing
> my head at Hari's feet.
> On the ninth day, Tuesday, in the month of Caitra,
> these deeds were illuminated in the city of Ayodhyā.
> On this day of Rāma's birth, the Vedas sing that all leave and
> go there for pilgrimage.[45]

---

42. *CM* 6.1, 8.1, 9.1, 16.1, 17.1.

43. See Ganeshbihari Mishra, Shukdevbihari Mishra, and Shyambihari Mishra, *Miśrabandhuvinod*, vol. 1 (Hyderabad: Ganga Granthagara, 1972; first published 1913, Hindi Granth Prasarak Mandali (Allahabad)), 272–73; Ramchandra Shukla, *Hindī Sāhitya Kā Itihās*, 9th ed. (Banaras: Nagari Pracharini Sabha, 1942), 326; and Ronald Stuart McGregor, *Hindi Literature from Its Beginnings to the Nineteenth Century* (Wiesbaden: Otto Harrassowitz, 1984), 195.

44. Philip Lutgendorf, *The Life of a Text: Performing the Rāmcaritmānas of Tulsidas* (Berkeley: University of California Press, 1991), 1.

45. *sādara sivahi nāi aba māthā baranauṃ bisada rāma guna gāthā*
saṃbata soraha sai ekatīsā karauṃ kathā hari pada dhari sīsā
naumī bhauma bāra madhu māsā avadhapurīṃ yaha carita prakāsā
jehi dina rāma janama śruti gāvahiṃ tīratha sakala tahāṃ cali āvahiṃ
|| *RCM* 1.34.2–3 ||
All references to the *Rāmcaritmānas* (*RCM*) are to the following edition: Tulsīdās, *Śrirāmcaritmānas*, ed. Hanumanprasad Poddar (Gorakhpur: Gita Press, 1966).

Cauhān's claim that he started the *Sabhāparv* on the same auspicious day that Tulsīdās says he began his *bhakti* Rāmāyaṇa is not a coincidence. Throughout his text, Cauhān makes it clear that he is emulating the *Rāmcaritmānas.* One prominent example of this is the metrical structure of Cauhān's poem. Several Bhasha narratives—including Viṣṇudās' fifteenth-century Mahābhārata, the *Pāṇḍavcarit*—are composed in *caupāī-dohā* (quatrain-couplet) meter. The *caupāī-dohā* stanza units of the *Mahābhārat*, however, which contain four to five *caupāī*s followed by a *dohā* or its variant, the *soraṭhā,* occasionally interspersed with verses in a meter called *harigītikā-chand* or "the meter of short songs to Hari," are undoubtedly inspired by the specific metrical format of the *Rāmcaritmānas.*[46] It is no wonder that recent editions describe Cauhān's work as being written in "the style of the Rāmāyaṇa created by Gosvāmī Tulsīdās."[47] By proclaiming that he began his *Sabhāparv* on Rāmnavamī, Cauhān firmly places his *Mahābhārat* in the same religious milieu as Tulsīdās' beloved *bhakti* poem.

Cauhān describes himself composing his text on Vaiṣṇava festivals in many of his prologues. He writes that he began the *Śalyaparv* ("The Book of Śalya") in 1667 CE on the tenth day of the month of Kārtik, which is celebrated in parts of North India as the day Kṛṣṇa vanquished Kaṃsa.[48] In Cauhān's *Śalyaparv,* while the Pāṇḍavas kill their maternal uncles Śakuni (the brother of their aunt Gāndhārī) and Śalya (the brother of their mother Mādrī),[49] Kṛṣṇa does not do much. The statement that Cauhān began this book on the tenth day of Kārtik, however, causes his audience to recall the day Kṛṣṇa killed his own maternal uncle, Kaṃsa.[50]

46. On the meter of the *Rāmcaritmānas,* see Lutgendorf, *Life of a Text,* 14–17.

47. See the title page of the 2015 Tej Kumar Book Depot edition.

48. *CM* 9.1. On the festival, see Tracy Pintchman, *Guests at God's Wedding: Celebrating Kartik among the Women of Benares* (Albany: State University of New York Press, 2005), 76.

49. *CM* 9.8, 9.11.

50. In the Sanskrit *Mahābhārata,* Kaṃsa is the cousin of Kṛṣṇa's mother, Devakī, and in the *Harivaṃśa,* Devakī is Kaṃsa's aunt. In the *Bhāgavatapurāṇa* and many other Vaiṣṇava *bhakti* compositions, however, Devakī is Kaṃsa's sister. See Benjamín Preciado-Solís, *The Kṛṣṇa Cycle in the Purāṇas: Themes and Motifs in a Heroic Saga* (Delhi: Motilal Banarsidass, 1984), 52.

The dates in the prologues of the *Droṇaparv* ("The Book of Droṇa") and the *Karṇaparv* ("The Book of Karṇa"), like the date in the *Sabhāparv*, are distinctly associated with Rāma. Cauhān states that he started the *Droṇaparv* in 1670 CE on the tenth day of the month of Āśvin, "that day Rāma left Laṅkā."[51] This is a clear reference to Vijayadaśamī, the day Rāma defeats Rāvaṇa. Vijayadaśamī also marks the end of Navarātri, the nine-day festival during which *Rāmlīlā* ("the divine play of Rāma") performances based on the *Rāmcaritmānas* are enacted throughout North India.[52] In the prologue of the *Karṇaparv*, Cauhān says that he began this book in 1667 CE on the fifth day of Āśvin, which is the fifth day of Navarātri.[53]

Yet it is not Rāma but Kṛṣṇa who plays a major role in the actual narratives of Cauhān's *Sabhāparv*, *Droṇaparv*, and *Karṇaparv*. In the *Sabhāparv*, Kṛṣṇa slays his insolent cousin, Śiśupāla, and saves Draupadī when the Kauravas try to disrobe her.[54] In the *Droṇaparv* and the *Karṇaparv*, Kṛṣṇa tells the Pāṇḍavas exactly how to defeat these two Kaurava generals.[55] The references to Rāmnavamī, Vijayadaśamī, and Navarātri in these three books thus explicitly incorporate the worship of Rāma into this otherwise Kṛṣṇa-centric Mahābhārata.

As seen in the *Sabhāparv*, Cauhān often invokes multiple different Hindu deities and sages in the opening verses of a single prologue. All eleven of his prologues, however, refer to some form of Viṣṇu. In the prologues to his final three books, Cauhān reaffirms his composition's identity as a Vaiṣṇava text. Cauhān tells his audience in the *Āśramavāsikaparv* ("The Book of Hermitage") that his Mahābhārata is about "when the lord of Śrī descended and bestowed protection."[56] In the *Muśalaparv* ("The Book of Clubs"), Cauhān announces that:

---

51. *jā dina laṅkā rāma payāne* || *CM* 7.1 ||

52. Multiple legends identify Tulsīdās as the founder of the *Rāmlīlā* tradition. See Lutgendorf, *Life of a Text*, 255–58. I should point out that there are some *Rāmlīlā* performances, such as the famous *Rāmlīlā* of Rāmnagar in Uttar Pradesh, that last for more than ten days.

53. *CM* 8.1.

54. *CM* 2.23, 2.58.

55. *CM* 7.51, 8.22.

56. *śrīprabhu jaba arake dai rākhā* || *CM* 16.1 ||

When King Aurangzeb, the lord of Delhi, was leader,
then Sabalsingh was the singer of the attributes of Hari.[57]

In a similar vein, in the prologue to the final book of his *Mahābhārat,* the *Svargārohaṇaparv* ("The Book of the Ascent to Heaven"), after describing how he called on Sarasvatī (the goddess of education and the arts) to help him write "the *līlā* of Hari," Cauhān states that:

In the pure and beautiful month of Agrahāyaṇ,
on the day of Wednesday, at the auspicious feet of Hari,
in Vikram Saṃvat 1781 (1724 CE), at that time, the story of
Hari was illuminated.
The entire world knows the form of Hari and all prostrate before
him as if planks.[58]

In contrast to the multiple episodes that focus on Kṛṣṇa in the narrative of the *Mahābhārat*, Cauhān's invocations barely mention this deity. Although the epithet Govinda (the master of cows) is found two times in the prologues,[59] unlike Villi's invocations or the Bhasha poems of sixteenth-century Kṛṣṇa devotees such as Sūrdās or Nandadās, Cauhān's invocations make no allusions to the stories of the charismatic cowherd of Vṛndāvana or praise the god in any detail.

Instead, the form of Viṣṇu that receives the most frequent and the most elaborate praise from Cauhān in his invocations is Rāma. The very first line of the *Āśramavāsikaparv* is:

Victory, victory to the best of the Raghu [lineage], the
illustrious Rāma
who fulfills all the desires of his devotees.[60]

57. *auraṃgaśāha dilīpati nāyaka sabalasiṃha taba hari guṇa gāyaka* || *CM* 17.1 ||

58. *agahana māsa punīta suhāvā budhabāra hari tithi śubha pāvā*
sambata satrahasai ikyāsī tāhi samaya harikathā prakāsī
hari ko rūpa sakala jaga jānā kari sabahina kahaṃ daṇḍa praṇāmā || *CM* 18.1 ||

59. *CM* 6.1, 17.1.

60. *jayati jayati raghubara śrīrāmā bhakta janana ko pūraṇakāmā* || *CM* 16.1 ||

While other deities and sages are usually extolled in less than half a line, Cauhān frequently dedicates entire quatrains to Rāma and other figures from the Rāmāyaṇa tradition. For example, in the prologue to the *Bhīṣmaparv* ("The Book of Bhīṣma"), he writes:

> I salute the feet of the lord of the Raghus (Rāma)
> whose attributes are sung of in the four Vedas,
> the beautiful protector of Ayodhyā, the lord of Sītā,[61]
> the friend of the poor, the one of the Raghu clan,
> the fortress destroyer.[62]

Just one line after this quatrain celebrating Rāma, Cauhān briefly pays homage to Hanumān (Rāma's beloved monkey devotee) before commending the author of the Sanskrit *Rāmāyaṇa*:

> Vālmīki creates the Rāmāyaṇa:
> the deeds of Rāma that destroy sin.[63]

Although this verse speaks of Vālmīki, the reference to the *carita* of Rāma in this line immediately reminds aficionados of Tulsīdās' Rāmāyaṇa of its title: the *Rāmcaritmānas*.

Cauhān continues to praise Rāma in the prologue to the *Droṇaparv*:

> I worship the feet of Rāma, the delight of the Raghus,
> the great hero, the destruction of the ten-shouldered one (Rāvaṇa),
> the one with long arms and lotus-petal eyes,
> the liberation of the courtesan, the hunter, and Ahalyā.[64]

---

61. Sītā is the wife of Rāma.

62. *kai praṇāma raghupati ke pāyana cāri veda jāke guṇa gāyana*
avadhanātha sītāpati sundara dīnabandhu raghuvaṃśa puraṃdara || *CM* 6.1 ||
While Puraṃdara (fortress destroyer) is a common epithet of the Vedic god Indra, the title can also refer to Viṣṇu or Kṛṣṇa. See Winand M. Callewaert and Swapna Sharma, *Dictionary of Bhakti: North-Indian Bhakti Texts into Khari Boli Hindi and English* (Delhi: D. K. Printworld, 2009), 1243.

63. *bālmīki rāmāyaṇa karatā rāma caritra pāpa ko haratā* || *CM* 6.1 ||

64. *bandauṃ rāma caraṇa raghunandana mahābīra daśakandha nikandana*
dīragha bāhu kamaladala locana gaṇikā byādha ahalyā mocana || *CM* 7.1 ||

In the second line of this quatrain, Cauhān mentions the courtesan Jīvantī and the hunter Vālmīki, two individuals whose lowly lives are redeemed after they chant *rāmnām* (the name of Rāma). The power of *rāmnām* is a major component of Tulsīdās' theology in the *Rāmcaritmānas*.[65] Tulsīdās dedicates ten stanzas[66] to the supremacy of Rāma's name in the opening prologue of his Rāmāyaṇa, in which he uses the stories of Vālmīki[67] and Jīvantī[68] to illustrate the omnipotence of *rāmnām*. By bringing up Jīvantī and Vālmīki in this invocation praising Rāma, Cauhān is able to allude to the potency of *rāmnām* in his own epic retelling. The prologues to the *Droṇaparv* and the *Karṇaparv* also both conclude with couplets in which Cauhān describes himself "worshiping the feet of the lord of the Raghus."[69] Recall that Cauhān claims that he began the *Droṇaparv* and the *Karṇaparv* during Vijayadaśamī and Navarātri.

In an earlier quatrain in the prologue to the *Karṇaparv*, Cauhān venerates Rāma alongside the prince of Ayodhyā's most well-known and dedicated devotee, Hanumān.

> I worship Rāmacandra, the ocean of attributes,
> the lord of Sītā, the splendor of the Raghu clan.
> No one understands his unfathomable magnificence.
> [Only] his greatest devotee Hanumān understands.[70]

This quatrain is one of five invocations to Hanumān in the prologues of the *Mahābhārat*.[71] Hanumān also has a significant presence in the narrative

65. For a detailed discussion of the use of *rāmnām* in this text, see Vasudha Paramasivan, "Between Text and Sect: Early Nineteenth Century Shifts in the Theology of Ram," (PhD diss., University of California, Berkeley, 2010), 39–42.

66. *RCM* 1.19–28.

67. *RCM* 1.19.3.

68. *RCM* 1.26.4.

69. *raghupati caraṇa manāikai* || *CM* 7.1, 8.1 ||

70. *bandauṃ rāmacandra guṇa sāgara sītāpati raghubaṃśa ujāgara*
mahimā agama aura nahiṃ jānā parama bhakta jānata hanumānā || *CM* 8.1 ||

71. *CM* 6.1, 8.1, 16.1, 17.1, 18.1.

of Cauhān's poem. Apart from Hanumān's meeting with his half-brother Bhīma[72] (which is also described in the Sanskrit epic),[73] Cauhān inserts multiple episodes into his retelling that feature Hanumān. At the end of his *Ādiparv* ("The Book of Beginnings"), Cauhān incorporates a story that is also found in the Sanskrit *Ānandarāmāyaṇa* (ca. fifteenth century) in which Kṛṣṇa saves Arjuna's life after the Pāṇḍava is humbled by Hanumān.[74] In Cauhān's *Bhīṣmaparv*, Hanumān attacks the elephant of Bhagadatta, the king of Prāgjyotiṣa and an ally of the Kauravas.[75] Hanumān then goes on to fight alongside Arjuna throughout the rest of the battle at Kurukṣetra.[76] While in the critical edition of the *Mahābhārata* Hanumān does promise Bhīma that he will reside in Arjuna's flag during the war,[77] he is noticeably absent from the battle itself in the Sanskrit text. Hanumān's participation in the Kurukṣetra war, however, does find a place in the *Hanumānbāhuk* ("The Arms of Hanumān"), a Bhasha composition attributed to Tulsīdās.[78]

As noted earlier, Cauhān regularly inserts episodes into the narrative of his retelling that focus on Kṛṣṇa. With the incorporation of scenes featuring Hanumān, Cauhān brings the world of Rāma into the Bhasha *Mahābhārat* as well. The eleven prologues in the *Mahābhārat* also help ensure that Rāma's story is part of Cauhān's *carita* of Kṛṣṇa. By announcing the composition dates of Rāmnavamī, Vijayadaśamī, and Navarātri, and inserting numerous invocatory verses dedicated to Rāma and other Rāmāyaṇa figures, Cauhān creates prologues that resonate with audiences of Rāma devotees and *Rāmcaritmānas* connoisseurs in North India.

---

72. *CM* 3.27–29. Hanumān and Bhīma are both the sons of the wind deity, Vāyu.

73. *MBh* 3.147–50.

74. *CM* 1.66–68. On this story in the *Ānandarāmāyaṇa*, see Philip Lutgendorf, *Hanuman's Tale: The Messages of a Divine Monkey* (New York: Oxford University Press, 2007), 230.

75. *CM* 6.25.

76. *CM* 6.40–44, 7.29, 8.14, 8.17, 9.4.

77. *MBh* 3.150.15.

78. *Hanumānbāhuk* 5. See Tulsīdās, *Hanumānbāhuk Saṭīk,* ed. M. P. Malviy Vaidya (Gorakhpur: Gita Press, 1994).

Conclusion: Larger Patterns of Retelling the Mahābhārata in Regional Languages

Despite the ubiquity of premodern retellings of the epic, few scholars have compared Mahābhāratas in regional languages.[79] The only theoretical work on these retellings is found in Sheldon Pollock's 2006 magnum opus, *The Language of the Gods in the World of Men*. Pollock argues that vernacular Mahābhāratas were literary representations of the political power of regional courts in premodern India.[80] This sweeping assertion is largely based on the opening prologues of Pampa's Kannada *Vikramārjunavijaya* (ca. 950), Ranna's Kannada *Sāhasabhīmavijaya* (ca. 1000), and Viṣṇudās' Bhasha *Pāṇḍavcarit* (1435), in which all three poets explicitly compare a courtly patron with one of the Pāṇḍava princes.[81] Pollock also makes a point of stating that Nannaya's eleventh-century portion of the Telugu *Mahābhāratamu* and Viṣṇudās' *Pāṇḍavcarit* were "entirely untouched by religious concerns."[82]

Like the regional Mahābhāratas of Pampa, Ranna, Nannaya, and Viṣṇudās, the Tamil *Pāratam* and the Bhasha *Mahābhārat* both claim to have been created in courtly contexts. In a preface (*ciṟappuppāyiram*) to the *Pāratam* attributed to Villi's son, Varantaruvār, Villi's patron is identified as a Koṅkar[83] chieftain named Varatapati Āṭkoṇṭāṉ.[84] At three different points in the *Pāratam* itself, Villi praises a "Koṅkar lord of the earth," a "Koṅkar king," and someone named "Āṭkoṇṭāṉ."[85] As noted earlier, Cauhān extols the

79. For two exceptions, see M. V. Subramanian, *The Mahabharata Story: Vyasa & Variations* (Madras: Higginbothams (Private) Ltd., 1967); and Kambalur Venkatesa Acharya, *Mahabharata and Variations: Perundevanar and Pampa; A Comparative Study* (Kurnool: Vyasaraja Publications, 1981).

80. Sheldon Pollock, *The Language of the Gods in the World of Men: Sanskrit, Culture, and Power in Premodern India* (Berkeley: University of California Press, 2006), 397.

81. Pollock, 360, 363, 395.

82. Pollock, 429. On the *Sāhasabhīmavijaya,* the *Mahābhāratamu,* and the *Pāṇḍavcarit,* see the chapters by Timothy Lorndale, Harshita Mruthinti Kamath, and Heidi Pauwels in this volume.

83. Koṅkar refers to Koṅku Nāṭu, a region in the western part of present-day Tamil Nadu.

84. *VP ciṟappuppāyiram* 18.

85. *VP* 1.8.69, 4.4.104, 8.1.90.

Mughal emperor Aurangzeb multiple times in his prologues. Cauhān also praises a king by the name of Mitrasen in the prologue of the *Droṇaparv* and describes himself performing his poem in the presence of both Mitrasen and Aurangzeb in Delhi in the prologue to his *Āśramavāsikaparv*.[86]

As I have shown in this chapter, however, while Villi and Cauhān place their Mahābhāratas in courtly milieus, both of these poets also make it abundantly clear that their retellings are steeped in local Vaiṣṇava religious traditions. Moreover, Villi and Cauhān are not the only ones who place Viṣṇu at the center of their regional retellings. Like several other premodern Mahābhāratas, Peruntēvaṉār's ninth-century Tamil *Pāratavenpā*—which is the earliest (albeit incomplete) regional retelling of the epic—claims a courtly patron who Tamil scholars have identified as King Nandivarman III of the Pallava dynasty.[87] Yet this Tamil Mahābhārata also clearly presents Māl as its hero, and Kamil Zvelebil points out that "at the beginning of every new portion of his book, the poet has an introductory stanza praising Tirumāl (Viṣṇu)."[88] Similarly, Vīranārāyaṇa, a local form of Viṣṇu in Karnataka, is the protagonist of Kumāravyāsa's fifteenth-century Kannada *Karṇāṭabhāratakathāmañjarī* and, as Shrinivas Ritti observes, Kumāravyāsa explains in his opening prologue that he composed this Mahābhārata "out of the urge to narrate [a] *Krishna-kathā* [story] which Krishna himself would appreciate."[89]

The invocations and prologues of the Mahābhāratas of Peruntēvaṉār, Kumāravyāsa, Villi, and Cauhān all suggest that there was a continuous centering of this epic around Viṣṇu throughout the Indian subcontinent. As we continue to study the many regional Mahābhāratas of premodern South Asia, it is imperative that along with examining the implications of courtly patronage claims in several of these texts, we also take into account and acknowledge the crucial role that different Vaiṣṇava devotional traditions played in the retelling of this epic narrative.

86. *CM* 7.1, 16.1.

87. See Venkatesa Acharya, *Mahabharata and Variations*, 61; and Kamil Zvelebil, *Companion Studies to the History of Tamil Literature* (Leiden: E. J. Brill, 1992), 68.

88. Zvelebil, 68. Also see Venkatesa Acharya, 71.

89. Shrinivas Ritti, "*Mahābhārata* in Early Kannada Literature," in *Mahābhārata: The End of an Era (Yugānta)*, ed. Ajay Mitra Shastri (Shimla: India Institute of Advanced Study, 2004), 362.

PART IV

Mahābhāratas of Modern South Asia

Chapter Fourteen

How to Be Political without Being Polemical

The Debate between Bankimchandra Chattopadhyay and Rabindranath Tagore over the *Kṛṣṇacaritra*

Ahona Panda

In Search of *Prajñā*

This instruction of dharma for you does not proceed solely from the scriptures alone. [It is] brought forth by *prajñā* (wisdom). It is the honey that the sages have gleaned. The king must make use of many kinds of wisdom. Therefore, the king's way of life does not proceed merely in accordance with a one-branched dharma. The kings who always engage in the performance of dharma will acquire the right intellectual insight and victory, O descendant of Kuru!—understand my words thus. . . . The kings who are the best with respect to intellect are the ones who when they seek victory actually get it. Thus the king must rely on dharma using his intellect . . . the dharma of kings is not given by any one-branched dharma. How can he who is weak

> have *prajñā* unless it is previously taught to him? He who does not know the two-faced nature of morality, when faced with a dilemma may fall into that, *so one ought to first understand the two-sidedness of prajñā, O Bhārata.*[1]

In the *Śāntiparvan* ("The Book of Peace," the twelfth book of the Sanskrit *Mahābhārata*), the great Kurukṣetra war is over, and a stricken Yudhiṣṭhira is trying to come to terms with a sovereignty achieved at the cost of the blood of his kin. He desires death, and his brothers along with Kṛṣṇa and various sages all offer him counsel, but he is unconvinced. The only person who can calm the troubled Yudhiṣṭhira is his dying granduncle Bhīṣma, to whom Yudhiṣṭhira plaintively lays out the question—What is a king?[2] To this question Bhīṣma has many answers, of which one is that the king, though hardly an intellectual, has to understand the manifold nature of dharma, and that it does not simply proceed unquestioningly from scriptural knowledge.[3] If political morality is a double-bind, then *prajñā* (true wisdom) involves the realization that one's own intellect (a critical nature) must judge the situation at hand.

My essay is not about the Sanskrit *Mahābhārata.* It is not even about Kṛṣṇa. Instead, it seeks to put two major Bengali political and literary figures of modern India in conversation with one another over their understanding of the figure of Kṛṣṇa, and therefore the *Mahābhārata,* in the late nineteenth century. Hence, this essay takes up the *Kṛṣṇacaritra* ("The Nature of Kṛṣṇa," 1886) by Bankimchandra Chattopadhyay (1838–1894)[4] and the rejoinder given to this book by Rabindranath Tagore (1861–1941) in

1. *MBh* 12.140.3–8 (emphasis mine). All references to the *Mahābhārata* (*MBh*) in this chapter are from *The Mahābhārata for the First Time Critically Edited*, ed. V. S. Sukthankar et al. 19 vols. (Poona: Bhandarkar Oriental Research Institute, 1933–66). All translations are my own unless noted otherwise.

2. *MBh* 12.56.

3. On one of the stories Bhīṣma tells Yudhiṣṭhira in the *Śāntiparvan*, see the chapter by Sally Sutherland Goldman.

4. Unless noted otherwise, all references to Bankim's *Kṛṣṇacaritra* (henceforth *Kṛṣṇacaritra*) in this essay are to the critical edition in *Baṅkima Racanābalī*, ed. Jogeshchandra Bagal (Kolkata: Sahitya Samsad, 1964), 407–583.

an 1895 review essay. By the end of the nineteenth century, Bankim (as Chattopadhyay was commonly known) was the most towering figure of the Bengal Renaissance, the first Indian novelist, and the writer of several critical essays, both serious and satirical. Toward the end of his life, Bankim's political views became somewhat more conservative, and by the time of his death in 1894, a younger generation of nationalist intellectuals had ascended.[5] Meanwhile, by 1895, Tagore was already an established poet and writer.[6] He was critically involved in certain streams of political activism at the time, especially in endeavors surrounding vernacular education and pedagogy, an issue that remained a lifelong concern.[7]

First published in *Sādhana* magazine in 1895, Tagore's review of the *Kṛṣṇacaritra* was later re-published in 1907 in a collection of essays in literary criticism entitled *Ādhunik Sāhitya* ("Modern Literature"). Together, Bankim's lengthy treatise and Tagore's short rejoinder generate a conversation between two distinct modern approaches to an early literary text. Bankim and Tagore agree that the Sanskrit *Mahābhārata* can be a guide to truth. For Bankim, the truth about the *Mahābhārata* is historical: it provides evidence of one true historical narrative about the exemplar of Kṛṣṇa. Tagore, however, posits the *Mahābhārata*'s truth as poetic, whereby facts and figures of the text are reinvented by a plurality of voices. This chapter studies the contrast between these two nineteenth-century interpretations of the *Mahābhārata* and traces the shadows of this debate in the twenty-first century. Is there a way to read the *Mahābhārata* that eludes us in the politically difficult environment of present-day South Asia?

---

5. For comprehensive biographies of Bankim see Sisir Kumar Das, *The Artist in Chains: The Life of Bankimchandra Chatterji* (Delhi: New Statesman, 1984); and Amiya P. Sen, *Bankim Chandra Chattopadhyay: An Intellectual Biography* (Delhi: Oxford University Press, 2008).

6. Tagore was the author of multiple Mahābhārata retellings, including the dance-drama *Citrāṅgadā* (1892) and the poems *Gāndhārīr Ābedan* ("Gāndhārī's Plea," 1897) and *Karṇa Kuntī Sambād* ("The Meeting of Karṇa and Kuntī," 1899).

7. For biographies of Tagore, see Krishna Kripalani, *Rabindranath Tagore: A Biography* (New York: Grove Press, 1962); and Sabyasachi Bhattacharya, *Rabindranath Tagore: An Interpretation* (Delhi: Penguin Books, 2011).

Kabitvamay Itihāsa (A Poetic History): Bankim's Ideological Project in the *Kṛṣṇacaritra*

Kṛṣṇa himself is God.[8]

—the *Bhāgavatapurāṇa*

In the 1880s, Bankim had entered the last phase of his literary career. This period is marked by his bitterly polemical views against Muslims, whom he believed were the social enemies of Hindus, in his novels *Ānandamaṭh* (1882), *Debī Caudhurānī* (1884), and *Sītārām* (1886). In his novels and his non-fictional treatises, *Kṛṣṇacaritra* and *Dharmatattva* ("The Essence of Dharma," 1888), Bankim laid the foundation of a politico-religious project that would argue for a nationalist selfhood in which the careful cultivation of the self, through training the senses and imposing physical and mental discipline, was undertaken for the higher good of the society (*samāj*). *Bhakti* (devotion) in this scheme was the selfless relationship between the self-monitoring ethical agent and the nation, which expected no rewards. The *Kṛṣṇacaritra,* following on the heels of *Dharmatattva,* plays an important role in Bankim's political project, as he explains in his own succinct blurb (*vijñapan*):

> What is mere theory in *anuśīlan* dharma (the dharma of self-cultivation) is embodied in the *Kṛṣṇacaritra*. The ideals that you come face-to-face with in *anuśīlan* (praxis), Kṛṣṇa's character itself is that ideal. First you explain theory, then you make it clearer with an example. The character of Kṛṣṇa itself is that example.[9]

The book itself is divided into seven parts corresponding to the various phases of Kṛṣṇa's life. While I focus on the introductory part, in which Bankim lays out his method and purpose for the *Kṛṣṇacaritra,* the following

8. *kṛṣṇastu bhagavān swayam* | *Kṛṣṇacaritra,* 407. This verse is from the *Bhāgavatapurāṇa* (1.3.28). See *Bhāgavata Purāṇa of Kṛṣṇa Dvaipayana Vyāsa*, ed. J. L. Shastri (Delhi: Motilal Banarsidass, 1983).

9. Bankimchandra Chattopadhyay, *Kṛṣṇacaritra*, eds. Brajendranath Bandyopadhyay and Sajanikanta Das (Calcutta: Bangiya Sahitya Parishad, 1941), 3. This *vijñapan* is not found in Bagal's edition of the text.

chapters embark on a philological reading of the various events of Kṛṣṇa's life. The model on which Bankim based his book is the *carita,* a genre in Sanskrit and vernacular literatures that narrates a eulogized biography of certain historical or mythological characters.[10] Earlier examples of this genre in Bengal include Ānanda Bhaṭṭa's biography of Ballāla Sena, the *Ballālacarita* (1510), and Kṛṣṇadāsa Kavirāja's early-seventeenth-century hagiography of the Vaiṣṇava poet-saint Caitanya, the *Caitanyacaritāmṛta*. Bankim's use of *carita* harnesses the cultural import of these earlier works. Moreover, he does not use the word *carita* (which is the more common spelling in Sanskrit texts) but instead uses the term *caritra* (broadly speaking, a more vernacular spelling of the term), which, in nineteenth-century Bengali usage, stresses the meaning "character" or "nature" rather than "deeds" or "life."

Bankim's characterization of Kṛṣṇa differs significantly from that which we find in the Vaiṣṇava *bhakti* traditions of the Bengal countryside. For centuries, Bankim laments, Bengalis worshiped Kṛṣṇa, built Kṛṣṇa temples, sang songs in praise of Kṛṣṇa and his beloved, Rādhā, and even taught their parrots to say "Rādhekṛṣṇa."[11] The Kṛṣṇa so popular and all-pervasive in Bengal—the Kṛṣṇa of the paramount Sanskrit Vaiṣṇava work, the *Bhāgavatapurāṇa*, and the *Padāvalī* lyrical tradition that was initiated by disciples of Caitanya in the sixteenth century—has become too commonplace, Bankim says, almost an unquestioned social reality. Kṛṣṇa is someone with whom most Bengalis live on a daily basis, present in every aspect of life, so common indeed that the mundane soon becomes the banal. He writes: "Most Hindus of Bhāratavarṣa (India), and all Hindus of Bengal, believe that Kṛṣṇa is an *avatāra* (incarnation) of God. 'Kṛṣṇa himself is God'—this is their firm belief."[12]

But what is the nature of the Kṛṣṇa that Bengal worships? Here, Bankim expresses a disgust with the Kṛṣṇa of the Bengali popular imagination—a child thief, a serial adulterer making young women lapse from the path of virtue, a cunning usurper on the verge of adulthood.[13] How

10. On two premodern poems that retell the Mahābhārata as the *carita* of Kṛṣṇa/Viṣṇu, see the chapter by Sohini Sarah Pillai in this volume.

11. *Kṛṣṇacaritra,* 407.

12. *Kṛṣṇacaritra*, 407.

13. *Kṛṣṇacaritra,* 407. Bankim's strategic choice of the warrior Kṛṣṇa has been discussed by Tanika Sarkar in *Hindu Wife, Hindu Nation: Community, Religion, and Cultural Nationalism* (Bloomington: Indiana University Press, 2001), 183.

could this be God? Bankim asks: "Can God have such a character? He who is essentially pure, He who purifies all, with whose very name we drive away all evil and impurity; is it appropriate that He will be sinful when he assumes a mortal body?"[14] Bankim bemoans the way Kṛṣṇa has been characterized and constructed over several centuries; he finds the banal mortality ascribed to a God unseemly. Bankim's project announces a moment of departure. What must be done with Kṛṣṇa now is *samālocanā* (criticism), despite Kṛṣṇa's stature as divinity.[15] The historical moment, after all, is one of objectivity; Bankim emphasizes that readers must not adopt his views without due consideration on their own part. He mentions that the late nineteenth century has witnessed a Hindu *dharmāndolan* (revivalist movement), and, more than ever, religion and custom must be held up to the light of criticism and scrutiny:

> This book has a specific purpose. I do not ask the reader to accept what I believe in, and neither is it my aim to establish Kṛṣṇa's divinity. In this book, I will only scrutinize his human character (*mānavacaritra*). Right now the *dharmāndolan* has gained some intensity. Within this *dharmāndolan* it is important that Kṛṣṇa's character is scrutinized at length. If we must hold on to the old, then we must understand what is worth holding on to. If we must do away with the old altogether, then we still must embark on a criticism of Kṛṣṇa; without discarding Kṛṣṇa, we cannot discard the old.[16]

There are two aspects of Bankim's exposition that I want to highlight in this essay. The first is the idea of *samālocanā*; *Kṛṣṇacaritra* marks the beginning of a clear philological method for Bankim. For Bankim, the project of textual criticism is clearly related to his understanding of the *Mahābhārata* as history.[17] The second issue worth foregrounding is Bankim's emphasis on

14. *Kṛṣṇacaritra*, 407.

15. *Kṛṣṇacaritra,* 407.

16. *Kṛṣṇacaritra*, 407–408.

17. Two important books that declare the *Kṛṣṇacaritra* as a crucial moment in the conceptualizing of historicity in colonial Bengal are Partha Chatterjee, *Nationalist Thought and Colonial World: A Derivative Discourse* (London: Zed Books for the United Nations University, 1993), 54–84; and Sudipta Kaviraj, *The Unhappy*

establishing Kṛṣṇa's *humanity*. We no longer inhabit *carita* as a biographical text in which man is almost godlike in heroic deeds; instead, in Bankim's new mythology, God must be made man. Here, the "historical" and the "human" are intertwined in a specific relationship: common positivist sense tells us that the divine cannot be historical. Yet at no point does Bankim depart from the paradox at the heart of the *Kṛṣṇacaritra* that Kṛṣṇa is both human and divine. It is in his human form that Kṛṣṇa is historical and accessible, an object of emulation. Bankim reminds the reader of *Kṛṣṇacaritra* of the ideal (nationalist) subject in the *Dharmatattva* (composed, he reminds the readers, between two editions of the *Kṛṣṇacaritra*): "man has some powers, I have named them *vṛtti*, humanity lies in their praxis, effervescence, and thus ultimate success. This is man's dharma. In the praxis, lies the harmony of all the *vṛtti*s . . . this is bliss."[18] Bankim admits that the praxis, effervescence, and harmony of the *vṛtti*s is almost impossible to achieve, yet:

> Above all these ideals, the Hindus have another ideal, in front of whom all other ideals become insignificant—from whom Yudhiṣṭhira himself learns dharma, whose disciple is Arjuna himself, of whose part is Rāma and Lakṣmaṇa (Rāma's brother), of such unequalled greatness of character that human language cannot enumerate its glories . . . To establish this principle through evidence is another reason why I have embarked on describing the character of Śrī Kṛṣṇa.[19]

Despite the paradoxical position in which no human language can describe the glories of the divine Kṛṣṇa, Bankim is intent on not only achieving this seemingly impossible task, but also on humanizing Kṛṣṇa by situating him historically. The desire for historicity necessitates a historical method. Taking the three bodies of texts that comprise the canonical life of Kṛṣṇa,

---

Consciousness: Bankimchandra Chattopadhyay and the Formation of Nationalist Discourse in India (Delhi: Oxford University Press, 1995), 72–106. While Chatterjee finds that historicizing Kṛṣṇa was important for Bankim within a scientific and rationalist framework in order to legitimize his larger political philosophy, Kaviraj speaks of a classicization of Kṛṣṇa in which Bankim constructs a rational theology through an exegesis of the *Mahābhārata* for a new national-popular mobilization.

18. *Kṛṣṇacaritra*, 408.

19. *Kṛṣṇacaritra*, 408.

he compares them to write a definitive "history." These texts in question are the *Mahābhārata,* the *Harivaṃśa,* and the *purāṇas*, of which he gives primacy to a section of the *Mahābhārata* as a point of origin, an urtext. That the *Mahābhārata* should be the originary text is determined by Bankim on the basis of the *Harivaṃśa* and the *purāṇas* declaring that they gloss the life of Kṛṣṇa that is not found in the *Mahābhārata* itself.[20] Therefore, for Bankim, here the first instance of the historical documentation of Kṛṣṇa is the *Mahābhārata,* in which the most authentic representation of a familiar god does not reflect the later degeneration found in the conceptions of the followers of Caitanya, who endlessly regurgitate Kṛṣṇa in the image of a lover. Nor is it a naughty god masquerading as a thieving child, as propounded by the stories of the *Bhāgavatapurāṇa*. Bankim's Kṛṣṇa is the *Mahābhārata*'s warrior statesman and householder king, a friend and strategist of the Pāṇḍavas.

Bankim is grappling with two ideas of historicity in his attempt to prove Kṛṣṇa as a historical figure. The first is a translational problem that he recognizes implicitly when speaking of *itihāsa* as history. Yet to the epics of the *Rāmāyaṇa* and the *Mahābhārata* he attaches a specific historicity that does not extend to any other texts in the Hindu canon. This is because these texts designated as *itihāsa* are *purāvṛtta,* "that which has occurred," an event or account or action of the past.[21] The greatest thorn in Bankim's side is the presence of supernatural and impossible elements in the *Mahābhārata.* He resolves this problem by fashioning the *Mahābhārata* as a civilizational text in line with the Western foundational histories by Thucydides, Herodotus, and Livy. The "great books" of any civilization, he argues, comprise foundational stories that combine the mythical with the historical, truth with fiction.[22] And yet history must be extricated by carefully separating the unhistorical or mythical from the historical. According to Bankim, there are two main problems in the project of *samālocanā*. The first is the Indian propensity to declare that certain texts are sacred, composed in Sanskrit five thousand years ago by great sages. Hence it is believed that the Vedas, the *Harivaṃśa,* and the *Aṣṭādaśapurāṇa*, being unchanged over the course of five millennia, stand above any scrutiny or suspicion.[23]

20. *Kṛṣṇacaritra*, 409.

21. *Kṛṣṇacaritra*, 410.

22. *Kṛṣṇacaritra*, 411.

23. *Kṛṣṇacaritra*, 409.

The second problem, Bankim warns the reader, is the fact that European scholars have embarked on the dubious nineteenth-century business of comparative philology.[24] Bankim's introduction lends fascinating insight into a non-Western appropriation of nineteenth-century positivist philology, whose ends Bankim despises but whose means he adopts for the cause of Hindu nationalism. His basic point of criticism against the European philologists is that they do not read the *Mahābhārata* as a historical text. Instead, they fashioned the *Mahābhārata* and the *Rāmāyaṇa* as examples of epic poetry because they were written in verse.[25] In particular, Bankim hates the philologists who he believes failed miserably at dating the *Mahābhārata*—the unfortunate German philologist Albrecht Weber, for instance, argued that the *Mahābhārata* did not exist in the time of Megasthenes since "Megasthenes says nothing of this epic."[26] Bankim counters this with a hilarious rebuttal—"Many Hindus have gone and visited Germany, and have written books. I have not come across Weber's name in any of them. Does it then mean that Weber *sāheb* never existed?"[27] Despite Bankim's hatred of European philologists, he still embarks on a philological project through which the *Mahābhārata* must be established as history.

Along with a yearning for factual historicity, at the heart of the *Kṛṣṇacaritra* lies one unresolvable paradox that Bankim must address in order to be taken seriously. This is the conflict between divinity and humanity. If Kṛṣṇa is God, how can he simultaneously be human? In a short section titled "Is it Possible for God to Descend to the Earth?" Bankim addresses these irreconcilable binaries of myth and history, natural and supernatural. He examines how contemporary philosophers and theologians discuss the idea of an immanent God in the nineteenth century. His discussion extends the *bhakti* theological terms *nirguṇa* (without qualities) and *saguṇa* (with qualities) to Western interlocutors. Importantly, he argues that the idea of a *saguṇa* God's ability to manifest in the world is evident in Herbert Spencer's turn from *nirguṇa* to *saguṇa*—("Something higher than Personality"[28]). Moreover, he cites the theologian Henry Longueville Mansel in order to argue that human beings do not have the capacity to understand a *nirguṇa*

24. *Kṛṣṇacaritra,* 409–10.

25. *Kṛṣṇacaritra,* 412.

26. *Kṛṣṇacaritra*, 413.

27. *Kṛṣṇacaritra*, 413.

28. Kṛṣṇacaritra, 432.

God in the first place. Behind the curtains of theology and historicity, however, lurks the shadow of an overwhelming desire to prove the human aspect of Kṛṣṇa. Let us now see why this is necessary.

The *avatāra* of Kṛṣṇa is the manifest human form of Viṣṇu; by using the conceptual framework of *avatāra*, Bankim connects the figure of Kṛṣṇa with a moral idea of man. The *avatāra* must preserve dharma, demonstrating how to preserve the moral fabric of society to lesser mortals. Citing the eighth verse of the fourth chapter of the *Gītā*, Bankim explains why Kṛṣṇa had to appear on the earth as human:

> To rescue the righteous, to destroy wrongdoers,
> To preserve dharma, I appear in the different ages.[29]

Dharma, then, is the moral imperative behind the connection of human and divine, the two Kṛṣṇas. In this short verse, dharma is still an abstraction. After all, what *is* dharma, and how do you "preserve" it? Can dharma be preserved and maintained by the Viṣṇu *avatāra* Kṛṣṇa killing his wicked uncle, Kaṃsa, and his insolent cousin, Śiśupāla? Or is there something more to the conceptual logic of *avatāra*?

The answer lies in the functional value of the *avatāra*, for which historicity lends a certain kind of legitimacy. If a historical Kṛṣṇa can be both human and perfect, then why cannot we? At one level, Bankim expresses more interest in questions of European and Eurocentric readings and receptions of the *Mahābhārata* and in the *Mahābhārata* as history. Then, at the second level, the exegesis gives way to his central ideological premise. Dharma consists in the comprehensive manifestation, development, harmony, and fulfillment of all our physical and mental capacities. Dharma is proportional to praxis, and praxis is proportional to karma (action). Therefore, karma is the main means to get to dharma. To act, and to act well, is the main means of dharma. He says, "This karma can be called *svadharmapālan* (duty)."[30] For the ordinary human being, however, it is difficult to act. One cannot learn how to act well through mere instruction; (good) action requires an exemplar. Bankim says, "That which is distant can only be learned through

29. *Kṛṣṇacaritra*, 433.

30. *Kṛṣṇacaritra*, 433.

an exemplar, not through instruction alone."[31] Here is our hero, our exemplar then: Kṛṣṇa, who serves as both an exemplar and a mirror in which the defeated colonial subject can look toward, and find, a better self. This exemplar must be retrieved as a human character out of the many layers of textual history, a history denied by European scholars as myth. By being extricated out of myth, Kṛṣṇa must be made human and historical.

Bankim cites a wide variety of Indological scholars who agreed that the Kurukṣetra war did take place in the distant past, such as H. T. Colebrooke, H. H. Wilson, Mountstuart Elphinstone, Francis Wilford, and Francis Buchanan. Their arguments that the Pāṇḍavas did not exist despite the reality of the great war perturbs Bankim, because the existence of Kṛṣṇa as a master strategist and warrior hinges on the existence of the former. Bankim argues that contemporaneous texts do not always validate the existence of historical figures. While there are Greek accounts of Alexander the Great's conquest of India, he says, there are no concomitant Hindu accounts corroborating the claims of Greek texts. Similarly, the rise of prophet Muhammad is not mentioned in the Hindu texts of that time in India, and neither do Bengali texts of Bakhtiyār Khaljī's time mention the great sovereign. Should the absence of names from contemporary chronicles necessarily be taken as a sort of inverted evidence?[32]

Bankim then identifies an additional problem. After collaborating with native scholars, many Western scholars work with translations. As the *Mahābhārata* moves further and further away from its original or originary version, scholars such as bureaucrat-historian Talboys Wheeler (1824–1897) argue that "The adventures of the Pandavas in the jungle, and their encounters with Asuras and Rakshasas [demons and monsters] are all palpable fictions . . ."[33] The solution, according to Bankim, is to realize that the palpable fictions are (of course) supernatural elements added by later scribes. Though Kṛṣṇa is God himself, he need not use any supernatural powers in his human *avatāra* form. With the *Kṛṣṇacaritra*, Bankim hopes to "show that Kṛṣṇa did not complete any task with any supernatural forces,

31. *Kṛṣṇacaritra,* 433.

32. *Kṛṣṇacaritra*, 418.

33. *Kṛṣṇacaritra*, 421.

or by going against any laws of nature."[34] Bankim's Kṛṣṇa, for the sake of his polemic, must be a human Kṛṣṇa.

Aitihāsik Kāvya: Tagore on the *Mahābhārata*

> In our view, the hero of the *Kṛṣṇacaritra* is not Kṛṣṇa, its main protagonist is independent thought.[35]
>
> —Rabindranath Tagore, "Kṛṣṇacaritra"

Tagore's 1895 review of the *Kṛṣṇacaritra* begins with a comment on the nature of colonial society that, deprived of actual political agency, has fallen into a state of uncritical navel-gazing. Western education has led to much political discussion and, in turn, to critical discussions of one's own society and religion. Compared to the Western subject, when the colonial subject considers his own civilization he finds it lacking; he experiences a certain self-doubt. It is perhaps unhealthy, Tagore points out, to be so self-hating and discontent, and therefore many defenses and accounts of Indian culture have been published by aggrieved Indian intellectuals.[36] Not that you could blame them, adds Tagore. Since social and religious life was so deeply embedded in the national character, the introduction of Western learning—which could change that very fabric—was obviously met with some resistance. It is not unnatural to proclaim, in glorifying defenses of *samāj* and dharma, that one's own civilization is the very best. The greatest fallout of colonialism, then, is the complete erosion of one's natural critical faculties.

Given that this is the trend when Bankim's *Kṛṣṇacaritra* emerges on the scene, Tagore opines that the work is a breath of fresh air in a milieu that constantly proclaims that the *śāstra*s are unquestionable. As Tagore says, "When even the learned people of this society are losing their sense of self,

34. *Kṛṣṇacaritra,* 435.

35. I am following "Kṛṣṇacaritra" in Rabindranath Tagore, *Ādhunik Sāhitya* (Calcutta: Visva Bharati Press, 1987), 71. The book was first published in 1907 as an anthology of Tagore's literary criticism.

36. Tagore, 69.

Bankim valiantly marks a return of an independent human intellect with the *Kṛṣṇacaritra*"[37] By viewing the *Mahābhārata* through the lens of historicity and by inaugurating a historical method that scrutinized the ancient text, Bankim, in Tagore's eyes, questions age-old beliefs while subjecting them to the logic of historical reason.[38] Entrenching such a critical method signals a disciplining, and not an endorsement, of an earlier popular nationalism. Tagore lauds Bankim's attempt completely to change the way in which religious belief functions in the Indian context, which encourages an inflexible and blind attachment to scriptural knowledge and to established customary rituals in the matter of worship. Tagore argues that in breaking out of that mold, Bankim encourages us to think of religion with self-awareness. Hence the *Kṛṣṇacaritra*'s second major contribution is to reverse the very understanding of what *śāstra* is: that which we term *śāstra* does not compel belief, but that which compels belief is called *śāstra*.[39]

Tagore argues that Bankim was a pioneer in inaugurating *itihāsa-samālocanā* (historical criticism) in the case of *Kṛṣṇacaritra*.[40] Yet he doubts the efficacy of Bankim's actual method. Tagore recognizes that no one before Bankim had embarked upon the difficult path of historicizing Kṛṣṇa. Therefore, Bankim is tasked with both the deconstruction of the various lives of Kṛṣṇa and also with Kṛṣṇa's subsequent reconstruction; before Bankim can conclude what is historical about Kṛṣṇa, he must determine what is *not* historical. Bankim never clearly marks the distinctions between the "historical" and the "not historical" in his chosen "historical" text, the *Mahābhārata*. So if what Bankim considers to be the "original" *Mahābhārata* were an authentic history, and if Bankim then goes on to argue that the text includes a vast number of later interpolations, then at which point does he clearly establish the absolutely authentic, and hence historical, portions? Tagore explains:

> Bankim primarily embraces the *Mahābhārata*. However, he has unhesitatingly proved that the *Mahābhārata* has many interpo-

37. Tagore, 70.
38. Tagore, 70.
39. Tagore, 71.
40. Tagore, 71.

> lations. However, he never established which was the original *Mahābhārata*. . . . He discovered three layers of the text. The first layer is composed in a vast and high poetic vein, the second less vast in scope and with some distortions and the third composed by many people according to their own wishes over a long period of time.[41]

Tagore adds the caveat that what is added over time is hard to separate from the original, since philological reading is entirely inferential (*ānumānik*). This inferential method, Tagore points out, never adequately addresses what construes evidence.[42]

And so Bankim's second major fallacy, according to Tagore, is understanding the *Mahābhārata* as the work of successive poets with different poetic styles and using analysis of poetic styles to study the evolution of the *Mahābhārata*. To think of one poet as superior to another is a subjective enterprise: even a single poet, Tagore argues, can be inconsistent. Hence, historical evolution is best judged through the evolution of language itself: "In terms of taste, poetic worth can appear differently to different people. Also, the same poet can have very different poetic styles in the same composition, such examples are not exactly rare. Hence, the difference in language is the main critical concern of the historian, not poetic style."[43]

Why indeed should historicity be the function of the poet? Great poetry and authentic history are not inherently intertwined: "Good poetry can be present in a good poet's work, but historicity does not depend on poetic worth. . . . on such ground, bad poetry can be more reliable for extricating history than good poetry."[44] There is one point on which Tagore agrees with Bankim: that the supernatural elements of the text are ahistorical, or, rather, that they are removed from the actual historical event and represent later additions. Tagore asserts that the knotty elements in Bankim's analysis are the portions of the *Mahābhārata* that Bankim concludes are incoherent with the rest of the text. Tagore's understanding of the plural-

41. Tagore, 72.
42. Tagore, 72.
43. Tagore, 72.
44. Tagore, 72.

istic nature of the *Mahābhārata* emerges here when he explains how an important man or a significant event will have a variety of popular accounts circulating in a land. He says: "A great man or a great event have a number of popular accounts circulating about them. Different poets construct these anew either by abandoning or by polishing these popular accounts."[45] By abandoning or filtering such accounts, different poets construct a variety of poems according to their own ideals. Some may construct Kṛṣṇa as a man imbued with divinity; others may paint him as a cunning politician. Both portrayals may be incomplete; despite being in conflict with one another, it is also probable that both have some truth attached to them. In reality, Tagore says, it is difficult to ascertain which portrayal is more dependable as history.[46]

At this point, Tagore's main contention surrounds the very question of the narrativization of history. To Tagore, history (if the *Mahābhārata* counted as history at all) is inherently tied to a notion of flux and uncertainty in which no singular position is "true" precisely because it is represented, and the poet is mediator. As Tagore points out, "Bankimbabu says from time to time that the words that Kṛṣṇa speaks in the *Mahābhārata* are not spoken by him, but express the poet's views on Kṛṣṇa. We need more evidence to claim that the poet's personal ideals were the historical ideals of the time."[47] If we must take the words of Kṛṣṇa to be universally and historically true, then we must compare them with other secondary or supplementary evidence, perhaps other poetic works of the same time period that express the same views. There is no such evidence.

A second point involves Tagore's reading of a *Mahābhārata* in which an ethos of great duty-driven action prevails. Rather than thinking that this is a historical Kṛṣṇa guiding an entire social world, one should note how the poet often makes other characters in the text profess the same ideals at different points of the narrative.[48] Tagore observes the structure of narrative instability characterizing the *Mahābhārata,* in which the truth value of testimony is constantly subverted and challenged:

45. Tagore, 73–74.

46. Tagore, 74.

47. Tagore, 74.

48. Tagore, 76.

> According to Bankimbabu's own evidence, we say that we have no originary *Mahābhārata* in our present time. The *Mahābhārata* available to us today has been told by Vyāsa to Vaiśampāyana, from the mouth of Vaiśampāyana is narrated to the father of Ugraśravas, then from father to Ugraśravas, and from Ugraśravas to some poet. Second, over time even this *Mahābhārata has seen the additions of many other people.*[49]

The *Mahābhārata* comprises both telling and retelling *ad infinitum*; the story is a conglomeration of voices within many historical moments.

This understanding of a plurality of voices within the storytelling cosmos of the *Mahābhārata* is key to Tagore's understanding of the *Mahābhārata*. If the poet functions as a historical witness, he also filters history. Why indeed should the poet stick to historical veracity as eyewitness, when his task is to compose poetry? Tagore says:

> It is well known that very few people are able to grasp the real form of the actual details of an event and convey it as it really unfolded. Fewer may possess the ability to construct a complete human character and history from fragmented details . . . To get to know a great personality is even more difficult. There is no doubt that the construction of an image of him from a distance or from past information is largely imaginary. By both proof and by inference, one man can have so many different portrayals that the *original* portrayal is apprehended differently by diverse people. History, by and large, depends on the inferences of the writer and the beliefs of the reader. In such terrain, it is not impossible that the writer's *anumān* (inference) may get closer to *actual history* than the historian's *anumān.*[50]

Here, Tagore counters Bankim by giving us a new paradigm in which to think of the *Mahābhārata* as a historical text. If Bankim constructs history as narrative (along the lines of Macaulay, Carlyle, Lamartine, and Thucydides), reading the *Mahābhārata* as poetic history (*kabitvamay itihās*), then Tagore

49. Tagore, 76–77 (emphasis mine).

50. Tagore, 79.

designates the *Mahābhārata* as historical poetry (*aitihāsik kāvya*).[51] This move signals a step wherein Tagore emphasizes once again that the great epics, the *itihāsas*, are also works of poetry, not just "history" (in the nineteenth-century positivist understanding of the word, which emphasizes conceptions of truth). In fact, Tagore is possibly referring to the flexibility of the Sanskrit terms themselves when he says, "Whether we get Kṛṣṇa's ideals from *itihāsa* or from *kāvya,* or in a mixture of *kāvya-itihāsa,* there is no need to excessively debate this. *Itihāsa* is not the words of the Vedas [i.e. infallible]."[52] The fallibility of a positivist notion of history is evident in his assertion that *itihāsa* itself may be questioned; nothing lies outside the purview of critical inquiry.

By framing the *Mahābhārata* as a mimetic text, one that narrates the perception of the witness but that questions the nature of this perception, Tagore takes a crucial step away from Bankim's simplistic formulation of the *Mahābhārata*'s historicity. Here, Tagore brings in a contemporary example from Victorian England. Rumored to be written by Robert Browning himself, the *Prose Life of Strafford* (1837) was originally written for John Forster and published under his name in his *Lives of Eminent British Statesmen.* This factual history of Thomas Wentworth, the Earl of Strafford, was outdone by Browning's play *Strafford: An Historical Tragedy*: "It is said that the Life of Strafford that Forster Sahib published was composed by Browning himself. The same poet composed a play *Strafford,* and it has been proved that this was more *true.*"[53] Just as Browning's play (a mimetic artifact) was historically more *true* than the *Prose Life of Strafford,* the *Mahābhārata* affords a similar exercise in the mimetic artwork approximating historical truth more than mere fact itself.[54] Having taken the chronicles of the Kurukṣetra war that

51. Tagore, 79.

52. Tagore, 79.

53. Tagore, 80.

54. Browning referred to this factual history, later discovered to be written by Browning himself, in the preface to his play, saying, "The portraits are, I think, faithful; and I am exceedingly fortunate in being able, in proof of this, to refer to the subtle and eloquent exposition of the characters of Eliot and Strafford, in the *Lives of Eminent British Statesmen* now in the course of publication in Lardner's Cyclopædia, by a writer whom I am proud to call my friend . . ." One hopes that they were indeed good friends, since he wrote it himself. Tagore possibly did not know that the future would bring about such a blurring of boundaries between *tathya* and *satya.* See *Strafford: An Historical Tragedy* (London: Longman, Rees, Orme, Brown, Greene, and Longman, 1837), iv.

were circulating at the time, what the poet of the *Mahābhārata* did was to collect these incomplete narratives and create a whole picture through the powers of the imagination. This is in no way less "true" than the historian's history (*aitihāsiker itihāsa*).

The criticism, then, is of the understanding of historicity as inherently premised on fact. Facticity is not equivalent to truth in Tagore's eyes, nor is mimesis untrue. One must remember, he says, that the poet is simultaneously concerned with both fact and representation. The poet is never merely an ancient historian, but something greater:

> *Tathya* is what is called fact in English, and *satya* (truth) is much greater than that. From a mound of facts, truth must be recovered with the powers of reason and imagination . . . truth only shines through in poetry through the radiance of the poet . . . to prove the historicity of the character of Kṛṣṇa in the *Mahābhārata* is quite a painstaking and unnecessary exercise. The famous antiquarian (James Anthony) Froude says, "A great personality's natural and easy greatness is outside the reach of prose; it is only to be described by the words of a poet. Whatever be the reasons for this, such is the truth. Poetry has this life giving force which prose lacks, this is why the poet is the greatest historian." From Froude's remarks we understand that the list of deeds of a great man are mere facts, his truth is his greatness; it is more necessary for the poet's gifts to convey that truth to the reader than the historian's research.[55]

There is a certain paradox for the *Mahābhārata* that Tagore set out at this point. He extricates it from the burden of facticity to which Bankim has subjected it yet argues that the *Mahābhārata* has some inherent truth value. This truth value emerges not despite but *because* of the work's status as mimetic artifact. This is an extraordinarily powerful argument that imbues poetry with some historical responsibility. *Itihāsa* should not be taken as absolute utterance. Yet it contains the kernels of some almost transcendental truth, the reality of human character outside the factual world.

He goes on to say that there is something whole and unfragmented about the matter of establishing the greatness of human character. You can

55. Tagore, "Kṛṣṇacaritra," 80.

prove the greatness of a certain character by taking bits and parts of the *Mahābhārata* and explaining them to the reader with reason and argument, yet you cannot use argumentation to diffuse this greatness through the heart of the reader. Here Bankim fails, according to Tagore, really to understand the essence of the *Mahābhārata*. In order to prove the text's historicity, Bankim embarks on the struggle for the burden of proof; in the process, he neglects to convey the whole picture of Kṛṣṇa. Thus Bankim, wanting to deconstruct the Kṛṣṇa who is available to the Bengali devotees, forgets many aspects of Kṛṣṇa's personality.[56] What one learns from Bankim's exposition is that between the Kṛṣṇa of customary belief and the "actual" Kṛṣṇa there might be a huge difference, but this difference should not be the basis of a polemic. Tagore writes, "Of the real Kṛṣṇa whatever seemed uncharacteristic, that was pushed aside. The poet of the *Mahābhārata* made his own (fictional) Kṛṣṇa far more real . . . the poet had retrieved a true and eternal Kṛṣṇa from history."[57] Tagore believes that Bankim has departed from the poet of the *Mahābhārata*: "By doing away with all the negative aspects of Kṛṣṇa's character in the *Mahābhārata*, we have complete doubt that Bankim has retrieved the ideal Kṛṣṇa even constructed by the ancient poet."[58]

Bankim's vitriol against European scholars of the *Mahābhārata* pains Tagore deeply. His disapprobation toward the "Western fools" is, in Tagore's opinion, a fundamental act of disrespect. Bankim's diatribe, Tagore argues, is better suited to the pages of a periodical than it is to a classic work. Tagore points out that this deep hatred is directed toward Western civilization or culture itself.[59] In his view, it flies in the face of any idealism, spiritual or intellectual, that Bankim feels for the Kṛṣṇa whom he fashioned as the greatest of men: "*mānavaśreṣṭha* . . . the vessel of forgiveness and valour, who despite being able does not embrace arms with or without having good reason to . . ."[60] To construct a text that analyzes this great character, and then to embark upon such a bitter criticism and denunciation of dissenters who hold different opinions, is an act that defeats the very purpose of the ideals that Bankim attributes to Kṛṣṇa.

56. Tagore, 85.

57. Tagore, 81.

58. Tagore, 85.

59. Tagore, 86.

60. Tagore, 86.

This is an important moment in Tagore's critique of *Kṛṣṇacaritra.* It signals a step away from historicity into the domain of the literary, from the *Mahābhārata* as a positivist historical text into a more complex domain in which the *Mahābhārata* acts as literary text. In Tagore's reading of the *Mahābhārata,* the construction of a *mānavaśreṣṭha* is an active and conscious choice both in the ambivalent past and in a bitter political present. This choice is made by the *authorial voice,* whether that voice represents a Vyāsa shrouded in mystery, the unnamed poets who contributed to the ongoing project that was the *Mahābhārata,* or indeed Bankim himself. For Tagore, if a text is literary—if it upholds the highest ideals of humanity or what it means to be human—then Bankim's attack on European critics goes against the very spirit of humanistic inquiry.

Tagore discusses one particular instance in the *Kṛṣṇacaritra* in which Bankim takes a potshot at Christianity:

> On listening to the curses of Śiśupāla, the Ideal Man (Kṛṣṇa) who instantiated the virtues of mercy, the greatest *yogin* did not reply . . . not an eyebrow did he raise at the abuse and nor did he call out like the Europeans, "Śiśupāla! Mercy is a great tenet of faith to live by! I forgive you!" He forgave his enemies silently.[61]

Tagore is horrified by the implicit comparison that Bankim raises in this passage between Christianity and Hinduism and by Bankim's desire to proclaim Hinduism as a superior religion. Not only does Tagore consider this dig at Europeans unnecessary, but he argues that it contradicts Bankim's construction of Kṛṣṇa as symbol of compassion and forgiveness. Where, Tagore asks, does Bankim find evidence of Europeans' national propensity to sing paeans to their own capacities of compassion during the act of forgiving? In fact, Tagore highlights many instances from the *śāstra*s wherein *brāhmaṇa*s brag about their compassion.[62]

---

61. Tagore, 87. This is a reference to Kṛṣṇa slaying his cousin Śiśupāla. In the *Mahābhārata,* Kṛṣṇa had earlier made a promise to Śiśupāla's mother that he would forgive one hundred insults by Śiśupāla. Yet after Śiśupāla offends Kṛṣṇa one hundred times, the deity beheads Śiśupāla (*MBh* 2.37–42). Tagore no doubt refers to Kṛṣṇa's long forbearance during the hundred insults.

62. Tagore, 87–88.

Tagore also critiques Bankim's views on the import of European literature to the colony. Bankim laments that despite the Hindu *purāṇa*s and *itihāsa*s, Indians read novels written by *memsahib*s (white women) and form literary societies around discussing them. Tagore finds it difficult to grapple with this cultural chauvinism when it comes to a discussion of literature. For Tagore, humanistic enterprise is premised on a certain universalism: "A book like *Kṛṣṇacaritra* should not just be written for modern Hindus, it is our duty to write it for all time, for all races of people," he explains.[63] "When one reads the *Kṛṣṇacaritra* one is constantly reminded that the ideals that must be established in the methodology prescribed by literature (*sāhitya*), Bankim has not followed that protocol."[64]

Tagore clearly sees through Bankim's ideological project, which realizes that it is difficult to establish the *Mahābhārata* as history and yet strives to do so. Tagore makes a crucial point here: the first poet (*ādi kavi*) of the text only perhaps partially believed in the divinity of Kṛṣṇa. He had witnessed him *historically* as man and therefore described both greatness of character as well as flaws or errors of judgment. Bankim, however, believes in the divinity of Kṛṣṇa and desires to imprint this divinity on the consciousness of the colonial Hindu reader.[65] Within this paradox lies the key to the puzzle that is Bankim's project. Tagore clearly identifies (as Bankim himself explains) that the *Kṛṣṇacaritra* is an exercise in presenting the *dharmatattva*, the essence of dharma, as living and embodied. For Tagore, this was no historical Kṛṣṇa—"The Kṛṣṇa that he desired to find was a Kṛṣṇa born out the desires of his heart . . . under such mental conditions, it is not possible for human beings to recover the ideals of any other (i.e., original) poet . . . Bankim was intent on discovering not a divine Kṛṣṇa but a very human Kṛṣṇa."[66]

In this very desire itself, Bankim fails. This failure, according to Tagore, is an act of misreading, a failure to apprehend the poetic qualities of the *Mahābhārata,* its status as literature or a mimetic object. He writes:

> The man that Bankim was searching for had no incompleteness, all his mental states were complete and in harmony. Thus this

63. Tagore, 87.
64. Tagore, 85.
65. Tagore, 82.
66. Tagore, 82.

> was an embodied theory . . . The creator of the *Mahābhārata* did not create a single character who was a theoretical proposition in human form, or just an ethical principle. This was the greatest indication of his poetic gifts. He even made his great heroes do unworthy things that lesser poets would not have the courage to do. Poets of lesser caliber have the power to build, but do not have the power to create; whatever they construct is always according to some conventions, they cannot keep any exception or self-conflict (within this narrative). The incompleteness of a great thing announces its greatness.[67]

This argument, in which representation is seen as a human field of endeavor, foregrounds the power of the *Mahābhārata* as a literary text. Second, Tagore raises the idea that flaw is an essential condition of human greatness. If, for Bankim, the task of reading the *Mahābhārata* is to arrive at the perfect human being, then, for Tagore, the *Mahābhārata* is an infinitely plural text whose greatness is marked by imperfection. To be human is to be flawed.

In keeping with this theme, Tagore provides two examples from the *Mahābhārata* that illustrate its difference from nineteenth-century Bengali novels. He argues that Draupadī and Karṇa are unfavorably compared to the pure and long-suffering figures who adorned the pages of the Victorian-Bengali novel. Yet no nineteenth-century character could match the original Draupadī, who, with all her flaws, rises above any prescriptive ethical formulation of how women should act. Nor could self-sacrificing modern literary heroes oppose the victorious protagonists, the Pāṇḍavas, and still effortlessly achieve immortality, as Karṇa does.[68] Only the creator of the *Mahābhārata* had the moral insight into human behavior to extricate Draupadī and Karṇa out of their flaws into something magnificent. Flaw was both downfall *and* redemption. What Bankim looks for is unity, and therefore he bowdlerizes the *Mahābhārata* and reconstructs a Kṛṣṇa in order to fulfill his own political ends. By Tagore's account, Bankim fails, in the process, to understand the cause of great literature and the power of mimesis. For Tagore, it is representation of the whole human being, the good and the bad, that creates empathy and beauty. As an essential com-

67. Tagore, 83.

68. Tagore, 84.

ponent of the very plurality of human beings, flaw can be a transformative element in human history.

The Reader's *Prajñā*

We currently live in an astonishing world in which right-wing political leaders declare that the Sanskrit *Mahābhārata* describes every amenity in the modern world (such as the internet)—everything except common sense.[69] Bankim's and Tagore's debate raises questions that we may find relevant in a world rife with tension between history and myth. So far, scholarly interest in the *Kṛṣṇacaritra* has highlighted its status as a unique encounter of *itihāsa* with history. What Sudipta Kaviraj calls Bankim's "rationalist cognitive criteria of historical enterprise"[70] is established firmly: the *Kṛṣṇacaritra* interrogates practices of reading. Yet what the *Kṛṣṇacaritra* ultimately reads is God.

I am more interested in the way in which Bankim emphasizes the other Kṛṣṇa, the Kṛṣṇa as man. Not just any man, but the *ādarśa* to be emulated, the perfect exemplar who must also be a mirror for a devastated and unachieving colonial subject. To defend this civilizational ideal, what Tagore calls the *nītisutra* or "embodied theory"[71] constructs the very opposite of a universal idea of man for whom dharma is to be the best one can be. Tagore reminds us that, on the contrary, man cannot and should not be perfect. For him, the *Mahābhārata* is a great text, a universal text, precisely because it problematizes the ethical, the human condition itself. When petitions and legal orders circulate against Western scholars of South Asian textual traditions such as Sheldon Pollock and Wendy Doniger, we are reminded of Tagore's great consternation at Bankim's polemic against

69. Twenty-first-century Hindu Right leaders have made many interesting claims about the historicity of the *Rāmāyaṇa* and the *Mahābhārata*, including statements that airplanes, nuclear weapons, and the internet existed during the time of the epics. For one example, see Alexis C. Madrigal, "An Indian Politician Claimed Ancient Hindus Invented the Internet . . . then the Indian internet laughed at him," *The Atlantic,* April 24, 2018, https://www.theatlantic.com/technology/archive/2018/04/india-ancient-internet/558725/

70. Kaviraj, *Unhappy Consciousness,* 82.

71. Tagore, "Kṛṣṇacaritra," 83.

European Indologists in the *Kṛṣṇacaritra.*[72] For Tagore, the singularity of the *Mahābhārata* lies in its plurality of poets, characters, and readers.

Tagore is wary of the explicit political project at the heart of the *Kṛṣṇacaritra.* In his discussion of the *Kṛṣṇacaritra,* Kaviraj cites Tagore on the *Rāmāyaṇa*: "Truth is what you create/write; whatever happens is not always true, poet, treat the land of your imagination as more real than Ayodhyā, the land of Rāma's birth."[73] Here, Kaviraj calls Tagore's understanding a non-cognivist truth of the literary text. In his critique of *Kṛṣṇacaritra,* however, Tagore develops a "non-cognivist truth" that simultaneously focuses on the very powers of cognition, *svādhin buddhi.* The poet is mediator, but the reader has the capacity to separate the historical from the unhistorical, the natural from the supernatural, the god from the man. The poet captures the zeitgeist through poetic consciousness, but great poets are not limited by parochialism or ideological constraints. That is the burden of the reader. A great poet, Tagore tells us, writes within a structure but can threaten to bring down that very structure itself. Great poetry—human greatness—does not search for a paltry unity.[74]

We could argue that this constant duality forms the basis of the *Mahābhārata*—"He who does not know the two-faced nature of morality, when faced with a dilemma may fall into that, *so one ought to first understand the two-sidedness of prajñā, O Bhārata!*" To read in itself is a political act. Bankim imagined a perfect and malleable reader for his *Kṛṣṇacaritra,* a subject who, while critical, must still be molded. Tagore warns us of the dangers of losing our powers of reasoning. He makes a plea for a different kind of humanist practice, centering on critical reading. The reader has to cultivate her own wisdom and see the two-sidedness of such a project. I argue that perhaps this sense of a critical wisdom can be traced back to one of the most politically charged sections of the *Mahābhārata*: when Yudhiṣṭhira grapples with the ethics of blood-splattered sovereignty which is *rājadharma.* In the

72. See Wendy Doniger, "India: Censorship by the Batra Brigade," *The New York Review of Books,* May 8, 2014, https://www.nybooks.com/articles/2014/05/08/india-censorship-batra-brigade/; and Manan Ahmed, "Why Hindutva Groups Have for Long had Sheldon Pollock in Their Sights," *Scroll.in,* March 4, 2016, https://scroll.in/article/804517/why-hindutva-forces-have-for-long-had-sheldon-pollock-in-their-sights

73. Kaviraj, *Unhappy Consciousness,* 83, citing Tagore, "Kṛṣṇacaritra," 84.

74. Tagore, 84.

stories of imperfect kings trying to forge an empire over the dead bodies of their loved ones, Tagore reads the essential condition of humanity: wisdom is recognizing our own limitations and precarious mortality. To search for a unifying narrative that allows for the reconstruction of an imagined and perfect tradition is to disregard such a conception of the human; it is not an adequately humanistic conception of literature. If there was an original or originary Kṛṣṇa, a human Kṛṣṇa, he was not perfect. The perfect Kṛṣṇa as an organizing principle is a modern creation, just one more reading of a great work of *aitihāsik kāvya.* It is Bankim's Kṛṣṇa.

Chapter Fifteen

The Epic and the Novel

Buddhadev Bose's Modern Reading of the *Mahābhārata*

Sudipta Kaviraj

Poets have told it before, poets are telling it now, other poets shall tell this history on earth in the future.[1]

—the Sanskrit *Mahābhārata*

The subtlest and cleverest teaching of the *Gītā* is that humanity has a need for God to some extent, but much greater is God's need for humanity.[2]

—Buddhadev Bose

1. *ācakhyuḥ kavayaḥ kecit sampraty ācakṣate pare* |
ākhyāsyanti tathaivānye itihāsam imaṃ bhuvi || *MBh* 1.1.24 ||
All references to the *Mahābhārata* (*MBh*) in this chapter are to the critical edition unless noted otherwise: *The Mahābhārata for the First Time Critically Edited*, ed. V. S. Sukthankar et al. 19 vols. (Poona: Bhandarkar Oriental Research Institute, 1933–66). This is J. A. B. van Buitenen's translation: *The Mahābhārata*, vol. 1, *The Book of the Beginning*, trans. J. A. B. van Buitenen (Chicago: The University of Chicago Press, 1973), 21.

2. Buddhadev Bose, *Mahābhārater Kathā* (Kolkata: MC Sarkar and Sons, 1974), 150. All translations in this essay are my own unless specified otherwise.

On the Contemporaneity Problem

Hans-Georg Gadamer states in his magisterial reflection on historicity that we must admit, though it seems strange, that Aristotle's works are our contemporary.[3] This statement is certainly true, but its truth needs some explication. Are they contemporary in the brute fact sense that his volumes are available in print? Or is it that there is some sense in which—though his current readers find something meaningful in his works—the way his works were meaningful to his readers in ancient times must have been different? Is intellectual history just a record-keeping of this perpetually shifting meaningfulness of texts that survive the obliteration by time? What is a contemporary reading of an ancient text? Are texts of philosophy, political theory, and literature affected differently by their ancientness?

On Buddhadev Bose

As Bengali literature began to be transformed in modernity, it raised a continual questioning about its own relation to the epic tradition, especially the Sanskrit *Mahābhārata*. Starting with Kaliprasanna Singha (d. 1870) and Ishwar Chandra Vidyasagar (1820–1891), major Bengali intellectuals such as Bankimchandra Chattopadhyay (1838–1894) and Rabindranath Tagore (1861–1941) produced proliferating commentaries on the meaning of the epic.[4] It is interesting to explore what each significant critic found meaningful in the *Mahābhārata*. A distinctive contribution to this long line of reflection about the epic came from the poet and critic Buddhadev Bose (1908–1974). A reflexive modernist, he participated in deep and at times bitter debates about the nature of "the literary" after Tagore. To expand the horizons of the literary, some critics turned toward modernist trends in European literature; some toward the premodern sensibilities of the epics. Bose was distinct because he turned in a sense to both and did

3. Hans-Georg Gadamer, *Truth and Method*, trans. Joel Weinsheimer and Donald G. Marshall (London: Continuum, 1975), 119–24.

4. On Bankim's and Tagore's interpretations of the *Mahābhārata*, see Ahona Panda's chapter in this volume.

not view these simultaneous "turns" as discordant. Bose was an unrepentant modernist. He believed there was no ontological escape from modernity and was therefore entirely unapologetic about re-reading the epic through the principles of an unstated and incontrovertible aesthetics of modernity. Interestingly, in neither the earlier reinterpretations by Tagore nor in Bose is there a prior explanation of why a historical text should not be read historically: modernity as a horizon of reading and aesthetic perception was taken primarily for granted.

On Modern Aesthetic Sensibility

What could be the meaning of modernity in literature and poetry? This was a central question to all of these Bengali intellectuals. In their view, as with their great European predecessors, modernity meant predominantly a rupture in the very constitutive language of aesthetics with which the artist sought to master the shocking new world of the experience of modernity. Modernity created a new social world; it was the task of literature to aesthetically capture and reflect upon that world. That experience (they would have agreed with Walter Benjamin) was so utterly new and disorienting that it required an entirely new language for aesthetic capture and reflection.[5] Bose's reading of the Sanskrit *Mahābhārata* implies—because he does not enter into a direct explication of these questions—that ancient stories must also be seen now through the criteria of a new aesthetic sensibility.

Mikhail Bakhtin's 1941 essay "Epic and Novel: Toward a Methodology for the Study of the Novel" provides a *problematique* of exploration that allows us to understand the logic of Bose's attempted displacement of the aesthetic reception of the epic. Bakhtin suggests a powerful binary distinction between the narrative logics of the epic and the novel—the paradigmatic narrative of modernity. In his well-known argument, Bakhtin asserts that epic heroes are narratively static, un-evolving figures who possess character

---

5. See Walter Benjamin, "The Work of Art in the Age of Mechanical Reproduction," in *Illuminations*, ed. Hannah Arendt, trans. Harry Zohn (London: Fontana, 1968), 240; and Walter Benjamin, "Theses on the Philosophy of History," in *Illuminations*, ed. Hannah Arendt, trans. Harry Zohn (London: Fontana, 1968), 264.

traits like bravery or cleverness or wisdom to an extraordinary degree. Such attributes exist in epic protagonists from the narrative origin and do not change; they are only tested by increasingly difficult trials.[6] This argument can used to interpret the Sanskrit epics as well.

In the Sanskrit *Rāmāyaṇa*, Rāma is extraordinarily heroic from the start. The episodes of his diegetic life are a series of tests of his fortitude and bravery, but these tests all essentially confirm his fundamental, always-existing heroism. As he grows into manhood and narrational fullness, these tests become progressively more difficult, but all of them are testaments to the abilities and dispositions which he carries in himself from the start. In his retelling of the Rāma story, the *Raghuvaṃśa* ("The Lineage of Raghu"), the Sanskrit poet Kālidāsa echoes this idea directly.[7] Thus Rāma is the greatest archer of his time from his adolescence; as a boy, he can kill the demoness Tāṭakā and destroy an army of demons in order to protect the sacrifices of the sage Viśvāmitra. Equally, in the Sanskrit *Mahābhārata,* Bhīma can subdue opponents from his childhood. Even when Bhīma is poisoned by his jealous cousins in the *Ādiparvan* ("The Book of Beginnings"), his superhuman strength allows him to survive.[8] In epic narratives, a process heightens the narrative pitch to a crescendo, as occurs in music, but there are no real surprises. We are not surprised when Bhīma kills Kīcaka and kneads his body into a ball of mangled flesh in the *Virāṭaparvan* ("The Book of Virāṭa's Court").[9] In the case of the slaying of Duḥśāsana in the *Karṇaparvan* ("The Book of Karṇa"), we are meant to be shocked by Bhīma drinking his enemy's blood and the inhuman eloquence of his anger, yet the surprise is a partly moral surprise at his crossing all conceivable limits

---

6. M. M. Bakhtin, "Epic and Novel: Toward a Methodology for the Study of the Novel," in *The Dialogic Imagination: Four Essays* by M. M. Bakhtin, ed. Michael Holquist, trans. Caryl Emerson and Michael Holquist (Austin: University of Texas Press, 1981), 34.

7. *kākapakṣadharam etya yācitas tejasāṃ hi na vayaḥ samīkṣyate* || *Raghuvaṃśa* 11.1 || "[The sage] asked for him though he had the curls of young boys; [because] among the great heroes age is no consideration." Kālidāsa, *The Raghuvamśa of Kālidāsa with the Commentary (the Sanjīvanī) of Mallinātha*, ed. M. R. Kale (Bombay: Gopal Narayen, 1922).

8. *MBh* 1.119.

9. *MBh* 4.21.

of humanity.[10] It is not a real narrative surprise, because it follows the logic of his character. Epic heroes represent types, not individuals. Qualities that they represent are fully aesthetically realized; there are no half-measures.

The hero of the modern novel for Bakhtin is marked precisely by the development of his character and profound indeterminacy.[11] A very talented young artist might become a famous painter or a tragic failure added to the human detritus of nineteenth-century Paris. The novel plays and builds on ordinariness and deep uncertainties in the trajectories of characters who are entirely deprived of the extraordinary, single-minded, typical perfection of the epic hero. In the novel, a hero's uncertain character makes readers wonder about what he will do at every subsequent turn. In a strange inversion, it is an ordinary life that is a life of real wonders. It wrings emotions from us because we suffer every time the hero fails a test that we expect him to pass; we exult when he surprises us with decisions of fortitude and nobility. Unlike the case of the epic hero, we cannot take anything for granted: we follow an ordinary life with suspense precisely because it is a life of surprises.

In addition, Bakhtin's famous analysis of Dostoevsky introduces the dimension of moral polyphony into our understanding of modern novels.[12] As every Dostoevsky character can usually advance a strong moral defense of the way they have undertaken their always-questionable acts, the moral complexity of the perspectivalist narrative draws the reader into its decisions' affective responses of disappointment, outrage, and indeterminacy of judgment. Famously, in Bakhtin's study of the aesthetics of novels, the reader is slowly constituted into a moral subject through the labor of navigating the imagined ethical predicaments of ordinary individuals who populate these plots.[13] Bakhtin's "Epic and Novel" contrast can serve as a way of entering the deep but surprising re-workings that Bose brings to a reading of the Sanskrit *Mahābhārata*. Bose implicitly believes that a modern reading must pass the epic story through the narrativistic aesthetic created by the modern novel. His reading unsettles traditional conventions because he clearly seeks a novelistic hero in the epic diegetic universe.

---

10. *MBh* 8.61.

11. Mikhail Bakhtin, *Problems of Dostoyevsky's Poetics*, ed. and trans. Caryl Emerson (Minneapolis: University of Minnesota Press, 1984), 38.

12. Bakhtin, 38.

13. Bakhtin, 10.

Bose's Reading of the Sanskrit *Mahābhārata*

Bose's implicit philosophical intuition cannot be faulted: of course, no modern reading of an epic can be innocent of aesthetic history. Every reading goes to the text with the burden of knowledge of all that has happened to literature. Such modernist readings can proceed in many directions. Bose's reading goes immediately to the heart of the problem. To continue to exist as a literary text, as opposed to a religious one—which in a sense it had ceased to do—the Sanskrit *Mahābhārata* must be valuable to a modern sensibility.

In modern times, the epic can exist in three forms. The first is as a religious text for those who want to draw its *śāstra*-like (treatise-like) lessons to supplement other *śāstric* knowledge—regarding the *Mahābhārata* as a fifth Veda. Presumably, such readers would focus on the *prabhusammita* (injunction) sections of the text where it "commands" us in an authoritative voice, such as Bhīṣma's discourses in the *Śantiparvan* ("The Book of Peace") and the *Anuśāsanaparvan* ("The Book of Instruction") or Kṛṣṇa's in the *Bhagavadgītā*. In modern times, some may read the *Mahābhārata* in its second mode, as an ancient epic—a text of *its* times—and try to understand the text temporally and historically in its own terms, which are recognized as quite different from literary values of the modern world. When they read the *Gītā* historically, these readers would seek to understand how a conception of Īśvara (God) is slowly separating itself from the common series of Vedic deities and assuming the figure of Kṛṣṇa in the *viśvarūpa-darśana* (vision of the universal form) section of the *Gītā*. Bose is interested in neither of these modes, but in a third kind of reading of the *Mahābhārata*, employing quite distinct internal aesthetic criteria. The reader of the third kind, like Bose, is a reader whose aesthetic sensibility is entirely and unapologetically modern, who is immersed (in the sense that he takes it for granted) in the peculiar and specific aesthetics of the novel, and who then returns to the *Mahābhārata* for literary enjoyment. What could such a reader find in the Sanskrit epic? And what does this new sensibility do to the aesthetic structure of the *Mahābhārata*?

Yudhiṣṭhira as the Central Figure

Sujit Mukherjee, the perceptive translator of Bose's *Mahābhārater Kathā* ("About the *Mahābhārata*," 1974) gave it the English title *The Book of Yud-*

histhir (1986), thus capturing the central theme of Bose's reinterpretation.[14] In a modern world, too, the *Mahābhārata* remains a gigantic, endlessly fascinating story of being human—but read now in a new, entirely modernist key. The *Mahābhārata*'s immensity and the fertility of the Indian philosophic tradition allows us to find philosophical arguments that place Yudhiṣṭhira as the central character of the epic.[15] To believe that Bose simply restates the case of the Dharmarāja (the king of dharma, an epithet for Yudhiṣṭhira), however, is a profound mistake. His arguments are entirely modern and utterly separate from such conventional interpretative judgments. Both the conventional reading and Bose's reading place Yudhiṣṭhira in the role of the hero—but for totally divergent reasons.

It will be instructive to state the premodern arguments for Yudhiṣṭhira's centrality and place Bose's arguments beside them; this juxtaposition will throw into sharp relief the differences between the two aesthetics. The first difference between the aesthetic apparatuses of early and modern times is the heavy focus in premodern aesthetics of the literal sense in *kāvya* (poetry). *Kāvya* was both poetry and verse because the literary in premodern times existed in a predominantly verse-poetic form. If we take this restrictive condition seriously, some of the appearance of limitedness in the early texts of the *alaṅkāra* (literally "ornament" or "decoration," a term for poetic figures) literary tradition becomes easily intelligible. Versification itself is ornamentation in a rather direct sense; and the *alam* in the *alaṅkāra* can refer (on this side of aesthetics) to a supplement in excess of the function of the bare informational communication. The literary utterance, if seen as *vakrokti* ("crooked speech"), is that whose *vakratā* (crookedness) can mean both the supplemental ornamentation of the words and also a semantic indirectness or bending. To refer to verbal supplementation as a kind of bending is inapt, so even the minimal, but highly suggestive, idea of what counts as *vakra* in literary utterance must be understood as something that lives within the realm of semantics. Clearly, a text like the *Mahābhārata*—

---

14. Buddhadev Bose, *The Book of Yudhisthir: A Study of the Mahabharat of Vyas*, trans. Sujit Mukherjee (Hyderabad: Sangam Books, 1986).

15. Since the Mahābhārata is so much part of the popular world of literature, it is important to note that at least in the Bengali popular reading of the epic, the question of the singular hero remains unsettled: Arjuna can answer the criteria in one sense, Kṛṣṇa in another, but the general understanding is that because of his personification of dharma, Yudhiṣṭhira is the hero of the narrative.

simply on account of its size, narrative complexity, and diegetic stratification—makes such simpler *alaṅkāra* aesthetic interpretation inadequate. Later interpretation theory, even after it introduced the immensely powerful and immensely problematic category of *rasa*, is not immediately able to set a clear path through the challenges that this text places before its analysts.[16] At first, the move of the Kashmiri *dhvanikāra* (the ninth-century literary theorist Ānandavardhana, who is termed the "*dhvani*-maker" because of his theory's focus on the concept of *dhvani*, or "implicature") to speculate that there must be a single dominant *rasa* in a text—however large, complex, or difficult that text may be—appears inadequate given the vastness of the text of the Sanskrit *Mahābhārata*, its repeated shifts of internal aesthetic register, and its diegetic complexity. There can be legitimate skepticism regarding the logical status of this "dominance' " of a single *rasa*: is it the *rasa* that runs through a dominant section of the narrative? Or is it the *rasa* that comes at the "end," cancelling and superseding the *rasa* registers that had been established earlier through a kind of teleological diegetic order—to "dominate" the story in this very different sense?[17]

Gary Tubb has analyzed at some length the interpretive position that Yudhiṣṭhira, not Arjuna, is the main protagonist of the Sanskrit epic.[18] The premodern argument for Yudhiṣṭhira is solidly based on aesthetic-theological grounds of traditional critical thought about epic narratives. The *Mahābhārata* is a vast and complex presentation of narrative and ethical subjects. Undoubtedly, the central moral concern of the narrative is

---

16. Two remarkable works have made it easier to understand this critical transition in Indian aesthetic theory: David Shulman, *More than Real: A History of the Imagination in South India* (Cambridge, MA: Harvard University Press, 2012); and Sheldon Pollock, ed. *A Rasa Reader: Classical Indian Aesthetics* (New York: Columbia University Press, 2016).

17. For an argument on this question, see Sudipta Kaviraj, "The Second *Mahābhārata*," in *South Asian Texts in History: Critical Engagements with Sheldon Pollock*, eds. Whitney Cox, Yigal Bronner, and Lawrence McCrea (Ann Arbor: Association for Asian Studies, 2011), 103–24.

18. He notes that "within the Sanskrit tradition, the awareness of the central role of Yudhiṣṭhira is so strong that even when another of the Pāṇḍavas has been made the focus of a later work of poetry, commentators are likely to persist in viewing Yudhiṣṭhira as the real protagonist in those poems." Gary A. Tubb, "*Śāntarasa* in the *Mahābhārata*," in *Essays on the Mahābhārata*, ed. Arvind Sharma (Leiden: E. J. Brill, 1991), 181.

the pursuit of dharma: defense of a complex, many-sided moral and social order which requires different types of individuals to play distinct kinds of roles. At the center of this narrative presentation, of course, is the idea that the social order depends crucially on two major social groups, *brāhmaṇas* (priests) and *kṣatriyas* (warriors), playing their proper dharmic roles. As the Hindu social order restricts *brāhmaṇas* mainly to contemplative and ritual functions, that responsibility to act to uphold the order of the world fell predominantly to the *kṣatriyas*. Among the *kṣatriyas*, too, there are internal role differentiations. To uphold dharma ideally, society required rulers who had a clear understanding of dharmic rules and the capacity for bold military action.

Startlingly, the *Mahābhārata* narratively splits these two desirable qualities of the ideal ruler and distributes them between the two main protagonists, Arjuna and Yudhiṣṭhira. Clearly, Arjuna is the great iconic hero of the military kind with his unequaled archery, unerring sense of fairness, and unflinching steadfastness in all military conflicts. In the division between Bhīma and Arjuna, who demonstrate two entirely different ideals of warrior-like qualities, the *Mahābhārata* characteristically uses the device of splitting (what is seen as) a single quality of the heroic warrior. This split is clearly shown through Arjuna being the repository of the more sophisticated and mental qualities of the great warrior. Bhīma, by comparison, is merely an intimidating wrestler. Bankim, long before Bose, had denounced Bhīma as a *raktapa rākṣasa* (blood-drinking monster).[19]

By splitting the heroic virtues between Arjuna and Bhīma, the *Mahābhārata* opens up the possibility of a characterological interpretation that is centered on Yudhiṣṭhira. It is in him that the dharma-discerning side of rulership is concentrated, though sometimes he carries it to excess, and Kuntī and Draupadī chide him for being too obsessed with hairsplitting cogitation on the subtle ways of dharma, which reduces him to an incapacity to act.[20] According to the premodern interpretive tradition, Yudhiṣṭhira can

19. Bankimchandra Chattopadhyay, *Kṛṣṇacaritra in Baṅkima Racanābalī*, ed. Jogeshchandra Bagal (Kolkata: Sahitya Samsad, 1964), 569–70. It is important to note, however, that some poets have retold the Mahābhārata with Bhīma as the central hero. For one example, see Heidi Pauwels' chapter in this volume.

20. While this episode is not in the critical edition of epic, it is in the vulgate recension (5.84–94). See *Mahabharata, Book Five: Preparations for War*, vol. 2, trans. Kathleen Garbutt, Clay Sanskrit Library (New York: New York University Press, JJC Foundation, 2008).

be viewed as the central heroic figure of the *Mahābhārata* because among the militaristic crowd of *kṣatriyas* he is the only one (with the exception of Bhīṣma) who is deeply concerned with the rules and ways of dharma. Even in the case of Bhīṣma, knowledge of dharma is passive rather than active. In most testing situations, except for one crucial one, Bhīṣma is shown as a repository of dharmic knowledge, but he is not shown as a "seeker" like Yudhiṣṭhira. Bhīṣma always knows what is true to dharma; Yudhiṣṭhira has always to search for it, but eventually, unfailingly, finds it. That is why he is Dharmarāja. This is the premodern dharmic reading which puts Yudhiṣṭhira at the center of the narrative structure. Bose's reading, however, is significantly different.

Yudhiṣṭhira as a Hero in Search of the Self

Bose recurrently refers to two modern Bengali "translations" of the Sanskrit *Mahābhārata*: the 1886 massive literal translation by Kaliprasanna Singha and the much more recent 1949 *saranubāda* (abridged translation) by Rajsekhar Basu (1880–1960). Bose notes the exceptional quality of Basu's "translation" and acknowledges that Basu, in his introduction to the work, also viewed Yudhiṣṭhira as a central figure of the *Mahābhārata*. It is useful to briefly analyze the logic of Basu's analysis. Basu also implicitly faces the basic interpretive question: how can modern readers find value in a story like the *Mahābhārata* coming from the deep past? His translation, Basu claims, follows the purpose of "making the whole *Mahābhārata* entertainingly readable *like a modern novel* while retaining the main course and features of the original narration."[21] The stories of the *Mahābhārata* are a strange mixture of the natural and supernatural; while reading "it seems we have come to a world of dreams."[22] But its enchantment, he says, has not been destroyed by the excessive load of supernatural phenomena.[23] If fictional characters are stretched too far, that disturbs literary enjoyment, because there are some limits to the ordinary reader's credulity. Basu believes that the aesthetic of the *Mahābhārata* goes in the direction of

21. Rajsekhar Basu, *Mahābhārata Saranubāda* (Kolkata: MC Sarkar and Sons, 1949), 2 (emphasis mine).

22. Basu, 3.

23. Basu, 4.

oversimplification: most of the main characters are sculpted and polished creatures. They do not have scratches or flaws. But Basu is clear about the main difficulty in a modern reader's enjoyment of the narrative: the reason behind narrative inconsistencies of the *Mahābhārata* is the addition of many legends. Characterological inconsistencies arise through the intervention of many composing hands and the difference between the artistic ideals of ancient and modern life.[24] Fortunately, Basu writes, such inconsistencies of character are not too numerous. In most cases, the men and women of the *Mahābhārata* are portrayed quite "naturally," that is, realistically; their conduct is not unintelligible to us.[25] A section of Basu's introduction presents short sketches of the main characters, rather than an overall analysis of their relative placements (as Bose does in his subsequent essay). Basu mentions all the major protagonists concisely, but I shall focus my discussion on Yudhiṣṭhira.

Basu points out that

> Yudhiṣṭhira is not as celebrated as Arjuna, but he is the hero and the central figure of the *Mahābhārata* . . . ordinarily, he does not engage in any action without a subtle analysis of the rights and wrongs of the case . . . Yudhiṣṭhira has an excessively developed sense of self; and as a consequence he constantly feels remorse by considering himself responsible for wrong-doing.[26]

Basu also believes that his "greatness is most clearly expressed in the last act. When he reached heaven, Indra uses a ruse to make a visit to hell. Yudhiṣṭhira thought his brothers and Draupadī were suffering there. Then, ignoring the temptation of paradise and requests from the Gods, he declared, 'I shall not return, I shall stay here.' "[27] By contrast, "Arjuna is endowed with all virtues (*sarvaguṇānvita*) and the foremost among the warriors of the *Mahābhārata* . . . He carries all the marks of the epic hero, because of this reason and excessive praise, he has become slightly unnatural."[28] Basu

24. Basu, 4.
25. Basu, 4.
26. Basu, 5.
27. Basu, 7.
28. Basu, 8.

thinks that Kṛṣṇa is the most mysterious figure in the *Mahābhārata* and that because of interpolations by many different authors, his character displays the largest number of inconsistencies.[29] Basu clearly designates Yudhiṣṭhira as the central pillar of the narrative edifice, but without specific reasons. From circumstantial evidence it seems that he also judges characters by their human credibility, using a kind of universalistic realistic standard of ordinary human behavior. Yudhiṣṭhira, for Basu, is a hero who conforms to the narrative demand for perfection: his blemishes make his character more credible and human. But, despite his tendency to agonize interminably about actual or intended action, his subtlety of reflection helps him reach ethical truths. He is a hero because he embodies this virtue.

The originality of Buddhadev Bose's new reading can come into clear relief against this context because, despite superficial similarities, Bose's judgment is very different. Bose's preface states that some of the specific questions in his reading emerged while teaching at the University of Indiana about eleven years before the publication of his study. One of his teaching subjects was a comparative discussion of the Greek and Sanskrit epics, with the *Iliad*, the *Odyssey*, and the *Aeneid* on one side and the *Mahābhārata* and the *Rāmāyaṇa* on the other. He found the task forbidding: "whenever I thought of the prose, I seemed to step back in fear; I thought always that I have not been able to prepare myself sufficiently; I did not have the resources to cross the enormous gap between the conception and the realization."[30] He also confessed that

> my style of writing is literary, or, because the term *literary* carries such a wide connotation, let us say, heavily focused on poetry and mythology which is close to the poetic. That is, the things that are incredible to the modern intelligence (but which even the most intelligent believed in in ancient times), I have not rejected them as "unrealistic," rather I have looked for its essence inside those mysteries *beyond the real*.[31]

Bose adds that he has tried "to show that the *Mahābhārata* is not some distant, grey static narrative: it flows through ordinary human life." Finally,

29. Basu, 10.

30. Bose, *Mahābhārater Kathā*, 10.

31. Bose, 7 (emphasis mine).

he signs off by saying that he received many questions about anthropology, sociology, and history from his readers, but those are beyond the terms he set for himself: "I am not a scholar [of the text], but a mere lover."[32]

Bose's analysis chooses a remarkable point of departure. In the *Vanaparvan* ("The Book of the Forest," which is also known as the *Āraṇyakaparvan*) on the last day of their exile in the forest, the five Pāṇḍavas go out in search of an elusive deer (which has a faint shadow of Rāma pursuing the enchanted deer in the *Araṇyakāṇḍa* ("The Book of the Forest") of the Sanskrit *Rāmāyaṇa*).[33] During this hunt, four of the brothers lose the deer, and come to a pond to drink water. A lone stork stands there and warns them not to drink water without answering the questions that he wants to ask them. Four of the Pāṇḍavas die when they refuse to answer the questions of this *yakṣa* (nature spirit) in the guise of the stork. Yudhiṣṭhira alone treats the stork with respect and, according to Bose's careful count, answers thirty-four distinct questions in order to return the lives of his impetuous and arrogant brothers.[34] The point at which Bose chooses to enter this vast narrative forest is selected with deliberation. This is one of the rare moments when the *kṣatriya* prowess of Yudhiṣṭhira's brothers, including the invincible Arjuna, is eclipsed by a crisis of a very different kind, and it is the ethical-philosophical capacity of Yudhiṣṭhira that saves them from destruction. This shift suggests that there are deeper destructions that cannot be fought only with the skill at arms. At the core of the epic, there is a layer of deep questions of this kind. The *Mahābhārata* is admittedly vast and inconsistent and quite evidently the creation of many authors of utterly unequal literary genius. Bose asserts that in the interest of their cultural self-defense, ancient *brāhmaṇa*s turned this text into an indiscriminate receptacle of everything: that is why to the modern mind "it is so problematic and misleading."[35]

To read the Sanskrit *Mahābhārata* does not mean that its reader must know every single episode. But this is not a faulty form of knowing. The *Mahābhārata* is conceived of as an answer to the world, and just as the world exceeds perfect knowledge, so does the epic. If we think closely, this is the way we know our world: we do not know every single grain of dust.

32. Bose, 11.

33. *MBh* 3.295–98.

34. Bose, *Mahābhārater Kathā*, 31–33.

35. Bose, 23.

Bose shows us that if we look at the vast expanse of the epic with a kinder aesthetic eye, we might be struck by the thought that the *Mahābhārata* might not be as incoherent or inconsistent as we think and we will discover a certain unity in the entire *Mahābhārata* story.[36] We will be frustrated if we expect the *Mahābhārata* to fit the criteria of a linear modern narrative. Yet if we alter our expectations, we will find a completeness that is circle-like. According to Bose, in order to impart this integrity or unity to the story, Vyāsa chose a single character who could be at the center of its refractions in various directions:

> I sense the presence of a single main protagonist in the *Mahābhārata*. And that leading figure or central character is not the celebrated winner of many battles or the hero of many women, Arjuna, or the figure with talent in all fields, superhuman [Kṛṣṇa] Vāsudeva; he is a calm, gentle, diffident, uncertain human being: he is Yudhiṣṭhira.[37]

But this is not an easy claim to establish. Yudhiṣṭhira's attraction is so faint that very few poets from Kālidāsa to Tagore have composed a poem or play centered around him.[38] We can clearly notice that he is not endowed with any of the qualities of an ancient epic hero and his "progress" through the narrative is very slow. He is the most negligible warrior among the Kuru clan and he is also an unfit descendant of great lovers such as Śakuntalā's husband, Duḥṣanta, and Bhīṣma's father, Śantanu. What marks him as different from all his brothers, for Bose, is his lack of confidence in his own powers. He is excessively dependent on advice. He is not the initiator of any serious action, except a titular one. He is only a bearer of consequences. He is never the actor, but a cipher.

Before the dice match in the *Sabhāparvan* ("The Book of the Assembly Hall"), we regard Yudhiṣṭhira as a faint but respectable character. Yet suddenly, at a particularly strange moment, we are stunned when we witness him being transformed into an insane obsessive gambler. Bose explains

36. Bose, 32.

37. Bose, 33.

38. Although, as Lawrence McCrea points out elsewhere in this volume, Yudhiṣṭhira plays a significant role in Māgha's seventh-century poem *Śiśupālavadha*.

that when we find him leaving for the forest untroubled by the condemnation of all, we do not know what to say of him—"insensitive or patient, unconscious or unattached, unnatural or lifeless. A question spurts in our mind: has he been turned to stone by this disaster, or has the disaster not touched him?"[39] As his character unfolds with his unperturbable peace, we realize that "Yudhiṣṭhira's love of dice is not exactly what European critics call a 'tragic flaw.' We remark that the defeat in the game of dice does not cause his fall; or the fall is merely worldly, not in his basic sense of the self. Instead of being devastated, his moral self becomes more developed and completed through the forest exile and the subsequent incidents of the war.[40] In other words, this not a Bakhtinian test that he passes unchanged, but an experience that transforms him. The aesthetic Bose is using is novelistic, not epic. Bose goes on to explain:

> It would not be an exaggeration to say that in some corner of his mind, in some secret unconscious, he had desired precisely this: this liberation—from the paradise constructed by Maya [the architect of the demons who constructed the palace of the Pāṇḍavas in Indraprastha], from the pomp and ceremony which bind people like chains, from a suffocating excess of wealth, and above all from political intrigues of the kind that led to the destruction of Jarāsandha and Śiśupāla. He desired a spell of time before the inevitable war—to live, to live like a human being/to live humanly.[41]

Thus, the real diegetic introduction of Yudhiṣṭhira begins with the *Vanaparvan*: "The *Vanaparvan* does not have much narrative intent; even if it is there, that is internal, unmechanical, *psychological*."[42] Bose follows this with an interesting comparison between the forest exiles of Rāma and Yudhiṣṭhira. Unlike Rāma, Yudhiṣṭhira does not take any interest in the enchanting beauty of the forest. He does not notice any remarkable creature or vegetation. He never gives any evidence of a love of nature; never

39. Bose, 38.

40. Bose, 38.

41. Bose, 42.

42. Bose, 186–94.

observes if the time is the rainy season or the spring: the world for him seems to be "season-less, bereft of color or fragrance."[43] What does he do in this long exile of twelve years? He listens. Bose informs us that

> To listen—that is his work, his vocation; the narrative happening in the *Vanaparvan* is this long endless listening. Slowly, there is a work that is going on in him: he slowly overcomes the grief over the dice game; but what is happening is that there is a new experience that is spreading through his self, almost like happiness. Slowly, with a secret and unexpressed joy, he is awaking within himself, he is becoming, coming to be himself.[44]

Bose does something strange through his reading. If we continue to use Bakhtin's analytic tools, Bose does not transform all characters of this epic tale into modern equivalents. He does nothing to alter the nature of the other figures who remain in their ancient artistic pose; he selects Yudhiṣṭhira and converts him into a reflexive modern individual—whose fragility is precisely his mark of greatness. Everyone around him remains the same, stuck in the characters they had been given at their birth: the Bakhtinian mark of an epic hero.[45] Yudhiṣṭhira alone turns the exile in the forest into a long learning process from the greatest teachers of his time. These lessons are not in military strategy or techniques or in *śāstraic* knowledge, but in reflexivity, self-development, in a search for the self and for an awareness of the world. Even the path of dharma is not easily or instantly accessible to him: his *progress* is always slow and gradual, through constant detours. Thus, for Yudhiṣṭhira, the great saying "the [correct] path is that which has been traversed by great people" is a dead-end in both its constructions—following great individuals or following the great majority of people.[46] Instead, he has to make his own way.

Bose's final characterization of Yudhiṣṭhira presents this argument with clarity.[47] Yudhiṣṭhira has accepted the limitations of mortality; there is no

43. Bose, 106.

44. Bose, 42–43.

45. Bakhtin, "Epic and Novel," 34.

46. *mahājano yena gataḥ sa panthāḥ*. This is found in Appendix I (32.65, B. 313.117) of the third volume of the critical edition of the Sanskrit *Mahābhārata*.

47. Bose, 186–94.

extremity in his character. He is the soul of dharma but is not blinded by it. He stands on that narrow and difficult ground where, even after all *śāstra*s have been mastered, there is still scope for doubts, and where, even after getting a thousand pieces of advice, certainty eludes you. In all these cross pressures, he has only one single resource, which is beyond all knowledge and all rules: a sleepless sense of pain that awakes in his heart. We generally call this conscience. Yudhiṣṭhira is that strange and incomparable creation of the Indian poetic genius. He is an actor but not a heroic one. He follows dharma but is not a dharmic hero. He is endlessly curious for knowledge, but not an instructor to anyone. Though naturally spiritual, he never engages in asceticism. We cannot, despite all our efforts, call him a *mahāpuruṣa* (great soul) or an epic hero. Bose points out that "Yudhiṣṭhira is a man, a mere human being, almost an ordinary householder on whose face all the responsibilities and the lines of pain of a human life are etched; and that is why he is unforgettable."[48] He adds that "Unlike Arjuna and Karṇa, he never gets a boon from any god; all his gifts and curses were latent within himself. How he made them flower and cohere and became a full human being—the *Mahābhārata* is an account of that history."[49]

Bose's reading of the *Mahābhārata* should not be confused with classical Sanskrit interpretations that put Yudhiṣṭhira at the center of the narrative; the philosophical justifications of these two readings are entirely different, and indeed almost opposed. The classical readings treat him as the narrative hero because despite his imperfections, Yudhiṣṭhira realizes the ideals of dharma to the extent humanly possible.[50] He is in that sense a Bakhtinian epic hero—an ideal man of some kind. Bose's reading is an inversion of this view. Intriguingly, his reading sees the *Mahābhārata* carrying forward a strange and fascinating contradiction. Surrounded by other characters, all of whom are epic according to Bakhtin's definition of the term, there is a single figure who defies that definition, who is entirely bereft of that ideal quality. He is the only character who is exactly like the central figures of a modern novel—whose character is not decided from the start, whose life is a mystery because of its deep undecidedness.[51] On Bose's distinctive reading, inside that vast expanse of an epic narrative, there is a carefully

48. Bose, 106.

49. Bose, 192. Emphases mine.

50. See Tubb, "*Śāntarasa* in the *Mahābhārata*," 181.

51. Bakhtin, "Epic and Novel," 37.

inserted *bildungsroman* tracing the journey through a real human life of a single character—of a fallible human being who defies the epic perfection of all the others. The *Mahābhārata* invites a modern reading because only a modern aesthetic intelligence can clearly discern this central story which stops its narrative endlessness from dissolving into chaos.

Modernity threatens to relegate all premodern thought (including its aesthetic) into an irredeemable obsolescence, condemning its narratives in particular for their uses of the supernatural, epic excess, and improbability. Nothing illustrates this tendency more clearly than the fate of the improbable. What was serenely accepted as evidence of the presence of a God who might appear ordinarily unavailable but who intervenes in serious crises with his assuring presence appears to modern readers as an instance of gullibility. The improbable and fantastic which abounded in literary works in premodern culture gradually shrink into designated corners of the modern literary field. It is only riding on the back of science that the fantastic can reappear.

After the rise of a modern literary sensibility from the time of Bankim, this kind of relentless effect of an impoverishing enlightenment is felt in Bengali literature. It takes a lamp to every dark corner of the soul and the world and banishes ghosts and deities and the divine in a process of harsh disenchantment. The *Mahābhārata* becomes the field of many of these battles of secularization. Already in the retelling of ancient tales by Ishwar Chandra Vidyasagar there is a clear avoidance of episodes of supernatural enchantment. Bankim, again, is a crucial figure. He undertakes most aggressively a task of rational selection—filtering out the supernatural, transforming all improbability into a register of the symbolic, in a relentless historical reduction—which was often so radical that it irked even modern writers like the young Tagore. But what happens in its aftermath is quite interesting. Despite the undeniable power of such reduction, Bose and Basu repeatedly recognize the force of Bankim's excisions. The Sanskrit *Mahābhārata*'s arrogant prophecy (cited at the outset of this chapter) retains its truth: this epic will be narrated by others in the future.

Bengali literary culture does not forget the epics, the *Mahābhārata* in particular. In an attempt to defy the curse of time (*kāla*)—its ability to degrade everything—Buddhadev Bose discovered a modern, or timeless, *bildungsroman* hidden in plain sight within the vast maze of the Sanskrit *Mahābhārata*. Instead of being rendered degraded and unintelligible, Bengal's modern literary culture learns how to find meaning in the *Mahābhārata* without repudiating its secularity. True to the improbable prophecy of its initial storyteller, the *Mahābhārata* continues to be narrated in an interminable, unconcluded future.

Chapter Sixteen

Draupadī, Yājñasenī, Pāñcālī, Kṛṣṇā

Representations of an Epic Heroine in Three Novels

Pamela Lothspeich

It is no secret that Indian writers in the modern era often find in the Mahābhārata a munificent muse. Some modern works retell the epic story in a condensed format, others reconstruct particular episodes, and still others allude to it in more layered ways. But when we consider the place of epic heroines in literary adaptations of the Mahābhārata and the Rāmāyaṇa over the last 150 years—and there are a considerable number of such works—we immediately notice some striking patterns. First, women in these works are often tasked with serving as signs of "Indian womanhood," "tradition" or "Hindu culture," and, as such, are brought to bear in socio-political discourses in the public sphere. What complicates this trend is the fact that public consensus about what these terms (and even the Mahābhārata itself) constitute has shifted over time and, in many ways, become more heterogeneous. Second, authors of modern literary works that foreground epic heroines are more likely to be women than men and to speak to women's lived experiences. While this trend may align with other developments in transnational feminisms, it does not, of course, signal a "universal" or homogenous sisterhood. Many feminist scholars have demonstrated as much.[1] Still, auto-universalizing has been a particularly entrenched mode of thinking among mainstream white, cisgender, middle-class Euro-American feminists, who presume that their ideas and ways of being in the world are or should be normative globally. As Nivedita Menon writes more generally with respect to the history of ideas and the "imperialism of categories,"

> The assumption is that the concepts emerging from Western (Euro-American) social philosophy necessarily contain within them the possibility of universalisation—the reverse is never assumed. Can, for instance, Julius Nyerere's concept of Ujamaa or the trope of Draupadi as the ambiguous figure of assertive femininity ever be considered relevant to analyse Euro-American experience? But Antigone can be made to speak about women and war everywhere.[2]

In this essay I discuss representations of Draupadī in three novels—all of them written by Indian women—that seem to embody the spirit of Menon's critique. Not only do they disrupt and rewrite inequitable gender and social scripts in the Sanskrit text (and contemporary society), but they do so in ways that are deeply generative and instructive. The three novels date from the latter half of the twentieth century to the beginning of the twenty-first: Jyotirmayi Devi's Bengali *Epar Gaṅgā, Opar Gaṅgā* ("This Bank of the Ganges, That Bank of the Ganges" (1968) published as "The River Churning"), Pratibha Ray's Oriya *Yājñasenī* (1984), and Chitra Banerjee Divakaruni's *The Palace of Illusions* (2008).[3] Taken together with broader cur-

---

1. See, for example, Amrita Basu, ed., *The Challenge of Local Feminisms: Women's Movements in Global Perspective* (Boulder, CO: Westview Press, 1995); Ali Mirsepassi, Amrita Basu, and Frederick Weaver, eds., *Localizing Knowledge in a Globalizing World: Recasting the Area Studies Debate* (Syracuse: Syracuse University Press, 2003); Chandra Talpade Mohanty, *Feminism without Borders: Decolonizing Theory, Practicing Solidarity* (Durham, NC: Duke University Press, 2003); and Ania Loomba and Ritty A. Lukose, eds. *South Asian Feminisms* (Durham, NC: Duke University Press, 2012).

2. Nivedita Menon, "Is Feminism about 'Women'?" *Economic and Political Weekly* 50, no. 17 (2015): 38.

3. All quotations from *Epar Gaṅgā, Opar Gaṅgā* and *Yājñasenī* in this essay are from the following English translations: Jyotirmayi Devi, *The River Churning: A*

rents in how Draupadī has been depicted in Mahābhārata-themed literature and performance over the last century and a half, these novels demonstrate the extent to which Draupadī serves as a multivalent figure in modern times, one that frequently ties into emancipatory narratives of social justice. My goal in this essay is not to interrogate how well these novels conform to any prescribed definition of feminism, but rather, from my subject position as a white cis female scholar from the U.S., to investigate how the novels themselves seem to offer alternative visions of two dominant narratives: first, that of the Sanskrit *Mahābhārata,* in all of its patriarchal bent; and second, that of feminisms offered up by white Euro-American scholars, who have historically—and maternalistically—sought to universalize their experiences and identities at home and abroad.

I selected these three novels not only because of their popularity but also because they were written at three different periods in modern Indian history. As such, they represent three moments in the wider historical arc of Indian feminisms and related activism. Of women's involvement in various and interrelated social and political movements Amrita Basu writes:

> The Indian women's movement not only comprises a number of movements but has emerged through its association with other important movements in India: the social reform movement of the late nineteenth century, the nationalist movement of the early to mid-twentieth century, the civil liberties movement of the mid-1970s, and the grassroots struggles of the rural and urban poor from the late 1970s on.[4]

The three novels discussed in this chapter speak in their own ways to Indian women's deep engagement in such movements. Devi's novel addresses the ideas and experiences of women in the immediate aftermath of Partition. All three novels, moreover, allude to the struggles and interventions of women themselves in the modern period. They reflect on Indian women's

---

Partition Novel, trans. Enakshi Chatterjee (Delhi: Kali for Women, 1995); and Pratibha Ray, *Yajnaseni: The Story of Draupadi*, trans. Pradip Bhattacharya (Delhi: Rupa & Co., 2002).

4. Amrita Basu, "Globalizing Local Women's Movements," in *Localizing Knowledge in a Globalizing World: Recasting the Area Studies Debate,* eds. Ali Mirsepassi, Amrita Basu, and Frederick Weaver (Syracuse: Syracuse University Press, 2003), 92–93.

rights, they respond to social conventions around sexuality and marriage, and they illuminate some of the socio-political issues most impacting women's lives.

A Draupadī Caught in the Chaos of Partition

Literature about Draupadī written in the colonial period (and written mostly by men) tends to coalesce around two poles. In most cases, she is either a victim of men's abuse or a glorified exemplar for contemporary women. The latter mode of representing Draupadī aligns with other kinds of colonial-era literature that were written expressly for women between 1850 and 1950—domestic manuals, cautionary social novels, women's magazines, and so on—which generally sought to shape and define Indian femininity. As the target of men's abuse, on the other hand, Draupadī figures prominently in many colonial-era reworkings of the Mahābhārata—fiction, poetry, and drama—in which her sexual harassment by the Kauravas and Kīcaka could deftly and covertly signal the colonial rape of Mother India.[5]

At the time of India's independence and the Partition of India, however, novelists, poets, and playwrights found new ways to retell or otherwise allude to the Mahābhārata, and for them, too, Draupadī was a potent force. The genre of Partition literature that emerged in the immediate aftermath of Partition and then underwent a resurgence toward the end of the twentieth century has done a great deal to articulate the gendered violence of that time. It has accomplished much of that affective work through references to Draupadī, and even more so through references to Sītā, the heroine of the Rāmāyaṇa. Works in this genre sometimes correlate Draupadī's abuse in the Mahābhārata, and Sītā's abduction in the Rāmāyaṇa (and the responses

---

5. See Purnima Mankekar, *Screening Culture, Viewing Politics: An Ethnography of Television, Womanhood, and Nation in Postcolonial India* (Durham, NC: Duke University Press, 1999), 224–56; Pamela Lothspeich, *Epic Nation: Reimagining the Mahabharata in the Age of Empire* (Delhi: Oxford University Press, 2009); and K. P. Khadilkar, *Globalization, Nationalism and the Text of 'Kichaka-Vadha': The First English Translation of the Marathi Anticolonial Classic, with a Historical Analysis of Theatre in British India*, trans. and ed. Rakesh H. Solomon (London: Anthem Press, 2014). On premodern depictions of Kīcaka, see the chapters by Harshita Mruthinti Kamath, Eva De Clercq and Simon Winant, and Heidi Pauwels in this volume.

of their menfolk), chillingly, with actual rapes, kidnappings, and forced marriages at the time of the Partition. Like the women on the ground in 1947, Draupadī and Sītā neither provoke their tormenters nor have a hand in the larger political dramas that unfold around them.[6]

In her Bengali novel *Epar Gaṅgā, Opar Gaṅgā*, Jyotirmayi Devi directly relates the plight of women during Partition with Draupadī. Grimly reflecting on the carnage of Partition, her narrator observes:

> The blood of one's own relatives was spilled in every house. People were reminded of shameful episodes when numerous Draupadis were disrobed and humiliated. After all, the easiest way to show off one's manhood is at the cost of helpless women like Sita, Draupadi, and the others.[7]

This novel, which was first published serially in the journal *Prabāsī* in 1967, was originally titled *Itihāse Strīparva* ("The Women's Book in History"), and the three parts of the novel (still retained) are named after the first, eleventh, and thirteenth books of the Sanskrit *Mahābhārata*: "Ādiparva," "Anuśāsanparva," and "Strīparva." In her English translation of the novel, Enakshi Chatterjee translates these titles as (respectively) "The Beginning," "The Imposition," and "The Women."

In the first part of the novel (corresponding to the first book of the *Mahābhārata*, which details the vast genealogical history of the warring cousins and sets up the main story), we learn of the Partition trauma of Sutārā, born into an orthodox Hindu family in a village in Noakhali district (now in Bangladesh). One night, a group of Muslims—including the family's own servants, Rahīm and Karīm—kill Sutārā's father, a schoolteacher, and abduct her sister. It is strongly implied that they rape Sutārā after she falls unconscious. They also set fire to the family's cow shed. Sutārā's mother, who jumps into a pond, is presumed dead. Sutārā then spends six months living with a kindly Muslim family, whose patriarch, Tamījuddin, had been

6. See, for example, Alok Bhalla's translations of Jamila Hashmi's "Exile" and Rajinder Singh Bedi's "Lajwanti" in *Stories about the Partition of India*, vol. 1, ed. Alok Bhalla (Delhi: HarperCollins, 1994), 39–66; "Piñjar" in Amrita Pritam, *Pinjar: The Skeleton and Other Stories,* trans. Khushwant Singh (Delhi: Tara Press, 2009); and the 2003 film adaptation, *Piñjar*.

7. Devi, *River Churning*, 68.

the headmaster at her father's school. There Sutārā mentally replays scenes from her night of terror, but she has no clear memories of her violation. Two key events from that night recall scenes from the Sanskrit *Mahābhārata*: her presumed rape evokes Draupadī's humiliation in the *Sabhāparvan* ("The Book of the Assembly Hall") and the burning of the cow shed echoes the burning of the house of lac in the *Ādiparvan* ("The Book of Beginnings").

In the second part of the novel, Sutārā—still separated from her family—essentially endures an extended exile, much as Draupadī does. First, Sutārā is forsaken by her three brothers, who, at this point, are living comfortably in Calcutta. Shunned by her relatives, especially by her eldest brother's mother-in-law and other elder women, Sutārā represents a burden and stain on the family. Devi is unsparing in her implicit critique of this orthodox mindset. She is sent off to a Christian boarding school, another imposed exile. Ultimately, however, Sutārā earns an M.A. in history (*itihāsa*—surely a reference to the fact that *itihāsa*, or "that which transpired," namely, history, represents a genre in which the Sanskrit *Mahābhārata* has traditionally been categorized), and ultimately gains employment as an instructor in a woman's school called Yājñasenī College. Yājñasenī ("daughter of Yajñasena," that is, Drupada) is, of course, a common epithet of Draupadī.[8] The irony here is that, having survived her own horrific trauma, Sutārā survives to tell her own history. Acerbically, the narrator notes that many female survivors of Partition and some of the college's other instructors are, like Sutārā, contemporary Draupadīs: "Since there was nobody to support them these Yajnasenis were forced to fend for themselves. Molested, without shelter, money or power, they were victims of Partition."[9]

The concluding part of the novel relates to the eleventh book of the Sanskrit *Mahābhārata*, in which the epic's women mourn (and praise) their deceased male relatives. The novel, however, does not end tragically. Sutārā, now an independent, self-made woman, spurns a marriage proposal from Azīzuddin, the eldest son of Tamījuddin. The novel frames Azīzuddin as a Karṇa-like character. That is, he is noble, but of the wrong family background; moreover, he serves as a constant reminder of her trauma. Sutārā then goes on an extensive pilgrimage through the Himalayas, which parallels

8. This epithet also reminds us that Draupadī was born from the sacrificial fire (*yajña*). As Ray's narrator says of her exceptional birth, "The sacrificial altar is my mother. Yajnasena is my father. So I am Yajnaseni." Ray, *Yajnaseni*, 5.

9. Devi, *River Churning*, 69.

Draupadī's final sojourn and ascent to heaven with her husbands in the two final books of the Sanskrit epic, the *Mahāprasthānikaparvan* ("The Book of the Great Journey") and the *Svargārohaṇaparvan* ("The Book of the Ascent to Heaven"). Just as none of her husbands shed a tear when Draupadī falls down, something on which the narrator ruminates,[10] Sutārā's family forsakes her. However, Devī's heroine ultimately receives and accepts a marriage proposal from her sympathetic brother-in-law, Pramod. In this way, the novel suggests that Sutārā moves beyond her "taint" and attains the best possible outcome in this orthodox Hindu world.

Epar Gaṅgā, Opar Gaṅgā is a powerful work that follows Sutārā's life from about age sixteen to twenty-eight, the same age a widowed Devi and mother of six began her writing career. The novel closes on a hopeful, romantic note, seemingly affirming the institution of marriage within normative *savarṇa* (caste-affiliated) Hindu society, but as Debali Mookerjea-Leonard has pointed out in her incisive reading of the novel, it was very radical for its time.[11] Moreover, whereas the anti-colonial literature of an earlier generation tended to equate the British with the Kauravas, *Epar Gaṅgā, Opar Gaṅgā* implicates certain parties—Hindu and Muslim alike—as moral transgressors. In the early scene where Muslims burn Sutārā's family's cowshed, Devi suggests that Rahīm and Karīm are like Duryodhana and Duḥśāsana, intent on killing Sutārā's family and stripping her. But later Devi's narrator notes that "Sutara was amazed to learn that Muslim women had had to face the same trauma [at Hindu hands]"[12]—a gesture of empathy toward Muslim women's experiences during Partition.

A Peacebuilding, Postcolonial Draupadī

When we turn to our broader post-1947 Mahābhārata novels, Pratibha Ray's *Yājñasenī* and Chitra Banerjee Divakaruni's *The Palace of Illusions*, we can see that they depart significantly from colonial-era reworkings of the Mahābhārata, which tend to portray Draupadī as a victim in need of saving. What is new about *Yājñasenī* and *The Palace of Illusions* is that, like

10. Devi, 107–109.

11. Debali Mookherjea-Leonard, "Quarantined: Women and the Partition," *Comparative Studies of South Asia, Africa and the Middle East* 24, no. 1 (2004): 33.

12. Devi, *River Churning*, 86.

many other novels in their mold, they are told in a first-person voice, which allows them to grant Draupadī a subjectivity that the Sanskrit *Mahābhārata*, with its many layers of chiefly male narration, does only on occasion. Here we recall Mikhail Bakhtin's essay from 1934–35, "Discourse in the Novel," in which he uses the terms "heteroglossia" and "polyphony" to explain the special narrative operations of the novel wherein the speech acts of diverse individual narrators and characters seamlessly enter into dialogue with one another and, at the same time, reflect *difference*—different social stations, genders, viewpoints, ideologies, ways of speaking, and so forth.[13] These ideas help us to better appreciate not only the structures of Mahābhārata-themed novels such as *Yājñasenī* and *The Palace of Illusions* but also their socially disruptive, ideological force *vis-à-vis* the classical Sanskrit *Mahābhārata*.

In *Yājñasenī*, Draupadī relays her story in a letter addressed to her *sakha* (friend and confidant) Kṛṣṇa on her ascent to heaven; thus the entire novel represents an extended flashback. The novel begins with a description of Draupadī's miraculous birth in the "Aryan heartland" during the *dvāpara-yuga,* the third of four eons in Hindu cyclical time. At the outset, Ray's Draupadī maintains that she is mortal, which immediately brings her down to earth—a significant point, given that many Mahābhāratas depict her as a goddess. "Time may transform me into a goddess," she says, "but I appeared on this earth with this body in human form."[14] When she is born, however, it is prophesized that she will facilitate vengeance against Droṇa for his insult to her father, Drupada, presumably through her marriage alliance with the Pāṇḍavas.[15]

The Draupadī of Ray's novel has little direct involvement in the war.[16] The war itself passes very quickly—it takes only about ten pages—and highlights the brutal killing of Abhimanyu, the deaths of Karṇa, Duḥśāsana, and Duryodhana (Draupadī's primary tormenters), the fate of Aśvatthāman, and the long lament of the Paṇḍava women. The vast majority of the novel

13. M. M. Bakhtin, "Discourse in the Novel," in *The Dialogic Imagination: Four Essays by M. M. Bakhtin*, eds. Michael Holquist, trans. Caryl Emerson and Michael Holquist (Austin: University of Texas Press, 1981), 259–422. Sudipta Kaviraj explores a related essay by Bakhtin in his chapter in this volume.

14. Ray, *Yajnaseni*, 4.

15. Ray, 8.

16. Ray, 388–90

takes place before the war, and it is in these pages that we hear of Draupadī's thoughts and feelings about her five husbands, Kṛṣṇa, Karṇa, and her mother-in-law, Kuntī. In the novel, Draupadī has a close relationship with Kuntī, whom she admires, and a complicated relationship with Karṇa, for whom her initial contempt ultimately softens into sympathy. He rescues Draupadī from drowning in a river; later, she saves Karṇa's life when he is bitten by a poisonous snake.[17]

Although Draupadī clearly has a romantic preference for Arjuna, she also has a special love for Kṛṣṇa as her confidant and guide. She eagerly awaits his visits, affectionately dotes on him, and writes poetry addressed to him. At a certain point she dreams that she is Kṛṣṇa's foster mother, Yaśodā, breastfeeding baby Kṛṣṇa. Yet the novel often presents Kṛṣṇa and Arjuna as one and the same: Arjuna inhabits the mortal body of their shared figure, while Kṛṣṇa represents the subtle body; their blue lotus feet are nearly identical in Draupadī's eyes.[18] Once Draupadī even mistakes a sleeping Kṛṣṇa for Arjuna.[19] Remembering when she learned from Kṛṣṇa that she was to marry Arjuna, Draupadī observes:

> That very moment I split into two. My subtlest essence merged into his deep blue radiant essence. My other portion remained as the body of Draupadi-of-the-*svayamvar* [*svayaṃvara* or "bride-groom-choice ceremony"], amid earthly pleasures, desires and anxieties in the royal palace of Panchal, waiting for Arjuna.[20]

On the surface, this vision sets up a love triangle, particularly because Ray induces us periodically to "forget" that Draupadī's love for Kṛṣṇa is of a higher order. And then there are the jealousies. Kṛṣṇa says he is jealous of Draupadī, fearing, he says, that "to *sakha* [Arjuna] you might become dearer than me."[21] Draupadī, meanwhile, is jealous of Arjuna's other wives—especially Kṛṣṇa's sister Subhadrā, though Draupadī eventually embraces her. For his part, Arjuna is jealous of his other brothers with whom he must share

17. Ray, 280, 324–25

18. Ray, 46, 189.

19. Ray, 191–92.

20. Ray, 25.

21. Ray, 273.

his wife: he even "tests" Draupadī by briefly pretending to love Subhadrā more than her.

What perhaps is most surprising about *Yājñasenī* is Ray's depiction of the historical lands of the *Mahābhārata* as being inhabited by two broad communities, Aryan and non-Aryan. The kingdoms of the Kurus and Pāñcālas are designated "*Āryāvarta*"—which makes the ruling class in this story decidedly Aryan. The Aryan community stands in contrast to a forest-dwelling *ādivāsī* (Indigenous or tribal) underclass, the members of which Ray calls Śabaras and Kirātas, whom the Pāṇḍavas run up against and ultimately befriend during their exile.[22] The novel also relays the well-known story of Ekalavya. In Ray's telling, Yudhiṣṭhira and Arjuna oppose Droṇa when he demands that Ekalavya cut off his thumb.[23] Yudhiṣṭhira, moreover, gives sermons on social equality and the brotherhood of Aryans and non-Aryans, praising Śabarī from the Rāmāyaṇa. Draupadī shares these sentiments, proclaiming that there should be "no distinction of class, caste, race. The injustice inflicted on Ekalavya will have to be made up here. There is enough cause for the Kirātas to hate the Aryans. But by binding them in chains of friendship we will bring about the great union of Aryans and non-Aryans . . ." She will lovingly serve non-Aryans from her own hands, she says, while Arjuna will "remove the used leaves of all."[24] Later in the novel, Draupadī saves the lives of two Śabara babies, nursing them (just as she does Kṛṣṇa, in her dream) after their mother is killed by a tiger. The novel even shows the Pāṇḍavas adopting elements of *ādivāsī* culture, such as their rituals, food, and dress. This scenario—Aryan elites engineering a political alliance and social contract with forest-dwelling indigenous groups through their beneficence—may, on the face of it, strike some as romantic and paternalistic. This novel of course centers elite characters and their concerns. Yet Ray's underlying intent in the novel seems to be geared toward advocating for gender justice and leveling social inequalities. At the same time, she does not let readers forget about the state's historically troubled relationship with *ādivāsī* communities.

Here we might recall that another author, Mahasweta Devi, wrote about a Santal tribal woman and the beleaguered state of indigenous peo-

22. Sucheta Kanjilal discusses a similar feature of two short stories by Mahasweta Devi in the following chapter in this volume.

23. On the details of Ekalavya's story, see Kanjilal's chapter in this volume.

24. Ray, 264.

ples in India four years earlier in her short story "Draupadī."[25] This short story—now canonical, thanks in part to Gayatri Spivak's 1987 reading of it, and her accompanying English translation—has led to public performances of women's empowerment and activism on various fronts. For example, Deepti Misri has shown how Heisnam Kanhailal's adaptation of Devi's short story into a Manipuri stage play in 2000 was likely the impetus for the ethnic Meitei women's naked protest against the Indian government in Imphal, the capital of the state of Manipur in northeastern India, in 2004.[26] There, women used their naked bodies to contest the Indian army's torture, murder, and rape of activist Thangjam Manorama while in the custody of the Indian Army's Assam Rifles Battalion. (She had been charged with militancy in connection with the separatist movement in Manipur.) Acknowledging the semiotic and political potency of the Meitei women's protest, Misri writes that "These defiant protests broadly challenge the rape script underlying the disciplinary violence of the state."[27] Yet Misri also warns that "particular ways of framing naked protest often tread the dangerous ground of appeals to good masculinity and protectionism."[28] In other words, within such a framework, cis women's bodies and sexualities still carry the burden and the stigma of social shame, and thus (in that binarist logic) require safeguarding by the good men.[29]

A "Bluer" and Bolder Draupadī

In the preface to *The Palace of Illusions*, Chitra Banerjee Divakaruni relates that she grew up hearing stories of the Mahābhārata yet wanted to retell

25. Mahasweta Devi, "Draupadi," ed. and trans. Gayatri Chakravorty Spivak, *Critical Inquiry* 8, no. 2 (1981): 381–402. For another analysis of this short story, see Ranjana Khanna, "In Search of a Voice for Dopdi/Draupadi: Writing the Other Woman's Story Out of the 'Dark Continent,'" in *Women's Lives/Women's Times: New Essays on Auto/Biography*, eds. Trev Lynn Broughton and Linda R. Anderson (Albany: State University of New York Press, 1997), 103–20.

26. Deepti Misri, "'Are You a Man?': Performing Naked Protest in India," *Signs* 36, no. 3 (Spring 2011): 603–25.

27. Misri, 622.

28. Misri, 623.

29. Misri, 619.

the story because she was "left unsatisfied by the portrayals of the women." She was bothered that they "remained shadowy figures, their thoughts and motives mysterious, their emotions portrayed only when they affected the lives of the male heroes, their roles ultimately subservient to those of their fathers or husbands, brothers or sons."[30] In contrast to Ray's "Yājñasenī," Divakaruni's Draupadī insists that everyone call her "Pāñcālī" ("woman of Pañcāla," her birthplace), which she says is "a name strong like the land, a name that knew how to endure."[31] Divakaruni's formula—having Draupadī tell the story of the Mahābhārata with encyclopedic detail, complete with running commentary—worked to make the novel nationally and internationally famous.

Validating one popular fan theory of the Mahābhārata, this Draupadī secretly harbors intense love for Karṇa.[32] In a recapitulation of the early South Asian literary trope of two characters falling in love before meeting, Draupadī hears stories about Karṇa from her maid Dhai Ma (*dāī māṃ*, "wet nurse"), grows intrigued, and only becomes more so upon seeing a painting of him. Yet at her *svayaṃvara*, Draupadī still humiliates Karṇa by questioning his birth—but only, she rationalizes, to save her brother, Dhṛṣṭadyumna, whom Karṇa is threatening to kill. Later, as a guest in Hāstinapura, she feels guilty for wanting to receive an admiring glance from Karṇa. Then dramatically, on the first night of the war, Draupadī overhears Karṇa admit to Bhīṣma that he is in love with her. It is only when the Pāṇḍavas ascend to heaven that we receive confirmation of Draupadī's own feelings on the matter. After Yudhiṣṭhira explains that Draupadī has

---

30. Chitra Banerjee Divakaruni, *The Palace of Illusions* (New York: Anchor Books, 2008), xiv.

31. Divakaruni, 42.

32. In some sources, including Sāraḷādāsa's fifteenth-century Oriya *Mahābhārata*, the twentieth-century Tamil chapbook *Pāṇṭavar Vanāvasam*, and the Marathi folk play *Jāṃbhūḷ Ākhyān*, Draupadī is forced to admit to the Pāṇḍavas and Kṛṣṇa that she is in love with Karṇa. This is also implied in Villiputtūr's fifteenth-century Tamil *Pāratam* and Kumāravyāsa's fifteenth-century Kannada *Karṇāṭabhāratakathāmañjarī*. See A. K. Ramanujan, "Repetition in the *Mahābhārata*," in *Essays on the Mahābhārata*, ed. Arvind Sharma (Leiden: E. J. Brill, 1991), 435 n5; Pathani Patnaik, "Sarala's Oriya Mahābhārata 'A Vox Populi' in Oriya Literature," in *Mahābhārata in the Tribal and Folk Traditions of India*, ed. K. S. Singh (Shimla: Indian Institute of Advanced Study, 1993), 180; and Devdutt Pattanaik, *Jaya: An Illustrated Retelling of the Mahabharata* (Delhi: Penguin Books, 2010), 184.

fallen because "she loved one man more than everyone else," and declares that man to be Arjuna, Draupadī drops this bombshell: "He [Yudhiṣṭhira] had spared me. He'd chosen kindness over truth and uttered, for the sake of my reputation, the second lie of his lifetime!"[33] She now realizes that Yudhiṣṭhira has known the truth all along: she loves their elder brother Karṇa best of all.

Ultimately, Divakaruni anoints theirs a spiritual love. Just as Draupadī is about to depart her mortal body, Kṛṣṇa appears. He tells her they are both divine. Then her body dissolves away and she attains her goal: "I am buoyant and expansive and uncontainable—but I always was so, only I never knew it! I am beyond name and gender and the imprisoning patterns of the ego. And yet, for the first time, I am Panchaali."[34] At this point Karṇa appears, and the three of them depart for a metaphorical palace—the only one, she says, she's ever needed: "Its walls are space, its floor is sky, its center everywhere."[35] In a metaphysical turn, Draupadī overcomes attachment to her senses and the desires of the mortal body, which the Upaniṣads (the esoteric works that cap the Vedic literary corpus) liken to a palace of nine gates (i.e., bodily openings). As Kṛṣṇa has earlier told Draupadī just before they built the (worldly palace) Indraprastha, "Already you live within a nine-gated palace."[36] By attaining *mokṣa* (spiritual liberation) Draupadī attains union with both Kṛṣṇa and Karṇa. Thus, this Draupadī prompts us to realize that the true "palace of illusions" is the body, not merely the magical palace that the divine architect, Maya, builds for the Pāṇḍavas at Indraprastha on the charred earth of the Khāṇḍava Forest.

Despite its occasional romantic and melodramatic moments, this novel also speaks about serious social issues that affect women in the real world. One of these issues is women's access to education (a topic that is also broached in Ray's novel). Divakaruni depicts Draupadī as a brilliant student who would rather surreptitiously attend her brother's academic lessons than learn the "sixty-four arts that noble ladies must know"—a nod to the sixty-four arts cited in the *Kāmasūtra* and referenced in other classical sources.[37] Another point of concern is women's free movement in

33. Divakaruni, *Palace of Illusions*, 348.

34. Divakaruni, 360.

35. Divakaruni, 360.

36. Divakaruni, 113.

37. Divakaruni, 29.

society. A woman "with a destiny to fulfill," Draupadī feels stifled within the confines of the palace: "With each lesson I felt the world of women tightening its noose around me."[38] Tellingly, women are Draupadī's most trusted mentors and authority figures: Dhai Ma, for example, confers upon Draupadī homespun wisdom and practical advice about navigating co-wives. A nameless sorceress, meanwhile, teaches Draupadī "unqueenly skills" such as how to dress hair, cook, heal, seduce, and speak up—skills she later puts to good use while living in King Virāṭa's palace.[39] Divakaruni further foregrounds Draupadī's special abilities in other ways. During the war, it is Draupadī, not Dhṛtarāṣṭra's charioteer Sañjaya, who receives the gift of divine sight that allows her to behold the war from afar, a narrative choice that reinforces Draupadī's position as the central subject. Divakaruni's Draupadī also displays a great deal of political acumen. Yudhiṣṭhira repeatedly consults her privately on issues of the state, and after the war it is Draupadī, not Yudhiṣṭhira, who uses her rhetorical skills to convince the war widows not to give up hope and to desist from committing suicide.

The Palace of Illusions also reflects on socially constructed double standards around gender and sexuality. When a sage prophesizes that Draupadī will have five husbands, Dhai Ma retorts, "You know what our shastras [*śāstra*s or "instructional texts"] call women who've been with more than one man, don't you? Though no one seems to have a problem when men sleep with a different wife each day of the week!"[40] The novel also shows that this Draupadī is aware of her own husbands' objectification of her for their own gratification. After Vyāsa mandates that she sleep with each husband one year in turn and grants a boon that she will become a virgin again at the end of each year, Draupadī states, "Like a communal drinking cup, I would be passed from hand to hand whether I wanted it or not. Nor was I particularly delighted by the virginity boon, which seemed designed more for my husbands' benefit than mine."[41] Like Devi's Draupadī, Divakaruni's protagonist is jealous of her husbands' other wives, especially Subhadrā, but she is also more aware of her husbands' motivations to marry

38. Divakaruni, 29. Also see *The Kamasutra of Vatsyayana*, trans. Wendy Doniger and Sudhir Kakar (New York: Oxford World Classics, 2002).

39. Divakaruni, 61.

40. Divakaruni, 42.

41. Divakaruni, 120.

these other women: "Sometimes there were political reasons, but mostly it was male desire."[42]

One interesting relationship broached in *The Palace of Illusions* (and rarely elsewhere) is that between Draupadī and her sibling Śikhaṇḍin (formerly Ambā).[43] When they first meet, Śikhaṇḍin—called Sikhandi (Śikhaṇḍī) in the novel—is already full-grown and presenting as masculine, although deemed female at birth. Corroborating a popular line of thought, he tells Draupadī how he became a man through the help of a *yakṣa* (a supernatural spirit) who in this telling "appeared in the sky with his burning demon sword. When he heard what I wanted [to become a man], he laughed and plunged it into me. The pain was unbearable. I fainted. When I awoke, I was a man"—a man who remembers "how women thought and what they longed for."[44] He did this, he says, in order to "kill the greatest warrior of our time [Bhīṣma]," which he plans to do with Draupadī's help.[45] Sikhandi also relates how he was the princess Ambā in a previous birth, concluding, "Wait for a man to avenge your honor, and you'll wait forever."[46] Draupadī takes an immediate liking to him and sympathizes with his suffering. She is also inspired and emboldened.

Although Draupadī is often called "Kṛṣṇā" (the dark one) in the Sanskrit *Mahābhārata* and elsewhere, popular artwork and TV adaptations[47] frequently depict her with a light or blue skin tone. Raja Ravi Varma's iconic nineteenth-century paintings of Draupadī, many of which feature scenes

42. Divakaruni, 151.

43. In the Mahābhārata tradition, Ambā was one of the three princesses in the royal house of Kāśī whom Bhīṣma abducted with the intent to marry them to his step-brother and the Kuru heir, Vicitravīrya. When Ambā informs him that she had intended to marry her beloved, Prince Śālva, Bhīṣma releases her. Subsequently, she is spurned by Śālva and (the celibate) Bhīṣma in turn. However, Ambā performs austerities to become a man so that she may mete out revenge against Bhīṣma. Reborn as Śikhaṇḍin, she does so, collaborating with Arjuna to slay him during the war.

44. Divakaruni, 46.

45. Divakaruni, 47.

46. Divakaruni, 49.

47. Among the most prominent Hindi TV adaptions are *Mahābhārat* (1988–90), *Draupadī* (2001–2), *Mahābhārat* (2013–14), *Dharmakṣetra* (2014–15), and *Sūryaputra Karṇ* (2015–16).

of her sexual humiliation at the dice game and in Virāṭa's court, also show her with very light skin.

At the beginning of her second chapter, "Blue," Divakaruni addresses Draupadī's skin color directly. Her Draupadī reflects:

> Perhaps the reason Krishna and I got along so well was that we were both severely dark-skinned. In a society that looked down its patrician nose on anything except milk-and-almond hues, this was considered most unfortunate, especially for a girl. It was clear that Krishna, whose complexion was even darker than mine, didn't consider his color a drawback.[48]

She goes on to marvel that Kṛṣṇa could tell such a girl she was "capable of changing history."[49] Ray, too, describes Draupadī's darkness in positive terms in *Yājñasenī,* but her Draupadī does not herself explicitly critique the social norms that guide people's reactions to her exceptional beauty. Rather, her criticism lies beneath the surface:

> People said of me—exquisitely beautiful! Amazing! Complexion like the petals of the blue lotus! Thick hair like the waves of the ocean, and large entrancing blue lotus-like eyes radiant with intelligence! . . . Father's court poets were exclaiming, 'Dark beauty, *Shyama* [*śyāma*]!'[50]

Divakaruni's Draupadī, by contrast, is more forthright: she implicitly critiques the beauty norms and colorism that, she suggests, hit "ordinary" women especially hard. In other words, Divakaruni uses her Draupadī to reflect on the larger social discourses of color, power, and imperialism in South Asia.

Divakaruni's affirming statements about Draupadī's skin tone resonate with social justice campaigns to combat anti-Black racism and colorism. In 2017 in Chennai, for instance, Bharadwaj Sundar and Naresh Nil developed the campaign "Dark is Divine" to critique the common practice of

48. Divakaruni, 8.

49. Divakaruni, 8.

50. Ray, *Yajnaseni*, 7.

depicting Hindu deities with light skin tones.[51] They created a calendar, which they promoted on social media, featuring photos of various gods and goddesses using seven models with skin tones representative of those of the Indian populace. Although the calendar does not feature "Kṛṣṇā" (Draupadī), it does include photos of Kṛṣṇa, Lakṣmī, Sarasvatī, Durgā, and Sītā. As Sundar explains, "Everyone here prefers fair skin. But I am a dark-skinned person and all my friends are dark-skinned too. So how do I identify with fair-skinned gods and goddesses?"[52] As another example (even earlier, in 2009), the non-profit organization Women of Worth, which is based in India, started a campaign called "Dark is Beautiful," for which actor Nandita Das has been a chief spokesperson.[53]

Conclusion

In literature written over the last 150 years, Draupadī is a fluid sign. In the novels considered here, she is a Partition survivor who rises above and prevails against the horror of her own gendered violence (*Epar Gaṅgā, Opar Gaṅgā*). She is an exiled princess who helps facilitate an imagined Aryan-*ādivāsī* alliance (*Yājñasenī*) and works to dismantle the hegemony of whiteness (*The Palace of Illusions*). As we have seen, one Draupadī studies and becomes a controller of her own history, while two other Draupadīs literally tell their own histories and, by and by, the history of *Bhārata-varṣa* (India). These works reframe the concept of the *pativratā*—the idealization of a woman's loyalty and devotion to her husband, and the social norms of chastity and monogamy that surround it—advocating, instead, for more egalitarian unions. Ultimately, these novels affirm what Rashmi Luthra says about the relevance of the Rāmāyaṇa and the Mahābhārata at the present moment: "Rather than being a dead-end, the epics and their characters are

51. Geetika Mantri, "Dark Is Divine: Chennai Duo's Photo Series Reimagines Gods with Dark Skin," *The News Minute,* January 2, 2018, https://www.thenewsminute.com/article/dark-divine-chennai-duo-s-photo-series-reimagines-gods-dark-skin-74071.

52. Geeta Pandey, "Dark Is Divine: What Colour Are Indian Gods and Goddesses?" *BBC*, January 21, 2018, http://www.bbc.com/news/world-asia-india-42637998.

53. "Dark is Beautiful: Our Story," Dark is Beautiful, http://www.darkisbeautiful.in/about/ Accessed August 24, 2020.

fertile ground for the enunciation of multiple feminisms and their various contradictions within the Indian context, and for the creation of common ground between feminists and Indian women at large."[54]

54. Rashmi Luthra, "Clearing Sacred Ground: Women-Centered Interpretations of the Indian Epics," *Feminist Formations* 26, no. 2 (2014): 137. On page 155, Luthra also notes that women artists, storytellers, and writers who bring the epics' women into new works risk "unintentionally becoming complicit with the politics of Hindu right-wing groups or appearing to be exclusivist of class and caste concerns." Yet Luthra advocates that women authors take those risks, so as not to abdicate "the cultural ground of the epics to inimical forces."

Chapter Seventeen

From Excluded to Exceptional

Caste in Contemporary Mahābhāratas[1]

Sucheta Kanjilal

As this book demonstrates, the story and the idea of the Mahābhārata have seen many interpolations and changes over the centuries. In contemporary India, adaptations keep this dynamic narrative tradition current. This chapter analyzes three recent tellings of the Mahābhārata that situate the epic within today's social and political climates by connecting characters and events from the Mahābhārata with contemporary efforts to advocate for social justice in India. First I examine two short stories by the Bengali author Mahasweta Devi (1926–2016), "Kuntī o Niṣādi" ("Kuntī and the Nishada Woman," 1999) and "Pañcakanyā" ("Five Virgins," 2000). These stories were translated into English in 2005 by Anjum Katyal and published in a collection titled *After Kurukshetra*. Then I turn to Kiran Nagarkar's four-act English play, *Bedtime Story*, which was published in 2015, even though Nagakar (b. 1942) originally wrote it in 1977. These Mahābhāratas—we might call them "contrapuntal" Mahābhāratas—spotlight characters from the epic

1. This essay draws from and builds on sections of the fourth chapter of my doctoral dissertation. See Sucheta Kanjilal, "Modern Mythologies: The Epic Imagination in Contemporary Indian Literature," (PhD diss., University of South Florida, 2017), 165–88.

who inhabit social identities that Brahmanical Hinduism has traditionally marginalized: individuals who belong to lower castes, particularly Dalits.[2] These works do not present lower-caste characters enacting every ideal of self-determination; their interpretations of the Mahābhārata do not reflect some sort of perfected vision of social justice. Rather, I argue, these works demonstrate how complicated it is to represent social marginalities within the narrative context of the Mahābhārata. Intentionally or not, Devi's and Nagarkar's compositions reflect (in certain respects) the very oppressive structures that they (in other respects) work to overturn. Devi's and Nagarkar's Mahābhāratas use the voices of lower-caste characters to critique mechanisms of social oppression, but they also mold these figures as exceptional; they are wise and idealistic even in the face of their marginality. Their primary role is to educate their co-characters about the ideals of social justice. It is worth noting that the major works that I analyze here were not written by individuals from marginalized communities; interpretations of the Mahābhārata by Dalits themselves form an important part of creative discourse on the epic today, and I make note of some of these works in the conclusion.

If the standard Mahābhārata narrative embodies the worldview of what scholars today call Brahmanical Hinduism—an elite, socio-normative religious culture that draws authority from certain canonical Sanskrit texts and the social structures that preserve them—then there is a way in which the very act of retelling the Mahābhārata underscores Brahmanical Hinduism as a hegemonic discourse. Dalit scholar and activist Kancha Ilaiah points out that even when adaptations of the Sanskrit epics adopt critical frameworks, they reinvigorate dominant narratives about Hinduism and Hindu culture that oppress alternative (that is, non-Hindu, non-high-caste) identities and communities.[3] In doing so, many of India's

2. The term *Dalit*, which means "oppressed" or "broken," functions as an empowering replacement for other derogatory terms that mean "untouchable" or "impure." Ramnarayan Rawat and K. Satyanarayana write that the term first gained traction in the 1970s thanks to the anti-caste activist group called the Dalit Panthers and has since been widely adopted by scholars, writers, and critics. See "Introduction: Dalit Studies: New Perspectives on Indian History and Society" in *Dalit Studies*. eds. Ramnarayan Rawat and K. Satyanarayana (Durham, NC: Duke University Press, 2016), 2.

3. Kancha Ilaiah, *Why I Am Not a Hindu: A Sudra Critique of Hindutva Philosophy, Culture and Political Economy* (1996; repr., Calcutta: Samya, 2007), 13.

modern Mahābhāratas (and Rāmāyaṇas, too) represent a certain complicity in maintaining or renewing Brahmanical Hindu hegemony. Stuart Hall contends that "No project achieves a position of permanent 'hegemony.' It is a process, not a state of being. No victories are final. Hegemony has to be constantly 'worked on,' maintained, renewed and revised."[4] Thus, while storytelling can bolster solidarities among those who experience oppression, not all stories produce or improve commonality; sometimes they serve as reminders of violent marginalization.

Critique from the Margins

The pervasiveness of the epic narratives has not been accepted uncritically by people who are not Hindus and particularly by those who do not belong to the upper castes. For instance, in his polemical book *Why I Am Not a Hindu* (1996), Ilaiah, who writes both in English and Telugu, reveals how the omnipresence of epic stories, whether in state-controlled textbooks or in the names of his classmates, underscored his position as a cultural outsider. Instead of valorizing a commonly held past, the presence of Sanskrit texts insisted on the centrality of Hinduism. The literary and philosophical content of the epics, no matter how engrossing, were secondary to Ilaiah's experience of its context: a religio-social order that had violently excluded and oppressed Dalits and many other marginalized groups.

Sharankumar Limbale—a Dalit author who writes in Marathi—suggests that the repetition of certain narratives, such as those that appear in the Sanskrit epics, is self-affirming for communities because retellings cement common knowledge and interests. Yet Limbale (among other Dalit writers) reminds us that not all communities' reiterated narratives earn the same cultural capital as retellings of the Mahābhārata and the Rāmāyaṇa do. Dalit narratives, Limbale argues, are considered "repetitious" in a way that retellings of the Sanskrit epics never are:

> There are TV serials based on the *Rāmāyaṇa*, books on the *Rāmāyaṇa* continue to pour in . . . No one says that this is all about the same thing because Rama is an important topic

4. Stuart Hall, "The Neo-Liberal Revolution," *Cultural Studies* 25, no. 6 (2011): 727.

> for them . . . But when Dalits write about themselves, it seems repetitious to these non-Dalits because it is not an important topic for them.[5]

Limbale asserts that it is valid for any community to evoke repeated experiences, whether they are lived, as in the case of Dalit oppression—"[O]ur touch is considered untouchable. Our colonies have been kept apart. We are expected to wear dirty clothes and use dirty language. Our culture is regarded as dirty,"[6] Limbale writes—or unlived, as in the case of epic adaptations. In this respect, Limbale commends Mahasweta Devi,[7] a writer and political activist whose Mahābhārata-themed works bridge the gaps between Brahmanical histories and tribal alterities by mining the epics to expose some of the origins of contemporary inequalities.

The View from the Forest in Mahasweta Devi's *After Kurukshetra*

Mahasweta Devi is certainly worthy of Limbale's praise. Fortified with decades of activism, her literary writing frequently sheds light on the inhumane treatment of marginalized people by the state and people in power. Although Devi's best known Mahābhārata-inspired work, her short story "Draupadī" (1980), has invited its share of critical discussants (such as Gayatri Spivak),[8] few scholars have explored Devi's other Mahābhārata short stories. Two of these stories, "Pañcakanyā" and "Kuntī o Niṣādi," present the lives of women characters in the Mahābhārata after the Kurukṣetra war has ended; they loosely correspond to the eleventh book of the Sanskrit epic, the *Strīparvan* ("The Book of the Women"). Unlike "Draupadī," however,

---

5. Sharankumar Limbale, *Towards an Aesthetic of Dalit Literature: History, Controversies, and Considerations*, trans. Alok Mukherjee (Delhi: Orient Longman, 2004), 146.

6. Limbale, 140.

7. Limbale, 138.

8. See Mahasweta Devi, "Draupadi," ed. and trans. Gayatri Chakravorty Spivak, *Critical Inquiry* 8, no. 2 (1981): 381–402.

which is set in modern India, these stories remain within the mythical universe of the Sanskrit *Mahābhārata*. This setting exhorts readers to challenge notions of an idealized Hindu past by using the voices of socially marginalized characters (some "new," some familiar from other Mahābhāratas) to expose the fissures and injustices in Brahmanical ideologies.[9] Therefore, the women characters in *After Kurukshetra* are not only upper-caste queens and princesses, but also women from lower-caste and tribal groups. Devi critiques the Sanskrit text from within, focusing specifically on the impact of upper-caste patriarchy on the lives of women.

In "Pañcakanyā," Devi decenters royal women in favor of commoners. While the title of this short story is an allusion to a Sanskrit invocation in praise of five virtuous women from the Sanskrit epics (Ahalyā, Tārā, Mandodarī, Draupadī, and Kuntī),[10] the narrative of Devi's story focuses on five lower-caste women. The women come from Kurujaṅgala (literally "the jungle of the Kurus"), a forest area that the story describes as lying outside the main areas of the kingdom. Through them, Devi's story critiques the strictures of widowhood for *kṣatriya* (warrior) and *brāhmaṇa* women. Uttarā, the young daughter-in-law of the Pāṇḍava brothers, mourns her husband Abhimanyu, who dies in the war.[11] Her grief is compounded by having to follow what Devi's text calls the "rigorous rules of widowhood" that are enforced by the *ācārya*s (religious elders).[12] When it is learned that Uttarā is pregnant with the kingdom's next heir, the five women are recruited to keep her company. The space of the forest allows the story to offer a contrasting portrait of women characters in the *rājavṛtta* (the circle of kings) with the voices of women characters in the *janavṛtta* or the *lokavṛtta* (the circle of commoners), the lower-caste community from which Uttarā's companions

9. Pamela Lothspeich discusses a similar feature in Pratibha Ray's Oriya novel *Yājñasenī* in her chapter in this volume.

10. See Pradip Bhattacharya, "Five Holy Virgins, Five Sacred Myths: A Quest for Meaning," *Manushi* 141 (2004): 4–12.

11. Please note that while I transliterate the names of terms and characters according to the International Alphabet of Sanskrit Transliteration (IAST) (e.g. *rājavṛtta,* Uttarā), the authors and translators discussed in this essay use more standard English spellings (e.g. *rajavritta*, Uttara).

12. Mahasweta Devi, *After Kurukshetra: Three Stories*, trans. Anjum Katyal (Kolkata: Seagull, 2005), 3.

emerge. The five forest women whom Devi's narrative conjures offer the story's upper-caste protagonist, Uttarā—and the reader alongside her—an alternative vision of widowhood.

Over and over again, the five women express an autonomy that Uttarā describes as unfamiliar: they are "from a totally different world."[13] Initially wanting no part in the doings of the *rājavṛtta*, the five women refuse to be subservient to Uttarā. They insist on social equality, agreeing to attend to Uttarā only if they are treated as "companions" and not "servants." As she interacts with them, Uttarā becomes fascinated with their social and familial customs, which help her understand how *rājavṛtta* customs are not always good for royal women. For instance, they encourage her to stay active during her pregnancy instead of resting, so that childbirth will be easier.[14] The forest women have far more freedom and agency than Uttarā does—they move about as they please without covering their heads and sing songs as loudly as they wish.[15] At one point, Uttarā marvels at the fact that the five women are given access to weapons for self-protection. When Uttarā muses that spears are a man's weapon, one of the forest women reminds her that they are a "woman's weapon too."[16]

Through her exchanges with the five women, Uttarā mourns not only her lack of freedom but also the youth that the upper-caste rules of widowhood have brought to an end: "the word 'widow' terrifies her . . . She can't recognize herself in the mirror. When was it that she laughed, played . . . ?"[17] Devi's story draws a pointed contrast between Uttarā's curtailed adolescence and the forest women's regenerative youth when the five women describe how, in their community, widows remarry:

> Our widows remarry and are respected by their families. They work alongside their husband, cultivating the land, working and storing crop. They never deny the demands of life in order to exist as mere shadowy ghosts . . . that's only for the rajavritta [*rājavṛtta*].[18]

---

13. Devi, 5.

14. Devi, 9.

15. Devi, 5.

16. Devi, 7, 10.

17. Devi, 14.

18. Devi, 24–25.

The "shadowy ghosts" of the women's description recall the idea that as an upper-caste widow, Uttarā is as dead as her husband. The forest women, on the other hand, find new life after widowhood: rather than obey the demands of the patriarchy, they obey only the "demands of life."

Through the voices of these five lower-caste women, the story links Uttarā's symbolic death at the hands of upper-caste patriarchy with the Bhārata men's "real" deaths in the war of Kurukṣetra, which the forest women similarly attribute to the moral failings of Brahmanical ideology. At the end of the story, the five women denounce the war and, in turn, the *rājavṛtta*'s conception of dharma: "This is not our dharmayuddha [war of dharma]. Brother kills brother, uncle kills nephew, shishya [*śiṣya*, "student"] kills guru [teacher]. It may be your idea of dharma but it's not ours."[19] Earlier in the story, the women vocalize a similar critique of the *rājavṛtta*'s discourse of dharma (though they use the terms "holy" and "righteous" as stand-ins for the term): "But such a war just for a throne? This, a holy war?! A righteous war?! Just call it a war of greed."[20] The women here emerge from a set of margins (the "Kurujaṅgala") that Devi integrates into the Mahābhārata story in order to offer a fresh critique of the epic's dominant, if endlessly scrutinized, ideology: dharma.

Another of Devi's stories, "Kuntī o Niṣādi," sets its protagonist, another upper-caste widow, in the forest as well. It narrates an exchange between Kuntī, the elderly mother of the Pāṇḍavas, and a Nishada (Niṣāda) woman. Present in both the epics and contemporary India, Nishadas are a forest-dwelling tribal community; readers of the epics will be most familiar with the term Niṣāda from the story of Ekalavya, which I discuss in the following section. When the story begins, Kuntī is living out her voluntary retirement from courtly life in a forest dwelling. Every day, she ventures out to the forest to gather firewood, which she plans to use for ritual purposes. During this time, she takes a moment to reflect and muse aloud about her life's regrets. One day, she spots a group of Nishada women. At first, Kuntī expresses fear and revulsion: "Kunti was trembling, terrified. Would they come closer? Their shadows may fall on the firewood for the sacred rites and defile it."[21] In narrating Kuntī's fear that the mere shadow of a Nishada woman would "defile" a piece of firewood, Devi evokes the

19. Devi, 26.

20. Devi, 3.

21. Devi, 33.

Hindu notions of ritual purity that have historically been among the most damaging to Dalits' lives.

Finally, one of the Nishada women approaches Kuntī and reveals that she has been eavesdropping on her confessions. Kuntī is shocked not only by the woman's physical approach, but by the fact that the woman speaks her language. (Recall Limbale's comment about the "dirty language" that many expect Dalits to speak.) Earlier in the story, Devi writes that Kuntī has "never tried to learn the language they speak"—perhaps because her life as a queen insulates her from people from lower-caste forest communities, who are, we learn, punished for approaching royals.[22] The Nishada woman responds to Kuntī's surprise at their shared language:

> Yes, I not only understand it but speak it too. Of course, you never thought of us as human, did you? No more than rocks, trees or animals . . . It hurts doesn't it, that a Nishadin [Nishada woman] should call you by name. Yes, I took your name. In the forest you are defenseless, Kunti [Kuntī]. They can't send in their soldiers to punish us.[23]

The Nishada woman's speech conjures an image of these women from the Nishada tribe emerging from the forest in quite a different manner from that in which the "five women" of the previous story do. The women of "Pañcakanyā" move physically from the forest to the court, but in this story, the Nishada women move imaginatively, not physically, away from the "rocks, trees or animals" from which Kuntī is asked to distinguish them. Here, perhaps, Devi suggests that reading characters who embody marginalized identities requires the reader to experience a certain imaginative transformation of her own. Placing lower-caste characters in stories that center on upper-caste characters only goes part of the way toward enlivening those lower-caste characters; readers have to be able to distinguish them from the background in order to individualize them and humanize them.

The space of the forest helps both women suspend traditional hierarchies and interact with one another. During her palace life Kuntī would not encounter, let alone speak with, a Nishada woman. In this case, the

22. Devi, 28.

23. Devi, 40.

forest becomes a space where they can interact as peers, unencumbered by class-related strictures or any male authority figure enforcing the same. In the remainder of the conversation between the two women, the Nishada woman presents Kuntī (and the reader) with a fresh interpretation of a major event in Kuntī's standard storyline, the pregnancy and childbirth that she experiences before she marries Pāṇḍu. Many Mahābhāratas play with the emotional tension that this event creates in the core Mahābhārata narrative. In Devi's work, the character of the Nishada woman offers a new perspective on this moment: she tells Kuntī that instead of being punished, unwed mothers in the *lokavṛtta* are celebrated for being in love and bringing new life to the world.[24] The Nishada woman links this invitation to "new life" with a vision of widowhood that echoes the language of the forest women's account of widowhood in the first story: "The Nishadin said with pride, we don't deny the demands of life. If we are widowed, we have the right to remarry. Those who wish can marry again."[25] Together, the two stories use voices that they attribute to women from lower-caste forest-dwelling communities to separate womanhood from the upper-caste *rājavṛtta*. These non-*rājavṛtta* figures reimagine women's primary responsibility as a call to follow "the demands of life," whether in creating new life (Kuntī's pregnancy) or in finding life after a death (Uttarā's and Kuntī's widowhoods).

Broadly, both stories bring marginalized voices to the forefront. Given that the Sanskrit epic revolves around the lives of upper-caste characters, this volume of stories performs the socially just work of giving voice to figures from marginalized groups that certainly exist in the world of the Sanskrit *Mahābhārata* (different kinds of forest-dwellers, lower-caste individuals, servants) but whose stories the epic leaves largely untold. But the stories in *After Kurukshetra* also share a more specific narrative framework: they tell stories about lower-caste women who reach across caste boundaries to lend emotional support to well-known, upper-caste characters. In both stories, lower-caste women awaken Kuntī and Uttarā to an alternative to the *rājavṛtta* way of life.

This shared feature, however, represents a limitation to the collection's ability to fully enact the literary form of restorative justice that many readers may desire from stories about characters whose social identities mark them as marginalized or oppressed. In each story, the *lokavṛtta* character's principal

24. Devi, 41.

25. Devi, 43.

role is to impart the virtues of *lokavṛtta* culture to the *rājavṛtta* character. The stories suggest too easily that lower-caste cultures are more socially just than royal ones. In the stories, the forest women speak about collective cultures that are romantically idealized. Although these figures make what many readers would consider to be valid critiques of gendered Brahmanical strictures, the reader learns little about these women as individuals.

In this manner, *After Kurukshetra* presents its lower-caste characters with what Spivak describes as "strategic essentialism:" when a group's interests and individual identities are temporarily essentialized in order to serve a larger political interest or goal.[26] Spivak herself shows ambivalence about this move. She notes in an interview that "strategic essentialism" may continue to feed essentialist readings of marginalized people if it is used incorrectly, becoming "a union ticket for essentialism."[27] In the case of Devi's *After Kurukshetra,* a monolithic Other is essentialized for a strategic political intention: to critique hegemony from the margins. The marginal figures themselves function more as instruments of critique than as fully-realized central subjects.

Re-reading Ekalavya in Kiran Nagarkar's *Bedtime Story*

Many contemporary Mahābhāratas valorize the figure of Ekalavya, the Nishada man whose archery skills outpace Arjuna's in a memorable story early in the Sanskrit *Mahābhārata.* In the Sanskrit epic, Ekalavya, the son of a Nishada king (*niṣāda-rājasya sutaḥ*), approaches Droṇa for lessons in archery, but Droṇa, thinking about the fact that Ekalavya is a Nishada (*naiṣādir iti cintayan*), turns him down "out of consideration" (*anvavekṣayā*) for his royal pupils.[28] Ekalavya prostrates at Droṇa's feet, departs, builds a mud statue

26. Gayatri Chakravorty Spivak, "Subaltern Studies. Deconstructing Historiography," in *The Spivak Reader*, eds. Donna Landry and Gerald MacLean (London: Routledge, 1996), 214.

27. Sara Danius, Stefan Jonsson, and Gayatri Chakravorty Spivak, "An Interview with Gayatri Chakravorty Spivak," *Boundary 2* 20, no. 2 (1993): 35.

28. *MBh* 1.123.10–11. All references to the *Mahābhārata* (*MBh*) are to: *The Mahābhārata for the First Time Critically Edited*, ed. V. S. Sukthankar et al. 19 vols. (Poona: Bhandarkar Oriental Research Institute, 1933–66).

of Droṇa, and practices under his symbolic tutelage. His exceptional skills are soon discovered by the Pāṇḍavas. Arjuna, whom Droṇa has promised that no archer will ever surpass,[29] brings Ekalavya to the teacher's notice. The two find Ekalavya: "his body caked with dirt, hair braided, dressed in tatters, bow in hand, ceaselessly shooting arrows."[30] In order to keep his promise to Arjuna, Droṇa makes a "cruel" (*dāruṇa*) demand: Ekalavya's right thumb as *guru-dakṣiṇā*, a formal price for his services as a teacher.[31] Ekalavya slices off his right thumb and presents it to Droṇa "with a happy face and unburdened mind."[32]

Recent reproductions of Ekalavya's story, such as Mahendra Mittal's Hindi comic *Ekalavya* (2016) and A. K. Lomhor's English novella *Eklavya: The Story of an Archer's Loyalty and Devotion* (2015), uphold Ekalavya's sacrifice as an example of masculine strength combined with obeisance. The cover page of Mittal's comic announces: "The complete life of brave archer Ekalavya, a rare example of *guru*-worship and *guru-dakṣiṇā* in history."[33] These retellings frame Ekalavya as exceptional: "exceptional" because Ekalavya demonstrates loyalty to his upper-caste teacher at great personal cost. Modern retellings of the Ekalavya story seldom criticize the fact that in the Sanskrit *Mahābhārata*, Droṇa prevents Ekalavya from sharing space with his upper-caste pupils and then orders him to maim himself.

Kiran Nagarkar's play *Bedtime Story* extends such a critique. The title of the play is a nod to oral storytelling traditions; in the first scene, a grandmother tells her grandson stories from the Mahābhārata to help him sleep.[34] The stories, however, quickly morph into nightmare-inducing scenarios filled with contemporary profanity and politically motivated

---

29. *MBh* 1.123.6.

30. *dadarśa maladigdhāṅgaṃ jaṭilaṃ cīravāsasam |*
ekalavyaṃ dhanuṣpāṇim asyantam aniśaṃ śarān || *MBh* 1.123.30 ||
This is J. A. B. van Buitenen's translation: *The Mahābhārata*, vol. 1, *The Book of the Beginning*, trans. J. A. B. van Buitenen (Chicago: The University of Chicago Press, 1973), 271.

31. *MBh* 1.123.35–36.

32. *MBh* 1.123.37. This is van Buitenen's translation in *Book of the Beginning*, 272.

33. Mahendra Mittal, *Ekalavya* (Delhi: Raja Pocket Books, 2016). This is my own translation.

34. Kiran Nagarkar, *Bedtime Story: A Play* (Delhi: Fourth Estate, 2015), 15–16.

violence. The play's characters include a taunting chorus and a group called "Hell's Angels" that terrorizes the audience. As retributive justice for violence against marginalized people, they gouge out a man's eyes and end the play by gassing the audience to death.[35] The play features provocative scenes that subvert stories from the Mahābhārata and lambast revered modern figures and institutions (Mahatma Gandhi, the Indian Army).

Bedtime Story reimagines several characters and scenes from the Mahābhārata. The episodes that present Ekalavya feature thought-provoking and sympathetic depictions of this character. The first episode, which reimagines the interaction between Ekalavya and Droṇa, connects the story of Ekalavya to the story of modern-day Dalit oppression. When Droṇa confronts Ekalavya for seeking his tutelage without permission, he calls him an untouchable: "A Bhil, a Mahar,[36] a leper. There's no place for subtle distinctions among untouchables."[37] Initially, Ekalavya offers to be his slave and suggests: "Make me do any kind of work. Keep me awake day and night. Make me clean up garbage, leftover, and shit."[38] Ekalavya's words recall the menial work that lower-caste people have been forced to do for centuries.

Yet Nagarkar's Ekalavya also challenges the story that has so often been told about him. When Droṇa demands Ekalavya's right thumb, Ekalavya fashions a thumb out of mud and hands it to him, wryly remarking, "Like guru, like gift."[39] Later in the scene, he warns Arjuna that Droṇa will go on to fight against Arjuna in the Mahābhārata's great war: "Beware the guru who discriminates between one student and another . . . Beware the guru who will betray you in your hour of direst need and join the enemy against you."[40] Nagarkar's Ekalavya resists the dominant reading of Ekalavya as obedient and subservient.

The real violence against Ekalavya comes later, when Nagarkar refigures the image of Ekalavya chopping off his thumb as Ekalavya being castrated

35. Nagarkar, 58, 96.

36. Bhils are an indigenous people from northwest India, while Mahars are a marginalized group from the state of Maharashtra in western India. Noted politician and social reformer B. R. Ambedkar (who also led the drafting of the constitution of India) belonged to this community.

37. Nagarkar, *Bedtime Story*, 19.

38. Nagarkar, 31.

39. Nagarkar, 30.

40. Nagakar, 31.

by an angry mob. In this scene, the characters are placed outside of mythic time: Ekalavya and Arjuna are medical students in modern-day India. Nagarkar develops the contrast between Ekalavya's famous martyrdom and Arjuna's privileged position under Droṇa's wing into a vivid and unforgiving depiction of anti-Dalit violence. The scene begins with Ekalavya and Arjuna as friends: Arjuna, caught having premarital sex with his fiancée, Draupadī, is being chased by her brothers and family members; to help protect Arjuna from the men, Ekalavya plans to hide him in the Mahar colony because, as he says, "nobody will dream of looking for you there."[41] His line highlights the reality that many modern Indian cities are still segregated based on caste. The mob nevertheless finds the two young men, turns on Ekalavya, and, representing a move that dominant cultural groups historically and globally use to maintain their positions of racial, social, and patriarchal privilege, accuse him of raping one of "their" women (in this case, of raping Draupadī, who, in the Mahābhārata, is sexually threatened more often by members of her own social class than by strangers): "You think you can step off the dunghill on which you were born, come into our town and rape our women?"[42] At the end of the scene, the crowd gags Ekalavya and castrates him. By representing the story of Ekalavya's thumb as a scene of castration, Nagarkar imagines Ekalavya's famous act not as a gesture of self-sacrifice but as a symbol of the brutal oppression of individuals from lower castes. This scene from *Bedtime Story* erases the idea of willing victimhood from the standard account of Ekalavya.

At the same time, the play preserves an idea that runs throughout the Sanskrit *Mahābhārata*'s version of the Ekalavya story, namely, that the Ekalavya character displays an unusual level of loyalty or trust toward people and ideas that eventually betray him. While Nagarkar's Ekalavya mistrusts Droṇa early on, he continues to demonstrate a certain belief in Arjuna's goodness even after his castration: when Ekalavya is ungagged, he calls out to Arjuna; Arjuna shakes his head and leaves with the others.[43] A different kind of betrayal occurs earlier in the drama, when Ekalavya entrusts Arjuna with the story of how he decided to pursue medicine:

41. Nagakar, 22.

42. Nagakar, 24.

43. Nagakar, 25.

> In my village, when an old cow or an ox died, someone would come over and holler to one of us untouchables, "Hey you, come and collect the carcass." I was seven when my mother got food poisoning eating such a cow. She vomited for two days and I settled down patiently, waiting for her to die. Somebody got hold of a doctor from the Christian mission. She lived. So did the doctor, in my heart.[44]

But Arjuna mocks this disclosure. He tells Ekalavya to "save this story for [his] autobiography," a reference to how the genre of autobiography has been one of the few ways for Dalit writers to enter the literary market in modern India.[45]

Bedtime Story parallels these personal betrayals with broader ideological ones. At a certain point, Ekalavya shares a belief in his upward social mobility: "Without me, my people will remain Mahars. Someone has to start a new generation."[46] The irony of this expression becomes clear when Ekalavya's castration prevents him from starting this "new generation." Later, during the castration scene, Draupadī's father reads Ekalavya's upward social mobility through the lens of the fraught history of caste politics and religious conversion in twentieth-century India:

> First it was that Mahatma Gandhi who filled their heads with ideas. Then came our spineless government, reserving all the best jobs for them. They're Mahars when it suits them. Otherwise they're Neo-Buddhists[47] . . . the bastards.[48]

---

44. Nagakar, 23.

45. Sarah Beth has shown that the autobiography has been a way for Dalit writers such as Omprakash Valmiki and Surajpal Chauhan to reclaim subjecthood in the literary and public sphere. See "Hindi Dalit Autobiography: An Exploration of Identity," *Modern Asian Studies* 41, no. 3 (2007): 545–74.

46. Nagarkar, *Bedtime Story,* 24.

47. Scholars such Raj Kumar Hans have written about Dalit people converting in large numbers to religions such as Buddhism, Sikhism, Islam, and Christianity to distance themselves from the oppression of mainstream Hinduism. B. R. Ambedkar converted to Buddhism in 1935, prompting many of his followers to do the same. See "Making Sense of Dalit Sikh History" in *Dalit Studies*. eds. Ramnarayan S. Rawat and K. Satyanarayana (Durham, NC: Duke University Press, 2016), 132.

48. Nagarkar, *Bedtime Story,* 25.

This accusation references the positive discrimination measures for historically disadvantaged groups—essentially the Indian version of affirmative action.[49] Dominant social groups, whose views Nagarkar uses Draupadī's father to voice, see reservations of government jobs (and positive discrimination measures in general) as a "reverse" discriminatory practice against them. Draupadī's father's line parrots the idea that by enraging individuals from dominant social groups even further, state measures to combat historical discrimination have actually *contributed* to violence against Dalit people. In rebuttal of this argument, Rupa Viswanath writes that upper-caste critics of the Dalit movement are in fact using positive discrimination as a new way to undermine Dalit self-determination. High-caste critics, Viswanath explains, insist that Dalits misuse reservations and play up "identity politics." Draupadī's father invokes this rhetoric when he accuses Dalits of being "Mahars when it suits them. Otherwise they're Neo-Buddhists." The angry mob claims that Ekalavya is taking unfair advantage of the system. As Viswanath points out, this kind of criticism detracts from Dalit activists' true intention, which is to ensure that the existing laws are rightly enforced.[50]

Although Nagarkar provides a sobering reminder of caste-based violence in this scene, modern Ekalavya's idealism—his dreams of upward mobility, his commitments to Arjuna despite Arjuna's untrustworthiness—also casts him as an exceptional marginalized character. In comparison, the re-imagined ancient Ekalavya who presents Droṇa with a mud thumb in the previous scene is more insurgent, though he, too, wisely predicts the future for the Pāṇḍavas. Like Mahasweta's characters, these Ekalavyas exist largely to enlighten their upper-caste counterparts. Nevertheless, the issues they highlight in the process are both current and controversial.

In the four decades since it was written, *Bedtime Story* has faced its own set of criticisms from the very kinds of conservative Hindus whose views Nagarkar incorporates into those of Draupadī's male relatives. Nagarkar had written the play in 1977 as both a political response to the Emergency[51] and

49. Several scholars have compared issues of discrimination based on race in America with those based on caste in India. For example, see Gyanendra Pandey, *A History of Prejudice: Race, Caste, and Difference in India and the United States* (Cambridge: Cambridge University Press, 2013).

50. Rupa Viswanath. *The Pariah Problem: Caste, Religion, and the Social in Modern India* (New York: Columbia University Press, 2014), 257.

51. The declaration of the Indian Emergency lasted twenty-one months between 1975 and 1977. Indira Gandhi, then prime minister of India, recommended that

a personal response to the "loss of naiveté" that he experienced after finding both journalism and academia lacking in integrity.[52] In the preface to the 2015 edition of the play, Nagarkar explains that even though stage directors (such as Shreeram Lagoo) had tried to generate interest in a production of the play shortly after Nagarkar had completed the work in 1978, several Hindu right-wing groups had worked to dismantle those efforts because they thought that the play was denigrating Hinduism. They threatened *Bedtime Story*'s writer, producer, director, and actors, bringing any efforts to stage it to a halt. ("None of these vociferous guardians of our culture had ever read [the play]," Nagarkar notes.[53]) In 1978, the play's script was sent to the Maharashtra Censor Board, who ordered seventy-eight cuts; the Board's criticisms ranged from ordering the author "[to remove from the play] the names of Buddha, Mahatma Gandhi" to accusing him of "distorting the original myths."[54] The play was finally staged in Mumbai in 1995 by the theatre group Abhivyakti and later by Vasant Nath in Cambridge in the UK and at the Edinburgh Fringe festival in Scotland. It would take another twenty years for the play to be published.

Press surrounding the release of *Bedtime Story* in 2015 suggests that the biggest factor in catalyzing the play's recent publication is a new generation of readers: those who read primarily in English and are unlikely to be aware of the play's counterparts in Marathi and Hindi literature.[55] These counterparts include Irawati Karve's Marathi study *Yugānta* ("The End of an Age," 1968), Vishnu Sakharam Khandekar's Marathi novel *Yayāti* (1978),

---

the president, Fakhruddin Ali Ahmed, declare a state of emergency in the country, granting her rule of decree. During the Emergency, civil liberties were suspended, curfew was applied, and leaders of the opposition were arrested. The chaos of the Emergency caused many people, including Nagarkar, to fear the decline of democracy and secularism in India.

52. Nagakar, *Bedtime Story*, 3.

53. Nagakar, 7.

54. Nagarkar, 6.

55. See Salil Tripathi, "When Kiran Nagarkar Said the Unsayable," *Live Mint*, February 28, 2015, http://www.livemint.com/Leisure/2izXvQjOpQm0hFGPz0vdIK/When-Kiran-Nagarkar-said-the-unsayable.html; and Ankush Arora, "Mahabharata Retold, with a Twist from Writer Kiran Nagarkar." *Reuters,* March 17, 2015, http://blogs.reuters.com/india/2015/03/17/mahabharata-retold-with-a-twist-from-writer-kiran-nagarkar/

Dharamvir Bharati's Hindi play *Andhā Yug* ("The Blind Age," 1954), and Mohan Rakesh's Hindi play *Ādhe Adhure* ("Half Incomplete," 1969).[56] In some ways, the publication of *Bedtime Story* today indicates that while the ideological dynamics of caste-based violence that this adaptation brings to light may be ever-present, a new crop of readers is eager to use the social and political realities of contemporary India to interrogate the perfection of an imagined Hindu past.

Conclusion: Writers from the Mahābhārata's Margins?

In the preface to *Bedtime Story*, Nagarkar makes a comment that seems to contradict his play's critique of the ways in which Mahābhāratas can be socially exclusive. He writes that there is a way in which the Mahābhārata is universal: "[The] Mahabharata is a living epic in the subcontinent. It's in the bloodstream of almost every Indian—Hindu, Muslim, Christian or Buddhist."[57] Nagarkar's idea of a universal Mahābhārata begs us to ask: How are writers and readers from marginalized groups forming their own relationships with the Mahābhārata? Devi and Nagarkar envision the intersection of the Mahābhārata with the experiences of lower-caste individuals in detail, but their works are written for (and produced by) individuals who belong to communities that are, by basic measures of education and wealth, elite. What about Mahābhāratas that are produced by and for individuals from marginalized groups?

A glance at the representations of the Ekalavya-Droṇa interaction by Dalit authors shows that their Ekalavyas are often more resistant and insurgent than the idealistic and noble Ekalavyas that writers such as Nagarkar and Mittal present. For instance, in the poem "Eklavyan" (2006), Meena Kandasamy, a Tamil Dalit poet who writes in English, urges Ekalavya to

56. For English translations of these works, see Irawati K. Karve, *Yugānta: The End of an Epoch* (Poona: Deshmukh Prakashan, 1969); Vishnu Sakharam Khandekar, *Yayati: A Classical Tale of Lust*, trans. Y. P. Kulkarni (Delhi: Orient Paperbacks, 2009); Dharamvir Bharathi, *Andha Yug*, trans. Alok Bhalla (Delhi: Oxford University Press, 2010); and Mohan Rakesh, *Halfway House*, trans. Bindu Batra, ed. Dilip K. Basu (Delhi: Worldview Publications, 1999).

57. Nagarkar, *Bedtime Story*, 4.

disregard the loss of his right thumb and prompts him to further militant action against "fascist Dronacharyas" with weapons of modern warfare: "you don't need your right thumb/to pull a trigger or hurl a bomb."[58] Similarly, Dalit author Omprakash Valmiki's seminal Hindi autobiography *Jūṭhan* ("Leftovers," 1997) illumines the modern difficulties of Dalit life by conversing with the epic imaginary. Valmiki recalls asking an upper-caste teacher why his community's lives are not documented in the epic. He points out that the teacher romanticizes Droṇa's poverty while ignoring similar problems Dalit people face. Angered that the Dalit student dares to see himself as an equal to Droṇa, the teacher "write[s] an epic on [his] body" by caning him.[59] Valmiki's autobiography reminds us of the ways in which seemingly innocent storytelling can be complicit in oppression and violence.

The variety of approaches to epic stories and characters by elite and Dalit writers reveals a continued interest in engaging with grand narratives such as the Mahābhārata. These writers and their subjects rarely share the same orientation toward the Mahābhārata, even if they share the same goals of social justice. Where elite writers such as Devi and Nagarkar use the narrative framework of the Mahābhārata to present marginalized individuals idealistically but purposefully, Dalit writers such as Illaiah, Valmiki, and Kandasamy use their own artistic talents to subvert, challenge, or even reject the epic narrative entirely. In this way, the Mahābhārata acts as a meaningful point of departure for a multivalent dialogue on the realities of caste-based injustice in modern India.

58. Meena Kandasamy, "The Flight of Birds," *Indian Literature* 50, no. 4 (2006): 99.

59. Omprakash Valmiki, *Joothan: A Dalit's Life*, trans. Arun Prabha Mukherjee (New York: Columbia University Press, 2003), 26–27.

Chapter Eighteen

A Long Time Ago in a Galaxy Far, Far Away

The Mahābhārata as Dystopian Future

Philip Lutgendorf

Episode IV: On the Absent Presence of Indian Science Fiction[1]

Before turning to this essay's principal subject—the recent appearance of three Mahābhārata tales as innovative Indian graphic novels set in a future interstellar civilization—I will consider the international literary and entertainment genre that these works inevitably invoke, and which has a distinct and culture-specific history that has generally not included the subcontinent of South Asia. By speculating on why this has been the case, I introduce themes to which I will return in my concluding section.

In the course of roughly four decades of academic engagement with various genres and mediated forms of modern South Asian popular culture, I have periodically pondered the striking absence of a genre that has

1. In my numbering of sections in this essay, I allude (as many readers will recognize) to the original trilogy of *Star Wars* films, whose epigram my title parodies and which I further discuss later in this section.

been extremely popular throughout the West during roughly the same period: science fiction. This absence has seemed especially notable to me in mainstream cinema, the dominant segment of which—Hindi-language films produced in Bombay (now Mumbai) and internationally branded for several decades as "Bollywood"—has otherwise been not only exceptionally prolific in its output but also notably aggressive in advancing a narrative and visual style that can appropriately be termed "surreal," that often freely mixes fantasy with realism, and that is well aware of and not averse to borrowing from popular Anglo-European films, especially those of Hollywood. In my critical engagement with a substantial number of films,[2] I have noted the use, by both the industry and its audiences, of genre labels such as "mythological," "historical," "crime thriller," "stunt film," and (the dominant genre since the 1940s) "the social," as well as stylistic designations invoked by critics and promoters, such as the "multi-starrer" and "*masālā*" film (the latter referring, in fact, to Hindi cinema's penchant for mixing standard international genre categories to produce a "spicy" blend of plot twists and emotional moods)—yet there has never been a category label for the "science fiction" (SF) film.[3] The apparent exceptions to this rule (for in India all rules have exceptions) are a very small number of movies that invoke SF imagery and conventions—such as the little-known 1967 film *Vahāṃ ke Log* ("Aliens," or, more literally, "The People From Over There"), which featured flying saucers hovering above Delhi's Jama Masjid mosque and an attack by apparent extraterrestrials. (In the end, though, the space-suited invaders proved to be from a hostile "neighboring country," and in fact appeared to be Chinese, doubtless alluding to their invasion of India five years earlier.) A full twenty years later, the more successful *Mr. India* (1987; remarkably, the versatile Shekhar Kapur cut his directorial teeth on this *masālā* potboiler) featured a bumbling violin teacher who stumbled upon an "invisibility bracelet," disguised as a wristwatch and invented by his deceased scientist father, which eventually allowed him (with the help of a golden statue of the Hindu monkey god, Hanumān, and a beautiful

2. See Philip Lutgendorf, "Notes on Indian Popular Cinema," accessed April 2018, https://uiowa.edu/indiancinema/; and Philip Lutgendorf, "Is There an Indian Way of Filmmaking?" *International Journal of Hindu Studies* 10, no. 3 (2006): 227–56.

3. Hereafter, I will use the acronym "SF," which is favored by Brooks Landon in his influential study *Science Fiction After 1900: From the Steam Man to the Stars* (New York: Routledge, 2002), xv.

young female reporter) to defeat Mogambo, a sadistic dictator planning to launch rocket attacks on Indian cities from his island stronghold.[4] Both of these films invoked visual conventions common in SF genre films internationally (such as hovering spacecraft and futuristic "control centers" with banks of flashing lights) and made modest use of the special effects possible in their day. It is notable, however, that neither film's narrative was set in the future—a point to which I shall soon return.

Science fiction is slightly better represented in modern Indian literature, with a smattering of stories and novels dating back to the late nineteenth century, and a modest output (and small but enthusiastic audiences of readers) during the twentieth century in some regional languages, especially Bengali, Marathi, and Tamil.[5] But there has never been anything like the vast output of popular SF characteristic of its so-called "golden age" in the United States (1930s–50s), epitomized by magazines like *Amazing Stories*, and also by films, television serials, and bestselling novels by writers such as Isaac Asimov, Arthur C. Clarke, and Robert Heinlein. This enormous and continuously evolving literature (now represented internationally as well) has allowed for the creative exploration of a great range of themes. Yet as one notable survey succinctly summarizes in its opening sentence, "Science fiction is the literature of change"[6]; that is, it is a branch of storytelling that embraces an ideology and mise-en-scène of (especially) technological advancement, which may be utopian and desirable, or (and this is especially characteristic of works produced after the Second World War) dystopian,

4. Sami Ahmad Khan, "Bollywood's Encounters with the Third Kind: A Critical Catalogue of Hindi Science Fiction Films," in *Bollywood and Its Others: Towards New Configurations*, eds. Sarwal Kishore and P. P. Patraj (Basingstoke: Palgrave Macmillan, 2014), 189–91.

5. For a survey of this literature (much of which dates to the final decades of the twentieth century and the beginning of the twenty-first), see *Muse India* 61 (May–June 2015), which is devoted to the topic. A pioneering work in the genre was the novel *Sultana's Dream* (1905), written in English by a Bengali woman, Rokeya Sakhawat Hossein, which depicted a futuristic feminist utopia of automated farms and flying cars, and in which patriarchal gender roles were reversed; see *Sultana's Dream, A Feminist Utopia and Selections from "The Secluded Ones."* (New York City: Feminist Press at CUNY, 1988).

6. Landon, *Science Fiction,* xi. Note also Landon's "working definition of SF" on page 31: "Science fiction is the literature that considers the impact of science and technology on humanity."

threatening, and even apocalyptic.[7] Given its sheer volume and breadth in the West, it has been called "the main literary tradition of the twentieth century,"[8] and (given its penetration of popular cultural forms, including television, cinema, comic books, and computer games) "the first truly multimedia genre."[9] Although, like all genre labels, "SF" gestures toward a loose set of audience expectations, not all of its practitioners and scholars are comfortable with the term. The celebrated author Robert Heinlein so disliked it that he preferred to label his work "speculative fiction," a term (conveniently reducible to the same acronym) that is now preferred by some academic scholars of the genre as well. Dubbed "the literature of the possible,"[10] this label encompasses works that may blur genre categories by, for example, incorporating features of "fantasy" fiction—a Western genre heavily indebted to Arthurian and Norse legend. Contrasting such "speculative fiction" to what he considers mainstream sci-fi, Brooks Landon observes that the former relies on "concepts [that] are anything but unfamiliar, drawing as they do on thousands of years of myth and superstition."[11]

Indeed, "speculative fiction" of a religio-mythical sort has an ancient South Asian pedigree, for this label might well be applied to the entire Sanskrit epic and *purāṇic* corpus as well as to its countless avatars in regional languages. This is a literature that prominently evokes (among other aesthetic moods) *adbhuta-rasa*, a term that emerges from the early Sanskrit literary theoretical corpus and that corresponds to (what Landon terms) "the sense of wonder so often identified as one of the most important aspects of SF."[12] In reading the Sanskrit *Mahābhārata*, for example, I have often been struck by its hyperbolic surrealism and "Cinemascope" special effects (albeit linguistically conveyed), as in the episode of the divine eagle Garuḍa's theft of the elixir of immortality in the *Ādiparvan* ("The Book of Beginnings"), or Kṛṣṇa's battle with the flying fortress of Saubha in the *Vanaparvan* ("The

7. Landon, xiii–xiv.

8. The phrase is attributed to sci-fi writer J. G. Ballard, but its source is not identified; quoted in Landon, xvii.

9. Landon, xiv, xvii.

10. Landon, 38.

11. Landon, xviii.

12. Landon, 18.

Book of the Forest," also known as the *Āraṇyakaparvan*). There is even a kind of dystopian futurism, epitomized by the sage Mārkaṇḍeya's account, in the same sub-book, of the *kali-yuga*—the fourth and most degraded epoch of cosmic time—although this dismal future, toward which the events of the epic are understood to be inexorably propelling the world, is also simultaneously the past of an ever-recurring cycle. With the advent of print technology in the nineteenth century, such literature began to circulate even more widely. It acquired additional traction in the early twentieth century, when tales of ancient epic and *purāṇic* heroes, often drawn from the Mahābhārata corpus but generally cast in a utopian or triumphalist mode, sometimes enabled authors to circumvent British colonial censorship policies and to produce, under the guise of "religious" narrative, veiled allegories of the anti-colonial struggle.[13] Interestingly, the same epic, now interpreted in the darker and more dystopian vein to which it so readily lends itself, became, in the post-Independence period, a favored source for playwrights and directors who crafted critiques of the failings of the new democratic regime—as in Dharamvir Bharati's famous Hindi drama *Andhā Yug* ("Blind Epoch," 1954).[14] I must also mention the contemporaneous flourishing of the Indo-Islamicate romance, which contained many of the same fantastical tropes (albeit transposed to a world of caliphs, jinns, and *parīs*, or female fairies) and which easily transitioned from the oral tales of Persian and Urdu-speaking storytellers (*dastān-goī*) and the illuminated manuscripts relished by the Mughal elite, to copious printed works such as the *Dāstān-e Amīr 'Hamza,* issued in forty-six enormous volumes by a press in Lucknow between 1883 and 1905.[15] The enduring popularity of such indigenous and traditional "speculative fiction"—which has assumed modern avatars through printed chap-books and graphic novels, feature films, television serials, animated cartoons, and newer digital media—suggests that such

---

13. See Pamela Lothspeich, *Epic Nation: Reimagining the Mahabharata in the Age of Empire* (Delhi: Oxford University Press, 2009).

14. See Aparna Bhargava Dharwadker, *Theatres of Independence: Drama, Theory, and Urban Performance in India since 1947* (Iowa City: University of Iowa Press, 2005), 186–203.

15. See Frances Pritchett, *The Romance Tradition in Urdu: Adventures from the Dāstān of Amīr 'Hamzah* (New York: Columbia University Press, 1991), 27.

traditional mythological and romance storytelling has largely occupied the niche for South Asian audiences that science fiction has, in modern times, arisen to fill in many other parts of the world. Indeed, it is worth noting here that Indian "mythological" films and TV serials have routinely used special effects that are comparable to those found in Western SF movies to depict such phenomena as flight (by individuals and aerial chariots), the teleportation of objects, and ray gun-like "divine weapons" (*divyāstras*) that streak across the sky to wreak destruction on enemies. The key difference, of course, was that the belief system that rendered such phenomena "possible" for Indian viewers was grounded in acceptance of the existence of divine and occult powers—which played a similar facilitating role to that of the discourse of a speculative "science" or futurism in the West.

Why did "speculative fiction" in South Asia long prefer, as a narrative strategy for mass entertainment, a timeless mythological realm or an immemorial and lost "golden age" to a scientifically-advanced future? Several explanations come readily to mind. Perhaps the most obvious is the fact of the enduring vitality of classical mythic and epic narrative on the subcontinent, kept alive (as so much scholarship of the past half century has emphasized) through several millennia via numerous oral and theatrical performance genres as well as through constant creative reiteration by literary authors. In short, mythology never died in South Asia; on the contrary, it remained alive, kicking, and ready to be reinterpreted to suit contemporary needs. By contrast, Western audiences, for whom classical mythology appeared to be dead and frozen, needed a new set of speculative tropes to satisfy their hunger for "possibility"—indeed, Landon characterizes Western SF as "in the process of creating myths grounded in science and technology."[16]

A second explanation lies in the concept of cyclical time, which is common to all the indigenous religious traditions of the subcontinent, and to which I have already alluded. The concept of recurring *yuga*s or "ages" and *kalpa*s (complete cycles of four ages) tended to short-circuit any teleology of change-as-progress by asserting that the most utopian epochs lay in the distant past and that subsequent world history was a sordid saga of continuous loss and decline.[17] Stock representations of the magical "technol-

16. Landon, *Science Fiction,* xviii.

17. On the development of *yuga* theory with particular reference to the *Mahābhārata*, see Luis Gonzalez-Reimann, *The Mahābhārata and the Yugas: India's Great Epic Poem and the Hindu System of World Ages* (New York: Peter Lang, 2002).

ogy" of lost *yugas* (such as the flying chariots and divine weapons already mentioned) contributed to the ease with which traditional chronology could be adapted to the newer iterations of the kind of home-grown "speculative fiction" I have been discussing.

But there is, I believe, a third explanation that is equally if not more compelling. It reflects the long shadow of a dominant colonial-era discourse that claimed the realm of science and technology as the monopoly of the West, especially of Great Britain. India was portrayed as backward and degenerate, incapable of catching up. Yet so-called Indological scholars simultaneously glorified its culture as a living museum of the archaic, and the subcontinent's pre-Islamic past as a "golden age" of high civilization. Nationalist discourse responded with an indigenized reverse-image of SF as it developed in the nineteenth- and twentieth-century West. Instead of looking ahead to a technologically advanced future, Indian speculative fiction situated "science" in a hyper-advanced past, with flying chariots and palatial carriages (*rathas* and *vimānas*) as mechanized airships and "divine weapons" (*divyāstras*) as incendiary (and, in time, atomic) bombs and missiles, and so forth. For Indian storytellers of the colonial and immediate post-colonial periods, an Indian techno-futurism (further discouraged by Gandhian Luddite austerity and Nehruvian socialist ideology) was difficult to imagine. The future, one might say, had already been colonized; the past, however, remained available for imaginative conquest.

This trend continues in the twenty-first century and is exemplified by literary works such as Amish Tripathi's extraordinarily popular "Shiva Trilogy" of fantasy novels (2010–13), which are set in an imagined "Meluhan" (Harappan) super-civilization, and also by such cinematic blockbusters as the two quasi-mythic *Bāhubalī* films (2015, 2017), now boasting of "world-class" CGI (computer-generated imagery). The mise-en-scène of both of these franchises suggests a neo-Fascist Hindutva ideology of a supposedly Aryan past in which Sanskrit-speaking "gods" populate the Indus Valley, and hyper-muscular heroes conquer the world beneath saffron banners. It is therefore no surprise that ministers of India's current Hindu-nationalist BJP government regularly assert that such marvels as the Rāmāyaṇa's flying fortress, the *puṣpaka*, are proof of the extraordinary achievements of technology in ancient India.[18]

18. See, for example, "Teach IIT Students About 'Pushpak Viman,'" *Outlook*, September 20, 2017, https://www.outlookindia.com/website/story/teach-iit-students-about-pushpak-viman-tell-them-about-indian-who-invented-plane/301966.

And yet, SF—which is to say, *science* fiction of a futuristic sort—has recently begun to take root in India, and the remainder of this essay will consider several literary and cinematic examples of it, all dating from after 1990, beginning with a Mahābhārata-inspired trilogy of graphic novels. What cultural trends enabled this turn toward a (now accessible) techno-future? George Lucas' original *Star Wars* film trilogy (1977, 1980, 1983)—the narrative premise of which I have already alluded to in my main and section titles—was, I suspect, one game-changer. Although the trilogy was not widely viewed in Indian cinema halls, its phenomenal and lasting popularity in the West came to have such an impact on the visual aesthetic of other films, novels, and video games during the last quarter of the twentieth century that it doubtless influenced several Indian artists. In its mythic ambitions, the trilogy's narrative of intergalactic struggle echoes certain themes and motifs of the Rāmāyaṇa, the story of which was reportedly told to director Lucas by comparative mythographer Joseph Campbell. In its pessimism about sovereignty—which it represents with an empire that has succumbed to the "dark side" of the Force that nurtures the cosmos—and its focus on fallen anti-heroes, the *Star Wars* trilogy resonates with the themes and motifs of the Mahābhārata. Moreover, its visual aesthetic eschewed some of the glossy futurism of earlier "space-operas" (from *Flash Gordon* to *Star Trek*) in favor of a somewhat shabbier future that was also already past (as epitomized in the series epigram, from which I have taken my title). The films evoke this past with neo-medieval tunics, robes, and helmets, with light-sabers that behave like swords, and with futuristic gadgetry that is simultaneously *jugāḍ* ("makeshift"—a beloved Hindi word applied to scrappy Indian improvisation), such as Han Solo's dilapidated spaceship, the *Millennium Falcon*, which somehow just manages to achieve light speed, or the obsolete-but-resourceful robots R2-D2 and C-3PO. If *Star Wars* contributed to the mainstreaming of SF in the West, it may also, for certain South Asian artists, have represented an aesthetic *setu* (bridge or causeway) capable of connecting timeless epic narrative with new realms of technological and consumer possibility that were opened up, for the burgeoning Indian middle classes, after the economic liberalization that began in 1990. During the same period, Indian success in one particular branch of technology—IT (information technology)—lent new confidence to futurist imaginings, as well as new, slick, and world-class imagery to their literary and cinematic avatars, such as the SF-influenced works I will examine in the next two sections of this essay.

Episode V: *The Kaurava Empire* Trilogy[19]

Campfire Graphic Novels, a series begun in 2007 as a division of Kalyani Navyug Media publishers and marketed in the United States by Random House, seeks to produce "books [that] are well researched, captivatingly illustrated, wonderfully written, and beautifully produced."[20] Their extensive catalog now includes the categories of Classics, Heroes (featuring historical figures such as Abraham Lincoln, M. K. Gandhi, and Martin Luther King Jr.), Mythology, Originals (new stories and characters), and History. The term "comics" or "comic books" is never used in their publicity materials, however, and even a glance at any of their books is enough to reveal that they are decidedly not (so to say) your grandfather's *Amar Chitra Katha*—the immense and popular Indian comic book series that began in 1967.[21] Campfire books typically run to one hundred or more pages, are produced on heavy paper stock, offer substantially more text on their pages (allowing for more complex plotting and character development), are aimed at a higher reading level, and feature an overall layout and quality of illustration that reflects international standards of graphic novel design. For example, in the Campfire catalog's mythology category, *Draupadi, the Fire-Born Princess* (2013) recapitulates the Sanskrit *Mahābhārata* narrative in considerable detail through the voice of its heroine. Interestingly, the story is framed as a flashback unfolding in the mind of the princess as she lies in the snow, freezing to death, having fallen during the Pāṇḍavas' final journey into the Himalayas—ultimately to be comforted, in its last pages, by Bhīma, who turns back to express his deep and abiding love for her. This narrative framing evidently draws (albeit without citation) on Irawati

---

19. I would like to express my warm thanks to Girija Jhunjhunwala, publisher of Campfire Graphic Novels, and to the company's marketing director, Sahadi Sharma, for generously supplying me with books and for permitting me to interview them in January 2017. I also thank artist Sachin Nagar, whom I interviewed (through Ms. Sharma's facilitation) in July 2017.

20. Campfire Graphic Novels, "Campfire Graphic Novels," accessed April 2018, http://www.campfiregraphicnovels.com.

21. On the history of this series, see Frances W. Pritchett, "The World of *Amar Chitra Katha*," in *Media and the Transformation of Religion in South Asia*, eds. Lawrence A. Babb and Susan S. Wadley (Philadelphia: University of Pennsylvania Press, 1995), 76–106; and Karline McLain, *India's Immortal Comic Books: Gods, Kings, and Other Heroes* (Bloomington: Indiana University Press, 2009).

Figure 18.1 The cover of *The Kaurava Empire*, Vol. 1: *Abhimanyu and the Conquest of the Chakravyuha*, 2014. *Source*: Campfire Graphic Novels, Kalyani. Navyug Media. Used with permission.

Karve's innovative meditation on Draupadī in her classic collection of essays on the epic, *Yugānta: The End of an Epoch* (1969).[22]

In 2014–2015, Campfire issued a series of three volumes titled *The Kaurava Empire*: "Abhimanyu and the Chakravyuha" (Vol. 1); "The Vengeance of Ashwatthama" (Vol. 2); and "The Loaded Dice of Shakuni" (Vol. 3).[23] The series reimagines the Mahābhārata war in the setting of an intergalactic empire during an unspecified future eon. Despite the common setting and shared imagery of the three volumes, each was intended (like *Draupadi, the Fire-Born Princess*) to serve as a stand-alone book, recapitulating much of the epic's so-called main story with a focus on a single character or episode—and with a particular sympathy (noted in the books' afterwords) for the losing side in the war, and hence for themes of tragedy and revenge, which are hardly unknown to the Mahābhārata tradition at large.

All three represented the collaboration of the same author and illustrator: Jason Quinn and Sachin Nagar, respectively. Quinn came to Delhi in 2013 from England, where he had once worked as a writer for Marvel Comics UK, to become Creative Content Head at Campfire, a position he held until 2015, when he returned to the UK. While in India, Quinn became fascinated by Hindu mythology and particularly by the Mahābhārata, which seemed to him especially adaptable to the format and conventions of graphic novels. Nagar is a versatile Delhi-based illustrator who had worked as a freelancer designing video games for the international market before taking a (likewise brief) staff position at Campfire; he subsequently returned to freelance work, though he continued to undertake additional assignments for Campfire. The stylistic range of his artistry—which Nagar achieves through hand-done illustration that is then colored and enhanced by computer—may be glimpsed by comparing the *Kaurava* series, with its vast cosmic setting and luminous, nebula-like color washes, with Nagar's grittier, sepia-toned illustrations for *Gandhi: My Life Is My Message* (2014; also written by Quinn, and drawing extensively on Gandhi's 1925–29

22. Irawati Karve, *Yugānta: The End of an Epoch* (Poona: Deshmukh Prakashan, 1969), 101–105. Other Campfire titles do often include a postscript by the author, which sometimes cites literary sources.

23. Please note that while I transliterate characters' names according to the International Alphabet of Sanskrit Transliteration (IAST) (e.g., Aśvatthāman) in this essay, the graphic novels of Quinn and Nagar use more common Indian English spelling of characters' names (e.g., Ashwatthama).

Autobiography), and also with his sunnier and more animé-like *Sundarkaand: Triumph of Hanuman* (2013, in collaboration with the writer Shyam Prakash), an adaptation of the beloved fifth sub-book of Tulsīdās' Avadhi *Rāmcaritmānas* (ca. 1574 CE).

The second book in the *Kaurava Empire* series, "The Vengeance of Ashwatthama," opens with a frame story set in a still more remote future, several thousand years after the Bhārata war has ended. Following a crash landing on a desolate "frontier" planet, a stranded female "sector governor" of a galaxy is saved from cut-throat bandits by a brooding, almost feral warrior with a bloody wound on his forehead. As the two wait for her to be rescued, the governor's strange companion asks her to listen to his story, revealing (to her astonishment) that he knew the legendary Pāṇḍavas and Kauravas and participated in the ancient Armageddon of cosmic civil war. Aśvatthāman's life then unfolds in flashback, following the outline of the central Mahābhārata story, but with a focus on the tale of Droṇa's falling-out with King Drupada, which leads the former friends fatefully to seek revenge on one another. Aśvatthāman himself grows up with friendly feelings toward both the Kauravas and their fatherless cousins, the Pāṇḍavas, and hence experiences an ambivalent sense of loyalty to the empire when (following the fateful dice match and the Pāṇḍavas' humiliation and exile) civil war erupts. The young man has a similarly ambivalent relationship with his own father and *guru*—for though he adores him, he is always conscious of his father's preference for Arjuna, Droṇa's most prodigious pupil. We repeatedly glimpse Aśvatthāman's jealousy, his pain at not being his own father's favorite, and his unsuccessful efforts to win Droṇa's love and approval.[24]

Though he is ultimately obliged to join his father on the Kaurava side in the battle, Aśvatthāman continues to have ambivalent feelings about the war and sympathy for the Pāṇḍavas—until his father's gruesome murder at the hands of Dhṛṣṭadyumna, who violates warrior dharma. This event, of course, ultimately pushes Aśvatthāman to commit the horrific massacre of the Sanskrit epic's *Sauptikaparvan* ("The Book of the Night Massacre")—the slaughter of the young survivors of Kurukṣetra—which is the climax of the graphic novel.[25] Then, after facing off with Arjuna and being cursed

24. Jason Quinn and Sachin Nagar, *The Kaurava Empire*, vol. 2, *The Vengeance of Ashwatthama* (Delhi: Kalyani Navyug Media, 2015), 32–33.

25. On this episode in the Sanskrit epic, see Robert Goldman's chapter in this volume.

Figure 18.2. Aśvatthāman's listener refuses to condone his crime. *The Kaurava Empire, Vol. 2: The Vengeance of Ashwatthama. Source*: Campfire Graphic Novels, Kalyani. Navyug Media. Used with permission.

by Kṛṣṇa, Aśvatthāman wanders the universe seeking to tell his story and expiate his crime—though, in the final panels, which return us to the frame story, his horrified listener can only confirm Kṛṣṇa's verdict and abandon him to his lonely fate.

As a contemporary contribution to Mahābhārata storytelling, *The Kaurava Empire* series has real interpretive merits. Its narratives are ingeniously and thoughtfully constructed: they accord with both a futuristic, intergalactic mise-en-scène and also with the basic details of the epic story. Its storylines probe the motivations of certain "dark" characters, both pivotal and relatively obscure (for example, Śakuni, the Kauravas' uncle, who explains the cause of his hatred for the entire joint Kaurava-Pāṇḍava clan, and a son of Duḥśāsana, who narrates, with considerable teenage angst, the killing of Abhimanyu) to contribute to an overall mood that is brooding and dystopian. The visuals, in contrast to the generally flat and garish look of earlier Indian comic books, are detailed, moodily evocative, and often strikingly beautiful. Quinn, who writes of his fascination with the Mahābhārata in an afterword to Vol. 1,[26] has clearly done a good deal of epic homework, including seeking out different versions of the story. His rendition of Śakuni's biography, for example, presented in Vol. 3, stands in stark contrast to the usual portrayal of this character as a one-dimensional villain; it includes motivational details (such as Śakuni fashioning his fateful dice from the bones of his father, who was murdered, according to this version, on Bhīṣma's orders) that are absent from the Sanskrit epic but that can be found in some regional and folk retellings.[27] He also evinces a talent for summarizing complex characters succinctly—important when writing a graphic novel—as in this précis of Vol. 2 of the series, which appears on its back cover:

> Ashwatthama, a man of peace and a man of war. A man torn between his love of two great families in the greatest civil war the universe has ever known. A man who does all he can to avoid war, but in the end, a man who fires the final shot. A man whose quest to avenge the death of his father costs him his

---

26. Jason Quinn and Sachin Nagar, *The Kaurava Empire*, vol. 1, *Abhimanyu and the Conquest of the Chakravyuha* (Delhi: Kalyani Navyug Media, 2014), 70–71.

27. Jason Quinn and Sachin Nagar, *The Kaurava Empire*, vol. 3, *The Loaded Dice of Shakuni* (Delhi: Kalyani Navyug Media, 2015). I am grateful to Robert Goldman for identifying this variant, which is also discussed in some detail by A. K. Ramanujan in "Repetition in the *Mahābhārata*," in *Essays on the Mahābhārata*, ed. Arvind Sharma (Leiden: E. J. Brill, 1991), 441–42.

> very humanity. Cursed to wander the universe forever, friendless and alone, this is the story of the vengeance of Ashwatthama![28]

There is also, of course, a surfeit of gory violence, which the books convey through video-game-like action sequences punctuated by orthographic sound effects ("AAIIEEE!" "KRAKOOM!" "THOOM!" "ZHAAP!"), but this feature is arguably appropriate to the epic's battle scenes; it also fulfills the expectations of Campfire's target audience. And despite its repeated iteration of the Mahābhārata plot, the series may perhaps be best appreciated by readers who are already familiar with the epic story and its characters, and who may experience the satisfaction of recognizing them in an unconventional setting—as in such earlier cinematic adaptations as the 1980 Hindi films *Kalyug* and *Ham Pāñc* ("We Five"), or 2010's *Rājnīti* ("Politics").[29] Indeed, certain important events are represented only visually, as when, for example, the series illustrates an apparently female archer (identified simply as a "shape-shifter") piercing Bhīṣma with multiple arrows—an image that alludes to, but does not directly recount, the backstory of Princess Ambā's quest for revenge on Bhīṣma through two lifetimes and a change in gender.[30]

But readers who appreciate the Mahābhārata as an *Indian* story may be put off by the cultural decontextualization of the trilogy's deep-space setting: a dark mise-en-scène of moody interstellar spaces, glittering cityscapes (suggestive of the retro-future metropolis of Ridley Scott's 1982 *Blade Runner*), and dramatically lit Wagnerian interiors. In this respect, I was reminded of the limitations of Peter Brook and Jean-Claude Carrière's nine-hour theatrical Mahābhārata from 1985, which bled the epic of its cultural context in order to present it as "the poetical history of mankind."[31] In the *Kaurava*

28. Quinn and Nagar, *Vengeance of Ashwatthama*.

29. On the two 1980 films, see Philip Lutgendorf, "Bending the *Bhārata*: Two Uncommon Cinematic Adaptations," in *Popular Indian Cinema and Literature: Recasting the Tradition*, ed. Heidi Pauwels (London: Routledge, 2008), 19–41.

30. Quinn and Nagar, *Abhimanyu and the Conquest,* 34–35.

31. Jean-Claude Carrière, *The Mahabharata: A Play Based upon the Indian Classic Epic*, trans. Peter Brook (London: Methuen, 1987), 3. For a trenchant critique of the failures of this attempt at intercultural "translation," see Robert P. Goldman, "The Great War and Ancient Memory: Modern Mahābhāratas and the Limits of Cultural Translation," *Visual Anthropology* 5, no. 1 (1992): 92–95.

Figure 18.3. "Hāstinapura" as capital of an intergalactic empire. *Abhimanyu and the Conquest of the Chakravyuha*, 2014. *Source*: Campfire Graphic Novels, Kalyani. Navyug Media. Used with permission.

Empire trilogy, a vestigial "Indian-ness" remains chiefly in characters' names, in occasional interjections in Hindi (as when Bhīṣma shouts "*Aakraman!*" and an asterisk guides readers to the emboxed footnote: "Attack!"), and in the unexplained *tilak*s (forehead-adorning marks of vaguely Vaiṣṇava or Śaiva provenance) that most of the characters wear. Ethnically, the majority of them appear to be Caucasian. and their garb is quasi (Western) medieval—with tunics and robes—though it is overlaid with heavy futuristic armor (suggestive of "Transformer" action figures) and helmets emblazoned with lurid heraldry (suggestive of biker clubs and heavy metal bands). There is indeed plenty of *adbhuta-rasa*, the sense of wonder and astonishment that is so important to both modern SF and early Indian storytelling: war elephants turn into monstrous mastodons, and the *makara* (crocodile) from which Arjuna rescues Droṇa becomes a gigantic, Godzilla-like dinosaur.

Ghaṭotkaca, Bhīma's half-*rākṣasa* son, appears as a fiery, bat-like apparition of gargantuan size, and his cataclysmic fall onto the Kaurava forces attracts special visual treatment, including a double-page spread in Vol. 2.[32] But apart from the identification of principal warriors as *kṣatriya*s (another term that is explained in a boxed note), there is no trace of social organization, *brāhmaṇa* priests, or of Hindu religious ideology or practice—aside from a rare invocation of dharma, which is glossed as "justice," and an occasional hooded "seer," such as the one who prophecies Droṇa's killing and looks like the evil Emperor of *Star Wars*.[33] Aśvatthāman is not possessed by Rudra/Śiva when he causes the carnage of the night massacre. Instead, the only Hindu god who appears in the trilogy is Kṛṣṇa, who—perhaps because the series depicts him from a predominantly Kaurava point of view—is pictured in a similarly eerie way. The Kṛṣṇa of the *Kaurava Empire* series is auspiciously blue-skinned, to be sure, but wears a vaguely pharaonic headdress (albeit with a peacock-feather insert) that frames his gaunt, somber face, giving him the appearance of a pastel-tinted version of Akhenaton, the ancient Egyptian king. He seems to lack any higher purpose in masterminding the Pāṇḍavas' morally dubious victory; rather, he presides over it as an impassive and spectral spectator.

32. Quinn and Nagar, *Vengeance of Ashwatthama*, 58–59, 60–61. See also Quinn and Nagar, *Abhimanyu and the Conquest,* 26–28. On Ghaṭotkaca in the Sanskrit *Mahābhārata*, see the chapter by David Gitomer in this volume.

33. Quinn and Nagar, *Vengeance of Ashwatthama*, 55.

Figure 18.4. Droṇa is seized by a monstrous reptile. *The Vengeance of Ashwatthama*. *Source*: Campfire Graphic Novels, Kalyani. Navyug Media, Delhi. Used with permission.

Figure 18.5. Kṛṣṇa visits the Kaurava court in an effort to avert war. *The Vengeance of Aswatthama*. *Source*: Campfire Graphic Novels, Kalyani. Navyug Media. Used with permission.

Futuristic gadgetry is depicted on nearly every page, but is only occasionally referenced in the text, as when Aśvatthāman notes the transparent "defence dome" that protects Pañcāla's capital from attack.[34] It is never "explained," and it need not be, since this kind of technology is doubly familiar to readers: not only does it reflect standard SF conventions, but it also represents a mere variant on what real technology has already given us. (This last point has led some in literary SF circles to claim that the genre has become obsolete, since we now patently live in the "future" that it once imagined.)[35] Neon green geometric tracings appear like holograms on

34. Quinn and Nagar, *Vengeance of Ashwatthama,* 36.

35. Landon, *Science Fiction,* 146–47.

Figure 18.6. Droṇa gives Arjuna the *brahmāstra*. *The Vengeance of Aswatthama*. *Source*: Campfire Graphic Novels, Kalyani. Navyug Media. Used with permission.

computer screens that float in cavernous war rooms; warriors scoot about the battlefield on snowboard-like flying platforms before being "beamed up" into hovering fortress-spacecraft; and wrist-worn video devices permit FaceTime-like conversations across the interstellar battlefield—as when, for example, the doomed Abhimanyu, trapped inside the *cakravyūha* (here, a luminous maze of concentric rings) has a final, tearful conversation with his pregnant teenage bride, Uttarā ("Tell our child about me. I'm sorry I'll never get to see his face").[36]

The epic's *divyāstra*s are formidably technologized. One example is the page-filling "Brahmastra" that Droṇa presents to Arjuna: "The most powerful weapon the cosmos has ever known. But remember it is not to be used except in the most dire situation, for its fire is enough to consume the planet."[37] Yet, as in the *Star Wars* films, more anachronistic weaponry persists in the pages of the series and is similarly unexplained; heads are lopped off with glowing swords and scimitars, and Arjuna eventually takes from his *guru* the title of "finest archer in the universe."[38] In what has become a great SF tradition, the future envisioned in *The Kaurava Empire* trilogy combines hyperbolic evocations of both our past and our present.

Episode VI: Ahead to the Future?

To return from the realm of intergalactic civil war to the broader cultural observations with which I began this essay, I will briefly consider the question: What is the future of futurism, and specifically of SF, in India? It seems to me that it is either bright or dark, depending on one's taste. On the one hand, factors that once hindered the Indian imagination from visualizing a techno-future have been gradually eliminated, as I have already suggested, by the neoliberal economy that has arisen since the early 1990s and that has led to the global transfer (and indigenous invention) of new technologies, especially in the cyber realm. The advent of CGI—which Hollywood producers now sometimes outsource to Indian programmers in Bangalore and Hyderabad—may be said to have leveled the playing field

36. Quinn and Nagar, *Abhimanyu and the Conquest,* 61.

37. Quinn and Nagar, *Vengeance of Ashwatthama*, 32.

38. Quinn and Nagar, *Vengeance of Ashwatthama,* 23.

in terms of what Indian artists and filmmakers can imaginatively project. This has led to a more globalized aesthetic in advertising, product design, graphic art, and in films of all genre categories, as well as, notably, to a modest number of big-budget films that have experimented, with some measure of success, with SF tropes.[39] Thus in *Koī . . . Mil Gayā* ("Encountering Someone," 2003), a stranded extraterrestrial named Jadoo (*jādū*, or "magic" in Hindi) befriends a developmentally disabled young man (played by Hrithik Roshan) and gradually empowers him to defeat bullies, woo a sweetheart, and outsmart government agents bent on capturing the alien. Though it clearly echoes the American film *E.T.* (1982) as well as an unproduced Satyajit Ray screenplay called *The Alien* (1967, one of many SF tales by the renowned "alternative cinema" director and an example of the small but feisty SF scene in twentieth-century Bengal), the film also incorporated Bollywood conventions and neo-Hindu tropes: the adorable, cartoon-like Jadoo, summoned from deep space by a computer that emitted the syllable *om*, sang a song and eventually turned the shy, childlike human hero Rohit into not only an intellectual genius but a dynamite dancer. Indeed, Jadoo gifted him with superhuman powers that would reappear in Rohit's son Krishna (also played by Roshan), who was featured in two CGI-heavy (but less successful) sequels, *Krrish* (2006) and *Krrish 3* (2013). The big-budget Tamil film *Entiraṉ* ("Robot," 2010, also released in Hindi), for its part, riffed on the *Terminator* franchise while giving South Indian superstar Rajinikanth the chance to play a double role as a future Chennai inventor and his Frankenstein-like android double, Chitti.

Perhaps the most ambitious such film (and reportedly the most expensive Hindi film ever made at the time of its release, in both 2D and 3D versions, in 2011) was *Ra One*, directed by Anubhav Sinha and starring Shah Rukh Khan, the leading male "superstar" of Hindi cinema during the 1990s and early 2000s. Its convoluted storyline, drawing on Hindu mythology as well as the conventions of cyber-gaming (and on American films such as *Tron*, 1982), features a computer game supervillain, invented by an Indian programmer living in London, who escapes from the virtual world into the real one, kills his creator, and unleashes havoc. At one point, he clones himself into ten forms, true to his name (the acronym for "Ran-

39. Khan, "Bollywood's Encounters," 191–200.

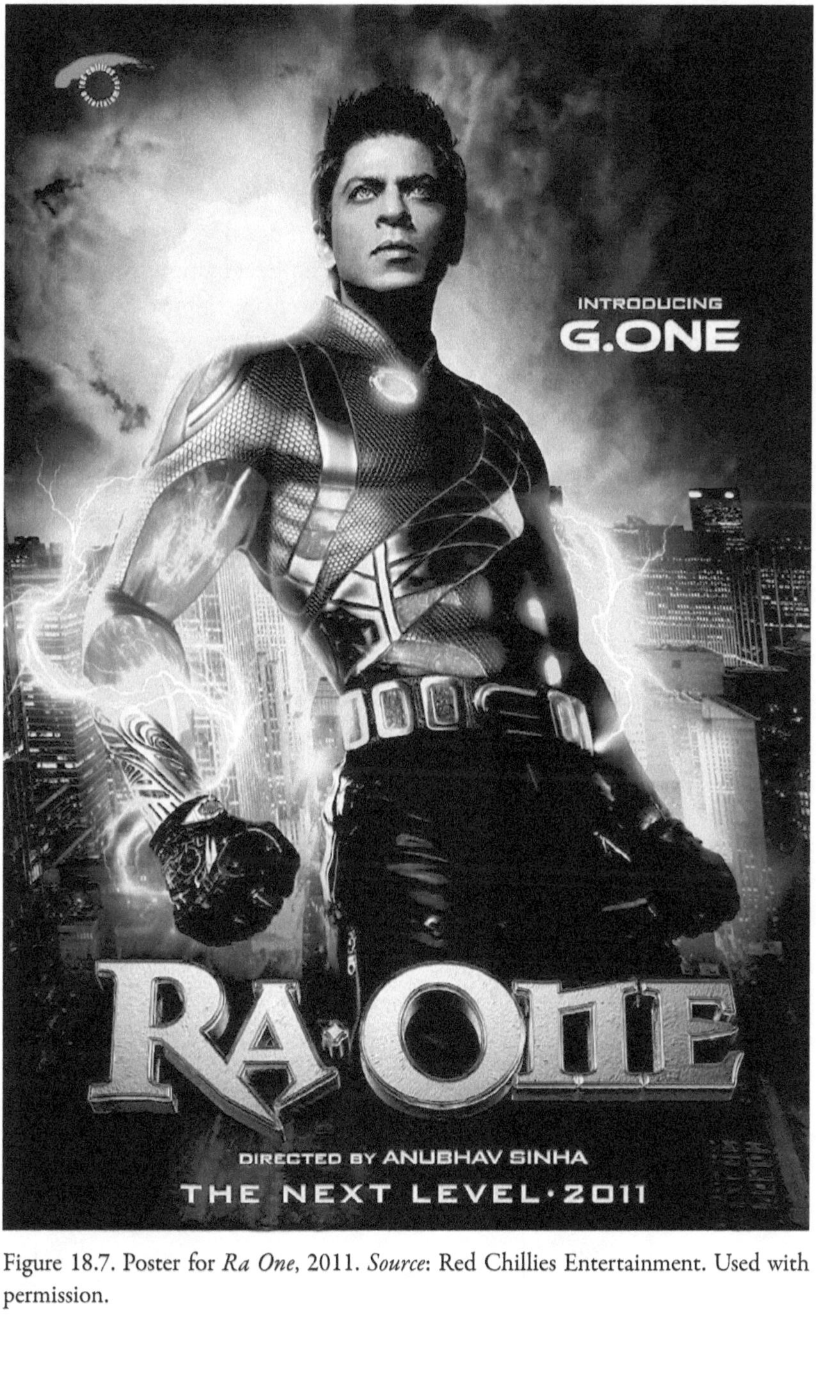

Figure 18.7. Poster for *Ra One*, 2011. *Source*: Red Chillies Entertainment. Used with permission.

dom Access Version One," but also *Rā-vaṇ* of Rāmāyaṇa infamy), only to be defeated by his virtual-world nemesis G-One (identified as both "Good One" and the Hindi *jī-van*, "soul" or "life"), who is a cyber embodiment of the dead designer. While the film looks decidedly global, its storyline remains (mildly) spiced with an Indian *masālā* that seeps through the coded names of the main characters.

But such films, like *The Kaurava Empire* trilogy of graphic novels, also seem to testify to the colonization of the Indian imagination by a new aesthetic hegemon: a truly globalized visual and narrative regime that permeates popular storytelling and that is, perhaps, most at home on the Internet. It glorifies hyperbolic musculature, militaristic machismo, techno-weaponry capable of unleashing apocalyptic violence, and the angst-ridden, usually male characters who wield it. And this potent new *masālā* mix, particularly when blended with a vague ideological and symbolic code that—to the extent that it is identifiable as "Indian"—is invariably "Hindu," seems to be yet another ominous portent of the future course of our present *kali-yuga*.

Bibliography

Primary Sources & Translations

Ānandavardhana. *The Dhvanyāloka of Ānandavardhana*. Edited by K. Krishnamoorthy. Dharwad: Karnatak University, 1974.

———. *The Dhvanyāloka of Ānandavardhana with the Locana of Abhinavagupta*. Translated by Daniel H. H. Ingalls, Jeffrey Moussaieff Masson, and M. V. Patwardhan. Cambridge, MA: Harvard University Press, 1990.

———. *Dhvanyāloka of Shri Anandavardhanacharya with the Lochan Commentary by Shri Abhinava Gupta*. 2 vols. Delhi and Varanasi: Motilal Banarsidass, 1973.

Āndhramahābhāratamu. Edited by G. V. Subrahmanyam. 15 volumes. Tirupati: Tirumala Tirupati Devasathanams, 2014.

Āndhraśabdacintāmaṇi: A Grammar of Telugu Literature in Sanskrit. Translated by Deven Patel and R. V. S. Sundaram. Mysore: Central Institute of Indian Languages, 2016.

Aurobindo. *Savitri: A Legend and a Symbol*. Twin Lakes, WI: Lotus Press, 1995.

Bandyopadhay, Sibaji, and Sankha Banerjee. *Vyasa: The Beginning*. Delhi: Penguin Books, 2017.

Basu, Rajsekhar. *Mahābhārata Saranubāda*. Kolkata: MC Sarkar and Sons, 1949.

Bhagavad-Gita with Eleven Commentaries. Edited by Pandit Gajanana Shastri Sadhale. 3 vols. Bombay: Gujarati Printing Press, 1935.

———. *The Bhagavadgītā in the Mahābhārata: A Bilingual Edition*. Translated by J. A. B. van Buitenen. Chicago: University of Chicago Press, 1981.

[*Bhāgavatapurāṇa*] *Bhāgavata Purāṇa of Kṛṣṇa Dvaipayana Vyāsa*. Edited by J. L. Shastri. Delhi: Motilal Banarsidass, 1983.

———. *Bhāgavata Purāṇa: Selected Readings*. Translated by Ravi M. Gupta and Kenneth R. Valpey. New York: Columbia University Press, 2017.

Bhalla, Alok, ed. *Stories about the Partition of India*. Vol. 1. Delhi: HarperCollins, 1994.

Bharati, C. Subramania. *Panchali's Pledge.* Translated by Usha Rajagopalan. Gurgaon: Hachette India, 2012.

Bharathi, Dharamvir. *Andha Yug.* Translated by Alok Bhalla. Delhi: Oxford University Press, 2010.

Bhāravi. *Arjuna and the Hunter.* Edited and translated by Indira Viswanathan Peterson. Murty Classical Library of India. Cambridge, MA: Harvard University Press, 2016.

———. *Kirātārjunīya.* Edited by Pandit Durgaprasad and Kashinath Pandurang Parab. Bombay: Nirnaya Sagara Press, 1895.

Bhyrappa, S. L. *Parva: A tale of war, Peace, Love, Death, God, and Man.* Translated by K. Raghavendra Rao. Delhi: Sahitya Akademi, 1994.

Bose, Buddhadev. *The Book of Yudhisthir: A Study of the Mahabharat of Vyas.* Translated by Sujit Mukherjee. Hyderabad: Sangam Books, 1986.

———. *Mahābhārater Kathā.* Kolkata: MC Sarkar and Sons, 1974.

Carrière, Jean-Claude. *The Mahabharata: A Play Based upon the Indian Classic Epic.* Translated by Peter Brook. London: Methuen, 1987.

Cauhān, Sabalsingh. *Sabalsingh Cauhān Kṛt Mahābhārat.* Edited by Ramlagan Pandey. Varanasi: Shri Thakur Prasad Pustak Bhandar, 2014.

———. *Sabalsingh Cauhān-Viracit Mahābhārat.* Lucknow: Tej Kumar Book Depot, 2015.

Chattopadhyay, Bankimchandra. *Baṅkima Racanābalī.* Edited by Jogeshchandra Bagal. Kolkata: Sahitya Samsad, 1964.

———. *Kṛṣṇacaritra.* Edited by Brajendranath Bandyopadhyay and Sajanikanta Das. Calcutta: Bangiya Sahitya Parishad, 1941.

Chokshi, Roshani. *Aru Shah and the City of Gold.* New York: Disney Hyperion, forthcoming 2021.

———. *Aru Shah and the End of Time.* New York: Disney Hyperion, 2018.

———. *Aru Shah and the Song of Death.* New York: Disney Hyperion, 2019.

———. *Aru Shah and the Tree of Wishes.* New York: Disney Hyperion, 2020.

Devi, Jyotirmayi. *The River Churning: A Partition Novel.* Translated by Enakshi Chatterjee. Delhi: Kali for Women, 1995.

Devi, Mahasweta. *After Kurukshetra: Three Stories.* Translated by Anjum Katyal. Kolkata: Seagull, 2005.

———. "Draupadi." Edited and translated by Gayatri Chakravorty Spivak. *Critical Inquiry* 8, no. 2 (1981): 381–402.

Divakaruni, Chitra Banerjee. *The Palace of Illusions.* New York: Anchor Books, 2008.

Gangopadhyay, Sunil. *Arjun.* Translated by Chitrita Banerji-Abdullah. New York: Viking Penguin, 1987.

[*Harivaṃśa*] *Krishna's Lineage: The Harivamsha of Vyāsa's Mahābhārata.* Translated by Simon Brodbeck. New York: Oxford University Press, 2019.

Homer. *Iliad.* Vol. 2, *Books 13–24.* Translated by A. T. Murray. Revised by William F. Wyatt. Loeb Classical Library 171. Cambridge, MA: Harvard University Press, 1999.

Hossein, Rokeya Sakhawat. *Sultana's Dream, A Feminist Utopia and Selections from "The Secluded Ones."* New York City: Feminist Press at CUNY, 1988.

Ilaiah, Kancha. *Why I Am Not a Hindu: A Sudra Critique of Hindutva Philosophy, Culture and Political Economy.* 1996. Reprint, Calcutta: Samya, 2007.

Jinasena Punnāṭa. *Harivaṃśa Purāṇa.* Edited and translated into Hindi by P. Jain. Delhi: Bharatiya Jnanpith, 1978.

Kālidāsa. *Abhijñānaśākuntala.* Edited by Narayana Balakrishna Godabole and Kasinatha Panduranga Paraba. Bombay: Nirnaya Sagara Press, 1883.

———. *The Raghuvamśa of Kālidāsa with the Commentary (the Sanjīvanī) of Mallinātha.* Edited by M. R. Kale. Bombay: Gopal Narayen, 1922.

[*Kāmasūtra*] *The Kamasutra of Vatsyayana.* Translated by Wendy Doniger and Sudhir Kakar. New York: Oxford World Classics, 2002.

Kandasamy, Meena. "The Flight of Birds." *Indian Literature* 50, no. 4 (2006): 99–101.

Karṇabhāra: The Trial of Karṇa. Translated by Barbara Stoler Miller. In *Essays on the Mahābhārata.* Edited by Arvind Sharma, 57–67. Leiden: E. J. Brill, 1991.

Karnad, Girish. *Yayati.* Delhi: Oxford University Press, 2008.

Karve, Irawati K. *Yugānta: The End of an Epoch.* Poona: Deshmukh Prakashan, 1969.

Khaḍagrāy. *Gopācal Ākhyān.* Edited by Harihar Nivas Dvivedi. Gwalior: Jivaji Visvavidyalay, 1980.

Khadilkar, K. P. *Globalization, Nationalism and the Text of Kichaka-Vadha: The First English Translation of the Marathi Anticolonial Classic, with a Historical Analysis of Theatre in British India.* Edited and translated by Rakesh H. Solomon. London: Anthem Press, 2014.

Khandekar, Vishnu Sakharam. *Yayati: A Classical Tale of Lust.* Translated by Y. P. Kulkarni. Delhi: Orient Paperbacks, 2009.

Krishnachandran, V. R. *Puruṣārtthākkūttu.* Trichur: Kerala Sahitya Akademi, 1978.

Kolatkar, Arun. *Arun Kolatkar: Collected Poems in English.* Edited by Arvind Krishna Mehrotra. Tarset: Bloodaxe, 2010.

Kulaśekhara. *The Subhadrādhananjaya of Kulasekhara Varma with the Commentary of Sivarāma.* Edited by T. Ganapati Sastri. Trivandrum: Travancore Government Press, 1912.

———. *The Sun God's Daughter and King Saṃvaraṇa: Tapatī-Saṃvaraṇam and the Kūṭiyāṭṭam Drama Tradition: Text With Vivaraṇa Commentary.* Translated by N. P. Unni and Bruce M. Sullivan. Delhi: Nag, 1995.

———. *The Wedding of Arjuna and Subhadrā: The Kūṭiyāṭṭam Drama Subhadrā-Dhanañjaya: Text with Vicāratilaka Commentary, Introduction, English*

Translation, and Notes. Translated by N. P. Unni and Bruce M. Sullivan. Delhi: Nag, 2001.

Kumar, Kirtana. *Shakuntala Remembered*. Unpublished manuscript. PDF file.

Kumudini. *Cillaṟaic Caṅkatikaḷ Limiṭeṭ*. Tricchi: Natesan Books Ltd., 1948.

Limbale, Sharankumar. *Towards an Aesthetic of Dalit Literature: History, Controversies, and Considerations*. Translated by Alok Mukherjee. Delhi: Orient Longman, 2004.

Lomhor, A. K. *Eklavya the Invincible: The Story of an Archer's Loyalty and Devotion*. Edited by Jasmine Grey. Digital Rainbow Publications, 2015.

Māgha. *The Killing of Shishupala*. Edited and translated by Paul Dundas. Murty Classical Library of India. Cambridge, MA: Harvard University Press, 2016.

———. *Śiśupālavadha*. Edited by Pandit Durgaprasad and Pandit Shivadatta. Bombay: Nirnaya Sagara Press, 1888.

[*Mahābhārata*]. *Sriman Mahābhāratam: A New Edition Mainly Based on the South Indian Texts*. Edited by T. R. Krishnacharya and T. R. Vyasacharya. 7 vols. Kumbakonam: Madhva Vilas Book Depot, 1906–10.

———. *Śrī Mahābhāratam with the Bhāratabhāvadīpa Commentary of Nīlakaṇṭha*. Edited by Ramchandrashastri Kinjawadekar. 6 vols. Poona: Chitrashala Press, 1929–36.

———. *The Mahābhārata for the First Time Critically Edited*. Edited by V. S. Sukthankar et al. 19 vols. Poona: Bhandarkar Oriental Research Institute, 1933–66.

———. *The Mahabharata of Krishna-Dwaipayana Translated into English Prose*. Translated by K. M. Ganguli. Edited by P. C. Roy. 12 vols. Calcutta: Bharat Press, 1883–96.

———. *A Prose English Translation of The Mahabharata: Translated Literally from the Original Sanskrit Text*. Translated by M. N. Dutt. 2 vols. Calcutta: Oriental Publishing Co., 1962. First published 1895–1905 by H. C. Dass, Elysium Press (Calcutta).

———. *The Mahābhārata*. Vol. 1, *The Book of the Beginning*. Translated by J. A. B. van Buitenen. Chicago: University of Chicago Press, 1973.

———. *The Mahābhārata*. Vol. 2, *2. The Book of the Assembly Hall, 3. The Book of the Forest*. Translated by J. A. B. van Buitenen. Chicago: University of Chicago Press, 1975.

———. *The Mahābhārata*. Vol. 3, *4. The Book of Virāṭa, 5. The Book of the Effort*. Translated by J. A. B. van Buitenen. Chicago: University of Chicago Press, 1978.

———. *The Mahābhārata*. Vol. 7, *11. The Book of the Women, 12. The Book of Peace, Part One*. Translated by James L. Fitzgerald. Chicago: University of Chicago Press, 2004.

———. *Mahabharata, Book Four: Virata*. Translated by Kathleen Garbutt. Clay Sanskrit Library. New York: New York University Press, JJC Foundation, 2006.

———. *Mahabharata, Book Five: Preparations for War*. Vol. 2. Translated by Kathleen Garbutt. Clay Sanskrit Library. New York: New York University Press, JJC Foundation, 2008.

———. *Mahabharata, Book Six: Bhishma*. Vol. 2. Translated by Alex Cherniak. Clay Sanskrit Library. New York: New York University Press, JJC Foundation, 2009.

———. *Mahabharata, Book Seven: Drona*. Vol. 1. Translated by Vaughn Pilikian. Clay Sanskrit Library. New York: New York University Press, JJC Foundation, 2006.

———. *The Mahābhārata: An Abridged Translation*. Translated by John D. Smith. London: Penguin Books, 2009.

———. *After the War: The Last Books of the Mahabharata*. Edited and translated by Wendy Doniger. New York: Oxford University Press, forthcoming.

Malliyarecana. *Kavijanāśrayamu*. Hyderabad: Telangana Sahityaparishodana Kendram, 2016.

[*Manusmṛti*] *Manusmṛti with the Commentary Manvarthamuktāvalī of Kullūka*. Edited by N. R. A. Kaavyatirtha. Bombay: Nirnaya Sagara Press, 1946.

———. *Manu's Code of Law: A Critical Edition and Translation of the Mānava-Dharmaśāstra*. Edited and translated by Patrick Olivelle. New York: Oxford University Press, 2005.

Mittal, Mahendra. *Ekalavya*. Delhi: Raja Pocket Books, 2016.

Mpu Kaṇwa. *Arjunawiwāha: The Marriage of Arjuna of Mpu Kaṇwa*. Translated by Stuart Robson. Leiden: Koninklijk Instituut, 2008.

Mpu Panuluh. *The Kakawin Ghaṭotkacāśraya by Mpu Panuluh*. Translated by Stuart Robson. Tokyo: Tokyo University of Foreign Studies, 2016.

Muḥammad Bihāmad Khānī. *Tarikh-i-Muhammadi by Muhammad Bihamad Khani*. Translated by Muhammad Zaki. Aligarh: Aligarh Muslim University, 1972.

Nagarkar, Kiran. *Bedtime Story: A Play*. Delhi: Fourth Estate, 2015.

Naidoo, Muthal. *W[orks] I[n] P[rogress] Theatre Plays*. South Africa: MN Publications, 2008.

Naïr, Karthika. *Until the Lions: Echoes from the Mahabharata*. Delhi: HarperCollins India, 2015.

Nair, M. T. Vasudevan. *Bhima: Lone Warrior*. Translated by Gita Krishnankutty. Delhi: Harper Perennial, 2013.

Nālāyirativviyappirapantam. Edited by P. P. Annangarachariyar. Kanchi: V. N. Tevanatan, 1971.

Nīlakaṇṭha. *Bhīma in Search of Celestial Flower: Nīlakaṇṭhakavi Kalyāṇasaugandhikavyāyoga*. Translated by K. G. Paulose. Delhi: Bharatiya Book Corporation, 2000.

Nītivarman. *The Kīcakavadha of Nītivarman with the Commentary of Janārdanasena*. Edited by S. K. De. Dacca: Dacca University, 1929.

Padmapurāṇa. Edited by J. L. Shastri, G. P. Bhatt, and N. A. Deshpande. Delhi: Motilal Banarasidass, 1951.

Pampa. *Vikramārjunavijaya*. Edited by Bellave Venkatanarayanappa. Mysore: University of Mysore Prasaranga, 2013. First published 1931, Kannada Sahitya Parishattu (Bangalore).

Pañcarātra. Edited by the Bhāsa Projekt Würzburg. *Multimediale Datenbank zum Sanskrit-Schauspiel*. 2007. http://www.bhasa.indologie.uni-wuerzburg.de/rahmen.html.

Patil, Amruta. *Adi Parva: Churning of the Ocean*. Noida: HarperCollins Publishers India, 2012.

———. *Sauptik: Blood and Flowers*. Noida: HarperCollins Publishers India, 2016.

Pritam, Amrita. *Pinjar: The Skeleton and Other Stories*. Translated by Khushwant Singh. Delhi: Tara Press, 2009.

Quinn, Jason, and Sachin Nagar. *The Kaurava Empire*. Vol. 1, *Abhimanyu and the Conquest of the Chakravyuha*. Delhi: Kalyani Navyug Media, 2014.

———. *The Kaurava Empire*. Vol. 2, *The Vengeance of Ashwatthama*. Delhi: Kalyani Navyug Media, 2015.

———. *The Kaurava Empire*. Vol. 3, *The Loaded Dice of Shakuni*. Delhi: Kalyani Navyug Media, 2015.

Raïdhū. *Harivaṃsapurāṇa*. Manuscript Jha 83. Shri Jaina Siddhanta Bhavan (Arrah, Bihar).

Rakesh, Mohan. *Halfway House*. Translated by Bindu Batra. Edited by Dilip K. Basu. Delhi: Worldview Publications, 1999.

Ranna. *Gadāyuddhasaṅgraha*. Edited by T. N. Srikanthayya. Bangalore: Vasantha Prakashana, 2015. First published 1949, Kavyalaya (Mysore).

———. *Sāhasabhīmavijaya*. Edited by B. S. Sannayya and Ramegauda. Mysore: University of Mysore Prasaranga, 1985.

Ray, Pratibha. *Yajnaseni: The Story of Draupadi*. Translated by Pradip Bhattacharya. Delhi: Rupa & Co., 2002.

Śaṅkarācārya. *The Upanishadbhashya*. Edited by Hari Raghunath Bhagavat. 2 vols. Poona: Ashtekar & Co., 1927–28.

Sawant, Shivaji. *Mrityunjaya: The Death Conqueror*. Translated by P. Lal and Nandini Nopany. Calcutta: Writer's Workshop, 1989.

Shakespeare, William. *Henry IV, Part 1*. Edited by Adam Frost. Mineola, NY: Dover Publications, 1997.

Somadeva. *Kathāsaritsāgara*. Edited by Jagadishalala Shastri. Delhi: Motilal Banarsidass, 2008. First published 1889 by Nirnaya Sagara Press (Bombay), edited by Pandit Durgaprasad and Kashinath Pandurang Parab.

Sreedharan, Chindu. *Epic Retold. #Mahabharata #TwitterFiction #Bhima #140 Characters*. Noida: HarperCollins Publishers India, 2014.

Sūrdās. *Sur's Ocean: Poems from the Early Tradition*. Translated by John Stratton Hawley. Edited by Kenneth E. Bryant. Murty Classical Library of India. Cambridge, MA: Harvard University Press, 2015.

Svayambhūdeva. *Riṭṭhaṇemicariya*. Edited by R. S. Tomar. 5 vols. Ahmedabad: Prakrit Text Society, 1993–2000.

———. *Riṭṭhaṇemicariu—Yādavakāṇḍa*. Edited and translated into Hindi by D. K. Jain. Delhi: Bharatiya Jnanpith, 1985.

Tagore, Rabindranath. *Ādhunik Sāhitya*. Calcutta: Visva Bharati Press, 1987.

Tharoor, Shashi. *The Great Indian Novel*. New York: Penguin, 1989.

Tulsīdās. *Hanumānbāhuk Saṭīk*. Edited by M. P. Malviy Vaidya. Gorakhpur: Gita Press, 1994.

———. *Śrirāmcaritmānas*. Edited by Hanumanprasad Poddar. Gorakhpur: Gita Press, 1966.

Udayasankar, Krishna. *Govinda: The Aryavarta Chronicles, Book 1*. Delhi: Hachette India, 2012.

———. *Kaurava: The Aryavarta Chronicles, Book 2*. Delhi: Hachette India, 2013.

———. *Kurukshetra: The Aryavarta Chronicles, Book 3*. Delhi: Hachette India, 2014.

Ūrubhaṅga: The Breaking of the Thighs. Translated by Edwin Gerow. In *Essays on the Mahābhārata*. Edited by Arvind Sharma, 68–83. Leiden: E. J. Brill, 1991.

Vālmīki. *The Rāmāyaṇa of Vālmīki: An Epic of Ancient India*. Vol. 4, *Kiṣkindhākāṇḍa*. Edited and translated by Rosalind Lefeber. Princeton, NJ: Princeton University Press, 1994.

———. *The Rāmāyaṇa of Vālmīki: An Epic of Ancient India*. Vol. 7, *Uttarakāṇḍa*. Edited and translated by Robert P. Goldman and Sally J. Sutherland Goldman. Princeton, NJ: Princeton University Press, 2017.

———. *The Vālmīki Rāmāyaṇa: Critically Edited for the First Time*. Edited by G. H. Bhatt and U. P. Shah, et al. 7 vols. Baroda: Oriental Institute, 1960–75.

Valmiki, Omprakash. *Joothan: A Dalit's Life*. Translated by Arun Prabha Mukherjee. New York: Columbia University Press, 2003.

Villiputtūr. *Villiputtūrār Iyaṟṟiya Makāpāratam*. Edited by V. M. Gopalakrishnamachariyar. 7 vols. Madras: 1963–68.

Viṣṇudās. *Mahākavi Viṣṇudās Kṛt Mahābhārat (Pāṇḍav-carit)*. Edited by Harihar Nivas Dvivedi. Gwalior: Vidya Mandir Prakasan, 1973.

Secondary Sources

Adluri, Vishwa. "Literary Violence and Literal Salvation: Śaunaka Interprets the *Mahābhārata*." *EXEMPLAR: The Journal of South Asian Studies* 1, no. 2 (2012): 45–68.

Adluri, Vishwa, and Joydeep Bagchee. *The Nay Science: A History of German Indology*. New York: Oxford University Press, 2014.

———. *Philology and Criticism: A Guide to Mahābhārata Textual Criticism*. New York: Anthem Press, 2018.

Arunachalam, M. *Ballad Poetry*. Thanjavur: Saraswati Mahal Library, 1976.

Ashton, Martha Bush, and Bruce Christie. *Yakṣagāna: A Dance Drama of India*. Delhi: Abhinav Publications, 1977.

Ate, Lynn. *Yaśodā's Songs to Her Playful Son, Kṛṣṇa: Periyāḻvār's 9th Century Tamil Tirumoḻi*. Woodland Hills, CA: South Asian Studies Association, 2011.

Austin, Christopher. "The Fructification of the Tale of a Tree: The *Pārijātaharaṇa* in the *Harivaṃśa* and Its Appendices." *Journal of the American Oriental Society* 33, no. 2 (2013): 249–68.

Austin, J. L. *How to Do Things with Words*. Oxford: Oxford University Press, 1975. First published 1962, Harvard University Press (Cambridge, MA).

Bai, B. N. Sumitra, and Robert Z. Zydenbos. "The Jaina *Mahābhārata*." In *Essays on the Mahābhārata*. Edited by Arvind Sharma, 251–73. Leiden: E. J. Brill, 1991.

Bailey, Gregory. "Suffering in the *Mahābhārata*: Draupadī and Yudhiṣṭhira." In *Inde et Littératures: Études Réunies par Marie-Claude Porcher*, 109–29. Paris: École des Hautes Études en Sciences Sociales, 1983.

Bakhtin, M. M. "Discourse in the Novel." In *The Dialogic Imagination: Four Essays by M. M. Bakhtin*. Edited by Michael Holquist. Translated by Caryl Emerson and Michael Holquist, 259–422. Austin: University of Texas Press, 1981.

———. "Epic and Novel: Toward a Methodology for the Study of the Novel." In *The Dialogic Imagination: Four Essays by M. M. Bakhtin*. Edited by Michael Holquist. Translated by Caryl Emerson and Michael Holquist, 3–40. Austin: University of Texas Press, 1981.

———. *Problems of Dostoyevsky's Poetics*. Edited and translated by Caryl Emerson. Minneapolis: University of Minnesota Press, 1984.

Bal, Mieke. *Narratology: Introduction to the Theory of Narrative*. Translated by Christine von Boheemen. Toronto: University of Toronto Press, 1985.

Bangha, Imre. "Early Hindi Epic Poetry in Gwalior: Beginnings and Continuities in the *Rāmāyan* of Vishnudas." In *After Timur Left: Culture and Circulation in Fifteenth-Century North India*. Edited by Francesca Orsini and Samira Sheikh, 365–402. Delhi: Oxford University Press, 2014.

Basu, Amrita, ed. *The Challenge of Local Feminisms: Women's Movements in Global Perspective*. Boulder, CO: Westview Press, 1995.

———. "Globalizing Local Women's Movements." In *Localizing Knowledge in a Globalizing World: Recasting the Area Studies Debate*. Edited by Ali Mirsepassi, Amrita Basu, and Frederick Weaver, 82–100. Syracuse, NY: Syracuse University Press, 2003.

Bedekar, V. M. "Studies in Sāṃkhyā: The Teachings of Pañcaśikha in the Mahābhārata." *Annals of the Bhandarkar Oriental Research Institute* 38, no. 3/4 (1957): 233–44.

Bednar, Michael. "Mongol, Muslim, Rajput: Mahimāsāhi in Persian Texts and the Sanskrit *Hammīra-Mahākāvya*." *Journal of the Economic and Social History of the Orient* 60, no. 5 (2017): 585–613.

Benjamin, Walter. "The Work of Art in the Age of Mechanical Reproduction." In *Illuminations*. Translated by Harry Zohn. Edited by Hannah Arendt, 217–52. London: Fontana, 1968.

———. "Theses on the Philosophy of History." In *Illuminations*. Translated by Harry Zohn. Edited by Hannah Arendt, 255–66. London: Fontana, 1968.

Beth, Sarah. "Hindi Dalit Autobiography: An Exploration of Identity." *Modern Asian Studies* 41, no. 3 (2007): 545–74.

Bhat, Subraya. *Gadāyuddhadarpaṇa*. Kasaragodu: Subraya Bhat, 1975.

Bhattacharya, Dinesh Chandra. "Vidyāsāgara's Commentary on the Mahābhārata." *Annals of the Bhandarkar Oriental Research Institute* 25, no. 1/3 (1944): 99–102.

Bhattacharya, Pradip. "Five Holy Virgins, Five Sacred Myths: A Quest for Meaning." *Manushi* 141 (2004): 4–12.

Bhattacharya, Sabyasachi. *Rabindranath Tagore: An Interpretation*. Delhi: Penguin Books, 2011.

Black, Brian. "Dialogue and Difference: Encountering the Other in Indian Religious and Philosophical Sources." In *Dialogue in Early South Asian Religions: Hindu, Buddhist, and Jain Traditions*. Edited by Brian Black and Laurie Patton, 243–57. New York: Routledge, 2015.

Bose, Mandakranta. "Staging *Abhijñānaśākuntalam*." In *Revising Abhijñānaśākuntalam: Love, Lineage and Language in Kālidāsa's Nāṭaka*. Edited by Saswati Sengupta and Deepika Tandon, 38–53. Delhi: Orient Blackswan Private Limited, 2011.

Bowles, Adam. *Dharma, Disorder and the Political in Ancient India: The Āpaddharmaparvan of the Mahābhārata*. Leiden: Brill, 2007.

Brockington, John. *Epic Threads: John Brockington on the Sanskrit Epics*. Edited by Greg Bailey and Mary Brockington. Delhi: Oxford University Press, 2000.

Brodbeck, Simon. "Analytic and Synthetic Approaches in Light of the Critical Edition of the Mahābhārata and Harivaṃśa." *Journal of Vaishnava Studies* 19, no. 2 (2011): 223–50.

———. "Husbands of Earth: *Kṣatriyas*, Females, and Female *Kṣatriyas* in the *Strīparvan* of the *Mahābhārata*." In *Papers of the 12th World Sanskrit Conference*. Vol. 2, *Epic Undertakings*. Edited by Robert P. Goldman and Muneo Tokunaga, 33–63. Delhi: Motilal Banarsidass, 2009.

———. "Solar and Lunar Lines in the Mahābhārata." *Religions of South Asia* 5, no. 1–2 (2012): 127–52.

Bronner, Yigal. *Extreme Poetry: The South Asian Movement of Simultaneous Narration*. New York: Columbia University Press, 2010.

Bronner, Yigal, and Lawrence McCrea. "To Be or Not to Be Śiśupāla: Which Version of the Key Speech in Māgha's Great Poem Did He Really Write?" *Journal of the American Oriental Society* 132, no. 3 (2012): 427–55.

Browning, Robert. *Strafford: An Historical Tragedy*. London: Longman, Rees, Orme, Brown, Greene, and Longman, 1837.

Brückner, Heidrun. "Manuscripts and Performance Traditions of the So-Called Trivandrum Plays Ascribed to Bhāsa: A Report on Work in Progress." *Bulletin d'études indiennes* 17–18 (1999–2000): 501–50.

Bryant, Edwin F. "Introduction." In *Krishna: The Beautiful Legend of God. Śrīmād Bhāgavata Purāṇa, Book X*. Translated by Edwin F. Bryant, ix–lxxviii. New York: Penguin Books, 2003.

Burnam, Reed Ethan. "Not Simply for Entertainment: The Failure of *Kahani Hamare Mahabharat Ki* and Its Place in a New Generation of Televised Indian Mythology." Master's thesis, University of Texas at Austin, 2010.

Butler, Judith. *Bodies that Matter: On the Discursive Limits of "Sex."* New York: Rutledge, 1993.

———. *Excitable Speech: A Politics of the Performative*. New York: Routledge, 1997.

Callewaert, Winand M., and Shilanand Hemraj. *Bhagavadgītānuvāda: A Study in Transcultural Translation*. Ranchi: Satya Bharati Publications, 1983.

Callewaert, Winand M., and Swapna Sharma. *Dictionary of Bhakti: North-Indian Bhakti Texts into Khari Boli Hindi and English*. Delhi: D. K. Printworld, 2009.

Carlson, Marvin. *The Haunted Stage: The Theatre as Memory Machine*. Ann Arbor: University of Michigan Press, 2003.

Case, Sue Ellen. "Classic Drag: The Greek Creation of Female Parts." *Theatre Journal* 37, no. 3 (1985): 317–27.

Chander, Romesh. "Vivid New Shades to Shakuntala." *The Times of India*. September 2, 1987.

Chatterjee, Partha. *Nationalist Thought and Colonial World: A Derivative Discourse*. London: Zed Books for the United Nations University, 1993.

Chowdhry, Prem. *Colonial India and the Making of Empire Cinema: Image, Ideology and Identity*. Manchester: Manchester University Press, 2000.

Cort, John E. "An Overview of the Jaina Purāṇas." In *Purāṇa Perennis: Reciprocity and Transformation in Hindu and Jaina Texts*. Edited by Wendy Doniger, 185–206. Albany: State University of New York Press, 1993.

Couture, André. *Kṛṣṇa in the Harivaṃśa*. 2 vols. Delhi: D. K. Printworld, 2015–17.

Cox, Whitney. "Sharing a Single Seat: The Poetics and Politics of Male Intimacy in the *Vikramāṅkakāvya*." *Journal of Indian Philosophy* 38, no. 5 (2010): 485–501.

Culp, Amanda Louise. "Searching for Shakuntala: Sanskrit Drama and Theatrical Modernity in Europe and India, 1789–Present." PhD diss., Columbia University, 2018.

Danius, Sara, Stefan Jonsson, and Gayatri Chakravorty Spivak. "An Interview with Gayatri Chakravorty Spivak." *Boundary 2* 20, no. 2 (1993): 24–50.

Das, N. K. "Adivasi Theatre Pandavani and Persona of Bhima in Folklore of Chhattisgarh-Gondwana Region." *Irish Journal of Anthropology* 18, no. 2 (2015): 78–90.

Das, Sisir Kumar. *The Artist in Chains: The Life of Bankimchandra Chatterji*. Delhi: New Statesman, 1984.

Dasgupta, S. N., and R. R. Agarwal. *History of Indian Philosophy*. Allahabad: Kitab Mahal, 1969.

Daugherty, Diane. "Subhadra Redux: Reinstating Female Kutiyattam." In *Between Fame and Shame: Performing Women—Women Performers in India*. Edited by Heidrun Brukner, Hanne M. de Bruin, and Heike Moser, 153–67. Wiesbaden: Otto Harrassowitz.

Davis, Donald Richard Jr. "Satire as Apology: The *Puruṣārtthakkūttŭ* of Kerala." In *Irreverent History: Essays for M. G. S. Narayanan*. Edited by Kesavan Veluthat and Donald Richard Davis, Jr., 93–103. Delhi: Primus Books, 2014.

Davis, Richard H. *The Bhagavad Gita: A Biography*. Princeton, NJ: Princeton University Press, 2015.

De Clercq, Eva. "Apabhramsha as a Literary Medium in Fifteenth-Century North India." In *After Timur Left: Culture and Circulation in Fifteenth-Century North India*. Edited by Francesca Orsini and Samira Sheikh, 339–64. Delhi: Oxford University Press, 2014.

———. *The Apabhramsa of Svayambhudeva's Paumacariu*. Pandit Nathuram Premi Research Series, Vol. 17. Mumbai: Hindi Granth Karyalay, 2009.

———. "The Jaina *Harivaṃśa* and *Mahābhārata* Tradition: A Preliminary Survey." In *Parallels and Comparisons in the Sanskrit Epics and Purāṇas*. Edited by P. Koskikallio, 399–421. Zagreb: Croatian Academy of Sciences and Arts, 2008.

De Clercq, Eva, and Tine Vekemans. "Rejecting and Appropriating Epic Lore." In *Jaina Narratives*. Edited by Peter Flügel. London: Routledge, forthcoming.

Derrida, Jacques. "Signature Event Context." In *Margins of Philosophy*. Translated by Alan Bass, 307–30. Chicago: University of Chicago Press, 1982.

Dhand, Arti. "Paradigms of the Good in the *Mahābhārata*: Śuka and Sulabhā in Quagmires of Ethics." In *Gender and Narrative in the Mahābhārata*. Edited by Simon Brodbeck and Brian Black, 258–78. London: Routledge, 2007.

Dharwadkar, Aparna Bhargava. *Theatres of Independence: Drama, Theory, and Urban Performance in India since 1947*. Iowa City: University of Iowa Press, 2005.

Doniger, Wendy. *The Hindus: An Alternative History*. New York: Viking Penguin, 2009.

———. "How to Escape the Curse: The *Mahabharata* Translated by John Smith." *London Review of Books* 31, no. 19 (2009): 17–18.

———. *Splitting the Difference: Gender and Myth in Ancient Greece and India*. Chicago: University of Chicago Press, 1999.

———. *The Woman Who Pretended to Be Who She Was: Myths of Self-Imitation*. New York: Oxford University Press, 2005.

Doniger O'Flaherty, Wendy. "Horses and Snakes in the Ādi Parvan of the *Mahābhārata*." In *Aspects of Essays in Honor of Edward Cameron Dimock, Jr*. Edited by Margaret Case and N. Gerald Barrier, 16–64. Delhi: American Institute of Indian Studies and Manohar, 1986.

———. *Śiva: The Erotic Ascetic*. New York: Oxford University Press, 1981.

Dvivedi, Harihar Nivas, ed. *Gvāliar ke Tomār*. Vol. 2. Gwalior: Vidya Mandir Prakasan, 1976.

Dwyer, Rachel. *Filming the Gods: Religion and Indian Cinema*. New York: Routledge, 2006.

Earl, James W. *Beginning the Mahābhārata: A Reader's Guide to the Frame Stories*. Woodland Hills, CA: South Asian Studies Association, 2011.

Fitzgerald, James. "Introduction." In *The Mahābhārata*. Vol. 7, *11. The Book of the Women, 12. The Book of Peace, Part One*, 100–42. Chicago: University of Chicago Press, 2004.

———. "Making Yudhiṣṭhira the King: The Dialectics and the Politics of Violence in the *Mahābhārata*." *Rocznik Orientalisticzny/Polskie Towarzystwo Orientalistyczne* 54, no. 1 (2001): 63–92.

———. "Nun Befuddles King, Shows *Karmayoga* Does Not Work: Sulabhā's Refutation of King Janaka at *MBh* 12.308." *Journal of Indian Philosophy* 30, no. 6 (2002): 641–77.

Flood, Finbarr B. *Objects of Translation: Material Culture and Medieval "Hindu-Muslim" Encounter*. Princeton, NJ: Princeton University Press, 2009.

Foucault, Michel. *The History of Sexuality*. Vol. 1, *An Introduction*. Translated by Robert Hurley. New York: Vintage Books, 1990.

Frasca, Richard Armando. *The Theatre of the Mahābhārata: Terukkūttu Performances in South India*. Honolulu: University of Hawaii Press, 1990.

Freeman, Rich. "The Literature of Hinduism in Malayalam." In *The Blackwell Companion to Hinduism*. Edited by Gavin Flood, 159–81. Oxford: Blackwell Publishing Ltd., 2003.

Gadamer, Hans-Georg. *Truth and Method*. Translated by Joel Weinsheimer and Donald G. Marshall. London: Continuum, 1975.

Garrett, Frances. *Religion, Medicine and the Human Embryo in Tibet*. New York: Routledge, 2008.

Geen, Jonathan. "The Evolution of Draupadī's Marriage in the Jaina Tradition." *Asiatische Studien-Etudes Asiatiques* 59, no. 2 (2005): 443–97.

———. "Jaina Origins for the Mahābhārata Story of Draupadī's Past Life." *Asiatische Studien-Etudes Asiatiques* 60, no. 3 (2006): 575–606.

———. "The Marriage of Draupadī in the Hindu and Jaina Mahābhārata." PhD diss., McMaster University, 2001.

Gerow, Edwin. "Abhinavagupta's Aesthetics as a Speculative Paradigm." *Journal of the American Oriental Society* 114, no. 2 (1994): 186–208.

———. "Bhāsa's *Ūrubhaṅga* and Indian Poetics." *Journal of the American Oriental Society* 105, no. 3 (1985): 405–12.

———. "Sanskrit Dramatic Theory and Kālidāsa's Plays." In *Theater of Memory: The Plays of Kālidāsa*. Edited by Barbara Stoler Miller, 42–62. New York: Columbia University Press, 1984.

Ghosh, Soumya Mohan, and Rajni Singh. "Demythologizing Draupadī: A Comparative Study of Saoli Mitra's *Nāthavatī anāthavat* ("Five Lords, Yet None a Protector") and Teejan Bai's *Draupadī cīrharaṇ*." *Archiv Orientalni* 82, no. 3 (2014): 511–28.

Gitomer, David L. "Can Men Change? Kālidāsa's Seducer King in the Thicket of Sanskrit Poetics." In *Revisiting Abhijñānaśākuntalam: Love, Lineage and Language in Kālidāsa's Nāṭaka*. Edited by Saswati Sengupta and Deepika Tandon, 167–84. Delhi: Orient Blackswan Private Limited, 2011.

———. "King Duryodhana: The *Mahābhārata* Discourse of Sinning and Virtue in Epic and Drama." *Journal of the American Oriental Society* 112, no. 2 (1992): 222–32.

———. "Rākṣasa Bhīma: Wolfbelly among Ogres and Brahmans in the Sanskrit *Mahābhārata* and the *Veṇīsaṃhāra*." In *Essays on the Mahābhārata*. Edited by Arvind Sharma, 296–323. Leiden: E. J. Brill, 1991.

———. "The 'Veṇīsaṃhāra' of Bhaṭṭa Nārāyaṇa: The Great Epic as Drama." PhD diss., Columbia University, 1988.

Goldman, Robert P. "Carried Away: Abduction and Marriage in Sanskrit *Itihāsa* and *Purāṇa*." In *Sanskrit Studies*. Vol. 4. Edited by Upendra Rao, 148–68. Delhi: D.K. Printworld, 2015.

———. "Gods in Hiding: The Virāṭa Parvan and the Divinity of the Indian Epic Hero." In *Modern Evaluation of the Mahābhārata*: *Professor R.K. Sharma Felicitation Volume*. Edited by Satya Pal Narang, 73–100. Delhi: Nag, 1995.

———. *Gods, Priests, and Warriors: The Bhṛgus of the Mahābhārata*. New York: Columbia University Press, 1977.

———. "The Great War and Ancient Memory: Modern Mahābhāratas and the Limits of Cultural Translation." *Visual Anthropology* 5, no. 1 (1992): 87–96.

Goldman, Sally J. Sutherland. "Against Their Will: Sexual Assault and the *Uttarakāṇḍa*." *Studies in History* 34, no. 2 (2019): 164–81.

———. "The Monstrous Feminine: Rākṣasīs and Other Others—The Archaic Mother of Bhāsa's *Madhyamavyāyoga*." In *On Meaning and Mantras: Essays in Honor of Frits Staal*. Edited by George Thompson and Richard K. Payne, 247–74. Moraga, CA: Institute of Buddhist Studies and BDK America, Inc., 2016.

———. "Sītā and Draupadī: Aggressive Behavior and Female Role-Models in the Sanskrit Epics." *Journal of the American Oriental Society* 109, no. 1 (1989): 63–79.

Gonzalez-Reimann, Luis. "The Divinity of Rāma in the *Rāmāyaṇa* of Vālmīki." *Journal of Indian Philosophy* 34, no. 3 (2006): 203–20.

———. *The Mahābhārata and the Yugas: India's Great Epic Poem and the Hindu System of World Ages*. New York: Peter Lang, 2002.

Gopal, B. R. *The Chalukyas of Kalyana and The Kalachuris*. Dharwad: Karnatak University Prasaranga, 1981.

Gopalakrishnan, Sudha. *Kutiyattam: The Heritage Theatre of India*. Delhi: Niyogi Books, 2011.

Granoff, Phyllis. "Mountains of Eternity: Raidhū and the Colossal Jinas of Gwalior." *Rivista di Studi Sudasiatici* 1 (2006): 31–50.

Habib, Mohammad, and Khaliq Ahmad Nizami, eds. *Comprehensive History of India*. Vol. 5, *The Delhi Sultanate*. Delhi: People's Publishing House, 1970.

Hacker, Paul. "Dharma in Hinduism." Translated by Donald R. Davis Jr. *Journal of Indian Philosophy* 34, no. 5 (2006): 479–96.

Hall, Stuart. "The Neo-Liberal Revolution." *Cultural Studies* 25, no. 6 (2011): 705–28.

Halperin, Ehud. *The Many Faces of a Himalayan Goddess: Haḍimbā, Her Devotees, and Religion in Rapid Change*. New York: Oxford University Press, 2019.

Hans, Raj Kumar. "Making Sense of Dalit Sikh History." In *Dalit Studies*. Edited by Ramnarayan S. Rawat and K. Satyanarayana, 131–51. Durham, NC: Duke University Press, 2016.

Hardy, Friedhelm. *Viraha-Bhakti: The Early History of Kṛṣṇa Devotion in South India*. Delhi: Oxford University Press, 1983.

Hawley, John Stratton. *The Memory of Love: Sūrdās Sings to Krishna*. New York: Oxford University Press, 2009.

Hellwig, Oliver. "Stratifying the Mahābhārata: The Textual Position of the Bhagavadgītā." *Indo-Iranian Journal* 60, no. 2 (2017): 132–69.

Hens, Sander. "Beyond Power and Praise: Nayacandra Sūri's Tragic-historical Epic Hammīra-mahākāvya as a Subversive Response to Hero Glorification in Early Tomar Gwalior." *South Asian History and Culture* 11, no. 1 (2020): 40–59.

Hess, Linda. "Marshaling Sacred Texts: Ram's Name and Story in Late Twentieth-Century Indian Politics." Academia. June 2020. https://www.academia.edu/43473803/Marshaling_Sacred_Texts_Rams_Name_and_Story_in_Late_Twentieth-Century_Indian_Politics. Previously published as "Marshalling Sacred Texts: Ram's Name and Story in Late Twentieth-Century Indian Politics." *Journal of Vaishnava Studies* 2, no. 4 (1994): 175–206.

Hiltebeitel, Alf. *The Cult of Draupadī*. Vol. 1, *Mythologies: From Gingee to Kurukṣetra*. Chicago: University of Chicago Press, 1988.

———. *The Cult of Draupadī*. Vol. 2, *On Hindu Ritual and the Goddess*. Chicago: University of Chicago Press, 1991.

———. *Dharma: Its Early History in Law, Religion, and Narrative*. New York: Oxford University Press, 2011.

———. "Draupadī's Hair." In *Essays by Alf Hiltebeitel*. Vol. 2, *When the Goddess was a Woman: Mahābhārata Ethnographies*. Edited by Vishwa Adluri and Joydeep Bagchee, 3–32. Leiden: Brill, 2011.

———. "Dying Before the *Mahābhārata* War: Martial and Transsexual Body-building for Aravāṉ." *The Journal of Asian Studies* 54, no. 2 (1995): 447–73.

———. "Krishna in the *Mahabharata:* The Death of Karna." In *Krishna: A Sourcebook*. Edited by Edwin F. Bryant, 23–76. New York: Oxford University Press, 2007.

———. "Not without Subtales: Telling Laws and Truths in the Sanskrit Epics." In *Argument and Design: The Unity of the Mahābhārata*. Edited by Vishwa Adluri and Joydeep Bagchee, 10–68. Boston: Brill, 2016.

———. *The Ritual of Battle: Krishna in the Mahābhārata*. Albany: State University of New York Press, 1976.

———. "Śiva, the Goddess, and the Disguises of the Pāṇḍavas and Draupadī." *History of Religions* 20, no. 1/2 (1980): 147–74.

Hopkins, Steven P. *An Ornament for Jewels: Poems for the Lord of Gods by Vedāntadeśika*. New York: Oxford University Press, 2007.

Horstmann, Monika. *Der Zusammenhalt der Welt: Religiöse Herrschaftslegitimation und Religionspolitik Mahārājā Savāī Jaisinghs (1700–1743)*. Wiesbaden: Otto Harrassowitz, 2009.

Hudson, Emily T. *Disorienting Dharma: Ethics and the Aesthetics of Suffering in the Mahabharata*. New York: Oxford University Press, 2013.

Hulin, Michael. *Sāṃkhya Literature*. Wiesbaden: Otto Harrassowitz, 1978.

Hymes, Dell. *Breakthrough Into Performance*. Rimini: Guaraldi, 2015.

Ingalls, Daniel H. H. "The Harivaṃśa as a Mahākāvya." In *Mélanges d'Indianisme à la mémoire de Louis Renou*, 381–94. Paris: Éditions de Boccard, 1968.

Jacobi, Hermann. "On Bhāravi and Māgha." *Wiener Zeitschrift für die Kunde des Morgenlandes* 3 (1889): 121–45.

Jain, Kundanlal. *Dillī-Jina-grantha-ratnāvalī: Dig. Jaina Sarasvatī Bhaṇḍāra, Nayā Mandira, Dharmapurā, Dehalī ke Saṃskṛta, Prākṛta, evaṃ Apabhraṃśa kī hastalikhita pāṇḍulipiyoṃ kī sūcī*. Delhi: Bharatiya Jnanpith Prakasan, 1981.

Jain, Rajaram. *Raïdhū Sāhitya kā Alocanātmak-pariśīlan*. Vaisali: Prakrt, Jainsastra aur Ahimsas-samsthan, 1974.

Jaini, Padmanabh S. "Bhaṭṭāraka Śrībhūṣaṇa's *Pāṇḍavapurāṇa*: A Case of Jaina Sectarian Plagiarism." In *Middle Indo-Aryan and Jaina Studies: Proceedings of the VIIth World Sanskrit Conference*. Edited by J. Bronkhorst and C. Caillat, 59–68. Leiden: E. J. Brill, 1991.

———. "A Purāṇic Counter Tradition." In *Purāṇa Perennis: Reciprocity and Transformation in Hindu and Jaina Texts*. Edited by Wendy Doniger, 207–49. Albany: State University of New York Press, 1993.

Jatavallabhula, Danielle Feller. "Raṇayajña: The Mahābhārata War as a Sacrifice." In *Violence Denied: Violence, Non-Violence, and the Rationalization of Violence in South Asian Cultural History*. Edited by Jan E. M. Houben and Karel R. Van Kooij. Leiden: Brill, 1999.

Jha, Pankaj Kumar. "Beyond the Local and the Universal: Exclusionary Strategies of Expansive Literary Cultures in Fifteenth Century Mithila." *The Indian Economic and Social History Review* 51, no. 1 (2014): 1–40.

Joshi, M. R. "Mahābhārata and Marathi Vernacular Writers." In *Mahābhārata: The End of an Era (Yugānta)*. Edited by Ajay Mitra Shastri, 367–80. Shimla: India Institute of Advanced Study, 2004.

Kamath, Harshita Mruthinti, and Velcheru Narayana Rao. "Introduction." In *Nandi Timmana. Theft of a Tree*. Translated by Harshita Mruthinti Kamath and Velcheru Narayana Rao. Murty Classical Library of India. Cambridge, MA: Harvard University Press, forthcoming.

Kane, Pandurang V. *History of Dharmaśāstra*. Vol. 5, Pt. 2. Poona: Bhandarkar Oriental Research Institute, 1962.

Kanjilal, Sucheta. "Modern Mythologies: The Epic Imagination in Contemporary Indian Literature." PhD diss., University of South Florida, 2017.

Karantha, K. Shivarama. *Yakṣagāna*. Delhi: Abhinav Publications, 1997.

Kaslival, Kasturcand. *Kavivar Bulākhīcand Bulākīdās aur Hemrāj* (Śrī Mahāvīr Granth Akādamī 6). Jaipur: Sri Mahavir Granth Akadami, 1983.

Kaviraj, Sudipta. "The Second *Mahābhārata*." In *South Asian Texts in History: Critical Engagements with Sheldon Pollock*. Edited by Whitney Cox, Yigal Bronner, and Lawrence McCrea, 103–24. Ann Arbor: Association for Asian Studies, 2011.

———. *The Unhappy Consciousness: Bankimchandra Chattopadhyay and the Formation of Nationalist Discourse in India*. Delhi: Oxford University Press, 1995.

Keith, A. B. *The Sāṃkhya System: A History of the Sāṃkhya Philosophy*. London: Oxford University Press, 1918.

Khan, Sami Ahmad. "Bollywood's Encounters with the Third Kind: A Critical Catalogue of Hindi Science Fiction Films." In *Bollywood and Its Others: Towards New Configurations*. Edited by Sarwal Kishore and P.P. Patraj, 186–201. Basingstoke: Palgrave Macmillan, 2014.

Khanna, Ranjana. "In Search of a Voice for Dopdi/Draupadi: Writing the Other Woman's Story Out of the 'Dark Continent.'" In *Women's Lives/Women's Times: New Essays on Auto/Biography*. Edited by Trev Lynn Broughton and Linda R. Anderson, 103–20. Albany: State University of New York Press, 1997.

Koskikallio, Petteri, and Christophe Vielle. "Epic and Puranic Texts Attributed to Jaimini." *Indologica Taurinensia* 27 (2001): 67–93.

Kripalani, Krishna. *Rabindranath Tagore: A Biography*. New York: Grove Press, 1962.

Kulke, Herman. "Jagannath as the state deity under the Gajapatis of Orissa." In *The Cult of Jagannath and the Regional Tradition of Orissa*. Edited by A. Eschmann, H. Kulke, and G. C. Tripathi, 199–208. Delhi: Manohar, 1986.

Lakshmikantham, Pingala. *Āndhra Sāhitya Caritra*. Hyderabad: Andhra Pradesh Sahitya Academy, 1974.

Lamb, Ramdas. *Rapt in the Name: The Ramnamis, Ramnam, and Untouchable Religion in Central India*. Albany: State University of New York Press, 2002.

Landon, Brooks. *Science Fiction After 1900: From the Steam Man to the Stars*. New York: Routledge, 2002.

Loomba, Ania, and Ritty A. Lukose, eds. *South Asian Feminisms*. Durham, NC: Duke University Press, 2012.

Lorndale, Timothy. "Epic Translation: Ranna's *Sāhasabhīmavijaya* and the Mahābhārata's Afterlife in Medieval Karṇāṭa." PhD diss., University of Pennsylvania, forthcoming.

Lothspeich, Pamela. *Epic Nation: Reimagining the Mahabharata in the Age of the Empire*. Delhi: Oxford University Press, 2009.

Luard, C. E., and Dwarka Nath. *Gwalior State Gazetteer*. 3 vols. Calcutta: Superintendent Government Printing, 1908.

Luthra, Rashmi. "Clearing Sacred Ground: Women-Centered Interpretations of the Indian Epics." *Feminist Formations* 26, no. 2 (2014): 135–61.

Lutgendorf, Philip. "Bending the Bhārata: Two Uncommon Cinematic Adaptations." In *Popular Indian Cinema and Literature: Recasting the Tradition*. Edited by Heidi Pauwels, 19–41. London: Routledge, 2008.

———. *Hanuman's Tale: The Messages of a Divine Monkey*. New York: Oxford University Press, 2007.

———. "Is There an Indian Way of Filmmaking?" *International Journal of Hindu Studies* 10, no. 3 (2006): 227–56.

———. *The Life of a Text: Performing the Rāmcaritmānas of Tulsidas*. Berkeley: University of California Press, 1991.

Madley, Benjamin. *An American Genocide: The United States and the California Indian Catastrophe, 1846–1873*. New Haven, CT: Yale University Press, 2016.

Mahadevan, Thennilapuram P. "On the Southern Recension of the Mahābhārata, Brahman Migrations, and the Brāhmī Paleography." *Electronic Journal of Vedic Studies* 15, no. 2 (2008): 43–147.

Mahawar, Niranjan. *Folk Theatre Pandwani*. Delhi: Abhinav Publications, 2013.

Mankekar, Purnima. *Screening Culture, Viewing Politics: An Ethnography of Television, Womanhood, and Nation in Postcolonial India*. Durham, NC: Duke University Press, 1999.

McCrea, Lawrence. "The Conquest of Cool: Theology and Aesthetics in Māgha's Śiśupālavadha." In *Innovations and Turning Points: Toward a History of Kāvya Literature*. Edited by Yigal Bronner, David Shulman, and Gary Tubb, 123–41. Delhi: Oxford University Press, 2014.

———. "*Śāntarasa* in the *Rājataraṅgiṇī*: History, Epic, and Moral Decay." *Indian Economic and Social History Review* 50 (2013): 179–99.

———. *The Teleology of Poetics in Medieval Kashmir*. Cambridge, MA: Harvard University Press, 2008.

McGann, Jerome J. "Theory of Texts." *London Review of Books* 10, no. 4 (1988): 20–21.

McGregor. Ronald Stuart. "An Early Hindi (Brajbhāṣā) Version of the Rāma Story." In *Devotion Divine: Bhakti Traditions from the Regions of India*. Edited by Diana Eck and Françoise Mallison, 181–96. Groningen: Egbert Forsten, 1991.

———. *Hindi Literature from Its Beginnings to the Nineteenth Century*. Wiesbaden: Otto Harrassowitz, 1984.

———. "A Narrative Poet's View of His Material: Viṣṇudās's Introduction to His Brajbhāṣā *Pāṇḍav-carit* (AD 1435)." In *The Banyan Tree: Essays on Early Literature in New Indo-Aryan Languages*. Edited by Mariola Offredi, 335–42. Delhi: Manohar, 2000.

———. "The Progress of Hindi, Part 1: The Development of a Transregional Idiom." In *Literary Cultures in History: Reconstructions from South Asia*. Edited by Sheldon Pollock, 912–57. Berkeley: University of California Press, 2003.

———. "Viṣṇudās and His *Rāmāyan-kathā*." In *Studies in Early Modern Indo-Aryan Languages, Literature and Culture*. Edited by Alan Entwistle and Carol Salomon with Heidi Pauwels and Michael C. Shapiro, 239–47. Delhi: Manohar, 1999.

McHugh, James. *Sandalwood and Carrion: Smell in Indian Religion and Culture*. New York: Oxford University Press, 2012.

McLain, Karline. *India's Immortal Comic Books: Gods, Kings, and Other Heroes*. Bloomington: Indiana University Press, 2009.

Mehendale, M. A. "The Critical Edition of the Mahābhārata—Its Constitution, Achievements, and Limitations." In *Texts and Variations of the Mahābhārata: Contextual, Regional, and Performative Traditions*. Edited by Kalyan Kumar Chakravarty, 3–23. Delhi: National Mission for Manuscripts, 2009.

Menon, Nivedita. "Is Feminism about 'Women'?" *Economic and Political Weekly* 50, no. 17 (2015): 37–44.

Minkowski, C. Z. "Janamejaya's *Sattra* and Ritual Structure." *Journal of the American Oriental Society* 109, no. 3 (1989): 401–20.

———. "Nīlakaṇṭha's Mahābhārata." *Seminar* 608 (2010): 32–38.

———. "What Makes a Work 'Traditional'? On the Success of Nīlakaṇṭha's *Mahābhārata* Commentary." In *Boundaries, Dynamics and Construction of Traditions*. Edited by Federico Squarcini, 225–44. Florence: Firenze University Press, 2005.

Mirsepassi, Ali Amrita Basu, and Frederick Weaver. eds. *Localizing Knowledge in a Globalizing World: Recasting the Area Studies Debate*. Syracuse, NY: Syracuse University Press, 2003.

Mishra, Ganeshbihari, Shukdevbihari Mishra, and Shyambihari Mishra. *Miśrabandhuvinod*. 2 vols. Hyderabad: Ganga-Granthagara, 1972. First published 1913 by Hindi Granth Prasarak Mandali (Allahabad).

Mishra, Mahendra Kumar. "A Hero of Mahābhārata in Folklore of Central India." In *Mahābhārata in the Tribal and Folk Traditions of India*. Edited by K. S. Singh, 157–70. Shimla: Indian Institute of Advanced Study, 1993.

Misri, Deepti. " 'Are You a Man?': Performing Naked Protest in India." *Signs* 36, no. 3 (2011): 603–25.

Mitra, Ananda. *Television and Popular Culture in India: A Study of the Mahabharat*. Delhi: Sage, 1993.

Mohanty, Chandra Talpade. *Feminism without Borders: Decolonizing Theory, Practicing Solidarity*. Durham, NC: Duke University Press, 2003.

Monier-Williams, Sir Monier. *Sanskrit English Dictionary*. Oxford: Clarendon Press, 1899.

Mookerjea-Leonard, Debali. "Quarantined: Women and the Partition" *Comparative Studies of South Asia, Africa and the Middle East* 24, no. 1 (2004): 33–46.

Narasimhacar, D. L. "Gadāyuddhada Ŏndu Padyada Arthavicāra." In *Pīṭhakĕgaḷu, Lekhanagaḷu*. Edited by D. L. Narasimhacar, 929–33. Mysore: D. V. K. Murthy Prakashan, 2015. First published 1971, D. V. K. Murthy Prakashan (Mysore).

Narayana Rao, Velcheru. "Coconut and Honey: Sanskrit and Telugu in Medieval Andhra." In *Text and Tradition in South India*, 152–74. Ranikhet: Permanent Black, 2016.

———. "Multiple Literary Cultures in Telugu: Court, Temple, and Public." In *Text and Tradition in South India*, 27–93. Ranikhet: Permanent Black, 2016.

Narayana Rao, Velcheru, and David Shulman. *Classical Telugu Poetry: An Anthology*. Berkeley: University of California Press, 2002.

———. *A Poem at the Right Moment: Remembered Verses from Premodern South India*. Berkeley: University of California Press, 1998.

Narayanan, Vasudha. *The Way and the Goal: Expressions of Devotion in the Early Śrī Vaiṣṇava Tradition*. Washington, DC: Institute for Vaishnava Studies, 1987.

Natarajan, Kanchana. "Gendering of Early Indian Philosophy: A Study of 'Samkhyakarika' " *Economic and Political Weekly* 36, no. 17 (2001): 1398–1401, 1403–1404.

Novetzke, Christian. *The Quotidian Revolution: Vernacularization, Religion, and the Premodern Public Sphere in India*. Columbia University Press, 2016.

Oberlin, Heike, and David Shulman, eds. *Two Masterpieces of Kūṭiyāṭṭam: Mantrāṅkam and Aṅgulīyāṅkam*. Delhi: Oxford University Press, 2019.

Olivelle, Patrick. "The Semantic History of Dharma: The Middle and Late Vedic Periods." *Journal of Indian Philosophy* 32 (2004): 491–511.

Orsini, Francesca. "Texts and Tellings: *Kathas* in the Fifteenth and Sixteenth Centuries." In *Tellings and Texts: Music, Literature and Performance in North India*. Edited by Francesca Orsini and Katherine Butler Schofield, 327–58. Cambridge, UK: Open Book Publishers, 2015.

Pandey, Gyanendra. *A History of Prejudice: Race, Caste, and Difference in India and the United States*. Cambridge: Cambridge University Press, 2013.

Paramasivan, Vasudha. "Between Text and Sect: Early Nineteenth Century Shifts in the Theology of Ram." PhD diss., University of California, Berkeley, 2010.

Patel, Deven M. *Text to Tradition: The Naiṣadhīyacarita and Literary Community in South Asia*. New York: Columbia University Press, 2014.

Pathak, Shubha. *Divine Yet Human Epics: Reflections of Poetic Rulers from Ancient Greece and India*. Hellenic Studies Series 62. Washington, DC: Center for Hellenic Studies, Harvard University, 2014.

Patnaik, Pathani. "Sarala's Oriya Mahābhārata 'A Vox Populi' In Oriya Literature." In *Mahābhārata in the Tribal and Folk Traditions of India*. Edited by K. S. Singh, 171–76. Shimla: Indian Institute of Advanced Study, 1993.

Pattanaik, Devdutt. Jaya: *An Illustrated Retelling of the Mahabharata*. Delhi: Penguin Books, 2010.

Patton, Laurie L. "How Do You Conduct Yourself? Gender and the Construction of a Dialogical Self in the *Mahābhārata*." In *Gender and Narrative in the Mahābhārata*. Edited by Simon Brodbeck and Brian Blackburn, 97–109. London: Routledge, 2007.

———. "*Samvada* as a Literary and Philosophical Genre: An Overlooked Resource for Public Debate and Conflict Resolution?" *Evam* 3 (2004): 177–90.

Pauwels, Heidi. "The Tomars' New Emotional Regime: Martial Hindu Identity?" *South Asian History and Culture* 11, no. 1 (2020): 23–39.

Peterson, Indira Viswanathan. *Design and Rhetoric in a Sanskrit Court Epic: The Kirātārjunīya of Bhāravi*. Albany: State University of New York Press, 2003.

Phillips-Rodriguez, Wendy J. "Unrooted Trees: A Way around the Dilemma of Recension." In *Papers of the 13th World Sanskrit Conference*. Vol. 2, *Battle, Bards and Brāhmins*. Edited by John Brockington, 217–29. Delhi: Motilal Banarsidass, 2012.

Pillai, Sohini Sarah. "Region and Religion in Retellings of the Mahābhārata." PhD diss., University of California, Berkeley, forthcoming.

Pinch, William R. *Warrior Ascetics and Indian Empires*. New York: Cambridge University Press, 2006.

Pintchman, Tracy. *Guests at God's Wedding: Celebrating Kartik among the Women of Benares*. Albany: State University of New York Press, 2005.

Pollock, Sheldon I. "Introduction." In *The Rāmāyaṇa of Vālmīki: An Epic of Ancient India*. Vol. 2, *Ayodhyākāṇḍa*. Translated by Sheldon I. Pollock, 1–76. Princeton, NJ: Princeton University Press, 1986.

———. *The Language of the Gods in the World of Men: Sanskrit, Culture, and Power in Premodern India*. Berkeley: University of California Press, 2006.

———. "*Rākṣasas* and Others." *Indologica Taurinensia* 13 (1985–86): 263–81.

———. "Rāmāyaṇa and Political Imagination in India." *The Journal of Asian Studies* 52, no. 2 (1993): 261–97.

———, ed. *A Rasa Reader: Classical Indian Aesthetics*. New York: Columbia University Press, 2016.

Preciado-Solís, Benjamín. *The Kṛṣṇa Cycle in the Purāṇas: Themes and Motifs in a Heroic Saga*. Delhi: Motilal Banarsidass, 1984.

Premi, Nathuram. *Jain Sāhitya aur Itihās*. Bombay: Hindi Granth Ratnakar, 1942.

Pritchett, Frances W. *The Romance Tradition in Urdu: Adventures from the Dāstān of Amīr 'Hamzah*. New York: Columbia University Press, 1991.

———. "The World of Amar Chitra Katha." In *Media and the Transformation of Religion in South Asia*. Edited by Lawrence A. Babb and Susan S. Wadley, 76–106. Philadelphia: University of Pennsylvania Press, 1995.

Quint, David. *Epic and Empire: Politics and Generic Form from Virgil to Milton*. Princeton, NJ: Princeton University Press, 1993.

Ramanujan, A. K. "Repetition in the *Mahābhārata*." In *Essays on the Mahābhārata*. Edited by Arvind Sharma, 419–43. Leiden: E. J. Brill, 1991.

———. "Three Hundred *Rāmāyaṇas*: Five Examples and Three Thoughts on Translation." In *Many Rāmāyaṇas: The Diversity of a Narrative Tradition in South Asia*. Edited by Paula Richman, 22–49. Berkeley: University of California Press, 1991.

———. "Where Mirrors are Windows: Toward an Anthology of Reflections." *History of Religions* 28, no. 3 (1989): 187–216.

Raveendran, P. P. "Fiction and Reception: Reconstructions of the Mahabharata in Malayalam." In *Reflections and Variations on The Mahabharata*. Edited by T. R. S. Sharma, 287–300. Delhi: Sahitya Akademi, 2009.

Rawat, Ramnarayan S., and K. Satyanarayana. "Introduction: Dalit Studies New Perspectives on Indian History and Society." In *Dalit Studies*. Edited by Ramnarayan S. Rawat and K. Satyanarayana, 1–25. Durham, NC: Duke University Press, 2016.

Richman, Paula. "Introduction: The Diversity of the *Rāmāyaṇa* Tradition." In *Many Rāmāyaṇas: The Diversity of a Narrative Tradition in South Asia*. Edited by Paula Richman, 3–21. Berkeley: University of California Press, 1991.

———, ed. *Many Rāmāyaṇas: The Diversity of a Narrative Tradition in South Asia*. Berkeley: University of California Press, 1991.

———, ed. *Questioning Rāmāyaṇas: A South Asian Tradition*. Berkeley: University of California Press, 2001.

———. "Silence in Muthal Naidoo's "Flight from the Mahabharath": Disrupting the Power of Categories in a South African play." *Tarikh: A Journal of History* (2011): 40–48.

———. "Why Did Bhima Wed Hidimbaa? A Comparative Perspective on Marriage to the Other." In *Reflections and Variations on The Mahabharata*. Edited by T. R. S. Sharma, 172–200. Delhi: Sahitya Akademi, 2009.

Ritti, Shrinivas. "Mahābhārata in Early Kannada Literature." In *Mahābhārata: The End of an Era (Yugānta)*. Edited by Ajay Mitra Shastri. 353–66. Shimla: India Institute of Advanced Study, 2004.

Rosen, Steven J. *The Jedi in the Lotus: Star Wars and the Hindu Tradition*. Huntingdon, UK: Arktos Media Ltd., 2010.

Sarkar, Tanika. *Hindu Wife, Hindu Nation: Community, Religion, and Cultural Nationalism*. Delhi: Permanent Black, 2001.

Sathaye, Adheesh. *Crossing the Lines of Caste: Viśvāmitra and the Construction of Brahmin Power in Hindu Mythology*. New York: Oxford University Press, 2015.

Sax, William S. *Dancing the Self: Personhood and Performance in the Pāṇḍav Līlā of Garhwal*. New York: Oxford University Press, 2002.

———. "Worshiping Epic Villains: A Kaurava Cult in the Central Himalayas." In *Epic Traditions in the Contemporary World: The Poetics of Community*. Edited by Margaret Beissinger, Jane Tylus, and Susanne Wofford, 171–82. Berkeley: University of California Press, 1999.

Schechner, Richard. *Performance Studies: An Introduction*. New York: Routledge, 2002.

Selby, Martha Ann. *Grow Long, Blessed Night: Love Poems from Classical India*. New York: Oxford University Press, 2000.

Sen, Amiya P. *Bankim Chandra Chattopadhyay: An Intellectual Biography*. Delhi: Oxford University Press, 2008.

Shalom, Naama. *Re-ending the Mahābhārata: The Rejection of Dharma in the Sanskrit Epic*. Albany: State University of New York Press, 2017.

Sharma, Arvind, ed. *Essays on the Mahābhārata*. Leiden: E. J. Brill, 1991.

Sharma, Chandradhar. *A Critical Survey of Indian Philosophy*. London: Rider & Company, 1960.

Sharma, Chinmay. "Many Mahabharatas: Linking Mythic Re-Tellings in Contemporary India." PhD diss., University of London: SOAS, 2017.

Shelat, Bharati. "Mahābhārata and its Study in Gujarati." In *Mahābhārata: The End of an Era (Yugānta)*. Edited by Ajay Mitra Shastri, 381–99. Shimla: India Institute of Advanced Study, 2004.

Shildrick, Margrit, and Janet Price. "Openings on the Body: A Critical Introduction." In *Feminist Theory and the Body*. Edited by Janet Price and Margrit Shildrick, 1–14. New York: Routledge, 1999.

Shukla, Ramchandra. *Hindī Sāhitya Kā Itihās*. 9th ed. Banaras: Nagari Pracharini Sabha, 1942.

Shulman, David. "On Being Human in the Sanskrit Epic: The Riddle of Nala." *Journal of Indian Philosophy* 22, no. 1 (1994): 1–29.

———. *The King and the Clown in South Indian Myth and Poetry*. Princeton, NJ: Princeton University Press, 1985.

———. *More than Real: A History of the Imagination in South India*. Cambridge, MA: Harvard University Press, 2012.

———. "The Serpent and the Sacrifice: An Anthill Myth from Tiruvārūr." *History of Religions* 18, no. 2 (1978): 107–37.

———. "Toward a Historical Poetics of the Sanskrit Epics." In *The Wisdom of Poets: Studies in Tamil, Telugu, and Sanskrit*, 21–38. Delhi: Oxford University Press, 2001.

Singh, Upinder. *Political Violence in Ancient India*. Cambridge, MA: Harvard University Press, 2017.

Smith, Frederick M. *The Self-Possessed: Deity and Spirit Possession in South Asian Literature and Civilization*. New York: Columbia University Press, 2006.

Smith, John D. *The Epic of Pābūjī: A Study, Transcription, and Translation*. Cambridge: Cambridge University Press, 1991.

Smith, W. L. "The Jaiminibhārata and Its Eastern Vernacular Versions." *Studia Orientalia* 85 (1999): 389–406.

Sondhi, Reeta. "Demystifying Shakuntalam." *The Economic Times*. July 5, 1987.

Spivak, Gayatri Chakravorty. "Subaltern Studies. Deconstructing Historiography." In *The Spivak Reader*. Edited by Donna Landry and Gerald MacLean, 203–37. London: Routledge, 1996.

Srikanthayya, T. N. "Gadāyuddhavū Svīkaraṇavicāravū." In *Ranna Kavi Praśasti*, 73–97. Bangalore: Kannada Sahitya Parishat, 1978. First Published 1928, Visvavidyanilaya Sangha (Mysore).

Subramanian, M. V. *The Mahabharata Story: Vyasa & Variations*. Madras: Higginbothams (Private) Ltd., 1967.

Sukthankar, V. S. "Studies in Bhāsa." In *V. S. Sukthankar Memorial Edition*. Vol. 2, Analecta. Edited by P. K. Gode. 82–184. Bombay: Karnatak Publishing House, 1945.

Sullivan, Bruce M. "Dying on Stage in the *Nāṭyaśāstra* and *Kūṭiyāṭṭam*: Perspectives from the Sanskrit Theatre Tradition." *Asian Theatre Journal* 24, no. 2 (2007): 422–39.

———. "Kerala's Mahābhārata on Stage: Texts and Performative Practices in Kūṭiyāṭṭam Drama." *Journal of Hindu Studies* 3, no. 1 (2010): 124–42.

———. "The *Mahābhārata*—Perspectives on its Ends and Endings." *International Journal of Hindu Studies* 15, no. 1 (2011): 1–7.

Sutton, Nicolas. "An Exposition of Early Sāṁkhya, A Rejection of the *Bhagavad-Gītā* and a Critique of the Role of Women in Hindu Society: The *Sulabhā-Janaka-Saṁvāda*." *Annals of the Bhandarkar Oriental Research Institute* 80 (1999): 53–65.

Talbot, Cynthia. *The Last Hindu Emperor: Prithviraj Chauhan and the Indian Past, 1200–2000*. New York: Cambridge University Press, 2016.

Tandon, Sunit. "A Directors' Play." *The Sunday Observer*. August 30, 1987.

Taub, Amanda. "Myanmar Follows Global Pattern in How Ethnic Cleansing Begins." *New York Times*. September 19, 2017. A4.

Tennyson, Alfred. *Idylls of the King*. London: C. Kegan Paul & Co., 1878.

Thapar, Romila. *Early India: From the Origins to AD 1300*. Berkeley: University of California Press, 2002.

———. *Śakuntalā: Texts, Readings, Histories*. London: Anthem Press, 1999.

Tharanatha, N. S. "Ranna: Itivṛtta, Paraśurāmacarita, Cakreśvaracarita." In *Kannaḍa Sāhitya Caritrĕ: Mūrunĕya Saṃpuṭa*. Edited by H. M. Nayak and T. V. Venkatachala Sastry, 570–605. Mysore: Institute of Kannada Studies, University of Mysore, 1976.

Thompson, M. S. H. "The Mahābhārata in Tamil." *Journal of the Royal Asiatic Society of Great Britain and Ireland* 92, no. 3/4 (1960): 115–23.

Tieken, Herman. "The So-Called Trivandrum Plays Attributed to Bhāsa." *Wiener Zeitschrift für die Kunde Südasiens und Archiv für Indische Philosophie* 37 (1993): 5–44.

Truschke, Audrey. *Culture of Encounters: Sanskrit at the Mughal Court.* New York: Columbia University Press, 2016.
Tubb, Gary A. "*Śāntarasa* in the *Mahābhārata*." In *Essays on the Mahābhārata.* Edited by Arvind Sharma, 171–203. Leiden: E. J. Brill, 1991.
Van Buitenen, J. A. B. "Studies in Sāmkhya (III)." *Journal of the American Oriental Society* 88, no. 2 (1957): 88–107.
Vanita, Ruth. "The Self Is Not Gendered: Sulabha's Debate with King Janaka." *NWESA Journal* 15, no. 2 (2003): 76–93.
Varadpande, M. L. *Mahabharata in Performance.* Delhi: Clarion Books, 1990.
Vasumati, E. Telugu *Literature in the Qutub Shahi Period.* Hyderabad: Abul Kalam Azad Oriental Research Institute, n.d., ca. 1960.
Venkatesa Acharya, Kambalur. *Mahabharata and Variations: Perundevanar and Pampa; A Comparative Study.* Kurnool: Vyasaraja Publications, 1981.
Venkatesan, Archana. "Speared through the Heart: The Sound of God in the Worlds of Tirumaṅkai." *Journal of Hindu Studies* 10, no. 3 (2017): 275–300.
Viswanath, Rupa. *The Pariah Problem: Caste, Religion, and the Social in Modern India.* New York: Columbia University Press, 2014.
Von Simson, Georg. "Text Layers in the *Mahābhārata*: Some Observations in Connection with *Mahābhārata* VII.131." In *The Mahābhārata Revisited.* Edited by R. N. Dandekar, 37–60. Delhi: Sahitya Akademi, 1990.
Wadley, Susan, ed. *Damayanti and Nala: The Many Lives of a Story.* Delhi: Chronicle, 2011.
Willis, Michael D. *Inscriptions of Gopakṣetra: Materials for the History of Central India.* London: British Museum Press, 1996.
Zarrilli, Phillip B. *Kathakali Dance-Drama: Where Gods and Demons Come to Play.* London and New York: Routledge 2000.
Zvelebil, Kamil. *Companion Studies to the History of Tamil Literature.* Leiden: E. J. Brill, 1992.

Contributors

Amanda Culp is a performance historian and dramaturg who specializes in Sanskrit drama and intercultural theater practice. Her research on Sanskrit theater in performance has been published in *Theatre Journal*, the *Routledge Companion to Scenography*, and the *Wiley-Blackwell Companion to World Literature*. For more on her work, please visit her website: amandalculp.com.

Eva De Clercq is associate professor of Indian language and culture at Ghent University, Belgium. Her research focuses on the literary heritage of the Jains, especially in Apabhramsha. Her translation of Svayambhudeva's *Paumacariu*, a Jain Ramayana in Apabhramsha, is published in the Murty Classical Library of India.

David Gitomer is a member of the DePaul University Department of Religious Studies. He has translated a number of Sanskrit dramas, including the *Vikramorvaśīya* and the *Veṇīsaṃhāra,* and written on Sanskrit aesthetics in epic and drama. He recently completed a translation of the *Bhīṣmaparvan* for the *Mahābhārata* translation series that is based on the epic's critical edition.

Robert Goldman is the William and Catherine Magistretti Distinguished Professor of Sanskrit at the University of California at Berkeley. He is the general editor and a principal translator of the *Rāmāyaṇa of Vālmīki*, the scholarly translation and annotation of the critical edition of the epic published by Princeton University Press. He is the author of *Gods, Priests, and Warriors: The Bhṛgus of the Mahābhārata* and numerous scholarly articles.

Sally J. Sutherland Goldman is a senior lecturer in Sanskrit at the University of California at Berkeley, where she has taught for many years. In 2012, she was awarded the Distinguished Teaching Award at Berkeley for her teaching and contributions to Sanskrit pedagogy. She is the co-author of *Devavāṇīpraveśikā: An Introduction to Sanskrit Language* (1980, 2004), co-annotator of the first book of the *Rāmāyaṇa of Vālmīki*, the *Bālakāṇḍa* (1984), co-author of the fifth book, the *Sundarakāṇḍa* (1996), the sixth book, the *Yuddhakāṇḍa* (2009), and the seventh book, the *Uttarakāṇḍa* (2017), and the author of numerous articles focusing primarily on issues of gender.

Sudha Gopalakrishnan is executive director of *Sahapedia*, an online encyclopedic resource on the arts and cultures of India, and was earlier the founder director of India's National Mission for Manuscripts. She was on the editorial team of the *Encyclopaedia of Indian Literature* and *Encyclopaedia of the Arts* (IGNCA) and has been on national and international committees on archives and libraries, intangible cultural heritage, and cultural policy. Her publications on Indian literature, performing arts, and aesthetic theory include *From the Comic to the Comedic: Traditions of Comedy from Bhasa to Shakespeare* (1993) and *Kutiyattam: The Heritage Theatre of India* (2010), and translations of *Krishnagiti* (1997), the *Rasasutra of Abhinavagupta* (2000), and the *Nalacaritam* (2001).

Nell Shapiro Hawley is preceptor in Sanskrit at Harvard University and a PhD candidate in South Asian Languages and Civilizations at the University of Chicago.

Harshita Mruthinti Kamath is Visweswara Rao and Sita Koppaka Assistant Professor in Telugu Culture, Literature, and History at Emory University. Her monograph, *Impersonations: The Artifice of Brahmin Masculinity in South Indian Dance* (2019), analyzes gender impersonation in the Telugu dance style of Kuchipudi. She has also co-translated the sixteenth-century classical Telugu text *Parijatapaharanamu (Theft of a Tree)* with Velcheru Narayana Rao, which will be published as part of the Murty Classical Library of India.

Sucheta Kanjilal is assistant professor of English and writing at the University of Tampa. Her research interests include novels and poetry of the British Empire, modern Hinduism, gender and sexuality, Hindi literature, and colonialism.

Sudipta Kaviraj is professor of Indian politics and intellectual history at Columbia University. His books include *The Invention of Private Life: Literature and Ideas* (2015), *The Imaginary Institution of India* (2010), and *The Unhappy Consciousness: Bankimchandra Chattopadhyay and the Formation of Nationalist Discourse in India* (1995).

Timothy Lorndale is a PhD candidate at the University of Pennsylvania. He works on Old Kannada and Sanskrit literature.

Pamela Lothspeich is associate professor of South Asian studies at the University of North Carolina at Chapel Hill. Her research focuses on the Indian epics, their presence in modern Indian literature, theatre and film, and postcolonial studies. Her current book project concerns the Hindi epic known as the *Rādheśyām Rāmāyaṇ*, and the theatre of *Ramlila*. She is the author of *Epic Nation: Reimagining the Mahabharata in the Age of Empire* (2009).

Philip Lutgendorf is professor emeritus of Hindi and modern Indian studies at the University of Iowa. Much of his research has focused on the Ramayana tradition in North India; he is the author of *The Life of a Text: Performing the Rāmcaritmānas of Tulsidas* (1991) and of *Hanuman's Tale: The Messages of a Divine Monkey* (2007). Current projects include a book on the cultural history of chai and a new translation of the *Ramcaritmanas* of Tulsidas, in seven dual-language volumes, for the Murty Classical Library of India.

Lawrence McCrea is the author of numerous papers on traditional Indian poetry, poetics, language theory, and hermeneutics. He has taught Sanskrit at the University of Chicago, Harvard University, and Cornell University, where he is currently professor in the Department of Asian Studies. He is the author of *The Teleology of Poetics in Medieval Kashmir* (2008) and co-author (with Parimal Patil) of *Buddhist Philosophy of Language in India: Jñānaśrīmitra on Exclusion* (2010).

Ahona Panda is a humanities teaching fellow in the Department of South Asian Languages and Civilizations and the College at the University of Chicago. Her research traces an intellectual history of philology in Bengal in the nineteenth and twentieth centuries and examines the political relationship between Hindus and Muslims through the lens of the language question. She writes fiction in English and Bengali and translates from Bengali into English.

Heidi Pauwels is professor in the Department of Asian Languages and Literature at the University of Washington in Seattle. Her publications include *Krishna's Round Dance Reconsidered* (1996), *In Praise of Holy Men* (2002), *The Goddess as Role Model: Sītā and Rādhā in Scripture and on Screen* (2008), *Cultural Exchange in Eighteenth-Century India: Poetry and Paintings from Kishangarh* (2015), and *Mobilizing Krishna's World* (2017). She is the editor of *Indian Literature and Popular Cinema* (2007), *Patronage and Popularisation, Pilgrimage and Procession* (2009), *Satire in the Age of Early Modernity* (with Monika Horstmann; 2012), and a special issue of the *Journal of the Royal Asiatic Society* on vernacular views of Aurangzeb (with Anne Murphy; 2018).

Sohini Sarah Pillai is a PhD candidate in South and Southeast Asian Studies at the University of California, Berkeley. She is a comparatist of South Asian religious literature and her area of specialization is the Mahābhārata and Rāmāyaṇa narrative traditions with a particular focus on retellings created in Hindi and Tamil.

Paula Richman is William H. Danforth Professor of South Asian Religions, Emerita at Oberlin College. In addition to three books on Tamil narrative, she has edited and contributed to three volumes on the Ramayana tradition: *Many Rāmāyaṇas: The Diversity of a Narrative Tradition in South Asia* (1991), *Questioning Rāmāyaṇas: A South Asian Tradition* (2000), and *Ramayana Stories in Modern South India: An Anthology* (2008). Currently, she and Rustom Bharucha are co-editing a volume of articles titled *Performing the Ramayana Tradition: Enactments, Interpretations, and Arguments.*

Simon Winant is a PhD student at Ghent University in Belgium. His research interests include Jaina narrative literature, the *Mahābhārata,* early *kāvya* authors, and historical linguistics.

Index

Abhijñānaśākuntala. See *Śākuntala*
Abhimanyu, 9, 57, 60n19, 68, 92, 112, 381; born, 137; and Uttarā, 347
abortion. *See under* fetuses
Ādāb al-Mulūk, 23
adbhuta-rasa. See under *rasa*
ādikāvya, 22–23
Ādiparv (Cauhān), 273
Ādiparva (Viṣṇudās), 245n35
Ādiparvan, 43–46, 57–58, 308, 329–330, 364
ādivāsīs. *See* tribal groups
aesthetic: of audience, 318; of battle, 56; of history, 310; of *kāvya*, 311; of modernity, 307, 311; of novels, 308, 310; of premodern epic, 307–308
After Kurukshetra (Devi), 343, 346–352
āgamas, 215–216
ahiṃsā, 39, 174
Airāvata (father of Ulūpī), 58
aitihāsik kāvya, 295
ākhyāna, xix, 2n1
Alambuṣa, 60, 68; fights Ghaṭotkaca, 60n19, 63, 65; kidnaps Subhadrā, 137; name, 60n19
alaṅkāra. *See* ornament
Alāyudha, 63, 65n36, 66, 68
Āḻvārs, 260, 261; Āṇṭāḷ, 263; layering *avatāras*, 262–264; Nammāḻvār, 264; Periyāḻvār, 260, 260–261; Tirumaṅkaiyāḻvār, 264
Amaracandrasūri, 213n1
Amar Chitra Katha, 28, 369
Ambā, 339n43; and Bhīṣma, 375; as Śikhaṇḍin, xxi–xxii. *See also* Śikhaṇḍin
Anadhītimaṅgalam, 139, 145, 147
Ānandavardhana, 12–13, 40, 312
Anasūyā, 155, 158, 161
Andhā Yug (Bharati), 27, 359, 365
ānṛśaṃsya, 39
Anuśāsanaparvan, 310
Apabhramsha, 4, 15, 25, 213–220 passim, 225, 226, 230n63, 234, 239n9, 243n29, 252, 253
apocalypse, 40, 49, 51
apsarases, 143–144, 248n43
Āraṇyakaparvan, 46, 58–59, 65, 67, 317, 319–320, 364–365
Āraṇyaparvamu (Ĕṟṟāpragaḍa), 195, 206–210
Aravāṉ: Arjuna, son of, 55n5; Irāvān, parallels with, 62, 66

Arjuna, 55, 92, 113, 115, 136, 142; as ascetic, 127; *ātmavān*; 94–95, 105, 108, 114; and Bhīma, 185, 313; as Bṛhannaḍā, xxi–xxii, 94–107 passim; as Bṛhannalā, 21, 91, 93–94, 101–114 passim; in core narrative, 7–9, 8n19; Droṇa's murder, 173, 176, 181–182; and Dvārakā residents, 49; and Ekalavya, 32–33, 353, 354–357; and Hanumān, 273; as hero, 313, 315; and Indra, 129, 187; and Irāvān, 57–63, 67; in Jain tradition, 226, 228; and Kauṇḍinya, 143, 149; in *Kaurava Empire*, 372, 381; and Khāṇḍava Forest, 46, 58n14; and Kṛṣṇa, 42, 99, 273; and *kṣatriya* dharma, 182–183; as mendicant, 143; modern tellings, 355–357; names, 108n31; postcolonial representations, 333–334, 337; Śiva and, 111–113, 115, 127, 173, 186–189; and Subhadrā, 137, 143; and Ulūpī, 67; as warrior, 107–108; weapons, 96–107 passim; Yudhiṣṭhira and, 103, 109–110
Arjunawiwāha (Kaṇwa), 23
Ārśyaśṛṅgi, 60–63; as Garuḍa, 61–62; slayed by Ghaṭotkaca, 65. *See also* Alambusa
artha, 5n13, 136
arthaśāstra, 126, 130, 132
Arthaśāstra (Kauṭilya), 139
Aryans, 334, 341
ascetic practice, 109–110, 112
Aśoka, 52, 174
Assamese, 4, 24
āśrama-dharma, 69, 71–72
Āśramavāsikaparv (Cauhān), 269–270
Āstīka, 44
asuras, 41, 50, 175, 289
Āśvamedhikaparvan, 67
Aśvatthāman, 9–11, 332; aided by *rākṣasas*, 65; in *Kaurava Empire*, 372–379; massacre of Kurukṣetra survivors, 372, 377; and Pāṇḍava lineage, 46–47; rumored dead, 176–180 passim
Aśvins, 8n18
Ātiparuvam (Villiputtūr), 259
ātman, 100n19, 101
audience, 99, 131, 269; "binocular vision" of, 164; caste identity and, 142; feminist perspective, 153, 157–158; Gaṇeśa as first, 4–5; Jain laypeople as, 234; of *Kūṭiyāṭṭam* performance, 135, 138, 142–143; modern, 151, 154; *Pañcarātra*, 94, 104, 111–113; *rasa*, evocation of, 156; of Śākuntala performances, 152, 159, 165, 167; Telugu-speaking, 196–197
Aurangzeb (Awrangzīb), 267–268, 270, 275
Aurva, 45
avatāras: concept, 288; layered representations, 262–264; 265–266

Babhruvāhana, 67n42
baladeva, 214
Balarāma, 48, 118; as advisor of Kṛṣṇa, 125–126, 131–132
Bankim. *See* Chattopadhyay, Bankimchandra
Basu, Rajsekhar, 314, 322; on *Mahābhārata*'s characters, 314–316
battle books, 46, 56–57
Bedtime Story (Nagarkar), 343, 353–359; delayed publication, 358; on Mahābhārata as universal epic, 359; right-wing critics, 357–358
Bengal, 280, 283

Bengali, 4, 24, 27
Bengali literature, 280, 283, 289, 297, 300, 311n15, 326, 329, 343, 363; and *Mahābhārata* (Sanskrit), 306; and modernism, 306–307, 310, 314; and modernity, 307, 322; translations, 314
Bengal Renaissance, 281
Bhagadatta, 185; elephant of (*see* Supratīka)
Bhagavadgītā (as category), 262
Bhagavadgītā (Sanskrit), 56, 71, 99, 104, 257, 260, 288, 310; Hindu worldview, 3; historical reading, 310; and Jñāndev on, 23; Kṛṣṇa's purpose in, 42; narrative, 9
Bhagavān (Kṛṣṇa), 266n38. *See also* Yudhiṣṭhira
Bhāgavatapurāṇa, 163, 257, 261, 283, 286
bhakti, 174, 267; and nationalism, 282, 287; types of, 260; Vaiṣṇava, 261
Bharata, 162
Bharatanāṭyam. See under dance
Bhārata War: battleground of, 43; end of *dvāpara-yuga*, 47; as mass-extinction event, 40–41; survivors of, 46
Bharati, C. Subramania: *Pāñcāli Capatam*, 27
Bharati, Dharamvir: *Andhā Yug*, 27, 365
Bhāravi: *Kirātārjunīya*, 18, 126–127
Bhārgavas: 44–45
Bhāsa, attributed to: *Dūtaghaṭotkaca*, 20, 91n1; *Dūtavākya*, 20, 91n1; *Karṇabhāra*, 20, 91n1; *Madhyamavyāyoga*, 20, 91n1; *Pañcarātra*, 11, 19, 21, 91–115 passim; *Ūrubhaṅga*, 20–21, 91n1, 153
Bhasha (*bhāṣā*). *See* Hindi, classical
bhāva, 75–78; term, 76n32, 81–82, 84; *vātsalya-bhāva*, 260
bhikṣuṇī (female mendicant), 72n15, 74, 84
Bhīma, xxiii, 17, 55, 56, 102, 238, 242, 244, 264, 272; and Arjuna, 313; conduct, 183; core narrative, 7, 9; as creator deity, 31; death of Irāvān, 62; and dice game, 184–185; disguised, 225, 251–252, 254n63; and Draupadī, 65, 184–185, 245n35, 250–251; and Duryodhana, 20, 127, 172; failures, 173, 183, 186; and Ghaṭotkaca, 59, 64; as hero, 308, 313; Hiḍimbā and, 31; in Jain tradition, 221–234 passim; and Karṇa, 183, 185–186; kingly model, 171–172, 245, 255; *kṣatriya* dharma, 172, 182–184, 186; modern representations, 369; murders Droṇa, 176; murders Hiḍimba and Bakāsura, 265; murders Jarāsandha, 128n24; murder of Kauravas, 183, 186; murders Kīcaka, 201, 246–251; in *Pāṇḍavcarit* chapters, 245n35; in *Paṇḍvānī*, 253; and *rākṣasas*, 64; in *Sāhasabhīmavijaya*, 25; and Supratīka, 185;in *Ūrubhaṅga*, 20; in *Virāṭaparvan*, 219, 231; worship in Chhattisgarh, 31
Bhīm Kavi: *Ḍaṅgvaikathā*, 11
Bhīṣma, xxi, 9, 10, 69, 92, 104, 140, 189, 264, 336, 338; and Ambā, 375; authoritative voice, 310; and dharma, 314; in Jain tradition, 228–229; and Yudhiṣṭhira, 280
Bhīṣmaparv (Cauhān), 271, 273
Bhīṣmaparvan, 17, 54–67
bildungsroman, 32, 321, 322

Bilhaṇa: *Vikramāṅkadevacarita*, 129–130, 132
bitextual poems. See *śleṣa*
body: constitution, 85, 86, 88; and gender (*see* gender); male, 84; ornamenting, 96–99, 106; possession, 74–84 passim; transformation, 73–74, 85–87; violation, 81–82
Bollywood, 10, 362, 382
Book of Yudhisthir (Bose). See *Mahābhārater Kathā*
Bose, Buddhadev: and *Mahābhārata*, 307, 309, 310–314, 316–323; *Mahābhārater Kathā*, 32, 310; modernist, 306–307, 310–311; style, 316; training, 316–317; and Yudhiṣṭhira, 314–319
brahmahatyā. See under *brāhmaṇas:* crime of killing
brāhmaṇas (Brahmins), 109–111, 138, 141, 146, 148, 313; and Aśoka, 174; crime of killing, 178, 182, 186; influence on *Mahābhārata*, 317; as king's companion, 110, 136, 149; as opposites of *rākṣasas*, 64
Brahmanical Hinduism, 344; critique of norms, 347–349
Brahmanical order, 80n53; 139–140
brahmāstra weapon, 47, 176
Bṛhannaḍā (Bṛhannalā). *See* Arjuna
Bṛhatkathā: in Jain Mahābhārata, 215, 216m, 229
buddhi, 74–77; meaning, 76n34, 81, 86
Buddhists, 52, 174, 356n47; 359
Bulākīdās: *Pāṇḍavapurāṇa* (Hindi), 218

Caitanya, 283, 286
Cākyār Kūttu, 138
Cākyārs, 141, 146
Cāḷukyas, 195; Kalyāṇi (Western), 171; Veṇgi (Eastern), 200
campaigning season, 241, 252, 255
Campfire Graphic Novels, 369
campūs, 18. *See also under* Nannaya
carita: genre, 283, 285; *kṛṣṇa-carita*, 26, 258, 262, 269; of Rāma, 271
caste: and language, 350; lower-caste representations, 344, 347–357; norms, 138, 141, 347–349, 350; purity, 349–350; reservations, 357; stereotypes, 146; violence, 354–355, 359
Cauhān, Sabalsingh, 8n18, 24, 26; *Mahābhārat* (Hindi), 253, 258–275 passim
Caüpaṇṇamahāpurisacariya (Śīlāṅka), 216
character development: feminist interpretation, 157; in modern vs. classical drama, 156–159
Chatterjee, Bankimchandra. *See* Chattopadhyay, Bankimchandra
Chattopadhyay, Bankimchandra, 306, 322; anti-Muslim views, 282; career, 281, 282; *Dharmatattva*, 282; and European scholarship, 287–289, 297, 298; and Hindu nationalism, 32; historicizing Mahābhārata tradition, 284–289, 291; Kṛṣṇa, representation of, 283–288, 297, 299, 301; *Kṛṣṇacaritra*, 32, 280–301 passim; nationalism, 282; philology of, 284, 287
Chhattisgarh, 31, 252
Citrabhāratamu (Cargoṇda Dharmanna), 11
Citrakathī tradition, 6n14

colonialism, 26–27, 219–220; Draupadī, representations of, 328; *Mahābhārata* in, 50; nationalist critique, 290; popular literature under, 299–300. *See also* nationalism
comedy, 246–255 passim; of the *vidūṣaka* (see under *vidūṣaka*)
coming-of-age story. *See* *bildungsroman*
commentary tradition: *Jayakaumudī*, 2n1; Nīlakaṇṭha and, 16
costume. *See* disguises
costume, in theater: *āśrama* clothing, 162; classical vs. modern, 158–159; gender and, 158
court cultures, 193, 274–275
cultural amnesia, 165–167
cultural chauvinism, 299
cultural memory, 162, 166–167
cyclical time, 47, 49, 51–52

Dalits: conversion, 356n47; interpretations of epics, 344–345; and reservations, 357; social exclusion, 345–346; term, 344n3; violence against, 354. *See also* caste
Damayantī, 11, 24
dance: *Bharatanāṭyam*, 161; -drama, 281n6; *Kathakaḷi*, xxiii, 160n20; *Kūcipūḍi*, 157, 160n20; modern, 29; *Yakṣagāna*, 11n24, 254n63
Ḍaṅgvaikathā (Bhīm Kavi), 11
Delhi Sultanate, 238, 243
desire, 4, 34, 37, 238, 246, 247, 299, 319, 337, 339. See also *kāma*
Devaprabhasūri, Maladhāri: *Pāṇḍavacarita*, 217, 234
Devi, Jyotirmayi: *Epar Gaṅgā, Opar Gaṅgā*, 326, 329–331
Devi, Mahasweta, 343–344; *After Kurukshetra*, 343, 346–352; "Draupadī," 334–335; "Kuntī o Niṣādi," 343, 346–347, 349–352; narrative, 347–349; "Pañcakanyā," 343, 346, 347
Dhanaṃjaya. *See* Arjuna
dharma, 2n1, 136, 244, 255, 314, 320–321; *brāhmaṇa* dharma, 349; humanity's, 285, 288, 301; as "justice," 377; and karma, 288; kingship and, 279–280; of *kṣatriyas*, 172, 173–174, 182–186, 189; Mahābhārata as guide, 38; nationalism and, 282; new vs. old, 174; as social order, 313; *varṇāśrama*, 174; and Yudhiṣṭhira, 180
Dharma (deity, Yudhiṣṭhira's father), 8, 179
dharmāndolan. *See* Hindu revivalism
Dharmanna, Cargoṇḍa: *Citrabhāratamu*, 11
Dharmarāja. *See under* Yudhiṣṭhira
dharmatattva, 299
Dharmatattva (Chattopadhyay), 282, 285
Dhṛṣṭadyumna, 9, 372; beheads Droṇa, 177, 181
Dhṛtarāṣṭra, 8–10, 55, 58n14; and Yudhiṣṭhira, 128
dice match, 8–9, 184, 189, 264, 318
disguises, 21, 92–114 passim, 137, 143, 225, 251
Divakaruni, Chitra Banerjee: *Palace of Illusions*, 326–341 passim
diversity (of Mahābhāratas), 3–7, 26, 53–54, 214, 235
doubled character, 91–102, 111–113

drama, xxiv, 151–167 passim; language in, 160; retelling epics, 153; and Western realism, 156. *See also* individual plays
Draupadeyas (sons of Draupadī), 9, 68
Draupadī, xxi, 57, 95, 211, 238, 245n35; achieves *mokṣa*, 337; as Amman, 6n14; in Bhārata War, 46; and Bhīma, 65, 201, 250–251; and caste critique, 355–356; colonial representations, 300, 328; complains to husbands, 250; and dice game, 8, 184; and Duḥśāsana, 183–185; and Duryodhana, 127; feminist engagement, 30, 32, 326, 337–338; in exile, 9; on film, 29n86; final journey, 10; five husbands, 333, 338; goddess cult in Tamil Nadu, 6n14, 24, 31, 55, 62n25; as human, 333; as Indraprastha queen, 6n14, 8; in Jain tradition, 215, 221–234 passim; as Kālī, 6n14; and Kīcaka, 201, 246–249; as Kṛṣṇā, 339–340; as *kuṟavañci*, 6n14; in *Mama's Boys*, 30; marriage, 8n19; modern representations, 327–342, 369; as Mother India, 220; and Muslims, 31; narrative significance, 8; as Pāñcālī, 336–337; in *Paṇḍvānī*, 253; in Partition literature, 328–330, 341; postcolonial representations, 30, 32, 331–342; sons, 68; South Indian forms, 6n14, 24, 31; and Subhadrā, 137; subjectivity, 332; *svayaṃvara*, 6n14; in *Virāṭaparvan*, 219, 231; at Virāṭa's court, 201; voice of, 202–203; as wife, 207–209; and Yudhiṣṭhira, 204–205, 313
"Draupadī" (Devi), 334–335, 346
Draupadi (painting by Balaji Srinivasan), 6n14
Draupadi, the Fire-Born Princess (2013), 369
Droṇa, 9, 264; attacks Pāṇḍavas, 176; Dalit representations, 359–360; and Ekalavya, 32, 352–357; in Jain tradition, 228–229; in *Kaurava Empire*, 372; murder of, 172, 176–181, 182, 189; postcolonial representations, 334; *rasa*, 177
Droṇaparv (Cauhān), 271, 275; dates, 269
Droṇaparvan, 65, 67
Drupada, 372
Duḥśalā, 29
Duḥṣanta. *See* Duṣyanta
Duḥśāsana, 7–9, 107, 109, 308; and Draupadī, 183–185
Dūṅgar Singh, 241–242; critique of, 249, 250; dates of reign, 242n24; as patron, 244–245
Durvāsas, 152
Duryodhana, xxii, 46, 92; and Alāyudha, 66; and Ārśyaśṛṅgi, 60; Bhīma defeats, 172; *brahmahatyā* accusation against Arjuna and Yudhiṣṭhira, 180–182, 186; core narrative; 7–10; and dice game, 184; in *Dūtavākya*, 20; Kaurava leader, 7; and Kṛṣṇa, 174–175; *kṣatriya* dharma, 172–173, 182, 189; as narrator, 172–173, 180–189; in *Sāhasabhīmavijaya*, 25, 171–190 passim; and Sañjaya, 176, 179; separation, experience of, 20–21; and Subhadrā, 137; in Uttarakhand, 31; and Yudhiṣṭhira, 10, 126–128, 178–179, 186

duṣṭavanitā. *See under* women
Duṣyanta: character, 151–152; costume, 158; in *Mahābhārata*, 164; name, 152n1; Śakuntalā displaces, 154, 159; voice of, 155
Dūtaghaṭotkaca, 20, 91n1
Dūtavākya, 20, 91n1
dvāpara-yuga, 41
Dvārakā, 48, 49, 124, 125; government, 126; Kṛṣṇa and, 118–131 passim
dystopias, 363; *kali-yuga* as, 365

eighteen: significance of, 3n7, 217
Ekalavya, 32–33, 104; Dalit representations, 359–360; in *Mahābhārata* (Sanskrit), 352, 355; modern tellings, 352–357; postcolonial representations, 334
Ekalavya (Mittal), 353
Eklavya: The Story of an Archer's Loyalty and Devotion (Lomhor), 353
"Eklavyan" (Kandasamy), 359–360
endings, 9–10, 40, 48–49, 92, 106, 151, 154, 165, 275, 312, 330, 349, 354, 355, 362
English: composition in, xxiii, xxiv, 15, 17, 27, 28, 32, 33, 343, 345, 353, 358, 359, 363n5; translation, 3n3, 73n20, 154, 165, 296, 310–311, 329, 335, 343, 359n56
Ensemble 86, 154–155, 158, 167. *See also Śākuntala* (1987 Prasanna production)
Epar Gaṅgā, Opar Gaṅgā (Devi), 326, 329; narrative, 329–331; translation, 329
epics, 57, 286; Bengali literature and, 322; comparative study, 286, 317; as genre, xxi–xxii, 2n1; and Jain tradition, 213; and the novel, 307; social exclusion and, 213; in Western traditions, 2n1, 286
epitomes, 18
Ĕṛṛana. *See* Ĕṛṛāpragaḍa
Ĕṛṛāpragaḍa, 191–192, 195, 210, 211; *Āraṇyaparavamu*, 195, 206–210; as Nannaya, 206; style, 206
ethnic cleansing. *See* genocide
exile. *See under* forest

father-son relationships, 59–60, 68
feminism: body, theories of, 70; classic works, critique of, 153; Draupadī, 30, 32; Euro-American, 326–327; Indian women's movement, 327; *Śākuntala* retelling, 155, 158. *See also under* audiences: feminist perspective
feminist critiques, 325–326
fetuses: abortion, 47, 47n33; stages of development, 85; survival of, 45; as weapons, 48–49
film, Mahābhārata in, 10, 11n24, 29–30, 205, 375
food, 147–148
forest: as exile, 9, 10, 127, 128, 317; and caste, 347, 349–352
forgetting. *See* cultural amnesia
frame stories, 5, 12n28, 28, 40, 42, 55–56, 74n26, 119, 161–162, 227, 229, 372, 373
future: as narrative backdrop, 363
futurism: popularity in India, 381

Gadāyuddha. See *Sāhasabhīmavijaya*
Gaṇapati. *See* Gaṇeśa
Gāndhārī, 8, 10, 245n35

gandharvas, 245n35, 249–250
Gandhi, Mahatma, 50, 354, 356, 358, 369
Gaṇeśa, 144, 147, 240, 266; as audience and scribe, 4–5, 34; and Pārvatī, 143–144
Gaṅgā, 57, 143–144
Ganguly, Rita: and classical theater at NSD, 160; *Tridhara* (1995 production), 154, 159–164 passim
Garhwal. *See* Uttarakhand
Garuḍa, 58; Ārśyaśṛṅgi takes form of, 61–62; immortality elixir, 364
gender, 17, 74n25, 100–101; in *Abhijñānaśākuntala*, 22; *āśrama-dharma* and, 72; and audience, 325; body, 70, 73, 74, 84–85, 88, 93–106 passim, 337; and caste, 347–352; costume in theater, 158; critique of, xx–xxii; embryo, 38; fetus, 85; hypermasculinity, 248–255 passim; indeterminate, 85n82; Kālidāsa and, 22; language, 70, 72; male, 84; and nationalism, 325; non-normative, 84; patriarchy, xxi, 80n52, 347, 349; performance of, xxi–xxii, 94–101, 112; politics, 153; sexuality, 338; sexual violence, 328–331, 341; transformation of body, 93–106 passim, 375; womanhood, 84, 100–101, 103, 105, 326. *See also* body
genocide, 17, 40, 46, 51, 52; and abortion, 47n33; Indra and, 41; Janamejaya's sacrifice and, 43; of Kauravas, 46–47; of *kṣatriyas*, 43–44; of *nāgas*, 43–44, 47; of *rākṣasas*, 45–46; of Somavaṃśa, 48
genre, xxi, 1–2n1, 255; autobiography (*see* autobiography); *campū* (see under *campūs*); *carita* (see *carita*); critique of, 156; drama (*see* drama); epic (*see* epics); in film, 362–364; graphic novels (*see* graphic novels); in Indian filmmaking, 362; *itihāsa* (see *itihāsa*); Mahābharata tradition as, 10–15; *mahākāvya* (see *mahākāvya*); *mārga*, 193; mythology, 29n86; *Paṇḍvānī* (see *Paṇḍvānī*); Partition literature (*see* Partition); *Prabandha Kūttu*, 138; science fiction (*see* science fiction); speculative fiction (*see* speculative fiction); tragedy, 154
Ghaṭotkaca, 55, 57, 68; and Bhīma, 59–60; in *Bhīṣmaparvan*, 17; birth, 65; in core narrative, 9, 11; death, 63, 68; in *Dūtaghaṭotkaca*, 20; fights Alambusa, 60, 60n19; and Irāvān, 59–60, 62–66; in *Kaurava Empire*, 377; kills Alāyudha, 66; in *Madhyamavyāyoga*, 20
Ghaṭotkacāśraya (Panuluh), 23
Gītā. See *Bhagavadgītā*
goddess cult. *See under* Draupadī
Gonds, 253; ballads, 24; Bhīma, descent from, 253
graphic novels, 28, 32, 361–384 passim
Gujarati, 4, 24
Guṇabhadra: *Uttarapurāṇa*, 216
Gupt, Maithilisharan: *Jayadrath Vadh*, 27; "Sairandhrī," 219
guru, 43, 165, 175, 182, 237n3, 248, 372, 381; betrayal of, 178–182, 349; *guru-dakṣiṇā*, 353–354
Gwalior, 25–25, 214, 224, 237–249 passim, 255; Fort, 220; Jain literary circles in fifteenth c., 219–220, 235, 243; Seths in, 243

Haḍimbā. *See under* Hiḍimbā
Ham Pāñc (1980), 30n87, 375
Hanumān, xxiii, 245n35, 271, 272–273, 362; and Arjuna, 273; meets half-brother Bhīma, 273
Harivaṃśa, 209, 257, 286; Kṛṣṇa in, 260; and *Mahābhārata*, 12–13
Harivaṃśapurāṇa (Jinasena Punnāṭa), 11, 214; about, 215n3, 216; inspires Raïdhū, 223–224, 234; and Svayambhūdeva, 234; title, 215n3
Harivaṃsapurāṇa (Raïdhū), 25, 214, 220, 252; Arjuna in, 226; composition, 221; inspired by Punnāṭa, 223–224; Kīcaka in, 221–225; moral cleansing of, 234
Hāstinapura, 49, 128, 153, 165
Hemacandra, 18n44, 217
heroes, 118, 127, 133, 136, 138, 142, 184, 186; epic, 307–309, 313, 318; modern, 309
heroines, 22, 142, 152, 154–167 passim, 325, 328, 331, 369
Hiḍimbā, xxiii, 31, 60, 64–65; 245n35; as Haḍimbā (local goddess), 31
Hindi, 4, 8n18, 11, 24–30 passim, 38, 213, 219, 353, 358–365 passim, 375, 377, 382; translation, 155
Hindi, classical, 213–224 passim, 228n52, 237–244 passim, 254, 255, 258, 265n34, 266–268, 270, 273
Hindu identity, 238
Hindu-Muslim relations, 243–244, 249, 255
Hindu nationalism, 3, 30, 32, 287, 301, 358, 367
Hindu revivalism, 284
historical criticism: and *śāstra*, 291
historical poetry, 295
history, 306; and *itihāsa*, 287, 301, 330; Mahābhārata tradition as, 284–289, 291–296; and myth, 286; Tagore and, 293–297
horse sacrifice, 10, 24, 67
householder, 32, 69–72, 78, 80, 84, 286, 321
humor, 138–149 passim, 175, 249–250, 252, 255

ideal ruler. *See* kingship
identities: confused, 142; fragmented, 19; and *rasa*, 177; social, 127, 145
Indian independence, 27–33, 219, 328. *See also* nationalism; postcolonial tellings
Indian Muslims, 31
Indra, 58n14, 59, 96, 137, 247, 315; and Arjuna, 187; and Karṇa, 20
Indraprastha, 8, 118–119, 127, 129, 337; Arjuna and Subhadrā, 137; Kṛṣṇa's arrival in (*see under* Kṛṣṇa)
internet: web-based Mahābhāratas, 29
inversion: of genre, 157, 159; of narrative, 92, 104, 115, 189; of norms, 136, 138, 140; of roles, 72, 77, 80, 88, 99, 103–104, 309; of source, 164; of themes, 189, 321
invocations: of Kṛṣṇa, 264; of Rāma, 265; of Viṣṇu, 258–259, 262, 264
Irāvān: 54, 67; as Ananta, 61; and Aravāṉ, 54–55, 62–63; battles Ārśyaśṛṅgi, 61–63; birth, 57–60, 63; death, 9, 57, 60, 62–63, 67–68; and Ghaṭotkaca, 59–60, 63–65; in Indra's heaven, 59, 67; "invention" of, 67; and *rākṣasa*s, 55, 63–66; story of, 17
Islamic cultures. *See* Indian Muslims

itihāsa, xix, 2n1, 396; as history, 287, 301, 330; and *kāvya*, 295; translation of, 286; *-samālocanā*, 291; and Vedas, 295

Jaiminibhārata, 24
Jainism: Hindu traditions, relationship to, 213
Jains, 52, 197n23–198n23; Digambaras, 8n20, 215, 220; merchants (*see under* Gwalior); narratives, 10, 25; Śvetāmbaras; 215; Śvetāmbara-Digambara divide, 225; Yāpanīyas, 227
Jain Universal History. *See* Mahābhārata, Jain tradition
Janaka, 69, 71–88
Janamejaya, 55; and snake sacrifice, 28, 43–44, 47
Jarāsandha, 128, 215, 245n35; in Sanskrit *Mahābhārata*, 215
Javanese, Old: *Arjunawiwāha*, 23; *Ghaṭotkacāśraya*, 23
Jayadrath Vadh (Gupt), 27
Jayakaumudī (Vidyāsāgara), 2n2
Jeyamohan, B.: *Veṇmuracu*, 30
jinas, 220, 244, 244n30
Jñāndev: *Jñāneśvarī*, 23
Jñāneśvarī (Jñāndev), 23

Kaïkaï (Kaikeyi), 230, 233
Kairātaparvan, 112–113
Kaḷarippayattu, 166
Kalhaṇa: *Rājataraṅgiṇī*, 19
Kālī, 6n14, 55n5, 144
Kālidāsa, 151–167 passim; *Abhijñānaśākuntala* (*Śākuntala*), 18; and gender, 22; *Raghuvaṃśa*, 308. See also under *Śākuntala* (Kālidāsa); *Śākuntala* (1987 Prassana production); *Shakuntala Remembered*; *Tridhara*
kali-yuga, 47, 166–167, 245n34; as dystopian future, 365; as present, 384
Kalyāṇasaugandhikam, xxiii
Kalyug (1980), 30n87, 375
kāma, 5n13, 80, 136
Kaṃsa, 117, 125, 261, 262; killed by Kṛṣṇa, 268; relations, 268n50
kanda (Telugu meter), 199, 200, 203, 211
Kandasamy, Meena: "Eklavyan," 359–360
Kaṅka. *See* Yudhiṣṭhira
Kannada, 4, 10, 27, 199, 200, 213, 274; Old Kannada, 171, 173, 180
Kaṇva: disciples, 155, 162
Kaṇwa, Mpu: *Arjunawiwāha*, 23
karma, 288; in Jain tradition, 221, 223, 231, 235
Karṇa, 104, 189; and Bhīma, 183, 185–186; bow, 186; in colonial literature, 300; core narrative, 9, 11; and Ghaṭotkaca, 63; in Jain tradition, 228; in *Karṇabhāra*, 20; and Kuntī, 185–186; in Partition literature, 330; postcolonial representations, 333, 336, 337; in Uttarakhand, 31
Karṇabhāra, 20, 91n9
Karṇaparv (Cauhān), 272; dates, 269
Karṇaparvan, 308
Karṇāṭabhāratakathāmañjarī (Kumāravyāsa), 10, 275
Karve, Irawati, 369–371
Kathakaḷi. *See under* dance
Kātyāyanī: rescues Subhadrā, 137
Kauṇḍinya, 139; and Arjuna, 137, 149; introduction of, 135, 142; and

kings, 149; narrative, 143–144; on poetic skill, 145; and Yudhiṣṭhira, 149. See also *vidūṣaka*
Kaurava Empire, 33, 371–381, 384; cultural decontextualization, 375, 377; setting, 372, 375, 379–380; language, 377; violence in, 372, 375; weaponry, 379–381
Kauravas, xix, 55–56, 92, 137n6, 240, 261, 269; ancestor of, 137n6; attempted genocide, 46–47; colonial representations, 328; core narrative, 7–10; in Jain tradition, 215; in *Kaurava Empire*, 372; Pāṇḍavas, alliance with, 11; perspective of, 19, 20, 25; and *rākṣasas*, 60; women, 6n14
Kavijanāśrayamu, 197n23–198n23
kavitrayamu (Trinity of Poets), 191; as translators, 196. *See also* Ĕṟṟāpragaḍa; Nannaya; Tikkana
kāvya, xix, 18; kingship in, 129; premodern aesthetics, 311
Kerala, 19, 136, 142, 148, 160n20, 166. See also *Kūṭiyāṭṭam*
Khadilkar, K. P., 219; *Kīcak Vadh*, 27
Khāṇḍava Forest, 46, 58n14, 337
Kīcaka, 25, 205, 214, 238, 244, 249, 308; Bhīma murders, 26, 245–252; colonial representations, 219, 220; and Draupadī, 201, 249–250; killed, 201; in *Virāṭaparvan* (Sanskrit), 219
Kīcaka (Jain tradition): becomes monk, 221–222; Bhīma and, 221–222, 229–233; brothers, 222, 233; cycle of rebirths, 223; death, 221, 232–233; and Draupadī, 221–223, 225, 229–233; and karma, 223, 235; Queen Sudeṣṇā in, 222n23; and Śvetāmbara-Digambara divide, 225; *yakṣa*, attempted seduction by, 222–223
Kīcakavadha (Nītivarman), 19, 254n63
Kīcakavadha episode (Viṣṇudās). See *Virāṭaparva* (Viṣṇudās); see also under *Pāṇḍavcarit* (Viṣṇudās)
Kīcak Vadh (Khadilkar), 27, 219–220
kingship, 71–73, 110, 117–118, 133, 241–242; advice, 126–128, 136, 140; avoidance of, as concept, 124; and dharma, 279–280, 302; and divinity, 133; ideal, 313; in *kāvya*, 129; and poetry, 193, 194; *rājaseva* (see under *puruṣārtha*); and royal power, 118, 128; sharing throne, 129–130; terminology, 124; violence and, 38
kirāta: Śiva disguised as, 187, 188
Kirātārjunīya (Bhāravi), 18, 126–127, 186; Arjuna and Śiva wrestle, 187n51
Kolatkar, Arun: *Sarpa Satra*, 28
Kṛpa, 46
Kṛṣṇa, 117, 137, 266; advisors, 125–126; and Arjuna, 9, 42, 46, 99, 273; army, 120; authoritative voice, 310; *avatāra*, 174, 262–264; Bankim's view on, 282–300, 303; Basu on, 316; in *Bhagavadgītā*, 50; Bhārata War, 46, 47; in *Citrabhāratamu*, 11; in colonial Bengal, 280–281, 283, 289; core narrative, 7–10; dharma, 174; as diplomat, 42; divinity, nature of, 175, 283–285, 287, 293, 299–300; and Draupadī, xxii, 9, 269; and Duryodhana, 174–175; in *Dūtavākya*, 20; as dwarf, 122–123; earthly form, 48–49; as god, 310; as Gopāla, 260; as Govinda, 270;

Kṛṣṇa *(continued)*
and *Harivaṃśa*, 12–13; historicity of, 285–286, 296–300; as human, 285–289, 293, 301–302; in Indraprastha, 130, 132; in Jain tradition, 215, 216, 227n48, 228; kills Kaṃsa, 125, 268; in *Kaurava Empire*, 377; killed, 10; in *Kṛṣṇacaritra* (see *Kṛṣṇacaritra* [Chattopadhyay]); lac palace fire, 265; in *mahākāvya*, 21; murder of Droṇa, 176–177; and Nārada, 121; and *pārijāta* tree, 123, 209; political status, 124, 128; postcolonial representations, 332–333, 337; protagonist, 257–259; *rājasūya* sacrifice, 128; and Rāma, 263; and religious nationalism, 282; revives Parikṣit, 10, 47; Satyabhāmā's husband, 206, 207; and Saubha fortress, 364; and Śiśupāla, 117, 120, 125–127, 269, 298; in South India, 39–40, 264; Tagore's view on, 290–303; Viṣṇu as, 288; in Yādava civil war, 48; yogic detachment, 56; youth, 260–262; and Yudhiṣṭhira, 21, 118–123, 128–133; 280
kṛṣṇa-carita. See under *carita*
Kṛṣṇacaritra (Chattopadhyay), 32, 280, 282–290; audience, 299, 302; and Christianity, 298; divinity, notions of, 283–285, 287, 299, 301; and historicity, 285–289, 291, 297, 301; and *śāstra*, 291
"Kṛṣṇacaritra" (Tagore), 280–281, 290–302
Kṛtavarman, 46, 48
kṣatriyas, 45, 242, 255, 313, 317; death in battle, 186n41; dharma, 25, 172–175, 182–184, 189; gender, 63, responsibilities, 110; slaughter of, 42, 43–46; social norms, 347
Kulaśekhara, 136–137; *Subhdrādhanañjaya*, 135–139, 142, 149; *Tapatīsaṃvaraṇa*, 137, 138
Kumar, Kirtana: plays Śakuntalā, 165; See also *Shakuntala Remembered* (2006 production)
Kumārapāla, 217
Kumāravyāsa: *Karṇāṭabhāratakathāmañjarī*, 10, 275
Kumudini. *See* Thatham, Ranganayaki
Kuntī, 245n35, 250, 313; childbirth, 351; core narrative, 8–11; in Jain tradition, 227n49, 228; Karṇa's vow to, 185; postcolonial representations, 333; and Subhadrā, 137; as widow, 349–352
"Kuntī o Niṣādi" (Devi), 343, 346; narrative, 349–352; women in, 349–352; See also *After Kurukshetra*
Kurukṣetra War, 6n14, 9, 10, 20, 41, 46–47, 49, 55n5, 62–63, 92, 172, 176, 348; aftermath, 280; as historical event, 289
Kūṭiyāṭṭam, 135–149 passim, 160n20; aesthetics, 142; language of, 138, 141, 142; Mahābharata tradition and, 21; *naṅṅyār*, 146; origins of, 137

lac palace, 8, 265
Lomhor, A. K.: *Eklavya*, 353
lower-caste characters. *See under* caste

Madhyamavyāyoga, 20, 91n1
Madhya Pradesh, 219, 237, 252
Mādrī, 8, 8n18, 9, 268

Māgha: *Śiśupālavadha*, 18, 21, 117–133 passim; and Bhāravi, 126n21; and *rasa*, 131
Mahābhārat (2013 film), 10
Mahābhārat (Cauhān): 26, 253; dating, 266–268, 269; Hanumān in, 271–273; Kṛṣṇa in, 258, 269, 273; and *Mahābhārata* (Sanskrit), 264–265; in *Paṇḍvānī*, 24; Rāma in, 259, 266, 269, 270–273; and *Rāmcaritmānas*, 268, 271–272
Mahābhārat (Doordarshan serial), 29
Mahābhārata (Bengali "translations"). *See* Singha, Kaliprasanna; Basu, Rajsekhar
Mahābhārata (Jain tradition): 235; *āgamas* and, 215–216; early and medieval versions, 214–218; languages of, 213; rejection of Sanskrit Mahābhārata, 227–228; sources for, 215
Mahābhārata (lower-caste tellings), 344–345, 359–360
Mahābhārata (Oriya, Sāraḷādāsa), 22, 336n32
Mahābhārata (Sanskrit), 53, 62, 66, 69, 96, 108, 118, 127–128, 139, 264; audience, 317–318; authorship: 58, 66n41, 67, 292, 298, 317; character inconsistencies, 315; composition, dates of, 1–2, 50, 287; critical edition, 16; duality, 302; frame stories and, 5, 28; Hindu nationalism, 301; as history, 284–289, 291–299, 301n69; and human nature, 311; hyperbolic surrealism, 364; ideal ruler, 313; inauspicious, 39; influenced by regional versions, 67; and Kālidāsa, 163; Kṛṣṇa introduced, 259; as literature, 298, 300–302; modern readings, 281, 305, 309, 310–311, 314–315, 321–323, 327, 332; multiplicity, 15–16; narrative inconsistency, 293–294, 318; Northern recension, 16; oral reception, 239; protagonist, absence of, 257–258; and *rasa*, 312; repetition in, 17; as *śāstra*, 310; Southern recension, 16, 57, 58n14; and supernatural, 314, 322; superstitions around, 194–195; in Telugu literary imagination (see under *Mahābhāratamu* [Telugu]); translation, 2n3, 4, 211; uniformity and, 17; urtext, 196, 209; as Veda, 310; vulgate, 16, women in, 209. *See also* titles of individual books
Mahabharata: A Play Based upon the Indian Classic (Carrière, 1985), 27, 375
Mahābhāratamu (Ĕṛṛāpragaḍa). See *Āraṇyaparavamu*
Mahābhāratamu (Nannaya), 191; 197–200
Mahābhāratamu (Telugu): 1, 2–3n3, 4, 22, 25, 191–212 passim, 274; *avatārika*, 199, 200; and *Mahābhārata* (Sanskrit) 194–197, 205–208; as *mārga*, 193; not translation, 211; opening, 197–199; orality, 201, 203; patron (*see* Rājarājanarendra); style, 201, 206, 208; vernacularization, 203, 210, 211–212; women in, 207–209. See also *Āraṇyaparavamu* (Ĕṛṛāpragaḍa); *Mahābhāratamu* (Nannaya); *Mahābhāratamu* (Tikkana)
Mahābhāratamu (Tikkana), 195, 200–206; *Virāṭaparvamu*, 201–205

Mahābhāratas (Tamil): 55n5, 62, 66. *See also* Bharati, C. Subramania; Peruntēvaṉār; Villiputtūr
Mahābhārata tradition: and Brahmanical Hinduism, 344–345; colonial adaptations, 328; comparative work, 274; contrapuntal, 343, 347–349; as muse, 325
Mahābhārater Kathā (Bose), 32, 316–321, translation, 310–311
mahākāvya, 13n28, 18, 21, 117, 124, 126, 187n51
Mahāprasthānikaparvan, 331
mahāpurāṇas, 216, 218; *See also under* individual titles
mahāpuruṣas, 214, 216
Mahars, 354–357
Malayalam, 4, 21–22, 23n54, 24, 28, 136, 228n52, 254n662; spoken by *vidūṣaka*, 138, 141–142, 146; and Sanskrit, 142
Malwa, 243, 244, 249, 250, 255
Mama's Boys, 30
Maraṇasamāhi, 216
Marathi, 4, 23, 24, 27, 192, 219, 336n32, 345, 358, 363
marriage, 224, 328, 330, 331; of Aravāṉ and Mohinī, 55n5; of Arjuna and Draupadī, 57; of Arjuna and Subhadrā, 136–137; of Bhīma and Hiḍimbā, 64; Draupadī's marriage, 8n20, 224n39, 225, 259, 332; forced, 329; and lineage, 146; of Pārtha [Arjuna] and Ulūpī, 57–58; purpose of, 146; responsibilities of, 151; Śakuntalā to Duṣyanta, 152; secret, 156; unlawful, 82
Mathurā, 117, 125
MBh. See *Mahābhārata* (Sanskrit)
Mēkkāntala, 144
micro-history, 26, 238
Mittal, Mahendra: *Ekalavya*, 353
modernism. *See under* Bengali literature
modernity, 307; Mahābhārata in, 26–33; and premodern, 322; and women's experiences, 327
mokṣa, 5n13, 10, 13, 71, 85, 136, 146, 337
Mughals, 23, 267, 275, 365
mukta, 69, 72–73, 80, 84
Muśalaparv (Cauhān), 269

Nagar, Sachin: *Gandhi: My Life is My Message*, 371; *Kaurava Empire*, 371
Nagarkar, Kiran, 343–344; *Bedtime Story*, 343, 353–359
nāgas, 43; and Irāvān, 57–58
Naidoo, Muthal: *Flight from the Mahabharath*, xx–xxiii
Naimiṣa Forest, 43
Naïr, Karthika: *Until the Lions*, 28
Naiṣadhīyacarita. *See* Śrīharṣa
Nakula, 7, 8, 8n18, 30, 229
Nala, 11, 23; Arjuna and, 100n19; as doubled character, 94
Nālāyirativiyappirapantam: Gajendra in, 265; Kṛṣṇa's youth in, 260–262. *See also* Āḻvārs
Nampūtiri community, 138, 147
Nannaya, 2n3; *ādi-kavi* of Telugu literature, 197; and *campū* style, 197; *Mahābhāratamu*, 197–200; patron (see Rājarājanarendra)
Nārada, 118, 120; and Kṛṣṇa, 121; and Pārvatī, 144; sacred thread, 124n14
Nārāyaṇa. *See under* Viṣṇu
Nārāyaṇa, Bhaṭṭa: *Veṇīsaṃhāra*, 19

National School of Drama (NSD), 155–156, 160
nationalism, 26–27, 281; Hindu (*see* Hindu nationalism); popular, 291; religious, 282, 285, 287; and speculative fiction, 367; women's movement, 327
Nāṭyaśāstra, 160
Nāyādhammakahāo, 214, 216, 224–225
Neminātha (Nemi), 11, 215, 216–218, 221, 229, 234
Nemināthacarita, 215, 218, 234
Nepali, 4, 24
nidāna, 213, 224, 225
Nīlakaṇṭha: defining terms, 74–79, 81; Indraloka visit, 59n15; southern recension, 54n4, 58n14; vulgate *Mahābhārata*, 16
niśācaras. *See rākṣasas*
Niṣāda (Nishada) community: 349–35
Nītivarman, 254n63: *Kīcakavadha*, 19
novels: aesthetics, 310, 314; Bakhtin and, 307, 309, 332; character, 321; graphic (*see* graphic novels); and narrative, 332; Partition literature (*see under* Partition); feminist critique, 325–342; Victorian-Bengali, 300

Orissa: Bhīma worship, 31
Oriya, 4, 22, 24, 32, 326, 336n32, 347n9
ornament, 56, 96–99, 102, 104–106, 110–111, 112, 114, 311–312

Palace of Illusions (Divakaruni), 326–341 passim
Pampa, 213n1; *Vikramārjunavijaya*, 22, 173, 177, 187, 274
Pampabhārata. *See Vikramārjunavijaya*
"Pañcakanyā" (Devi), 343, 346; narrative, 347–349; women in, 347–350. See also *After Kurukshetra*
Pāñcālas, 38, 176, 334
Pañcarātra, 11, 19, 21, 91--115 passim
Pañcaśikha, 71, 78
Pāṇḍavacarita (*Pāṇḍavapurāṇas*), 215, 216, 217, 234
Pāṇḍavas, xix, 92, 98, 102, 118, 132, 185, 223, 261, 264, 337; alliance with Kauravas, 11; ancestor of, 137n6; as antagonists, 173, 189–190; birth, 41; and colonial literature, 300; core narrative, 7–10; court, 129; deer hunt, 317; departure from world, 49; heroism, 203; and historicity, 289; in Jain tradition, 215–216, 217, 229–230; in *Kaurava Empire*, 372; *kṣatriya* dharma and, 175, 182–183, 189; name, 7–8, 108n31; perspective of, 19; sisters, 28; survive Bhārata War, 46, 47; victory, 172, 174; at Virāṭa's court, 93, 108n31, 200–205, 246
Pāṇḍavcarit (Viṣṇudās), 172n3, 214, 221, 224, 225, 268; Arjuna in, 226; comedic elements, 246–248; context for composition, 238, 241, 244–245, 255; emotional appeal, 238, 240; *Kīcakavadha* episode, 237–238, 245n35, 246–252; martial character, 240–241, 245, 252, 255; name, 237n2; and *Paṇḍvānī*, 252–254; patron, critique of, 250, 255; as performance, 239, 246–247, 251, 255; preface, 240; and Sanskrit *Mahābhārata*, 239, 253–254; Sanskrit preamble, 239

Pāṇḍavlīlā, 8n18, 172n4, 252
Pāṇḍu, 7–8, 41, 227, 241, 351
Paṇḍvānī, 24, 239, 252–253; tribal associations, 253–255
Panuluh: *Ghaṭotkacāśraya*, 23
Parāśara: destruction of world, 45–46
Pāratam (Villiputtūr), xvii, 24, 26, 254n63; context of composition, 274; Draupadī, 336n32; Kṛṣṇa in, 258–266; and *Mahābhārata* (Sanskrit), 264; Māl in, 262; South Indian landscape, 262
Pāratavenpā (Peruntēvaṉār), 22, 228n52, 275
parigraha, 78–87 passim
pārijāta, 123, 209
Pārijātāpaharaṇamu (Timmana), 209
Parikṣit, 10; death and *nāga* genocide, 44, 47; Kṛṣṇa restores to life, 47
Partition, 328; literature, 327–331; women and, 327–331
Pārvatī, 266; and Arjuna, 112, 187; Gaṅgā, rivalry with, 143–144
pāśupata weapon, 187–189
pativratā. *See under* women
patriarchy. *See under* gender
performance, 94, 99–102, 107–108, 205; and kingship, 242, 255; *Kūṭiyāṭṭam* (see *Kūṭiyāṭṭam*); manuals, 138; public; 238; in Tomar court, 237–256 passim
performance studies, 26, 100, 238
performance traditions. *See* dance; theater
Persian, 4, 23, 24, 243, 365
Peruntēvaṉār: *Pāratavenpā*, 22, 54, 228n52, 275
philology. *See under* Chattopadhyay, Bankimchandra
Piracaṅkam Pāratam: and *Pāratam*, 24
poetics, xix, 12–14, 192; Sanskrit, 200, 206; Telugu, 203
poetry: and audience, 302; and history, 292–296; meter, 197, 199–200, 203, 268; modern, 28–29. See also *kāvya*; *mahākāvya*
postcolonial tellings, 30, 32, 331–342
Prabandha Kūttu, 138
Prabhāsatīrtha, 137, 143
Prāgjyotiṣa, 185, 273
prajñā: 279–280, 301–302
Prakrit, 4, 160, 213, 224; and Apabhramsha, 218; Ardhamagadhi, 214; Maharashtri, 216; spoken by *vidūṣaka*, 138
prāsa, 203, 204n42
Prasanna: *Śākuntala* (1987 production), 155–159
prativāsudeva, 214, 215, 216n7
pregnancy, 10, 47, 48, 146, 151, 347, 381
Priyaṃvadā, 155, 161
prose-poems, mixed. *See campūs*
Pulastya, 46
Punnāṭa, Jinasena: *Harivaṃśapurāṇa*, 11, 214–216, 234
purāṇas, 2n1, 13n28, 286, 299; genre, 239n6, Jain tradition, 213, 214–216, 229
Puruṣārtha Kūttu, 136, 139, Day One, 141–143; Day Two, 143–145; Day Three, 145–147; Day Four, 147–149; Day Five, 149
puruṣārthas (goals of life), 136, 139, 147; inverted, 140; *mokṣa* as, 146; *rājaseva* as, 140, 149; versus reality, 141; *vañcanam* as, 145–147; *vinodam* as, 145–147. See also *Puruṣārtha Kūttu*

Pūtanā, 259–261; as Kṛṣṇa devotee, 261

Quinn, Jason: *Gandhi: My Life is My Message*, 371–372; *Kaurava Empire,* 371

Ra One (2011), 382–383
racism, 340–341
Raïdhū, 239n9, 243n29, 252; biography, 220; inspired by Punnāṭa, 223; *Harivaṃsapurāṇa*, 25, 214, 220–22, 234
rājadharma. See under kingship
Rājā Hariścandra, 29
Rājarājanarendra, 195, 198, 199, 206; details of rule, 200
rājaseva. See under kingship
rājasūya, 118–120; and Kṛṣṇa, 128
Rājataraṅgiṇī (Kalhana), 19
rājavṛtta, 347–349, 351–352
Rājnītī (2010), 30, 375
Rajputs, 241, 249, 254; descent from Pāṇḍavas, 252; Rajputization (process), 246, 249
rākṣasas, 76; battles, 55, 60, 65–68; *brāhmaṇa*s, opposites, 64, 66; clan, 65n36; genocide of, 45–46; and Ghaṭotkaca, 62–65; and Irāvān, 63; Kaurava, 60; Pāṇḍavas, hatred of, 65; in *Rāmāyaṇa*, 64
Rāma, 51–52, 247, 267, 345; *avatāra* of Viṣṇu, 124n16, 266; as hero, 308; Yudhiṣṭhira, comparison with, 319
Rāma Jāmadagnya (Paraśurāma), 44–46
Rāmāyaṇa (Jain tradition), 227, 229
Rāmāyaṇa (Sanskrit), xix, xxiii, 38, 257, 271, 302, 308, 317; compared with *Mahābhārata*, 51
Rāmāyaṇa traditions, xix–xxi, 247, 271, 345; Dalit interpretations, 345; diversity of, 53–54; heroines in, 325, 328; Hindu nationalism and, 30; as history, 286, 301n69
Rāmcaritmānas (Tulsīdās), 267–268, 269; model for *Mahābhārat* (Cauhān), 268, 271–273, 372
Ranna, 213n1; *Sāhasabhīmavijaya*, 25; 171–189 passim, 274
rape. *See* sexual assault
rasa, 131, 156, 177, 312; *adbhuta-rasa*, 364, 377; *hāsya rasa*, 246; and identity, 177; interpretation theory, 312; *śānta-rasa*, 13
Rāvaṇa, xix, 83, 247, 231, 247; and Śiśupāla, 124n14
Ray, Pratibha: *Yājñasenī*, 326, 331–335
Razmnāmah, 23
repetition: in Sanskrit *Mahābhārata*, 17; and mirroring, 20; in Dalit narratives, 345
revenge, 17, 237–256 passim, 371; Ambā, 339n43; cycle, 64; Draupadī and, 219; Kīcaka, 222; *rākṣasa* killings, 63, 66
Riṭṭhanemicariu (Raïdhū). *See Harivaṃsapurāṇa* (Raïdhū)
Riṭṭhaṇemicariu (Svayambhūdeva), 25, 214; audience, 234; first Jain Mahābhārata, 217; frame story, 227; Kīcaka in, 229–233; language, 234; patron Dhavalaïya, 234; structure, 226; Sanskrit *Virāṭaparvan* and, 229, 233, 234; Tribhuvana contributes, 226; violence in narrative, 234; Yaśaḥkīrti completes, 219, 226
royal power. *See* kingship

royalty. *See* kingship
rūpa, 73, 79, 85, 87–88. *See also* body
Ruru, 44

Sabhāparv (Cauhān), 266; date, 266–269
Sabhāparva (Viṣṇudās), 245n35
Sabhāparvan, 318, 330
sacrifice: self-, 62: and world order, 49. *See also* snake sacrifice
Sahadeva, 6n14, 7, 8
Sāhasabhīmavijaya (Ranna), 25, 213n1, 274; dating, 171n2–172n2; dharma in, 174; Draupadī's molestation in, 185; and *Mahābhārata* (Sanskrit), 173–189 passim
"Sairandhrī" (Gupt, 1927), 219
Śaktin: killed by *rākṣasa*, 45
Śakuni, 8, 92; killed, 268
Śākuntala (1987 Prasanna production): casting, 155; comparison, use of, 164; Duṣyanta and Śakuntalā reunite, 159; feminist nature of production, 155n8; genre, critique of, 156; Kālidāsa, departs from, 157, 159; review, 158; Śakuntalā in, 155–157
Śākuntala (1995 Ganguly production). See *Tridhara*
Śakuntalā (character), 11, 248n43; as agent, 159; audience perspective, 157; compared, 167; costume, 158; evolution, 155; in *Mahābhārata*, 165, 167; personality, 152–163 passim; popular representations, 163; voice, 155–156, 166
Śākuntala (Kālidāsa): *Abhijñānaśākuntala* (full title), 151, 154, 167; adapted, 153–154, 167; Duṣyanta and Śakuntalā reunite, 159; feminist corrective, 22; language in, 160n18; and *Mahābhārata* (Sanskrit), 152–153, 155
Śalya, 9, killed, 268
Śalyaparv (Cauhān): date, 268; Kṛṣṇa in, 268
Samantapañcaka, 43–46
Sāmba, 48
sāṃkhya, 69, 71, 76–77, 78n40, 85n78
saṃsāra, 34; in Jain tradition, 231, 234
Saṃvaraṇa, 137
Sañjaya, 55–56; as audience, 172, 179; dice game, 184; and Duryodhana, 176, 179; praises Bhīma, 185
Sanskrit, 160; cosmopolis, 192; and gender, 326; history of, 192; homogenous voice, 17; Jain Mahābhārata tradition, 213; and Malayalam, 142; meter, 203; in modernity, 22; in multilingual works, 160n18; prosody, 198–199, 200; and Telugu, 191–211 passim
Śāntiparvan, 69, 140, 280, 310
Sāraḻādāsa: Oriya *Mahābhārata*, 22
Sarasvatī, 198, 270, 341; martial aspect, 240
śārdūla meter (*śārdūlavikrīḍita*), 197–205 passim
Sarpa Satra (Kolatkar), 28
sarpasattra. *See* snake sacrifice
śāstras, 2n1, 50, 139, 290, 321, 338; and compassion, 298; and epics, 310; and historicity, 291
sattva: meaning, 74–86 passim
satya: and *tathya*, 296, 395n54
Satyabhāmā: Draupadī, dialogue with, 206–209; and *pārijāta* tree, 209; in *Pārijātāpaharaṇamu*, 209
Satyāśraya, 171–172; as Bhīma, 172

Satyavatī, 29
Sauptikaparvan, 65, 68, 372
Sāvitrī, 11
science fiction, 33; absence in Indian films, 361–362; and colonial rule, 367; in Indian literature, 363; rising popularity, 367; term, 364; in United States, 363
selfhood, 94, 101–115 passim; body and, 103–106, 111; fragmented, 92, 101, 109, 111, 113
sexual assault, 3, 25, 79–84, 219, 246, 330; and caste, 355; and Mother India, 328; Partition, 329; by state forces, 335
sexuality: female, 72–73, 80, 84
Shakuntala Remembered (2006 production), 154; actor's roles in, 165; audience, 164, 167; and *Bhāgavatapurāṇa*, 163; departs from Kālidāsa, 162–163, 165; Duṣyanta in, 164, 167; language in, 165; and *Mahābhārata* (Sanskrit), 163–165; Śakuntalā in, 166–167; *sūtradhāra* in, 165, Vyāsa in, 165
shape-shifting. *See* body: transformation
Śikhaṇḍin, xxi–xxii, 9; postcolonial representations, 339
Śīlāṅka (Śīlācārya), 216
Singha, Kaliprasanna, 306, 314
Śiśupāla, 124n16, 269; death, 118; and Kṛṣṇa, 117–133 passim, 298; as sun, 124
Śiśupālavadha (Māgha), 18, 117–133 passim; and Bhāravi, 126n21; kingship, idea of, 21; and *rasa*, 131
Sītā, 231, 241, 247, 271, 272; modern representations, 163; in Partition literature, 328–329
Śiva, 104, 145, 266, 267; Ardhanārīśvara, 112; Arjuna and, 111–113, 127, 173, 186–189; and Gaṇapati, 144, 147; Pārvatī and, 112; wives' rivalry, 143–144
śleṣa, 18, 111, 113, 115; and fragmented identities, 19; narrative perspective, 19; *vidūṣaka* recites, 145
smṛti, 49
snake sacrifice, 28, 43–45
social justice, 327, 334, 344
society, disintegration of, 19–20, 33, 144–145
South India, 6n14, 54n3, 171n2, 192, 205, 210, 217, 260, 262, 266
speculative fiction: as political critique, 365; setting, 363–366; and South Asian literature, 364
Śreṇika, 227–229
śrī (glory/prosperity), 110
Śrī (Lakṣmī), 122, 131, 265, 269
Śrīharṣa: *Naiṣadhīyacarita*, 18, 194
Śrīnāthuḍu, 194
Srinivasan, Balaji: *Draupadi*, 6n14
Śrīvaiṣṇavas, 260, 261, 262
śruti, 49
Star Wars trilogy, 33, 361n1; aesthetic, 368; influence in India, 368; and Rāmāyaṇa, 368
Strīparva (Devi), 329
Strīparvan, 77n39, 346
Śubhacandra: 229; *Pāṇḍavapurāṇa*, 217, 217n9, 234
Subhadrā, 136; abducted, 137; and Arjuna, 137; identity confused, 142; postcolonial representations, 333, 338
Subhadrādhanañjaya (Kulaśekhara), 135–136, 139, 149; dating of,

Subhadrādhanañjaya (continued) 136n3; in *Kūṭiyāṭṭam* repertoire, 21–22, 137–138; *vidūṣaka* in, 142
Sudeṣṇā, 246–248, 249; Draupadi and, 205
suicide, 40, 137, 222n23, 338
Sukosalacariu, 221
Sulabhā, 69–88; meaning, 72
Suparṇa. *See* Garuḍa
Supratīka, 183, 184–185
sūtradhāra, 157, 165
Svargārohaṇ (Viṣṇudās), 245n34
Svargārohaṇaparv (Cauhān), 270
Svargārohaṇaparvan, 331
Svayambhūdeva: Digambaras and, 227; frame story, use of, 227; Jain Mahābhārata tradition and, 234; *Nemināthacarita* (*Harivaṃśapurāṇa*), 134; Paümacariu, 226, 227; possible Yāpanīya identity, 227; *Riṭṭhaṇemicariu*, 25, 214, 217, 226–233
Śvetāmbaras. *See under* Jains

Tagore, Rabindranath: 306, 322, career, 281; and European scholarship, 297–299; "Kṛṣṇacaritra," 32, 280–281, 290–302; *Mahābhārata*, historicity of, 291–292, 294–295; *Mahābhārata*, Kṛṣṇa in, 297; *Mahābhārata*, as literature, 298–300; *Mahābhārata*, narrative instability, 293; *Mahābhārata*, as poetry, 292–296, 302; *Mahābhārata*, supernatural elements of, 292; and religious difference, 298; retellings, 281n6; and translation, 295
Takṣaka, 44, 58n14
Tamil, xxiii, 4, 11n24, 14, 22–31 passim, 228n52, 254n63, 336n32, 363, 382; Aravāṉ, 62; Mahābhāratas in, 54, 55n5, 66, 67, *Pāratam*, 258–266 passim, 275, 277
Tamil Nadu, 4, 6n14; and Draupadī worship, 24, 31, 55, 274n83
tapas. *See* ascetic practice
Tapatī, 137n6
Tapatīsaṃvaraṇa: in *Kūṭiyāṭṭam* repertoire, 137–138
tathya: and *satya*, 296, 395n54
television dramas: in Hindi: 29, 339n47; *See also Mahābhārat* (Doordarshan TV serial)
Telugu, 4, 2n3, 3, 11, 24, 25, 30; audience, 196–197; Dalit literature, 345; history of, 191–192, 210–211; *Mahābhārata* (see under *Mahābharatamu*); *mārga* (see under *mārga*); meter, classical, 199–200, 203; prosody, 197, 199, 200–203; and Sanskrit, 25, 191–211 passim; women in classical literature, 207–209
Terukkūttu, 6n14; *Pāratam*, drawing on, 24
Thatham, Ranganayaki (pseud. Kumudini), xxiii
theater: adaptation of, 153; tradition, 252. *See also* performance; performance studies; performance tradition
Tikkana, 191–192, 195, 200, 210, 211; *Mahābhāratamu*, 25, 195, 200–206; *naṭakīyata* style, 201; orality of tone, 201, 203; *Paṇḍvānī*, contrasted with, 254; Viṣṇudās, contrasted with, 246.

See also Virāṭaparvamu and *see also under* vernacularization
Tilak, Lokmanya B. G.: and *Mahābhārata*, 50
time, cyclical, 47, 166–167, 332; and speculative fiction, 366
Timmana, Nandi: *Pārijātāpaharaṇamu*, 209
tīrthaṅkaras, 214, 227
Tomar court (Gwalior), 224, 238; Delhi Sultanate and, 243–244; *kṣatriya* identity, 255; literature, 244, 249; and Malwa, 244, 250; Pāṇḍava genealogy, 241; tribal associations, 254, 255
tragedy: as genre, 154–155, 161, 167; as theme, 371
transgender: community, 55n5; individuals, xx–xxii
translation, 211; iconic, 196, 208; indexical, 196
tribal groups, 37, 334, 335, 349–352, 254; contrast with Aryans, 334; descent from Bhīma, 253; Ekalavya and, 32, 104; and Tomar dynasty, 253–255
Tridhara (1995 production), 154; classical format, 159–160; comparison, use of, 164; costume, 162; Duṣyanta in, 161, 162; Duṣyanta and Śakuntalā reunite, 162; Kālidāsa, departs from, 160–161, 162; Śakuntalā in, 160–162; Sanskrit, use of, 160; stage set, 160, 161
Triṣaṣṭilakṣaṇamahāpurāṇasaṃgraha, 216
Triṣaṣṭiśalākāpuruṣacaritra (Hemacandra), 217
Tulsīdās: *Hanumānbāhuk*, 273; *Rāmcaritmānas*, 267–268, 271–272
Turōṇaparuvam (Villiputtūr), 264
Twitter. *See* internet

Uddhava, 118; advisor of Kṛṣṇa, 126, 131–132
Ugrasena, 48, 125
Ugraśravas, 43–45, 117
Ulūpī, 28–29, 67; and Arjuna, 67; as mother of Irāvān, 57–58, 60, 66
universal monarch. See *rājasūya*
Uṇṇimañjarī, 146–147
Until the Lions (Naïr), 28
untouchability. *See* Dalits
Urdu, 4, 365
Ūrubhaṅga, 20–21, 91n1, 153
utopias, 363; anti-colonial allegories, 365
Uttarā, 10, 47, 98–99, 108n31, 114, 347–349, 351, 380
Uttarakhand, 8n18; Duryodhana worship in, 31; Karṇa worship in, 31
Uttarapurāṇa (Guṇabhadra), 216

Vādicandra: 229; *Pāṇḍavapurāṇa*, 218
Vaiśaṃpāyana, 43, 55
Vaiṣṇavas, 260–261, 268, 275, 283
Vaiśravaṇa, 147
Vālmīki: author (see *Rāmāyaṇa* [Sanskrit]); hunter, 272
Vāmana. *See under* Viṣṇu
Vanaparva (Viṣṇudās), 245n35
Vanaparvan. See *Āraṇyakaparvan*
vañcanam. See under *puruṣārthas*
varṇas: mixing of, 82
varṇāśrama dharma, 174
Vasiṣṭha: dissuades Parāśara, 45

vāsudeva (figure in Jain literature), 214
Vasudeva (Kṛṣṇa's father), 215
Vedas, 41, 83, 286; and *itihāsa*, 295; Mahābharata as, 2n1, 310
Vedic era: challenges to, 52
Veṇīsaṃhāra (Nārāyaṇa, Bhaṭṭa), 19, 92n2
Veṇmuracu (Jeyamohan), 30
vernacular, xxiv, 7, 27, 194, 237, 252, 254, 281; Bengali, 283; "cosmpolitan vernacular," 192–194; Jain literature, 218; meter, 199; and Sanskrit tradition, 196–212 passim, 246, 237–239, 283; Mahābhārata retellings, 22, 192, 255, 273, 274
vernacularization, 24, cosmopolitan vernacular and, 192–194; non-linear, 209; power, 194; Telugu and, 192–194, 197–199, 210–211; Tikkana's verse, role of, 203, 211–212
veśyas, 140, 146
viḍḍhi (buffoon), 146
vidūṣaka (jester), 135–136, 138; comedic role, 136, 138–141, 145–148; feasting, 140, 147; friend of Arjuna, 142; and "imagined interlocutor," 140–141; inversion of norms, 138; language of, 138; as mediator, 145; role, 139, 141–142; and performance of *Puruṣārtha Kūttu*, 139–149 passim; Shakespeare's Falstaff, 141; in *Subhadrādhanañjaya*, 21–22; translator, 142. See also *Kūṭiyāṭṭam*
vidūṣakastobham, 142n13
Vidyasagar, Ishwar Chandra, 306, 322
Vidyāsāgara: *Jayakaumudī*, 2n2
Vijayanagara, 209, 211
Vikramāṅkadevacarita (Bilhaṇa), 129–130, 132
Vikramārjunavijaya (Pampa), 22, 53n1, 173, 177, 185–188, 195–196, 213, 274
Villiputtūr (Villi), 24, 26; name, 260n12, 261; *Pāratam*, 258–266, 274
vinodam (amusement). See under *puruṣārtha*s
violence, xx, xxi, 3, 37–38, 42, 47, 49, 50–51, 234 360; caste, 354–355, 357, 359; genocide (*see under* genocide); in graphic novels, 375, 384; internecine, 38–40, 47; kingship and, 38; magical, 60; *Rāmāyaṇa* and, 38; as sacrifice, 49; sexual (*see under* sexual violence); state, 49–51, 335; Vedic understanding, 49; in Western literature, 38
Virāṭa, 9, 11, 112, 200, 201; 219, 231, 233, 238, 246; cattle, 97–98, 107; court, 93–95, 101, 107, 108; as Vairāṭa (Vairāḍa), 225
Virāṭaparva (Viṣṇudās), 237–238, 245n35, 246–252
Virāṭaparvamu (Tikkana). See under *Mahābhāratamu* (Tikkana)
Virāṭaparvan, 5–6, 21, 92–115 passim;, 204, 219, 222n23, 229, 230, 308
Viṣṇu, 257, 258, 275; *avatāras*, 61, 262–264, 265–266; Gajendra, salvation of, 265; as Kṛṣṇa, 41, 240, 288; Kṛṣṇa, contrast with, 175; Narasiṃha, 124n16, 240, 264; Nārāyaṇa, 264; Vāmana, 263
Viṣṇudās, 172n3, 214, 221; Nāth Yogī, 237n3; *Pāṇḍavcarit*, 26, 221, 224, 225–226, 237–256, 268, 274; *Svargārohaṇ*, 245n34
Viṣṇupurāṇa, 257; Kṛṣṇa in, 260

Viśvāmitra, 308
Vīṭṭumaparuvam (Villiputtūr), 263–264
Vṛndāvana, 259, 261, 263
Vṛṣṇis, 10; death of, 48–49
Vyāsa, xxii, 4, 13, 17, 28, 37, 38, 43, 152, 227n49, 229, 266, 294, 298; father of Dhṛtarāṣṭra, 227n49; name, 200; postcolonial representations, 338; protagonist, choice of, 318; in *Shakuntala Remembered*, 165; Viṣṇudās acknowledges, 239

war books. *See* battle books
widowhood: upper-caste norms, critique of, 347–352
wilderness. *See* forest
women: avoidance of, 247–248; as bad wives, 208; as *duṣṭavanitā* (evil-minded), 207; as *pativratā* (virtuous and married), 207, 209, 211; social issues, 337–338. *See also* feminism; gender

Yadus (Yādavas), 47–48
Yājñasenī (epithet for Draupadī), 330
Yājñasenī (Ray), 326, 331–335; *ādivāsīs* in, 334; Aryans in, 334; narrative, 332–335
yakṣas, 75–76, 222–223, 245n35, 317, 338
Yaśaḥkīrti, 219, 239n9. *See also* *Riṭṭhaṇemicariu*
yati, 198, 200, 204n42
yoga, 72–76, 81, 174
YouTube. *See* internet
Yudhiṣṭhira, 40, 57, 69, 310, 92, 100, 102, 103, 109–110; and Arjuna, 109–111; army of, 120; as Bhagavān, 109n33; Bhīṣma and, 280; *bildungsroman*, 32; as a *brāhmana*, 109–111; brothers, 120, 128; core narrative, 7–10; and dharma, 285, 313–314, 321; as Dharmanandana, 181; as Dharmarāja, 43, 245; and Dhṛtarāṣṭra, 128; dice match, 9, 184, 264, 318; and Droṇa, 173, 176, 180; and Draupadī, 204; and Duryodhana, 8, 10, 126–127; exile, 128, 319–320; hell, visits, 315; horse sacrifice, 10, 24; in *Jaiminibhārata*, 24; in Jain tradition, 215, 219, 223, 229, 231–232; as Kaṅka, 109n33; Kauṇḍinya and, 149; as king, 8, 110, 118–130 passim, 280, 302; and Kṛṣṇa, 21, 118–123, 128–133, 280; lies, 177–179, 182; as modern, 320–321; postcolonial representations, 334, 336; as protagonist, 311–313, 315–318, 321; *rājasūya* sacrifice (see *rājasūya* sacrifice); Rāma, comparison with, 319; reaches heaven, 10; reputation, 178, 180–181; in *Svargārohaṇ*, 245n35; tells truth, 177; and *yakṣa*, 317
yugas, 366; transition between, 44, 47. *See also* time, cyclical

www.ingramcontent.com/pod-product-compliance
Lightning Source LLC
Chambersburg PA
CBHW020257240426
43673CB00039B/624
* 9 7 8 1 4 3 8 4 8 2 4 0 8 *